VIRGINIA GLEANINGS IN ENGLAND

VIRGINIA GLEANINGS IN ENGLAND

Abstracts of 17th and 18th-Century
English Wills and Administrations
Relating to Virginia and Virginians

A Consolidation of Articles from
The Virginia Magazine of History and Biography

BY LOTHROP WITHINGTON

Indexed by Thomas L. Hollowak

Baltimore
GENEALOGICAL PUBLISHING CO., INC.
1980

Excerpted and reprinted from
*The Virginia Magazine of
History and Biography*
With added Preface and Index
Genealogical Publishing Co., Inc.
Baltimore, 1980
Copyright © 1980
Genealogical Publishing Co., Inc.
Baltimore, Maryland
All Rights Reserved
Library of Congress Catalogue Card Number 79-90754
International Standard Book Number 0-8063-0869-9
Made in the United States of America

PREFACE

 HE LONG SERIES of articles published in *The Virginia Magazine of History and Biography* under the title "Virginia Gleanings in England" was inspired by Henry F. Waters' celebrated "Genealogical Gleanings in England," published in *The New England Historical and Genealogical Register* between 1883 and 1899, and collected and published in book form in 1901 in two volumes. Indeed, "Virginia Gleanings" was originally based on materials accumulated by Waters but not submitted for publication in the *Register* because of their bearing on Virginia. Utilizing Waters' manuscript notes, Lothrop Withington commenced publication of "Virginia Gleanings" in the issue of the *Magazine* for January 1903 (Volume X), continuing his contributions right up to the time of his death on the *Lucitania* in 1916. The last issue of the *Magazine* in which his name appeared as primary contributor of "Virginia Gleanings" was that for January 1916 (Volume XXIV). For the next three years the series was entrusted to Leo Culleton, although it was apparently based on materials left by Withington at the time of his death. The series was eventually concluded by Reginald Glencross, whose contributions appeared sporadically in the *Magazine* until July 1929.

Throughout the course of the series' publication the editor of the *Magazine* was the noted genealogist William G. Stanard, and it is Stanard's hand that is evident in the scholarly annotations which accompany the abstracts of wills and administrations. Stanard's achievement in developing material supplementary to Withington's is remarkable in itself, and to him must go a good portion of the credit for the success of the series as a whole.

The complete "Virginia Gleanings" series, assembled here in book form for the first time, consists of eighty-five articles, the bulk of them contributed by Lothrop Withington. While not as massive a work as Waters' *Genealogical Gleanings*, the series is no less important, especially for the light it sheds on relationships between English and Virginia families, and consolidation is no more than the series deserves. The articles are reprinted here in the order in which they appeared in the *Magazine* and represent no critical judgment or selection on the part of the publisher.

GENEALOGICAL PUBLISHING CO., INC.

NOTE

A N ATTEMPT was made in 1948 to revive the "Virginia Gleanings" series, but only two articles under this heading were in fact published (Volume 56, Nos. 1 and 3). As these contributions were not an integral part of the original series they have been omitted from the present volume.

Virginia Gleanings
In England

VIRGINIA GLEANINGS IN ENGLAND.

In 1879, Mr. Henry Fitzgilbert Waters, in company with Mr.
J. A. Emmerton, issued the results of a tour in England, "glean-
ing" notes concerning early New England families. This attracted so much interest that in 1883, under the auspices of the
New England Historic-Genealogical Society, a committee was
formed to support Mr. Waters in a general search in England
for early New England families. This arrangement with Mr.
Waters nominally lasted until January, 1899, although for a long
interval the research was at the sole charge of Mr. James Junius
Goodwin, who at all times was the leading contributor to the
fund. To Mr. Goodwin all interested in early American genealogy owe a debt only second to that due to Mr. Waters. The
New England Society soon began to reap great credit from the
remarkable work of Mr. Waters in England, as published in
their *Register*, the most striking cases being the settlement of
the Washington and Harvard pedigrees. Finally, in 1901, two
years after the conclusion of the work of Mr. Waters in England, the New England Society issued all of the printed "Gleanings" in two bulky volumes. Although credit for the support of
Mr. Waters' work in England is due to certain leading members
of the New England Society, especially to the tireless energy of
Mr. J. T. Hassam, ably sustained by Mr. W. S. Appleton, the
late John Ward Denand and W. H. Whitmore, the New England Society, as a body, never did anything in the matter, and
charged the voluntary committee for the expense of printing the
"Gleanings" of Mr. Waters, now universally acknowledged as
the most important matter which has appeared in the *New England Historical and Genealogical Register* since its foundation,
1847. Early in the period of Mr. Waters' work there arose
complaints in Boston concerning the space given by him to
Virginia matters, there being naturally in the early English
records a richer harvest of such references than to New England.
Consequently, Mr. Waters was obliged to put aside great numbers of these Virginia references with his mass of unpublished
notes, exceeding in bulk his published ones some four or five

From Vol. X, No. 3 (Jan. 1903), p. 291.

fold. These notes at his departure from London, Mr. Waters turned over to me to collate, continue, cross-reference, and utilize in every way for the public benefit. As I began my researches among English records as a youth in 1874, like him I have naturally accumulated a mass of English notes, including many Virginia matters. Interested from boyhood in the many ramifications of my own ancestry, and in all of the four or five hundred pioneer families of Old Newbury, in Massachusetts, I soon found myself extending in all directions, and often to Virginia, It is now a great pleasure both to Mr. Waters and myself to be able to utilize jointly these Virginia references in our notes, which I shall cull out from time to time for the Virginia Historical Society.

LOTHROP WITHINGTON,

30 Little Russell Street, W. C., London.

JAMES ASHTON, of Stafford county, Virginia, gentleman. Will dated 18 August, 1686; proved 8 September, 1686, in County Court; proved 14 July, 1687, in Prerogative Court of Canterbury. Cosen John Ashton, Haberdasher in Rustall Street, Covent Garden, London, that seat or tract of land, undisposed, which formerly belonged to my brother, John Ashton. Cosen John Foster, of Wozbridge, Cambridgeshire, gentleman, that Plantation called Chatterton on the River side, and that tract of land belonging to my 550 acres. Godchildren Sarah Mattershed, Rich: Elkin, Eliz: Sabastian and John Rosier's daughter, each a heifer with a calf by her side. Rose Fitzhugh, daughter of Col. William Fitzhugh, two heifers and two calves. William King and his wife two heifers and two calves. William King to be employed on the plantation where I live. John Harvey two heifers and two calves. Samuel Haywood, ditto. Ric: Elkin 100 acres of land adjoining upon John Grigsby of the ¼ Divdt. William Fitzhugh, Samuel Hayward, and John Harvey, executors in trust. Freight taken for me by Mr. Thomas Storke of London, merchant. Sarah Fermer, now servant, a heifer when free. John Ashton and John Foster, executors. To Dr. William Bankes 20s. to buy him a ring. Others.

Foot, 90.

[James Ashton was J. P. for Stafford county, Va., in 1680, and in 1690—as appears from the Northern Neck Land Grant Books—owned a tract of land which he had inherited as the heir of his brother, John Ashton, to whom it was bequeathed by Col. Peter Ashton, who had patented it in 1658.

Col. Peter Ashton was a member of the House of Burgesses for Charles City county in 1656, and for Northumberland 1659 and 1660; sheriff of the last-named county, 1658, and member of the "Committee of the Association of Northumberland, Westmoreland and Stafford" in November, 1667, then having the title "Colonel." He was very probably of the family of Ashton, of Spalding, Lincolnshire, descended from the Ashtons of Chaderton or Chatterton, Lancashire. (Hence the name of his estate "Chatterton," King George county, Va., now the home of a branch of the Tayloe family.)

Col. Peter Ashton died in or before 1671, leaving a will dated 1669, by which he gave his brother, James Ashton, of Kirby-Underwood, County Lincoln, Eng., his estate of Chatterton on the Potomac, and to his brother, John Ashton, of Lowth, Lincolnshire, 2,000 acres adjoining Chatterton.

The will of John Ashton, of Stafford county, was dated September 6, 1682, and proved in old Rappahannock county January 26, 1682. Gave wife Elizabeth his whole estate "if she will come over and live heare"; if not £20 sterling per annum or £150 down, as she might choose. To Thos. Bunbery and wife £5. To Capt. John Ashton, 20 shillings. Appointed his brother, James Ashton, sole executor, and bequeathed to him his whole estate (subject to the provisions made), and if he die without heirs, then to his cousin, John Ashton, of Russell Street, "at the Adam and Eve," London.

The Capt. Jno. Ashton. named in Jas. Ashton's will, was son of Charles Ashton, who was J. P. of Northumberland at the time Col. Peter Ashton was sheriff, and was ancestor of the Virginia family of the name.

There is on record in Stafford county a deed dated January 12, 1705, from John Foster, of Wishback *als*. Woodbridge, in the Isle of Ely, county of Cambridge, Eng., to Elisha James, of the City of Bristol, mariner, conveying for a consideration of £135 sterling, a plantation of 550 acres in Stafford county, commonly called Chatterton, which was devised by Peter Ashton to James Ashton, of Virginia, and by him devised to the said John Foster ; and also a statement that Mr. John Ashton, a co-legatee of Chatterton, had renounced his claim.—EDITOR.]

NATHANIEL AXTELL, now or late of St. Peter's, near borough of St. Albans, Herts (to travel in New England). Will dated 17 August, 1639; proved 12 June, 1640. Thomas Buckingham, of Queen Epioth, in New England, [i. e., Virginia], husbandman. Richard Miles, of Queen Epioth. Mr. Peter Pridden, minister of God in New England. My two brothers, Thomas and Daniel Axtell. My three sisters, Jeane, Anne and Sarah.

Coventry, 82.

JOHN ADKINS, the elder, of Chard, Somerset, merchant. Will dated 16 July, 1636, mentions grandchild born in Virginia.

Pile, 110.

SAMUEL PARTRIDGE, late at Rapah Hannocks, in Virginia. Admon 31 July, 1676, to Sarah Partridge alias Wilson, natural and lawfull sistered De bonis grant January, 1689–90.

1650 JOHN BOYS, bound for Verginia.

59 Pembroke.

ROBERT PERRY, 1652. Nephew Robert Perry, son of sister Elizabeth Perry, living in Virginia.

243 Bowyer.

[See *Waters' Gleanings* page 921, with Mr. Brown's note. The above was given Mr. Waters by Mr. Gerald Fothergill.]

ZACHARY CUSTIS, late of Kingston Hull, died at Accomack, in Virginia. Admon to father Joseph Custis.

Admon Act Book, 1685, folio 93.

[See *Waters' Gleanings*, page 700.]

JOHN BROOKS, of Stepney, died in Virginia. Admon 5 July, 1684, to widow Mary.

Admon Act Book, 1684, folio 110.

WILLIAM CAVENDISH, EARL OF DEVONSHIRE. Will dated 17 June, 1628; proved 1628. Shares in Virginia and Somer Islands to wife until son William come to full age of 21 and then to him.

Barrington, 68.

CHARLES BOYLE, EARL OF ORRERY. Will dated 6 November, 1728; proved 3 May, 1732; mentions William Bird, of Virginia.

Isham, 236.

[Wm. Byrd's epitaph refers to his friendship with "the learned and and illustrious Chas. Boyle, Earl of Orrery."—ED.]

JOHN BRITTEN, of Hadleigh, clothier. Will dated 17 July, 1636; proved 1 Feb., 1636. Wife Elizabeth. Daughter Margaret, wife of George Goodday. Youngest, William Britten, all my stock and adventure with the company of merchants trading for Virginia and Bermudas. Son Lawrence Britten, Daughter Mary Maxie (her children); Daughter Sarah (her children); Youngest daughter, Sarah Goodday; Thomas Welham, my sister's son; said sister Driver; eldest son, Thomas Britten, deceased; his wife Sibill, now wife of John Alablaster; eldest son, his son John Britten, Houses, &c., in Debbenham, Suffolk.

14 Goare.

VIRGINIA GLEANINGS IN ENGLAND.

Communicated by Mr. LOTHROP WITHINGTON, 30 Little Russell street, W. C., London (including "Gleanings" by Mr. H. F. WATERS, not before printed)

(CONTINUED)

THOMAS COLLINS, Cittizen and Barber Chirurgion of London. Will 12 June 1657; proved 15 October 1657. To be buried in the church of St. Katharine neare the Tower where my late Wife and Daughter Rebeccah lie buried. To my grand child Rebeccah Collins the lease of that messuage on Tower wharfe London wherein I lately dwelt and I give unto her £300 at twenty or marriage. To my grand child Elizabeth Collins the lease of that other messeuage in Wapping, Middlesex, and I give her £300 at twenty one or marriage. To my grand children Thomazine and Ann Collins £300 a piece at twenty one or marriage. My grand children to marry with the consent of their

From Vol. X, No. 4 (April 1903), p. 405.

5

father and mother. To my grand child Birkenhead Collins £300 at his age of twenty-one. To my grand child Thomas Collins his heirs &c. for ever all those my freehold lands in the parish of Hessen, Middlesex; also to him £300 at twenty one. To the poor of St. Katherine near the Tower of London £5, also 20s. for bread. To the poor of the liberty of Dullidge in the parish of Camberwell, Surrey £3. To my Son's Servants Edmund Woollham £5 and to Margerie French £3. To Richard White and Sarah White his wife £8. To Thomas White sonne unto Richard White £5 at fourteen. To my kinsman Thomas Downe if he return home from sea and demand it £5. To my kinsman James Seaward, Sonne of my late Sister Anne Collins als. Seaward, now dwelling in Virginia. £50, provided he come over to England and demand it. To my kinsmen and friends Master Alexander Hughes, Master Thomas Wilcox, Master Alexander Eaton, Master Edward Nunne, Master Robert Earle, Master William Baker, Master John Malby, and Master John Broughton, to each of them a ring the value of four nobles. To Company of Barbers Chirurgions of London a piece of plate. Residuary legatee and executor: Sonne Phillipp Collins. Witnesses: Joane Clarke, her mark, Henry Faucon, Robert Earle, scrivener.

Ruthen 373.

[The name Seward is found at an early date in Isle of Wight and Surry counties. John Seward had a grant of 300 acres of land in the county of Warrosquoiacke (Isle of Wight) July 1st, 1635, and had numerous other grants. He was Burgess for Isle of Wight in 1645. In 1665 "Mr. John Seward" was granted 1,500 acres, called "New Hemington," on Seward's creek in Isle of Wight, which had been formerly granted to his father, John Seward, in 1649. In 1672 John Seward of the city of Bristol, merchant, and James Seward, of the same place, the former the eldest son and heir of John Seward, late of said city, merchant (but who died in Virginia), conveyed to William Bressie of Virginia a tract called "Levy Neck," Isle of Wight county. There is in Isle of Wight the will of a John Seward, dated November 30, and proved February 9, 1650; but not recorded in Isle of Wight until 1705, in which he bequeaths portions of his estate to his sons John and James and his wife Sarah, and mentions a will "at home in Bristol." This was evidently the first John Seward and the James mentioned may have been the one named in the text. It is possible, though not probable, that the person named may have been a James Seward, son of William Seward of Surry county, who is named

in his fathers will, dated March 16, 1702-3. William Seward was a tith-
able in Surry in 1668.—ED.]

JOHN ALLEN of London being now bound for Virginia in the
parts beyond seas. Will 13 November 1673; proved 14 January
1674-5. To my brother Peter Allen all that my messuage &c
called the Peacock in Cornehill in the parish of St. Michael in
Cornehill London now occupied of one Richard Wise, for his
life, chargeable with the yearly payment of 40s. to my Aunt Ann
Tarsy the wife of Thomas Tarsy, for her life. In case my
said brother Peter Allen marry and have issue male then I desire that his eldest son be called after my name and after the
decease of the said Peter Allen I give my said messuage unto
such eldest son of the said Peter, but for want of such issue to
my executors in trust that they receive the rents and dispose of
the same for the best use of such of the children of my sister
Rachel Hewitt, the wife of William Hewett of London, merchant,
as shee hath or may have. Whereas there is due to me from John
Fuysting wine cooper living in the Warner Street in Amsterdam in
Holland 3000 guilders Flemish money amounting to £300 which
I have deputed my trusty friend Dirrick Van Pas of Amsterdam
merchant and Timothy Harmer citizen and haberdasher of London to receive to and for my use, I do give to the Poore
children of Christ Hospital in London £10, and to poore of
parish of St. Katherin Coleman, London, £10. To my
niece Mary Allen the daughter of my brother William Allen,
deceased £10. To the youngest son of my vncle in law Thomas
Tarsy living at my death £10. To Timothy Harmer and to
Helena his wife and to Francis Harmer and Elizabeth his wife,
each of them 20s. To friend Paul Wheeler £5. To kinsman
John Vanheeck and Sarah his wife, to Captaine Thomas Howell
in Virginia and his wife of Mary Land 20s. apiece. Touching the
money due to me out of the estate of my cousin Mistriss Mary
Beswick deceased I give one full fowerth part thereof to my
friend Francis Harmer and the other three parts to my executors to be disposed of by them amongst poor aged men and women. Residuary legatees and executors: Timothy Harmer Fran-.
cis Harmer and Paul Wheeler in trust for some of the children
of my sister Rachel Hewitt. Witnesses: William Abbott William Harmer Joshua Watmough. Commission 14 June 1688 to

7

William Harmer brother and administrator of Timothy Harmer deceased, Francis Harmer and Paul Wheeler now also deceased.

Dycer 2.

[The only Thomas Howell whose name appears in any of our records at all near this period is one who was granted 100 acres in Isle of Wight on April 28, 1702.—ED.]

ROGER ABDY, London, merchant. Will 5 October 1641; proved 3 September 1642. My body to be buried in the afternoon with a moderate expense in the parish church of St. Andrewe Vndershaft London, by the grave of my late father att his feet. To the several parishes of St. Andrewe Vndershaft and St. St. Dionice Backchurch in London, St. George the Martir in the burrough of Southwark, Surrey, St. Giles without Cripplegate, St. Leonards in Shoreditch, and St. Mary Matfellon als Whitechapel, Middlesex, for the use of the poor, £120. Several bequests to hospitals, &c &c. To tenne poore boyes, children of Freemen of London, for putting apprentices, £100. Also £120 to be bestowed upon twenty more poore boyes and girles to be taken vpp out of the streets of London as vagrants and transported either to Virginia, Newe England or any of the Westerne plantations. To company of cloth workers £40, &c. To 60 poore men and 40 women gowns as mourners if I die in England, &c. To every one of my Foure Brethren viz., Sir Thomas Abdy, Mr. Robert Abdy, Mr. John Abdy, and Mr. Nicholas Abdy £2000 apiece. To my Brother in lawe Mr. John Bromston and Mrs. Alice Bramston his wife my Sister £500, and if they die then amongst such of their sons as shall live to be twenty one and to such of their daughters as shall live to be twenty one or married. To my four own brethren before named and to my sister Dame Maria Abdy the wife of my brother Sir Thomas Abdy and to my said brother Bramston and my sister his wife £10 apeece. To my Neece Rachell Abdy daughter of the said Sir Thomas Abdy £20. To my Nephew and Neece Anthony and Abigaill Bramston two of the children of my said brother and sister Bramston £20 apeece, and to my Neeces Marie and Bridgett Bramston the other two children of my said brother and sister Bramston £10 apeece. To Mrs. Rachaell Corselis £10. To my cousin Mr. William

8

Meggs and Mr. James Meggs £5 apeece. To my cousin Mr. Humfrey Abdy £100. To my cousin Antony Daniell £50, and I will to the rest of his brothers viz., Henry, Walter and Humfrie Daniel £10 apeece at twenty one. To Abigaill Daniell and Elizabeth Daniell the sisters of the said Antony Daniell £10 ditto. To Millicent Shaw £20. To Dr. Ouldsworth and Dr. Westfield £10 apeece, it being my desire that one of them preach at my funeral if I die in England. To my friends Mr. Roger Vivean and Mr .Richard Millward £20 apeece. To Mr. Adam Bowen £10. Residuary legatees and executors my two eldest brethren the before named Sir Thomas Abdy and Robert Abdy. Whereas my late deceased father Antony Abdy, late of London, Alderman, did by his will devise all that his messuage then and now used for a tavern called by the sign of the Antwerpe near the Royal Exchange in London to mee the said Roger Abdy and my heirs male, for default of such issue to the right heirs of him the said Antony Abdy, I leave, &c. Witnesses: Roger Paigan, William Loue, and John Merrick, scrivener.

Campbell 108.

[The very practical philanthropy of Roger Abdy had been anticipated by the corporation of the city of London which at an earlier date sent boys to Virginia.—ED.]

HENRY ARCHER, parish of St. John, Hertford, co. Hertford, Gentleman. Will 19 October 1723; proved 21 January, 1723. My body I would have buried in All Saints church yard, Hertford. To John and Elizabeth Archer his Wife, my Brother and Sister and Thomas Archer their Son, £50 apeice. To my cousin William Mails of Barton in the clay, Bedfordshire, and James his brother at Palloxhill and Elizabeth their Sister and to Daniel Mailes Child £20 apeice the child to have hers paid at 21 or marriage. To Couzen William and Thomas Mails, one or both living at Sandon, Bedfordshire, £10 apiece. To John Archer my couzen in Queen Street London, Daniel his brother, Jno. Denshaw his nephew, his sister Sarah at Greenwich, £10 apeice. To Mary Hoppy my niece and each of her Children £10 apeice. To George Maynard my godson and Sarah Maynard his Sister, the children of Mr. John Maynard, Virginia merchant in little St. Hellens, London £100 apeice. To Anne and Mary Tuffnell my couzens children of my couzen John Tuffnell late of Bayford co. Hertford £10 apeice. To the Rev. Mr. Affabel Battel and Mr. Thomas Powell, Organist of Dullwich £5 apeice. To Thomas Spicer my Couzen who lately lived with Mr. Siggens of Sacomb £10 and to William Godson 20s. To Johanna Mails my Kinswoman who liveth with me £500. To Mathew Mails living at Statfold in Bedfordshire £100 to have the interest during his life and after his decease to go to his Son Mathew Mails of London. To John the Infant of my Nephew Thomas Archer of Hertford £200 and his Grand Father Newton to be guardian. To these six widows living in Hertford viz., the widow of Robert Gold, Widow Want, Widow Greenel, Widow of John Ulph, Widow Welch at neighbour Sebthorps, Widow Half head, 20s. apeice, and the remainder of my money I give to my kinsman James Mailes and for all my freehold estate I give the same to my said Kinsman James Mailes who now liveth with me and after his death to go to my Nephew Thomas Archer and his heirs male and for want of such to the right heirs of my Father Thomas Archer for ever. Witnesses: Samuel Parrish, R. Battel, Ann Newman. Commission 8 november 1748 to William Burton the surviving executor named in the will of the said James Mailes deceased.

Bolton 1.

JOHN NORTON, Christ church, Surrey, Cordwainer. Will 7 June 1676; proved 22 January 1677-8. To wife Elizabeth best featherbed, bolster &c. To my wife £30 a year out of my tenements which I hold of Esqre Cape situate in the parke to hold to her for the term of the lease. To my wifees Kinsman Nicholas Straine £5. To Nicholas Hoysted my brother in law and father of my Executor £5 and to the wife of the said Nicholas Hoysted £5. To my brother George Norton 20s. To every of the children of the said Nicholas Hoysted 20s. To Katherine Straine my kinswoman £5. To Margery Kempe now in Virginia (couzen of my former wife Margery) in case shee be liveing and come to require the same £5 a year for her life out of the lease of my dwelling house &c. that I hold of Eliz: Primate. To James Griffin at the Barge house I remitt the £10 debt that he oweth me and I give to his wife and Children £10. Residuary legatee

10

and executor: Kinsman John Hoysted. Witnesses: Thomas Rone his mark, Fra: Bunting.

Court of Delegates Register 2 (1670–1681). fo. 234.

[Proved by sentence, not mentioned in Register. In the "Long Acts" for 1676-1677 of the Prerogative Court this will is the subject of contention in case of Norton against Saxby.—L. W.

There were two families of Kempe of early settlement in Virginia, one in Middlesex and Gloucester, and the other in Lower Norfolk and the counties formed from it. William Kempe was living in Virginia in 1624, with his wife Margery and son Anthony, who was born December 12, 1623. He was Burgess for the Upper Parish of Elizabeth City in 1629-30. He was probably ancestor of the Kemps of Princess Anne and Middlesex.—ED.]

WILLIAM WATERS of Northampton County in Virginia. Will 3 July 1720; proved 22 October 1722. To my son William Waters all that plantation wherein I now live and to his heirs and for want of such heirs to ——. My plantation on the North side of Hungers Creek I give to my said son William and to his heirs for ever. To my said son William Gold Seal Ring, Scruetore, chist of Drawers, English Table in Hall Chamber, Looking Glass, Wicker Chair, &c. To said son William all my negroes male and female, except one boy called Amsbury which I give to my Grand Son Thomas the Son of Zerrub^le Preeson and Margaret his Wife. To my Grand Daughter Isabell the Daughter of the said Zerrub^le and Margaret £25 to be laid out in female negroes. To son William Waters all my stock of creatures. To daughter Margaret Preeson a large silver salt marked W ^W I also my white woman servant and her daughter Mary during the time they have to serve me and my servant man John Robins to son William. To Robert Baynton £10. Rest of goods, Tobacco unshipt &c., two thirds to son, one third to Daughter (having had already). To Son William Sloop Isabell, Platt belonging to her, and two Mast Boat. To Son William and Zerrub^le Preeson eight part of Sloop Dolphin. Estate in Gt. Britain to Son and Daughter equally. Executor: Son William Waters. Witnesses: Robert Baynton, James Locker, clerk curate Northampton. Commission 21 October 1757, to Anthony Bacon, administrator of the goods of the said William Waters, the son deceased for the use of William Waters the son of the said William Waters the executor aforesaid now residing at the city of Williamsburg in Virginia, for that the said executor died intestate no residuary legatee being named in the will, and Margaret Kincade formerly Preeson (wife of —— Kincade) daughter and together with the said executor only next of kin of the testator dying without taking out letters of administration.

Marlboro' 205.

[For notes on this family of Waters see this *Magazine* I, 92, 93; II, 179; IX, 210, 428, 429.—ED.]

ANNE MACON, St. Botolph, Algate, London, widow. Will 7 September 1699; proved 3 August 1700. To Mr. Gideon Macon now living in Virginia and to his wife to each of them a ring of 20s. apiece. To Gideon Macon his son my silver tankard &c. To Ann Macon daughter of Gideon Macon the elder my silver porringer. To Martha my six silver spoons. To Mary Elwenn, spinster, all my wearing linen and my best hood &c. To Sarah Freckelton a black flowred silk Petticoate which was her sisters. To Mr. John Baldwin and his wife to each of them 20s. for gloves.

Rest to son in law Robert Freckelton, executor, and I desire my friend Mr. John Baldwin will see this my will executed.

Witnesses: John Shaw, John Goodyer, Ath Lake.

Consistory of London Register Redman (1670–1720) fo. 94.

[Gideon Macon who is believed to have been a Huguenot or of Huguenot descent, was living in New Kent county, Virginia, as early as 1682, and was a member of the House of Burgesses for that county in 1696. His daughter, Martha (named in the will), married, January 31, 1703, Orlando Jones, of King William county, and died May 4, 1716. Their daughter, Frances Jones, born August 6, 1710, married Colonel John Dandridge, and was the mother of Mrs. Martha Washington. Gideon Macon, of North Carolina, father of the distinguished Nathaniel Macon, speaker of the United States House of Representatives, member of the United States Senate, is stated to have been a native of Virginia, and was no doubt a descendant of Gideon Macon named above. See *William and Mary Quarterly*, VI, 33-36; V, 192-197, and *Virginia Historical Society Collections*, XI, 86.—ED.]

RICHARD FRANCIS late of the parish of St. Andrew Holborn, but dying at York Town in the Island of Virginia. Admon. 31

December 1742 to Susannah Francis, relict of deceased.

Ditto, Register Dodson (1720–1751), fo. 88.

JAMES MOIR late of Norfolk in Virginia, Batchelor. Admon.
4 September, 1747 to Robert Moir father of deceased.

Ditto, fo. 176.

EDWARD CHAMBERLAINE, Island of Barbadoes. Will 20 July
1673, proved 13 October 1676. If I die in the Barbadoes I desire my body to be buried in St. Phillips church yard in the said
island near my daughter Butler Chamberlaine and my brother
Captain Richard Chamberlaine. To my wife Mary Chamberlaine
the one third of all my messuages in Barbadoes or in England
for her llfe, and at her death to my two sons Sagrave and Willoughby Chamberlaine, To my two sons my other two thirds
of all my messuages &c. Executors: my wife Mary and my
sons Sagrave and Willoughby Chamberlaine. My wife to manage my whole estate and guard my children till my son Sagrave
be twenty one. My daughter Butler and my daughter Tanquerville to be educated as gentlewomen at some school in England.
My wife to pay my said son Sagrave at the age of twenty one
years £1000, and my said son Willoughby the like sum at twenty
years, my daughter Butler Chamberlaine £2000 at eighteen, and
likewise to my said daughter Tanquerville Chamberlaine £2000
at eighteen. I will that my son Sagrave pay my daughter Butler
£1500 and my son Willoughby pay my daughter Tanquerville
£1500. To my brother William Chamberlaine 10,000 lbs. of
sugar a year. To my nephew John Chamberlaine ditto and the
whole proceed of the negroes and rume &c. I sent with him to
Virginia. To my nephew William Chamberlaine 20,000 lbs. of
sugar at twenty three. To my nephew Marmaduke Chamberlaine 30,000 lbs. of sugar at twenty two. To my niece Susanna
Chamberlaine ditto at twenty two. To my nephew James
Broughton and my niece Ann Broughton 20s. To my nephew
John Leer and my niece Elizabeth his wife 20s. each. To my
brother and sister Gay and to every one of their children 20s.
each. To my mother Butler, my brother George Butler and my
sister Butler his wife, my brother Ramsey and sister Raysey his
wife, my brother Daniell and sister Daniell his wife, 20s. each.

13

To my sons in law George and Robert Green, mourning. Overseers: Friends Colonel Samuell Barwick and Colonel William Sharpe, Mr. John Witham and my brother Mr. George Butler. Witnesses: John Hawkesworth, George Green, Robert Legard, John Witham. Commission 7 October 1695 to Willowby Chamberlaine Esq. brother of Segrave Chamberlaine, late of St. James Garlickhithe, London, deceased.

Commissary of London, Register 1695, fo. 214.

[There is no evidence that the nephew, John Chamberlaine, settled in Virginia. He was probably on a trading voyage.—ED.]

VIRGINIA GLEANINGS IN ENGLAND.

Communicated by Mr. LOTHROP WITHINGTON, 30 Little Russell street, W. C., London (including "Gleanings" by Mr. H. F. WATERS, not before printed.)

(CONTINUED)

HENRY ARMISTEAD, late of Carolina County in Virginia Colony beyond seas, Esq., deceased, a widower. Administration 10 December 1748 to Edward Hunt, attorney of William Armistead, Esq., son of the defunct, now residing in Virginia.

P. C. C. Admon Act Book, 1748.

[Henry Armistead, son of Colonel John Armistead, of Gloucester county, member of the Council, lived on the Pianketank river, Gloucester, at a place called "Hesse." He married Martha (baptized November 16, 1685), daughter of Major Lewis Burwell, the young lady with whom Governor Nicholson was so much infatuated. In 1733 he was sworn county lieutenant of Caroline, and must have resided during the latter portion of his life in that county. He had issue: 1. William, of "Hesse," who married, in 1739, Mary, daughter of James Bowles, of Maryland, and sister of Mrs. Eleanor Gooch–Lewis; 2. Lucy, married Thomas Nelson, of Yorktown, Secretary of Virginia; 3. Martha, married Dudley Digges; 4. Robert. See Armistead genealogy, *William and Mary Quarterly*, Vols. VI, VII, and VIII.].

HUGH BALLANTYNE, late of Henrico County on James River in Virginia, bachelor, deceased. Administration 24 January 1735–6 to his brother George Ballantyne.

Dittto, 1736.

From Vol. XI, No. 1 (July 1903), p. 68.

MATTHIAS JOB BANKS, late of Virginia, but at the Island of Jamaica, deceased. Administration 27 March 1738 to Jonathan Collet, Esq., a creditor, Judith Banks widow the relict being first cited and not appearing, and Hannah Riggs, wife of Richmond Riggs, sister of the defunct, first renouncing.

Ditto, 1738.

THOMAS BAYTOP senior, late in Virginia, widower, deceased. Administration to Daniel Baytop, uncle and guardian of Thomas Baytop a minor son of defunct, 19 January 1691-2. This grant expired at full age of said Thomas Baytop and new grant made 25 September 1699.

Ditto, 1692, folio 5.

[From deeds, &c., recorded in York county, it appears that Thomas Baytop, merchant, emigrated from Staplehurst, Kent, England, in 1679, and settled in Gloucester county, Va. He married Hannah ——, and died in 1690, leaving one child, Thomas Baytop (born 1676), who married ——, daughter Dr. David Alexander, of York county, and has numerous descendants. For a partial account of the family see "Descendants of John Stubbs," by W. C. Stubbs, Ph. D., pp. 95-96.]

SAMUEL BLAYDES, late of Virginia, bachelor, deceased. Administration 27 June 1683 to Richard Booth a creditor.

Ditto, 1683.

RICHARD BRAY, late of Rappahannock River in Island of Virginia. Administration 20 November, 1691 to Elianor Daniell his sister.

Ditto, 1691, folio 201.

[The nuncupative will of Richard Bray was dated April 9, 1690, and proved in Lancaster county in the same month. He leaves most of his property to his widow, Ann. "Then mayest go to England and live like a gentlewoman," "only I give the boy Ned a mare and gun, and some small things to begin with, because I brought him out of his native countrey, and hee farther said he had no Relacon but the boy Ned and a sister that had two daughters, but he said he will give them nothing when he dyed, but they might shift as heed done before them." There is on record in Richmond county a deed dated June 5, 1699, from Edward Bray, of that county, nephew and heir of Richard Bray, deceased, to John King, of Bristol, Eng., mariner. This Edward Bray was, of course, the "Boy Ned," mentioned in the will.]

WILLIAM BRENT, late of Virginia, but in parish of St. James, Clarkenwell Middlesex, deceased. Administration 3 February 1709–10 to his relict Sara Brent.

Ditto, 1710, folio 28.

[William Brent, of "Richland," Stafford county, Va. (son of Giles Brent, of Stafford county, and grandson of Giles Brent, first of Maryland and afterwards of Virginia), fell heir, by the deaths of relatives, to the estates of Stoke and Cossington, Somersetshire, and went to England in 1708 to recover his inheritance. He married, May 12, 1709, Sarah Gibbons, of Box Parish, Middlesex, Eng., daughter of William Gibbons, and sister of Sir John Gibbons, M. P., for Middlesex. William Brent died in England December 26, 1709, and his widow came in January, 1719, to Virginia, where not long afterwards she married Rev. Alexander Scott, of Overwharton Parish, Stafford county. William and Sarah Brent had one child, William Brent, of "Richland," born March 6, 1710, and died 1742, who was ancestor of the family of Brent of "Richland." In September, 1744, the Virginia Assembly passed an act authorizing Peter Hedgman, executor of the younger William Brent, to pay out of the rents and profits of his estate £300 sterling and interest, which had been borrowed by the said William Brent the younger to prosecute an appeal before the Privy Council in England (which had been decided in his favor) for a large parcel of land in the Province of Maryland.

A genealogy of the Brents is contained in the *Richmond Critic.*]

JOHN BRIDGE ALS BRIDGES, lately in Virginia, deceased. Administration 2 March 1637 to George Warren his kinsman.

Ditto, 1636–1638, folio 159.

ROBERT BRISTOW, late of Virginia in America, bachelor, deceased. Administration 10 October 1755 to his sister Rachel Bristow, spinster, James Bristow the father renouncing.

Ditto, 1755.

MILDRED BROOKES, late of Gloucester County in Virginia, spinster, deceased. Administration 11 November 1748 to her brother Thomas Brookes.

Ditto, 1748.

THOMAS BULLEN, late of Virginia, bachelor, deceased. Administration 11 May 1691 to his brot her Arthur Bullen. The warrant says that he died in Virginia three years ago.

Ditto, 1691, f. 77.

ANNE CANDLER, late of Virginia beyond seas, spinster, deceased. Administration 14 December 1733 to her brother John Candler.

Ditto, 1733.

ANNE CHAPMAN, late of Virginia, deceased. Administration 17 August 1716 to John Weeton, attorney for John Chapman now in Virginia, son of the defunct.

Ditto, 1716, folio 156.

WOOLLEY COBB, late of Virginia in America, deceased. Administration 19 December 1732 to his father John Cobb.

Ditto, 1732, folio 273.

GEFFREY FLOWER, late of Virginia beyond seas, bachelor, deceased. Administration 1 February 1725–6 to Noblett Rubock, attorney for Lucie Flower, now in Ireland, mother of the defunct.

Ditto, 1726, folio 21.

[In Abingdon churchyard, Gloucester county, is the tomb of Geffrey or Jeffrey Flower, with arms: *sa. a unicorn pass., or on a chief ar.*, and the following inscription :

" Here Lyeth the Body of
Mr. Jeffrey Flower,
Who departed this Life Sept'br ye 2d, 1726
Aged 38 years."

He died intestate, Peter Whiting being administrator in Virginia.]

JOHN NORBURY, late on the Island of Virginia, bachelor, deceased. Administration 19 August 1748 to his sister Arabella Norbury, spinster.

Ditto 1748.

JOHN CORNELIUS, late of H. M. Ship Colchester, bachelor, deceased. Administration 9 May 1704 to Nicolas Smith, attorney for Isaac Cornelius, now at Virginia, brother of the defunct.

Ditto, 1704, folio 102.

JOHN CORNELISON, late of Virginia, bachelor, deceased. Administration granted 11 November 1682 to Andrew Anderson, principal creditor.

Ditto, 1682.

GEORGE CROSSE, late of Virginia beyond seas, deceased. Administration 18 January 1699–1700 to his relict Sarah Crosse.

Ditto, 1700, folio 12.

JOHN CURTIS, late of Virginia, bachelor, deceased. Administration 14 August 1684 to his brother Alexander Curtis.

Ditto, 1684.

JOSEPH CUSTIS, late in Virginia, deceased. Administration 19 February 1655 to Edward Miles, principal creditor.

Ditto, 1656, folio 38.

JOSEPH DALTON, late at Virginia, deceased, bachelor. Administration 8 July 1720 to his brother Benjamin Dalton.

Ditto, 1720, folio 152.

TERENCE DANIEL, late of Virginia over seas, bachelor, but in Dublin deceased. Administration 11 November 1709 to his cousin (consobrino) Patrick Donnelly.

Ditto, 1709, folio 221.

ISAACK DAVIES, late in Virginia, deceased. Administration 9 December 1658 to Thomas Davies his father.

Ditto, 1658, folio 344.

WILLIAM DURLY late of Nancemond in the County of Nancemond in Virginia, but deceased in St. Martins-in-the-Fields, Middlesex. Administration 13 November 1741 to William Parker, attorney for Mary Durly, the relict, now residing at Nancemond. Second grant 22 December 1753 to James Stockdale, attorney for Mary Durly, the relict, now residing in Virginia, a former grant in November 1741 to William Parker having expired with his death.

Ditto, 1741 and 1753.

ELIZABETH ELKIN, late of Barbadoes, but at Virginia in parts beyond seas, spinster, deceased. Administration 28 August 1752 to her brother John Elkin.

Ditto, 1752.

CATHERINE EVERIGIN, late of the Island of Virginia, spinster. Administration 15 November 1698 to brother William Everigin.

Ditto, 1698, folio 212.

RCHARD FARMER, late of Virginia, but on board the Quaker Ketch on the high seas, bachelor, deceased. Administration 15 May 1689 to Daniel Porter, principal creditor.

Ditto, 1689.

JOHN FOISSIN, late in Virginia, bachelor. Administration 10 December 1694 to Abraham Palmentier, cousin (consobrino.)

Ditto, 1694, folio 225.

SAMUEL FRY, late in Virginia, bachelor. Administration 12 March 1655–6, to Anne Fry, natural lawful mother.

Ditto, 1656, folio 55.

JOHN FREEMAN, late of Virginia in America, bachelor, deceased. Administration 20 July 1739 to his sister Charity Freeman.

Ditto, 1739.

ISAAC GILES, late of Virginia, bachelor, deceased. Administration 10 November 1730 to his sister Rebecca, wife of John Lowe.

Ditto, 1730.

ROBERT GAYLARD of Virginia, bachelor deceased. Administration 24 April 1657 to Mary Gaylard, widow, his mother.

Ditto, 1651.

RICHARD GLOVER, late of Virginia, widdower, deceased at sea in the ship Maryland. Administration 21 August 1684 to his brother Charles Glover.

Ditto, 1684.

[Among other deeds from the same person recorded in Rappahannock county, Va., is one dated June 5, 1677, from Richard Glover, of Farnham Parish, Rappahannock county, gent., conveying 350 acres. Mary, his wife, joins in the deed. October 13, 1670, Richard Glover, citizen and ironmonger of London, appointed John Smith, of Rappahannock in Virginia, his attorney. It is probable that this Richard Glover is the son of the person of the same name, whose widow, Mary, died in 1661. Her will, proved that year, refers to her deceased husband's estate beyond seas. See *Waters's Gleanings*, I, 776. In Thurloe's *State Papers* is mention of a Richard Glover, who traded to Virginia during the Commonwealth and Protectorate.]

WILLIAM GOOCH the younger, late of the Colony of Virginia in the West Indies, Esq., deceased. Administration 10

January 1743–4 to Robert Cary, Attorney for the relict Eleanor Gooch now residing in Virginia.

Ditto, 1744.

[William Gooch, Jr., son of Sir William Gooch, Bart., Governor of Virginia, married Eleanor, daughter of James Bowles, of Maryland. Mrs. Eleanor Gooch married, secondly, Warner Lewis, of "Warner Hall," Gloucester county.]

THOMAS GOODRICH, late of Virginia, infant. Administration 20 November 1703 to Sir Abstrupus Danby, Knight, uncle by mother's side and next of kin.

Ditto, 1703, folio 211.

[Sir Abstrupus Danby, of Masham, Yorkshire, was Knighted at Kingston, August 30, 1691, and was M. P. for Alborow 1699. He was son of Christopher Danby, of Farnley, Yorks., and Anne, daughter of John Culpeper (brother of the first Lord). Sir Abstrupus Danby married Judith, daughter of Abraham Moon, of London, merchant. She died January 15, 1702, and was buried at Masham Church (Le Neve's *Book of Knights*).

An Abraham Moon settled in Lancaster county before 1654, bringing with him his wife Ann, and died in 1655. His only child and heir is stated in the records to have been Mrs. Elizabeth Hazlewood, who died without issue. See this Magazine, V, 252. There were two families of Goodrich settled in Virginia at an early date, one in Rappahannock and the other in Isle of Wight; but the Thomas Goodrich of the text has not been identified.]

JOHN GOSWELL, late of Virginia in America, bachelor, deceased. Administration 10 September 1734 to his sister Elizabeth Goswell, spinster.

Ditto, 1734.

THOMAS HAYWARD, late of Rivo Rapahanack in Virginia, but in ship William and Mary on high seas, bachelor, deceased. Administration 8 October 1698 to Charity Britton als Hayward, wife of John Britton and relict of Thomas Hayward, defunct, mother of defunct.

JOHN HAYWARD, ditto, bachelor. Administration ditto.

Ditto, 1698, folio 184.

JOHN HILL, formerly of Virginia over seas, but late of Newent in Gloucester. Administration to Gravell Smither, sister's son and next of kin, 30 March 1720.

Ditto, 1720.

MARY HOOKER, late in the Island of Virginia, deceased. Administration 12 October 1682 to Oliver Gregory, cousin (consobrino) of the deceased.

Ditto, 1682.

THOMAS HUBBARD, late of Virginia beyond seas, bachelor, deceased. Administration 20 September 1697 to brother Edward Hooker.

Ditto, 1697, folio 161.

CHARLES HUTTON, late of Plexen in Virginia, bachelor, deceased. Administration 8 September 1722 to his nephew (ex fratre) John Hutton, Jane Hutton, mother of the defunct, having first renounced.

Ditto, 1722, folio 188.

MARTHA JONES als IRONMONGER, late wife of John Jones senior, deceased, late of Virginia. Administration 29 November 1681 to Elizabeth Evernden als Ironmonger, wife of Anthony Evernden, aunt by the mother's side of John Jones junior, now beyond the seas, son of the deceased.

Administration (same date) on estate of ANNE RUMNEY als IRONMONGER deceased granted to ditto, natural sister. Deceased described as of St. Botolph's Bishopgate, widow.

Administration (same date) on CORDEROY IRONMONGER, late of Virginia, bachelor, deceased, to ditto, natural sister of deceased.

Ditto, 1681.

[A deed from Mordecai Cooke, of Gloucester county, dated September 27, 1786, recorded in Westmoreland county, recites that William Ironmonger, of Gloucester, by his will dated August 30, 1695, left his land in Potomac Neck to John, son of Mordecai Cooke, and father of Mordecai Cooke, party to this deed. The land in question contained 600 acres.

On July 2, 1652, Mrs. Anne Bernard obtained a grant of 1,000 acres in Gloucester, at the head of Jones's creek. The headrights were: "Mr. Richard Barnett [Bernard], Mrs. Anna Barnett, Ellinor Corderoy, Eliza Barnett, Corderoy Barnett, Richard Barnett, Wm. Corderoy, Edw'd Corderoy, Wm. Ironmonger, Fra. Ironmonger, Eliza Ironmonger," and nine others.

In Chester's *London Marriage Licenses* is given the license for "Richard Bernard, of Petsoe, Bucks, Gent., widower, aged 26 years," to marry "Anna Corderoy, aged 22, daughter of —— Corderoy, Esq., at St. Andrew's in the Wardrobe."

There is in Lancaster county a deed, dated January 1, 1665, from William Ironmonger, of Gloucester county, conveying the plantation in Lancaster, where the said Ironmonger lately lived.

Elizabeth, his wife, relinquishes dower and appoints her brother, Mr. Robert Jones, her attorney for the purpose.]

GEORGE KNIGHT, late of Virginia, bachelor, deceased. Administration 23 May 1684 to his sister Frances Bayley als Knight, now wife of Charles Bayley.

Ditto, 1684.

MARY KNIGHT of Virginia. Administration 26 June 1686 to Catherine Shawe als Knight wife of Richard Shawe, not admonished by Elizabeth Knight natural mother, also deceased. Former grant June, 1685.

Ditto, 1686, folio 102.

ADEN LEY, ESQ., late of York Town in Virginia and Captain of Colonel Marge's regiment of Foot at Goree, deceased. Administration 28 May 1762 to his relict Mary Ley.

Ditto, 1762.

ELIZABETH LLOYD als CARTER, lately in Richmond, Virginia. Administration 19 October 1694 to John Lloyd, gent, husband, &c.

Ditto, 1694, folio 201.

[John Lloyd, of Richmond county, was J. P. for that county in 1692, and in 1693 was recommended to the English government as a gentleman of estate and standing suitable for appointment to the Council. He married about 1693 Elizabeth, only child and heiress of Col. John Carter, Jr., of Lancaster county. Mrs. Lloyd only lived a short time, and died without issue. In 1694, her husband was appointed administrator of her father's estate. John Lloyd returned to England about 1700, and there is on record in Richmond county, Va., a power of attorney from him, as "John Lloyd of the City of Chester, Esq.," to his "worthy kinsman," Griffin Fauntleroy, of Virginia. He was son of Colonel William Lloyd, of Rappahannock county, Va. See this Magazine, II, 235-238, V, 160-161.]

THOMAS LUCAS JUNIOR, late of Virginia, bachelor, deceased. Administration 7 July 1675 to John Lucas, cousin and next of kin.

Ditto, 1675.

[On October 6, 1675, Thomas Hawkins, of Rappahannock county, obtained a grant of 2,611 acres on the south side of the Rappahannock river, including a tract of 1,676 acres, on which Mr. Thomas Lucas, Sr., and Mr. Thomas Lucas, Jr., had lived and died, and the latter leaving no heir, the land was found to escheat. This Lucas, Sr., gent., patented 600 acres in Lancaster county in 1652, was Burgess for Rappahannock 1657-8, and died in 1673. His will, proved March 14, 1673, names only one son, Thomas Lucas, who doubtless was the person named in the text. See this Magazine, I, 36, 61, 62.]

ROBERT MILWARD, late of Yanoak juxta Swinnards Bay, James River in Virginia, bachelor, deceased. Administration 8 July 1718 to Marmaduke Carver, principal creditor, Mary Dudley wife of John Dudley and Anne Gilbert wife of Wm. Gilbert, sisters of defunct, first renouncing.

Ditto, 1718, folio 134.

JAMES NEDHAM, lately in parts of Virginia overseas, bachelor. Administration 14 January 1677 to George Nedham, Esq., brother and next of kin, as to goods unadministered by Barbara Nedham, his mother, now also deceased. Prior grant February last.

Ditto, 1678, folio 3.

EDWARD NOWELL, late at Virginia, bachelor, deceased. Administration 26 July 1689 to Elizabeth Quint, attorney for Edward Nowell, now in Cornwall, father of deceased.

Ditto, 1689, folio 113.

TOBIAS NORTON, late in Virginia, deceased. Administration 13 December 1658 to Joane Norton his widow.

Ditto, 1658.

ANNE PARSONS, late of Virginia, spinster, deceased upon the high seas. Administration 28 November 1702 to her brother Thomas Parsons.

Ditto, 1702, folio 215.

NATHANIEL RHODES, late of Virginia, bachelor, deceased. Administration 18 September 1697 to his brother James Rhodes, his mother Ester Rhodes, widow, renouncing.

Ditto, 1697, folio 166.

REV. MOSES ROBERTSON, late of the parish of St. Michael in county Northumberland in Virginia, America, deceased. Administration 15 April 1752 to Newton Keene, guardian of John Willoughby Robertson, a minor, one of the children of the deceased, for his use, as well as for the use of Moses Robertson and Frances Robertson, infants, the other children of the said deceased, Susannah Robertson, widow, the relict, dying without having taken administration.

Ditto, 1752.

[Sarah Willoughby, of Norfolk county, daughter of Thomas Willoughby, in her will dated January 19, 1738, makes a bequest to her cousin (nephew), John Willoughby Robertson, son of Rev. Moses Robertson, of St. Stephen's Parish, Northumberland county. Rev. Moses Robertson was minister of St. Stephen's 1743 1752.]

GEORGE REEVE, late of Virginia. Administration 23 April 1689 to brother Charles Reeve.

Ditto, 1689.

[GEORGE REEVES, of the Island of Virginia, Merchant, now residing in England. Will 1 November 1675; proved 26 April 1689. Executor to pay to now wife £500, as by obligation of even date in £1,000 to James Johnson of St. Sepulchers, London, Gent, and James Cary, Citizen and Salter. Rest to such children as I may have by said wife, and, in case, I have no children, then to my brother Charles Reeves, executor. Witnesses: James Johnson, Jo. Jackson, James Cary, John Midgley, Scr. Proved by executor, previous administration as intestate being annulled. Ent. 53.—L. W.

There is an entry in the Middlesex records of a suit in 1697 by John Curtis and Frances his wife, administrator of Erasmus Withers, vs· Charles Reeves executor of George Reeves, who was administrator of Frances Reeves.

In Middlesex county on April 2, 1689, the will of Mr. George Reeves, Jr., was presented for probate, but Captain Oswald Cary, Mr. Christopher Robinson, and Mr. Henry Wareing, the executors named in the will, disavowing the execution thereof, the sheriff was ordered to summon witnesses to more fully prove it. No further action appears, but not long afterwards Phebe, widow of George Reeves, who had married Lieutenant John Smith, of Middlesex, was appointed administratrix.

By deed recorded in Middlesex and dated September 20, 1707, Charles Reeves, of the parish of Stepney, and county of Middlesex, England, heir to George Reeves, of Virginia, deceased, conveyed to Gawin Corbin, of Middlesex county, Va., gentleman, 500 acres, patented by John

Appleton in October, 1664, and by him sold to Thomas Reeves, and from the last named descended to Frances and George Reeves, and now to the above named Charles Reeves, surviving heir.

George Reeves was for a number of years a resident of Middlesex county.]

HENRY ROSSE, late of Potomack River in Virginia, widower, deceased. Administration 15 August 1700 to his sister Eunice Thistelwheate, widow.

Ditto, 1700, folio 170.

JONATHAN SAUNDERS, clerk, late minister or rector of the parish of Lenhaven in Princess Anne county in Virginia, deceased. Administration 15 December 1702 to Jonathan Matthews, attorney for the relict Mary Boush als Saunders, now wife of Maximilian Boush, now in Virginia. [Intestate died 2 years ago. See warrant.]

Ditto, 1702, folio 243.

[Rev. Jonathan Saunders was minister of Lynhaven Parish, Princess Anne county, in 1695. On March 6, 1700-1, his widow, Mary (who had before been the widow of Thomas Ewell), qualified as his administratrix, he dying intestate. She was married a third time to Maximilian Boush. We are indebted to Edward Wilson James, of Norfolk, for the following abstract of the will of John Saunders, mariner, son of Rev. Jonathan Saunders. It is of record in Princess Anne county :

Will made Feb'y 16, 1733-4, recorded June 5th, 1734. Capt. John Saunders To wife Mary two negroes George & Jurien; to daughter Mary negro woman Nell and child Roben; to son Johnnathan negro woman Benebo and child Issaker; to dafter Margret negroes Jude & Tone; to child my wife is bearing negro Isble; to son Johnnathan the mannood plantation I live on 250 acres and the plantation formerly called Joseph Smiths 100 acres, and "Seaven acres of Land which is in England in Isseks" [Essex]; also half a dozen Silver Spoons & a quart Tankard, also one dozen of Silver Spoons between my two Dafters Mary & Margret Saunders. To dafters each a feether bed & firniture; to Son Johnnathan the large Looking Glass. The remainder of his estate after his debts had been paid to his wife. Wife & Arthr Sawer "Execkutors." From Princess Anne County records.]

VIRGINIA GLEANINGS IN ENGLAND.

Communicated by Mr. LOTHROP WITHINGTON, 30 Little Russell street, W. C., London (including "Gleanings" by Mr. H. F. WATERS, not before printed.)

(CONTINUED)

JOHN SANDFORD, late of the Island of Virginia, deceased. Administration 1 June 1704 to William Sandford jun'r, guardian of John Sandford, a minor, son of the deceased.

Admon. Act Book, 1704, folio 128.

[A John Sandford, who was born about 1649, patented several tracts of land, amounting in all to 3,297 acres, between 1675 and 1688. He was a justice of the first court of Princess Anne county in 1691. On March 1, 1692–3, administration on his estate was granted to his widow Sarah. He was a merchant, and in 1673 had given a power of attorney to his brother Samuel Sanford, merchant. Dorothy Tucker, of Exeter, England, widow, by her will dated May 13, 1693, and proved in the Archdeaconry Court of Exeter, June 30, of the same year, left certain houses to her brother John Sandford, of Virginia. On February 6, 1694-'5, Mrs. Sarah Sandford, above mentioned, through her attorney, her brother Henry Woodhouse, confirmed deed of gift to her sons Cowson and Henry and daughter Sarah. See *William and Mary Quarterly* IV, 15–17. Of course there is no positive proof that this John Sandford is identical with the person of the same name whose administration is given above.]

JOHN SAYER, lately in Island of Virginia. Administration 10 March 1685–6 to Thomas Arnall, principal creditor.

Ditto, 1686, folio 50.

JOHN SCRIMGEOUR, late Rector of Rectory of Nominie in county Westmorland in Virginia, bachelor, deceased. Administration 9 January 1692–3 to William Scrimgeour, natural brother and heir.

Ditto, 1693, folio 12.

[On account of the loss of all the church records of Westmoreland, Bishop Meade was unable to give the names of the early ministers. The administration of the Rev. John Scrimgeour supplies one name.]

From Vol. XI, No. 2 (Oct. 1903), p. 144.

ROBERT SHARPE late of Rappahannock River in Virginia, but at Stepney, Middlesex, deceased. Administration 20 October 1666 to his brother Abraham Sharpe.

Ditto, 1666, folio 190.

THOMAS SHARPE, late in Virginia deceased. Administration 26 March 1677-8 to Hugh Noden, principal creditor.
[These letters brought back and renounced and new grant April 1679.] Ditto, 1678, folio 31.

WILLIAM SHORTRIKE, late in the Yorke Old Fields in Virginia deceased. Administration 21 June 1669 to his relict Rachel Melton als Shortrike, now wife of Anthony Melton.

Ditto, 1669, folio 62.

REV. WILLIAM SKELTON, clerk, late of Virginia in America, but deceased in St. Andrew Wardrobe, London. Administration 17 August 1739 to his relict Sarah Skelton.

Ditto, 1739.

WILLIAM SWALE, late of the City of Chichester, but deceased at Virginia in America. Administration 20 November 1734 to his sister Elizabeth Howson, widow, ——— Swale, the relict, dying before taking out administration.

Ditto, 1734.

ANDREW THOMSON, late of the City and County of Elizabeth in Virginia, bachelor, deceased. Administration 9 April 1724 to his brother Alexander Thomson, M. D.

Ditto, 1724, folio 86.

[Perhaps the person whose administration is here given is the same as Rev. Andrew Thompson, whose tomb, formerly on "Pembroke" farm near Hampton, the site of the early church of Elizabeth City, has now been removed to the churchyard of St. John's, Hampton. The inscription is as follows:

" Here lyeth the Body of the
Reverend Mr. Andrew Thompson
who was born at Stone hive in
Scotland & was minister of this
Parish seven years and departed
this life the 11th of September 1719
in ye 46th year of His Age, bearing
the character of a sober Religious
Man."]

27

JOHN TOULSON, late of Ackamack, Virginia, bachelor. Administration 9 September 1656 to his brother Wm. Toulson.

Ditto, 1656.

[John Toulson, or Towlson as the name was then spelt, appears from the records of old Accomack, now at Northampton Courthouse, to have been a prosperous carpenter, ship builder and farmer. On October 25, 1637 there is an order for him to view and report on certain work. In 1638 is reference to a pinnace he had built and in which he had a half interest. On September 20, 1641, a certificate that he was entitled to patent 450 acres of land. There is a power of attorney dated February 7, 1641, from John Towlson, of Accomack, carpenter, to Thos. Cooke, of the same, gentleman. In 1642 it is stated that he had always been a resident in the house of Captain William Stone, afterwards governor of Maryland.]

MARIA TOWNSEND, late of Newton or Higham Ferrers in county Northampton, widow, but at Virginia deceased. Administration 7 November 1694 to Geoffrey Jeffreys, Esq. and John Jeffreys, Esq. principal creditors.

Ditto, 1694, folio 205.

[Mary, or Maria, Townshend, was widow of Colonel Robert Townshend, of Stafford county, Va. (who died in 1675), and daughter of Needham Langhorne, of Newton Brownshall, Northamptonshire, England. After her husband's death she resided for a time in England, and there is on record in Virginia a power of attorney from her dated at Newton Brownshall. Colonel Robert and Mary Townshend had issue, to survive, two daughters: 1. Mary, who married John Washington, Jr., son of Lawrence Washington, the immigrant, and has many descendants; 2. Frances, married (I) Francis Dade of Stafford county, and has many descendants; (II) Captain John Withers, no issue, it is believed, by this marriage, though Captain Withers had a daughter and heiress, who in 1699, was the wife of Richard Fossaker, of Stafford county; (III) in 1699, Rice Hooe, and has many descendants. See *Virginia Magazine of History and Biography*, IX, 173, 174; IV, 427-429; Hayden's *Virginia Genealogies*, 516-522, 731-734, 716-719.

In the visitation of Hertfordshire, 1634 (Harleian Society), is a pedigree of "Langhorne of Bedford," which begins with William Langhorne, of Bedford [born about 1560], whose eldest son was Robert—marriage or descendants not given—and whose second son William, was father of William Langhorne, of the Middle Temple, 1634, who married Lettice, daughter of Eustace Needham, of Little Wymondley, Hertfordshire. In the same visitation is the pedigree of Needham, of Little Wymondley and Wilwyn, from which it appears that John Needham, of Wymondley (of the third generation in the pedigree), had a daughter Margaret, who married Robert Langhorne, of Bedford, and a granddaughter, Lettice, as above, who married William Langhorne. Doubtless Needham Langhorne was a descendant of Robert or William.]

RICHARD WALSH, late of Virginia in the West Indies, deceased. Administration 23 April 1742 to his relict Mary Walsh.
Ditto, 1742.

ALEXANDER WHITAKER, crossing the seas to Virginia. Will 16 February 1610; proved 4 August 1617. Sister Susanna Lothrop £5. I owe Christopher Levite, a linen draper of the city of York, £5. 1. 0. Cosen Anthony Culverwell owes me £16. Cosen Mr. William Gouge, clark of Blackfryars, overseer. Brother Samuel Whitaker £24 and all moveables and sole executor. Sister Marie Clarke, wife of Reindolph (?) Clarke, £5. Brother William Whitaker £5. Sister Francis Whitaker £5. Brother Jabez Whitaker £5. Needy poor £5. Cosen William Gouge £2 to buy him self either a ring or books. Brother Samuel and his heirs my bill of adventure to Virginia. Witnesses: Richard Culverwell, Caleb Gowge.

Commissary of London, Reg. 23, folio 75. Also registered in Weldon, 95.

[Alexander Whitaker, "the Apostle to Virginia," was born at Cambridge in 1585, was M. A. of that University about 1604, and had a good parish in the north of England, but gave it up to become a missionary to Virginia. He came to the colony with Dale in 1611, was preacher at Henrico in 1612 and later, living in 1614 at his parsonage, Rock Hall, on the south side of James river, in what is now the county of Chesterfield; was minister of Bermuda Nether Hundred in 1616, and was drowned before June, 1617. He is commonly stated to have baptized and married Pocahontas; but Mr. Brown thinks the Rev. Mr. Bucke performed the latter ceremony. Whitaker, however, appears to have been a friend of John Rolfe, and there is really no positive evidence as to who was the minister on the two occasions referred to.

Alexander Whitaker was the leading minister of Virginia in his day, and it is worthy of note that he belonged to the early Puritan section of the Church of England. It may be suggested, in passing, that possibly the "low church" type, which has always prevailed in the Episcopal Church in Virginia, may have originated in the form of belief held by one who was so largely instrumental in founding the established church in the colony.

Mr. Whitaker was son of Rev. William Whitaker, D. D. (1548–1595), the eminent Puritan divine and master of St. John's College, Cambridge, who was a son of Thomas Whitaker, of Holme, Lancashire, and his wife, Elizabeth, a sister of Alexander Nowell, Dean of St. Paul's. All of the connections of the family were strongly Puritan in belief. The first wife of Dr. William Whitaker, and the mother of Alexander Whitaker, was a daughter of Nicholas Culverwell, merchant, of London. Her brothers, Ezekiel and Samuel Culverwell, were noted Puritan preachers. Her sisters were Cecilia, who married Lawrence Chaderton, Master of Emanuel College, Cambridge, also a noted Puritan, and ————, who married Thomas Gouge, and was mother of Rev. William Gouge, D. D., likewise a distinguished Puritan divine.

Dr. William Whitaker married, secondly, the widow of Dudley Fenner, a Puritan, who died in exile.

Whitaker's "Good News from Virginia," published in London in 1613, was one of the first books written in Virginia. It has never been entirely reprinted, though portions are given in Brown's *Genesis* and Neill's *Virginia Company*.

Purchas printed in his "Pilgrimes," "Part of a tractate written at Henrico in Virginia by Master Alexander Whitaker, Minister to the Colony there, which was governed by Sir T. Dale 1613." A letter dated Jamestown, August 9, 1611, from Alexander Whitaker, to Rev. William Crashaw, was printed in the *Richmond Standard* February 4, 1882, and reprinted in Neill's *Virginia Vetusta*. Another letter from him, written in 1614, and addressed to his cousin "M. G." (*i. e.*, "Master Gouge," Rev. Wm. Gouge), is appended to Hamor's "True Relation." Mr. Neill, without any reason, doubts the genuineness of this letter.

There can be no doubt that the brother of Jabez Whitaker, named in the will, was Captain Jabez Whitaker, who was a member of the Virginia House of Burgesses in 1623 and of the Council in 1626, and married a daughter of Sir John Bourchier. William Whitaker, who was Burgess for James City, 1649–1659, and chosen member of the Council in the last year, may have been of this family.]

WILLIAM BEARD. Will 20 December 1636; proved 27 October 1646. To my poor dear sister in Rye, Dorothy Beard, 40 s the year for life. To my sister Docke in Rye 20 s. To a new church at James Cittie in Virginia five hundred waight of tobacco. To my wicked wife, Margarett Beard, £5. To Mr. Kempe, the King's secretary, my nest of boxes. To Lawrence Mones my best cloke and £5. My servants to have all my clothes, &c. Executor, Mr. Alexander Chill, merchant, at Billingsgate in London, to pay all my debts here in Virginia, which is to the estate of Thomas Crowe £13, &c. Overseers:

Mr. William Barker, Mr. William Swan, Mr. Edward Sherly, and to each three hundred waight of tobacco. To Joves Mones and Elizabeth Mones a spoon apiece. Witnesses: Thomas Baryhard, Thomas Locke.

Twisse, 140.

[The new church referred to was the first one entirely of brick built at Jamestown. It is believed that the substantial foundations now to be seen adjoining the tower at Jamestown are those of this "new church." "Mr. Kemp, the King's secretary," was Richard Kemp, secretary of State of Virginia. William Barker, mariner, was one of the proprietors of Martin's Brandon. William Swan was the immigrant ancestor of a well known family in Virginia and North Carolina.]

NATHANIEL BRADDOCK, citizen and mercer of London, bound on a voyage to Virginia in parts beyond the seas in the good ship called the Merchant Hope of London. Will 10 July 1635; proved 31 May, 1636. Whereas my brother-in-law John Rooke standeth bound to me for payment of threescore pounds of 1 January ensueing the death of my father John Braddock, out of said sum I give to John Rooke, son of said John, £20, to be put out till his age of 21. To John More, son of my brother Valentine More, £20 at 21 to remain in the hands of my executor, he paying to Susanna Moore, mother of the said John, 32 s. per annum; if he die, then to sister Susan More for life, then to John Rooke the son. To my brother John Braddocke £5 and £5 to my sister Rebecca Braddocke. Rest of said threescore pounds to brother-in-law John Rooke. Residuary legatees: my brother John Braddocks, sisters Sara Rooke, Rebecca Braddock, and Susann Moore. Executor: Brother-in law John Rooke. Witnesses: Robert Hanson, scrivenor, William Salesbury, Barnard Osler, his servants.

Pile, 55.

[In Hotten's "Emigrants" in the list of passangers in the ship Merchant Hope, which left England for Virginia in January, 1635, appears the name of "Nat. Braddock," aged 31.]

GEORGE BARTLETT of London, citizen and Pavior. Will 31 January 1659–60; proved 22 March 1659–60. My daughter-in-law Elizabeth Westcoate now residing in Virginia. Mary Taylor, daughter of William Bartlett, deceased. My cosen Mary Bartlett, daughter of Thomas Bartlett, deceased. Elizabeth Ambler, widow, executrix. Her son George Ambler. Overseers: my loving friends Mr. George Hooper and Mr. John Braynte.

Nabbs, 5.

JOHN BEDFORD of York Hampton Parish, Virginia late of Stepney, county Middlesex. Will 4 December 1708; proved 13 September 1716. Sole legatee and executrix: wife Mary Bedford. Witnesses: Robert Harrison, John Lester.

Fox, 174.

[In the records of York county, Va., appears the indentures, dated March 24, 1695–6, of Mourning Cooper with John Bedford. John Bedford was appointed headborough for Hampton parish May 25, 1696.]

JOHN TAYLOR of Knightsbridge, Westminster, bricklayer. Will 20 April 1641; proved 31 May 1641. Sister Elizabeth wife of Thomas Slye and her children. Sister Jane Taylor. Son Samuel Taylor now in Virginia and his wife Mary and daughter Elizabeth. Daughter Dennis wife of Thomas Grover. Daughter Elizabeth wife of Nicholas Broadway.

Evelyn, 52.

JOHN ATKINS the elder of Chard, Somerset, merchant. Will 16 July 1636; proved 18 November 1636. To be buried in the churchyard of Chard. To the parish church of Chard 6 s. 8d., to the poor of same 10 s. To Edward Atkins my eldest son and heir certain rooms, parcell of my now dwelling house in Chard. To wife Katherine during her widowhood rest of said dwelling house. To said Edward Atkins and heirs all those my goods mentioned in the schedule which are to remain in my said dwelling house forever, and wife to have use during widowhood. Said Edward Atkins my son to pay unto Francis Atkins my son 40 s. To William Atkins my son one feather bed &c. To Hannah Ford my daughter my best silver bole and 5 s. To Elizabeth Smith my daughter 5 s. &c. and all other my goods in my dwelling house in Old Chard now in occupation of John Key. To John Atkins my grandchild son of John Atkins my son who was born in Virginia, if living, £100, but if he come not to England or die before 21, then to Edward, William and Francis my sons. To son Edward Atkins and William Atkins

£40 each and to son Francis £160. To Edward James, my son-in-law £10. To Thomas Atkins, Robert Atkins, and Nicholas Atkins, my brothers, 40 s. apiece. To Sara Selwood my sister £5. To Elizabeth Webb my sister-in-law 20 s. To William Lea of Winslade, county Devon, gent, William Atkins the elder my brother, and Gilbert Drake my brother-in-law £130 for the use of my daughter Katherine Wills, if she survive her husband, if not then to her child or children at 21 or marriage. To son Edward and William Atkins £30 for the use of the poor of Chard. Overseers: brother William Atkins the elder, Gilbert Drake, and Abraham Furser. Residuary legatee and executrix: wife Katherine. Witnesses: Raphe Owsleyes, William Legg, Thomas Pitts, scrivenor.

Pile, 110.

ROBERT BELL, citizen and skinner of London. Will 16 January 1656–7; proved 16 February 1656–7. To be buried in parish church of St. John Baptist, London, near my wife. To my brother John Bell £5, and to every one of his three daughters £20 at 21 or marriage. Whereas I purchased of William Burges, gentleman, certain old tenements in Hounsditch, London, which are since demolished and upon which ground I have built four new houses and out of the same have secured an annuitie of £34 unto my mother-in-law Elizabeth Bidwell during her life, now I give the overplus of the said rents to my brother John Bell for the education of his son and my nephew John Bell the younger and to his heirs forever. To so many of the children of my deceased sister Amy Atkins, late wife of Richard Atkins, as are living when I die £10 at 21 or marriage. To said mother Elizabeth Bidwell £10. To my kinswoman Philadelphia Bickley, daughter of my cousin Anne Bickley, £20. To my kinsman Francis Bickley, son of my said cosen Anne (now at Virginia) £20. To friend Mr. Laurence Withers £10. To friend Mr. Francis August my liverie gown and hood and to him and his wife £15. To Mr. Edward Gregorie, scrivenor, and his wife £15. To their son Edward Gregorie the younger £20. To my aunt Mary Terry of Ansford county Kent £10. To friend Edward Higgins of Deptford £10. To my wife's goddaughter Mary Cox and her brother John Cox, children of my friend Mr.

Peter Cox, vintner, £20. To godson Robert Beale, son of friend Robert Beale, dyer, £10. To the wife of said Robert Beale the elder £5. To my late servant Edward Mitchell £10. To Mr. Witham, minister of said parish, £5. To John Wild, D. D., £10. To friend Stephen Turner, merchant, £5. To Mary the wife of Jethro Chelsham, vintner, £5. To the following friends a ring, viz: Deputie Charles Mynne, Captain Tasker, Mr. Thomas Rose, Captain Henry Creech, Mr. Robert West, Mr. Francis Carpenter, Mr. Richard Carpenter, Mr. Daniel Belt, Mr. Thomas Boyleston, Mr. William Jarary (?), Mr. Robert Beale, Mr. Mathew Bellingrock, Mr. Peter Cox, Mr. Robert Story, Mr. James Blackaby, Doctor Croydon, Mr. Christopher Stacy (?), Mr. Samuel Reeve, Mr. Thomas Hackett, and Mr. Pennant of Skinners' Hall. To the poor of Wandsford in the parish of Stibbington, county Huntingdon, where I was born, £5. Whereas I took letters of administration of the goods of my deceased uncle Humphry Bell for the use of his daughter Anne Bickley, I desire my executor to be ayding to my said kinswoman. Residuary legatee and executor: Mr. Richard Chapman of Bread Street, London, Silkeman. Witnesses: Richard Bates, Stephen Turner, Edward Mitchell, Mary Vallence, Edward Gregory, scrivenor.

Ruthen, 72.

[Though the name Francis appears frequently in the family of Bickley, of Attleborough, baronets, the one named in this will cannot be identified. In Chester's *Marriage Licenses, Westm. and Vic. Genl.* is given the license, dated July 24, 1693, for the marriage of Nevill Hall, of Kennington, Kent, Gent., aged 22, and Mrs. Philadelphia Bickley, aged 20, of Great St. Bartholomew, London, both parents dead.

Joseph Bickley, fourth son of Sir Francis Bickley, Bart., came to Virginia before 1703, and his eldest son William succeeded to the title. In the announcement of his death in 1771, the *Virginia Gazette* calls him Sir William Bickley, Bart. The title as now vested in the heirs of Sir William's son Joseph who removed to Tennessee in 1820.

In the calendar of the House of Lords Manuscripts, 1643–47, published with the Sixth Report of the Royal Commission on Historical Manuscripts, are several petitions from Anne Bickley, widow of John Bickley, late of London, draper. On February 17, 1643–'4, she states that by order of September 9th preceding, the estate of her deceased husband had been "sequested into the hands of Sir John Nulls, for payment of debts and the maintenance of herself & children."

In January, 1644-'5, Nulls expressed a wish to be released from the business, and Mrs. Bickley petitioned that her father Humphrey Bell, and Levinus Hopper might be appointed trustees in his stead.]

RICHARD ATTERBURY of London, fishmonger (apparently resident in Virginia). Will 24 July 1637; proved 28 June 1638. To brother Stephen Atterbury, 20s for a ring. To brother Francis Atterbury, £10. To brother in law Thurstone Tone, 20s for a ring. To my sister Mary Toone, Dorothie Atterbury, and Elizabeth Atherbury, wife of Francis Atterbury, rings. To friend John Robins of the back River, planter, 500 waight of tobacco. Overseer: John Robins. Rest to brother William Atterbury of London, grocer, executor, except as follows: To Elizabeth Atterbury of Milton, two small siluer shallops; to Mary Toone of Coling, trough, one purse, and pinpillowe; to my sister Dorothie, one siluer seale and one small Ring with a Rubie Diamond Cutt almost fower square wch Mr. Neale did take to Accomacke to mend for me. A true coppie of original remayning proved in Virginia. Test. E. Horsell.

Lee, 71.

[John Robins, who was appointed overseer of the will, came to Virginia in 1622, and settled in Elizabeth City county, which he represented in the House of Burgesses in 1646. He was ancestor of the Gloucester and King William family of the name. See this MAGAZINE, II, 187 and 316.]

WILLIAM AYLWARD late of Virginia, merchant. Will 6 November 1701; proved 20 February 1706-7. All estate in England and Virginia to friend Mr. Robert Cary, living in Watling streete, London, executor. Witnesses: Edward Garrett, Elizabeth Lane, William Scorey, not. pub. [Probate Act Book says "late of Virginia, merchant, but in the Kingdom of France, bachelor, deceased"].

Poley 24.

JOHN ATKINS of Virginia. Will 3 September 1623; proved 2 October 1624. To be buried in vsuall buryinge place by James Citty. Whereas I stand indebted to seuerall persons heare in Virginia as in England, and there is owinge to me in this country about 6000 waight of tobacco this cropp for goods sould, as by my booke of Accompts, &c. Now I entreate Mr. Luke Boyse of the neck of land to administer, gather in Cropp, satisfie debts in this country, and send into England enough for creditors there. As to rest of estate I remitte to Mr. Luke Boyse what he is indebted. To Peter Stafferton all household stuffe except one wainscott chaire to Mr. Davison. To Mr. Christopher Davison, 100 waight of tobacco, and remitt what he owes. Am covenant with Peter Stafferton for 1000 weight of tobacco this cropp and one third my Cropp of corne. Rest to brother William Attkins, dwelling neare the Beare in Bassinghall. Witnesses: Christopher Davison, Peter Stafferton. Vera Copia. Ed. Sharples, cleric. Administration to brother William Atkins. Administration 28 August 1626 to brother Richard Atkins, during minor estate of Elizabeth, George, Anne, and Lee Atkins, children of William Atkins, deceased, administrator. 1 June 1627 administration to brother Humfrey Atkins on estate of John Atkins deceased over seas left unadministered by brother Richard Atkins, now also deceased.

Byrde, 84.

[Luke Boyse came to Virginia in 1619 and was a member of the House of Burgesses in 1623-'4. Peter Stafferton was a member of the House of Burgesses for Elizabeth City in 1639. Christopher Davison was secretary of State of the colony. Edward Sharpless was the clerk of the council, who was sentenced to have his ears cut off for showing the records of the Burgesses and Council to the three commissioners, who in 1624, had been sent over to Virginia by the King to oppose the Virginia Company.]

ANNE ASHTON late at Virginia, deceased. Administration 31 August 1704 to her husband Charles Ashton.

Admon Act Book 1704, folio 168.

[Ann Ashton, whose maiden name is believed to have been Burdett, was the first wife of Charles Ashton, who was a member of the House of Burgesses for Westmoreland county, 1702-1705. He was grandson of Charles Ashton, the immigrant of this family, who was living in Northumberland county as early as 1660. Charles and Ann Ashton, have many descendants. Old tombs in Westmoreland bear the family arms, *a mullet on a bend.*]

FRANCIS AMIAS of Gosnarch in Lancashire, gent. Will 28 November 1620; proved 6 July 1622. Uncle Walter Wentworth, Esq. Sister in law Bridget Fleetwood. To brother Pawle Amias

lande in Gosnarch of the Lardge measure and of anchient rent of
11s. per annum, paying to Vncle Walter Wentworth, Esq. all
dues. To brother Paule also a judgment of £200 in common
Pleas against Sir Richard Houghton of Howaghton tower,
county Lancaster, Knight, and Barronett to pay £100, provided brother pay debts and give to my mother, if living, and
to brethren Peter and Thomas, and to my sister Bruen, rings,
and ditto to Uncle Walter Wentworth, to Christian Amias his
wife, and sister in law Bridgett Fleetewood. "Item. I doe bequeathe vnto the said Paule Amias halfe the benefit of my now
adventure into Virginia as will appeare by bill of adventure nowe
left in the handes of my vncle Walter Wentworth." To brother
Thomas Amias other half of Adventure to Virginia. Executor:
brother Paule Amias. Witness: Robert Fitzhugh.

Savile, 67.

JOHN ANDREWES of Cambridge, merchant. Will 7 September 1609; proved 4 June 1616. Codicil 21 March 1610. Understanding of the death of my son John Andrewes in Virginia. A
right in a house in Long Lane, London. Wife Easter. Son
William at 21. Sons Francis, Richard, and George. Three
daughters Easter, Elizabeth, and Sara Andrewes.

VIRGINIA GLEANINGS IN ENGLAND.

Communicated by Mr. LOTHROP WITHINGTON, 30 Little Russell street, W. C. London (including "Gleanings" by Mr. H. F. WATERS, not before printed.)

(CONTINUED)

ANNE WATERS of St. Sepulchres, London, widow. Will 29 September 1697; proved 4 July 1700. Son John Waters, who for divers years past hath been gone to Virginia, 5s and no more. Son Samuel Waters, and Margaret his wife, 10s apiece. Daughter Elizabeth Overton, now in Virginia, 10s, and William her husband, 10s. Son-in-law Mr. William Goodwin, 10s. for a ring. Brother-in-law Caleb Millett, 10s. Son Thomas Waters, residuary legatee, and he the sole Executor.

Noel, 108.

[John Waters, the son, settled, first, in Gloucester county, Va., and afterwards in Old Rappahannock. On Sep. 26, 1678, he had a patent for 140 acres in Kingston parish, in the former county, and a year or two later one for 500 acres, which included the first patent. On October 25, 1688, a patent was issued to "Mr. Robert Yard," and "Mr. John Waters," for 900 acres on the south side of the Rappahannock river, which had been formerly granted to Epaphroditus Lawson, had become the property of Robert Paine as marrying Lawson's daughter, and been deserted by Paine.

In 1684, John Waters, together with his horse, having been impressed along with a number of others, by order of Colonel John Stone, to bring down corn and lumber belonging to the Rappahannock Indians, from their fort to the river side, was paid for nine days' service.

In the years 1684, 1685, &c., John Waters appears in the records of Rappahannock in connection with various business transactions. On October 2, 1684, "Mr. John Waters" and "Mr. Samuel Perry" bound themselves in the sum of 30,000 pounds of tobacco to William Lake, to deliver the estate of Thomas Harper to the court or its order. December 3, 1684, certificate was granted to Mr. John Waters for 750 acres of land for the importation of fifteen persons, himself among the number. December 2, 1685, Mr. John Waters was granted administration on the estate of Samuel Dudley, clerk, who died intestate. In 1685-6, he was attorney for Captain John Purvis, a merchant-captain, who was long in the Virginia and London trade.

From Vol. XI, No. 3 (Jan. 1904), p. 305.

Several deeds made by him are in the records of old Rappahannock:
1. John Waters, of Rappahannock county, Va., planter, November 2,
1682, conveying to John Savage 200 acres on the south side of Piscation
[Piscataway] creek, Rappahannock county, which was purchased by
said Waters of William Thornton and Richard Glover; 2. John Waters,
of Rappahannock county, April 7, 1686, to John Savage, of Kingston
parish, Gloucester, 200 acres in Rappahannock, part of the land purchased of Thornton and Glover; 3. John Waters, of Rappahannock
county, gent , and Arabella, his wife, August 5, 1686, conveying 200
acres to George Brooks, being part of the land purchased of Thornton
and Glover.

October 11, 1692, a power of attorney from Mr. John Waters to Mr.
James Baughan was recorded, and on December 12, 1693, John Waters
brought suit against Henry Picket for improper seizure by the latter of
certain goods of Waters', while Waters was out of the country. It appears from the records that John Waters was too sick to appear at court
during the summer of 1694, and probably died intestate during the fall
of that year. On March 11, 1694 [5], a quietus was granted to Mr.
Henry Williamson, administrator of John Waters, deceased, in regard
to a debt to the estate of Christopher Robinson, and on December 10,
1695, John Waters, administrator of John Waters, deceased, returned an
inventory.

We are indebted to Judge W. J Leake, of this city, a descendent of
William Overton, for the following note:

The following is a copy of the Overton register, copied from the book
Josephus:

William Overton, born December 3rd, 1628, in England.   Married
Mary Waters, November 24th, 1670   Emigrated to America.
Elizabeth, their daughter, born June 28th, 1673.
William Overton, their son, born Augst. 14th, 1675.
Temperance Overton, their daughter, born March 2, 1679.
Samuel Overton, their son, born Augst. 14, 1685.
James Overton, their son, born Augst. 14, 1688.
Barbara Overton, their daughter, born Feb y 5, 1690.

Barbara Overton married *John* Winston.
Barbara Overton Winston died Octo. 30, 1766.

The above is a *copy* of a *copy* made by Wm. S. Pryor (a descendant
of *Barbara Overton Winston*), in August, 1821.

This *Josephus* is mentioned in Barbara Overton Winston's will, a copy
of which you will find in Mr. Isaac Winston's manuscript

This *Josephus* was burned at "Courtland" a few years ago, when the
house of the late Wm. Overton Winston, dec'd, was destroyed by fire.

Liber No. 7, p. 78.

Dated 23rd April, 1681. Henry Chicheley, Gov'r, to *William Overton* and *Eben Jones.*

Forty-six hundred acres lying in New Kent (now Hanover), on South side of Pamunkey River, on Falling creek, &c., for transportation to the Colony of 92 persons. Among the 92 names attached you find *William Overton* and *Elizabeth Overton.*

Liber No. 8, p. 121, dated 29th Octo., 1690.

Francis Nicholson, Lt.-Gov., to *William Overton* and *John Lydall.*
837 acres lying in St. Peter's Parish, New Kent Co. (now Hanover), above main fork of Pamunkey, next above a dividend of land granted Jonathan Norwood and Ambrose Clare, late in the tenure of Sam'l *Ousteen.* Beginning at a white oak at Mouth of a small *Pritt* on ye South side of Western Branch of the Pamunkey [South Anna] & then down south side, &c.

(This is land on which Barbara (Overton) Winston resided at her death in 1766.)

For importation of 17 persons, names attached.]

THOMAS TOMLINS of Bartholomew the Great, citizen and grocer of London. Will 10 July 1665; proved 26 September 1666. To brother-in-law Francis Camfield, citizen and grocer of London, all my plantation or dividend of land in Mockejacke Bay, parish of Ware, county Gloucester, in Virginia, about 300 acres, which I bought of said Francis Camfield, and water mill in Crane Creek is said parish. To sister Lettice Draper, wife of Matthew Draper, copyhold tenements in Wormeley, Herts. Cozen Judith Millsopp, her daughter. Brother Jonathan Tomlins. Brother Samuel Tomlins. Brother John Tomlins. Little cosen ———— Tomlins, eldest daughter of brother John. Sister Patience Camfield. Little cosen Jacob Camfield, son of brother John. Cosen Hanna Camfield. Sister Judith Pope. Aunt Joane Willmore. Kinswoman Judith Butcher. Kinsman Hugh Vessey. Richard Camfield a witness.

Mico, 136.

["Mr. Francis Campfield" had a patent for 314 acres in Gloucester county, adjoining his own land, April 10, 1668. "Campfield," in Gloucester, doubtless derived its name from him.]

MARK GLOCESTER als WARKMAN, citizen and grocer of London. Will 20 April 1670; proved 28 April 1670. Wife Elizabeth. Son Mark at 21. Daughter Elizabeth at 21 or marriage. Brother Edmund, Thomas, Robert, and Joseph, and sister Christian, Anne, Sarah, and Mary. To brother Robert who I believe is in Virginia, my estate there.

Penn, 40.

["Mr. Marke Warkman" was granted on April 20, 1684, a dividend of land called Pampetike, 908 acres in New Kent county, on the north side of Pamunkey river, in Pamunkey Neck, beginning at the mouth of Goddin's creek or swamp, a little below Goddin's Island. &c., purchased by one —— Booth, of the [Indian] Queen of Pamunkey, after whose death the said land was granted to his son, Robert Booth, by an order of Assembly, dated April 25, 1679, and by said Robt. Booth assigned to said Mr. Marke Warkman. This grantee was evidently the son of the testator. Among the old records in the State Library is a complaint against a mill built about 1682 by Thomas Claiborne and Mark Warkman.]

EDWARD BRADDOCK, Esq., Major General of H. M.'s forces, and Commander in Chief of an expedition now fitting out for America. I give, devise, and bequeath, all my ready money, securities for money, plate, linen, furniture, and all other my personal estate and effects whatsoever &c. unto my two good friends, Mary Yorke, the wife of John Yorke, Lieutenant in the Royal Regiment of Artillery, now on duty at Gibraltar, and John Calcraft of Brewer Street in the parish of St. James, Westminster, Esq., to be equally divided, &c. These two joint executrix and executor.

Paul, 233.

[The famous commander of the English forces at "Braddock's Defeat," born about 1695, died of wounds, at Great Meadows, July 13, 1755.

WILLIAM ANGELL, citizen and merchant taylor of London. Will 16 July 1635; proved 17 Februrary 1636. To be buried in St. Mildred in Poultry. Wife Anne. Cosen Richard Angell and and my godson William Angell his son. Brother James Angell. Cosen Richard to provide for my brother as before. Wife's sister Susan Downes, widow, and her daughters Beatrice, Mary, and Elizabeth Downes. Robert Downes, son of Edward Downes.

Kinsman John Elvins the younger who now liveth with me.
Sister Judith Pope which dwelleth in Ireland. My friend Henry
Kersey, and to his son now in Virginia.

Goare, 26.

[A Henry *Kersley* was living at Elizabeth City, February, 1623.

ANNE ANGELL of St. Bartholomew Exchange, widow. Will
16 March 1640–41; proved March 31 1641. Sister Susan Downes
of London, widow, and Hester Townge her daughter and Elizabeth Atkins her daughter and Beatrice Downes her daughter
and Mary Ashe another daughter. John and Robert Downes
her sons. (Others.)

Evelyn, 33.

ROBERT PARKER. Will 13 November 1671; proved 4 April
1673. Wife and fellow traveller Jane. Son George and Son John.
Ungrateful son John Martin 13 pence (his wife Abigail my daug-
ter). Daughter Margaret Parker. Daughter Anne Parker.
Daughter Constance Parker. My grandfather John Parker and
father lie buried in church of St. Laurence, Southampton.
Land in Bosham and Meadhurst. Plantation in Virginia. Mr.
John Wise in Accomake.

Pye, 49.

[This Robert Parker and his wife, Joan, were in Virginia, as appears
by the records of Northampton county, in 1654. There is on record in
Isle of Wight a power of attorney, dated May, 1661, from Robert Parker, of Northampton county, Va. The records show that Robert Parker
was brother of George and John Parker, ancestors of the well-known
family of the name, of the Eastern Shore of Virginia. See this Magazine, Vol. VI, 412–418, for account of descendants of George Parker.

FRANCIS KESTON of London, All Saints Barking, going to St.
Christopher's. Wife Elizabeth executrix. Mr. Richard Wright.
Poor of Great Bowden, Leicestershire. Uncle Richard Kestin.
Sister Elizabeth Kestin. Brother Thomas Kestin in Virginia
£4 to be laid out in goods.

Carr, 7.

JOSEPH JOHN JACKMAN of Surrey County Collony of Virginia, gent. Will 27 April 1714; proved 27 May 1714. Mother
Catharine Jackman. Godson Josiah John Halliman 100 acres

south side of Notoway river in Isle of Wight county commonly called Joseph's Mount. Brother William Jackman. Children of sister Mary Harris. Brother in law Richard Slade and Catharine his wife and daughter Mary Slade. Sister in law Catharine Allen and cosen John and Arthur Allen. Wife Mary.

Aston, 98.

[Joseph John Jackman appears to have settled in Surry county, Va., about the year 1700, and to have been a man of some property. On June 6, 1700, Joseph John Jackman, gent., of Surry county, and Elizabeth, his wife, sold to John Wilson, of London, merchant, for 30,000 ℔ of tobacco, 400 acres on Lawnes creek, Surry. This land probably was the property of Mrs. Jackman. In 1700, J. J. Jackman was assessed with 19 tithables. On December 22, 1706, Samuel Swann, of North Carolina (formerly of Surry), sold to J. J. Jackman for £450 sterling, the plantation of Swann's Point, 1,650 acres. In February, 1706, he sold this estate to George Marable, of James City county for £250.

Joseph John Jackman was appointed a justice of Surry in 1702, and sheriff in 1705. He married, first, Elizabeth, widow of Captain Robert Canfield, or Caufield, and daughter of Arthur Allen, who came to Virginia before 1649, and settled in what is now Surry county. Her brother Arthur Allen, was speaker of the House of Burgesses. He married, second, Mary.]

MICAJAH LOWE, late of Charles Citty County in the Collony and Dominion of Virginia, but now of Carshaulton, county Surrey, merchant. Will 20 January 1702-3; proved 17 March 1703-4. To my uncle Micajah Perry a gold ring and to my mother in law Mr. (sic) Elizabeth Hamlin a gold ring. To my sisters Susanna Lowe, Johanna Jarrett, and Mary Lowe, to each of them a ring. To my friends Capt. Christopher Morgan and Capt. James Morgan each a ring. Residuary legatee: Wife Sarah Lowe. Executors: my said uncle Mr. Micajah Perry and my said wife. Witnesses: Sarah Barnes, Joseph Cooper, Robert Dalley, Thomas Dewbery. Proved by Micajah Perry with power reserved.

Degg, 53.

[In 1700, and for many years before and after, the London house of Perry, Lane & Co., were the greatest English traders with Virginia. About this time the firm was composed of Micajah Perry, Thomas Lane and Richard Perry. Peter Perry, the brother of Micajah, was at one time their resident agent in Virginia, and it is probable that Micajah

Low may also have held this position. The firm long represented in England the business interests of William and Mary College. A Micajah Perry was Lord Mayor of London in 1729. It is probable that the mother-in-law, Elizabeth Hamlin, was the wife of a member of the family resident in Charles City and Prince George, whose immigrant ancestor was Stephen Hamlin.]

GEORGE MANFEILD of Verginia in the parts beyond the seas, merchant, now at London. Will 21 May 1670; proved 27 July 1670. To my three sisters, Anne Sumner the wife of Francis Sumner, Mary Swann the wife of Collonell Thomas Swann, and Margaret Oldis wife of ———— Oldis, £10 apiece. To my cousin Elizabeth Tanner, widow, £10. To my uncle Mr. John Beale, citizen and grocer of London, £20. To my nephew Francis Sumner, son of aforesaid Francis Sumner and Anne, all my lands &c. &c. and all the rest of my goods at age. Executor: My said uncle John Beale. Witnesses: Charles Barham, David Gryer, Phillip Peirson.

Penn, 92.

[In Surry county, on March 16, 1676, Colonel Thomas Swann was granted administration on the estate of Francis Sumner, deceased.

"Mr. John Sumner" was granted 67 acres in the upper parish of Nansemond county, April 14, 1670. John Sumner and John Stallenge were granted 1,000 acres in the upper parish of Nansemond at a place called Orapeake, April 19, 1683. In 1742, the town of Suffolk, Nansemond county, was laid out on the land belonging to Jethro Sumner, gent., of Nansemond, and Margaret, his wife, who was daughter of Daniel Sullivan, of Nansemond county.

General Jethro Sumner, of Warren county, N. C., was born in Nansemond county, Va., about 1730, died about 1790. He served with distinction throughout the Revolution, rising to the rank of brigadier general. The ordinary accounts which state that his father was an Englishman, William Sumner, who settled near Suffolk, Va., about 1690, are no doubt erroneous. General Sumner was probably a descendant of one of the earlier Sumners, named above.

Mrs. Mary Swann was the last wife of Colonel Thomas Swann, of "Swann's Point," Surry county, a member of the Virginia Council, and not long after his death married Captain Robert Randolph, or Randall, who was sheriff of Surry in 1688. In 1681, Mrs. Mary Swann made a power of attorney to her "brother," William Edwards, so it is probable that Edwards was a second husband of one of the other sisters named in the will. For Swann family, see this Magazine, III, 154.

It is probable that Mrs. Margaret Oldis was the wife of William Oldis, who was assessed with nine tithables in Surry in 1669, and with three in 1673. She must have been a second wife for there is in Isle of Wight an assignment, dated 1665, from William Oldis and Jane, his wife. There is on record in Isle of Wight a deed dated June 5, 1668, from Valentine Oldis, citizen and apothecary, of London, to his brother, William Oldis, of James river, in Virginia, merchant.

Charles Barham, the witness to the will, was a vestryman of Lownes Creek parish, Surry, in 1661, and was sheriff of the county in 1673. In the will of John Barnes, Surry, March 7, 1690–91, is a legacy to his kinsman, Robert Barham, son of Charles Barham, late of Merchants' Hundred, deceased. It is probable that the family of the name in the same section of Virginia descends from Charles Barham.]

ELIZABETH LLOYD of Elizabeth River in Lower Norfolk in Virginia, widow. Will 19 February 1656–7; proved 15 June 1657. To my friend Lieutenant Colonel Thomas Lambert two thousand pounds of tobacco. To Mr. William Davies one thousand of ditto. To Mr. William Shipp 40s. To Mr. Richard Pinner's sonne, my godchild, one haifer with a calf. To Mr. Sayer's sonne, my godchild, ditto. I will that Nedd a molatto shall be a free man at the expiration of his time with Mr. Sanderson. To Rachell Lambert, daughter of said Thomas, £5 for a gowne and £5 more to pay for her passage into Virginia, and my executor to pay this money to James Matts of Bristoll, attorney. Whereas I have given to Mr. Nicholas Hart seaven thousand pounds of tobacco for looking after my business in Virginia, I give him five thousand pounds more of ditto. Residuary legatee and executor: brother in law Thomas Eauens of Kilkenny in Ireland, gent, for the use of my sister Mary Eavens his wife, he paying to Dr. Collins of Bristol all money due to him. Overseers: Lieut. Col. Thomas Lambert and James Matts. Witnesses: William Pyner, Jane Mansfield, Sara Matts, James Matts.

Ruthen, 249.

[Mrs. Lloyd was the widow of Cornelius Lloyd, of Lower Norfolk county, who settled there in 1641, or earlier, was lieutenant-colonel of the militia, and a member of the House of Burgesses for several sessions between 1642 and 1653. There is among the records of Lower Norfolk a suit in September, 1654, by Elizabeth, widow of Lieutenant-Colonel Cornelius Lloyd. In 1655, she, from love and affection to Philemon Lloyd, son of her brother-in-law, Edward Lloyd, of Maryland, conveying to him certain claims and personal estate. See this Magazine, V, 212–213.

Thomas Lambert was a prominent early settler of Lower Norfolk, burgess, sheriff, &c. Richard Pinner gave his name to Pinner's Point, and this, together with Lambert's Point, which derived its name from Thomas Lambert, are two well known shipping places at Norfolk, Va.]

JAMES BOWKER of St. Peter's parish, New Kent, Virginia. Will 10 March 1702–3; proved 17 November 1704. Brother Edward Bowker of London. Sister Madam Barbara Lyddall. Friend John Lyddall. Brother Ralph Bowker's children. Brother Ralph, executor.

Ash, 224.

[Rev. Ralph Bowker was minister of St. Stephen's parish, King and Queen county, 1704-5, and probably other years. A marriage bond was issued in Spotsylvania county, November 29, 1744, to Parmenas Bowker and Anne Stevens. There is also on record in Spotsylvania a deed, dated December, 1751, from Bowker Smith, of Cumberland county, and Judith, his wife, conveying 150 acres, part of a tract patented by Ralph Bowker, clerk, of St. Stephen's parish, King and Queen county, and by him bequeathed to his daughter, Anne Smith; the said patent having been renewed in May, 1729, by Bird Bowker, and by him bequeathed to Bowker Smith.

"Madam Barbara Lyddall" was probably the wife, and John Lyddall the son of Captain George Lyddall, who patented land in New Kent in 1654, commanded a fort on the Mattaponi river in 1679, and died a very old man, in St. Peter's parish, New Kent, January 19, 1705. It seems probable that he was a son of Thomas Lyddall, of England. See Keith's *Ancestry of Benjamin Harrison*, 25, 26, and Water's *Gleanings*.]

EDWARD EWELL of St. Peter the Apostle, Isle of Thanet, Kent, Yeoman. Will circa 1722. I give to the heirs of James Ewell, late of Annok Creek in Accomac county on the eastern shore in Virginia £10 to be shared equally.

Arch. Canterbury, register 84, folio 24.

[Thomas and James Ewell patented 200 acres in Princess Anne county, April 6, 1699. James appears to have gone later to the Eastern Shore. The family of Ewell has up to the present time been represented on the Eastern Shore of Virginia and Maryland.]

WILLIAM AYLWARD late of Virginia, merchant, now in London. Will 6 November 1701; proved 20 February 1706-7. Sole legatee and executor: Mr. Robert Cary, living in Watling street, London. Witnesses: Edward Garrett, Elizabeth Lane, William Scorey, notary.

Poley, 24.

SIR THOMAS SMITH of London, Knight. Will 30 January 1621–2; proved 12 October 1625. Skinners. Virginia Company. Wife Dame Sarah Smith. Son Sir John Smith. Nephew Thomas Smith of Ostenhanger, Kent, Esq., son and heir of my late brother Sir John Smith, deceased. Nephew Thomas, son of brother Sir Richard Smith. Nephew John Smith, son of late brother Robert Smith, deceased. Nephew Thomas Fanshawe, son of Lady Fanshawe. Sister Mrs. Joane Fanshawe. Nephew Sir Thomas Butler and Oliver Butler, sons of sister Ursula Butler. Nephew Sir Arthur Harris, son of late sister Alice Harris. Children of late sister Katharine Hayward als Scott. Children of late brother Henry Smith, deceased.

Clarke, 107.

[Sir Thomas Smith, the first treasurer of the Virginia Company, of London, and at the head of that corporation until May, 1619. He was born about 1558, and died September 4, 1625. For a careful and detailed biography of this distinguished man who had so much to do with the settlement of Virginia, see Brown's *Genesis*, II, 1012–1018.]

ARTHUR PETT, master of Ship Unitie of London. Will 30 August 1609; proved 19 March 1609–10. Sick aboard the Ship Blessing of Plymouth, Captain Robert Adames of Limehouse, master, now riding at anchor before St. James Town in Virginia. Mother now wife unto Richard Nottingham of Ratcliffe. Brother William Pett. Brother William Welch. Wife Florence Pett. Daughter Elizabeth Pett (under 10). Wife Florence Pett and Thomas Johnson of Ratcliffe, mariner, now master of the Lyon of London now riding in this port of St. James Towne, executors. Father in law Richard Nottingham, overseer. Witnesses: Thomas Johnson, Robert Addames, William Milward.

Commissary of London, register 21 (1607–1611), folio 235.

[Arthur Pett was a member of the Virginia Company under the second charter, in 1609. He was probably a member of the Kentish family of Pett, so closely connected with English naval affairs in the 16th and 17th centuries.

The ships *Blessing*, *Unity* and *Lion* were in Sir George Somers' fleet,

47

which left Plymouth for Virginia on June 2, 1609, was scattered by a great storm, and some of the ships wrecked on the Bermudas, while those named reached Virginia.

This will shows that the Captain Adams, of whom there is a notice in Brown's *Genesis*, II, 812, and who made seven voyages to Virginia between 1609 and 1614, and was afterwards in the service of the East India Company, was, as Mr. Brown suggests, Captain Robert Adams.]

THOMAS DEACON of St. Savior's, Southwark, yeoman. Will 15 May 1652; proved 14 October 1652. To be buried in parish church of St. Saviors. Cosen Magdalen Causon ot Enfield. Cosen Alice Crew of London, widow. Cosen William Graves, a chaundler living in Tower street, London. Cosen Thomas Deacon, a planter in Virginia. Wife Margaret Deacon.

Bowyer, 166.

[Thomas Deacon, aged 19, sailed for Virginia in the *Assurance*, in 1635.]

CAPT. THOMAS COVELL, citizen and skinner of London. Will 21 December, 1643; proved 7 February 1643-4. To be buried in Barking church, London, with father and mother and children. Tenements in Wargrave, Berkshire. Cosen Richard Young, citizen and haberdasher. Wife Hellena and cosen Richard Young messuages, tenements, &c. in Virginia, Barbadoes, &c. Children Thomas and Frances. Poor of Havering, Essex, where I now live.

Arch Essex, register Whitehead (1637–1652), folio 136.

HENRY SMITH of Watford, Herts. Will proved 15 February 1666. Brother Richard Smith of Norton, county Northampton, £5. Brother William Smith in Virginia, £5. Sister Elizabeth Wills of Long Buckly £5. Sister Joane Smith of Welton 20s for a ring. Sister Thomazine Smith 20s. for a ring. Cosens Amy and Elizabeth Smith, daughters to brother Thomas Smith, deceased £5. Cosen Thomas Smith, son to brother Thomas Smith, £10. To cosen John Cosford, son of John Cossord, £10. Son John Smith £500, to be put out for his best advancement and £500 at 21 with the interest. Child my wife now goes with, £500. Executrix· wife Sarah. Overseers: James Hayes, Esq. and my brother Mr. Thomas Blackmore.

Carr, 29.

[Of course it is impossible to speak with certainty of a William Smith. William and John Smith, sons of Robert Smith, of Yeocomico, had a grant of 500 acres on Acquacond (Aquia), in 1658. Henry and William Smith, sons of Mr. Toby Smith, deceased, of Lancaster county, had a grant of 1,600 acres on Rappahannock river in 1664. William Smith had a grant of 590 acres in Westmoreland county in 1667; another of the name, a grant of 400 acres in James City county in 1659; another one a grant of 300 acres in Isle of Wight in 1657 and 1661, and still another William Smith, "Son and heir of Thomas Smith, *als* Hins-man," had a grant of 400 acres in Northampton, which had been assigned in 1643 to Sarah Smith, mother of said William.]

WALTER FLOOD of London, carpenter. Will 13 January 1635–6; proved 22 January 1635-6. John Furnell jr., son to John Furnell of London haberdasher. Mary Furnell, daughter to to John Furnell. Estate in Virginia. Bridget and Margaret Davis, daughter of Thomas, husband of Margaret Davis. Judith Weane, daughter of William Weane, husband of Joane Weane of Southwark, weaver. A feather bed and boulster which is in Virginia I give and bequeath unto Francis Warner of Virginia.

Arch London, register 8, folio 101.

JOHN UNETT of London. Will 14 July 1622; proved 18 October 1622. St. Anne Blackfriars. Only son John Unett (now in Virginia) lease of house in Blackfriars formerly granted to me for 1 & 20 years by Alexander Clover of London, deceased. Also £20 in money in one year. Cosen Water Long Nearest allies and kindred in Ashillworth, Gloucester. Kinswoman Margaret Heyward £6 in one year &c.

Arch London, register 6, folio 89.

THOMAS BUTLER, minister of God's Word. Will 20 November 1636; proved 25 July 1637. Friends Captain Thomas Flint and Mary his wife. Mrs. Mary Barnett wife of Mr. Thomas Barnett. Peter Hull. Legacies to be paid by my executrix in England upon receipt of the first tobaccos out of Virginia. Wife to be executrix of all. Mr. Thomas Barnett and Peter Hull overseers here. Cosen Mr. William Broome and friend Mr. Christopher Irons, both living in Gracious Street. Witnesses: Thomas Flint and Thomas Pratt.

Goare, 107.

[Thomas Butler, "Clarke and Pastor of Denbie" (Warwick county, Va.), as he is styled in a patent to him, dated June 11, 1635. He married Mary, widow of John Brewer, citizen and grocer, of London, who at the time of his death, in 1635, was a resident of Virginia and a member of the Council, and whose will has been printed in *Waters' Gleanings*. See this Magazine, III, 182–184.

Thomas Flint, gent., came to Virginia in 1618, and settled in the present Warwick county. He was several times a member of the House of Burgesses, and was alive in 1647. Thomas Barnett (or Bernard), was an early settler in the same section, and was Burgess for Stanley Hundred, September, 1632, and for Warwick River, January, &c., 1641. Peter Hull was Burgess for Isle of Wight, October, 1644. In 1663, he had a grant of 400 acres in Isle of Wight, part of a tract of 1,100 acres formerly granted him and others in 1651.]

VIRGINIA GLEANINGS IN ENGLAND.

Communicated by Mr. LOTHROP WITHINGTON, 30 Little Russell street,
W. C. London (including "Gleanings" by Mr. H. F. WATERS,
not before printed.)

(CONTINUED)

WALTER WALTON. Will 30 November 1649; proved 17
August 1650. Mr. Alexander Ewes and Mr. Richard Lawson
to be my executors in the behalf of my mother, Johane Walton,
living in Spoford in the parish of Spoford, Yorkshire, England.
They to pay all my debts demanded in this my voyage in the
adventure now in Verginney bound for Maryland, and I give
power to John Underhill and Benjamin Cowell of the said ship
to receive what is due me. One servant that I brought over
sold for twelve C tobacco. Henry Dagord for one sute and
cloke three C tobacco. John Smith, a passenger, 30 ℔s tobacco. Simon Asbe 27 ℔ tobacco. Nathaniel Foord 9 ℔ tobacco. Mr. Walker 374 ℔ tobacco. Henry Dagord 9 ℔ tobacco.
Witnesses: Thomas May, Peter Walker, John Addams, Miles
Cooke, Richard ———. Proved by Richard Lawson, with
power reserved.

Pembroke, 139.

EDWARD GOLDSTONE of Lymehouse in the parish of Stepney, Middlesex, mariner. Will 8 July 1663; proved 14 July
1663. To my two brothers Thomas and Charles Goldstone 5 s.
apeece. To my four sisters, Margaret Hedge, Mary Angell,
Suzann Mundy, and Alice Goldstone 5 s. apeece. To my father
Edward Goldstone and Susannah his wife 5 s. apeece. To wife
Sara Goldstone and to my daughter Sàrah Goldstone (or if my
said wife be left breeding with another, to that child the part of
her portion) all due to me in Holland and also the house occupied by my said father in Woodbridge, Suffolk (father to enjoy
said house for his life), and also my full eight part of the ship
Susan, and also all money now in the hands of the Alderman
John Jeffereyes and Mr. Thomas Colclough, merchants, Mr.
Peter Noy, and Mr. Edmond Graygoose, for tobaccoes sold to

them and all such debts dues &c. owing to me in Virginia in parts beyond the seas, as appears by accompt in my attorneys hands, Mr. David Fox of Virginia. Residuary legatees: wife Sarah Goldstone and daughter Sarah Goldstone. To the poor of Stepney £4. Executors: wife Sarah and Malachi Harris, D. D., rector of Farthingho in Northampton. Overseers: Edward Bartlett, ropemaker, Runceford Waterhouse, ship chaundler. Witnesses: Henry Bonner, Reuben Fisher, William Facett, Robertes Rose, scrivenor.

Juxon, 93.

[John Jeffreys or Jefferys, and his nephews, were, for a long period, leading London merchants in the Virginia trade.

Edward Jeffreys, of Brecknockshire, had issue: 1. Ann, married Morgan Jones, of Landvillo Ar. Vaen; 2. John, of London, tobacconist, born 1614, *d. s. p.*, November 5, 1684, and was buried at St. Andrew Undershaft. His epitaph is in *The New View of London*, p. 122. He left most of his great estate to his nephews, Sir Jeffrey Jeffreys and John Jeffreys; 3. Watkyn, who was the father of: (*a*) Sir Jeffrey, of London, who was knighted at Kensington, October 20, 1699, was sheriff of London in the same year, was alderman for Portsoken Ward, and died October 25, 1709. He married and left children; (*b*) John, of London, merchant, and of Richmond, Surry, where he died October 20, 1715. He was several times M. P. for Brecon, Radnor, and Marlborough. He married and had issue. (Le Neve's *Pedigrees of Knights*, pp. 470–471.)

Thomas Colclough was also a London merchant largely interested in the Virginia trade. He may have been a brother of George Colclough, who was a member of the House of Burgesses for Lancaster county, March, 1658-'9.

David Fox was of Lancaster county.]

FRANCIS WEST of the city of Winchester, county Southampton, Esq. Will 17 December 1629; proved 28 April 1634. Being desirous to make provision for Jane, my now wife, one of the daughters of Sir Henry Davye, knight, in case she outlive me, my wife to sell my lands, plantations &c. in England or in Virginia (except jewells, plate, &c.) for the best rate, and she to have the whole profitts thereof till son Francis West accomplish his full age of 21, and then he to have the one half of my said estate. Residuary legatee and executrix: my said wife Jane.

Overseer: said Sir Henry Davye, knt.   Witnesses: Tho: South, Tho: Hill.

Seager, 33.

[Francis West, born October 28, 1586, was a son of the second Lord Delaware and brother of Thomas, third Lord Delaware, and of Captain John West, governors of Virginia. He was a member of the Virginia Company; came to the colony with Newport about July, 1608, and was elected to the Council in August, 1609. In January, 1610, he returned to England, but came back to Virginia in the latter part of the same year, and succeeded Percy, when he left, as Commander at Jamestown. He held this office many years, and, also, that of member of the Council, to which body he belonged, continuously, from 1619 to 1633. On March 22, 1622, the Indians killed two men men on his plantation at Westover, about a mile from "Berkeley Hundred." In November, 1622, he was commissioned Admiral of New England; went there in May or June and again in August. He was in New England in September, but appears not to have remained long, as he was back in Virginia in February, 1624, where he was living at "West and Shirley Hundred Island." In the next year he was living in Elizabeth City, where the widow of his brother, Nathaniel West, and her infant son lived with him. About November, 1627, he was elected Governor of Virginia, and continued in office until March 5, 1629, when, being chosen to go to England as the agent of the colony, Dr. John Pott was elected Governor in his stead. During his stay in England he resisted the planting of Lord Baltimore's proposed colony within the limits of Virginia. He returned to Virginia prior to December, 1631, and was present at a meeting of the Council February, 1633 This is the last appearance of his name in the Virginia records. His will was evidently made during his visit to England as agent for the colony. Therefore his election as agent must have taken place in March, 1628-'29. It is very probable that he died in Virginia. The probate of the will gives the first information in regard to the year of his death.

In annotating a will of one of the Wests it may be well to add that in Matthews' "Year Books of Probates P. C. C.," it is stated that on September 8, 1630, the will of Nathaniel West, citizen and mercer, of London, was proved by his brother Francis West. This was probably the Nathaniel West, sometime of Virginia.]

RICHARD BIGGS of West and Sherley Hundred in the Cuntrey of Virginia. Will 10 September 1625; proved 9 August 1626. To wife Sarah and my son Richard Biggs all my lands, goods, &c. &c. except three hundred pounds waight of tobacco, which I give to my friend Samuell Sharpe, and six acres of land which I give to my sister Rebecka Rose, adjoining to the now dwelling house and lying by the swamp side next to Christopher Woodward's ground. Witnesses: Thomas Pawlett, Samuell Sharpe. Proved by Sarah Biggs, relict &c.

Hele, 106.

[The census printed in *Hotten's Emigrants* shows, among the inhabitants of West and Shirley Hundred, in January, 1624, the "Muster" of Richard Biggs. It includes Richard Biggs, age forty-one (at the date of the census), who came in the ship *Swann*, in Aug., 1610; Sarah, his wife, aged thirty-five, who came in the *Marygold*, in May, 1618; Richard, their son, aged three years; Thomas Turner, his cousin, aged eleven, who came in the *Marygold*, in 1616, and Susan Old, his cousin, aged ten, who came in the *Marygold*, in 1616. There were also four servants.

Richard Biggs had apparently lost two children within the preceding year, for the list of people living at West and Shirley Hundred in 1623, gives Biggs and his wife, and sons William, Thomas, and Richard.

The census of 1624–5 also gives the "Muster" of Rebecca Rose, widow, living at West and Shirley Hundred. She was fifty years old and came in the *Marygold*, in May, 1619, and her muster included Marmaduke Hill, aged eleven, and John Hill, aged fourteen, who came in the same ship.

Samuel Sharpe was a member of the House of Burgesses from Charles City in 1619, and for The Neck of Land, October, 1629.

Christopher Woodward, born 1594, came to Virginia in 1620, and was member for Westover in the House of Burgesses in October, 1629. There is on record in Henrico county, a deed, dated 1705, from Samuel Woodward, of Boston, Mass , son of Samuel Woodward, of Charles City county, Va. (who died in 1680), and his wife, Sarah, daughter of Robert Hollam.

Thomas Pawlett, born 1578, came to Virginia in 1618, was a member of the House of Burgesses in 1619, appointed member of council 1641, and died 1644. He acquired the Westover plantation. 2,000 acres, by patent, dated January 15, 1637. By his will, dated January 12, 1643-4, he left this estate to his brother, Sir John Pawlett. His brother, Chidiock Pawlett, is also mentioned in the will.]

WILLIAM WRAXALL of the cittie of London, joyner. Will 3 September 1629; proved 17 June 1630. On a voyage to Virginia in parts beyond the seas. Sole legatee and executrix: wife Anna Wraxhall, towards the releife of herself and Mabell Wraxhall my daughter. (Signed) William Raxhall (Sealed).

54

Witnesses: John Warner, scrivenor, Ric: Armestrong, Henry Wilkinson.

Scroope, 52.

TOBIAS BOXE, being bound to goe a voiage to St. Christophers in the good ship called the Hopewell of London, cooper. Will 15 December 1628; proved 15 December 1629. To Annis Barker (sic) of London, spinster, fortie-six pounds of tobacco in the hands of Leanard Huitt, quartermaster of the good shipp called the Indeavor of London, bound from Virginia, which he received of George Ayers, plaunter in Virginne. To the said Annis all my clothes and pay. I bequeath all other goods to the said Agnes Barber (sic) and make the said Annis my sole executor. Witnesses: James Man, Josian Man. Proved by Agnes Barber.

Ridley, 110.

THOMAS COX late of Nansy Mumm on the bay in Virginia, bachelor. Administration 3 June 1697 to Father Richard Cox. 15 March 1697–8 grant of administration on above to Mary Tinkerson als Cox, sister of the deceased, on the goods &c. unadministrated by the " brother " (sic.) Richard Cox, now also deceased.

Admon Act Book 1697, folio 104 and ditto 1698, folio 52.

GEORGE HOLCROFT late of Virginia, bachelor, deceased. Administration 29 December 1666 to his father Michael Holcroft.

Admon Act Book, 1666, fo. 223.

THOMAS JONES late of Virginia, bachelor, deceased. Administration 10 November 1724 to his father Richard Jones.

Admon Act Book, 1724, fo. 228.

JOHN MOODY late of the Island of Virginia, deceased. Administration 14 September 1681 to Susan Poynte, mother of Rebecca Moody relict, during the absence and for the benefit of the said Rebecca Moody.

Admon Act Book, 1681.

ROBERT WALTON als Wanton late of Virginia. Administration 22 June 1670 to John Tayloe principal creditor, Elizabeth Walton als Wanton renouncing.

Admon Act Book, 1670.

[The will of Robert Walton, dated January 14, 1669, was proved in Northumberland county, July 19, 1671. By it he gave most of his estate to his wife, his son Charles, and his daughter, all then in England, and legacies to his sister, Mrs. Frissie Mathew, and his brother, Mr. Thomas Mathew, of Northumberland county, Va. It is probable that the testator was the same person as the Robert Walton of the text, and that administration was granted before the will was produced for probate. Thomas Mathew was the author of "T. M.'s" account of Bacon's Rebellion. See this Magazine, I, 201-202.]

JOHN BEHEATHLAND. Will undated; proved 22 October, 1639. About to go to my mother at Virginia, and having some small means coming to me from my grandfather Mr. Richard Beheathland deceased, do leave all unto Charles Beheathland my kinsman, being my guardian. Witnesses: Pollider Pen, Samuell Eslake, Thomas Voyley. Administration to Charles Beheathland, sole legatee named, &c.

Harvey, 157.

[This unusual surname was represented in Virginia at the time of the first settlement. Robert Beheathland, gentleman, came in the first ship which landed at Jamestown in 1607. During the period 1607–1609 his name appears frequently in *Smith* as taking an active part in the affairs of the colony. In 1620 a petition was presented to the Royal Council for Virginia by many of the first personal adventurers and planters (who were ready to return if a favorable response was made) asking that some person of distinction be appointed Governor of Virginia to succeed Lord Delaware. Among the signers was Captain Robert Beheathland.

In 1655 there was recorded a deed from Major John Smith and Beheathland his wife. John Smith was, as the records show, the assumed name of Francis Dade, who before his death took again his own name. No reason for this disguise has ever been discovered. Mrs. Beheathland Dade married, secondly, Major Andrew Gilson and has many descendants by each marriage.]

ROBERT PERRY, of the City of Bristoll, clerke. Will 24 Aprill 1652; proved 2 July 1652. To be buried in Cathedral church of Bristoll. To the poor of St. Michaells parish in Bristoll 40 s. To the poor of St. Augustine's parish 40 s. To the poor of St. Peter's parish 40 s. To my kinswoman Temperance Morgan, wife of Richard Morgan of Chepstow £20. To my kinswoman wife of Richard Morder of Chepstow £20. To my nephew Robert Perry, son of my sister Elizabeth Perry, living in Virginia, £10. To William Webb, son of kinsman William Webb £10 at 21. To cosen Richard Jones and his wife 20s. each. To brother-in-law William Bentley and his wife 20s. each. To Robert Bentley my godson £5 at 21. To cosen Phillipp Hill and his wife 20s. each. To my kinswoman and goddaughter Marrian Medowes, the wife of Marrian Medowes (sic) £20., and two tenements purchased from Mrs. Cary als. Lavington and her son. To my wife Elizabeth Perry my fower other tenements and one purchased of Mr. Thomas Browne, provided she pay unto Mrs. Mary Taylor of Bristol City, widow, for life, and then to the heirs of John Taylor late an alderman of the said city, 31s 4d yearly. To servant Anne Cadell £5. I desire Mr. Henry Jones, minister of St. Stephens, to preach my funeral sermon, and to him 20s. To friend Mr. Richard Pownell, clerke, 40s. Residuary legatee and executrix: wife Elizabeth. Overseers: friends George Williamson, clerke, and Christopher Large, gent, and to each 10s. To my old servant Joane Horwood 20s. To servant John Massie after the death of my wife, my organs and some of my music books. Witnesses: Anthony Potter, Anne Capell, Richard Pownell, and Richard Orchard, notary public.

Bowyer, 243.

EDWARD AISHLEY, late of Ratcliff, at Virginia beyond seas, deceased. Administration 18 August 1656 to James Shawe, ye guardian of Elizabeth Aishley, a minor, only child.

Admon Act Book, 1656, fo. 202.

THROCKMORTON TROTMAN of London, merchant. Will 13 October 1663; proved 24 October 1664. To my cosin Edward Trotman his daughter in Virginia £50, and to her mother £20. To my cosin Margarett Suffingam and each of her children £50. To cosin Anna Haynes her children (she being dead) £30 each. To cosin Edward Trotman secondary £100, and to each of his children by Susan Watts excepting Edward the eldest £100. To cosin Sara Page £200, and to each of her chiidren £100. To sister-in-law Ann Sellwin £30, and to my sister-in-law Susan Trotman £50. To my old cozen Sara Pope, widow of Stinch-combe, and to her children £10 each. To cosin Sybell Hunt £200, and to each of her children £100. To said cosen Sybell all my linen wearing and tableing. To cosin Nathaniel Hill, son of Jo: Hill deceased, £20. To Cosin Edward Meyners, lately my cosin Edward Trotman his servant £30, and to his mother £30. To Thomas Haynes, grocer, of Bristoll £20. To Margaret Benlose widow £20, and the £20, her son Richard oweth me. To Mathew Tindall of London, trader in cloth, £10. To Judith Goidd, widow, sister Trotman's sister, £10. To my sister Sellwyn's daughter, An Trenner, £10. To Richard Trotman of Cam, clothier, the grandchild of Edward Trotman of the Steps at Cam, £20. To John Archer once my servant £100, To Mr. James Baber my father at Hamberoe £150. To Mr. Thomas Goodyeare, one of the Lady Mowlson's servants, £50. To Mrs. Abigail Loyd my tenant and to her two daughters, Abygall and Sara, £10 each. To the company of Merchant Adventurers of England, £600. To poor of Mary Butha parish in London £30. To Thomas Ward, silke wever in little moore-fields, £20. To cosen Joseph Dorney, son of Thomas Dorny of Vly, deceased £30. To cosen Margaret Trottman, sister to cosen Thomas Trotman, hosier, £10. To Mr. John Dogett, merchant in bush Lane £20, and the two books called Mercater Atlas to the company of Haberdashers of London. To the poor of the parish of Cam in Gloucester where I was born £30. To poor ministers put by their employment, £500 to be given, £5 to a man, to those whom the following shall appoint, viz: Mr. Joseph Carrill, Mr. Slater late of Wapping, Mr. Antony Palmer and Mr. Helmes dwelling in Moorefields, Mr. Thomas Brooks formerly on Fishstreet hill, Mr. —— Barker of ditto, Mr. Venning formerly at St. Tulye, Mr. —— Cocking, teacher near Soper lane, and Mr. Carter who used to exercise at Great Allhallows. To the aforesaid nine ministers I give the inheritance of the house I now live in with adjoining lands now possessed of Mrs. Loyd as also ten houses bought of Antony Selfe held by lease of Sir Edward Barckham. Residuary legatee and executors: brother Samuell Trottman and cousin Edward Trotman the son of Edward Trotman (my brother's son). If Edward Trotman be not of age, I appoint Thomas Trotman the hosier in Soper Lane to be his guardian and I give him £50. My executors to pay my bro. two thirds, my cousin Edward Trottman junior, one-third of the annuitie to my sister-in-law.

Hyde, 29.

LUKE JOHNSON of Virginia, planter. Will 25 June 1659; proved 1 August 1659. To my uncle John Turton of West Bromwich, county Stafford, gent, and James Carie, citizen and salter of London, my executors, 20 s. To Elizabeth, the wife of said James Carie, 20 s. To friends Mr. John Banester and Elizabeth his wife, 40 s. To my loving godson John Banister, son of John Banister of Yorke River in Virginia, planter, one cowe. To my godson Robert Bryen, son of Robert Bryen of Virginia, planter, one cowe. Residuary legatee: Anne Johnson, my wife. Executors: my uncle John Turton and friend James Cary. Witnesses: Richard Morton, Pr. Stedman, servant to Thomas Russell, scrivenor.

Pell, 450.

[James Cary, a London merchant, engaged in the Virginia trade, had a son Oswald Cary who came to the colony and settled in Middlesex county. There is recorded in that county a bill dated June 23, 1690, drawn by Oswald on James Cary and signed "yo'r dutiful son Oswald Cary." Oswald Cary was commissioned sheriff of Middlesex, April 30, 1690. In 1691 Mr. Randolph Seager had married Ann, the relict of Cary, and in that year Captain John Purvis recorded a power of attorney from Mr James Cary, of London, merchant, authorizing him to bring suit againt Seager and wife, who was the administratrix of Captain Oswald Cary. In May, 1698, James Smith and Ann his wife, daughter and heiress of Oswald Cary, deceased, brought suit in Middlesex court against Samuel Gray, clerk (minister of Christ Church parish), who had married the relict of Randolph Segar, she before being the relict of Oswald Cary. An account of some of the descendants of James and Ann (Cary) Smith is given in the *William and Mary Quarterly*, IX, 45, 46.

John Banister, Thomas Foote and John Boarham had a patent, dated November 25, 1653, for 350 acres on Horn Harbor creek (Gloucester county), adjoining the lands of Mrs. Morrison, Mr. Armistead, Mr. Hall, Henry Singleton, John Trage, and Edward Morgan. Mrs. Elizabeth Banister had a grant of land in Gloucester in 1679. In the grant reference is made to her son John Banister and her deceased husband John Banister. It might have been supposed that the son was John Banister the naturalist, who lived in Charles City county were it not for the fact that a fragment of the records of that county has an entry showing that on April 9, 1661, Thomas Chappell appeared in the court of Charles City and acknowledged that he had received from James Wallis, who had married the relict of Lieutenant John Banister, deceased, a legacy which had been bequeathed in Banister's will to a child of Chappell's.]

RALPH VIZER, late of the City of Dublin in Ireland, merchant, and now of Bristoll. Will 30 July 1667; proved 5 September 1667. To be buried in the parish church of St. James, Bristol, Mr. Horne, minister of said parish, to preach my funeral sermon, and to him 40 s. To wife Bridgett Vizer all that my house in St. Patrick's street in Dublin possessed of Mr. Thomas Cooker, merchant, and also the little house in Bull Alley possessed of Mr. William Alison during so many years which I have to come; the rest thereof, after decease of wife, I give to son Barnard Vizer. To wife Bridgett my two houses in Cockhill in Dublin possessed of John Amos and Widow Walch for so many years to come; the rest, at her death, to son Raphill Vizer. To said wife my messuage in St. Thomas street, Dublin, wherein I lately dwelt, during term to come; the rest to son William. To said wife £500. To son William £100. To son Raphill £100. To son Henry Vizer, now or late resident in Virginia, if living, £100. To brother Nicholas Vizer £3 annually for life. To grandsons Thomas and Robert Vizer, sons of Thomas Vizer, deceased, £10 apiece at 21, and if they both die, then to my granddaughter Susanna Vizer, their sister. To said granddaughter Susanna Vizer £150 at 21 or marriage. To son Barnard's two daughters, Bridgett and Sara, £10 apiece at 21 or marriage. To son William my little house next door to my late dwelling in St. Thomas street possessed of Elianor Cavanagh. To Alice Vizer, my now apprentice, £10 at 21 or marriage. Residuary legatee and executrix: said wife Bridget. Overseers: friends Thomas Smart, glazier, and Abraham Saunders, chaundler. To the poor of St. James aforesaid, 20 s. Witnesses: John Harrys, Francis Payne, Richard Williamson, Not. Pub.

Carr, 121.

RICHARD CLARKE, Virginia, widower. Administration 25 August 1686 to daughter Margaret Howard als Clark, wife of John Howard.

Admon Act Book, 1686, folio 130.

JOHN WHITE, vicar of Cherton als Cheriton, Wilts. Will 1 February 1669–70; proved 6 February 1671–2. To be buried near wife. Forgive all debts from Brother Goodwin, Cozen Lapworth, Samuel Roman of Woodborough, and Henry Lighe, and to all such my brothers-in-law and sisters who are deceased. To my deceased brother's children in Virginia, his eldest son John White, £5, his whole sister 50 s., and the rest of his children 50 s. To sisters Judith and Margaret all Goods and household stuff at Culnes Aylwins, but 20 markes due in those parts to Margarett, shee discharging the Heriot to the Lord. Money due from Richard Gipps to be paid to his now wife Jane. To children of Sister Joane Lupworth deceased 20 s. apeice. To Cousine Phyllis Broadhurst £60 her father John Broadhurst owes. To nephew Edward Broadhurst £10 yearly for 80 years, if he so long live, viz: 50 s. quarterly toward his Releife and maintenance at Oxford or e sewhere, to be paid out of lands at Bushton or out of goods if hee shall come and demand &c. Whereas Deede made mee by sister Anne Beale to recouer debts from George Beale and John Beale and Robert Constable, and George and John not to be found, the securitie for 50 s. half yearly from Robert Constable for 8 years assigned to said Sister Anne, my heires to provide houseroom &c. for my aged deare sister, and if she outlive the 8 years to have all necessaries for life in my new house at Bushton. To grand Nephewes Trinepotes, Charles and Samuell Broadhurst £20 apeice at 21. Of £10 owing by Richard Barnes (whose wife is lately deceased), 50 s. each to his children my godchildren William and Mary and the other £5 to the releife of my godchildren Jane Bridges and Mary Bridges (who both are deafe and dumbe). To six poore men and women of Cherton six large white woollen wastcoats worth 40 s. Rest to Nephew and Neice John Broadhurst and Phyllis Broadhurst his nowe wife. Overseers: Sister Anne Beale and executor's sons Trinepotes John and Edward Broadhurst. Witnesses: Francis Smith, Anne Smith.

Eure 23.

[It is of course difficult to ascertain positively the name of the brother who had lived in Virginia, but it seems probable that he was Rev. William White, who was a parish minister in Lancaster and York counties.

Thomas Brice, of Lancaster county, by will, dated April 24, and proved May 19, 1657, gave his whole estate in England and Virginia to his wife. On the last date Lancaster court made an order in regard to Brice's estate in favor of his widow, Martha, and on the same date was recorded a marriage contract between her and William White. In December, 1657, is reference in the Lancaster records to Mr. William White, clerk, and Martha, his wife. The will of William White was dated January 25th, and proved February 12, 1658, in Lancaster. His legatees were his sons John, William, and Edward, daughter Deborah, and daughter-in-law [step-daughter?] Mary Alford. There is recorded in York county the will of Martha White, widow of William White, of York county, minister of York parish, dated Sept. 14, and proved January 24, 1658. She makes a bequest to her husband's two children, Jeremiah and Mary White, "now living in London," and makes Mr. Jeremiah White, minister, and "Mr. Hulett," trustees for these children. The differences in dates and names of legatees in the two wills are perplexing, but Martha White, of York, was certainly the widow of William White, of Lancaster. This fact is proved by a comparison of her will with a deed in Lancaster, dated March 3, 1660, in which it is stated that the land given Martha White, widow of William White, by her former husband, Thomas Brice, was given by the said Martha to the son and daughter of said White, and that by order of the Governor and Council this land was ordered to be sold to pay a debt to Jeffreys and Colclough, and notice thereof being given to Mr. John Jeffreys and Mr. Thomas Colclough, and to Mr. Jeremiah White and Mr. George Hewit, guardians of the said White children, it was sold to Lieutenant-Colonel Edward Carter, of Nansemond county, for £330 sterling. The land contained 1,650 acres.

There appears to be no Chereton or Cherton in Wiltshire, though there is in the adjoining Hampshire. If there is any historical account of Chereton, Hampshire, we should be glad to know what is said of Rev. John White.

Could Rev. Jeremiah White, who was evidently resident in England, have been Cromwell's wellknown chaplain of that name, who was born in 1629, and died in 1707? The *Dictionary of National Biography* does not give the father or the birthplace of the latter.

Foster's *Alumni Oxonienses* gives the following in regard to two nephews of Rev. John White. Though Mr. White seems to have been a man of some property, his Broadhurst nephews were evidently in an humble station in life:

"Broadhurst, Edward, son of John, of Cherington, Wilts., pleb. Magdalen Coll., matric. 24 March, 1669-70, aged 16; chorister 1672-4; B. A. 13 Feb., 1673-4; M. A. 1676; usher of the College School 1677-83, brother of the next named.

"Broadhurst, Samuel, son of John, of Cherington, Wilts., paup., Magdalen Coll., matric. 16 July, 1687, aged 17; B. A. 1691; rector of Weston Birt., co. Gloucester, 1695."]

VIRGINIA GLEANINGS IN ENGLAND.

Communicated by Mr. LOTHROP WITHINGTON, 30 Little Russell street, W. C. London (including "Gleanings" by Mr. H. F. WATERS, not before printed).

(CONTINUED)

RICHARD MAHIER now of London but late of New England in America mariner. Will 4 March 1720 | 21; proved 4 July 1721. To wife Mary Mahier, daughter of Captain Savage of Cherrystone, Eastern Shore of Occomack County in Virginia, the next proceed of ⅜ of my cargo which I brought to London, which shall appear visible by the account of sale, and ⅜ of the Hull of the Ship Friendship of which I was late Master, the effects of which I desire my executor John Lloyd to ship for New England in America and consign them to James Bowdwine merchant in Boston, also the amount current of my beloved friend James Bowdwine aforesaid merchant which was drawn sometime in July last, which lies in trust at my good friend's Mary Pyke, widow, near the Salutation in Boston, also 204 oz. of Spanish silver in the hands of the said Mary Pyke, widow, of which I have her promisary Note enclosed with other papers in a lether left in the hands of Mr. John Marshall, living with the aforesaid James Bowdwine, merchant, also a bond from Captain Ebinezer Wentworth of £114 neat money with all the interest due thereon, also a bond from Abigail Jervis, widow, of £100 neat money &c. &c., also a bond from Mary Hues, widow (£125) &c. which three last persons liveth at Boston aforesaid, and also such goods and effects which I have already sent over to her and which she hath now in possession. Item I give to my nephew Richard Mahier one bond of £50 neat money upon Solomon Townsend of Boston, Blacksmith, also two suits of Broadcloth cloaths, one stript Holland westcoat and Breeches, one pair silk stockens, two pair worsted ditto, three calico shirts, two Bagg Holland ditto, and one pair silver buttons. To my nephew John Mahier, son of my brother John Mahier of the Island of Jersey in the county of Hampshire, 600 crowns. To my nieces Mary and Elizabeth Mahier, daughters of said John

---

From Vol. XII, No. 1 (July 1904), p. 83.

Mahier, 100 crowns. To my loving sister Katherine Renoff late
Mahier 400 crowns. To my loving sister Mary Woden late
Mahier 100 crowns. To my loving friend Mary Pyke aforesaid,
widow, £5. To my loving friend Sarah Bass of Boston, widow,
mother of said Mary Pyke, £5. To my loving friends James
Bowden aforesaid merchant and Anthony Todder £2 5 s o d each
to buy them mourning rings. To my friend James Lloyd of
Boston aforesaid muck [sic in original]. To the poor of the
two parishes of the Island of Jersey in the county of Hampshire
aforesaid 100 livers to be equally divided and to be paid to the
several and respective churchwardens of each parish for the time
being for the use of said poor. To the poor of my native parish
of St. Johns in the Island of Jersey aforesaid 200 livers. All
rest &c. to my nephew Richard Mahier of Boston in New England, mariner. Friend John Lloyd of London, merchant,
executor, and manager of my adventures in Great Britain and
Island of Jersey, and friends James Bowdwin of Boston, merchant,
and Anthony Todder of same place, merchant, my executors
and managers of my affairs in New England or any other parts
in America. Proved by John Lloyd.

Buckingham, 135.

[Captain Savage was a member of the old Eastern Shore family of
the name—the only family in Virginia tracing in a direct male line to one
of the first party of settlers in 1607.]

GEORGE MORDANT of Fellingham, county Norfolk, gent.
Will 31 December 1627; proved 2 November 1633. I bequeath
my estate into the hands of my friends, my nephew Henrie
Mordant, Esq., my brother Talbott Pepys Esq., my neighbour
Raph Ward of Suffield, gent, and Thomas Utbert of How,
gent., whom I make my executors. To Lestrange my eldest
son my annuitie of £50, being for payment of £500, out of the
manor of Winslow in Hempsteed in Essex, I give the same
£500 to him at 24, and if he die then to my three younger sons
John, Henry, and George beside their portions. To Mary my
daughter my annuitie of £50 and also £500 due to me out of a
marsh of my brother Castles being in Thulton Norton and Rav-
ingham at 21. To Robert Mordant my second son all my lands
in Barton, Beeston Leemes, Beeston Kibballs, Smalborow, Neats-

head, and Irsted, as I purchased of Clement Poyd, now in occupation of Peter Burton. I give the said and tenement [sic] in Barton to Robert my son at 25, paying out thereof to Nicholas Benwell and Grace his wife till his age of 25, £3 a year to Nicholas and 40 s a year to Grace his wife [erased]. If I dont surrender the copyhold lands I hold of the several manors then being molested by Strange his brother, then I will that Lestrange pay to Robert, if he be henderance or else not. To John Mordant, my third son, £300 at 24. To Henry my fourth son all my adventure in Virginia, also £300 at 24. To George my fifth and youngest son £300 at 24. To Lestrange my eldest son two of my best beds, a chest of lynnen by the assignement of my sister Bedingfield, and all plate as his grandmother Riches gave him, also my wife's wedding ring. To Mary my daughter my great iron chest with her mother's clothes, with my sugar box that was her grandmother Pleyters which was given to my wife. To George the silver cup M^ris Utber his godmother gave him. To my brother Castle 40 s. To my nephew Sir Robert 20 s and to his son Charles 20 s. To Nephew Henry Mordant 40 s a year and to his wife my neece a nagg. To my Ladie Reynolds 20 s. and to every one of her children 10 s apiece. To my neece Cleere £3. To Mr. Alden of London 20 s. To my sister Castle 20 s and to my cousin Tallemage 10 s and to my neece Frances his daughter 10 s. To sister Bedingfield 40 s. To godson Edmund Bedingfield 20 s. To brother Pepys if he be overseer or executor 40 s yearly till son Lestrange be 24, and to his son Roger my godson 20 s. To Mr. Raphe Ward my neighbour on like conditions 40 s yearly as aforesaid. To Mr. Utber likewise 40 s yearly on said conditions. To his son Thomas my godson 10 s. To Mr. Henrie Monting 20 s. To George Pilkington my godson 10 s. To my mayd servant Mary Hayward 10 s yearly. To Edward Turner, Grace Benwell's nephew, 5 s yearlie till Lestrange be 21. ([In margin.] "This legacie to Edward Turner I have paid 20 s., and discharged upon my will at his departure 19 January 1628.") To Robert Payne 10 s yearlie till Lestrange be 21. To Mr. Startuy [? Starlin] if I be there dwelling at my death 10 s. To the repairing of the church of Fellingham 6 s 8d. To the poor of North Walsham till eldest son be 24, 400 furres out of the close I have in Worsted parish of Mr. Rant to be made at my cost. To cousin Thomas Bull of Worsted 10 s. To Peter Burton my servant past and now my tenant a cloak and to my godson two weather hoggs. To William Merton my servant 10 s yearly till Lestrange be 24. To the poor of Barton 5 s yearlie till son Robert be 24. I give John Moy his indenture, also 30 s. I give Peter Burton his wife 10 s that is my tenant at Barton. To the poor at Little Massingham 40 s to make a pump at the pond head and to the poor of the parish yearly 5 s till eldest son be 24. If I be buried in the chancell in my wife's sepulchre in Heyden, then to that parish 20 s. Witnesses: Thomas Bull, Robert Payne, William Starlin. Proved by Henry Mordant and Talbott Pepys.

Russell, 95.

[George Mordant or Mordaunt was evidently a brother of Sir Le-strange Mordaunt, who was created a baronet in 1611 and died in 1627, and uncle of Sir Robert Mordaunt, who succeeded his father in the title and died in 1635. A Lestrange Mordaunt was in Virginia in the seven-teenth century, but the exact reference to him is not now at hand.]

THOMAS MACKIE. 1719 April 30. Testament dative of Thomas Mackie of Langtounsyde, merchant in Glasgow, who died in November last, given up by Thomas Edgar, nephew to the defunct and son of James Edgar in Carmuck, and by the said James Edgar as administrator for his said son, and by Thomas Martine, son to Thomas Martine in Lands, procreated between him and Jonet Edgar his spouse who was neice to the defunct and procreated between the above James Edgar and —— Mackie his sister german, and the said Thomas Martine as administrator to his said son, as executors dative. At the call-ing whereof appearance was made for Thomas Edgar, merchant in Dumfries, and James Anderson, merchant in Glasgow, who produced a Will made by the defunct in their favor, but re-nounced the same in favor of the above executors. The defunct's estate consisted of debts due to him for merchant goods, tobacco, &c. and among other things a she-ass run out of milk with a he-colt valued together at £3 6 s 8d ; a silver-hilted sword worth 24 s sterling; a silver watch with a silver stamp fixed to the rib-bon valued at £4 sterling; and a sea-chest containing some old decayed drugs. The whole being £661 10 s 10 d sterling. His

Testament is dated at Glasgow 4th October 1718, and in it he appoints Thomas Edgar, merchant in Dumfries, and James Anderson, younger, merchant in Glasgow, his sole executors. He leaves to his nephew Thomas Edgar, son to James Edgar in Carmuck, £500 sterling; to Janet Rae, his niece, daughter lawful to William Rae living in Langtounsyde, with what is due to him by James Hillhouse, merchant in Bristol, and every other person in Bristol; and due to him from his partnership with John McWilliams, merchant in Philadelphia, to Thomas Martin, son to Thomas Martin in Lands, procreated between him and Jonet Edgar his neice, daughter to the said James Edgar in Carmuck, £100 sterling. He appoints his executors to educate Robert Eskridge, son of Captain George Eskridge of Virginia, at the grammar-school of Wood end where he now is, and afterwards in university and other learning and to pay the expenses of his education and board until he is sixteen years old, when he is to receive £30 sterling and be sent back to his native country whence he was brought under the defunct's care. But if his father wishes to recall him before, then he is only to receive the £30. His executors are to recompence themselves out of his estate for their pains and trouble. There is also a Deed of Renunciation by the said executors in favor of the legatees. Confirmed as above at Glasgow 20th April 1719, and James Edgar and Thomas Martin aforesaid are cautioners.

Glasgow Testaments, volume 48.

[Col. George Eskridge, of "Sandy Point," Westmoreland county, was a successful lawyer, and represented his county in the House of Burgesses in 1706, 1714, 1720, 1722, 1723, 1726, 1727-8, 1730 and 1732. In his will dated October 27 and proved November 25, 1735, he names his son Robert. Colonel Eskridge was for a time guardian of Mary Ball, the mother of George Washington, and it is probable that her great son was named after him. Col. Eskridge has many descendants, but the family genealogy gives no account of the son Robert, except that he is said to have studied medicine abroad and that his wife was name Jane.]

SIR JOHN ZOUCH, knight. Will 30 August 1636; proved 4 December 1639. To sonn John Zouch all land in Virginia, my watch, all bookes, my Armore and quilted coates and all my gunns because I cannot conveniently give him any more because I have been at so great charge with my plantation, having laid out about £1200 and such moneys as he hath adventured with me about the iron works, being £250, hath been lost, and much more of my owne, by reason that divers that promise to ioyne with us in that designe and did vnderwrite great sumes and did neglect the performance of it. To daughter Isabella Zouch my servantes, horses, plate, and all other goods in Virginia not before disposed to my sonn to £400 and any more to be divided with her two sisters, my daughters Elizabeth and Mary. I doe not give Isabella more [not] because I love her more than her sisters, but because shee hath adventured her life in soe dangerous a voyage. To daughters Elizabeth Zouch and Mary Zouch moneys in hands of Sir Thomas Hutchinson and due from Mr. Thomas Leake, of Little Leake, assigned me by Mr. Bispam, and a lease made to Mr. Emanuell Odingsells by said Mr. Leake. If anie daughter die before marriage, then to others, &c. "My daughter Bette I bequeath to my euer honored kinswoman and Noblest freind the Lady Theophila Coke, whom I doe desire to receive into her service and continue her in it while she deserues soe greate an honor." Executors: Sir Thomas Hutchinson and Mr. Gilbert Ward. Desire worthie friends Sir John Biron, Sir Edward Leech, and Mr. David Ramsey, if daughters want necessities, to assist them, &c. Witnesses: James Mason, George Baker, Thomas Waite, Thomas Lewis. Administration to son John Zouch, executors renouncing.

Harvey, 198.

[Sir John Zouch, of Codnor, Derbyshire, and his son John Zouch, Esq., were long engaged in colonial enterprises. Sir John, who was knighted at Belvoir Castle, April 23, 1603, made an engagement, dated October 30, 1605, with Captain George Weymouth, by which Zouch was to furnish and equip two ships which Weymouth was to command on a trading, fishing and exploring voyage to Virginia. This plan was put an end to by the granting of the charter of the Virginia Company. In 1631 he was appointed by the King one of the commissioners to devise a new plan of government in Virginia. He went to Virginia in 1634, with his son John (who was a member of the Virginia Company in 1623 and in that year received from the Company a grant of land in Virginia) and a daughter. In addition to a plantation the father and son attempted to set up iron works, which, as an entry in an old record says, "Came to nothing, their partners failing them." Sir John Zouch was an intimate

friend and confidant of Matthews and others of the party in Virginia op-
posed to Governor Harvey, and on his return to England about April 3,
1635 (as shown by a letter from Harvey), seems to have carried the statement of the grievances of the popular party.

Governor Harvey in a paper dated December, 1635, describing his
principal opponents, gives as "Reasons why Sir John Zouch should not
be made one of the Councell in Virginia, nor be permitted to returne
thither againe:

"1. Sir John Zouch is observed to be of a factious disposition, and of
the Puritan Sect. And its probable that all these stirs which have hap-
pened in Virginia had bin fermented by him, for he arrived there about
the beginning of November, 1631, and immediately he consorted himself with Mathewes and the rest of the faction, and in December following they fell to consult and contrive the complaint against Sir John
Harvey, which his Majesty hath heard and sent them into England by
Sir John Zouch, and gave him £500 to beare his charges in the Nego-
tiation.

"2. It appeares by Young Mr. Zouch, his Letter to his father that Sir
John Harvey was removed to make place for Sir John Zouch to be Governor of Virginia."

Though the date 1631 is given in the printed copy of Harvey's paper,
it is evident that it should be 1634.

The letter from his son, referred to, is printed in Neill's *Virginia
Carolorum*, p. 118, &c. In it he says: "The Countrey prayeth for you
both [some words illegible] you come Governor. My sister and all of
your friends are very well."

An extract from an old court record shows that Sir John Zouch's will
was put on record in Virginia.

No accessible records contain information as to the later history of
John Zouch, the son, and his sisters.

In Henrico county there is recorded a deed, dated April, 1681, from
Wm. Byrd, Esq , to Richard Kennon, gent., conveying 657 acres at
Roxdale [still a well-known farm in Chesterfield county, on James
river], formerly the property of Sir John Zouch, Knight ; but escheated
and afterwards granted to Abel Gower, who sold to Byrd. This land
was probably escheated, because abandoned by Zouch or his heirs.]

ALEXANDER WINCHELSEY, unprofitable servante of God.
Will 15 July 1620; proved 10 May 1621. To Thomas Daye
of Lymehouse, Ship-Carpenter, 50 lbs. of Tobacco to be paid
in London. To Anne Ravelin, dwelling at Tower-hill, 40s.
To Mrs. Ravelin goulde ringe left with her husband. To
Thomas Jarvis his wife, of Lymehouse, in Nightingale Lane, as
much Grograine as will make her a gowne. To Richard Woodes,

dwelling at Lymehouse in Ropemakerfeildes, 10 lbs. of Tobacco and a suite. To William Danyell, Surgeon of this shippe, 5 lbs. of Tobacco and a suite of clothes of white cut canvas and a hatt in my chest. Executor: Mr. Thomas Ravenett. To Mr. Edgar, the preacher at Stepney, 20s. To my hostis, her boy, 1 Barbery Ducket and rest to her and all things in her house, onlie a Barbery strappe to hang a ponnyarde to Master of this ship Mr. James Brett. To my nephew Walter Winchelsey 200 lbs. Tobacco and benefit of wages. Overseers: Mr. James Brett, John White, Benjamin Jewer, to receive all Tobacco owing in Virginia. Rest owing in Virginia and that owing by Robert Parton to Richard Domelawe. Witnesses: William Danyell, Richard Domelawe.

Dale, 40.

[A William Ravenett lived in James City in 1623, and had a grant of 150 acres in the " County of Denbigh " (now Warwick), in 1635, and of 250 acres in Warwick in 1636.]

PETER HOOKER, of London, Tallow chandler, intending a voyage to Virginia in good Shipp the Globb of London. Will 6 August 1636; proved 22 November 1639. To the poore of Chilcombe, county Southampton, 20s. out of my adventure, when adventure doth returne into England, to my Aunt Stroud £3, to cousen Anne Hooker my Vnckle Richard's daughter £3, to her brother Richard 40s, to Henry Hooker my Vnckle Peeter's sonne 40s at 21, to his brother Nicholas Hooker ditto, to Sibell Hooker Vnckle Peeter's daughter 20s, to Richard Wood his children Hannah, John, and Samuell 20s. apece. If Aunt Stroud die, then to her sonne and his wife. If anie of my poore kindred die, then to others. To brother John Hooker all goods left in his hands and £30 out of adventure. If brother John die, to his sonn John Hooker. Rest to brother Edward Hooker, executor. Overseers: Vnckle Edward Hooker and cusen John Wood. Witnesses: Edward Hooker, Richard Potter, George Strettin.

Harvey, 187.

THOMAS PROCTOR, cittizen and haberdasher of London. Will 9 October 1624; proved 6 November 1624. To be buried in church of greate Allhallowes in London. To sonn Samuell

coppyhoulds of " Dunmowe Pryorata " and " Dunmowe parva,"
in little Dunmowe, Essex, and also coppyhould " Harris
Landes," &c , in Muche Wakeringe, Essex.   To wief Jane one
full eighte parte of good Shippe called the Tyger, of London,
nowe gone on a voyadge (by Godisgrace) to the Streightes,
also recognizance of Statute staple by Henry Hayes of Wans-
worth, Surrey, in Kinges Bench for debt of £200, also debt of
£120 in Virginia in hands of my brother John Proctor, also all
Platt, Apparell, Implements, &c., also £50.   To brother John
Proctor £130 in his handes as a Stocke above £120 above.   To
Father in lawe William Squier £10.   To godsonne Thomas
Squier, sonne of Joseph Squier, £10.   To loving Vncle and
friende William Graye of London, Plumber, and aunte Mary
Graye, his weif, £50 each.   To poore of hamlett of Lymehouse,
Middlesex, £5.   Uncle William Graye to be guardian of sonne
Samuell till 24.   Rest to son Samuel, paying legacies above
with bonds of £100 each due by Mr. Williamole, Mr. Burdett,
and Mr. Startute.   Executor: Vncle William Graye.   Witnesses: Thomas Pennent, Scrivenor, John Gray.   2 November,
——, administration to Jane Proctor als. Squire relict of Thomas
Proctor, late of Stepney, deceased, during minority of son Samuel Proctor, not administered by William Gray, executor, deceased.

Bryde, 117.

[Mr. John Proctor received a patent for land in Virginia from the
Virginia Company on July 5, 1623, on condition that he would carry
over 100 persons.   A few days later it is recorded that he intended to
send over £50 worth of supplies for the relief of his plantation.   He was
a member of the Company.   In 1625 his name appears among those
who had received grants in the corporation of Henrico.   On account
of the massacre this section of the colony had been abandoned, and
Proctor and his wife were living on James river in the present Surry
county, not far from Jamestown.

It is probable that he was in England at the time of the massacre and
that it was his wife who held out against the Indians as described by
Smith : "Mistress Proctor, a proper, civil, modest Gentlewoman, did
the like [held out against the Indians] till perforce the English officers
forced her and all them with her to goe with them, or they would
fire her house themselves ; as the Salvages did when they were gone,
in whose despight they had kept it and what they had, a month or three
weeks after the massacre ; which was to their hearts a griefe beyond

comparison, to lose all they had in that manner, onely to secure others pleasures.''

The census of 1624–5 (*Hotten*) states that there were then living at Pace's Paines (in the present county of Surry) John Proctor, who had come in the *Seaventure* in 1607, and Allis, his wife, who came in the *George* in 1621.

It is possible that Proctor's Creek, in the county of Chesterfield, marks the place of John Proctor's early grant in the corporation of Henrico, and that a family of Proctor, once resident in Surry, descended from him.]

VIRGINIA GLEANINGS IN ENGLAND.

Communicated by Mr. LOTHROP WITHINGTON, 30 Little Russell street,
W. C., London (including "Gleanings" by Mr. H. F. WATERS,
not before printed).

(CONTINUED)

OTHO THORPE of the parish of All Hallows the Wall in London, merchant   Will 28 June 1686; proved 13 July 1686.   To my neice Hannah Thorpe, my brother's daughter, three hundred pounds, to be paid unto her out of goods and estate in Virginia.   To my cousin John Grice living in Virginia, his two eldest children and their heirs my plantation in Virginia called Tuttis Neck.   All the rest of my estate in Virginia to my cousin Thomas Thorpe and his wife Katherine for their lives, and next to my wife Frances for her life, lastly to my right heirs.   The residue to my wife and she to be sole executrix.

Lloyd, 102.

[We are indebted to the *Wm. and Mary Quarterly*, IX, 209, &c., for the following note on the Thorpe family:

"George Thorpe, Esq., was the son of Nicholas Thorpe, of Wanswell Court, Gloucestershire, by his first wife, Mary Wikes, alias Mason, niece of Sir John Mason, a councillor of state, and was grandson of Thomas Thorpe and Margaret Throckmorton.   In 1618 he formed a partnership with his kinsmen and connections, Sir William Throckmorton, John Smith, of Nibley, and Richard Berkeley, to found 'a new Berkeley,' in Virginia.   He was a manager of the college lands in Virginia and a great friend of the Indians.   He had been a gentlemen pensioner, a gentleman of the king's privy chamber, M. P. for Portsmouth, 1614, and member of the council of the Virginia Company.   He was massacred by the Indians at Berkeley, March 21, 1622.   He was twice married, first to Margaret, daughter of Sir Thomas Porter, on July 11, 1600, who died *s. p.*, and secondly to Margaret, daughter of David Harris, who died in 1629.   Their son, William Thorpe, was also twice married, his first wife (married in 1636), being Ursula, daughter of John Smith, of Nibley.   There was a Richard Thorpe, who died in York county, Va., in 1660, who mentions his sons Richard and George, wife Elizabeth, and kinsman, Major Otho Thorpe.   These sons probably died unmarried, as the will of Richard Thorpe, of Marston parish, dated March 12, 1669, gives his whole estate to his father-in-law (step-father), Otho Thorpe. The widow, Elizabeth Thorpe, when about to marry Otho Thorpe, made a deed to her sons, Richard and George Thorpe. Major Otho Thorpe was a justice of Yorke county and major of militia. He suffered severe losses during Bacon's Rebellion. He married three times, first, Elizabeth, widow of Richard Thorpe; secondly, Dorothy, widow of Samuel Fenn, who died October 27, 1675; and thirdly, Frances ———, who survived him, and married John Annesley, gent., of Westminster, England. Major Thorpe appears to have died without issue, in the parish of All-Hallows-the-Wall, London, giving his property to his nephew, Captain Thomas Thorpe, niece Hannah Thorpe, and cousin, John Grice. Captain Thomas Thorpe died October 7, 1693, aged forty-eight, and his tombstone is in Bruton churchyard, Williamsburg. He probably left no children, since in a deed, in 1699, Hannah Thorpe, who married John Pell, a cooper, of London, calls himself Major Otho Thorpe's 'right and lawful heir.'

Otho Thorpe, of Virginia, was certainly the Otho Thorpe who was baptised in the parish of St. Martins-in-the-Fields, London, on August 16, 1606. He died in 1686–7. The Thorpe entries in the register establish his relationship with Captain George Thorpe. This latter had an Indian lad whom he trained to learning. He copied the draft of the patent of Berkeley Hundred sent to the Governor, Sir George Yeardley. Among the burials reported in the register of St. Martins-in-the-Fields, is *George Thorp, homo Virginiae, September 27, 1619.*

FROM THE REGISTER OF THE PARISH OF ST. MARTIN'S-IN-THE-FIELDS, COUNTY MIDDLESEX, ENGLAND.

Gulielmus Thorpe, buried June 18, 1567.

Joannes Thorpe and Rebecca Greene, married Sept. 15, 1592.

Elizabeth Thorpe, baptized May 30, 1593.

Maria Thorpe, baptized November 24, 1594.

Rebecca Thorpe, baptized Jan. 25, 1595.

Katherine Thorpe, baptized December 11, 1597.

Gulielmus Thorpe, baptized November 7, 1600.

Thomas Thorpe, baptized June 23, 1598.

Mr. George Thorpe and Mrs. Margaret Porter, married July 11, 1600.

Johannis Thorpe, baptized Jan. 28, 1601.

Johannis Thorpe, baptized March 26, 1602.

Richard Thorpe, baptized Oct. 6, 1603.

Rebecca Thorp, buried June 22, 1604.

Johannis Thorpe and Margaret Ann Sherry, married Sept. 16, 1605.

Otho Thorpe, baptized Aug. 16, 1606.

Rebecca Thorpe, fil. Johannis, baptized Dec. 27, 1608.

Ellina *Tharp*, fil. John, baptized July 30, 1611.

John Lynch and Elizabeth Thorp, married Sept. 17, 1611.

Richard Thorp, buried March 2, 1614.
Margaret Thorp, baptized February 13, 1613.
Infans George Thorp, buried January 12, 1617.
Georgius Thorp, baptized September 10, 1619.
Rebecca Thorp, buried April 7, 1617.
Richard Thorp, Gen., buried June 3, 1619.
Georgius Thorp, *homo Virginianae*, buried September 27, 1619.''

The following epitaphs are on tombs in Bruton churchyard:

Here lyeth in Hope of a Joyfull
Resurrection the Body of Capt.
Thomas Thorp of Bruton
Parish in the Dominion of Virginia
Nephew of Maj. Otho Thorp
of the same Parish who Departed
This Life the 7 day of October
Ano 1693 Aged 48.

———

Katherine Thorp
Relick of Cap't Thomas
Thorp Nephew to Major
Otho Thorp Formerly
Inhabitant of this Parish
after a Pilgrimage of Forty
three yeares in a Troublesome
World Lay Down here to
Rest in hope of a Joyfull
Resurrection obiit June 6, 1695.]

Sir Thomas Hewet, knight. Will 30 January 1623 | 4;
proved 11 February 1623 | 4. To be buried in church of Olde
Jurye in London, and executor to bestowe 299 Markes vpon a
Tombe, and to poore of parish of olde Jurie where I was borne
rent charge of £5 out of my landes called "Bakes" in Goldhanger, Essex. Messuages in Horne church, Goldhanger, and
elsewhere in Essex, and certain coppie holdes in Essex, and
coppie holdes (already surrendered) in Kentish Towne helde of
Mannor of Tottenhall, Middlesex, and lease for certaine lives of
house lately built adioyninge to house nowe or latelie Fishbornes
and Brownes neere or in Lothburie, London, with gardaine and
entry, all to brother Sir William Hewett for use of this will.
Lands in Ireland, some of inheritance in fee simple and some
leasehold, and two shares of adventure in the Bermudas and

alsoe an adventure of £75 in Virginia or a share of Lands for said £75, and other profits in Bermudas and Virginia which lands in Ireland I alsoe purpose to convey by deed (if God permitt mee tyme) and also all shares in the Bermudas and Virginia, and whatever else I possess in Ireland or anie of the said Bermudas or Virginia (except covenantes with John Cope touching certain Lands in Ireland of £1300 onlie) all to my naturall sonne William Curwen als Hewett and his heirs male, or in default to my said brother Sir William Hewett, but Anne Curwen mother of said William Curwen als Hewett to enjoy £30 per annum for life out of lands in Ireland, brother Sir William Hewett to take rents till William Curwen als Hewett is 21. Lands bequeathed to brother Sir William to be sold for debts in schedule and for legacies. Whereas not being truly enformed of my estate and for some other causes which my present sicknes admitts not abilitie to examine, if sufficient estates made as by stricknes of Lawe requisite, beseech Lord Keeper or Lord Chancellor of England and ditto of Ireland for time being to decree according to intent of this will. To poore at buriall £20. To Nephewe Sir John Hewett Baronet ringe of £5. To sister Ladie Hewett wife of brother Sir. William £200. To Companie of Clothworkers for a dinner £30. To Sir Roberte Wiseman, knight, £30. To children of brother Sir William Hewett £10 apiece. To Mr. Ralph Freeman, Sheriffe of London £10 for ringe. To Mr. Thomas Ferrers £50. Sir Richard Wiseman, knight, Mr. Thomas Wiseman, and Mr. John Wiseman £10 apiece. To cozen John Hewett and Samuel Hewett £10 apiece. To servants George Burdett, Mathewe Parret, Henrie Fortescue, William Fortescue, and George Shelton £10 apiece. To Elizabeth Mathewes £30. To Captaine Thomas Aderly lyving in Ireland £40. To fifty poore menn fifty goundes of 20s. Rest to brother Sir William Hewett, executor. Overseers: friends Sir Roberte Wiseman and Mr. Thomas Ferrers. Witnesses: Robert Wiseman, Richard Wiseman, J: Delden, Antho: Cliffe, William Stisted.

Dale, 8.

[Sir Thomas Hewit, cloth worker, was a member of the Virginia Company under the third charter and subscribed and paid £75. He was also a member of the East India Company, was knighted at Theo-

balds, December 15, 1613, and was master of the company of clothworkers in 1619. He was a son of William Hewit or Hewet, Esq., who
died in 1599, aged seventy-seven, and was buried in St. Paul's, London.
The nephew, Sir John Hewet, was of Headley Hall, Yorkshire, and
was created a baronet October 11, 1621. The title is now extinct.]

THOMAS WHAPLETT. Will 6 January 1635 | 6; proved 7
July 1636. To sister Rebecca Whaplett, executrix, all my
porcion, remayning in the chamber of London. Whereas friend
John Redman has paid £300 lbs. of tobacco for a plantation
for me, he to have £18 sterling or as much more as 300 lbs. of
Tobacco yeelds in England. Executor in trust in Virginia:
friend John Redman. To vncle Thomas Whaplett 40s. for a
nagg. To John Redman ditto, he to pay debts I own here in
Virginia, etc. Witnesses: Abraham Peate, Mathewe Martin,
Thomas Andrewes. 3 November 1636. Administration to Ralph
Gregge, late husband of special executrix Rebecca Whaplett als
Gregge deceased, reserving to John Redman.

Pile, 82.

[Thomas Whaplett, aged twenty-one, was a passenger on the ship
Globe, of London, which left that port for Virginia in August, 1635.
Hotten, 120.]

ROBERT FILBRIGG, citizen and Scrivenor of London [St.
Dunstans in the East. Probate Act Book.] Will 4 July 1638;
proved 10 July 1638. To cozon Margaret Newman widdowe
£4 and her daughter Ann Newman £4. To William Walford,
Vpholster, best blacke cloth cloake to weare in remembrance of
mee. To old William Robson 20s. To William Lowe for his
pains 40s. To friend John Wilkinsonne, Shoemaker, £10. To
my brother John Filbrigg now Resident in Virginia £10. Rest
to brother William Fillbrigge, executor. Overseers: John Wilkinsonne, William Lowe. Witnesses: Thomas Lowd, James
Garrett, Thomas Brady, scrivenor.

Lee, 87.

JOHN POWELL, citizen and clothworker of London. Will
30 July 1624; proved 17 December 1624. To poorest of Clothworkers Company £5. To wife Anne lands in London or elsewhere. To brother Thomas Powell 40s. To kinsmen Joseph Rogers, William Miller, and kinswomen Sara Browne and cosin Judith

Rawlins £3 each. To my cosin now being in Virginia the son of my uncle David Powell 40s. To freind Richard Asope, Scrivenor, 40s. To neare kindred 12d each. Rest to wife Ann, executrix. Overseers: brother Thomas Powell and Cozen William Miller. Witnesses: Hen. Burnley, Scr., William Wood, Nathaniell Draper, Edward Drake.

Byrde, 112.

JOHN PARRY inhabiting in Virginia. Will [nuncupative] 24 March 1637 | 8; proved 30 July 1638. To Samuell, Mr. Minifrey his servant, his coopers tools, one suit of Clothes, and one shirt. To John Martin one shirte and other old clothes. To Stephen Pendle shirt and Convase clothes. To Raphe Hvnter, groome his Bedd pillow and rugg. To brother William Parry his wages. Witnesses: Joseia James, Ralph Hunter groome, and others.

Lee, 87.

[John Parry, aged twenty-seven, was a passenger in the ship *Primrose*, which left Gravesend for Virginia in July, 1635. (*Hotten*, 115.) George Menifee was a wealthy merchant and planter.]

CAPTAIN ROBERT SMALLAY of Bermoda Hundred. Will 19 December 1617; proved 15 November 1621. To my man Christopher Hardyn three Barrells of Indian Corne. To my man Thomas Chapman fifty waight best Tobacco. To my man Richard Kyes 5 yardes of kersey, 2½ barrells of Corne Indian. To my man Thomas Oge 3 barrells of Corne Indian. To wife Elizabeth house and grounds at Bermoda Hundred, 2 cowes, 3 cowe calves, 1 bull cowe, 1 sowe, and rest of goodes, certaine notes in my Trunck to receive Tobacco for other men and notes of Mr. Peers with Ensign Chaplyn and Prokter. Mr Prokter is to pay £20 of best Tobacco for corne he had of Leuveten' Bartlett. Sir Thomas Dale oweth me for 63 lbs. of Tobacco at 3s, 4d; I am to have of Thomas Chapman 400 lbs. of Tobacco at Henrico. To Cáptain Samuel Argall, Esq., now Gou'nor of Virginia, executor, 2 yoke of Oxen when my Tobacco hath paid for them. Witnesses: Henry Richardson, John Downeman. Administration to Elizabeth Smallay, relict, &c., Samuel Argall renouncing.

Dale, 19.

[This will is of especial interest because it is the earliest known which includes a bequest of land in Virginia owned by an individual. In 1614 or 1615, says Hamor: "Dale hath alotted to every man three English acres." (*True Discourse*, p. 17.) This was the beginning of private ownership of land in Virginia, and doubtless Captain Smalley's tract was one of these three acre alotments. John Rolfe's *Relation* states that in 1614-15, Captain Smaley commanded at Henrico in the absence of the chief officer, Captain Davis. On October 21, 1621, Elizabeth Smalley, widow, having petitioned the king against Captain Argall, pretending that he detained from her certain goods to the value of £500, and being referred by his majesty to the council for Virginia, now petitions the Company to hear the cause. Mrs. Smalley afterwards retracted her charge against Argall; but still later stated that he had forced her to write the retraction by refusing to relinquish the administration on her husband's estate, unless she did as he wished. No final action seems to have been taken by the company.]

WILLIAM THOMAS of Lantwit Maior. Will 15 January 1647 | 8; proved 6 June 1649. To church of Landath 10s. To church of Lantwit 40s. To poore of Lantwit 40s. To my wife's children by her first husband £10. To wife during widowhood 13½ acres of land, viz: 5½ we call the Abeles Field, 6 acres we call the Marlpit, and 2 acres adjoining to little Abeles Field on North side of the Hills, but if she marry, only 7 acres for life, viz: 6 acres at Marlepitt and 2 acres of the White Close adjoining the wayside. If wife be with child, then to child 27 acres, house &c. bought of my brother and Originall lease from Mr. Edward Stradling to old Liddon assigned me by my father, also £500 worth of lands and grounds due me in the West Indies and the continent of America, and all due in Walse and all goods in West Indies or any other place specified. If I have noe child, then lands, except those specified to wife, to brother Lamorock Thomas, and in default of issue to brother Alexander Thomas, and his eldest, then second son. Of goods in West Indies, one half to brother Lamorock Thomas in consideration of bond due and one half to wife. To wife's mother £5. To poore in parish of Landwit 20s. yearly if I and brother Lamorock have no issue. To wife during widdowhood house I live in &c. and rest of houses to brother Alexander Thomas. Executor: brother Alexander Thomas. Overseers: cozen Alexander Yeoreth

79

and friend Thomas Walker.   Witnesses: John Lloyd, William
Tobie, Jane Rawder.

JOHN CREED of Martyns Hundred, Virginia.   Will 29 Janu-
ary 1633 | 4; proved 18 April 1635.   To sister Joane Perryor
£5 due from brother Cutbeard Creed.   To my master Francis
Clarke £5 for debt sealed by me under age.   Rest to my mas-
ter Thomas Faussett, executor.   Witnesses: Thomas Ward,
Christopher Edwards.   Administration to Anne Fassett wife of
Thomas Fassett now dwelling in Virginia.

Sadler, 34.

[Thomas Fossett was among the people living at West or Shirley
Hundred island, in February, 1623. Francis Clarke, aged twenty-
eight, was a passenger on the ship *Transport*, of London, which sailed
for Virginia in July, 1635.]

JOHN PAYTON of Ham Green, parish Portbury, Somerset.
Will 23 February 1697 | 8; proved 4 August 1699.   To wife
Jane Payton and four children William, John, Thomas, George,
all estate &c., wife and Kinsman Mr. Joseph Cox, attorney,
with advice of Mr. Joseph Wade to imploy estate.   Being now
sick on board ship Sarah, Capt. John Miller commander, if it
please God to call me, Mr. Edward Foye now merchant on
board to take care of my interest on board, and if it arrive
safely at Virginia where bound to dispose of all goods and collect all moneys due me in the country of Virginia or Maryland
for my wife and children, and friend Captain John Miller to assist.
Executrix: wife Jone Payton.   Overseer: Mr. Joseph Cox of
Hamgreen, and if he die, Mr. Joseph Wade of Parish of St.
George, Marriner.   Witnesses: John Miller, Timothy Bayly,
James Lilliwhite.

Pett, 137.

[Abraham Persey, who came to Virginia in 1616, was cape merchant
(or treasurer), of the colony and member of the council. See this
magazine, I, 187, 188.]

ABRAHAM PERSEY of Persey's Hundred, Esq.   Will 1 March
1626 | 7; proved 10 May 1633.   Executrix: wife Francis Persey.
Overseers in Virginia: Mr. Grevell Pooly, Minister, and Mr.

Richard Kingmill of James Citty Island. Debts in England and Virginia to be paid. Debts in Tobacco in Schedule. Overseer in England: Mr. Delyonell Russell, Merchant, of London. Land by patent &c. to be sold, also land due for transport of servants since my going to England in March 1620, for which I have not taken up one foote of lande, of which the number of men will appear by their indentures, of women about eight. Executrix to sell all estate in Virginia, servants, cattell, hoggs, corne, Tobacco, &c. To sister Judith Smythe in England £20. To overseers Mr. Pooly and Mr. Kingmill each 300 lbs of tobacco. To friend Mr. Delyonell Russell in England £30. To Nathaniel West, sonn of dearly beloved wife Frances Persey, £20 at 21. To wife one third of estate. To two daughters Elizabeth Persey and Mary Persey one twelfth. To Mr. Russell one half of estate in best tobacco for use of said children &c., but if either of daughters marry without consent of their mother in law or of said Mr. Russell one half of their portion to my brother John Persey. Daughters to remain in custody of Mr. Russell. No witnesses. Administration of Abraham Persey late of Persey's Hundred in Virginia to daughter Mary Hill als Persey, relict Frances Persey being dead.

Russell, 41.

THOMAS CLARKE of parish and county of York in Virginia in America. Will 16 April 1666; proved 10 May 1670. All lands as heir unto Edward Clarke of Thriploe near Foulemere, Cambridgeshire, my late father deceased, in hands of William Deering of Thriploe in open court by me elected Guardian, as also all other lands particularly one House, orchard etc. in possession of Richard Farrowe in Thriploe conveyed by me by deed of guift to Mr. Peter Temple 12 December 1665, I doe freely give unto my Loueing Friend Peter Temple. To sister Susanna Clarke if living, three acres in Meldred. To sister Mary Clarke piece of land called New Ditch. Rest to Peter Temple, executor. Witnesses: Johnathan Newells, Robert Hawlin, John Baskerville.

Penn, 57.

[Rev. Peter Temple, minister of York parish, York county, Va., received a grant of land December 24, 1665. He married, in 1669, Mary,

81

widow of Lieutenant-Coloney Thomas Ludlow, of York county, and later returned to England. On November 6, 1686, as " Peter Temple, of Sible Henigham, in the County of Essex, Clerk," he, together with his wife, made conveyance of her interest in a tract of land in York county, Va., which had belonged to her first husband. There is also recorded in York a deed, dated February 26, 1693, from Peter Temple and Mary, his wife, to Lambeth, in the county of Surrey, Eng. Rev. Peter Temple had a son, Captain Peter Temple, of York county, who married Anne, daughter of James Bray, Esq., member of the council of Virginia, and died in 1695.

Jonathan Newell was a prominent merchant residing in York and James City counties as early as 1661. He died in 1679, and the appraisement of his estate included " Bookes—63 Bookes of several sortes, 6 pay Bookes, some large." Among the servants were "4 Turkes at £95." The estate was a large and valuable one. His widow, Elizabeth, was administratrix.

"John Baskervyle, gent.," was clerk of York county in 1667, and other years. He married Mary, daughter of Lieutenant-Colonel William Barber, of York county, and had issue: George, Elizabeth, Magdalen who married Joseph White; Sarah, Rebecca, and Mary, who married John Batten. John Baskervyle died 1674-5, and the inventory of his estate includes "a p'cell of English Bookes, £3; a p'cell of Latine Bookes, £1." He died intestate. The will of Mary Baskervyle, his widow, was dated July 12, 1693, and proved in York, June 25, 1694. She left her daughter, Mary Batten, "my lined Gowne and Muzling cornit" (a cornet was a lady's headdress); to daughter Magdalen White her mourning ring; to daughters Rebecca and Sarah Baskervyle her two ewes and lambs; to son George Baskervyle her negro boy Frank; remainder of estate equally between George, Sarah and Rebecca.

Possibly the Baskervills of Mecklenburg county are descendants of John Baskervyle.

The will of Thomas Clarke was proved and recorded in York, April 24, 1666. On April 25, 1666, Jonathan Newell and John Baskervyle came into court and made oath as witnesses to a deed, dated December 25, 1665, from Thomas Clarke, of York parish, York county, son and heir of Edward Clarke, of Thriploe, Cambridgeshire, Eng., lately deceased, conveying to his " loving friend " Peter Temple, a messuage at Thriploe, lately in the occupation of Richard Farrow, deceased. The witnesses swore that this deed was made by Thomas Clarke, deceased.]

HENRY HENDERSON neare Yorke River in the county of Kent of Virginia, Planter. Will 10 March 1673 | 4; proved 3 November 1674. To wife Susanna all my Plantations, Land, Tenements neare York River in Virginia and all other estate in

Virginia or England.   Executor my friend and kinsman Richard Stone of St. James, Clerkenwell, Phisitian, and to him two hogsheads best Tobacco my plantation in Virginia affords. Witnesses: Will: Ridges, Tho: Reynolds, scrivenor.

Bunce, 126.

NATHANIEL WEST, Cittizen and Mercer of London.   Will 17 July 1630; proved 8 September 1630.   Having noe child, goods in two parts according to laudable custom of London, one half to wife Jane, other one half as follows: To poor of St. Ethelborough 40s.   To uncle Thomas Williamson £20.   To Aunt Anne Williamson £20.   To cozen George Williamson £100. To Cozen Elizabeth Williamson £50.   To Cozen Richard Williamson £20.   To brother David Woodroffe and sister Anne his wife £20.   To cozen Frauncis West sonn of Ingram West £20. To cozen William Williamson 40s. for ring.   To Anne Woodroffe and David Woodroffe, children of brother David Woodroffe, £10 each.   To John West and Anne West, children of brother Francis West, ditto.   To sister Margaret West, now wife of said brother Francis West, one large Persian carpett. To Aunt Anne Williamson, one lesser ditto.   To sister Anne Woodroffe one ditto.   Rest to Brother Francis West, executor.

Scroope, 78.

[Mr. Withington kindly made these abstracts at the editor's request, as it was thought the testator might have been the Nathaniel West of Virginia.   This idea proves to be incorrect.]

Communicated by Mr. LOTHROP WITHINGTON, 30 Little Russell street,
W. C., London (including "Gleanings" by Mr. H. F. WATERS,
not before printed).

(CONTINUED)

SAMUEL LEONARDE. Will proved 3 February 1618 | 9.
Auspicate sacrasancta Tria de Ego Samuel Leonarde filius
Johannus Lennard at Elizabetha (quas honoris causa nomine)
sciens morte mihil certius horavero mortis mihil incertius esse
Kalendis martis Anno salutis millessimo sexcentessimo decimo
septimo aetatis meae sexagessimo quinto ineunte hoc meum tes-
tamentum facio," &c. "Having thus witnessed my faith :
To brethren Sir Frauncis Eure, Sir Thomas Gresham, and Sir
Marmaduke Darell, knights, and to my loving sonne in law
Thomas Hobbes, Esq., all estate in Kent as by indenture 18
July 1617 to bring up my children, advance sonns at 21 &c.
Dame Elizabeth my wife to receive rents, as each to have £1000
&c. To my sonne Covert Lennard all sommes of money ad-
ventured into Virginia and newe found land. To each daugh-
ter a gold ring of 10s. with "Inhumia potius quam Impudicia,"
earnestly charging them to bestowe themselves in marriage with
consent of theire mother, and my sonne Hobbes. To the right
honorable Lord Bergavenny, my loving brothers in lawe Sir
Fra: Eure, Sir Walter Covert, Sir Thomas Gresham, and Sir
Marmaduke Darell, and my loving sonne Thomas Hobbes,
Esq. gold ringes of 20s. with "Hodie mihi Cras tibi" engraven.
To my honorable neice the Ladie Gray, my loving mother in
law the Ladie Slanye, my loving sisters the ladie Gresham, the
ladie Darell and the ladie Weld, golde rings at 20s. with "Mori-
endo vinetis." To sonn Stephen all bookes and armor with my
bases and sleeves of purple velvet. To poore of Westwickam
40s. To servauntes Fraunces Morden, Richard Phillipps, and
Ralphe Wollam 40s. and rest of servaunts 10s. apiece. To wife
Elizabeth Lennarde use of all plate and household stuffe.
Executors : wife, sonne Stephen, and sonne in lawe Thomas

From Vol. XII, No. 3 (Jan. 1905), p. 297.

Hobbes. Children every Sabbath to frequent the "assemblces of godes people" &c. To Master and fellow of Emanuell College, Cambridge, to present a godlie and learned preacher to Westwickam, Kent. To a sermon on 5th of November on infernall and damnable treason plotted by limes of that antichristian archiheriticke of Rome 20s. yearlie out of lands in Eurith and Dockmeade in Heese. To be buried in the lords chappell in Westwickam church. Overseers : Sir Thomas Gresham and Sir Marmaduke Darell, Knts. No witnesses.

Parker, 13.

[Samuel Lennarde, of West Wickham, Kent, son of John Lennarde, of Knole, in the same county, was knighted in 1603, and was a member of the Virginia Company under the third charter, when he paid £62. 10. He was ancestor of the Lennards of West Wickham, baronets, now extinct. His sisters were Elizabeth, who married Sir Francis Eure, Chief Justice of North Wales; Timothea, married Sir Walter Covert, of Slaugham, in Sussex, a member of the Virginia Company; Mary, married Sir Thomas Gresham, of Fitzey, in Surrey (kinsman and heir of the famous Elizabethan merchant), and Anne, who married Sir Marmaduke Darrell, of Fulmer, Berkshire, also a member of the Virginia Company. As Lady Darrell's oldest brother was named Sampson Lennarde, it is possible that Sampson Darrell who lived in Virginia in the latter part of the seventeenth century, was a descendant.]

JOHN FISHER, citizen and Barbersurgeon of London. Will 8 July 1634: proved 10 October 1634. To be buried in parish church, St. Giles Cripplegate. To now wife Isable lease of house I now live in in Golding Lane, Cripplegate, held of bridgehouse at £4 per annum, of which 15 years to run, for her greate love and affection, and if she die to Moses Fisher, my brother James Fisher's son. To brother James Fisher gold ring. To sister Catherine 20s, my late apprentice William Fletcher put over to Mr. Adam Thorowgood who sent him over to Virginia, and am to receive for his services £50 waight of Tobacco yearly for Adam's term of five years from May last, which to use of wife Isabel, Isabel Fisher, my brother James Fisher's daughter and Eliah Easton the youngest, whom I keep. Goods to wife Isable for life, then to sister Catherine's children. Executor : wife Isable. Overseers : Mr. William Neede of

London, milliner, and Mr. Henry Hickman of London, salter. Witnesses : Thomas Sparkes, Edward Flower, John Hughes.

Dean and Chapter of St. Paul's, register E, folio 19.

[Adam Thoroughgood was of Lower Norfolk county. See this magazine, II, 414, *et seq.*]

JOHN ASHLEY, late of Virginia in partes beyond ye seas, deceased. Administration 15 May 1657 to Christopher Rowe ye Grandfather and Curator to Joane Ashley a minor ye naturall lawful and onely child.

Admon Act Book, 1657, folio 47.

[An imperfect record of a patent shows that a John Ashley and John Hamper were granted 1,000 acres in Virginia on March 10, 1653. A John Ashley was granted 240 acres on Nantypoyson creek, Lancaster county, June 13, 1662.]

MARY BAGG als Butler late of Washington, county of Westmoreland in Virginia. Administration 11 September 1717 to her husband John Bagg clerk.

Ditto, 1717, folio 182.

[John Bagge received his bounty for the cost of his passage, as a minister, to Virginia November 13, 1717. He came first to the colony in 1709, in deacon's orders; but was allowed to take charge of St. Anne's parish, Essex. In 1717 he returned to England for priest's orders, and again became minister of St. Anne's (*Meade's Old Churches and Families of Virginia*, I, 396). He died in 1726, and his inventory, on record in Essex, includes books, valued at £22. 1.

There is recorded in Essex, a deed, dated October, 1714, from John Bagge, of St. Anne's parish, Essex, clerk, and Mary, his wife, late the widow of Samuel Thacker. John Bagge married a second time, and again a wife whose name was Mary. The will of John Bagge, of St. Anne's parish, Essex, clerk, was dated November, 1724, and proved in Essex, June, 1726. His legatees were his wife Mary, cousin Edmund Bagge, £100 sterling, sisters Ann Coughlin and Mary Kely, nephews William and John, sons of brother Leonard Bagge, and nephews Edmund and William, sons of brother Luke Bagge.

The will of Mary Bagge, of St. Anne's parish, widow of John Bagge, was dated in August, 1726, and proved in Essex, in September of the same year. Her legatees were Mrs. Elizabeth, wife of Captain Thomas Waring, and their eldest daughter Betty; her cousin Penelope Manly, and her nephew Edmund Bagge, who was appointed executor.

The will of Edmund Bagge was dated January, 1733, and proved in

Essex, May, 1734. His legatees were his wife Katherine, and son, Robert Bagge.

There is on record in Essex a power of attorney from Andrew Bagge, of Start, county Waterford, Ireland, gent., authorizing the conveyance of his interest in the lands of John Bagge, late of Virginia, clerk, and also a deed, dated March, 1737, from John Bagge, of Ardmore, county Waterford, Ireland, only son and heir of Leonard Bagge, late of Kilbree, in said county, deceased, and surviving executor of the will of John Bagge, late of Virginia, clerk, conveying his interest to Andrew Bagge, of Start, county Waterford, gent., son of Luke Bagge, of the same place.]

JOHN BOYSE late of South River in Virginia, bachelor, deceased. Administration 4 January 1709 | 10 to Edmund Hunt, principal creditor.

Ditto, 1710, folio 3.

JAMES BRIGHOUSE late in the island of Virginia in parts beyond seas, bachelor, deceased five years ago. Warrant for administration 19 June 1683 to Elizabeth Brighouse the mother.

Ditto, 1683.

[Colonel John Stringer, George Brighouse, and Robert Foster patented, August 14, 1672, 2,100 acres in Northampton county, on the seaboard side in Foster's Neck.]

JOHN BURGIS late of Virginia beyond seas, widower, deceased. Administration 23 July 1712 to his son William Burgis.

Ditto, 1712, folio 139.

COPE DOYLEY senior, late of Virginia beyond seas, widower, deceased. Administration 1 June 1713 to his son Charles Doyley, a former grant (January 1705) to Robert Doyley uncle (patrus) and guardian of the said Charles Doyley and of Cope Doyley, junior, sons of the defunct having expired.

Ditto, 1713, folio 153.

COPE DOYLEY, junior, late of Virginia, bachelor, deceased. Administration 1 June 1713 to his brother Charles Doyley. (Another grant in November, 1714.)

Ditto, 1713, folio 155.

[Rev. Cope Doyley became minister of Bruton parish, Williamsburg, Va., in 1697, and remained until his death in October, 1704. The parish register shows that his wife, Elizabeth, died in 1701, and his daughter, Elizabeth, in 1700-1. He had two sons, Charles and Cope, who survived him. In July, 1709, Robert D'Oyley, clerk, petitioned the Queen in council, stating that he was administrator of his brother, Cope D'Oyley, late rector of Williamsburg, deceased, and guardian of the latter's two sons, Charles and Cope, minors; that they were possessed of land and personal property, but were detained in Virginia. The said children were by the order of Governor Nicholson put under the care of the court of York county; but about a year afterwards Benjamin Harrison found means to get hold of them, and now kept them both among negroes to hinder petitioner's agent from having anything to do with them; that the said Harrison was appropriating their money to his own use and that in consideration of their lost education and that all their relations were in England, he prayed that they might be sent over and put under his care.

The matter was referred to the Board of Trade, who in turn referred it to the Solicitor-General. The latter, in his opinion, stated that the laws of Virginia had made very good provision for the children, and that the Attorney-General of Virginia (who was also the petitioner's agent), must have it in his power to do them right. He also said that petitioner, as next heir, could not be their guardian. Rev. Robert D'Oyley said, in reply, that he did not wish to be made legal guardian, but asked that the eldest boy be brought before the Governor in Virginia and allowed to exercise the choice of coming to England or not. (Sainsbury MSS.) Harrison's side of the case does not appear. It is probable that the Rev. Cope Doyley had left only a small estate and that York Court had bound the boys to Benjamin Harrison.

Rev. Cope Doyley, son of Charles, of Southrop, county Gloucester, gent., matriculated at Wadham College, Oxford, 10th March, 1675-6, aged sixteen; B. A. from Merton College, 1680. Foster (*Alumni Oxonienses*), states correctly, that he was a brother of Robert, but incorrectly, that he was buried at Southrop in 1741.

Robert Doyley, the petitioner, brother of Rev. Cope, matriculated at Wadham College, 10th March, 1675-6, aged fifteen, scholar 1677, B. A. 1679, M. A. 1682, fellow 1686, subwarden 1692, rector of Fryaning, Essex, 1688, and of St. Margaret Roding, Essex, 1705, until his death, 10th April, 1733. In 1732 he gave £3,000 to "the corporation of the sons of the clergy."]

ROBERT DYER late of Mock Jack Bay in Virginia, bachelor, deceased. Administration 5 September 1718 to his sister Sarah wife of John Mercer.

Ditto, 1718, folio 166.

WILLIAM GLANVELL late of Virginia in parts beyond the

seas, deceased.   Administration 23 September 1668 to Alice
Glanvell relict.

Ditto, 1668.

WILLIAM HAWES late of Virginia in the West Indies, bache-
lor deceased.   Administration 25 February 1730 | 1 to his bro-
ther Henry Hawes.

Ditto, 1731.

MARY HOOKER lately in Virginia.   Administration 12 October 1682 to Oliver Gregory cousin and next of kin.

Ditto, 1682, folio 139.

ARTHUR JACKSON late of Quary crick in Potomack River in
County Stafford, Virginia, bachelor, deceased.   Administration
12 July 1712 to his father Arthur Jackson.

Ditto, 1712.

WILLIAM KITTS late of Yorke River in County Gloucester in
Virginia, bachelor, deceased.   Administration 15 September
1710 to his sister Elizabeth Kitts.

Ditto, 1710, folio 184.

ISAAC SEDGEWICKE late of Virginia beyond seas, bachelor,
deceased in parish of St. Catherine Creechurch, London.   Administration 7 March 1710—11 to his brother Thomas Sedgewicke.

Ditto, 1711, folio 47.

[Isaac Sedgwicke, of York county, Va., was a lawyer, and in 1687-8,
and probably in other years, was deputy clerk of the county.   His
brother, William Sedgwick, was clerk of York, 1692, 1701, and doubtless before and after these dates.   In William Sedgwick's will, which
states that he was "of York County, late of burlen hall, Linkingshier,"
and was very sick, £10 sterling is bequeathed to brother Thomas Sedgwick for a mourning suit, and the rest of estate given to his brother
Isaac, who is made sole executor.   William Sedgwick's will was probably written in haste by an illiterate person.]

WILLIAM SHIRLEY (late Secretary to the late Honorable
General Edward Braddock in America) Esq. bachelor, deceased.
Administration 22 January 1757 to his father William Shirley
Esq.   The aforesaid William Shirley Esq. on the same date

89

takes out administration of his son John Shirley late captain of 50th Foot, commanded by the Hon. William Shirley, Esq.

Ditto, 1757.

[William Shirley was killed at Braddock's defeat, in 1755. He was a son of William Shirley, who was twice governor of Massachusetts.]

WILLIAM SLATTER late of the Town of Norfolke in Virginia, but deceased at Kingston in Jamaica, a bachelor. Administration 17 May 1760 to his brother the Rev. Thomas Slatter, clerk, Elizabeth Slatter, widow the mother having renounced.

Ditto, 1760.

NICHOLAS WARE late of Rappa Hannock in Virginia, deceased. Renunciation of administration of estate August 1662 by Anne Ware, relict.

Court Act Book [PCC. Admon Act Book for year 1662 being lost.]

[Nicholas Ware lived in Rappahannock county. On January 3, 1661, a certificate was recorded in Rappahannock Court that Mr. Nicholas Ware, merchant, had that day signed a power of attorney to Mr. John Ware, of Rappahannock. There is also among the Rappahannock records a bond from Nicholas Ware, "now resident in Rappahannock county, in Virginia, merchant," to John Vassall, of Barbadoes, merchant, in the amount of 17,234 pounds of tobacco, to secure the payment by Ware to Vassall of 8,617 pounds of tobacco for four good negroes.]

WILLIAM WATERS late of the County of Northampton in Virginia, deceased. Administration 21 October 1757 to Anthony Bacon, attorney of William Waters now residing at the City of Williamsburg in Virginia, son of the defunct,—Burton, formerly Waters, widow, the relict dying without having taken administration.

Admon Act Book, 1757.

[The William Waters on whose estate administration was granted in 1757, was the son of William Waters, who died in 1722, and whose will is given in this series of "Gleanings" (*Va. Mag.*, X, 411, 412). William Waters, of Williamsburg, the son of the first named, died in that city in May, 1767, and left an only chily, Sarah, who married, on May 12, 1768, David Meade, of Nansemond county.]

JOHN MYNTERNE, Manigo in Virginia. Will 15 March 1617 | 8, proved 16 January 1618 | 9. To wife while a widow £20, but if she marry said £20 to cosen Elizabeth Wills, daughter of John Wills. To Mary Raddon my gould Ring and my whissell. To Henry Raddon my frame platt. To wife 1¾ shares of the "Content," while a widow, she paying debts. To brother Samuel Mynterne best suite with cloake and hatt, pare of silke stockings and green silk garters and beste sherte. To brother William a silk doblett and hose, paire of black silk garters and worsted stockings. To John Wynter my David's crosse staffe. To my boye George Lang my long cape, one waistcoate, one Dublett and 20s. To William Leane, servant to my father one suit of clothes of Mellye cloathe. To Thomas Gee, my brother in lawe, one fustian Dublett, one payer of Mellye hose and one sherte. To Owen Pomerye one Straightes platt which is at home. To John Davies of Foye my shirte cape. To John Stanings the coverlet I have here, one crosse staffe which is broken, with a book called the Seamans callender. To George Cheltnam three pair of platt compasses, two falling Bandes. To my brothers Nathaniel and Bynger Mynterne two handkerchers to each. Witnesses: John Wynter, Owen Pomerye, William Clement. Administration to relict Alice Mynterne. No executors named.

Parker, 7.

OWEN WYN, gent. Will 12 January 1609 | 10; proved 10 May 1611. To brother Lewys Wyn £50. To sister Catherine £60. To sister Elizabeth £60. To sister Gwin £60. To sister Margaret £60. To sister Marseley £60. To sister Meddanny £60. To brother John Wynn £60. To foster brother Thomas ap Robert ap Evan £20. To foster sister Gwellian £20. To daughter Elizabeth Gwynn gotten vppen Bridget Toye all landes I bought in Connystreets county of Hartfordshire [sic] and £20. To Ann Tompson £20. To cozen John Edwardes £60. To cozen Richard Hughes £60. To cozen John Edwardes's children £100. To sister in law Eleanour verch John ap Robert that married my elder brother £20. Executors· cozens John Edwardes and Richard Hughes. I leave statutes and bonds for these legacies in hands of faithful cozen Richard Hughes. Of tenements left by my father as they fall out of lease, the first to foster brother Morgan ap Robert, second to his sister Gwenlian ap Robert and rest to my poore sisters and brothers. Plate to cozens John Edwards and Richard Hughes. To brother Lewys Wyn all my adventure in Virginia. To Bridget Toy the mother of my base daughter £20. To Elyzabeth verch Harry £20. To sister in Lawe Rose Wynn, brother Rowland Wynn his wife £10. To brother William Wyn his wife to be divided to his children begoten by him £10. To all officers of the Kinges Butterye and Seller to every yeame a ring of 20s. with my name Ingraven to come to my funeral if I dye within twenty miles of London. No witnesses:

Wood, 47.

[It would seem that Mr. Brown (*Genesis*, II, 1055), has made a mistake in his identification of the Owen Wynne, who was a member of the Virginia Company.]

JAMES WHITE of London. Will 2 May 1609; proved 12 January 1610 | 11. Purpose to travaile beyounde the seas. Refer to account with Sir William Fleetwood of Great Missenden, Bucks, knight. To brother William White adventures for Virginia (i. e. £25 in hands of Sir William Fleetwood). To sister Mary White £50. To cosen William Fleetwood son of said Sir William Fleetwood £10. To cosen Henry Fowles son of Sir David Fowles of London, Knight, £10. To friend Robert Paine now servant of David Fowles of London £10. To Thomas Davyes of Newerne, county Montgomery £4 14s. od. Residue to sister Mary White, executrix. Witnesses: Jacob Bonamye, Griffin Myllynton, Thomas Dudley, Tho: Davyes, Robert Payne.

Wood, 1.

[James White, gent., was a member of the Virginia Company under the second charter, and subscribed £25. Sir William Fleetwood, of Missenden, Bucks, was a member of the Virginia Company under the third charter, and subscribed and paid £37. 10. He was long member of Parliament for Bucks, and died in 1630.]

JOSEPH MAYE of the Strand, Middlesex, gentleman. Will 5 March, 1631 | 2; proved in February 1635 | 6. To poore cf the Savoy parish 20s. To sister Susan £10. To sister Ester ringe of 20s. To Cozen Beniamine Cleland £5. To cozen Thomas Maye, brother Nathaniel's sonne £30, or if he die in the warres to his dafter. To cozen Cornelius Maye £5 as his Uncle Phineas Maye thinks fitt, but if [he] die at sea, give his sonne that was borne in Virginia. To cozen Mathyas's children £30. To cozen Thomas Collins £5 and all his sisters ringe of 20s and ditto to his wife. To [cozen] William Collins and wife ditto. To my [cozen] Jayn Primrose £5 and her sister Elizabeth Maye 40s. To younge man at Tavestock called Joseph Maye [£3 erased] 2s. To a Goldsmith wife in Exon Mary Ratcliffe £5. [To John Mercer £8 and a suite of Parell and cloak, erased]. To George Raymond [my mare, erased] great feather bed. Executor: brother Phineas Maye. To kinsman Manuell Maye [40s—erased] 20s. Lett brother Phineas remember brother Mathias children and my cozen Thomas Maye. To brother Collins a ring of 20s. To cozen John Beane ditto of 10s., and to cozen John Sherman 10s. Witnessed 20 November 1635. Witnesses: Edward Fotherstone, Thos. Maye, Nuncupative codicil reduced legacies and annulled some. Witnesses, ditto.

Pile, 9.

[Cornelius Maies, aged twelve, was a passenger in the ship *Safety*, which left England for Virginia in August, 1635. Cornelius and Elizabeth May and Henry May, a child, were living at Elizabeth City, Va., February 16, 1623. In the census of 1624-5, the "muster" of Cornelius May, at Elizabeth City, only included himself, aged twenty-five, who had come in the *Providence*, in 1616. He had patented 100 acres at Blunt Point, on James river.]

EDMUND JENNINGS in county York, Esq. Will 10 March 1756; proved 24 March 1756. To poor of parish where I die £5. To Mr. James Buchanan, Merchant in London, one of executors, £1300 in special trust to pay £1200 to Mrs. Sibila Cowcher, widow. To said Mrs. Sibila Cowcher all cash and moneys, to be in bar of all claims to estate. To Mrs. Anne White, spinster, balance of £100. If moneys in England not sufficient, executors to call in securities. To Honorable Colonel Richard Corbin of Virginia in North America £1700 in trust to pay to my daughter Ariana Randolph the interest without control of her husband, and after her death said money to my grandson and god son Edmund Randolph, if he survive his mother, but if not, then to my said daughter's children and grandchildren surviving. To my nephew Edmund Jennings of the Province of Maryland, four such negroes as he shall choose among my stock of negroes on my plantation in the freshes of Patuxent River, Ann Arundell Co., & also all the plantation utensils, cattle & horses; but as to the land itself with the houses, I only give it to him for his life. To servant William Russell year's wages and woollen apparell. To Honorable Cecilius Calvert, Esquire, William Sharpe, Esquire, Mrs. Chester of Bristol, widow, Mrs. Russell, wife of James Russell of City of London, merchant, Honorable Philip Ludwell of Colony of Virginia, Mrs. Corbin, wife of aforesaid Colonel Corbin, John Tayloe of Virginia, Mrs. Brice, wife of John Brice of the City of Anapolis in Province of Maryland, Esquire, Stephen Bordely, Esquire, Elizabeth Bordely, spinster. Mrs. —— Harris, widow, of Kent county in Maryland, daughter of my late wife Ariana Jennings, Mrs. —— Harris, widow of James Harris, Esquire of ditto, deceased, Mrs. Shipping, widow, sister to my late wife, William Bordely, John Bordely, Matthias Bordely, and Beale Bordely, all of Maryland, Margaret Beckwith, Elizabeth Beckwith, Robert Porteus, Nanny Porteus his daughter, Edward Thompson of Helbury in county of York, esquire, and his Wife, a mourning Ring each. Rest to son Edmund Jennings. Executors: son Edmund and Mr. James Buchanan. Trustees for managing estates in Maryland and Virginia : Colonel Richard Corbin and John Brice. Witnesses : Alexander Sutherland, Jon^{tia} Fleming, Lewis Clutterbuck. Codicil Cash to Mrs. Cowcher to be free of travelling and other expenses. Witnesses: ditto.

Glazier, 72.

[*The Curio*, a short-lived New York periodical, contained a chart pedigree of the family of Jennings, or Jenings, as it was later generally written, of England and Virginia, and gave as its source " The Heralds College, London, England." This is a rather general reference; but there can be no doubt of the genuiness of the pedigree. Letters contemporary with President Edmund Jenings, of Virginia, state that he was a son of Sir Edmund Jenings, of Ripon, Yorkshire.

The following is, with some slight omissions, a copy of the pedigree:

"The House of the Jennings's, of Silsden, was called Jennings's Hall, & they are said to have raised themselves by being Stewards to the Cliffords" (Earls of Cumberland).

.... d'r of ......=Peter Jennings of Silsden=Eliz. d'a of ....
　　First wife.　　　｜　　Parker in the parish of Kildwick. Married at Kildwick 13 Jan., 1558, in Craven in Comit: Ebor [Yorkshire].

｜ ｜ ｜　　　　｜
Sons　　Peter Jennings of Silsden=Anne d'r of .... Baldwyn
&　　　in Co. Ebor: Died 1 Sp't'r ｜ of Crane-énd, in Marton in Co: Ebor.
dau.　　1651.

｜　　　　　｜　　　　　｜
Peter Jennings,　Edmund Jennings,　Jonathan Jennings=Eliz'h d'r &
A. M. d. unm:　A. M. died un-　of Ripon, died　co-heir of Giles
9 July 1623 aet　married 4th March　24th Aug't 1649.　Parker of New-
25 ann:　　1624.　　Barrister at Law.　by in Com:
　　　　　　　　　　　　　　Ebor:

｜　　　　　　　｜
Christ.=Elizabeth=Henry Wat-　Sir Edmund Jennings=Marg't d'r of
Hodson. Jennings kinson,　of Ripon, Knt. aet ｜ S'r Edw.
　　　　LL. D.　38 ann: 15 Augt 1665.　Barkham of
　　　　Chancellor　Representative in　Tottenham
　　　　of York.　Parliament for that　High Cross
　　　　　　Borough 1660, 1661,　in Co: Midd.
　　　　　　1678, 1680, Sheriff of　Knt & Bart.
　　　　　　the C'ty of York 1675.　& of South
　　　　　　Ob. *circ.* 1687 bur'd at　Acre in Nor-
　　　　　　St. Clements Ch.　folk.
　　　　　　Temple Bar, London

｜
Sir Jonathan Jennings Knt:=Anne d'r of S'r Edw'd
Elected Representative for ｜　Barkham.
the Boro' of Ripon, where
he resided, in 1688 & again
in 1690 being the same year
appointed Sheriff of the
City of York.

｜
Peter Jennings of Ripon,
admitted to Grays Inn
Nov. 1687. Made will May
28, 1707 & left Edmd J. of
Lincoln's Inn his heir.

｜　　　　｜　　　　｜
a　　　*b*　　　*c*

95

a	*b*	*c*

Elizabeth mar. S'rRoger Beckwith of Aldborough [And was mother of S'r Marmaduke Beckwith Bart., who was appointed by his uncle, President Jennings, Clerk of Richmond Co Va, where he died at an advanced age, leaving sons & daughters]

Jonathan Jennings of Ripon, Esq. aet 10 ann. 15 Augt 1665 Representative in Parl't for Ripon with his uncle Sir Jonathan in 1690 & (with others) in 1695 & 1698. Died unmarried.

Edmund Jen-=Frances 5th
nings Esq. aet | d'r of Henry
6 ann. 1665, | Corbin of Vir-
Settled in Vir- | ginia, by Alice
ginia & was | his wife d'r of
President of | Rich'd Elton-
the Council | head in Com.
there. Resided | Lanc: which
on his estate in | Henry was 3d
Virginta w'ch | son of Thos.
was called | Corbin of Hall
Ripon. | End in Co:
| Warw: Engd.
| She died in
| Londn 22Novr
| 1713. Bur'd in
| St. Clements,
| East Chap (2
| D 14-105b.)

Eliz: ux: Robt. Porteus of York Gt. Ob. 20 Jany 1754 aet 60, bur'd in St Martin's Coney St't York M. S. (Mother of Beilby Porteus, B'p of Chester) [and, after 1787, of London]

[Frances married Charles Grymes of "Morattico," Richmond Co Va & was ancestress of Genl R. E. Lee].

Edmund Jen-=Ariana d'r of
nings Esqr Sec- | ..... Broadley.
retary of the | [Incorrect. She
Province of | was widow of
Maryland,Ob.at | Thos Bordley of
Bath 3d March | Md. & dau of
1759 aet. 59 ann., | Matthias Van-
buried there. | derheyden.]
[The testator
above.]

Some other children died young.

Ariana=John Randolph, Attorney General of Virginia .. L'r'g 1778

Edmund Jennings late of Lincolns Inn, Esqr, l'v'g in 1778. Had sold all his Yorkshire Estates; but had large possessions in Virginia.

Edmund Jenings, of "Ripon Hall," York county, Va., was born 1659, and died December 5, 1727. He came to Virginia in 1680; was Attorney-General in 1684, &c.; was appointed to the Council in 1701, and remained a member until his death. On January 1, 1701-2, he was appointed Secretary of State, and from June, 1706, to August 23, 1710, as President of the Council, he was Acting-Governor. He resigned his position as Secretary about 1713, to go to England (as letters in the Sainsbury Abstracts, Virginia State Library, relate), to obtain an estate, which fell to him on the death of an elder brother; but was reappointed Secretary in 1720. Later he would again have become Acting-Governor, but was set aside on account of feeble health.

His son, Edmund Jenings, the testator above, was admitted an attorney in the Baltimore County Court, March, 1723-4, and was one of the representatives for Annapolis in the House of Burgesses of Maryland, 1728-32; took his seat as a member of the Council, October 21, 1732, and attended until 1752; was commissioned Secretary of the Province, March 20, 1732-3, and resigned that office in 1755. He married Ariana, widow of Thomas Bordley, Esq., July 2, 1728. (We are indebted to Dr. Christopher Johnston, of Baltimore, for data in regard to Edmund Jenings, 2d.)

Though the chart and other accounts say that Edmund Jenings, 3d, died (according to one account, in 1819), unmarried, it seems certain that he did marry, and have children. In a pleasant letter, written from London, June 28, 1769, to William Lee, he speaks humourously of an intended trip to Wales, &c., with his "two little Indians." In 1769, he presented to "The Gentlemen of Westmoreland county," a portrait of Lord Chatham, which for many years hung in the hall of the House of Delegates, in Richmond. (For correspondence on this subject see *Virginia Historical Register*, I, 68-76.) The letter book of Richard Corbin (copy now in collections of this Society), shows that Edmund Jenings and his father had loaned large sums of money to persons in Virginia, which in the hard times just preceding the Revolution, Colonel Corbin had much difficulty in collecting. Writing to one creditor he stated that Mr. Jenings was about to dock the entail on his Yorkshire estates.]

VIRGINIA GLEANINGS IN ENGLAND.

Communicated by Mr. LOTHROP WITHINGTON, 30 Little Russell street, W. C., London (including "Gleanings" by Mr. H. F. WATERS, not before printed).

(CONTINUED.)

CHARLES ANTHONYE of the parish of St. John Zacharie of London chiefe Grauer of the Kinges Maisties Mynt and of his Seales. Will 24 October 1615, proved 21 November 1615. To wife Elizabeth lease of dwelling house and childbed Lynen. To children Thomas, Richard, Charles, James Andrewe, Edward and Mary each 100 markes, to sons at 24 and daughter at 21 or marriage, and if any child die two thirds of the 100 markes to other children and one third to my wife if living. To eldest sonne Thomas all goldsmiths tooles worke presses patterns and prints of Seales and all Bookes and papers. Allso my Seale Rynge, when Goods praysed wife to take what she pleases according to custom of the Cittie, etc. Forgive brother Francys Anthonye debtes except what accrue in three years, etc. As great part of my estate ys out of my handes and cannot be disposed of as I have formerly done I ordayne when yt please god to send yt viz. my fyve partes of waterwork at Broken Wharfe and £137 adventure into the Sommer Islandes, also £137 adventure to first colonye into Virginia, and £22.16 | adventure in the second colonye into virginia all of which one fourth to wyfe Elizabeth, one fourth to sonne Thomas Anthonye and two fourths to my children living. Rest to sonne Thomas Anthonye executor. Overseers: Brother in law Samuel Arnold. Witnesses: John Leighe, Jehanne Brusell. Administration 15 September 1623, widow Elizabeth Anthonye of estate left unadministered by son Thomas Anthonye executor now deceased.

105, Rudd.

[Charles Anthony, goldsmith, was a member of the Virginia Company under the second charter, subscribing £37.10, and paying £137.-10. He was also a member of the North West Passage Company. Was second son of Derrick Anthony, "chief graver of the mynt and seals to King Edward II, Queen Mary and Queen Elizabeth." He was engraver for King James, Prince Henry, the mint, &c., and is believed to have engraved the seals for the Virginia Companies. Mr. Brown believes that Dr. Francis Anthony, the celebrated "empiric" (or quack) physician, who joined the Virginia Company in May, 1617, was his brother. His sister, Elizabeth, married Richard Yardley, fishmonger, of London. (Brown's *Genesis*, II, 814.)]

WILLIAM ATKINSON of London gent. the younger. Will 5 May 1609; proved 27 August 1613. Determined by god's permission to travail beyond the Seas to Virginia. Debts being paid, all to William Atkinson of London Esquire my natural Father. Thomas Atkinson of Penrith Countie of Cumberland, and Raphe Atkinson of Woburn Deyncourte in the Countie of Buckingham, Gentlemen. Witnesses: Humfrey Shepperd, Browne Salkins, William Williams.

Capell, 77.

[He was probably a son of William Atkinson, counsellor at law, who was a member of the Virginia Company under the second charter, and cousin of Richard Atkinson, who was clerk of the Company in 1609. Brown's *Genesis*, II, 818.]

FELIX FORBY of Norwich, Hosier. Will 8 December 1660:
proved 10 January 1660 | 61.   To Wife Ursula £10.   To sonne
Benjamin Forby now in Virginia 40s for as much as he hath
done unworthily by me and forsaken the Faith of the Church of
England.   To son John Forby £40.   Freeholds in Worstead
and North Walsham, Norfolk, to be sold by executors and friend
Mr. Roger Smith.   So long as my daughter Jane shall continue
in Virginia, executors to remitt yearly 50s of merchantable
goods fitt for women, soe long as she live in Virginia, but if she
come to England £20 in lieu thereof.   To Mr. Alexander Burnett to preach a sermon at my funeral 20s.   Rest to son in law
Richard Coates and Martha his wife, executors.   Witnesses:
Wm. Thrower, Bridgett Gibson, John Burrage, publiq. notary.

May, 4.

PHILIP MALLORY, lately resident in Virginia and now in London, clerk.   Will 23 July 1661; proved 27 July 1661.   To be
buried by Captaine John Whitty, one of executors.   To nephew
Roger Mallory all Plantations in Virginia.   To mother Mrs.
Elizabeth Mallory and my brother Mr. Thomas Mallory £10
each.   To Nephew Thomas Hawford £10.   To erecting and
building a college in Virginia £20.   To sister Tucker and sister
Lepington £5 each.   To Mrs. Isabell Whittie £5.   To aforesaid Captain John Whittie £5 and £10 for black mourning.   To
my nurse Anne Hobson £10.   To Minister that Preaches at
Funerall as executors think fit.   To niece Frances Pidgeon ten
head of cattell to be delivered in Virginia.   Rest in England
and Virginia to nephew Richard Mallory.   Executors: Roger
Mallory and Captain John Whittie.   To cosen William Mallory
£20.   Witnesses: Warham Horsmonden, Benjamine Sheppard,
scrivenor.

May, 114.

[Philip Mallory, son of Thomas Mallory, Dean of Chester, was born
in 1617, and was matriculated May, 28, 1634, at Corpus Christi College,
Oxford.   He was B. A. from St. Mary's Hall, April 27, 1637; M. A. January 16, 1639-40, and was rector of Norton, county Durham, from 1641
to 1644, when he was ejected by the Parliamentary authorities.   He is
said to have gone with Prince Rupert's fleet to the West Indies (Foster's
Oxford Matriculations and Walbran's *Genealogical Account of the*

Lords of Studley Royal in Yorkshire, Surtees Society, Vol. 67). Rev. Philip Mallory was, of course, a loyalist.

The date of Mr. Mallory's arrival in Virginia is not known, but in 1656 he was one of the most prominent ministers of the Colony, and by resolution of Assembly in December of that year, was appointed, togethe. with Mr. John Green, to examine all ministerial candidates for parishesr (*Hening* I, 424). In March, 1659-60, he was paid 2,000 pounds of tobacco for officiating at the two last Assemblies, and was desired to preach at the next Assembly (*Ib*, 549). At the session of March 1660-61, the Assembly adopted the following resolution:

"Whereas Mr. Phillip Mallory hath been eminently faithfull in the ministry and very diligent in endeavoring the advancement of all those meanes that might conduce to the advancement of religion in this country, *It is ordered* that he be desired to undertake the soliciting our church affaires in England, & that there be paid him as a gratuity for the many paines he hath alreadie and hereafter is like to take about the countreys business the sume of eleaven thousand pounds of tobacco, to be paid the next levy (*Ib*. II, 34).

Philip Mallory officiated, as a minister, in York county September, 1660, at the celebration of the restoration of Charles II, (*William and Mary Quarterly* I, 196,) and probably performed the same office at Jamestown. He must have died almost immediately after landing in England.

Mr. Mallory was evidently a man of learning, piety and high character, and these qualities, as well as his royalist politics, seem to have made him a favorite with the Virginia people. He married Catherine, daughter of Robert Batte, Vice-Master of University College, Oxford; (Batte pedigree, Visitation of Yorkshire, 1665) but had no issue. Several of Mrs. Mallory's family, the Battes, settled in Virginia.

The Mallorys were an ancient and distinguished family, long seated at Studley Royal in Yorkshire. Accounts of the family are given in Walbran's work already referred to; the Visitation of Yorkshire, 1564, etc., Harlean MSS. 1394, 1420, etc. Sir William Mallory, of Studley, married Ursula, daugter of George Gayle, of York, and had numerous children. In his will, 1586, he names, among others, his son Thomas. This was Thomas Mallory, D. D., Dean of Chester, and rector of Davenham and Mobberley, Cheshire. Dean Mallory married Elizabeth, daughter of Richard Vaughan, Bishop of Chester, and died at the deanery house, April 3d, 1644. He had the following children: 1. Richard, of Mobberley, eldest son, married and had issue; 2. William, baptized at Davenham, August 4, 1606, knighted 1642, died without issue; 3. Thomas (of whom later;) 4 George, curate of Mobberley in 1632, married Alice, daughter of Thomas Strethill of Mobberley, settled in Ireland and had many children; 5. John, baptized at Davenham, May 4, 1612; 6. Avery; 7. Everard; 8. Philip (the testator above); 9. Jane, wife of

John Halford, of Davenham, Eng., (this is evidently the "Hawford" of Rev. Philip Mallory's will. His niece, Elizabeth, daughter of Richard, married her first cousin, Richard Halford. It appears from Omerod's *Cheshire*, Vol. II, p. 329, and from a land grant in Virginia, 1668, to Thomas and Henry Batte, that Thomas Halford or Holford, a son of John and Jane, came to Virginia); 10. Katherine (Martha ?) married John Batte, of Okewell, Yorkshire. He, too, came to Virginia; 11. Elizabeth, baptized at Davenham, January 6, 1608, married at Mobberley, September 13, 1642, Thomas Glover, rector of West Kirkley; 12. Mary, married Edward Wyrley, youngest son of Humphrey Wyrley, of Hampshire Hall, Staffordshire, and rector of Mobberley after the Dean's death. (See Omerod's *Cheshire*, Vol. I, 329. Earwaker's *East Cheshire*, Vol. II; *The Cheshire Shief*, Vol. II).

Thomas Mallory named above as son of the Dean of Chester, was baptized at Davenham, August 27, 1605, matriculated at New College, Oxford, October 15, 1724, B. A. May 7, 1628, M. A. January 17, 1631-2. He was appointed rector of Easington, Oxfordshire, 1632, and on May 14, 1634, was presented by Richard Mallory and Bishop Foster of Sodor and Man, to the family living of Northenden, Cheshire. On the outbreak of the Civil war he was ejected as a royalist and his rectory was sequestered, with his other estates. His wife and six young children seem to have remained in the rectory and had money granted them in his absence. He, himself, was one of the small band of Royalists garrisoned in Robert Talton's mansion, Wythensham, near Northenden. After more than a year's siege the house surrendered to the Parliamentarians. Mallory was probably imprisoned. In June 1660, he petitioned Parliament to secure the profits of his sequestered living until the title could be determined. On July 6, 1660, he petitioned the King (*Dom. State Papers*, 58) for presentation to the rectory of Haughton, diocese of Durham, stating that he served the late King in the war and his present Majesty in the late abortive attempts of the Cheshire gentlemen. The matter was referred to Doctors Shelton, Earles and Morley and they reported in his favor. There is a certificate (58, 1) by Bruno Ryves, Dean of Chester, and three others in his favor. On July 30, 1660, he was made canon of Chester, and created D. D. on December 1, 1660. In 1662 there was a dispensation for him to hold the meetings of Eccleston (Lancashire) and Northenden. He died at Brindle near Eccleston in 1671. The second Dr. Thomas Mallory was twice married, first, Jane, who died February 12, 1638; second, Mary (according to the Dictionary of National Biography; but in his will his last wife is named Frances.

We are indebted to Lieutenant-Colonel John S. Mallory, U. S. A. for the following copy of the will of Dr. Thomas Maliory (son of the Dean and brother of Rev. Phiiip), which was recently obtained from the probate register of Chester.

In Nom. Din. Amen. I Tho. Mallory, D. D., & Rector of Eccleston in ye Countie of Lancaster being weake of body but of perfect mynde & memory make this my last Will & Testam't. Imp'r'is I deliver up & com'end my Sp'r't into ye hands of my gratious Redeemer J. Christ leaving my body to be buryed by my executrix hereafter named in ye Chancell of Eccleston before named in the night as the late B'p of Chester was. As for that small parcell of goods & chattells wch the providence of the Almighty hath bestowed upon me I dispose of in manner & forme as followeth: First I give unto Frances my deare wyfe the sume of two hundred & fifty powndes to make up that sume of money wch is in her nephew Dr. Millingtone's hands foure hundred poundes. As also the bed and clothes wch belong unto it whereon we have laine since or intermarriage & and all her wearing apparrell, rings, jewels & my Stone horse. I'tm. I give & bequeath unto my sonne Thomas in Virginia the sume of twenty shillings to buy him a ring; to my sonne Roger Mallory in Virginia ye some of five pounds. To my sonne John Mallory Drugster in London the sume of twenty shillings to buy him a ring. To my daughter Mary Forde the like sume. To my daughter Jane Stamp the sume of an hundred ponnds to be paid unto her within 6 months after my decease or before in case she be married, again w'th the consent of my executrix. To my daughter Susanna the sume of twenty pounds & upon better deliberation thirty pounds more. It'm. I give & bequeath to ye poore of Eccleston the sume of five pounds. To ye poore of Northen the like sume. To my servants Jo Ravenscroft, James Charlton, Mary Kennyon, Anne Potter, if they continue in my service till my decease to each the sum of twenty shillings for their good and faithfull service. Item. my mynde & will is that the forementioned four hundred pounds wch is my bequest to my dear wife Frances Mallory extend no further than to the use & occupation & at her decease to be divided among my children that shall be alive viz an hundred pounds to my sonne Thomas in Virginia & the rest to such of my children as she in her discretion shall thinke most to diserve & want. Lastly I appoint & constitute my wife Frances afores'd sole executrix of this my last will & Testam't. Given under my hand & Seale the 10th day of July 1671——— Tho: Mallory [L. S.]——

In ye presence of——Tho. Whittingham Jun'r X ——I. R——

Memoran—that these words of leaving a hundred pound to my sonne John were expugned in presence of us——Tho Whittingham——Mary Kenion——

Her
Anne X Potter,
Mark.

Proved in the Consistory Court of Chester on the 21st of November, 1671, and also on the 19th of May, 1674.

A number of the Mallorys apparently came to Virginia at the same time. Under a land grant to Thomas and Henry Batte, April 1668, appear as "head rights," Philip Mallory, Nathaniel Mallory Sr., Nathaniel Mallory, Jr., William Mallory, Thomas Mallory, Elizabeth Mallory and Roger Mallory. Of course the date does not indicate that these persons came in 1668.

Captain Roger Mallory, the son of Dr. Thomas Mallory, and named in the two wills which have been given, received a grant of land in 1660; but probably had been in Virginia a few years before. He settled in that part of New Kent county, which was afterwards King and Queen and King William, was a justice of the last named county in 1680 (and no doubt long before), and of King and Queen in 1690. If he was the Roger Mallory who was a justice of King William in 1705, he was a very old man. In the records of Elizabeth City county appears under date of August 16, 1680, a power of attorney from Ann, wife of William Mallory, to her "father-in-law," Captain Roger Mallory of New Kent county, authorizing him to release her dower (expectant) in certain lands there. William and Ann (Wythe) Mallory were the ancestors of the Mallorys of Elizabeth City, &c.

Thomas Mallory, the other son mentioned in Dr. Thomas Mallory's will as being in Virginia, was doubtless Thomas Mallory of Charles City ceunty, who, in a deposition made in 1676, gave his age as 40 years. As Charles City then included Prince George, it is probable that he was the father of Francis Mallory, who was sheriff of Prince George in 1705, and whose will, proved August 11, 1719, is of record in that county. It seems that this Francis Mallory was ancestor of the family of the name in Prince George, Brunswick, &c.

John Mallory, the "drugster" of London, the other son of Dr. Thomas Mallory, was probably the father of John Mallory, merchant of London, whose will was dated in 1747. He gave most of his estate to his wife, Mary, for her life, and after her death, to the children of his brother, William Mallory, near Jamestown in Virginia, of his sister, Elizabeth Balmol [?], of his brothers Roger, Thomas and Charles, of his sister, Quarles, and of his cousin, Francis Mallory of James river. The testator died in 1752, and his widow in 1754, and the heirs were advertised for in the English newspapers of the time.]

JOHN PARKER. Will 13 December 1699; proved 5 August 1701. To Elias Wilson, Senior, one of Negro women named Maria with her future increase or £15. To Terence Webb his freedom, £10 worth of goods, my shallop with all sayles, my gig, etc., my wearing apparell and 25s. due from John Foster.

To John Upton's children, if any of them appearse, 5,000 lbs. of Tobacco, that is to say, of the John Upton who dyed at my House. To John Burkett my saddle and bridle and the 20s. he oweth to his daughter Margaret Burkett. To John Jones, son of Nebuchudnezor Jones, one Mare and Colt branded on buttock I. P. To Richard Fancy suite of Apparell. Mr. William Colston to have care of Thomas Parker son of Thomas Parker deceased and deliver 2,000 lbs. of Tobacco which I gave vntill he shall thinke fitt to deliver it. To Rawleigh Travers and Tho. Beale gold rings at discretion of Mr. William Colston, executor. Virginia : Proved on oaths of Thomas Dickenson and Francis Newman in court of County Richmond 3 January 1699 | 1700. Test: William Colston, Clcm. Vera copia, William Colston, clecm. Administration P. C. C. by John Purvis, attorney for William Colston, executor of John Parker of Virginia, deceased overseas.

Dyer, 116.

[It appears from the records of Richmond county that Elias Wilson, married, in 1701, Mary, daughter of William Lane, and widow of Alvin Montjoy of the same county ; that he left by his said wife one son, Elias; that Elias Wilson, Sr.'s, will was dated December 23, and proved Feb. 5, 1706 ; and that Elias Wilson, Jr., died at the age of fourteen, and that Henry Wilson was his heir. Mrs. Mary Wilson married, thirdly, Joseph Belfield.

William Colston was the clerk of Richmond county, and ancestor of the family of the name in Virginia.

For the Travers family see *William and Mary Quarterly*, IV, 27, 203. The Thomas Beale referred to was the third of the name. William Colston had married his mother, Anne, widow of Captain Thomas Beale, of "Chestnut Hill," and daughter of Major William Gooch, of the Virginia Council, whose tomb remains near Yorktown.]

WILLIAM BURRELL of Virginia, planter. Will 14 July 1648; proved 5 August 1648. To Sister Anne Karmichell her two youngest daughters £5 apeice. To brother John Burrell soe much lockering Cloth as will make him four shirts. Rest, in consideration of debt due, to brother in lawe Richard Kelley, executor. Witnesses: Rich. Watson, Rich. Browne.

Essex, 126.

RICHARD EYRES of Barmondsey, Surrey, citizen and leath-
erseller of London. Will 8 August 1646; proved 16 February
1647 | 8. To be buried in East end of Barmondsey church yard.
To William Sowter als Salter, citizen and merchant taylor, £5
I owe of his wife's portion. To his wife Sarah Meel Salter 20s.
To his two daughters Johane and Rebecca 5s. apiece. To wife
Alice freeholde dwelling purchased of Sir William Withins of
Eltham, Kent, kt., and Dame Marie his wife for life of Alice,
then to Sarah Meel Sowter als Salter above named, reserving
£40 which I give to Sarah wife of William Clapham of Virginia
and her children. Rest to wife Alice, executrix. Witnesses:
James Hallam, Thomas Boyden, William Rheanes.

Essex, 18.

[The following grants appear in the Virginia Land Office: (1) Henry
Lee and William Clapham, 250 acres on Crotoman river, August 20,
1650 ; (2) William Clapham, 1,100 acres on the south side of Rappahannock river, August 20, 1650 ; (3) "Mr. George Clapham," 670 acres on
the south side of York river at the narrows. He was a head-right and
Roger Penn another, December 24, 1652. William Clapham, of Wanes-
quoiake (Isle of Wight), planter, made a deed to Roger Bagnall, August 3d, 1635. William Clapham, Sr., with five tithables and William
Clapham, Jr., with seven were residents of Lancaster county in 1654.
"Mr. William Clapham, Sr.," was one of the collectors of the levy at
this time, and William Clapham, Jr., had been chosen vestryman of the
Lancaster north side parish on April 1, 1652.]

GEORGE HARRIS of Westover, Charles Countie in Virginia,
in parts beyond the Seas. Will (nuncupative) 24 March 1672 |
3. Henry Martin, John Royston and Anne Dunken being in
the room ; proved 20 August 1674. To wife £1,600 with all her
Clothes, Rings, Jewells, and plate. To my sister £250. Rest
to brother Thomas. To John Royston grey sute. To Henry
Martin black stuffe sute. To this poor wench Nann (meaning
Ann Dunken) who hath taken care of me in sickness 360 lbs. of
Tobacco Mr. Gower oweth me. Witnesses: John Roch als
Royston, Anne, wife of William Gower. Administration to Sa-
rah Greenden als Harris, relict and chief legatee [sic].

Bunce, 100.

[Royston has been a name long represented in Virginia. William Gowers patented 300 acres in Northampton county at Deep creek, March 27, 1656, and on February 23, 1663, 600 acres in Accomac.

Sarah, widow of George Harris, married again Thomas Stegg, Jr., Auditor of Virginia, and Thomas Grendon, who died in 1685. She got into trouble by her ardent support of Nathaniel Bacon. See this *Magazine*, I, 441, 442.]

RICHARD DEWIN, citizen and cordwainer of London. Will 19 July 1647; proved 23 September 1647. To two grandchildren John and Thomas Dunmore, children of daughter Mabel Dunmore deceased, 40s. apiece. To kinswomen Anne, wife of John Rapley, and Alice, wife of John King, 20s. apiece. To kinswomen Joane, wife of —— Cole of Redding, weaver, and Sarah, wife of William Cowley now resident in Virginia, 10s. apiece. To other kinsfolk living 12d each, if they demand it. Rest to wife Alice Dewin, executrix. Overseers: William Lippincott and Edward Quicke. Witnesses: Thomas Phillipes, Thomas Homes, Hen. Ring, Scr. [St. Botolph Aldgate—Probate Act.]

Fines, 190.

[William Cowley, aged twenty, was a passenger on the ship *America*, which sailed from London for Virginia in June, 1635.]

WILLIAM PRIOR. Will 21 January 1646 | 17 ; proved 15 April 1647. To eldest daughter Margaret my whole part of Ship Honor and £591 sterling. To daughter Mary £500 sterling. To eldest son of brother in law Jasper Clayton £100; to rest of children of said Jasper Clayton £100. To wife of Richard Kempe, Esq. £50. To Richard Bennet, Esq. £30. To Captain Thomas Harrison, captain of Ship Honor, £30. To Captain Thomas [Harwood] £30. To eldest daughter Margaret whole divident of land where I live. To daughter Mary rest of lands in Virginia. To Mrs. Mary Kirton £100. If not soe much more in England to pay legacies, Tobacco to be sent home this year from Virginia etc. Rest to daughters Margaret and Mary, executrixes. Overseers and Feoffees in trust: friend Jasper Clayton, brother in law Captain Thomas Harrison, Captain

107

Thomas Harwood and Thomas Harrison. Witnesses: John Rose, Will. Hockaday. Administration to Jasper Clayton.

Fines, 73.

[William Prior or Pryor was a justice of York county from 1633 to his death in 1646. His will was proved and recorded in that county January, 1646. See this *Magazine*, III, 184.]

JOHN LATHBURY, Cittizen and Pewterer. Will 9 September 1654; proved 26 July 1655. To brother Thomas Lathbury 5s. To brothers Robert Kirkham and Richard Kirkham 5s. apiece. Rest to John Drury citizen and pewterer of London. Witnesses: John Peart, Nathaniel Hudson, Scrivenor, William Parker.

[Late of London, but at Virginia deceased.—Probate Act Book 1655, folio 257.]

Aylett, 313.

[There are in the Virginia Land office various grants to persons named Leatherbury or Letherbury of about the date of this will; but none to a John.]

VIRGINIA GLEANINGS IN ENGLAND.

Communicated by Mr. LOTHROP WITHINGTON, 30 Little Russell street, W. C., London (including "Gleanings" by Mr. H. F. WATERS, not before printed.)

(CONTINUED)

DANIEL LLUELLIN of Chelmsford, Essex, planter. Will 6 February 1663 | 4; proved 11 March 1663 | 4. Lands, tene-

From Vol. XIII, No. 1 (July 1905), p. 53.

ments, hereditaments in Charles county in upper part of James River, in Virginia, to wife Anne for life, then to son Daniel Llewellin. Ditto as to goods, but to daughter Martha Jones his sister two seasoned servantes. Also to son Daniell Lluellin best suite, cloake, coate and hatt, second best hatt with silver hatband, all Linnen, and my sayle skinn Trunck. To friend Mary Elsing of Chelmsford, spinster, for care, one of best white ruggs and my new peece of Dowlas, saving sufficient for a winding sheet to bury mee. To Mary Deerington of Chelmsford, widow one of worst white ruggs. To daughter Margaret Cruse 40s. for ring and to her husband ditto. To son in law Robert Hallom ditto. To master Chr. Salter living in Wine Court without Bishopgate and Anne his wife 10s. each for gloves. Goods sent over this spring and summer to be sold for debts due. Rest to son Daniel. Executors: Thomas Vervell of Roxwell, Essex, gent, James Jauncy of Cateaton Streete, London, Merchant, Giles Sussex of Thames Street, London, Hottpresser, and Master William Walker of Colchest:, Essex, Shopkeeper. To be buried in parish church of Chelmsford neare the Reading deske and friend Doctor John Michelson to preach. Witnesses: Robert Lloyd, Tim Code senior, scrivenor.

Bruce, 31.

[Daniel Lluellin, or Llewellyn, of Chelmsford, Essex, England, came to Virginia in or before 1642, and settled near Shirley, in Charles City county. On August 7, 1642, he patented 856 acres, bounded by the land of Mrs. Heyman, the upper branches of Turkey Island Creek, the lands of Mr. Aston and Joseph Royall, and the river. Robert Hallome was a head right. Later he received several other grants in the same neighborhood. Daniel Llewellyn was a justice of the peace for Charles City, a captain of militia, and member of the House of Burgesses for Henrico county at the sessions of March, 1642-'3, and October, 1644, and for Charles City at the sessions of October, 1646, November, 1652, March, 1654-'5, March, 1655-'6, and December, 1656. He married Anne, widow of Robert Hallam, or Hollam.

The patent of 1642 was re-granted in 1666 to Daniel Llewellin, "son and heir of the aforesaid Captain Daniel Llewellin." The son, according to the records of Henrico county, was born in 1647, and, in 1677, calls himself the "son-in-law" of Captain John Stith. The daughter, Margaret Cruse, may have been the wife of Captain James Crews, of Henrico, who was hung for his participation in Bacon's Rebellion, though Crews was unmarried at the time of his death. See this magazine, IV, 122-123.

Robert Hallam was living at the Neck of Land (in the upper parts) in February, 1623, and at the census of 1624-'5 was aged twenty-three, and is stated to have come to Virginia in the *Bonaventure* in August, 1620. The census includes him as one of the servants in the "muster" of Luke Boyse at Neck of Land, Charles City. That the term "servant" did not always mean, as used in this census, a menial, is shown by the fact that on June 7, 1636, Robert Hallam had a grant of 1,000 acres in Henrico adjoining the land of Edward Osborne, and lying on the river "right over against a creek called the fallen creek" [Falling Creek, Chesterfield county], Hallam had a re-grant of this land on November 1, 1637, and on May 6, 1638, there was granted to Anne Hollam, widow, and to the heirs of Robert Hollam, deceased, 1,000 acres in Henrico, lying on the river, extending towards Bremo and Turkey Island, and adjoining the lands of Mr. Richard Cocke and John Price—the said tract being due to them by sale from Arthur Bayly, merchant.

In the *William and Mary Quarterly*, VIII, 237-245, are printed a number of letters (copied from an old Charles City record book), dated in 1655-'7, and addressed to Daniel Llewellin, the elder, by various relations in England.

These letters show the Hallams to have been of Essex, England. One of the correspondents was William Hallam, of Burnham, Essex, salter, a brother of Robert Hallam, the elder, of Virginia. Another brother was Thomas Hallam, dead in 1656, who had a son, Thomas Hallam, salter, of London, who made a voyage to Virginia in 1657. Margaret, widow of Thomas Hallam, Sr., married William Mason, another of the correspondents. Robert Hallam, Jr., of Virginia, was living with the Masons. They speak highly of his character and appearance, and state that he had been bound to one Wood, a prosperous tailor, who had married Ann, daughter of Thomas Hallam, deceased. Samuel Woodward, of Charles City, who died in 1680, married Sarah, daughter of Robert Hallam, and had a son, Samuel, who was living in Boston, Mass., in 1705. There is recorded in Henrico a deed dated June, 1691, from John Gundey, of Gloucester, and his wife, Anne, daughter of Mr. Robert Hallam, conveying to Captain William Randolph a tract of land at Turkey Island. Daniel Llewellin's daughter, Martha Jones, may have been ancestress of the family in Amelia, Prince George, &c., in which Llewellin was frequently a Christian name.]

JOHN HOWETT of Elixabeth Cittie in Virginia in parts beyond the seas, Planter, bound on a voyage to Virginia. Will 6 September 1654; proved 28 July 1659. To wife Elizabeth Howett if living and vnmarried contrary to now report from Virginia

one third of my estate of Tobacco etc. To brother and all kindred 1s each. Rest to friend Mr. Thomas Howett, Citizen and
cooper of London, executor. Witnesses: Robert Earle, scrivenor, Prior Henry Fancin.

Pell, 425.

WILLIAM THOMAS. Will 2 January 1655 | 6; proved 19 Oc-
tober 1660. To wife Judith Thomas three parts of estate, but
if she depart her life, which God forbid, to her sister Francis
Henshaw the third, and another third to Thomas Jones here in
Virginia, and last third to Sarah Jones late wife of Richard
Jones; and to said Sarah the fourth part given to wife, but if
Sarah depart life while she stayeth in Virginia or in twelve
months, then her fourth part to Thomas Bigge, etc. To god-
child Mr. Garrett Farrellchild two cowes and three sowes. To
Thomas Bigge one Cowe and Suite of Broadcloth. Thomas
Jones to dispose of estate till order from Proprietors and send
home good Tobacco this year. Executrix: my wife. Over-
seers: the Court. Estate to be sold at Cry. Witnesses: Ben
Sidway, John Richards.

Nabbs, 195.

[Benjamin Sidway, of Surry county, married Mary, widow of Benjamin Harrison, first of the name. By order of court, Capt. Benjamin Sidway sold on January 16, 1652, a tract of land belonging to
Peter, "orphan of Benjamin Harrison." Captain Sidway was appointed
a justice of Surry in 1652. The will of Mrs. Mary Sidway was dated
March 1, 1686-'7, and proved May 29, 1688. Her principal legatees
were her sons, Benjamin Harrison and Thomas Sidway. Thos. Sidway, by his will, proved December 3, 1695, left most of his estate to
his wife, Jean. He apparently had no children.]

RICHARD KEMPE of Kich-neck [Rich-Neck] in Colonie of
Virginia, Esquire.

Berkeley, 455.

[Richard Kemp, Secretary of State of Virginia. He seems to have
been a brother of Sir Robert Kemp, of Gissing, Bart.]

[Printed in full in Va. His. Magazine, II, 174-175. The
official copying clerks at Somerset House work as mere ma-
chines and have a most annoying way of omitting the proper
references to the verbatim wills which they copy from the

old registers, for which venerable records they have not the least reverence, covering them with their own scrawls to mark off their hack jobs. Worse than this, lately several precious old illuminations in the manuscript have been slashed out of the fine old Elizabethan register, Langley, of the Prerogative Court of Canterbury.—L. W.]

JOHN BLY. Will 3 January 1662 | 3; proved 16 May 1664. Release £40 I was to have at my mother's death. Release £80 and £50 in hands of Master Richard Booth, Merchant, to be shared as by order left in hands of brother Giles Bly. Release brother William of £20. Desire £3 to be paid for silk rugge I received from Richard West of money in hands of Brother Giles, and release him the rest. To wife produce of 50 Hogshead of Tobacco shipped home for England in the Fredericke, as also shipped upon said joynt Cargoe. Desire shipped this present year for England, if Tobacco may be procured, 220 Hogshead, and my Third conveyed to wife in such goods she shall desire. To wife Goods and Household stuff I brought over this yeare to furnish my house and desire her father to make satisfaction to her of £120 for goods I bought for her this yeare in England. To wife all Rings and Watches, Deskes, and Trunckes and Chests, only one large chest to Master William Bough Junior, and one middle sized ditto to brother George Hunt, and in case he desires to returne to England, at his returne to be paid by wife the produce of 10 hogshead of Tobacco. Produce of 60 Hogsheads, whereof 40 are to shipp home this yeare by the Frederick, to be divided to my Mother, Brothers, and Sisters, and other 20 when they arrive in England. Goods amounting to £26 left last yeare in hands of father in law Abraham Wood, Esquire, besides other things, to be returned to wife if she desires. To Master Christopher Branch, senior, for writing my will one good Hogshead of Tobacco. To Christopher Branch, junior, for care in sickness ditto in such goods as he like of this yeare. To wife all Tobacco received by bills and bonds. Executrix: wife Mary Bly, to be advised by her father. Executor in England: brother Giles Bly, to be advised by Richard Booth, merchant. Witnesses: Thomas Branch, John Gardner. Proved 23 March 1662 | 3 before the Governor and councill. Test: Fra: Kirkham, copia vera F. K., Clerke to Hon¹ Governor and councill of Virga. Hen. Randolph, Not. Pub. Proved by Giles Bly as to goods in England.   Bruce, 46.

[A John Blyth received a grant from the Virginia Company in 1623. William Baugh, Sr., was justice of Henrico 1656, 1669, &c. He was born not later than 1612, and died in 1687, when his will was proved in Henrico. He has many descendants. His son, William Baugh, Jr., died before him. See this magazine VII, 424, for a note on Baugh. In addition to the grants there mentioned, the following should be included (1) Assignment, June 13, 1636, of a patent to John Baugh, of Varina, planter; (2) John Baugh, gent., 250 acres on Appomattock river, adjoining the land lately belonging to Mr. Abraham Pearcey, May 11, 1638; (3) John Baugh, gent., of 100 acres in Bermodo Hundred, in Henrico county, 80 acres, part thereof, bounded on the north by the land lately belonging to John Arundel, S. E. by the Bay of Appomattock, W. S. W. by Powell's Creek and N. E. by Conecock Path; 4 acres bounded on the N. N. E. by James River, E. S. E. by the land of James Usher, S. S. E. by the land of Michaell Maysters, W. N. W. by the land of William Sharp; 16 acres lying in Bermodo Hundred Neck, bounded on the south by the land of Joseph Royall, N. N. E. by the swamp, and N. W. by the land of Michaell Maysters, July 24, 1645; re-grant August 6, 1650; (4) Col. Robert Pitt, and Mr. William Baugh, 1,800 acres in Isle of Wight on a branch of Blackwater Swamp, February 18, 1664; (5) Col. Robert Pitt, Captain Joseph Bridger, and Mr. William Baugh, 3,000 acres in Isle of Wight, including 1,200 acres of the land formerly granted to Pitt and Baugh, March 21, 1664.

Abraham Wood, member of the Council and Major-General of Militia. See this magazine, III, 252.

The Branches were descendants of Christopher Branch, of Kingsland," Henrico, Burgess 1639. For a notice of a part of this very numerous family see the *Richmond Critic*.

Francis Kirkman was long Clerk of the Council. It may be mentioned, by the way, that the editors of the first volume of the *Calendar of Virginia State Papers* read his signature "Fra." as "Ira."

Henry Randolph, a half brother of the poet, Thomas Randolph, came to Virginia in 1642, and was Clerk of the House of Burgesses from 1660 to his death in 1673. He was uncle of William Randolph, of "Turkey Island." See this magazine, III, 261; XI, 58, and *William and Mary Quarterly*, October, 1895. In March, 1661-'2, the Assembly appointed Henry Randolph notary public for the colony (*Hening*, II, 136), and he is stated to have held the office until his death. He was succeeded by Thomas Ludwell, and he in turn by Robert Beverley (*Hening*, II, 456, 457).]

113

Robert Bristow of the parish of Gabriel Fenchurch, London, Merchant. Will 20 September 1700; proved 29 November 1707. To be interred in the family burying ground in Tabernacle Alley belonging to the parish of Gabriell Fenchurch or in burying ground in or near Bunhill Feilds. To poore of Brinstead, County Southampton, where I was born, £10; to poore of Micheldever in said county £5. Executors to pay to loving wife in case she survive and not otherwise £4000 as by marriage agreement as in recognizance in Court of Common Pleas at Westminster 24 November 1680 in lieu of her third as a Freeman's Widow of London; also to wife a necklace of pearls, diamond ring, and gold watch presented her before marriage. To my daughter-in-law Catherine Bristow, widow of my dear son Robert Bristow lately deceased, £1000 in trust for my granddaughter Avarilla Madgwick, wife of William Madgwick of London, Merchant, or to Avarilla's children if she die, and said Avarilla to release personal estate for pretence to custom of London, etc. To my granddaughter Katherine Baily £500 at 21, and in case of her father Arthur Baily Esq'r pay to said Avarilla Madgwick £500 and discharge her real estate of £500 part of £1000 payable in right of her mother his late wife, then to said Katherine Baily £500 more, she to release as other granddaughter is directed to. To William Blanchard and John Blanchard, sons of my sister Jane Blanchard, £20 each. Release to John Stevens son of sister Alice Alice [sic] Stephens two bonds of £95. To Ann Blanchard, Widow, relict of nephew Thomas Blanchard, £20. To my six granddaughters the daughters of my said son Robert Bristow deceased, viz: Katherine, Avarilla, Elizabeth, Anne, Frances, and Rebecca Bristow £1000 each at 21, etc. To granddaughter Katherine Bristow £100 more at 21 or marriage. To grandson William Bristow all my land in the parish of St. Mary Overeys in the Burrough of Southwark purchased of Mr. John Lorain, being the Talbott Inn and other houses leased at £240 per annum, and in default of issue of said William Bristow to my grandson John Bristow, then to my grandson Robert Bristow. To grandson John Bristow, youngest son of said son Robert Bristow, lands at Brittlewell in Hundred of Rocheford, Essex, lately purchased of Thomas

114

Werg, Esq'r, being the Moiety of Mannor of Earls Hall and Lordshipp of Brittlewell and Farm lett to William Ferrys, and Rectory lett to Thomas Short, all of £180 per annum, other Moiety whereof belongs to Mr. John Chambers, and also 120 acres in parish of East Wood Bury, Hundred of Rocheford, of annual value of £30, in default of issue of John, to grandsons William and Robert. To my grandson Robert lands and all money and debts owing to me in Virginia, in default of issue the same to my grandson William Bristow, in default, to my grandson John Bristow. To my daughter-in-law Katherine Bristow, the said William Madgwick, and Benjamin Woolley of Mortlack Gent all the lands in the hundred of Rocheford, Essex, which I purchased of the Right Honoble Daniel Earle of Nottingham, in trust for my grandson Robert Bristow with remainder as aforesaid. My daughter-in-law Katherine Bristow to be executrix until she marry or the said Robert, William, and John Bristow are 21, then they to be executors with granddaughter Katherine Bristow. Residue of estate other than in Virginia to 6 granddaughters children of son Robert Bristow. If any except Robert claim under custom of London, legacies to be void. If Robert claim, said claim to be charged out of his legacy. To my wife and daughter-in-law £20 each for mourning. To my said son-in-law Arthur Baily and said William Madgwick £10 ditto. To each of my servants £5 ditto. Codicil, 3 April, 1707. Whereas I have bought the Mannor of Havering in Parish of Hornechurch, Essex, and several Farms in Essex from John Woolley, merchant, to my daughter-in-law Katherine Bristow and Lawrence Hatsell of London, Scrivener, in trust for the nine children of my said daughter-in-law, the same, to be sold and the money to be equally divided among the said nine children of my said daughter Bristow by Mr. Robert Bristow, my son, her Husband, deceased. Witnesses to both will and codicil. Edward Northey, William Lang, Ja: Gibbon. Proved 21 March 1743|4 by John Bristow, Esquire, one of the grandsons and surviving executors, reserving to other surviving executors William Bristow and Katherine Bristow, grant to Katherine Bristow Widow expiring by reason of said John Bristow attaining age of 21.   Poley, 275.

[In *Burke's Landed Gentry*, edition of 1847, is a pedigree of the family to which the testator belonged. It states that Robert Bristow, Esq., second son of Robert Bristow, Esq., of Ayot, St. Lawrence, Hertfordshire, was born in 1643, and settled in Virginia, about 1660 (as stated in *Byshes Visitation of Herts.*, 1669). In Virginia he purchased in 1663, and following years, various estates in the counties of Lancaster, Gloucester and Prince William (which was then Staf-ford). He married in Virginia, Avarilla, daughter of Major Curtis. Returning to England about 1680, he became a merchant in London, and acquired a considerable fortune, and purchased estates in London and elsewhere. His only son, Robert Bristow, Esq., associated with him in business, was also very successful, and bought property in Sussex and Essex. He was M. P. for Winchelsea in the Parliaments of 1698 and 1700. The family seems to have been one of considerable wealth and social standing.

This account is borne out by our records. Robert Bristow received the following grants: (1) One thousand acres on Fleet's Bay, Lancaster county, formerly granted to Humphrey Tabb by patent, March 22, 1654, and by Thomas Tabb, son and heir of the said Humphrey, assigned to Philip Mallory, and by said Mallory assigned to Bristow and Edmund Welsh, who sold his share to Bristow, September 29, 1663; (2) 398 acres in Gloucester, on North River, in Mockjack Bay, and adjoining the lands of Harris, Thomas Morris, Major Curtis, and Mr. Richard Young—288 acres, part thereof was formerly granted to Mrs. Avarilla Curtis April 4, 1661 (being part of a grant of 410 acres), and by the said Avarilla assigned to "the said Mr. Bristow's husband" (evidently "Mr. Bristow, her husband," is meant); October 25, 1665; (3) 184 acres in Gloucester, on Ware River, adjoining his own land and that of Harris, May 7, 1666. After his return to England he became a partner with Brent and others, about 1689 in the purchase of 30,000 acres in Stafford, now in Prince William, called Brent Town or Brenton. Bristow Station, well known during the Civil War, doubtless derives its name from the Bristow estate in Prince William, which remained in the possession of the family until the Revolution, when it was confiscated.

Robert Bristow evidently returned to England about 1677. In the report of the Bacon's Rebellion Commissioners on the sufferers in that insurrection, made October 15, 1677, they say: "Major Robert Bristow, a Gentleman of a good estate and an Eminent sufferer in his stock, Provision, Armes, Ammunition, Mr'chts Goods & considerable Quantitys or Strong Liquors, as also in his person by being kept a prisoner until Bacon's death and after, he hath had a general knowledge of most passages relating to the late unhappy Troubles, and is able not only to justify most Particulars of our Narrative, But also is a person very fitt & necessary to be examined to divers particulars in the generall & personall Grievances. Being a man of good understanding in the Virginia affaires and one of Integrity and moderacion, soe that wee could wish hee might bee sent where there shall bee occasion & use of him in any of the aforesaid affaires being now an Inhabitant in Tower Street, London, Agt. Barking Church."

Robert Bristow married Avarilla, daughter of Major Thomas Curtis, of Gloucester, and Avarilla, his wife. They also had a daughter, Sarah Curtis, born in Ware Parish, Gloucester, August 16, 1657, who married, first, William Halfhide, and secondly, Richard Perrott, of Middlesex county.]

FRANCIS HOUGH of St. Peters the Poor, London, merchant. Will (nuncupative) 25 July 1648; proved 27 July 1648. Eldest son William to be sent over to Virginia. To mother Mrs. Christian Stockwood £150, and sister Mrs. Elizabeth Stockwood £50. To children William, John, Jane, and Anne Hough, all Tobaccos, money, goods, etc. in England, Virginia, or elsewhere. Estate of Tobacco due in Virginia to be received by friend Mr. Richard Preston. Profits of severall plantations in Virginia to be divided to four children till eldest son William is 21 and fit to manage same, then plantations to two sons William and John. Eldest son William Hough to be educated, bred up, and made fitt to be sent over to Virginia to manage those plantations for best use of himself and his brother John Hough, and younger son John Hough to be likewise educated in England for managing such affairs as shall be transported from eldest son out of Virginia to said youngest son in England. Witnesses: Thomas Billiard, gent, Thomas Potter, Grocer, Ann Hill, and others. Administration to Anne Cooke, grandmother of William, John, Jane, and Ann Hough, children of Francis Hough deceased, during minority. Administration 6 September 1667 to John Hough, Jane Hough als Andrewes, and Anne Ferrick als Hough, children of deceased, former grant to Anne Cooke having expired.

Essex, 117.

[Francis Hough, or Huff, as it was sometimes spelt phonetically, came to Virginia in the *Swan* in 1620, and at the census of 1624-'5, when he was twenty years old, was living at Elizabeth City. He assigned a patent for 50 acres in Elizabeth City in 1632. On January 3, 1633, he conveyed to Henry Coleman, of Elizabeth City, 60 acres there, formerly granted to Christopher Windmill, deceased, and due Hough as marrying his widow. On November 12, 1635, he patented 800 acres at the first creek on the south side of Nansemond River, and extending to the mouth of the river. December 26, 1636, he made a bill of sale for rights for 300 acres to Humphrey Swan. On May 17, 1637, he obtained four patents, aggregating 1,500 acres, in Nansemond or Upper New Norfolk (see this magazine, VI, 189). He was a member of the House of Burgesses for Nutmeg Quarter February, 1632-'3, and in October, 1645, during the Indian War, was a member of the "Council of War" for the "Associated Counties" of Isle of Wight and Upper and Lower Norfolk. There is an entry in the Lower Norfolk records, March 4, 1647-'8, of certain bills, &c., delivered to Mr. Francis Hough "by God's p'vidence bound for England."]

FRANCIS ROCKETT, late of Parish of Goochland, county of Henrico, province of Virginia, now of St. John Wapping, London. Will 6 June 1748; proved 21 April 1749. To William Fettiplace of St. John aforesaid, victualler, executor, my tract of land in Goochland adjoining to Inskatt Creek, county Henrico, Virginia, in America, with all Houses, Furniture, Wood Undressed. Witnesses: Frans Seede, Will: Skeets.

Lisle, 120.

[From this family, "Rocketts," the port of Richmond, derives its name.]

PHILIP CHESLEY, county York, Virginia. Will 18 December 1674; proved 10 May 1675. To brother Mr. Daniel Wilde 12s for mourning ring. Ditto to sister Margaret Wilde, brother Alexander Walker, sister Walker, cozen Francis Mitton, Fitz William Lawrence, Robert Bee, and Elizabeth Bee. To Esquire Ballard my seale ringe. To Daniel Parke Esq. one mourning ring of 20s. To cozen Hugh Hardy one hogshead of Tobacco. To Mr. William Dingley, cozen Mathew White, Mr. Jno. Wilde, cozen Henry Wilde, cozen John Hardy, cozen Edward Highings, cozen John Highings, and to every person whose surname is Chesley Inhabiting in Welford in Gloucestershire, each one hogshead of Tobacco year after demise. To two persons whose surname is Aplewhite living in Vpham in Gloucestershire ditto each. To poore of Welford £10. To wife Margaret Chesley all personal estate. To nephew Philip Chesley Plantation in New Kent

County with servants, cattle, and household goods. To nephew William Chesley ditto at Queenes Creek. Nephews Philipp and William to be sent for vp to London and put to Schoole to learne to write and cast up Accompts. Four years and after sent over to Virginia to be disposed at discretion of executrix during her life. Cozen Richard Turner to be sent home for London, his passage paid and a suite of Apparell given him att London and 20s. to beare expenses into Gloucestershire. My negro Joseph to serve eleven years and noe longer. Executrix wife Margaret Chesley. Witnesses: Daniel Parke, Fitz William Laurence, Anthony Hatch.

Dycer, 44.

[Captain Philip Chesley, of Queen's Creek, York county, who probably emigrated from Welford, Gloucestershire, was a church warden of Bruton Parish in 1674. His will is of record in York county. He obtained the following grants: (1) Four hundred acres on the east side of Chickahominy River, in James City county, adjoining the lands of Mr. Robert Holt, Mr. Felgate and James Crockett, on Little Neck Creek, June 7, 1650; (2) Robert Wild and Philip Chesley, 100 acres in York county, in Hampton Parish, beginning at the Mill Swamp, at the head of Queen's Creek, October 11, 1653; (3) Philip Chesley and Nicholas Meriwether, 1,000 acres on the northeast side of Skiminoe Swamp, adjoining the land of Wild and Chesley and the Rickahock Path, June 7, 1655; (4) Philip Chesley and Daniel Wilde 750 acres in York, on the southwest side of York River, and on Skiminoe Swamp, adjoining Rickahock Path, June 10, 1654.

In 1610 Lord Delaware appointed Mr. Robert Wild a clerk of the store at Jamestown. His property was appraised in York county, November 24, 1647. In 1655 Robert and Daniel Wild were living in York county, and the former died before 1662, leaving land in York county to the other. Daniel Wild was sworn J. P. April 24, 1660, and married Margaret (died February 12, 1675), widow of William Stephens, cooper, and had an only child, Margaret, who married Captain John Martin, of Stepney, mariner. Philip Chesley married Daniel Wild's sister, Margaret (*William and Mary Quarterly,* IV, 4).

Thomas Ballard and Daniel Parke were members of the Council.]

119

Communicated by Mr. LOTHROP WITHINGTON, 30 Little Russell street, W. C., London (including "Gleanings" by Mr. H. F. WATERS, not before printed.)

(CONTINUED)

THEODORE GULTSTON, of St. Martyn Ludgate Hill   Doctor of Medicine. Will April 26 1632; Proved 1 June 1632. To my father William Gultston and my mother Elizabeth his wife, £20 each. To my sister Elizabeth Allen widow. £20. To his wife Ellen's two sisters. £20 each. To my sister Dorothy Hill £10. To my brother Nathaniel Gulston, £20. To my sister, Martha, £10. To ———— Whitworth, grocer, Old Bayley, £10. For a lecture of Physicke, College of Physicians, London, £20 yearly. To be distributed amongst my kindred, £500. To my cosin Ellis Sotherton, £20, his wife, Rachel, 20s each to buy rings. To my sister ———— Stubbes, £5. To Stephen Barkham, £20. To Abraham Allen, my sister's son, £10. To John Toomes Apothecary, £10. To my friends Drs. Yonge, Gettaker, Nathaniel Sute, Mr, Foxley, Ministers, £3 each. To Sampson Kerrill, son of William Kerrill, deceased, £5. To Elizabeth Ayres, my maid servant, £5. To the parson, curate and lecturer of St. Martyns, £5 each. To the parson for a funeral sermon, £4. To the poor of Said Parish, £20. Lease I hold or Deane and Chapter of St. Paul's to the 6 younger sons & daughters of my Brother John, after my wife's death. Executrix wife Ellen. Overseers: Ellis Sotherton and Stephen Basleham. To my wife Ellen, my rectory of Bardwell, Suffolk; after her decease to my nephew Richard Gurton. Lands in Warwickshire, one-fifth to my godson, Theodor Gurton, the remainder to my brother John's children. Witnesses: Jenkyn Griffith, Thomas Hodgkin, To St. Paul's Cathedral, £20.

Audley, 64.

[Dr. Theodore Gulston was a celebrated London physician, and a prominent member of the Virginia Company. He was born in 1572, studied at Merton College, Oxford, where he took his doctor's degree, April 30, 1610, was fellow (Dec. 29, 1611,) and Censor of the College of Physicians, and practised with great success in London. In 1616 he frequently entertained Sir Thomas Dale and Uttomakin, Powhatan's counsellor, who had been sent to England. On June 14, 1619, Dr. Gulston was appointed on the committee of the Virginia Company in regard to the college. On Dec. 15, 1619, he bought ten shares of land in Virginia from various persons. He was made one of the King's Council for the Company in England, on July 8, 1620, and in July 1621, he recommended Dr. Pott for appointment as physician-general of Virginia. Dr. Gulston was distinguished as a Greek and Latin scholar, and translated several works from Greek into Latin. He married Helen, daughter of George Sotherton, a merchant-tailor and M. P. of London, and died May 4, 1623. See Brown's *Genesis* and *First Republic.*]

WILLIAM PARKE. Will 13 November 1633; proved 18 August 1634. To my youngest son Daniel Parke, £100. To my wife Sarah Parke, £150. If my wife marry again, her husband give security on behalf of my eldest son William to Francis Columbell of London and Nathaniel Fulden of London. To James Stone of London, Merchant, 50s. To Daniel Bourche, Purser of the good ship Blessinge, 25s. To Adam Thorowgood of Virginia, gent., 50s worth of commodities. Executor: my son William Parke. Witnesses: James Stone, Thomas Rey, John Felgate, Daniell Boulcher.

Seager, 75.

[Neither the will nor the probate act gives the residence of the testator, though the latter states that he died beyond seas. There is good reason to believe that he died in Virginia, and that he was the father of Daniel Parke, the elder, of that colony, whose will will appear later in this series. That the family of William Parke was in Virginia is shown by the fact that many years after his death, the land due for the emigration of members of his family to the Colony was taken up. Under a patent, dated 1655, for land in York County, appear the names of William Parke, Mrs. Sarah Parke, and William Parke, Jr., as head-rights. William Parke was witness to a deed in York County, in 1652, to Daniel Parke. Daniel Parke, Sr., was born, according to a deposition about 1628.

The epitaph of Daniel Parke, Sr., and the will of his son, Daniel Parke, Jr., state that the family was of Essex, England. Morant's *Essex* II, 309, gives an account of a family of Parke, resident in that county, from the time of Edward III, to that of Charles I, and the Visitation

121

of Essex 1634 (*Harleian Society*) has a pedigree of four generations of the family; but though the name William appears he does not seem to be identical with the testator above.]

JOHN THOMPSON of Surrey County, James River, Virginia. Will 27 January 1698/99; proved 16 March 1698/99. To my sister Katherine Paine, wife of Robert Paine, £50. To my sister Elizabeth Catlet, wife of William Catlet, £50. To my Brother William Thompson, £100 when 21. To my Brother Samuel Thompson, all my lands, Slaves, etc., failing him to my Brother William. To my friends Thomas Haistwell, Coll. Harry Hartwell, Major Arthur Allen, and Captain Francis Clements, a Ring to each of them. All the rest to my Brother Samuel Thompson. Executor: Samuel Thompson. Executors in trust: Thomas Haistwell and Coll. Henry Hartwell. Witnesses: John Burgis, Anne Bradley, Wm. Storey, Notary.

Pett, 50.

[The first of the testator's family of whom anything is known, was Rev. William Thomson, or Thompson, who became minister of Southwark Parish, Surry county, Virginia, in or shortly before 1662. It is possible that he was a son of Rev. William Thompson, one of the three pastors who were sent about 1642 or 1643 from New England to minister to the Virginia dissenters; but who soon returned home and died at Braintree, Mass., Dec. 10, 1666, aged 68. There was (a high authority states), a William Thompson, of New London, who is believed to have been a son of the New England minister. Rev. William Thompson, of Surry county, Va., bought property in New London.

On August 16, 1675 the County Court of Surry put on record that "On ye parte of Mr. William Thompson now after 13 years experience, wee report him an Orthodox faithfull & painfull minist'r of a quiett, sober & Exemplary Life & Conversation becoming his function unreproachable." On August 1, 1661, William Thompson, of Surry county, minister God's word, gave a general power of attorney to George Jordan. There is a deed, dated November 1, 1673, from William Thompson, Clerk, and Katherine, his wife. In or before 1690 he became minister of Washington parish, Westmoreland county. There is recorded in Surry a deed dated August 4, 1690 from William Thompson, of Westmoreland county, for 150 acres, and appointing his sons, Samuel and John Thompson, of Surry, his attorneys. Also, in Surry, another deed, dated Dec. 2, 1690, from William Thompson, Clerk, of Westmoreland county, conveying to —— Bagge, 150 acres in Surry, which had been granted to said Thompson, April 20, 1684. Katherine, wife of William Thompson, Clerk, of the parish of Washington, Westmoreland, joins in a deed, April 19, 1690. These items enable us to fill gaps in the lists of ministers of Southwark and Washington. Mr. Thompson is not mentioned in Meade's *Old Churches*.

Rev. William Thompson and Katherine, his wife, had issue : (1) John, (2,) Samuel, (3,) William, (4,) Katherine married Robert Payne, (5,) Elizabeth, married William or Robert Catlett.

John Thompson, the testator above, was born, according to a deposition, about 1661. He was a member of the House of Burgesses, for Surry, at the Sessions of March 1692-3, April 1695, April 1696 and September 1696. He married Elizabeth, widow, first of John Salway, of Surry, (whose will dated April 10, 1678, left her his whole estate with reversion to his next of kin in England,) and second, of Joseph Malden of Surry. *Surry Records*.

There are two wills of John Thompson in record of Surry. The earliest was dated August 2nd, 1698, and proved Nov. 7, 1699. He gave his brother Samuel Thompson £50 sterling, and brother William Thompson £50 sterling. To wife the labor of his slaves during her life—after her death they go to his brothers. If brother Samuel should desire to return and live in Surry, he was to have the plantation called Gilberts, on condition that he paid testator's executrix 20 shillings per annum during her life. To his two brothers and Mr. Robert Paine and Mr. Robert [*sic*] Catlett 25 shillings each for a ring. To wife, all estate given her by the will of Mr. John Salway. Remainder of estate to wife, Elizabeth, and she appointed executrix.

It is evident that soon after the date of the will just given, Mrs. Elizabeth Thompson died, and that her husband went at once to England. The will which is given in the text was proved and recorded in Surry, May 14, 1702. It begins : "I, John Thomson, of James River, in Virginia, merchant, at present in London, very sick."

Samuel Thompson, another son of Rev. William Thompson, was a member of the House of Burgesses for Surry, at the sessions of August 1701, May 1702, June 1702, August 1715 and April 1718 In March, 1682, Mr. Samuel Thompson had married Mary, daughter and heiress of Major William Marriott, of Surry. (*Surry Records.*) The will of Samuel Thompson was dated Sept. 20, 1720, and proved in Surry May 17, 1721. Legatees : brother William Thompson, nephew Samuel Thompson, cousins, [nephew,] William Moseley, cousin Samuel Thompson, cousins Katherine, William and John Thompson, William and Mary Moseley—to William Marriott, "my seal ring, that was my wife's father's ring," cousin Robert Payne, wife Mary, and brother William Thompson, executors.

William Thompson, the third son (named above) of Rev. William Thompson, was born according to a deposition about 1662. He died in 1731 or 1732, and by will recorded in Surry bequeathed his property to his children, Samuel, John, Katharine and Hannah, and grand-children, Samuel and Mary.]

ROBERT THROCKMORTON, of Paxton Parva, County Huntingdon. Will 1 March 1698/99; proved 3 May, 1699.

Pett, 83.

[Robert Throckmorton was a son of John Throckmorton, formerly of Ellington, Huntingdonshire, England, and afterwards of Virginia. Robbert, the testator, was born in Virginia, in 1662; but returned to England and died at Paxton Parva, Hunts., March 9, 1698-9. A picture of his tomb in the church there, and a copy of the inscription are given in the number of this Magazine, cited above. The Virginia Throckmortons descended from his brothers, Albion and Gabriel, who remained in the Colony. For Throckmorton genealogy, documents, &c., see *William & Mary Quarterly* II, 241; III, 46,142,240,280; IV, 128, 202; V, 54 and *Virginia Magazine of History and Biography* V, Nos. 4, and VII, numbers 1 and 3. Mr. C. Wickliffe Throckmorton of 503 5th Avenue, New York City, is preparing an elaborate history of the Thockmortons of England and America.]

[Abstracts of this will are printed in *Virginia Magazine of History and Biography*, VIII, 85, 86, and *Wm. & Mary Quarterly*, III, 48.]

PETER EFFORD. Will 24 August 1665; proved 2 October 1665. To my daughter and son Nicholas Efford, all my real and personal estate here, or in the plantation of Virginia. To them all my tobacco in custody of Mr. John Curell of Abchurch Lane and Mr. Jonathan Smith in Bow Lane. To my son Nicholas, and Sarah my daughter, £100, equally between them; if they die, to my kinsman Mr. Tirrell, Prebend of Winsor. John Weldon, minister of Newington, and Albertus Skinner, gent., executors, to give me as decent a burial as my distemper will permit. Witnesses: William Cocke, Joane Baker, Joane Wooding.

Hyde, 113.

[Peter Efford resided in York county, Va., where his will was proved Oct. 2nd, 1666. On Feb. 10, 1660 "Mr. Peter Efford" had a grant of 900 acres in the counties of James City and York, lying between Powhatan Swamp [which extends to James River] and Queen's Creek [running into York River,] adjoining the land of Bradshaw, Vardy, "Mr. Kemp, Esq," and Richard Ford—400 acres of said land bought by Efford from

John Barker, the assignee of John Bromfield, the assignee of Captain John Shepard, and Lucy, his wife, the assignees of Captain David Maunsell, under whose name and that of Lucy Webster, the original patent of 1000 acres, was granted January 9, 1640, and re-granted to the said Shepard, March 20, 1650, and the other 500 acres due said Efford for the transportation of 10 persons into the Colony.

Sarah Efford, his only surviving child, married Samuel Weldon, J. P. for James City county, who was doubtless a son or brother of Rev. John Weldon mentioned in the will. In 1692-3 Mrs. Sarah Weldon "widow of Major Samuel Weldon," brought an action of ejectment by Poynes Weldon, her attorney. Her husband, Major Samuel Weldon, of London, came to Virginia in 1675 as factor for Philip Foster, of London, merchant, and settled in James City county. The family of Weldon was long a resident in Virginia and North Carolina. Samuel Weldon, of James City county, married in 1725, Elizabeth, daughter of Daniel Allen, and widow of Robert Cobbs, of York county. He removed to Chesterfield county, and his will names his children (under age,) Daniel, Benjamin, (who received lands in Goochland,) Samuel, Elizabeth and Priscilla, son-in law Roderick Easley, wife's daughters Sarah Jones and Martha Richardson, and her grand-children, Allen Willie and Charlotte Jones, (Mrs. Weldon had by her marriage with Robert Cobbs, two daughters, Sarah, who married Robert Jones. Jr., of Sussex county, Va., who emigrated to North Carolina, and was Attorney General of that colony. and Martha, who married Dudley Richardson. Mrs. Jones was the mother of the distinguished Allen and Willie Jones.)

Benjamin Weldon, of Southampton county, Va., in his will dated August 5, 1755, and proved Feb. 9, 1756, names his brothers Daniel and Samuel Weldon, sisters Elizabeth and Priscilla, and cousins Allen, Willie and Martha Jones, and appoints Robert Jones and Gray Briggs, executors.

In 1749 Daniel Weldon was one of the North Carolina Commissioners to run the boundary line with Virginia, and Samuel Weldon, was member of the North Carolina Convention of 1776. The city of Weldon, N. C. is named after the family. (See *William & Mary Quarterly* II, 121.)

Efford was a family name in the Channell Islands—Guernsey and Jersey. See Foster's *Alumni Oxonienses.*]

WILLIAM GUY, Citizen and Haberdasher of London. Will 14 November 1665; proved 29 November, 1665. To be buried in the parish churchyard of St. Mildred, Breadstreete, London. To my brother, Robert Guy, 40s. to buy him a ring, and £6. To my said brother Robert's eldest daughter by his first wife, £50. To my said Brother's son William Guy, £50, and to his son John Guy, £50. To my sister Sarah Tailton, £100. To my daughter in law Elizabeth Nowell, £20.

To Joseph Drewe, my accompt and £20. To my friend Roger Martin, £5. To my friend John Martin the elder, £5. To my kinswoman Abigail How, £5. To Elizabeth Biscoe, £5. To my sister Ann Fisher's two daughters, Sarah and Martha Fisher, £20 each. To my friend William Browne, Ribbon weaver in Shoreditch, £5. To my cousin John Gate, at present in Virginia, £40. To my friend William Allen of London, Merchant, and Anthony Field, my executors, £20 each, and, if any be left, £50 to my sister Sarah Tarlton, the rest amongst the children of brother Robert Guy and sister Anne Fisher. Witnesses: Wm. Blanchard, John Martin, junior, Wilbeard Watts, Anne Martin.

Hyde, 140.

SPARKS MARTIN of Withy Bush House, County Pembroke, Esqr. Will 12 September 1786; proved 3 August 1787. All my manor of Pendergast, with all Royalties, Profits, etc., from lands in County Pembroke, Haverfordwest, County Middlesex, City of Bristol, or elsewhere in Great Britain, to my sister Elizabeth Phelps for life, subject to charges made upon certain of my estates through the will of my late wife Martha Martin, to be held in trust by Right Honble. Richard (Phillips) Lord Milford of Kingdom of Ireland and the Right Honble. William (Edwards) Lord Kensington of Kingdom of Ireland, to preserve to her use the said estates, and after her, to her son Thomas Phelps, and his eldest son in succession, failing him, to John Phelps, second son of my said sister Elizabeth, and his heirs, failing him, to my brother Henry Martin, who went to Virginia, in America, many years ago, and his eldest son in succession, failing him, to my Brother John Martin, who also went to Virginia many years ago. Whoever inherits to take the arms and name of Martin. To my housekeeper Mary Probert, £100 a year for life. To Elizabeth Probert her sister, £5 a year for life. To Martha Jones, £5 a year for life. Executrix: Elizabeth Phelps. Witnesses: Thos. Ormes, junior, Hannah Wills, Joseph Wills, all of Charles Square, Hoxton.

Major, 170.

[In the printed Journal of the Virginia House of Delegates covering the period, is an entry of a petition received January 12, 1784, from James, Lord Clifden, and Edmund Perry, Esq., Speaker of the House of Commons of Ireland, in behalf of certain persons interested under the will of Col. John Martin, deceased, in a certain estate which was escheated, and also a petition of George Martin to the same effect. The petitions are not now among the legislative files for 1784 in the Virginia State archives, and it is probable that they were withdrawn for use at a later session. Unfortunately there are no printed journals accessible for a number of years after, so that it is impossible to learn anything more in regard to the petitions.

James Ager, of county Kilkenny, Ireland, (created Baron Clifden in 1776 and Viscount in 1781), married March 20, 1760, Lucia, eldest daughter of John Martin, Esq., (she died July 26, 1802), and widow of Henry Boyle, youngest son of Henry, first Earl of Shannon ; and Edmund Sexton Perry or Pery (1719-1806), Speaker of the Irish House of Commons, 1771-1785, and created Viscount Pery in 1785, married in 1756, Patty youngest daughter of John Martin, Esq. What was the relation between these ladies and Col. John Martin, of Virginia, does not appear, though it is evident that it was on their account that the Virginia Legislature was pe titioned As Sparkes Martin made two Irishmen his trustees, it seems probable that his brother, John Martin, was the Col. John Martin, of Virginia.

Col. Martin, of Virginia, was a member of the House of Burgesses or Caroline county, at the sessions of November 1738 and May 1740, and for King William county, at the sessions of Feb. 1752, Nov. 1753, Feb. 1754, Aug. 1754, Oct. 1754, May 1755, Aug. 1755, Oct. 1755 and March 1756. He died during the last session.

All the records of King William have been destroyed, and all those of Caroline except the court proceedings, ("Order books") but from the latter a few notes can be gleaned. John Martin was J. P. for Caroline in 1732. On Nov. 10, 1738, John Martin, Jr., qualified as an attorney. On Oct. 17, 1752 was recorded a deed from John and George Martin, of the city of Bristol, merchants, (by John Martin, gent, of Virginia, their attorney), to Thomas Turner, gent.

In the *Virginia Gazette*, Jan. 27, 1750-51 (Cited in the *William & Mary Quarterly* XII, 74) is an advertisement signed by John and Samuel Martin, of King William county, announcing the proposed sale of the house and land, where Col. John Martin lately lived in Caroline county, containing 2700 acres, and in the same paper for Dec. 8-15, 1738, is advertised a reward for the return of a silver pint cup, fluted on both sides, which had been stolen from Col. John Martin, of Caroline county. It had engraved on it his coat of arms, "a chevron between three half moons."

At "Clifton," Caroline county, is a tomb with the following epitaph, (*W. and M. Q.*, XI, 146).

"Interred beneath this Stone,
lyes the Body of Mrs.
Martha Martin, wife of Col.
John Martin, of Caroline
County, and daughter of
Lewis Burwell, Esq., of Gloss-
ter county, who departed this
life the 27th of May 1738, in
the 36th year of her age & left
three sons & four daughters."

It is evident that, at the time of the Revolution some or all of Col.
Martin's sons were residents of Great Britain, or were Tories. In the
Virginia Council Journal 1777-78 is an order in regard to the estates in
Goochland counties, of heirs of Lewis B. (doubtless Lewis Burwell,) and
Samuel Martin, who were British subjects.]

JOHN HANDFORD of Ludlowe, County Salop, Esqre. Will
17 September 1669; proved 24 January 1669|70. To my
son John Handford, gent., my manor of Shobden, and the
avowson of said Parish in County Hereford. All my estates
in Ledicott, nether Shobdon, East Hampton, Ap Hampton,
Hill Hampton als Newton Byton, and Betgatt, sold by one
Barnecombe Wissmore by indenture inrolled in Chancery,
dated the 7 June, 1658, or, however, I doe enjoy the same, to
his heirs male, and after, to the females, failing his issue, to
Tobias Handford, gent., now living in Virginia, one of the
sons of Hugh Handford, late of London, deceased, and then
to his eldest sons in succession, and for want of such issue.
the tithes of Shobdon for an augumentation to the minister.
and the property to maintain a preaching minister, and the
rest, in case my said son and the said Tobias die without issue,
to Walter Handford of Wollashall, County Worcester, Gent.,
and his heirs male in succession, failing him, to the right
heirs of me the said John Handford. To my son all my
bookes of Divinity, History, etc., except those my wife uses
as her own. To the minister who preaches my funeral sermon, 40s. To Sir Walter Williams of Upton Bishopp, County Hereford, Bart., Sir John Winford of Ashley, County
Worcester, Knt., the Lady Winford, his wife (my wife's sister), and to Mrs. Mary Williams, another of my wife's sisters,
and to her kinswoman Mrs. Eleanor Williams, £5 each. To

every servant living with me at my death, 40 s each. All the rest not bequeathed I give to my wife. Executors: Sir Walter Williams, Bart., Sir John Winford, and my wife. My son to be left at school till he can enter one of the Honourable Societies of the Inns of Court to study Law. To the poor of Ludlow, £3. Witnesses: Richard Wright, Jo. Edwardes, Henry Browne, John Browne.

Penn, 6.

[The testator evidently belonged to a family seated at Wallashall, in the parish of Nafford, Worcestershire, but which had representatives in other parts of England. In Nash's *Worcestershire*, II, 180-182, is an account of the family at Wallashall. Thomas Hanford or Handford (stated to be descended in the 8th generation from Sir John Hanford, of Cheshire), named Margaret, daughter and co-heiress of William Higford, of Nafford, and had issue: I, Margaret, married Thomas Copley, of Norton: 2, John married Anne, daughter of Richard Rake: 3, Catherine married —— Whittington, of Norgrave. John and Anne (Rake) Hanford were the parents of Francis Hanford, (living *temp.* Charles I), who married Elizabeth, daughter of Walter Gifford, of Chillington, and was the father of Walter Hanford, who married Frances, daughter of Sir Henry Compton, Knight of the Bath. Walter and Frances (Compton) Hanford had issue: 1, Compton who married 1st—Chaumont and had no issue, and 2d—Slingsby: 2. Edward, who was the father of Charles Hanford, of Rid Marley. Compton and — (Slingsby) Hanford had issue: 1. Edward married Elizabeth Hurst, of Haverhill, Essex ; 2, Charles: 3. Elizabeth. Edward and Elizabeth (Hurst) Hanford had issue: 1. James: 2. Edward: 3. Charles: 4 Eleanor. The name appears to have been spelt, indifferently, Hansford, Hanford or Handford. Sir Humphrey Hansford or Handford, of London, was an active member of the Virginia Company, and John Hansford, of London, merchant tailor, was also a member. See Brown's *Genesis*.

Tobias Hansford, named in the will, lived in Gloucester county, Va. On Jan. 8, 1666, Tobias *Hansford* had a grant of 324 acres in Ware Parish, Gloucester, beginning at a point at the mouth of Deep Creek, in Mockjack Bay, and running down the bay and then along Christopher Robins's land to the mouth of Finches' Creek. On the same date "Mr. Tobias Handford" had a grant of 324 acres in Gloucester, on the Eastern side of Wolf Creek, beginning at the mouth thereof—a marsh dividing this land from that of Col. Augustine Warner, &c.—150 acres, part thereof, was granted to Col. John Walker, Esq., by patent dated March 15, 1651, and 174 acres, the remainder, taken up. On Oct. 24, 1673, Philip Ludwell, Tobias Handford and Richard Whitehead renewed a grant of 20,000 acres in New Kent county, on the southside of Mattapony river—due for the importation of 400 persons into the Colony.]

129

MOTTRAM WRIGHT of Milend, St. Dunstan's, Stepney, County Middlesex, Merchant. Will 8 October 1700; proved 10 October 1700. To my daughter Frances Wright, £100 and 700 acres of land on north side of Rappahamack Creeke, in Virginia. To my son Mottrom Wright, £600 and all my lands, etc., in Virginia (except the said 7000 acres), and 6 negroes. To my cousin John Wright of Puttomack River, in Virginia, £50 of England. To each and every other of my children born of the body of my wife Ruth Wright, 20s. apiece and noe more. The rest and residue to my two children Frances and Mottrom; if they die, to go to my cousin John Wright. My son Mottrom to be brought up in the Church of England. Executor: Mottrom Wright. Overseer: Captain John Pyrvis. Witnesses: J. Sharpe, A. M., James Berouth, Hannah Bradley, Thomas Quilter, N. P.

Noel, 189.

[The testator was a party to one of the very few legal separations of husband and wife which appear in the early records of Virginia.

The family of Wright was, like so many others in Virginia, of London origin. Richard Wright, of London, a merchant or master of a ship in the Virginia trade, is recorded as carrying tobacco from Virginia to Holland in 1653. This is of record in Northumberland county, a contract, dated May 29, 1656, between Richard Wright, of London—"being homeward bound," to transport 60 hogsheads of tobacco. A little later Wright settled in Virginia, and was a justice of Northumberland in 1659. He married Ann, daughter of Col. John Mottram, of Northumberland county, (she afterwards married David Fox) and died in 1663. His will is preserved in a much mutilated record book in Northumberland. He gives his wife Anne, one half his land Machodoc and Potomac rivers—"that is the half that joins my brother Spencer (Nicholas Spencer, Esq., of Cople parish, Westmoreland county, Va., and formerly of Cople, Bedfordshire, England, Governor of Virginia, &c., who had married Frances, daughter of Col. John Mottram), with reversion at her death to his son Francis Wright. To wife two negroes (named.) All of the English servants, negroes, not otherwise bequeathed, and rest of personal estate in Virginia and Maryland, to be divided into three equal parts, of which wife is to have one part and his three children the other two parts. To son, Mottram Wright, all his land on Elk Run, Maryland. To my *** land lying **.—** Francis **.—** for discharging education all my money in England **. To daughter ** land in the freshes of Potomac. To my brother*** land at **. To my brother Nicholas Spencer, and sister Mrs. Frances Spencer, and brother John

Mottram, each a ring.   Brothers Spencer and Mottram, overseers.   Cousin Mathew Merriton, of London, merchant, an overseer in England, dated Aug. 16, and proved in Northumberland, Dec. 10, 1663.   The inventory of the personal estate of Mr. Richard Wright was recorded March 10, 1663-4, and was appraised at 23,334 lbs. tobacco.

Before March 12, 1684, Mottram Wright, the testator above, and the son of Richard Wright, whose will has been given, married Ruth, daughter of Robert Griggs, a well-to-do planter of Northumberland county, and widow of John Mottram, Jr., who was uncle to Mottram Wright. An uncle's widow was within the prohibited degrees of affinity, and it seems strange that such a marriage should have been solemnized under English jurisdiction, but such the records show, was certainly the case. After at least ten years of marriage, and after giving birth to children, Mrs. Wright appears to have become horrified at the sinfulness of her union, and secured a separation.   There is on record in Lancaster county, a bond dated Oct. 12, 1694, reciting that Mottram Wright married Ruth Mottram, widow of Major John Mottram, who was the said Mottram Wright's mother's brother, ''which marriage was incestious and unlawful,'' and had been the occasion of the said Ruth's departing from her husband ''choosing rather to lead her life in banishment from her friends, country and estate, than continue any longer in that sinful marriage,'' therefore said Mottram Wright agrees that said Ruth shall live separately and apart, and to pay her a suitable alimony, and that the daughter be had in marriage with her shall be put to school where he shall think fit.   There is on record in Lancaster, the marriage contract, dated Dec. 11, 1701, between Robert Gibson and Mrs. Ruth Wright, widow of Mottram Wright.

Of course such a marriage as that between Wright and Mrs. Mottram would now be legal.

Mottram Wright, Jr. died without issue, and most of his father's estate passed to the daughter, Frances, who married Joseph Belfield, of Richmond county.   Mottram Wright's will (above) was also recorded in in Lancaster to July, 1701.]

HENRY WOODHOUSE of parish of Linhaven, County of Lower Norfolk, Virginia. Will 29 January 1686|7; proved 24 July 1688. To my eldest son Henry Woodhouse, my plantation I now live on, being 500 acres. To my second son Horatio Woodhouse, my plantation called Moyes land. If the survey of my land run into Noyes neck, he to have it. To my son John Woodhouse, my land next to land of Richard Bonney whereon Richard Dobbs dwells. To my two sons Horatio and John, my land I bot of Mr. William Bassnett, Senior, lying in woods by John Swell's lands. To my son Henry Woodhouse, my two Negroes, Roger and Sarah by name. When my children Horatio and John are at age, and my daughters Elizabeth and Luce 16, the rest of negroes to be divided among them. To my daughter Mary the wife of William More, Negro woman called Kate, 2,000 lbs. of Tobacco, £10, and 3 silver spoons. To my daughter Sarah, wife of Earon More, £10, 2,000 lbs. of Tobacco, and 3 silver spoons. the money being due from Mr. Thomas Minnford. All the rest between Henry, Horatio, John, Elizabeth and Luce. Executor: Son Henry, he to plant an apple orchard in the next two years. Witnesses: William Cornick, Mala Thruston.

Exton, 102.

[Henry Woodhouse, the testator, was son of Henry Woodhouse, of Lower Norfolk county, Va., who died in 1655, and grandson of Capt. Henry Woodhouse, Governor of the Bermudas 1623-26. The last named was second son of Sir Henry Woodhouse, of Waxham, Norfolk, England. For accounts of the Woodhouse family, and will of Henry Woodhouse, who died 1655 as well as that of Rev. Horatio Woodhouse, Rector of Collingtree, Northamptonshire, England, who was also a son of Governor Woodhouse, and who died in 1697. See *William & Mary Quarterly* I, 227-232, II, 262-264, V, 41-44, and Vols. I-IV, *Lower Norfolk County Virginia Antiquary*. The name is still prominently represented in Princess Anne county, a part of old Lower Norfolk.]

THOMAS BLAGRAVE of Westminnster, gent. Will 14 May 1686. proved 4 December 1688. To my wife Margaret Blagrave, my house and land in Teddington, County Middlesex. To my kinsman Thomas Blagrave, £40. To my kinsman Ambrose Searle, £10. To my kinsman John Goodwin, £20, and forgive what he owes me. To my kinswoman Anne Williams, in Virginia, £5. To my Kinsman Henry Johnson, £5. To my Kinsman John Blagrave, my brother Anthony Blagrave's youngest sonne, £5. To the poor which shall be near at my interment, 20s. All the rest to my beloved wife Margaret Blagrave, whom I make executrix. Witnesses: John Clayton, Elias Silvester, Tho. Jennings.

Exton, 106.

[There have, apparently, been several families of Blagrave, or Bla-grove, in Virginia. A. Henry Blagrave, was a justice of Lunenburg county, prior to the Revolution, and Rev. Benjamin Blagrove, son of John, of Oxford, England, *pleb.*, matriculated at St. Mary Hall, Oxford, Oct. 15, 1764, at the age of 18, came to Virginia in 1772, (Foster's *Alumni Oxonienses*, and Fothergill's *Emigrant Ministers*). He became Minister of Southwark parish, Surry; took the American side during the Revolution, and was a member of the Surry Committee of Safety in 1776.

John Blagrave, son of Anthony Blagrave, of Berks, *Arm.*, who matriculated at Magdalen College, Feb. 1, 1731–2, aged 19, may have been the nephew John, named in the will.]

EDWARD DEWALL of Warrasquoyke, servant to Symon Cornocke of the same. Will 11 November 1636; proved 23 November 1640 ["Edward Dewell, of Warwicke Squeake, in Virginia, defunct," in sentence.]. To Symon Coornocke of War-rasquoyke, in Virginia, one Messuage being an Hoast-house or Inne in a Towne called Redding, County Berks, England, in the parish of Saint Maries, in Minstrell Streete, now or late in the tenure of Richard Marcombe, my uncle, as tenant to mee, given to me by my father George Dewell in his life time being the signe of the Rose, and also all houses and money left me by my mother, Joane Duell. Executor: Symon Cornocke. Witnesses: John Army, Nicholas Spackman, William Clappum. Sentence, same date, for will in cause between executor Simon Curnocke and brother Humphry Dewell, claiming to be administrator.

Coventry, 139.

[This will gives an unusual, though not unique instance, of a servant owning lands or houses.]

ELIZABETH DRAPER of London, Widow. Will 17 August, 1625; proved 3 September 1625. To my son Vincent Draper, in lieu of his child's pte., £150. To my grandchild Darcis Draper, daughter of said Vincent, £150 when 18 or day of marriage, her Aunt Sara Symons to have the education of her. If she die, one-half to her father and the other half to her said aunt. To my grandchildren Elizabeth and Mary Peirsey, daughters of my sonne-in-law Abraham Peirsey, merchaunte, resident in Virginia, £100 apiece when 18 or marriage; if they die, the money to be divided between the said Vincent and Sara. To Abraham Peirsiey a ring of value of 30s. To my son in law Thurston Symons, one Ringe value 30s. To Mrs. Cowley, my cosen, 30s. to make her a Ringe. To my god-daughter Elizabeth Cowley, one Ring with eight Dyamond Stones in it. To my daughter Elizabeth Peirsey one dyamond Ringe. To Mary Peirsey one Dyamond Ringe set after the Duch fashion. To Darkis Draper, one Opell Ringe with sixe Opelle stones of several colours in yt. To my cosen Smythson, 20s., and to his wife, 20s., and his daughter Elizabeth, 20s. To the poore of St. Clements neare Candlewicke streete, in London, wherein I nowe dwell, 50s. To John Peirsye, 13s, 4d. To Mr. Price, Clarke of St. Clements paryshe. 20s. To Netherwood, the sexton of same p'sh., 10s. To Katherin Ruter, my mayde servant, 50s. To Robert Mincharde, Scrivener, 13s., 4d. All the rest to my executors in trust for my daughter Sara Simmons, her husband and Thurstone Symons not to have any claim (he, notwithstanding his pretensions of giving up his vile and lewd courses, having wronged me). Executors: my lovinge Cozens Mr. Richard Berisford, marchante of London, that sometime dwelt uppon Newe Fyshstreet Hill, London, and ——— Warriner, merchante, dwelling in Mark Lane, in London. Mem. of Scrivener, Robert Mincharde, that the said testatrix did order me to draw up her will in the aforesaid manner in the presence of Katherin Ruter.

Clarke, 93.

[Abraham Persey or Piersey, who died in 1628, was a member of the Council, and was reputed to be the wealthiest man of his day in Virginia. He married twice, his first wife, evidently the daughter of Mrs. Draper, was the mother of his two children, Elizabeth and Mary. His will was printed in full in Neill's *Virginia Carolorium*, 404-406, and an abstract from the P. C. C., given in the Magazine XII, 177-178. See also this Magazine I, 187-188]

VIRGINIA GLEANINGS IN ENGLAND.

Communicated by Mr. LOTHROP WITHINGTON, 30 Little Russell street, W. C., London (including "Gleanings" by Mr. H. F. WATERS, not before printed.)

(CONTINUED)

RICHARD BARNABE, London, Marchant, bound on a voyage by God's grace to the East Indyes with good shipp or vessell named the Mary of London of the burden of One Thousand Tunnes or thereabouts. Will 19 January 1630 | 1; proved 11 July 1636. To be buried neere late wief in church of St. Katherine Coleman, London. All to daughters Elizabeth Barnabe and Mary Barnabe, executrixes. Overseers: brothers in lawe Mr. John Boulteel, Clarke, and George Rookes, Marchant, goodes to remayne in their hands till daughters are 21; if either die, or refuse said [sic] Samuell Fortre to join with surviver or Refuser, and if Samuel Fortre die or refuse, then my brother in lawe Samuel Gatre vncle of my children to ioyne etc. etc. Whereas £600 given by will of Mrs. Anne Gatree late of London, widdow, etc. dated 5 December 1627 given to said daughter Elizabeth and Mary and due to me if they die before marriage or 21, whereof £200 is in charge of Mr. John Fortree, £200 in hands of said Samuel Fortree and £200 in hands of said John Boulteel, three of executors of will of said Anne Gatree: To Loving brother John Barnabe resident in Virginia and Planter there £100, and my brother James Barnabe resident in Virginia £100, to be paid to them if living, or if dead to their sons and daughters. If none be living, then to children of said brother in law George Rookes, Merchant. To sister Elizabeth Rookes £30, and to her seven children £70, viz. George Rookes the younger £20 and residue of £50 to others, at 21 to sons, and to daughters at 21 or marriage. To sister Martha Barnabe, sometime wief of John Sargenson, vintner, deceased £30, and, to her sonn William Sargenson £20 at 21, or if he die, to children of John Boultell. To sister Katherine Clarke £30, and to her son Robert at 21 and daughter Katherine at 21 or marriage £10 each etc. To Anne Barnabe, daughter of uncle John Barnabe,

From Vol. XIII, No. 3 (Jan. 1906), p. 303.

nowe wief of —— Edwards, Merchant, £50, and if dead, to her children. To sometyme servant Elizabeth Rivers als Marsh £20. Residue of £600, viz: £130 to Masters and Wardens of Company of Drapers of London (whereof I am a brother) to pay £10, yearly, viz: £5 for some godly and vertuous Preacher to preach five sermons yearly in church of St. Katherine Colman neere billeter lane, London, whereof one sermon on New Yeares day at 20s per sermon and 12d weekely upon Sabbath day in bread to poore of parish of St Katherine Colman and 20s a year on New Yeares daye and to Sexton at same time 3s. for ever; and to poore of St. Martin in Vintry in London 10s upon New Yeares day forever; and to poore of Lambeth ditto, for the love I beare said parishes and places for that my late deare wife and her mother and my Chrisome Child lye interred in same parish church of St. Katherine Colman, and for that two of my children lye interred in parish church of St. Martin in the Vintry, and three of my children lye interred in parish church of Lambeth. As to £100 left to my children by their aunt Jane Cuthbert due to me in case they dye, £50 in hands of said James Fortrie and £50 in hands of said John Boulteel, I give to sister Mrs. Mary Boulteel £30, to god daughter Elizabeth Boulteel £50 at 21 or marriage, and John Boulteel the younger, god son of my late dear wife Ann Barnabe, £20 at 21, and if they die, to the other children of John Boulteel. To cousin Mary, wife of John Chaundler, £10. To good wife Vale of Hadley neere Barnett, sometymes nurse of my daughter Mary, £6-13s-4d if lyving. To Nurse Abbott, widdowe, dwelling in the parish of Creechurch neere Algate, £3-6s-8d. Rest to twoe brethren John Barnabe and James Barnabe, yf lyving, and yf dead, to their children yf lyving; yf dead, then to children of my said brother George Rookes. If daughters Elizabeth and Mary die, said Samuel Fortrie, John Boulteel senior, and George Rookes to be executors. Witnesses: James Merrifield, William Taylor, Robert Minchard Not. Pub. "Appendix to will made in England by me Richard Barnaby, Merchant. In good shipp Hart now bound for England, viz: To friend Captain Richard Swanley one Japan Cutter and one paire of Buffe gloves. To friend Thomas Robinssonne merchant one Capp wrought with silke and gold and one capp of lynnen with needle worke purles. To nephe George

Rookes imbroidered girdle with silver buckles. To apprentice Willm Curtis his freedome and liberty, also 1 cloth sute, 1 peece of white damaske, 3 little batting bands, 1 paire of shoes and 1 paire of slippers. To Samuell Lathorppe now Chirurgeon of the shipp Hart 1 woollen cloth cote and 1 silver spoone. To William Pearce chirurgeon's mate 1 cloth sute, 1 pewter seringe with a silver pipe. To Richard Foster, Barber, 1 pare of Bayes Breeches, 1 pare of cloth stockings, 1 pare of shoes, and 1 pare of slippers. To Henry Hayman one red woollen capp. To George Swanley one cloth capp with gold lace. To John Swanley 'The Practis of Piety.' Rest for daughters Elizabeth Barnabe and Mary Barnabe in trust to Samuell Fortrie and John Boulteel. Overseers: Captain Richard Swanley and Mr. Thomas Robinsonne. 24 April 1635. Witness: James Mathew, purser's mate. Administration to sister Elizabeth Rookes als Barnabe during minority of Elizabeth Barnabe and Mary Barnabe.

Pile, 84.

[The census of Virginia, 1624-5, gives the " Muster " of John Barnabe, at Elizabeth City. It includes himself, aged 21, who came in the *London Marchant* in 1620 (Notten's *Emigrants*, p. 247.)—Ed.]

GEORGE RUGGLES of the University of Cambridge, Master of Artes. Will 6 September 1621; proved 3 November 1622. To the the poor of the towne of Lavenham, County of Suffolke, where I was borne, 20 markes. To the poor of Parish where I shall be buried £5. To him that shall preache at my buriall £5. To the two prisons in Cambridge £5 between them. To the Chapple of Clarehall 20 marks to buy a silver bason to be used at the Communion for the collection of the Poore. " Item. I further give and bequeath unto Clarehall in Cambridge aforesaid one hundred pounds to be Payed within one yeare nexte after my decease to the intent that it may alwaies remayne in parte of their stocke to be imployed for the better makinge of provision at the best handes for the benefitt of the said Colledge and the students in it And that at their Audits or accompte once a yeare I will that the one hundred poundes be alwaies brought in and tituled by the name of George Ruggles one hundred Poundes." To Clarehall Library all my books whatsoever the Master and fellowes shall think fittinge. The rest of my books to the children

137

of Mr. Toddy Pallyvicine. All my papers and paper books to be burned. To my sisters Mary Dardes and Sara Liminall, both living in the City of Westchester, £100 each. To all my sister's children £10 each. I give and bequeath £100 towards bringing up the Infidell's Children in Virginia in Christian Religion, to be disposed of by the Virginia Company. To Mrs. Jane Pallavycine, wife of said Toby, plate to value of £10. To my loving Aunt Mrs. Alice Vigoris of Ipswich, to Mr. Henry Coppinger the elder of Lavenham, to Mr. William Greenhalt sometyme my schoolmaster, 40s. each for ringes, To my friends of Clarehall, Augistine Linsell, D. D., Thomas Winston, Doctor of Physicke, Thomas Parke, D. D., Mr. William Lake, Mr. Thomas Parkinson, Mr. Nicholas Ferrer, Mr. Samuell Linsell, and Mr. James Harley, 40s. each for ringes. To my friends Mr. Edward Mannesty, Mr. John Sherman the elder of Cambridge, and Clement his wife, and their son Mr. John Sherman the younger, and to Mr. Thomas Sherman thelder, 40s. apiece for rings. To Mr. John Crane and Mr. Thomas Wake, both of Cambridge, to Mr. William Parker of Sproughton neare Ispwich, and to Mr. Thomas Lake of London 40s. each to make them ringes. To Mr. William Bryarte of London Merchant 40s. To my friend Myles Goulsborrow and his heires 20 nobles. To John Briggs, some times my poor scholar, £3. To Sir Edmond Varney, Knighte, dwelling in Buckinghamshire, an especiall friend of Mr. Toby Pallavicine, Plate to the value of £5. All the rest to Mr. Toby Pallavicine and his heirs. Executor: Sir Edmond Varney. Witnesses: Tho. Abbott, Scr. East Smithfield, Co. Middx, John Johnson, Tho. Boden, servant to said Scr.

Savile, 101.

[George Ruggle or Ruggles, son of Thomas Ruggle, of Suffolk, was born November 13, 1575, and entered St John's College, Cambridge, in his fourteenth year. He received his A. M from Trinity in 1597, and in 1598 became a Fellow of Clare Hall. In 1614, during a visit of King James to the University, a Latin comedy by Ruggle was performed by the students, and received great applause from the King. In 1619 he retired from the University, and Secretary Ferrar, of the Virginia Company, states that from that time until his death his labors were almost entirely given to the Company and to the cause of English colonization.

He was thought to be the author of a treatise on planting which the Company sent to Virginia for the Councillors to read. He died in 1622, and in his will bequeathed £100 for the education of Indian children in Virginia. *A Life of George Ruggle*, by J. S. Hawkins, was published in London in 1787.—Ed.]

GEORGE HAWKER of the Parish of St. Martains Ludgate, London, Combemaker. Will 20 November 1657; proved 15 January 1657-8. To my mother Ann Hawker 5s. To my sister Ann Knight 5s. To my brother Edward Hawker living in Virginia 1s. All these legacies to be paid within one month of my decease by my executrix, my loving wife Martha, to whom I bequeath all the remainder of my estate, my debts and funeral expenses being paid. Witnesses : William Trigge & Fran : Bartlett Scr. att Holborne Conduitte, Grace Davenish.

Wootton, 3.

CORNELIUS WATTES, of St. Cuthbertes in the City of Wells, in the County of Somersett, Vintener. Will 3 January 1640-1, proved 2 October 1640. To be buried in the Churchyard of St. Cuthberts. To John Davis of Shipton Mallet and his wife one Arrisoe Coverlett and a blew Rugg and twoe siluer wine boles and 40s. a piece to buy each of them a ring. To Margarett Davies, daughter of said John Davies, 40s. To William Watts, which is now in Virginia, my house next below the Ashe-in-the-well and £10. If he dothe not returne again, my son Edward Watts to have the house but not the money. To the Church of St. Cuthberts 10s. To the people of Thalmeshouse of Bp. Bubwith's and Bp. Stil their foundations 10s. All the rest to my wife Ann Watts and Edward Watts my son and Anne Watts my daughter whom I make executors. Witnesses: Richard Deane, Clarke, Willm Sherman, John Oldford.

Coventry, 129.

[William Watts and Richard Davis patented, July 30, 1638, seventy-five acres on Queens Creek, adjoining the lands of Robert Booth and Lieutenant Popeley ; due as follows : Fifty acres for the adventure of said Watts and wife, the second year, to Charles River, and twenty-five acres for the adventure, the second year, of the said Davis to Charles River.

The " adventure " refers to the bounty in land offered tho se who would settle on Charles (now York) river, then a frontier of the Colony. See grant to John Chew, July 6, 1636, reciting an order of Council of October 8, 1630 (this Magazine V, 341–342). Queens Creek flows into York River not far from Williamsburg.—Ed.]

RICHARD PHILLIPS of the City of Bristol, Marriner, being bound to Sea. Will 3 January 1703-4 proved 20 December 1704. One half of my goods and personal estate to the children of my uncle John Phillips in Virginia equally between them, and the other half to Hannah Cockayne, Spinster, daughter of Thomas Cockayne of the said City, victualler. Executor : Jeoffry Peniell of said City, Linnendrapen, Witnesses ; Margaret Lewis, J. Freke.

Ash, 239.

[There was a John Phillips, of Lancaster county, who may have been the uncle referred to. On January 1, 1652, he was made Clerk of the county, and at the same time, commissioned Sheriff, "because the county was then in its infancy, and could not afford a subsistence." The County Court was held in his house in August, 1653. No doubt, the records of Lancaster county could give more details in regard to him, and as to his children, if he left any. The records of this old county are quite complete, and the files of vellum bound books is unbroken ; but the county authorities deserve severe condemnation for leaving these most valuable records in a room with a brick floor and without fire, where it is so damp that they have very perceptibly faded within the past few years.

John Phillips, referred to, had the following grants :

(1) John Phillips, 240 acres on the north of Rappahannock, adjoining the land of George Eaton, March 2, 1652 ; (2) John Phillips, 100 acres in the county of Lancaster on Powells Creek, March 3, 1652 ; (3) Mrs. John Phillips, 400 acres in the county of Lancaster on the north of Rappahannock at the head of a dividend, formerly surveyed for Captain Daniel Gookins, by "the side of a mountain" [this probably means a hill], and on the west bank of Cassatawomen river, July 13, 1653 ; (4) John Phillips, 250 acres in Lancaster north of Rappahannock, July 13, 1653 ; (5) John Phillips, 100 acres in Lancaster north of Rappahannock, adjoining his own land and that of Evan Griffith, July 13, 1653 ; (6) John Phillips, 200 acres in Lancaster on south of Rappahannock, and on "Barham or Burnham Creek or Sunderland," lying at the head of a dividend of 200 acres in the possession of Edward Boswell, and adjoining the land of Evan Davy and Den. Conier, September 3, 1653 ; (7) John Phillips, 200 acres in Lancaster, south of Rappahannock at the

head of 300 acres surveyed for Mr. David Fox, and adjoining the land of Thomas Browne, Oliver Carver and Mr. Richard Parrett, September 2, 1652 ; (8) John Phillips and John Batts, 500 acres on the north side of the freshes of Rappahannock in Lancaster county, about 14 miles above the " Nanzemun Towne," adjoining 100 acres surveyed for John Weyre, September 7, 1654 ; (9) John Phillips, 300 acres on a branch of Occupason Creek and on a creek called Wassanasson, said land formerly granted by patent to Richard Coleman, January 11, 1652, and by him relinquished and now granted to Phillips, June 14, 1655 ; (10) Thomas Meads and John Phillips, 1000 acres on the south side of the freshes of Rappahannock, opposite a tract of 1400 acres surveyed for Richard Coleman, September 7, 1654 ; (11) John Weyre, John Gillet, Andrew Gilson and John Phillips, 4000 acres on the south side of the freshes of Rappahannock, about twelve miles above Nanzemun town, and on Weyre's creek, September 7, 1654 ; (12) Sarah Phillips and Lt. Col. Moore Fauntleroy, 250 acres in Lancaster on the north of Rappahannock, due them by virtue of letters of administration on the estate of Mr. John Phillips, deceased and formerly granted to him July 13, 1653, now regranted January 5, 1656.—Ed.]

EDWARD CHANDLER of Ware, County Hertford, Draper. Will 8 May 1650 ; proved 24 April 1657. To my wife Elizabeth Chandler my houses in Ware, one wherein I now life, the one purchased of Will Beecke of London, Linnen Draper, the other of John Geates, Bricklayer, of Hunsden, for life, and after her decease to my son Edward Chandler, failing him, to my son John, failing him to my son Noah. To my said wife houses in Hartford and Buchery Green, lately purchased of Will Beeke and John Brett, Linen Draper, of London, and after her deathe to my son Edward. To my son John Chandler house in Drad Lane in tenure of Edward Gillett, bought of William Burchett and Thomasine his wife, and £20. To my son Noah the Barne and garden in Drad lane, which I bought of Mr. Will Love, and two closes in Annoell March, bought of Elizabeth Challis, widow, sometime the wife of Nicholas Slater. To my daughter Susan Chandler £80. To my daughter Mary Holly 40s. To my son Danial Chandler £10 to be paid him or sent over in commodities to Virginia and to my daughter Sara Chandler, now in Virginia, £5. To my youngest daughter Rebecca £30. To my daughter Martha £20. Household stuff to my wife for life, and after her decease to my children, Susan, Martha, Rebecca,

Edward, Job, and Noah. To my son Edward all debts owing me, the wares in my shops at Hartford and Ware, my maults in the Mault Lought and barley Lought, and all my money in the house except £60 which my wife is to have, and he to pay her £20 of the payment of £80 to my daughter Susan. Executors : Elizabeth my wife and Edwarde my sonne. Witnesses : William Love, Mary Randall.

Grey, 63.

JOHN SEWARD of Bristoll, Merchant (being bound to sea). Will 16 September 1650; proved 23 May 1651. To my youngest daughter Rebecca Seward £300. To my second daughter Mary Seward £250. To my eldest daughter Sarah Seward £250, and to my wife's daughter (by her former husband) Brigitt Eyton £50, all when 21 or married. To my eldest son John Seward £200 when 21. To my son James Seward £250 when 21. If any die, their shares to go to survivors. My farm in Butcombe, county Somerset, to my wife during widowhood, and after her decease to my son John, he to pay £20 yearly to my son James. The house I now dwell in situate in parish of St. Leonard, Bristol, bought of Mr. John Griffith of Winterbourne, clerke, to my wife, and after her decease to my son James. Lands at Bevington and Baddington, County Somerset, held by lease from Mr. Bamfield, to my said daughter Sara. My plantation called Levenecke (1350 acres), Isle of Wight County, Virginia, to my son John. My Plantation called Blackwater in said County (1600 acres) to my son James. All horses, servants, merchandize in Virginia to my said two sons. To the poor of St. Thomas in Bristol 50s. To the poor of Redcliffe 50s. All the rest to my executrix, my wife. Overseers : William Carey of London, mch't., Francis Yeoman of Bristow, gent Walter Stephens the younger of Bristoll, Mercer, Witnesses : Francis Yeoman, Not. Public, Matthew Wolfe, Den. Long, John Hellier.

Grey, 98.

[See this Magazine X, 406.]

EDWARD PORTEOUS. Will 23 February 1693-4 ; proved 24 October 1700. To the poor of Petsoe Parish where I now live £8. To Mary Cox and her children all the debt her deceased

142

husband owed me and £4 more. To George Major, Senior, £5.
To James Murr two cowes, to his sister Rachell two cowes and £4.
To the poor of Newbottle parish in Scotland where my fathers
estate is £8 to be remitted to my friend Mr. James Fowlis in
London, and by him to be sent to my sisters for distribution.
To William Allen one cow. To John Gardner and his wife one
cow, and to Nathaniel Mills a cow and a calfe. To Mr. Thomas
Buckner and his wife £10. To Mr. David Alexander and his
wife £10. To my sister Mary, wife of Mr. Thomas Lowny, £20.
To my sister Isabell £25. To my sister Elizabeth £20. To
my sister Christian £25. To my wife my horse Jack, silver
Tankard, and Caudle Cupp, and household stuff, and the time
that my English Servant Betty hath to serve, and my negro girl
Cumbo. My estate not to be valued, but my wife to have one
third, the rest to my son Robert. My property and estate in
Virginia to my son Robert and his heirs, £16 out of £20 that
was my Brother John's to be sent to Mr. James Fowlis for the
use of my said sisters; if he is dead, to Jeffery Jefferies, to whom
I give 20s. My fathers estate in Newbottle, Scotland, incum-
bered with debt and in the arangement of my brother in law
Thomas Lowny, said estate to be redeemed for my son Robert.
The produce of my plantations to be sent to England every
year. Executor: Captain John Smith, to whom £9 and 20s. to
his Lady. Witnesses: Sarah Buckner, Richard Bradshaw.

Noel, 107.

[Edward Porteus was living in Gloucester County, Virginia, in 1681,
where he was a vestryman of Petsworth (commonly called Petsoe) parish.
In 1693 the Governor included him in a list of " gentlemen of estate and
standing suitable for appointment to the Council," which he sent to
England. Edward Porteus was, however, not one of those appointed.
He married the " Relict of Robert Lee," who left £7 to the poor of the
parish. " Violet Banks, on York River and Poropotank Creek, is the
modern name of the house of Edward Porteus, the emigrant. It is an
old square brick building, two stories and a half, with four rooms to the
floor. Though abandoned, it still retains the fine panelling and interior
carving of the long past." (*William and Mary Quarterly*, III, 58–59.)
His tomb, on which the inscription is not entirely legible, remains at
this place. It is :

"Here lies the Body of Edward Porteus
of Petsworth Parish, Gloucester County,
Merchant, Departed this life the * * *
169* in the *** Year of his Age,
leaving only Sir Robert to
Succeed him."

(*William and Mary Quarterly*, III, 28.)

The son Robert Porteus, born 1679, died August 8, 1758, lived at "New Bottle," now called "Concord," in Gloucester. Hodgson, in his life of Bishop Porteus, says that the Bishop had "a singular picture which, though not in the best style of coloring, was yet thought valuable by Sir Joshua Reynolds as a specimen of the extent to which the art of paintings had at that time reached in America, and he himself very highly praised it as exhibiting a faithful and interesting representation of his father's residence."

Robert Porteus was appointed to the Couneil in 1713, and remained a member of that body until he removed to England sometime between 1725 and 1730. He settled in the city of York, and afterwards at Ripon. To the latter place he was probably led by the fact that his wife was Elizabeth (died January 20, 1754, aged 80, buried at St. Martins, Coney street, York), daughter of Edmund Jenings of "Ripon Hall," Virginia, and formerly of Ripon, Yorkshire.

In Ripon Cathedral, on the wall of the south aisle of the choir, is a mural tablet with the following inscription :

"Near this Place
Are deposited the Remains
Of Robert Porteus, Esquire,
A Native of Virginia, and a Member of His Majesty's Council,
Or Upper House of Legislature in that Province,
From thence he removed to England,
And resided first at York, afterwards at this Town,
Where he died August 8, 1758,
Aged 79 years."

Robert Porteus was the father of Beilby Porteus, born at York May 8, 1731, died May 14, 1808, successively Bishop of Chester and London. Ed.]

VIRGINIA GLEANINGS IN ENGLAND.

Communicated by Mr. Lothrop Withington, 30 Little Russell street, W. C., London (including "Gleanings" by Mr. H. F. Waters, not before printed.)

(Continued)

Hugh Nelson of Penrith, Co. Cumberland, gent. Will 13 December, 1708. Proved 16 February, 1708–9. All land and houses in Penrith unto the Reverend Richard Holme of Lowther Co Westmoreland and Robert Wilson, Thomas Nelson and Thomas Fisher all of Penrith in trust for the use of my wife Sarah Nelson for life, and then I give (the Shops and Warehouses called Redmans excepted) to the said trustees for the use of my eldest son now living Thomas Nelson he to pay my sons John Nelson, Hugh Nelson, and to my daughters Dorothy wife of George Wilkinson and Bridget Nelson £300. If he make default, in such case I give the whole to said trustees (except the house and shop called Redmans) for the use of my son John, he to pay the said £300 If he make default, to my son Hugh. If all fail, the estate to be divided amongst them all. To my grandson William Nelson now in Barbadoes, £20 (having formerly laid out and payd upon the account of his father £500, to be paid when he is 21. To my grand child Sarah Wilkinson £20. To my grand child Dorothy Wilkinson £20. To my servants Samuel Denny and Ellenor Robinson 20s. each. The house &c called Redmans formerly mortgaged to William Nelson my father, and all the rest of my goods to Sons John and Hugh and Daughters Dorothy and Bridget my joint executors.

Overseers aforesaid trustees. Witnesses : Jos. Langhorne, John Sandson, Geo. Sandson

Consistory Carlisle Filed Will.

[Thomas Nelson, the son who is named in the will, emigrated to Virginia and settled at Yorktown. He became a man of influence and acquired a large estate. He married, 1st, Margaret Reade and, 2nd, Mrs. Frances Tucker née Houston. He was the father of Wm. Nelson,

From Vol. XIII, No. 4 (April 1906), p. 402.

member Council and acting governor, and of Thomas Nelson, Secretary of State and last President of Council under Colonial regime. Thomas, son of Wm. Nelson, was the well-known signer of the Declaration of Independence, Governor of Virginia, and Commander of the militia of the State at the siege of Yorktown. The tomb of the emigrant remains in the churchyard at Yorktown, and bears the following arms : *Per pale argent and sable, a chevron between three fleus-de-lis counterchanged. Crest. A fleus de-lis per pale argent and sable* and the following epitaph :

Hic Jacet

Spe certa resurgendi in Christo

THOMAS NELSON, Generosus

Filius Hugonis et Sariæ Nelson

de Penrith in Comitatu Cumbriæ

Natus 20'mo die Februarii Anno Domini, 1677

Vitæ bene gestæ finem implevit

7 mo. die Octobris, 1745.   Aetatis suæ 68.—ED.]

HUGH NELSON of Penrith, Co Cumberland.   Will 1 September, 1734; proved 23 October, 1734.   To my cousin William Bleamire of Penrith, the elder, Brazier and to my nephew William Cookson of Penrith, grocer, all my lands in Penrith bequeathed to me by my Uncle John Nelson.   I also give them all debts, note books, a legacy left me by my father Hugh Nelson in trust to be sold and conveyed to my Brother Thomas Nelson of Yorktown in Virginia, America, to be distributed among such of the children of my late brother George Wilkinson of Penrith deceased, by my sister Dorothy, now wife of William Richardson of Penrith aforesaid.   Witnesses : William Wilkinson, William Barton, Dorothy Cookson.

PETER MOULSEN of London, gent.   Will 29 May 1674, proved 30 June 1674.   To be buried in Little St Bartholomew, behind the South door of the Church where I used to sit.   My funeral charges not to exceed £20.   To my Brother Foulke Moulson, who is now beyond the seas in Virginia, if he be living, £200 of English money, he to come to England for it, and give a legal discharge.   If he be living at my death, and shall not come over within two years with a full determination to live and die in England, only £100.   If he die first, £100 to my three nieces, Anne Roades, widow, Margaret Pommell, wife of ———— Pemmell, and Mary Cary, wife of Mr. Daniele Cary, and

£100 to my friend Mrs. Margarett Blague, my executrix. To nephew Peter Moulson of Warton als Waverton £100. A lease I hold of P. Dutton Esqre, in occupation of said Peter and niece Ann Roades, to said Peter Moulson. To Ann Roades, cattle, sheep, cows, etc., household stuff and furniture, and £66 13s. 4d. To Margarett Pemmell £50. To Mary Cary £66. 13s. 4d, and I forgive her and her husband Daniel a debt of £150. To Dame Moulson, mother of said Peter, £10. To Margarett Harding, wife of Mr. Edward Harding, £10. To him and his two sons Edward and William £4 apiece. To Thomas Yates, another of said Margarett's sons, £10. To Richard Mills, Treasurer of St. Bartholomew's Hospital, 40s. To Edward Arryes 40s. To Mr. John Haynes 20s. To said Mr. Richard Mills and the Governor of said Hospital for the use of poor £30. To Churchwardens of Parish of Warton in Chester where I was born £20. To poor of Little St. Bartholomews 40s. To Dr. John Micklethwaite 40s. To my friends Nicholas Raynton, Thomas Raynton, George Raynton, and Lady Rye 20s. each. To Mr. William Cawthorne £10. To Christopher Cawthorne £3. 6s. 8d. To Mrs. Margarett Yarward 20s. To Mrs. Margaret Blague £150, and all the rest and residue. Witnesses: Thos Cooke, John Haslipp, Wm. Cawthorne.

Bunce, 74.

[Edward Moalsen was granted 50 acres in York county on North branch Chisman's Creek, adjoining the lands of William Hawkins and Samuel Tucker, November 25th, 1657. Renewed to him March 18, 1662.—ED.]

WILLIAM GOUDREY of Londen, gent., now bound forth to Virginia. Will 7 July 1637; proved 24 April 1638 and 2 July 1638. Being bound for Virginia in the ship "Rebecca" of London. To my sister Susan Jepson, wife of Robert Jepson, £5. All the rest to my mother Anne Preston. Executors: My mother Anne Preston and William Palmer of London, Merchant taylor. Witnesses: William Jennison, John Dewer, servant to John Wheatley Scr., John Lewin.

Lee, 47.

WILLIAM QUICKE, Citizen and Grocer of London. Will 26

October 1614; proved 21 January 1614-5. [Printed in *Waters's Gleanings*, p. 20.]

Rudd, 1.

[William Quick, Grocer and Apothecary of London, was a member of the Virginia Company under the second charter and paid £62. 10s.—Ed.]

THOMAS STACIE of Maidstone, County Kent, gentleman. Will 31 August 1619; proved 13 September 1619. To my nephewe William Joye (sonne of my brother-in-lawe Roberte Joye) all my lands, tenements, situate and being in Virginia, to him and his heirs for ever. To the said Roberte Joye all my Goods and chattels in whose hands soever as well in England as in Virginia or elsewhere, which said Roberte Joye I make my executor. Witnesses: Tho: Ayerest, Thomas Skelton.

Parker, 88.

[Wm. Joy was living at Elizabeth City at the time of the census of February, 1623. Thomas Stacy was a member of the Virginia Company, and paid £25. "Mr. Robert Stacy" was Burgess for Martin's Brandon in the first Virginia Assembly in 1619.—Ed.]

EDWARD FLEETWOOD of London, gentleman. Will 9 November 1608; proved 19 December 1609. To my mother £50. To my brother William Sergeant £50. To my Brother Francis Fleetwood £50. To my Kyneswoman germaine Elizabeth Howse £50. To my cosen Sir Fleetwood Dormer, Knt., £50. To my lovinge friend and hoste Robert Brett, Shomaker, £20. To my sister the Lady Cordelia Fouls £100. Rest to my Brother Sir William Fleetwood of Great Missenden, County Bucks, Knight, executor. A Remembraunce of such things as I lefte with Mr. Robert Brett at my departure for Virginia, the eighth of Maye A. D. 1609. My bookes in a presse of the said Mr. Bretts, An Emptie Truncke, and An Emptie Deske, a Cipresse Cheste, A broad sworde, A rapier and dagger, A Bagge of Instruments for Sea, Gown, yellow Cloathe, A Stuffe case Anglerodd, A Waynskott chiste to be given my Kinswoman Elizabeth Howse if I die. A Celler of Glasses which my cosen Edward White left with me at his goyng to spruceland. Edward Fleetwood.

Dorset, 116.

[Edward Fleetwood, Esquire, was a member of the Virginia Company under the second charter and paid £62. 10s. He was son of Sir William Fleetwood, Recorder of London. His brother, Sir William, was long M. P., and was a member of the Virginia Company. The cousin, Sir Fleetwood Dormer, was of Lee Grange and Purton, Bucks, and died February 1st, 1638–9. He was the father of another Sir Fleetwood Dormer, of Arle Court in Gloucestershire, who emigrated to Virginia (Burk's *Extinct Baronetage*.) By deed December 26, 1649, John White, of James Parish in Virginia, merchant, sold (in consideration of 15,000 pounds of tobacco and cask) 1,000 acres near the Falls of James river, called "My Lord's Island," "Prince's Island," and other lands adjoining to Fleetwood Dormer, gent. The witnesses to this deed were Thomas Lunsford, Philip Honywood and John Meare, two of them certainly officers in the King's army, but recently come to Virginia. On March 18th of the same year Dormer sold this land to Robert Lesley of James City, rector, later the land, which included parts of the present sites of Richmond and Manchester, passed to the Steggs, and later to the Byrds. This will is especially interesting as giving an instance, of which there were no doubt many examples of the influence of a membership in the Virginia Company on the settlement of Virginia.—ED.]

NATHANIEL BUGGE, of Branderton, County Suffolk, Clerke. Will undated; proved 24 April 1656. To Mary Bugge, my wife, my goods, etc. To Joseph Bugge, my kinsman, my house in Tenderinge, to pay to George Bugge of London £60, 40s a year to Marie Bugge widow of Samuel Bugge deceased, and £40 to increase the portions of sixteen of my kinsmen and women. To Samuel Bugge, son of Samuel Bugge deceased, my house at Tender: he to pay to Joseph Bugge his brother £40 and £40 to the portions of the rest of my kindred. To Joseph Bugge, my Brother, my house at Laxfield, he to pay £140 to my kindred. My house at Titshall to be sold by my executors, and the money to be equally divided amongst these following : To Thomas Bugge, son of Thomas Bugge, deceased, now in Virginia, if he shall come over to give a discharge; Jane Puckle (wife to Richard Puckle) and Sara Bugge, children of Thomas Bugge; Marie, Sara, Joanna, and ——— Bugge, children of Samuel Bugge, deceased; Anne and Frances, daughters to John Bugge; Nathaniel and John Bugg, children of John Bugg whoe deceased at Birch in Suffolk 1653; and Nathaniell Maxwell, Samuel Maxwell, Sara Twisse (wife of Samuel Twisse), and Rebecca

149

Maxwell, children of Richard Maxwell and Sara my sister. To Nathaniell Bugge, son of John Bugge deceased, my house in Batisford, he to pay to Nathaniel Bugge, son of Thomas Bugg, £100 and to Sara Maxwell, my sister "The some of Five of good and lawful money of England." To Joseph, my Brother, all my ready money, to pay my funeral charges and to give £5, half to the Poore of Nedam Market, half to the other poor in the Town. Executor: my Brother Joseph Bugge. No witnesses.

Berkeley, 114

[Samuel Bugg died in St. Peter's Parish, New Kent county, Va. September 13, 1716. An account of his descendants is given in *William and Mary Quarterly*, Vol. X, 271-272.—ED.]

RICHARD WHEELER, citizen and Inholder of London. Will 3 February 1656-7; proved 5 January 1657-8. To my grandchild Richard Moye £150, and to his Brother John Moye, now residing in Virginia, £50; if either die, the portions to go to the survivors of them, the said John to come to England to receive his legacy, or it will not be paid. To my sister Margarett Wheeler the sum of 40s. a year for life. To my Cozin Stephen Wheeler of Chelsey £8 and to his son Arthur Wheeier 40s. To my kinsman John Langford 40s., and to his son Cecill 20s. To Katherene Freeke and her son John Freeke 20s. apiece and to her daughter 10s. To my kinsfolks Thomas, Ann, and Elizabeth Kelsey 40s. each, and to Simon Kelsey, who lives with me, £3. To these four Kelsies household stuff value of £4. To Joane Wheeler, my brother's daughter 40s., and to the now wife of Richard Smith my kinswoman 20s., and to her son Hayes my godson 40s. To my brother in law Hitchcock in Wiltshire 10s., to his three sons 5s. each, and to his daughter 10s. To George Cooke and Arthur Cooke his brother 12d. each out of my property called "the Cocke in the hole" in Moorefields, London, after the above legacies are paid, as follows: To my grandchild Richard Moye £16 per annum; to Susan Kelsey, who formerly lived with me and whom I brought up from Childhood, a house in tenure of one John Francklin. All the rest to my brother in lawe George Kelsey, with £5, and £5 per annum as long as my Lease doth run. Executor: said

George Kelsey.   Overseers: My Cosen Stephen Wheeler and
William Cunningham of Moorefields; victualler.   Wittnesses:
William House, John Slater, William Hall Scr.

Wootton, 2.

[John Moye, son in-law of Richard Wheeler, lived at Linhaven in
lower Norfolk county, Va., and died 1645. At August Court, 1645,
Robt. Davyes was ordered to sell the estate of John Moye, deceased,
for the benefit of his creditors and orphans. At the next Court the inventory was recorded. There are other records of these Moyes and of
Richard Wheeler in later records of the county.—ED.]

SUSANNA FARLEY, of St. Stephen in Coleman Streete, Lon-
don, widdow. Will 17 March 1655–6, proved 10 April 1656.
To be buried in St. Stephen Walbrooke, beside my husband
Humphrey Farley. To son William Farley, apprentice at Worcester, a lease of the house in Walbrooke London. To my son,
Thomas Farley a court cupboard, 5 chaires, etc., in possession of Henry Robinson, of Black Friars, Taylor. To his wife
Joyce, a black gown. To my daughter Susanna, the wife of
Charles Gregory of Virginia, a bed and belongings. To my
daughter Anne Mitchell, wife of Peter Mitchell, my wearing apparell. To my sister Jane Pickering, my small Hooper ring of
gould. To my sister Bridget Shippey my redd clothe petticoate,
and her husband John, my best hatt. To their daughter
Susanna, my goddaughter, my Turkey moihair petticoate. To
my cousin Mary Harvey, widow, my nightgown and a furr petticoate. All the rest (except my books to Thomas Farley my
son) to my Brother John Shippey, Citizen, Tyler, and Bricklayer
of London. Executor. Said John Shippey. Witnesses: John
Vaughton, Mary Vaughton, John Alsope Scr., Isabell Smith,
Anne Breesford.

Berkeley, 125.

DANIEL HOPKINSON. Will 21 November 1636: proved 8 April
1637. My Brother Joseph Clifton to be my executor and attorney
to pay wages and receive money, tobacco, etc. from Virginia,
and appoint seamen etc. for the ship Tristam and Jane. To wife
Sarah my share in said ship. To my father Clifton and Mother
Clifton two bever Hattes. To my mother Katharine Hopkinson a bever hatt, to my brother Abraham a bever hatt, to my

brother Joseph Clifton a bever hat, and to my brother Michael Markland my surgery chest. To my brother and sister Lole two bever hats; my ring to my sister Barbary Clifton. To Mr. Reeves the freighte of two tunne of goods homeward bound. To Mr. Hart the same and 25s to buy him a ring. Witnesses: Robert Reeves, Thomas Mant.

Goare, 52.

JOHN RINGE of London, Yoeman, being bound for Virginia in the Ship the Greate Hopewell. Will 31 August 1636: proved 19 April 1637. To my Brother Matthew Ringe, plummer, of the Strand, London, one half of my goods, etc., and to Thomas Fluellinge, livinge att the Pottashe quarter in Virginia, the other half, except as follows: To my friend Master Richard Atkins, three hundred weight of Tobacco, and my gold signet ring; to Mrs. Abigail Atkins, his wife, my Drumme cupp of silver; to Margaret Burnett, wife of Robert Burnett, my silver spoone; to Raphael Shemans, Chirurgeon of said ship, my bible and 20s. Exeeutors: Matthew Ringe my Brother, and Richard Atkins. Witnesses: Edward North, Richard Hayne, William Baulke, N. P.

Goare, 54.

[Joseph Ring, merchant of York county, was born 1646, and died February 26 in 1702-3. He lived at "Ringfield," where his tomb bearing his arms remains He left a iarge and valuable estate. For notice of the family see *William and Mary Quarterly*, VI, 148, 149.—ED.]

VIRGINIA GLEANINGS IN ENGLAND.

Communicated by Mr. LOTHROP WITHINGTON, 30 Little Russell street,
W. C., London (including "Gleanings" by Mr. H. F. WATERS,
not before printed.)

(CONTINUED)

LEWIS PHILLIPS of Town and County of Huntingdon, Gent.
Will 24 August 1668; proved 3 March 1669-70. To be buried
in parish church at Brampton under the stone where Alice the
first wife of my deceased brother John Phillips was buried in
1640. Ty my Kinsman and godson Lewis Phillips, son of my
nephew John Phillips eldest son of my eldest brother John Phillips who was slain in the service of that Holy King and Martyr
Charles the First, my lands in Brampton and to his heirs for
ever, failing to my nephew Thomas Phillips, failing him to my
cousin Albion Throckmorton, failing him to the right heirs of
me the said Lewis Phillips, whoever gets to pay every year for
ever four or five days before the feast of St. Thomas the Apostle,
being the Annual day of my birth and of my late dear wife's
decease, to the Churchwardens and overseers of the poor 30s.
To my sister Patchenson £5. To her daughter Dowse £3. To
her husband 40s., and to each child of theirs living 40s. To my
sister Margarett Phillips, the widow of my Brother John Phillips, 40s. To my niece Alice Brownsmith £5, to her husband
40s., and to every child of hers living 40s. To my sister Dann,
formerly the wife of my Brother Henry Phillips, 40s. and to her
daughter Hester Phillips £5. To my Nephew John Phillips
£5; to his now wife 40s. To Judith Phillips, widow of my
nephew Charles Phillips, £10. To my old friend Mr. John
Tryme of Wisbeech 40s., and to his wife 20s. To my cousin
Dorrington 40s. and all my billet wood that shall be left;
and the other wood to my Landlord. To my old servant Robert
Browne 20s., to his wife 10s., to his son 10s., and to his daughter
Sarah 10s. To my godson Lewis Alcocke £5. To my godson Lewis Barton 5s. To my godson Lewis Throche, being

From Vol. XIV, No. 1 (July 1906), p. 82.

fatherless and motherless, £10. To my godson Phillips Bludwick £5 and two silver spoons his mother hath of mine. To my
late servant Mr. James King £5 and my old gray nag, or other
horse I die possessed of, with Saddle, Saddle cloth, and bridle,
and I desire him to assist my executor. To my cousin John
Brownsall £5. To my sister Alice Throckmorton £20. To
my Brother Gabrieli Throckmorton in Ireland, his wife, and
children £10. To my Brother Edwyn Sandys of Wilburton,
Isle of Ely, 40s. To my aforesoid cousin Albion Throckmorton £20. To my cousin Robert Throckmorton £10. To my
cousin John Throckmorton in Virginia £5. To my cousin Mr.
Henry Reede and his wife £5, and 40s. to every child living at
my decease. To my cousin Cadwallader Powell £10, and to
his sister Mary £10. To my cousin John Jackson and his wife
£5. To Mrs Jane Rous, Kinswoman and god-daughter to my
wife, 40s. To my cousin Anne Bowes, wife of Henry Bowes
my least silver Cuppe. To my Landlord Bludwick 20s. with all
the shelves, hangings, curtains, and tables in my Study, and in
my outward Chamber, except the great Presse of Pistols, Coates
of Armes, and pewter Scoterne, Bookes, and writings, and the
Keye and Desk. The Great Armes, Rushy Chayres and 12 of
the best other chairs to my godson Lewis Phillips; the rest of
my chairs to my said landlord, as well as other furniture in
James's chamber. To my Landladie Mrs. Bludwick 20s. and
all the goods of mine she has in her custody, The use of the
Tankard shall be for the Clubbe as long as it shall continue. To
my landlord's sons Richard and William Bludwick 10s., and
every servant dwelling with them at my decease 5s. Whereas
to secure a debt I paid £80 for a copyhold (the said debt being
due to Mr. Edward Bedell Esq.) from one Fox, bought in the
names of my cousin Robert Eusam deceased and my aforesaid
Cousin Robert Throckmorton, besides other charges and a
letter of Attorney from Mr. Ravenscrofte, the said copyhold
being in Alconbury Weston, the said Mr. Edward Bedell to
pay all charges, besides the £80 to my godson Lewis Phillips,
before it is released to him. To the poor of Huntingdon £5.
To the Poor of Backden 40s. To my cousin Mr. Lynson Gun-
ton, Clerk, or Mr. Samuell Eynsworth, 40s. to preach my
funeral sermon. Rest to my godson Lewis Phillips. To Mr.

Halley, guardian and executor, £10. My godson Lewis Phillips to go to Wisbesch School to my old master Trisney, or his son who is to have the school after him, then, if capable, to Cambridge University for Master of Arts; if not capable, to be clerk to an Attorney, where my study will benefit him; if capable of neither, to be put to some Trade. Witnesses : John Nagus, Will: Jeay, Ben: Sheppeard, Samuel Backler.

Penn, 39.

[Alice, sister of the testator, married Robert Throckmorton, Esq., of Ellington, Huntingdonshire, and was the mother of John Throckmorton who settled in Virginia, see this Magazine XIII, 195.—ED]

EDWARD IRBIE, Citizer and Grocer of London. Will 27 February 1616–17; proved 24 March 1616–17. To my wife Catherine all my lands in London or elsewhere in England for life, then as follows : To my son Edward house in the Minories without Aldgate of London, now in tenure of Marthias Rutton, gent., two houses in the parish of St. Michael upon Cornhill, one in tenure of Richard Pope, merchant, and the other my dwelling house and shop. The rest of my houses, etc., to my son John. To my son Edwarde £20 a year when he is 21. To my son John £20 a year when 21. Such annuities and houses to be in satisfaction of their parts, according to the custom of the Citie. If my son Edwarde agrees, he to have the property known by the sign of the Horne in Southwark, County Surrey, now in tenure of William Stubbes, white baker, and Richard Hynde, Salter, To my daughter Anne my house in St. Saviours Southwarke held by indenture, given me by one Mr. Riche of Horneden Esqr deceased, and £250. To my daughter Winifred my house near Holborn, held by indenture from Mrs. Pype, and £200. To my daughter Catherine house in Bond Alley, East Smithfield, in tenure of Water Davies, Brewer, and one in Minories als Hounsditch, in tenure of Hugh Bell, sometime in occupation of Mrs. Evans, a poor almswoman (who paid no duty, but I gave Mr. Francke £20) and £200. To my said son John £50 toward Placing him. To Mr. Doctor Archbold 10s. To the Curate of the parish church 10s., upon condition he shall let my wife choose the Preacher for my funeral sermon. To the Clark of said Parish 6s. 8d. To the Sexton 5s. To

155

the Children of Christ's Hospital, for their paines to attend my body to the grave, £3. To the poor, in twopenny doles, £5, the Beadles to be paid out of same. To my Brother in law Rafe Yardlie and his wife £5. To my Brother in law Richard Hine and his wife £5. To my Brother Yardlie's two children 40s. apiece. To my brother Hine's Father 40s. To relieving three poore prisoners out of Ludgate and the other two Compters of London £3. To my wife and children mourning for them all. A Running Banquette to be held to entertain my friends and neighbors who follow my bodie. My Executors to pay to my Brother in lawe George Yardlie, now in Virginia, £40, so that he ratifies an indenture made by me and his Brother Rafe. Executrix : my wife Catherine. Overseers : Uncle George Sayre and Nicholas Reeve. Witnesses : Nicholas Reeve, Scr., William Manley, servant to the said Scrivener, Thomas Taylor, Edward Pierce, servant to said Scrivener.

Weldon, 134.

[Edward Irbie married Ann, sister of Sir George Yeardley, Governor of Virginia. See Brown's *Genesis*, II, 1065. Mr. Brown states positively that Sir George was a son of Ralph Yeardley, citizen and merchant-taylor of London. Mr. T. T. Upshur in his *Sir George Yeardley* (Nashville, 1896), says that the Governor was son of William Yeardley, of Yeardley, Staffordshire, but gives no details of proof. From the various references which occur in contemporary writings it is almost certain that Sir George was a son of the merchant-taylor.—ED.]

STEPHEN FOX Att Sea. Lattitude 24 degrees. 7^{br} ye 9th 1662. Aboard ye Restauracion. Loveinge Brother. These Certifie you we sett sayle from New England the 5th August, encountered two storms, lost our mastes, thrown overboard fish and mickrell and pipestaves & 3 horses drowned, one of which was betwixt your selfe and my brother Thomas soe that yow have lost all, as well as my Brother Thomas and myselfe and Peter. I knowe not whether I have saved any thing or noe till I come to some Port & I hope yow paid the £3. 3s. I charged to yow from Deale. I have sent 50 or 60 or 70 cwt of Tobacco in one Captain Thomas Carter's hands at Nuncemund in Jeames River. I had a servant run away in Virginia, that makes mee not knowe what Quantitie of Tobbacco is in Captaine Carter's hands. Lett my Brother Peter, my sister Mary, and My

Brother William have it. Captain Jno. Whitty, who uses Virginia, knowes the man, and will bring it home, which will be £70 or £80 apiece, and £70 or £80 amongst you all for mourninge. I am in hast the shipp being under saile. Your loveing Brother Stephen Fox. Administration 20 October 1663, to Brother John Fox.

Juxon, 119.

[Captain Thomas Carter, of Nancemond, was doubtless the person of the name who lived afterwards in Lancaster.—ED.]

JOHN CHEESEMAN of St. Mary Magdalen, Bermondsey, county Surrey, gent. Will— December 1663; proved 2 May 1665. My Property held of Hellen Norwood, Norcourt, or Norcote, in Southall, Eling als Zeling, old Brentford, and new Brentford, County Middlesex, all these to my wife Margarett, she to bring up my and her grandchild Anna Cheeseman till marriage or till of age 24 June 1670, after her death to said Anna, and failing her, to my brother Edmond Cheeseman, then to his two sons Edmond and Thomas, these to pay to their sisters £200 apiece. My Property at Braban in County Kent to the heirs of my deceased nephew Thomas Cheeseman, my eldest Brother's son. All my lands in County Gloucester in Virginia to my said Grandchild Anna, and failing issue, to nephews Edmond and Thomas aforesaid. The lease of my dwelling house after wife's death to my deceased nephew Thomas's son Thomas. To Elizabeth Byme, widow, 20s. a year. To my maid servant Ellinor Harvill £10, and to her sister Elizabeth Harvill 20s. a year for 6 years. To the poor of St. Mary Magdalen £10. To the Poor widowes of Redriffe £5. Rest to my wife Margaret, unless she marry again, then to Grandchild Anna. Executrix : Wife Margaret. Overseers and executors in trust : Mr. James Betts of London, Grocer, Mr. Robert Skrine, Citizen and Iremonger, Mr. John Harrison of Stepney, Mariner, and Mr. William Turner. Witnesses : Rich: Childe, Jonathan Monday, Lewis Andrews.

Hyde, 46.

[John Chisman, or Cheesman, came to Virginia in 1621, was in 1624 living in Elizabeth City and was aged 27. He was then a lieutenant in the militia. He subsequently removed to York county, where he was a commissioner (justice) in 1633, &c., was a member of the House of Burgesses 1642-3, and appointed to the council in 1652. He returned to England in or before 1661. His brother Edmund Chisman, who was living at Elizabeth City in 1624, aged 22, also settled in York county, where his will was proved Feb. 4, 1678. His son Edmund Chisman, Jr., was arrested for taking part in Bacon's Rebellion, and died in prison. See *William and Mary Quarterly*, I, 89-98. The will of Mrs. Margaret Cheesman, widow of Col. John, the testator above, was printed in *Waters' Gleanings*, I, 691. Berry's *Heraldry* gives the arms of Cheesman of Kent.—ED.]

ROBERT GOSNOLD of Earleshall, County Suffolk, Esq. Will 15 August 1615; proved 1 November 1615. To be buried at Oteley, near my wife. To Elizabeth Keene, my daughter, the wife of Thomas Keene, £8 a year. To my son Anthony Gosnold my house in Swillon called Eales. To my son Thomas Gosnold £200. To my grandson Robert Gosnold all moveable goods in the house at Otely, with the horse mill, brewing house, Dayrie goods, etc. To Anthony Gosnold, my grandchild, nowe in Virginia, £100, if he shall return within one year after my decease. To Henry Keene my grandchild £20. To Thomas Keene my grandchild £20. To my son John Gosnold £500 which he owes me for buying his office at the Court. To John Joanes my house in Otely in occupation of Francis Butterhall. To Anthony my son a piece of ground in Otely nowe in lease to Daniel Walton. To my executors, towards the performance of this will, lands I bought of my son John Gosnold, unless he pay then £400. Executors: Son Anthony and Mr. Francis Cornwallis of Earleshall. Witnesses: Robert Gosnold, John Cornwaleys, Francis Fowkes, Robert Grimble, Richard Webster.

Rudd, 101.

[Anthony Gosnold, "the younger," was a member of the Virginia Company. Two persons named Anthony Gosnold, doubtless father and son, went with the first planters to Virginia. Brown says (*Genesis*, II, 904), that the younger Anthony went to Virginia in the first expedition with his father and uncle—Bartholomew Gosnold must have been meant as the uncle. But a "Master Anthony Gosnol" was drowned in Virginia, Jan. 7, 1609. Therefore the son Anthony, to whom a bequest was made in 1615, could not have been the one who went to Virginia in 1606-7.—ED.]

[Mr. Lea included this will in his Gosnold notes printed in

the *New England Historical and Genealogical Register*, Vol. lvi, p. 405, (October, 1902), but by some extraordinary slip he missed the reference to the grandson in Virginia. I hope this will help in his search for the great Bartholomew, the patriarch of all Massachusetts pioneers.—L. W.]

CHRISTIAN WILHELME, of St. Olave's Southwarke Surrey, Gally-pot-maker. Will 8 March 1629–30; proved 9 April 1630. To the Poor of St. Olave's £5. To my wife Alkin all the leases, goods, etc., I had with her when shee and I were first married. To Christian my son one half of the lands in the Pallatinate beyond the Seas, the other half to Mary my daughter wife of Thomas Townsend. To my son Christian £200. "Whereas I am a great adventurer to Virginia and other parts beyond the seas and have a great stocke with Sir John Harvie Knight and other company touching sope-ashes and pott-ashes," etc., the profits to be divided equally between my son Christian and son-in-law Thomas Townsend. As my son Christian is now beyond the seas my son-in-law Stephen Poore to be attorney, he to have 40s. in every £100. To my wife's son John Townsend £5, and his daughter Marie £20. Residuary Legatee and Executors : Thomas and Mary Townsend. Overseers : Mr. Timothius ——, clarke, Stephen Poore. Witnesses : John Freebody Scr., Alex. Mouce, Stephen Poore, Ursula Arnold.

Scroope, 39.

WILLIAM POPPLETON. Will 9 April 1632; proved 6 July 1632. To poor of parish of St. Giles Cripplegate, London. 6s. 8d. All the rest of my lands etc. in Virginia as well as elsewhere to William Thorowgood, gent, Richard Buffington, and Will'm Emerson, whom I make executors. Witnesses : Edward Fuller, Clerke, Edw. Cater, Henry Guly.

Audley, 81.

THOMAS MALLORY, D. D. [Printed in full in this Magazine XII, 401.]

Bunce, 74.

BENONY EATON of St. Mary Magdalen, Bermondsey. Will 1 June 1675; proven 31 May 1677. My estates in Virginia and

England to be sold, and one-half to my children Ruth and James Eaton and the child my wife now goeth with when 21 or day of marriage, or survivors; if they die, one half of their portion to my relations, and the other half to my wife Deborah. The other half of my estate to my wife Deborah Eaton; and a house in Great Yarmouth given me by my father to go to my children. To my mother Dinah Eaton £5. To my Mother Deborah Buckwell 40s. To my mother Sarah Slaughter 40s. To my Brother John Eaton 40s. To my first wife's daughter Mary Wilmore 40s. Executrix : Wife Deborah Eaton. Overseers : Mr. Thomas Peacock of Buttolph Wharf, London, Wharfinger. Mr. William Laite, Senior, of the Same, Cheesemonger, Mr. James Buckwell of St. Mary Magdalen, Bermondsey, Surrey, Shipwright, and my Brother Joseph Eaton of St. Mary Magdalen, Surrey, Mariner. Witnesses : Samnel Bosworth, Bartholomew Hopkins, John Fuller, Scr.

Hale, 47.

VIRGINIA GLEANINGS IN ENGLAND.

Communicated by Mr. LOTHROP WITHINGTON, 30 Little Russell street,
W. C., London (including "Gleanings" by Mr. H. F. WATERS,
not before printed)

(CONTINUED)

ELIZABETH HOWE, of St. Giles Cripplegate, London,
Widow. Will 18 April 1677; proved 30 May 1677. To my
son in law Edward Hill, now of Virginia, £5 which Mr. Baker a
mercer in St. Lawrence Lane, London, owes me of £140 in
hands of Mr. Edward Whitechurch, an Apothecary in Walbrooke, London, shortly to be increased to £150, and also a
necklace of Pearle, two gold rings, one with a Table Diamond
and one with a Rose Diamond: to my Granddaughter Elizabeth
Hill the Table Diamond Ring, to my granddaughter Henrietta
Maria Hill my necklace of pearle, and to my granddaughter
Sara Hill my Rose Diamond Ring. To my daughter and their
Mother, Elizabeth Hill, a Gold seal ring. To my said grandchildren £150. My son in law Edward Hill to come over to
England, or his executors to receive the legacies. To my
grandchildren not specified a gold Hoop ring each. To my
daughter Elizabeth Hill all my brass, Pewter, Bedding, etc. The
rest among my grandchildren. Executors: Edward Hill and my
maid Sarah Alcorne. Witnesses: Henry Palmer, Tho. Luckett,
scr.

Hale, 49.

[Mrs. Howe had evidently been formerly the wife of Sir Edward
Williams, whose daughter Elizabeth married Edward Hill, of "Shirley,"
Charles City county, Va. See this Magazine X, 107. The portraits of
Col. Edward Hill and Elizabeth his wife are at "Shirley," as are their
funeral escutcheons, the only ones remaining in Virginia. Mrs. Howe
was an ancestress of General Robert E. Lee.]

RICHARD YOUNG, Citizen and Cooper of London. Will 7
October 1665; proved 24 November 1665. My estate to be
divided into three equal parts, one third to my wife Millicent

From Vol. XIV, No. 2 (Oct. 1906), p. 171.

Young, one third to my fower children, John, Samuel, and Elizabeth Young. To my son Samuel my dwelling house in Marke Lane, London, he paying for it out of his share. My son John to rebate £350 out of his share, it having been paid him to trade with. My son Richard to take in satisfaction of his share my plantation which I hold jointly with Dorcas Price, widow, lying att Mock Jacke Bay, neare Yorke River in Virginia. To Sarah and Samuell Young, children of said son John Young, £20 apiece when 21. To my sister Elizabeth Wagden, wife of Anthony Wagden, 40s. quarterly till £80 be paid. To each of the children of my said sister £5. To Susan Power, wife of ———— Power, daughter of Ambrose Young, my deceased brother, £10. To Mary and Anna, two other daughters of said Ambrose, they being married, £10 each. To Sarah, another daughter of said Ambrose, £10. To William Wagden, son of said Anthony, and apprentice to my son John Young, £30. To Mrs. Dorcas Price, widow, my wife's daughter, £10. To her four children, £5 each. To Mr. Robert Fox, mariner, and his wife Ann, 40s. apiece. To ———— Burnham, widdow, late wife of Thomas Burnham, 40s. To the Company of Coopers of London, £50, and £10 for a piece of Plate; to George Eyers, Upper Beadle of said Company, or to the then Upper Beadle of said Company, 20s. To the Company of Distillers, London, £10; to Joseph Brooks, or Upper Beadle of said Company, 10s. To the poor of Parish of St. Steyning, London, £5. To the poor of the parish of Ingolsby, County Lincoln, where I was borne, £5. To the poor of Hambleton, County Rutland, £5. To John Butler, the elder, Citizen and Fletcher of London, £5. To Captain Arthur Bayly of Upper Shadwell, County Middlesex, £5. If my son Samuell marry ———— Ive, daughter of George Ive of Hall Pavington als Hullington, County Wilts, gent, then I revoke £120. Overseers: John Butler and Captain Arthur Bayly. Executor: my son John. Witnesses: Hugh Rich, Jno. Poultney, servant to John Butler, senior, ser.

Hyde, 145.

[A Richard Young had several grants of land in Warwicksqueake and its successor Upper Norfolk in 1636-43. It is not known whether this person was the same as the testator. But on June 20, 1665, "Mr. Richard Young, Senior," patented 1700 acres in Gloucester county, 900

162

of which were in Ware parish, adjoining the land of Thomas Todd, and on the west side of Cow Creek at the head of Ware River, and 800 in Ware parish on North River, beginning at the mouth of Back Creek, and adjoining the 900 acres and the land of Thomas Todd, the said 1700 being within the bounds of 2400 acres granted to Edward Dawber, Nov. 25, 1642, and by the heirs of the said Dawber, sold to Mr. Richard Young and John Price, of London, by deed dated June 17, 1659, "said Price dieth and Mr. Young as survivor enjoyeth." The land granted to Dawber was in right of his wife Margaret, daughter of Sir Thomas Gates.]

ROBERT WYNNE of Jordans Parishe of Charles City County in Virginia. Gent. Will 1 July 1675; proved 15 August 1678. To be buried in Jordans Church as near as possible to my son Robert. My estate in England as follows: To my eldest son Thomas Wynne one farm in Whitestaple Parish in Kent near Canterbury, and commonly called Linebett Banckes; if he die, to my son Joshua, and if he die, to my daughter Wodlief. To my son Thomas two houses in Canterbury in St. Mildred's Parish in the same form as the said farm. To my youngest son Joshua Wynne one house and Oatmeale mill lying in Dover Lane without St. George's in Canterbury, commonly called the Lilly Pott, and two houses adjoining where a Ropemaker and one Rawlins were formerly tenants. Touching my estate in Virginia, to my son Thomas all the cattle of his own mark except one cow called Moll which is to be killed for provision; to my son Joshua my plantation called Georges withall the Tobacco houses; to my daughter Woodlief one servant of Fower yeares to serve the next shipping after my decease; to my grandchild and godson young George Woodlief one filly foal. All the rest of my Estate in Virginia and England to my wife and executrix, Mary Wynne. Overseers: Thomas Grendon, Merchant, and my son in law Captain Francis Poythres. Witnesses: Tho. Brome, John Burge.

Reeve, 89.

[The testator, Captain Robert Wynne, was, in his day, one of the most influential men in Virginia. Beginning his service a representative for Charles City county at the sessions of March, 1657-8, and March, 1659-60, he was during the entire existence of Virginia's "Long Parliament" 1661-1674, Speaker of the House of Burgesses. It would appear from his will that he married a widow Poythress. The Woodliefs are believed to be descendants of Captain John Woodlief, who came to Virginia in 1620 to take charge of the well-known Berkeley plantation, in regard to which the "Smith of Nibley Papers," now in the New York Public Library, give so much interesting information. Robert Wynne's sons were living and married early in the 18th century. Thomas Wynne, gent, of Prince George county, was living in 1707, and then aged 50. In November of the same year, he, together with Agnes his wife, made deeds, recorded in Surry, to his daughter Mary Melone, and his son Robert Wynne. Major Joshua Wynne and Mary his wife, deeded a tract of land in Surry in 1708. In that year he was a justice of Prince George county. These brothers are believed to be ancestors of the Wynnes of southern Virginia.]

DANIEL PARKE of London, Esquire. Will 11 August 1677; proved 16 September 1679. To my son Daniel Parke all my Plantations and Negroes in Virginia, and to the heirs male; failing heirs male, to the heirs at law, providing they take the name of Parke; failing his issue, to my eldest daughter and her heirs, they also to take the name of Parke. To my daughter Evelring Parke £1500 of lawful money of England when she is 18 or day of marriage. To my daughter Rebekah Parke £1500 when 18 or married. To my daughter Jane Parke £1500 when 18 or married. If any die, to the survivors of them. All money remaining in England and coming from the sale of Tobacco and profits of Shipping to be put into the Chamber of London for my said daughters' benefit. To my friends Coll. Edward Carter, Mr. Michaiah Perry, Mr. Thomas Lane, James Bray, Esq., and Mr. Robert Cobb, £5 apiece to buy them rings with. All the rest of my estate in Virginia and England to my son and sole executor, Daniel Parke. Executors in trust for England: Coll. Edward Carter, Michaiah Perry, and Thomas Lane. Executors in trust for Virginia: James Bray and Robert Cobb. Witnesses: Rowland Place, junior, Samuel Pettit, John White, servant to Hen: Faucon, scrivener. ["Sometime of London Esquire, but now in Virginia in the parts beyond the sea deceased."—Probate act book.]

King, 120.

[Daniel Parke, doubtless a son of William Parke, whose will was printed in this Magazine XIII, 192, seems to have been in Virginia when a child. He was born, according to a deposition, about 1628, and probably lived for a time in England. He was in Virginia in 1652, was a justice of York county 1653, and sheriff 1659; was a Burgess for York county in 1666 and doubtless at other sessions of that long Assembly; was sworn as member of the Council June 21, 1670, was Secretary of State 1678-79, and was at the same time Treasurer. He married, in or before 1658, Rebecca, widow of Bartholomew Knipe, of Virginia, gentleman, and daughter of George Evelyn. On Nov. 25, 1658, a renewal patent was granted to Robert Bourne and Daniel Parke, gentlemen, for 580 acres in York county on the south side of York River, adjoining the lands of Richard Ford, Thomas Smith, the Rickahock path &c., formerly granted them on Oct. 8, 1655. Daniel Parke, his wife, &c., headrights. On March 24, 1662-3, Captain Daniel Parke was granted 528 acres in James City county on the west side of Rickahock Path, and on the cart path that goes from Mr. Sorrel's to Mr. Barker's, adjoining the land of Col. Pettus, the path that goes to Chickahominy Gate, &c., sold in part to said Parke by Christopher Harris, and in part by Mr. Robert Sorrell.

On the wall of Bruton Church, Williamsburg, is a tablet with the following inscription :

"Near this Marble Lyes
ye HON'BLE DANIEL PARKE
of ye County of Essex Esq who
was one of his Ma'ties Counsellors
and some time Secretary of the
Collony of Virg'a he Died ye 6th of
March Anno 1679
His other Felicityes were crowned by
his happy Marridg with REBBECKA
the Daughter of GEORGE EVELYN
of the County of Surry Esq she dyed
the 2d of Ianuary Anno 1672 at Long
Ditton in ye County of Surry and
left behind her a most
hopefull progeny."

It should be noted that the counties named in this epitaph are English, not Virginian.

One of the "hopeful progeny" was the noted (or notorious) Col. Daniel Parke, who was born in 1669, was appointed to the Virginia Council in 1692, removed to England where he purchased an estate in Hampshire and was elected to Parliament; but was unseated for bribery, then entered the army and distinguished himself greatly at Blenheim as one of Marlborough's aids. In recognition of his gallantry the Duke sent him to England with the first news of the victory. A fac simile of the brief note has been published in one of the lives of Marlborough. Parke was then appointed Governor of the Leeward Islands, and was murdered in a riot at Antigua, Dec. 7, 1710. A copy of his will is in the

"Byrd Title Book," Virginia Historical Society. Two fine portraits of Daniel Parke the younger, by Kneller, are in Virginia, one at "Brandon," which descended through the Byrd family, and another at Washington-Lee University, the property of the Lees, which came through the Custis family. The younger Daniel Parke married —— Ludwell, and had two children, Lucy, who married Col. Wm. Byrd, of "Westover," and Frances who married Col. John Custis]

RICHARD FEILDING. Will 16 July 1666; proved 22 June 1667. [Abstract printed in this Magazine XI, 455, 456].

["Richard Feilding of Bristol, now beyond the Seas."—Probate Act.]

JOHN SMITH, Citizen and Cooke of London. Will 20 April 1672; proved 5 July 1672. To my eldest son John Smith £30 a year for 12 years from my decease and £10. To my daughter Marie Smith, wife of my said son John Smith, £20 a year for 12 years, all the bedding and furniture of the Great Room, and also of the room in which my sister Anne Poynter now lodgeth, and all my plate. To my grandchild Thomas Smith, sonne o my said son John Smith, £300 when he is 21; to my granddaughter Anne Smith, daughter of my said son John Smith, £300 when 21 or married; to my grandchild John Smith, son of my son John Smith, £300; or to the survivors of them when 21. If they all die, money as follows: to their father John Smith £225; to my granddaughter Abigail Pouchin, daughter of my son in law George Pouchin, £225; to her brother George Pouchin £225; all out of the £900 after the decease of said three grandchildren. To my granddaughter the said Abigail £150 when 21. To the said George her brother £150 when 21. To my granddaughter Bethia Smith, daughter of my son William, £225, being part of the said £900, if my said three grandchildren die. My executors to take my sister Anne Poynter to live with them, or to pay her £15 a year for life. To Allen Whore, now in Virginia, £10, in case he shall return into England within six months next after my decease. To my maid servant Elizabeth Wilshem £20. All the rest to my executors, my son William Smith and my son in law George Pouchin, to be guardians to my said grandchildren Thomas, Anne, and John Smith. Overseer: my friend James Windus.

Witnesses: James Windus, Scr., Edward Cole, Robert Stamper, his servants. [No parish in probate act].

Eure, 93.

JOSEPH HAYES, parish of Ware, County Gloucester in Virginia. Will 26 December 1677; proved 8 June 1678. To James Taylor one suite of Cloath, Hatt, and Stockens which are in the hous. To Sarah Collier my cow and yearlings and Calf. All the rest of my estate to my wife and sonne and do make them executors. To John Greene my Coate and Breeches I have now wearing. I doe empower my good Friends James Taylor and Mr. Mordecai Cooke, my Trustees, to settle all accounts with my master in Virginia, and after my debts satisfied, the remainder to be sent home to England. Witnesses: John Bartlett, John Greene.

Reeve, 64.

JOHN MARTIN, of Stepney, County Middlesex, Marriner. Will 20 October 1684; proved 23 October 1684. Whereas I am indebted to divers persons for several sums of money and more especially to Micaiah Perry of London, Merchant, and Thomas Lane of London, Merchant, in the full sum of £300, all my estate in England and my two plantations in Virginia to be administered by the said Micaiah Perry and Thomas Lane till all debts be paid; then the surplus to go to my wife Mary, who is to take care of my daughter Margaret by my former wife; when said daughter is 18 or marryed, she is to have the estate in Virginia. Witnesses: Samll Sandford, John Rogers, Joseph Burley.

Hare, 128.

[Capt. John Martin was long the master of a ship in the Virginia trade. Mariners in this trade frequently owned land and servants in Virginia. His first wife was Margaret, only daughter of Daniel Wild, of Virginia, by whom he had an only child Margaret, who, as Margaret Martin, spinster, of Cheshunt, Herts., England, sold in 1703, 470 acres in Virginia.]

ROBERT FANNING of Barking neere Tower Street, London, Tayler. Will 29 May 1672; proved 7 July 1672. To be buried in Parish Church of Barking aforesaid. My three houses at the Horse-ferry in Westminster, County Middlesex, under the yearly rent of 20s., granted from one Mr. Dauis the farther-

167

most house westward in possession of ———, to the Master and Governors of Christs Hospital for the use of the poor of said Hospital; to my loving mother Elizabeth Fanning the other two houses, and after her decease to my Kinsman John Fanning now in Virginia, and son of James Fanning deceased; if he die before my mother, I give one of the houses to John Burges, the other to the children of my sister Mary or the survivor of them. To my neice Sarah Swetnam, daughter of my brother in law ——— Swetnam, my house on the Mill-banke at Westminster whereof Mr. Gentle is now tenant. To my godson Abraham Parrat my silver chafing-dish, my silver Sugar-dish, and my silver Porringer. To John Browne that went into Virginia with Mr. Allen and John Fanning aforenamed £50. To my friend Robert Moulton, son of Robert Moulton of Dover, £10 for a ring; if he be dead, to my sister Katherine Ebourne, to whom I give £10. To my sister Elizabeth Bryan £5. To my sister Mary Etherington 1s; to her four youngest children £20 to be paid to my brother in law John Etherington. To the parish of Uxbridge, County Middlesex, £5. To the Parish of Barking £5. To my friend Anthony Standford my great Looking-glass now standing in my chamber. All the rest of my household stuff to my mother. To my servant George Saunderson all the Things of my trade. To my man Phillip Pritchard all my coarse shirts and £10. To Mr. Robert Tirrell £10. To Mrs. Fortuna Fanning, widow, £10. To Mrs. Haddocke, wife of Mr. Richard Haddocke, beltmaker, 40s. To my loving friends Mr. Thomas Allen, Mr. Thomas Carter, Mr. Edward Weldon, Mr. John Parrat, Mr. Richard Spire, Mr. George Hudson, 20s. each. Executor and residuary legatee: John Burges in St. Mary Axe. To John Daniell his cane staffe and 10s. To Sir John Kempthorne's son Rupert, my ivory George on horseback. To Arthur Miles, Scrivener, my best Hatt. Witnesses: Tho: Brottrell, Will: Houlding, Arthur myles, Scrivener.

Eure, 76.

JOHN SARGENT, of St. Mary Magdalens, Bermondsey, county Surrey, Weaver. Will 17 July 1701; proved 9 October 1701. I forgive my son-in-law William Batey £320 he owes me. To my grandson John Batey, son of said William, £150. To my grandson Benjamin Batey £150. To my grandson William Batey £150. To my granddaughter Elizabeth Batey £268. To my grandson John Voll, son of my daughter Rebecca Tyre (now wife of Jame Tyre of New Kent on the South Side of Yorke River in Virginia) by Jacob Voll, deceased, her late husband, £150. To my granddaughter Rebecca Voll £268. To my granddaughter Elizabeth Tyre £268. To be paid when boys reach 21 and girls at marriage or 18 years old. To Willian Dorrell of the parish of Creedchurch, London, weaver, £5. To Zachary Dorrell, senior, £5 and 10s. he oweth me. To my servant Dorothy Cook £5 and a bed with the furniture. To the poor of St. Mary Magdalens £5. To Margaret Marriott, widow, 20s. to buy a ring in remembraunce of me. All the rest to my friends Samuel Enderby, Senior, and John Washford, both tanners, in trust for my two daughters Elizabeth Batey, wife of the said William Batey, and Rebecca Tyre aforesaid. Assistants to my executors and overseers: John Rous and Joseph Rous, Scriveners on London Bridge. Witnesses: Samuel Enderby, junior, Sam'l Board, Matthew Fryer, all in Long Lane, Southwarke. Codicil 29 September 1701. £20 to be spent on my funeral and all money left after payment of charges to be divided amongst my two daughters. Witnesses: Edward Besst. Tho. Welham, Notary Public. Codicil 28 September 1701. Revokes Samuel Enderby and John Washford as executors and appoints John and Joseph Rouse in their place. Witnesses: Sam'l Board, Tho. Welham, Notary Public. Codicil 26 September. My granddaughter Rebecca Voll to have only £209, Elizabeth Tyre only £209. The money taken away from them to be paid to my 8 grandchildren, share and share alike. Witnesses: Tho. Stringer, Sam'l Board.

Dyer, 143.

THOMAS LEE, mariner. Will 8 October 1700; proved 2 January 1702–3. Now bound to Virginia in the ship Levitt, Captain Bagwill, commander. All wages, money, lands, goods, and estate whatsoever to my honoured father Francis Lee. Executor: My Landlord Thomas Cornelius. Witnesses: Henry Hinde, Thomas Ruddell, Jno. Cornelius. [Probate granted to the father Francis Lee of the will of Thomas Lee, deceased, H. M. S. Draggon, Thomas Cornelius, executor having renounced.]

Degg, 10.

["Mr. Francis Lee" was a justice of Northumberland county, Va., in 1673. There is in Middlesex a deed dated April 10, 1677, from Erasmus Wethers and Frances his wife, of Middlesex, to Francis Lee, of Buttolfe Lane, London, merchant, and in the same month a deed from "Francis Lee of Butolphe Lane in London, citizen, and formerly an inhabitant of Dividing Creek [Northumberland county] in Va." There is a power of attorney, dated May 18, 1684, from George Lee, of London, merchant, to his son Francis Lee, empowering him to collect money due from the estates of Daniel Wild and Captain John Martin. And also, recorded in Middlesex, Sept. 3, 1699, a power of attorney from Francis Lee, citizen and merchant, of St. Dionis Backchurch, London, to William Churchill of Virginia.]

VIRGINIA GLEANINGS IN ENGLAND.

Communicated by Mr. LOTHROP WITHINGTON, 30 Little Russell street, W. C., London (including "Gleanings" by Mr. H. F. WATERS, not before printed.)

JOHN FOXALL of Washington parish in Westmorland County. Will 10 February 1697–8; proved 31 August 1704. To Robert Volkes and Sara Elliott all my estate real and personal in the Kingdom of England in Bromingham in Warwickshire for ever. I give my Watermill to James Volkes and John Elliott junior for ever. I give my plantation at the head of Popes Creke unto Susan Cornock. To Elizabeth Volkes my plantation in Essex County. To James Volkes my horse and furniture. To Mary Elliott my Mare, and colt to Martha Elliot, and further I do appoint my loving brother Caleb Butler to be my whole and sole executor. Witnesses: Richard Cradunck, Ann Webster, Humphre Lee.

Ash, 162.

["Mr. John Foxhall" was living in Westmoreland county in 1670. There is recorded in that county, under date of 1673, a deed from the wife and attorney of John Foxhall, of Pope's Creek, Westmoreland, to her daughter Martha Foxhall. His wife and child evidently died before

From Vol. XIV, No. 3 (Jan. 1907), p. 301.

him. His will was proved in Westmoreland March 30, 1678. Though John Foxhall apparently left no descendants, the name has frequently appeared as a baptismal one in the distinguished family of Parker. "Bromingham" of the will was Birmingham, and "Volkes" is intended for the old Westmoreland family of Vaulx, now extinct in the male line. Butler and Elliott were also well known Westmoreland names.]

JOHN WARNSLEY of the parish of St. Olaves Southwark, county Surrey, outer bound in the Jefferies for Virginia. Will 10 November 1694; proved 27 May 1698. Powers of attorney to William Glassbroke in the same parish and county aforesaid, Victualler, to whom I give all I possess and execution of this my last will. Witnesses: William Moore, George Hoffield, Matt Gibbes. [John Warnsley, deceased, of the ship Jefferyes, but in H. M. S. Reserve. Probate Act Book.]

Lort, 134.

EDMUND MORECROFT of Virginia, Merchant. Will 18 December 1638; proved 20 June 1639. To my sister Anne Thurmer £20. To John Thurmer the younger one heifer of three years old. To Elizabeth Thurmer, my goddaughter, one two yere old heifer. To Joan Thurmer a Bull Calfe. My sisters Elizabeth and Marie Morecrofte, executors, to enjoy all my goods whatsoever in England or Virginia, and my Brother-in-John Thurmer and Robert Hatt and Cornelius Lloyde to administer my estate here in Virginia on their behalf and also to take accompte of Mr. William Thomson what is due to me in fowerths or seuenths. To Brother in law John Thurman £30. To Robert Houlde £10. Mr. Jeremia Blackman and William Church to sell my goods in the stores. Witnesses: In Virginia: Nicholas Stallings, Richard Handson, John Webb.

Harvey, 162.

[Edmund Morecroft patented 500 acres on Chickahominy River, in James City county, about two miles up Pynie Point Creek, May 29, 1638.]

EDWARD NOTT Esquire, Lieutenant and Governor General of the Colony of Virginia, being forthwith bound thither. Will 28 Aprill 1705; proved 28 November 1706. To my niece Ann Leighton £500. To the poor of Town of Newcastle upon

Tine £20. To the poor of Richmond in Surrey £20; and, subject to the payment of the said three legacies, I give my dear sister Sussanna Leighton my seven army debentures, left by me in the custody of my kinsman Archibald Hutcheson, of the Middle Temple, London, Esquire, amounting to £2056.2s.od. To my brother in law Colonel Nathaniel Blakiston £500, and to the said Archibald Hutcheson £50. Rest to my sister and executrix Sussanna Leighton. Witnesses: Edw: Porter, Tho: Watson, Wm Martin.

Eedes, 240.

[Edward Nott, who had been a major in the English army, came to Virginia in August, 1704, as Lieutenant Governor to the sinecure Governor, the Earl of Orkney. He is stated to have been a mild, benevolent man, and as a successor to the tempestuous Nicholson, was welcomed. For an account of his short administration see Campbell's *History of Virginia*, 375-376. He died August 26, 1706, aged 49 years. The General Assembly of Virginia erected a monument over his grave, which still remains in Bruton Church-yard, Williamsburg. See *Virginia Historical Collections*, Vol. XI, 73.]

THOMAS STARKE of London, Merchant. Will 13 January 1705-6; proved 4 March 1705-6. To my wife Sarah one full third part of my estate; if the ⅓ does not amount to £2000, then I give her all my estate in county Suffolk lying in the Hundreds, during her life, after her decease to my son John Starke for ever; if the ⅓ does amount to £2000, then said estate to go to my son immediately. Also I give her all her Jewels, pieces of gold, Gold watch, a large silver salver, a candle, Cup and Cover. To my son John Starke all my estate in Virginia, consisting of 5 plantations, £500, and the Diamond Ring I ware. To my daughter Mary Sherman £200 and all moneys she owes me. To son John after debts are paid 1-5 of my personal estate and after wife's ⅓ is deducted. To daughter Sarah Starke £300 and 1-5 of my personal estate. To my daughters Martha Starke 1-5 of my personal estate. To my daughters Francis and Elizabeth 1-5 part each of my personal estate. To my daughter Sarah a large guilt spoon and two broad gold pieces which were my aunt Dennis's. To my daughter Martha one broad gold piece which was my Aunt's. To my Daughter Francis an old Nobb Spoon. To Francis Lee and William Downer £10 each

to assist my wife and son. Executors: Wife and son. Overseers: said Francis Lee and William Downer. Witnesses: Anne
Stephens, W. Ford, Jno. Hodgkin, Jeffery Bass.

Eedes.

[John Starke, merchant, of New Kent county, patented 484 acres in
that county (now in King William and King and Queen) on October 30,
1686. The boundary line began at the said Starke's landing, running
thence to Apostequicke Swamp, and along the land, formerly Col.
Abrahall's, to the Mattapony River, &c. The land was formerly granted
to Mr. Richard Barnehouse, Sr., deceased, and upon the petition of his
son and heir Richard Barnehouse, Jr., for a survey, it was made by Col.
John Lewis and George Morris, surveyors, in the presence of a jury,
May 10, 1673, and the said 484 acres were sold by Mr. Richard Barnehouse, Jr., to Mr. John Starke, and afterwards confirmed to him upon
order of the General Court in a suit depending between said Starke and
Major William Wyatt, &c.

There is a power of attorney in York county, dated 1713, from Sarah
Starke, widow of Thomas Starke, of London, merchant, and Frances
Lee, of London, for sale of lands in King William county, formerly New
Kent, belonging to John Starke, of London, now on a voyage to the
East Indies. John Starke, of Hanover county, and Ann Wyatt were
married May 25, 1735. It is probable that all of these people were
related, as Hanover had been part of New Kent. See *William and
Mary Quarterly*, V, 256, &c.]

WILLIAM HOLMES. Will not dated; proved 16 February
1648-9. This being my last will I doe give my son William
Holmes £50. To my son Robert £30. If either of them
should dye the other to have his share. If it should please God
to take us all three out of this life, then I give my Sister Parkinson £10, my Sister Grabe £10, my Sister Coxce £10, and I give
£10 to my kinsman Mathye Holmes's two children, to pay to the
Master of the Ship if he will lett them goe to Vergenia, and 40s.
to buy them some cloathing, but if they do not go they are to
have nothing. To Mr. Nicklis 10s to make him a ring and to
his wife 10s. for a ring. To Oliuer Holmes £10 and to Richard
Grabe £10. To my Brother James Parker 40s. who dwells near
Canterbury. To the poore at Lugden 40s, to be given them
in bread, before Christmas and Neuers Day, as the rector and
overseers shall see fit. To Mrs. Janson, my good country
woman, 20s. Executors: Oliuer Holmes and Richard Grabe.

Witnesses: Richard Graybee and Elizabeth Walker. [Deceased in Parts beyond the sea.—Probate Act Book.]

Fairfax, 24.

EDWARD DIGGS. Will 28 August 1669; proved 30 June 1686. Now bound upon a Voyage for Virginia do make my wife Elizabeth Diggs my sole Executrix and doe give her £1200, and all the rest of my estate except the following legacies. To all my children, being four boys and four girls, £250 each, the profits of ⅔ of my plantation till my eldest son is 24. Guardians and executors, in case of my wife's death, Sir William Houell, Coll William Willis, Mr. John Jefferies, and my cozen Dudley Diggs. Witnesses: Jo: Diggs, Will Diggs. The 16th of June, 1675. This will proved in Court by the oath of William Diggs and a probate granted the Executrix and ordered to be recorded. This is a true copy of the abovesaid will, from the Records in the Secretary's office. Test Edw. Harrison. per E: Chilton official Clerk. 15 May 1685. The above writing is a true copy of the will of Edward Diggs Esqr. taken of from the Records, as appeares by the Certiff of the Clerke of the Office, William Cole, John Page.

Lloyd, 73.

[Edward Digges, the testator, was son of Sir Dudley Digges, of Chilham, Kent, England, Master of the Rolls, and was Governor of Virginia. For an account of his descendants in Virginia, see *William and Mary Quarterly*, Vol. I. The "cozen" Dudley Digges, one of the executors, was doubtless his nephew, son of his eldest brother, Thomas Digges, of Chilham.]

THOMAS PUTNAM, aboard the Increase, bound for Virginia. Will 29 December 1647; proved 20 May 1659. I make my wife Dorothy my executrix. To my son Thomas Putnam £20 out of £43.9s due to me by my father William Putnam's will, dwellingham shire [sic] in Chessam parish, remainder of said money to Dorothy my wife, she to pay Sara Miller at Holburne Barre in middle Rowe £5 and To John Salter £4.16s due to me from Henry Bolton of Saint Clements Church, unto Mr. Coxyn, Chirurgeon aboard the Ship, 20s. He to take care of my wife and child. Witnesses: Arthur Bromwell, John Bigge. [Letters of administration granted to John Smyth, husband of Dorothy

Smyth alias Putnam, late wife of said testator. Thomas Putnam the elder to administer during the absence of said Dorothy and Thomas Putnam the son of said deceased (now both in Virginia beyond sea).—Probate Act Book.]

Ruthen, 197

PETER CHAMBRELAN, thelder, of London, Chirurgeon. Will 29 November 1631; proved 16 December 1631. To the poore of the French Church in London £5. To the poore of All Hallows Stayning in marke Lane, London, 40s. To the poor of Downe in County Kent 40s. To Mr. Nett, vicar of said parish, 20s. To the poor of Dionis Backchurch in London where I now live 40s. To Esther Cargill, eldest daughter of my daughter Esther, £200. To the rest of my daughter Esther's children, that is to say, Jane, William, and Margaret, £200 each, said children in Scotland. To Thomas Cargill, eldest son of my said daughter, all my property in Downe, Crodon, Keston, and ffarneborowe, County Kent., my bookes, and my watch. To Anne Cargill, my grandchild, my New English Bible and the Diamond ring I had from Queen Anne To my Brother Simon Chambrelan of county Kent my furred coats. To Peter Smith my godson, now in France, £60. To his brother Robert Smith, now in Virginia, £40. They to claim said legacies within 8 years after my decease. To my cozen Abraham Chambrelan the younger my house clocke. To my three servants Thomas Price, George Crawley, and Francis August, my shop books, and all moneys owing me therein, and all stuff in my shop except Confectio, Alcarnus, Ambergrice, muske, Civett, and Pearle. To my two woman servants £3 each. To my Grandchild Anne all the rest and residue of my estate whatsoever. Executors: my friends Mr. Richard Legge, Merchant in Tower streete, London, and Mr Abraham Chambrelan, Merchant in Breadstreete, London. Overseer, Mr. Abraham Chambrelan thelder, Merchant. Witnesses: John Davies, Scr. Edward Ridley, Cittizen and leather seller of London, Fran: Harrison, servant to the said Scr.

St. John, 130.

[See a sketch of his life in the "Dictionary of National Biography."]

ROBERT MIDDLETON. Will 3 April 1627; proved 18 July

1627. To my brother William Middleton of Lamton, in York-shire, all goodes, to wit one Trunck where in is certain goodes and money, one suit, one Cloake, a girdle, a pair of gloves, A Pettrass ring, a venis looking glasse of Ebonie, also £6 in the hands of Edward Lane, Pulley maker, dwelling in Shadwell, £7 due to me from Alexander Normans of Saint Katherines, Cooper, also all due to me in the plantacion, whereof is Mas-ter, Peter Andrewes. My friend Thomas Baab and Richard Lowther to be overseers and receive the above for the benefit of my brother, William Niddleton. [Deceased in Virginia —Pro-bate Act.]

Skynner 78.

GEORGE RICHARDS of London, Weaver. Will 14 June 1690; proved 15 June 1694. To be buried by my deare wife in Ald-gate Church. All debts in England or Virginia to be paid. I doe order that whereas about 18 years since I did enter several tobbs in the custom house, London, and in the farmers time which I judge was to the value of about £80 or £90 which the Waiters of severall Virginia Shipps did order me to post short of what I ought and should have done, and likewise about 12 years since when the King had it in his hands to the value of about £50 or £60 and about 10 years since to the value of 8, said sums to be returned to the rightful owners. To my bro-ther Edward Richards, eldest son, who is now at Oxford, £20 per annum towards his bringing up for four years and £100. To his eldest daughter and her sister Elizabeth, who is now an apprentice near the New Exchange, £100 each when 21. To his other 3 children £50 each. To my brother in law Mr. John Nevoyes two eldest sons, John and Edward, £50 apiece. To my neice Barbara Wittall, my sister Barbara Phillpott's daugh-ter, £50, and to her children living at the age of 16 £20 each To the poor of St. Buttolphs, Aldgate, £50. to buy land and houses, the profits to be given to the poor. To Christ Hospita £200. To the poor of Weavers Hall, London, £50. To the poor of Holy Roods in Southampton, where I was born, £5 To the poor of Lambeth £5. To my wife's father, and her mothe and sister, and her husband, and to Captain Phillip Foster who was my master, £10 each. To William Lydyerd, my porter, £5

To my daughter Sarah Richards £1800 when married.   All the
rest to my son Phillipp.   I judge I am at this time worth above
£8000.   Executor: my son Phillip.   Witnesses: William Ly-
deard, John Warr, Thomas Nevey.

Box, 138.

[The species of fraud in the tobacco trade described by this penitent
sinner was doubtless common in London.]

HENRY GERRARD.   Will 20 July 1689; proved 11 March
1692-3.   To my daughter Elizabeth Bayley 20s. to buy her a
ring.   To William and Elizabeth Bayley, my grandchildren, each
of them a mare filly the first that falls and shall live to be wean-
able with their increase.   To Thomas Peters, the son of John
Peters, deceased, A Cow and a Calf to be putt into the hands of
Mr. Hennery Harman provided he keeps the boy.   To George
Peters a heifer called Crooks Heifer.   To Margaret Osborne the
250 lbs of Tobacco she was indebted to me for a Gowne and desire she may be paid 600 lbs of Tobacco which is her full wages.
To Ferninando and Nicholas Gerrard, my two sons, all the rest
of my estate, also all the money or goods which may be
recovered in England.   To Jacob Bayley, my Son in law, two
Barroes four years old each.   Overseers: Capt. Nicholas Wyatt
and John Tirrey.   Witnesses: Mathew Adams: Will Jennings.
After the signing and sealing of the in mentioned will I the said
Henry Gerrard doe make this my last bequest (vizt) Item I give
to my Godson Francis Wray a Cow Calf.   Test the mark of
William Jennings.   Charles City county, in Virginia.   October
3 Anno 1689.   Oath of William Jennings.

Coker, 51.

[Captain Nichols Wyatt was a well known citizen of Charles City
county, and John Tirrey, of Surry.]

MICHAELL MUSGRAVE of the parish of Pienketanck in the
River of Rappehannock in the County of Midlesex, Virginia.
Will 21 December 1697; proved 26 January 1697-8.
[Printed in full in this Magazine, XIV, 93.]

Lort, 15.

VIRGINIA GLEANINGS IN ENGLAND.

Communicated by Mr. LOTHROP WITHINGTON, 30 Little Russell street,
W. C., London (including "Gleanings" by Mr. H. F. WATERS,
not before printed.)

(CONTINUED)

FRANCIS HANNSWORTH. Will 11 April 1656; proved 28
February 1656–7. To John Hamond one hogshead of Tobacco.
To Thomas Wilkinson of Rosewell in Virginia one Case of
Waters. To Elizabeth Ramsey, daughter vnto Thomas Ram-
sey of Virginia 15s. for a ring. To Francis Wheeler and his
wife 20s. for gloves. To Master John White and his wife 20s.
The rest of my estate vnto three of my neerest of Kindred in

From Vol. XIV, No. 4 (April 1907), p. 419.

Fatel Thrope in County Lincoln or thereabouts; if they do not come or appear, then I give the rest of my estate to John Creed of Virginia, Planter. To Michaell Tillard a bedd and rugg and all other things I have in a bag in the Shipp Phillipp. Witnesses : Michael Tyllyard, Edw. Symons. Debts Master Hannsworth oweth. To Robert Williams of Virginia £2 12s. To an old Man for a Coate to be paid for it be not gott againe and my passage. Nuncupalive Codicil, same date, of francis Hannsworth late of St. Sepulchres, London, deceased. He having made no executor, desired Master John White to take up the 14 hogsheads of Tobacco in the ship Phillip and with the proceeds pay his legacies. Witnesses : Edward Symons, Mary Tilliard.

Ruthen, 59.

[The Rosewell, where Thos. Wilkinson lived, was no doubt the place afterwards well known as a seat of the Page family. Thomas Wilkinson had several grants of land (1) 500 acres on the South side of Potomac at the mouth of Matchotack river, August 18, 1650. Among the headrights were "4 Indians Trans.[ported] by Mr. Gerraid;" (2) 320 acres on both sides of a creek flowing into Rappahannock river, about 2¼ miles above the land of Richard Coleman, 1653; (3) 6,000 acres above the head of Potomac Creek, adjoining the land of Mr. Merewether, now in the tenure of Nicholas Russell, January 10, 1658, renewed to said Wilkinson March 18, 1662.

Thomas Ramsey (sometimes spelt Ramshawe in the old records), was a member of the House of Burgesses for Warwick river at the session of February, 1631–2 ; for Gloucester, March, 1654–5, March, 1655–6, December, 1656, and March, 1657–8. Captain Edward Ramsey, possibly his son, was Burgess for James City, 1663 and 1666, and possibly other years of that long Assembly. On March 18, 1662, Thomas Ramsey had a patent for 1,000 acres in Gloucester county, on the North-east side of Mattapony river, adjoining the lands of Ralph Green, Thos. Bell and Captain Abrell, patented by Col. John West, May 27, 1654, and assigned to Ramsey by "Captain West, son of Colonel West, Esqr."]

HUMPHREY HAWKER, liveinge in the parishe of Bowe in Cheapside in the Warde of Cordwayner. Will undated; proved 16 November 1647. To my daughter Dorothie in Virginia if shee be liveinge five poundes. To her daughter that was borne in England £20. To the next to eldest £5. To my maid nowe liveinge with me called Abigall £5. For my funerall £3.

Executors : Mr. John Oresbie and Mr. Henrie Hodges. To
Elizabeth Muse 40s. Witnesses : Richard Harris, Henrie
Hodges, Roberte Woodford.

Fines, 234.

GEORGE MENEFIE of Buckland in Virginia, Esquire. Will
31 December 1645; proved 25 February 1646–7. To be buried
at discretion of my wife in parish Church of Weston [Westover].
All debts in Virginia to be satisfied. All Tobacco or money
debts in England to be transferred to my books, "The shipp
Desire now lyeinge before Buckland may with all possible expedition be dispatched way for England, and to bee part loaded
with what Tobacco is ready here above, and receive the remainder of her ladeinge belowe, vizt, tooe hundred Hoggsheads on
the partable account" 100 hoggshead my own account and the
rest by discretion of a note to be found in a small book of
tobacco shipped and to be shipped. My 100 hogsheads and
also my part in the ship Desire and cargo, and my 1-16 part of
the William and George be consigned to Captain Peter Andrews,
he to give an exact account to my heirs and executors. To my
daughter Elizabeth Menefie all my land at Weston, att James
Citty, and at Yorke River. To my brother John Bishopp, the
money he owes me, and one-third part of my crop of Tobacco
made the last summer at my plantation of Buckland. My sheep
at Buckland to be a joint stock between my daughter Elizabeth,
and my son-in-law Henry Perry. To Mr. Jo. James £20 and
1000 lbs of Tobacco, he to preach a sermon at my funeral. To
Mr. Jo. Converse, Chirurgeon, 2000 lbs of Tobacco. To my
brother Roger Booker £50, he to assist Humphrey Lister in
collecting my debts. To Jo. White, Merchant, £50, provided
he continue one year longer in Virginia and collect my debts as
formerly. Tobacco not able to go in the Desire to be sent in
the Flower of London Goods consigned in the William and
George to be returned in Kind. Everything to my wife and
daughter. Executrix and guardian to my daughter; my wife
Mary. Tobacco due to me from Captaine Tho. Varvell shall be
satisfied by Mr. Walter Aston. Satisfaction to be made to Mr.
Humfrey Adlington for his care in my business concerning
Chamberlaine, by Captaine Peter Andrews. Overseers : friends

Captain Peter Andrews, Richard Bennett, Esq. Witnesses :
Howell Prise, Humfrey Lister.

Fines, 31.

[George Menifie came to Virginia in 1625, was Burgess for James City
County, 1629, and member of the Council, 1635–1646. He was one of
the wealthiest men of his day in the Colony, and was probably the
leading merchant. In 1634 he lived at "Littleton," or "Littletown,"
not far below Jamestown. His large garden here "contained fruits of
Holland and Roses of Provence." His orchard was planted with
apple, pear and cherry trees, and he cultivated here the first peach
trees introduced into America. Around the house grew, in the fashion
of the times, rosemary, thyme, and marjoram. He took a prominent
part in the deposition of Governor Harvey. Later he removed to
"Buckland," an estate of 8,000 acres in Charles City County. His only
child, Elizabeth, married Captain Henry Perry of Charles City County,
member of the Council. They left two daughters and co-heiresses:
Elizabeth, who married John Coggs, gent., of Rainslip, Middlesex, Esq.,
and Mary, who married Thomas Mercer, stationer, of London.

The site of old Westover Church, near the house at "Westover," still
contains a number of tombs formerly in or near the old building. The
name John James supplies information as to one of the early ministers of
the parish. John Bishop was an early resident of Charles City County,
as was Walter Aston. Howell Price was once clerk of the county.]

ARTHUR BULKELY of the City of London, merchant, bound
for the Plantation of Virginia in the parts of America beyond
the seas, and shipt in the good ship the "Blessing" of London,
whereof is Master, Mr. William Simmory. Will 4 August
1638; proved 3 November 1645. All my estate whatsoever to
my brother Thomas Bulkely of City of London, Merchant,
executor of this will. Witnesses : Hen. Kighte, Ser. to John
sen'r Warner, Scrivener, Samuel Leadbetter. [Arthur Bulkely,
Citizen of London, Merchant, deceased in London.—Probate
Act Book.]

Rivers, 145.

ELIZABETH VINCENT of St. Andrews Holborn, in the Suburbs
of London, Widow. Will 28 August, 1660; proved 14 November 1660. "Whereas my late husband William Vincent did
give to vnto mee or otherwise appointe for mee the Sume of One
hundred Poundes Sterlinge out of such goodes and Estate as
hee had in Virginia which is yett remaining in the handes of

Thomas Edmunds, Planter there, or of William Daynes who I Authorized to Receive the same for mee" I give the said sum and all other goods and all profits from the estate of my said late husband or otherwise to my good friend Mr. Benjamin Wyche, appothecary, dwelling in Holborne, London. He to give £10 to my kinswoman Elizabeth Anderton, £10 to my Kinswoman Love Meredith liveinge in Virginia, and 40s. to her brother Henry Meredith, as legacies from mee. Residuary Legatee and Executor : said Benjamin Wyche. Witnesses : Francis Orton, Elizabeth Orton, Jo. Houghton, Nory Publique.

Nabbs, 301.

[William Vincent patented 640 acres in Northumberland County, on the North side of Dividing Creek and on the Bay, adjoining the land of James Willis and John Waddy, April 3, 1651.]

WILLIAM WOOTTON. Will 13 October 1653; proved 12 May 1656. "Virginie this 14th of March 1653-4. Most deare and loveinge sister my kind love to you and my cosen Fatwell, hopeinge of your welfare and desireing it as my own. These are to certifie you that wee came well to our porte, God bee praised, not without trouble and a great deal of danger, Sister I have sent to Mr. Gough Thirty hoagsheads of Tobacco to dispose of them for mee, which I hope will be to your advantage, but if hee bee not payd in that monie which hee ought mee, hee shall not dispose of this tobacco, but if hee has payd in the money then lett it remaine for him to dispose deare Sister. I desire that if God shall deale otherwise with mee then the continuance of life. For the produce of the Tobacco which I have now sent home I desire that my Aunt Wintower may have five pounds layd out in ringe for her and Thirty pound I give to your selfe" £30 to my Sister Barber, £10 to my Sister Gaward, £10 to her husband, £10 to my Brother Arthur, the rest between my sister Phillipp and sister Sharpham; if they get more than £10 each, give £10 to Mr. Pale and £5 for the poor to whom Mr. Pale shall think fit "Here is an enclosure for Captain Grig if Mr. Gough be dead. Respects to Mr. and Mrs. Paule, tell their maid I cannot hear of her brother from want of his Masters name, but I will make sale of the token and give her the proceeds, your loving Brother William Wotton.

Direct your letter to Mr. ffriers house Liveinge in Chichen homine river neare James Cittie in Virginia. Will of William Wootton written with my own hand 13 October 1653, bound for Virginie." A bond in hands of Mrs. Phillipp Winter of £80 due from Giles Gough. To my sister Mary Meredith £30 of same. To my sister Susanna Barber £50 of said bond. If I return from Virginia this will to be void. Witnesses : John Steevans, Richard Jenings.

Berkeley, 163.

[The name of William Wootton does not appear in the land grants; but Richard Wootton, patented, in partnership with John Lewis, 100 acres in Deep Creek, Warwick county, part of 1,000 acres patented by James Merryman, and assigned by Mr. Merryman, April 30, 1647; and by himself, 300 acres in Northumberland at the head of Upper River, April 1, 1651. Thomas Wotton, gentleman, was one of the first settlers in Virginia in 1607.]

PHILIP NOYE of Burian, now of St. Just, in Cornwall. Will 4 March 1649–50; proved 8 June 1650. To the poor of parish of Fellacke where I was born 20s. To the poor of Burian 20s. To the poor of St. Just where I now live 20s. "Whereas my brother Joseph Noye did adventure with mee when I went for Virginia the sum of Fifty Foure pounds whereof hee hath as yett had noe returne" my will is that the said sum be paid unto him out of my manor of Trena and 2s. more as a legacy. To my brother in law John Ellis of Madren 20s. To my brother in law John Wallis 20s. To my sister Barbara Gayre, widow £10. To my sister Anne the wife of John Ellys £10. To my sister Sarah Wallish wife of John Wallish £10. To Phillipp Gayre daughter of my sister Barbara Gayre £100, if she die during minority or before marriage, to remain to her sister Sarah. To the other two children of my sister Barbara Gaire £10 each. To Anne Ellis daughter of John Ellis £50. To Anne and Phillipp Wallis daughters of my brother in law John Wallish £50 each. To Mr. John Leay 40s. To Martine Harvey, son of Martine Harvey, 50s. My one half of the manor of Treva, house in Sellan bean in Sancrett parish in tenure of John Chirgwine, and a house in Burian Church Town in tenure of one John Marten, and one annuity of 16s. 8d. out of the lands and Barton of Bortemall, all which I give to my mother Sarah

Noyes and her heirs for ever for the payment of my debts and legacies. To the servants at my death in my brother Wallishes house 5s. apiece. Executrix: Mother Sarah Noyes. My brothers in law, John Wallish and John Ellys to assist her. Witnesses: Mich. Fleminge, Johan Wallish, Barbara Geare.

Pembroke, 98

[This a cousin german of the famous attorney general William Noye, and is mentioned in the 1620 Visitation, but this adds much to the account given by Colonel Vivian.—L. W.]

WILLIAM MERCER, Citizen and Haberdasher of London. Will 24 March 1653–4; proved 28 March 1654. To be buried in St. Michall in the Querne where I now live. To my Brother Burrandine Mercer, now living in Virginia, £50, and to his two daughters £25 each, or the survivor of them to have the whole. To my brother in law James Fleetwood, Doctor in Divinity, £20; to my sister Martha his wife £50. To my mother Mistress Mary Mercer £10. To Dr. Fleetwood and his wife Martha £10 each for mourning. To my two Neeces and goddaughters Anne and Elizabeth Fleetwood £50 apiece. To my nephews Maximilian Fleetwood, Arthur Fleetwood, and John Fleetwood £25 each. To my neeces Bridgett Fleetwood and ——— Fleetwood, now living at Giles Chalfont, £25 each. To my neece Mary Perry £25. To my Brother in law William Perry £10. To Margarett my maid servant £10. To Six Batchelors, my good friends, to carry my corpse to church, 20s. each. To Master Poole, minister of Said St. Michaells, £5, and £5 for a sermon at my funeral. To the parish clerke 20s. To the sexton 10s. To the Porters and Water bearers that shall plye neere the Conduite 2s. each. My executor to pay £300 advanced to Virginia, but not to be enforced to pay any other debts or legacies till he recovers my debts at home and abroad. Executor and residuary legatee: my brother Walter Mercer. Witnesses: Moses Atkinson, Tho. Thorne, Notii Public.

Alchin, 22.

WILLIAM STOCKEMAN of Barford, County Wilts, Esquire. Will 21 July 1655; proved 6 October 1658. All my freehold lands in Barford I give to my brother Joseph Stockeman for life, after his decease to his son William Stockeman and the heirs male of his body; in default, to the second son of the said Joseph; in default to the 3rd, 4th, 5th and so on in their respective ages and seniority, also my lordship of Hampworth in the same manner; also my land called Whithorne Hill which I hold by lease in the same manner while the lease shall run, also my lands in White parish, my farm of White house parish of Langford in the same manner, as above lands of Barford, My interest in the farm of Cuttenham which I hold for two lives I give absolutely to my said Brother Joseph. To my cousin Gerret Edington now in Virginia, if he be living at the time of my death, £200. To my cousen Henry Greene and his sister Mary Greene £100 apiece. Executor : my brother Joseph.

Ruthen, 484.

[Garret Edington. This is undoubtedly the same person as "Jerrard Errington," who on September 6, 1654 (renewed to him June 6, 1657), patented 500 acres in the freshes of Rappahannock above Nansemond town, opposite the land of John Weyre.]

[Mr. Withington was not able to read the proofs of this instalment.]

VIRGINIA GLEANINGS IN ENGLAND.

Communicated by Mr. LOTHROP WITHINGTON. 30 Little Russell street,
W. C., London (including "Gleanings" by Mr. H. F. WATERS,
not before printed)

(CONTINUED)

JOHN WESTHROPE of London, Merchant.   Will 24 September-
ber 1655; proved 12 June 1658.   To the Church of Martimber
in Virginia 2000 lbs of **Merchantable Tobacco and Caske** toward
the Repairing or the building up of a new Church, provided
always the said Church be built upon the same ground or place
the said Church now stand on; also 1000 lbs of Tobacco and
Caske to contain the same to bye a Communion Cupp, also my
Great bible, and a book called Bishop Andrews' sermons, both
in my house in Virginia.   To my father Master John Sadler 4
Cowes I have in Virginia.   To Thomas Cooper, sonne of Walter
Cooper in the Mayne neer James Towne in Virginia, 1 cow I
have in Virginia.   To Joshua Clarke my servant 6 years (that
is to say) the 6 last years of the 20 years he is bound to me.
To my other servant Thomas Smith 1 year of his tyme.   All
my goods in England, and on the ship called the seaven sisters
bound for Virginia, Captain Abraham Reade, and all the rest of
my estate in Virginia, amongst my sisters, Anne Beckford, wife
of Edmond Beckford, Frances Henshawe, wife of Edward Henshawe, gent, Bridgett Bickerton, wife of Richard Bickerton, and
Dorothy Gibson, wife of Marke Gibson, and Judith Thomas,

From Vol. XV, No. 1 (July 1907), p. 56.

wife of William Thomas. Executors: Edward Henshawe, gent.,
and Edmond Beckford, gent., my loving Brothers. Witnesses:
Tho: Henshawe, Joseph Crake, Robert Overinge.

Berkeley, 233.

[In the Land Office appears the following grants: (1) "Mr. John
Westropp" 1,500 acres lying about the mill at Wards Creek, Charles
City County Aug. 30, 1650. (2) "Major John Westhrope," 600 acres
on the south side of James River in Charles City County, on the branches
of Birchen Swamp, being part of the old town adjoining the lands of
William Short and Mr. Sparrow, Nov. 24, 1653. At the date of these
patents the present Prince George County was included in Charles City.
These grants were near Brandon.

Brandon Parish still has the cup purchased in accordance with the
provisions of the will, and the tomb of Westhrope's wife, with the date
obliterated by time, remains in the parish. The "father," John Sadler,
who is referred to was no doubt John Sadler of London, a part owner
Martin's Brandon, whose will is printed in *Waters* I, 621. No doubt
John Westhrope married a daughter of John Sadler, but she died before
her father without issue, and is therefore not mentioned in this will.

Walter Cooper patented on April 30, 1639, 350 acres in James City
County at and near Powhatan swamp bridge, lying north by east on
said swamp, and southerly on the neck of land, all places near Jamestown.]

THOMAS MATTHEW, formerly of Cherry point, in the parish
of Bowtracy in the County of Northumberland in Virginia, Merchant. Will 6 May 1703: proved 28 February 1706-7. "My
body I desire may be buried if I shall dye in or about London
as neare to my dearly beloved Son William as it can be laid in
the Church of St. Dunstan in the East." If I dye possest of any
estate in England after my debts be paid, to be divided amongst
my three children, John, Thomas and Anna. Lands in Stafford
County, Virginia, to my said three children, John, Thomas and
Anne Matthew. Estate in County of Northumberland, Cherry
point, in Virginia, as follows: One-half to my son John,
other half to Thomas and Anne. My Brother in law Captaine
John Cralle and my old and faithfull servants Mr. James Gunn
and Mary his wife have manifested great faithfulness and industry to me, both in Virginia and since I cam thence, so they to
live peaceably in the houses they now inhabit. Executors: my
sons John and Thomas. Witnesses: Tho. Hughes, Mary Boyes,
Nicholas Boyes, Mary Middleton. Poley, 40.

[Thomas Mathew of Northumberland County, Va., a member of the House of Burgesses at the session of June, 1676, and the author of "T. M." 's account of Bacon's Rebellion. There is no evidence that he was in any way related to the family of governor Samuel Mathews. For note on Thomas Mathews see this Magazine, I, 201, 202.]

HENRY BASKERVILLE, citizen and Fishmonger of London. Will 26 February 1675-6; proved 19 May 1676. To my Brother Thomas Baskerville and wife £12 for mourning. To my Brother Thomas Hund and wife £12 for mourning. To my Brother Thomas Cowper and wife £12 for mourning. To my sister Gregg the sum of £6. To my Brother Randall Baskerville £6 for mourning and £5 per annum for life. To my goddaughter Katherin Baskerville £10 for a peece of plate. To Mr. Thomas Edge and Mr. William Jenkyns, ministers, £5 apiece. To my Brother John Baskerville in Virginia £10. To Joane Eaton and Mary Morley, maidservant to my Brother Lawrence Baskerville, £3 apiece. To Mr. Henry Aston and wife and to my cosen Swetenham 20s. apiece to buy them Rings. To my friends Mr. Hugh Noden, Mr. Thomas Yates, Doctor William Vaughan, Mr. Charles and Mr. John Hearle, Mr. Richard Knewstub, Mr. Richard Malcher, Mr. Thomas Jackson of Bromfield and Mr. Thomas Cowles, being all my countrymen, 10s. each for a Ring. All the rest to my executor and brother Lawrence Baskerville. Witnesses: Richard Malcher, Tho: Cowles.

Bence, 47.

[Lord Clarendon, in his memoirs, speaks of the usually large families of the Cheshire gentry, and of the small portions given to younger sons, for that reason many of them became merchants and tradesmen. We have here an instance of this sort. In the last edition of Omerod's *History of Cheshire* III, 717 &c., is a genealogy of "Baskervyle, of Old Withington. From Booth's pedigrees and the visitations, with additions [and corrections from the Plea and Recognizance Rolls, charters, wills and] from the parochial registers, and an original pedigree communicated by John Glegg Esq.". The pedigree begins with John de Baskervyle, Knight, grantee of a moiety of Old Withington in 1266, and continues through eleven intervening generations to Thomas Baskervyle of Oulde Withington, gent, born 1566 and baptized at Goosetrey, died in 1625, and burried at Goosetry; married secondly, Dorothy, daughter of Ralph Adderly of Blackhaugh in Coton, Stafforshire, gent. She died Jan. 2, 1602, and was burried at Goosetry.

They had a son John Baskervyle of Ould Withington, Esq., baptized at Goosetry, Feb. 25, 1599, died Feb. 16, 1661 and was buried at Goose·try. He married Magdalen, daughter of George Hope, of Queen's Hope, County Flint, and of Dodleston, County Chester. She died April 19, 1669.

John and Magdalen Baskervyle had issue: I, George, son and heir apparent, *d. s. p.* 1649, under age, buried April 30, at Goosetry; II. Thomas, of Old Withington and Blackden, born 1632, baptized at Goosetry, but called 18 years of age in September 1663 in the visitation; buried at Goosetry December 11, 1676 (tombstone, but not in register), married first Elizabeth, daughter and heiress of John Lightborn of Salford (and had one daughter Katherine, who *d. s. p.*); married secondly Margaret daughter of Hugh Hassall of Lightsecke, County Salop, she was buried at Goosetry July 20, 1671; II, Lawrence, married Katherine, niece of Ralph Godwyn, and had a son Randle in 1669, who was living in 1682; IV, Randle, born 1635, baptized at Goosetry, living in 1669; V, John, born 1635, baptized at Goosetry, living in 1669, (Thus, was John Baskervyle or Baskerville of Virginia); VI, Henry, baptized at Goosetry November 10, 1646, died 1676, and burried there. (The testator above); VII, Rebecca; Elizabeth; IX Katherine wife of Thomas Hand of Chester and Broughton, gent; X, Mary; XI, Mau'-din; XII, Elizabeth, married Thomas Cooper.

Omerod (*Cheshire* III, 133) states that in the Chapel of Goosetry is a flat stone with the inscription "Thomas Baskervyle, of Withington, Esq., buried 11, December 1676. Mary, widow of John Baskervyle, Esq., his son, and daughter of Edmond Jodrell, Esq., buried February 17, 1758, age 90."

And also on an old wooden tablet suspended in the vestry:

"John Baskervyle of Old Withington in the County Palatyne of Chester, who took to wife Magdalene, daughter of George Hope of Queen's Hope, in the county Flint, Esq. He had six sons, viz: George, who died in his minority, Thomas, Lawrence, Randle, John and Henry, and six daughters, viz: Rebecca, Elizabeth, Magdalene, deceased; Katherine, Mary, and Elizabeth surviving. He died ye sixteenth day of February Anno Domini M D C L XII, and about the sixty third year of his age."

The arms of the family are: Baskervyle: *Argent, three hurts,* quartering *argent, a chevron gules between three squirrels segant of the second, impaling* Hope (with nine quarterings) *argent, a chevron engrailed sable, between three storks sable, legged gules.*

On another tablet in Goosetry chapel is the following inscription:

"Here lyeth the body of Magdalen, daughter of George Hope of Dodleston, in the county palatyne of Chester, esq., the relict of John Baskervyle of Old Withington in the said county palatvne of Chester, esq., by whom she had yssue several sonnes and daughters; she died the ixth day of April, in the year 1670, aged 66 years."

It will be observed that Henry Baskerville names in his will his brothers Thomas, Randall, John and Lawrence, and his brother-in-law Thomas Hund (Hand in the pedigree) and Thomas Cowper, thus completing beyond doubt the identification.

John Baskervyle, or Baskerville, named in the will, settled in York county, Virginia, before 1667, and was for a number of years clerk of its court. He died in 1675, and the inventory of his estate includes "a parcell of English Books," valued at £3, and "a parcell of Latin Books," £1. He married Mary, daughter of Lt.-Col. William Barber, of York county, and had a daughter Mary and a son George. On Nov. 29, 1714, George Baskervyle, of Bruton parish, York county, sold a tract of 350 acres, together with his dwelling, &c., formerly belonging to John Baskervyle, grandfarther of the said George Baskerville. The George Baskerville (son of George, and grandson of John, the immigrant), who sold his home in York county in 1714, doubtless moved higher up the country, though exactly where is not known. Several persons of the name who are believed to have been his sons settled in what is now Cumberland county. John Baskerville was vestryman of Southam parish, Cumberland, in 1755. There is on record in Cumberland county a deed dated October 22, 1753, from George Baskerville, of Cumberland parish, Lunenburg county, conveying land in Cumberland county The will of Nowell Baskerville, dated January 9, 1750, and proved in Cumberland county February, 1750, bequeathed his whole estate to his brother George Baskerville. In 1770, in Cumberland county, Richard Baskerville married Martha, daughter of Bennett Goode. The will of John Baskerville, of Cumberland county, was dated January 16 and proved September 22, 1788. He left the estate where he lived, 730 acres on Willis's River, 4 slaves, horses, cattle, furniture, &c., to his brother Samuel, and 13 slaves to his brothers George, Richard and William Barber Baskerville, and to his sisters Mary Bass and Magdalen Trabue To his brothers George, 100 acres "where he now lives." There is a brief and (as to English origin) incorrect account of the family in Goode's *Virginia Cousins*, 233, 234.]

THOMAS BUTCHER of Madhurst, County Sussex, gent. Will 22 July 1646; proved 15 September 1646. To the poor of Madhurst £6. To my neices Marie and Elizabeth Butcher, daughters of my deceased Brother John Butcher, £10 apiece when 18. To my Brother Anthony 20s. To Deborah his wife £5. To my two nephews Edward and John Butcher £10 each. To my sister Elmott, wife of Walter Monde, £5. To my sister Mond's four children £40 each out of my lands at Bennenden in Kent, and £40 apiece to her two former sons Abell and Thomas Bridge. To my sister Shelbury £5. To Henry, Rachell, and Ann Shelburie £5 each. To Marie, wife of William Lucke of Durgates, use of £100 for life, then to Thomas, Luck her second son; if he should die before my neice, then to marie his mother, then to his brother Richard, then to his Brother Edward, then to his sister Mary. To my neice Ann, wife of David Holland, £100 ditto, then to her second son, then to her daughter Ann. To Anne and Elizabeth Delton, daughters of my uncle William Delton, £5 each. To •Margaret their sister, wife of Mr. Thomas Swanne, now resident in Virginia, £5, if shee live to come over into England. To my cozen Elizabeth Mills in Southwarke 10s. To my neice Alice, daughter of John Jeffery, £5; to her sister Dorothy 40s. To my cozen Mary, late wife of William Osborne of Burmish, Labourer, £10. To her sister Elizabeth, wife of Beniamin Weston of Tyhurst, labourer, £30. To Jeane, wife of my cozen Baker of Beyham, £3 for piece of plate. To my cozen Elizabeth, wife of Solomon Wenborne, 20s. for ring. To Mr. Thomas Saunders ditto. To my godson Thomas Saunders his son £5 for plate. My house and land at Benenden, Kent, now in tenure of Edmond Jones, to Mary Butcher, my wife, for life, after her decease to John Butcher, second son of my brother Anthony Butcher, he to pay the legacies to Abell and Thomas Bridge and Walter, Henrie, Jane, and Elizabeth Monde. My lands at Beckley and Northam in Sussex, now in tenure of Richard Ive, to my said wife for life, then to John Butcher, youngest son of my brother Anthony, failing him to his Brother Edward, failing him to the right heirs of my deceased Mother Joane, etc., etc. All the rest to my executrix, my wife Marie. Overseers: Brother Mr. John Dyne, Cozen Mr. Thomas Dyne of East Greensted, gent. Witnesses: Peter Braviour, Clericus, Thomas Saunders, William Brian.

Twisse, 125.

[Several persons of the name Butcher are mentioned in Berry's *Kentish Families*. Richard Butcher, of Wye, married in 1685 Martha daughter of Richard Champneys, Esq, of Biddenden. George Butcher married Ursula, daughter of William Swan, of Wye, and sister of Sir

Francis Swan, of Denton Court, who was knighted in 1608. The latter had a son William Swan, who may have been the emigrant to Virginia.

Col. Thomas Swann, of "Swann's Point," now in Surry county, Virgiaia, the person named in the will, was long a prominent man and was member of the Council. See this Magazine, III, 154, &c.]

JOHN HUDSON of City of Bristol, Clothier. Will 24 January 1715–6; proved 13 October 1725. To be buried in parish of Temple als Holly Cross as near my wive's grave as possible. My house in Temple street in said parish to my grandson George Martin for life, he to pay to my great grandson Hudson Martin £5 a year, he to have the house when George Martin dies. To my great grandson Hudson Martin my house in Temple Street where Mr. Lippiatt doth now dwell; if he die, to my grandson Henry Martin, and, upon his decease, to my great grandson Roger Martin. To my grandson George Martin a house in the horse-fair in parish of St. James in said City, my Inn called the George Inn in Bedminster, County Somerset, also all lands I bought of Mr. Hancock and Mr. Viger, also my house in Backstreet in St. Nicolas in tenure of William Rayney, and also all property in Bedminster, to him and his heires, and in default of such issue to my great grandson Hudson Martin, in default to the heirs of my grandsons Henry and George Martin. To my grandson Henry Martin my houses in Cheese lane in Parish of St. Philip and Jacob, then to my great grand son Hudson Martin, in default to great grandson Roger Martin. To my grandson Henry Martin my house in Redcliff street in tenure of —— Driver, Tobacconist, after his decease to my granddaughter Mary Martin and to great grandson Hudson Martin joyntly. To my grandson Henry Martin my house in Backstreet in tenure of Widow Gayner. To my servant Mary Jenkins that part of my dwelling house where in John Martin now lives, for life, also the bed she lies on. To be spent in bread for the poor when I am buried 40s. To my sister Elizabeth Gilbert £5. To my brothers David and Matthew Hudson and my son-in-law Roger Martin and Mr. Richard Sharke of Haverfordwest and to my cousin John Hudson one guinea each. My plate equally between my two grandsons Henry Martin and George Martin. To my friends Mr. Thomas

Hollister and my cozen Martin Jnnys 40s. apiece. The rest to my two grandsons George and Henry Martin, whom I make joint executors. Overseers: Friends Thomas Hollister and Martin Jnnys. Witnesses: Benj. Randolph, Joseph Little, Jonathan Clarke. Codicil 21 March 1716-7. Revoke bequest of houses in Cheese lane to Henry Martin. Witnesses: Tho: Edward, Jonathan Clarke. (2nd Codicil 29 December 1716.) My late brother William Hudson, Planter of Virginia, owed me at the time of his death £76 and upwards, and his plantation descends to me lawfully as heir at law to my said brother, and whereas I have appointed Mr. Thomas Godwin of Virginia aforesaid, merchant, and Mr. Abraham Lewis of Bristoll, Mariner, my lawful Attorneys, I bequeath the same to my grandsons Henry and George Martin, and to my great grand-daughter Mary Martin daughter of said Henry Martin, for ever, subject to payment of £5 apiece to my Brothers David and Matthew Hudson. To the minister of the parish of Temple 20s. to preach my funeral sermon. Witnesses: John Rich, Joseph Little, Joseph Holt.

Romney, 212.

[The name Hudson has been numerously represented in Virginia, though the place of residence of the William Hudson named in the will can not be ascertained. Foster's *Oxford Matriculations* shows that Hudson Martin, son of Henry, of Bristol, gentleman, entered Jesus College March 26, 1728, aged 17, received B. A. in 1731 and M. A. in 1734. He was, of course, the person named in the will. Hudson Martin, who lived in Albemarle county, Virginia, prior to the Revolution, served in that war as a lieutenant in the 11th Virginia regiment. His descendants lived in Amherst county.]

JEREMY ROBINS of St. Martins in the Fields, Fringweaver. Will 4 September 1671; proved 3 October 1671. To my son Richard Robins £5. To my grandson Jeremy Robins, son of my said son Richard, £5. To my daughter Mary Robins £5. To my daughter Rebecca Robins, now in Virginia, £5, to be paid within one year next after my decease if in case shee shall arive backe from Virginia into London. To my son Jeremy Robins £5 when he shall come back from Virginia into London. All the rest of my goods, estate, etc., to my dear and loving wife Sarah Robins, whom I make my executrix. Witnesses: Tho: Prettyman, William Rose, Tho: Gilbert, Scr.

Duke, 124.

WILLIAM SAKER of Surrey, gent. Will 1 December 1627; proved 7 December 1627. To be spent for my burial in a decent manner 100 marks. To my nephew Christopher Saker and his heirs my house and estate in Lambeth. If he die before he is 21, my cosen John Rayner and his heirs to have the same. To my neece Dorothy Saker £150. To my servant Thomas Gregory, if he returne alive out of Virginia into England, £50. To Mris Machett a pece of plate which she hath in her custody of the fashion of a Cocke and to Mr. Matchett 2 cwt. of my Virginia Tobacco. To Mr. Thomas Clarke £10, and to Mr. John Upton the elder £16 which he owes me and £5. Executors: Sir Thomas Jay of the Precincts of the Blackfryers, London, Knight, and Nathaniel Finch of Grayes Inne. Witnesses: C. Hastings, Benjamin Jeay.

Skinner, 117.

WILLIAM WHITE, citizen and Haberdasher of London, parish of St. Brides. Will 20 November 1676; proved 18 December 1676. To my wife Anne the lease of the wharfe and piece of ground adjoining White-Fryers Docke in St. Brides which I hold of George Arnold Esquire, upon which I have built a Brewhouse, now in occupation of one John Day, also upon which Wharf I have built a crane and other buildings, also all goods had with her in Marriage. To my sonne Thomas White all that Debt which is owing by my brother John White now in Virginia beyond the seas, and £10. I give him noe more because he hath already had more than can accrew to him by the custom of the City of London. To my daughter Elizabeth, wife of Mr. George Saunders, my house at Collier Rowe, parish of Hornechurch, Essex. To my son William White the land I hold by lease from one Mr. Hancock. To my son in law Mr. George Saunders 20s. All the rest to my executors, my son William White and daughter Elizabeth Saunders, and doe hope they will not differ about it. Witnesses: Jasper White, Wm. Warne, Henry Duke his servant.

Bence, 158.

VIRGINIA GLEANINGS IN ENGLAND.

Communicated by Mr. LOTHROP WITHINGTON, 30 Little Russell street, W. C., London (including " Gleanings " by Mr. H. F. WATERS, not before printed).

ANTHONY YONGE, citizen and Grocer of London. Will 23 February, 1635-6; proved 1 December, 1636. My attorney Mr. Thomas Cely to recover my debts and give account to Mr. John Gase in little Eastcheape and my brother Mr. William Yonge. To said Mr. Thomas Cely, merchant of London, 1000 lbs. of Virginia Tobacco. To Captaine Samuel Matthewes 500 lbs. of Tobacco. To Denby Church 500 lbs. To Thomas Hunson, my servant, 300 lbs. of Tobacco. To the church of the newe Poquoson 500 lbs. of Tobacco. I acquit Thomas Downum of all debts. My will left in the hands of Thomas Adison to be void. To Thomas Curtis and Mr. William Petty both of the newe Poquoson, Planters 200 lbs. of Tobacco each. To Mr. John Carter of the Newe Poquoson, Virginia, chirurgeon 100 lbs. of Tobacco. Mr. William Cely to take charge of the bills of lading for tobacco shipt abord Mr. Kinge shippe. Witnesses: Thomas Curtice, John Carter.

Pile, 118.

[It is probable that Anthony Yonge's place of business in Virginia was at Kechoughtan, the later Hampton. This portion of the colony was quite thickly settled at an early date. This will contains the earliest notices of Denbigh Church, Warwick county, and New Poquoson Church, York county.

Most of the persons named in the will were well known residents of the lower Peninsula. Thomas Celey, or Ceeley, the London merchant, was no doubt the person of the name who was a member of the House of Burgesses from Warwick River in 1629 and 1639. A deed of record in Elizabeth City county shows that he had a son, Thomas Ceeley, alive in 1698. It was, probably, the son who was sheriff of Warwick in 1663. The son sold in 1691 and 1695 to Col. Wm. Wilson the land in Elizabeth City county which, afterwards as "Ceeleys," was a well known residence of the Carey family. Thomas Ceeley, the second, had a son, Charles, who was living in Elizabeth City county, and then had a wife, Jane. Captain Samuel Matthews was of Warwick county, and was afterards governor. Thomas Curtis was born in 1600, and came to Virginia in the "Flying Hart" in 1621. In 1624 he was in Daniel Gookin's "Muster" at Newport News. Though the census includes all of Gookin's men under the head of "servants," it is evident that Curtis was a freeman. He later settled in Gloucester county, when, as Major Thomas Curtis, he patented large tracts of land. His descendants have been numerous in Gloucester, Middlesex, Spottsylvania, etc. See this Magazine, V, 344, XIV, 92. Thomas Addison was living at Elizabeth City in 1623.]

RICHARD FASSAKER, of Stafford County, in Virginia. Will 16 June, 1676; proved 24 July, 1676. Now on board the Raphannocke, Merchant bound for England and having by will, left in Virginia, disposed of my estate excepting what I have on board the Raphannocke Merchant. I desire my friend Mr. Samuel Phillips to sell whatsoever belongs to me on board and return the proceeds to Virginia to Mr. Robert Hall and to Mr. Edward Tomason, trustees to my will in Virginia for the benefit of my children, and also to buy three mourning rings of 10s. value and give one to Captain John Plover, one to himself, and one to Mr. George Brent the Posey I would have prepared be to follow me. Witnesses: Samuel Coldham, Wm. Bowie.

Bence, 90.

[Richard Fossaker was an early settler in Stafford county, and was a justice in 1664, and sheriff in 1667. One of his sons was Richard Fossaker, who was a Burgess for Stafford in 1702-'3. In or before 1693, Richard Fossaker married the widow of Thomas Hatherway, of Stafford, and in 1699 he was the husband of the daughter and heiress of Capt. John Withers, of Stafford. On April 14, 1692, John Fossaker and Elizabeth his wife, of Rappahannock county, one of the daughters and coheiresses of Mr. George Mott, of the same county, made a deed for land.]

ANNE CHEYNEY, widdow of parish of Katherine Cree church, London. Will 28 May 1663; proved 4 October 1667. To be buried either in the Chancel in Creechurch or at my pew dore. To the poor of sayd Parish of Katherine Cree church £10. To the clerk and Sexton of said Parish 20s. each. If I be buried in Creechurch I give the minister 40s. I give £10 to be bestowed in Bibles to be given to such as want them. To the poor of

West Ham in Essex £5. To my Cozen Mr. Bartholomew Harrison £50 and all the money he owes me. To my couzen Mr. Matthew Harrison £50 and all he owes me. To my said cozen Mr. Bartholomew and Matthew Harrison to be equally divided between them a Furniture for a Bed. White Curtain and Vallans, 2 Boulsters, 2 Pillows, one Redd Rugg, one white Blankett, 6 chayrs and stools. To my couzen Bartholomew a gold Ring with cornelion stone cutt for a seale, and my couzen Matthew Harrison my watch. I acquit the son and hayre of my couzen John Harrison deceased of all the money my said couzen owed me at his death. To the 3 children of my couzen John Harrison 40s. each. To Mrs. Elizabeth their mother my pearle necklace. To my couzen Mrs. Sarah Taylor £20. To my couzen Mrs. Lettice Hoxton my silver plate trencher. To my couzen Mr. Robert Waddis 40s. To my 3 couzens Mr. Thomas, Mr. Bartholomew and Mrs. Alice Feriman 40s. each. To my couzen Thomas Feriman's son Thomas and his daugher Susan 40s. each, and to his daughter Mary £5. To my couzen Mrs. Alice Twittie £5 and to her daughter Magdalene 40s. To my couzen Thomas Gwinne and his wife £5 each. To my Cozen Matthew Billingsbee £5. To my couzen Anna Roe £5 to be sent out in suitable things to Virginia. To my couzin Pilgram £5. To my cousin Zacheus Ewell £5. To my cousins Mathew and Thomas Pindar each of them £5. To my cousin John Ewell's wife that was, one bond of £30 that her husband and Mr. Colman was bound to mee before her husband's death. £20 to the congregation I am a member of to be paid to Mr. Legatt. To Mr. Nye £10. To Mr. Loader £10. Mr. Yates £10. Mr. Greenhill 40s. Mr. Foord £10. Mr. Spucogg £5. Mrs. Gray a silver sugar dish. Mrs. Clark and Mrs. Sumner 20s. apiece. Mrs. Campion 40s. Mrs. Rolfe 40s. Mr. John Allen £10. Mr. James, Mr. Joseph, Mr. Benjamin Allen 40s. each. Mrs. Mary Allen £20. To Mrs. Smyth the least stone pott with silver and gilt lide. To Mr. Ashbourne and his wife £2. To Mr. Thrayle £10. To Mrs. Thrayle £10. also my silver pint pot. To Mrs. Foster £5. Betty Foster 40s. Mrs. Barber £5. Mrs. Maselin, Goodwife Dandy, Gudwife Turner, Goodwife Dun 20s. each. My mayd Isabell Cocks £3. To any other servant living with me at my decease 40s. All my linen not bequeathed to my friends, my couzen Taylor, Mrs. Campion, Mrs. Thrayle, Mrs. Foster and some of them to Mrs. Smyth and my maid servant. £150 to be bestowed on my funeral. All the rest to my friend and executor Mr. John Gray. Witnesses: Daniel Trissell, George Whitehead.

Com. London, 1670, folio 254.

[Anna Roe was probably wife of Edward Roe, who obtained the following grants of land: (1) in partnership with John Lewis, 550 acres in Lancaster (now Middlesex) on the branches of Pianketank Swamp. The "Mattapony path," and "Mr. Potter's land" mentioned as boundaries, June 29, 1663. (2) 250 acres in Lancaster at the heads of the branches of the Beaver Dams, "that issueth out of Pianketank River," "Cheescake path towards Matchepingo." (3) "Mr. Edward Roe" 250 acres in Gloucester adjoining his own land where he lives, May 27, 1665.]

RICHARD RICHMOND, Cittizen and Leatherseller of London. Will 15 April 1684: proved 23 January 1684-5. [Printed in Waters' Gleanings, 325.]

Cann, 9.

[A "Mr. Robert Richmond" patented on Oct. 21, 1684, 600 acres on the west side of Cypress Swamp, in Lynhaven parish, Lower Norfolk county.]

RICHARD WILLIAMSON, Citizen and Merchanttaylor of London. Will 30 June 1646: proved 5 December 1646. To my loveinge Brother Roger Williamson Residinge in Virginia the summe of twenty shillings of lawfull English money, and I doe forgive him all the money which he owes me. To all the children of my said brother £5 equally amongst them. To my cousen Thomas Williamson £3 and my long blacke cloth Cloake. To my cousen Alice Williamson (his sister) £3 and I forgive her all the money she owes me. To my cosen Anne Nightingale (to whom I have given a porcon in marriage) 5s. To my cousin Sarah Williamson £20 when 21 or married. The lease of my new dwelling house and all the rest of my estate whatsoever to my wife Mary Williamson my executrix.

Witnesses: Edward Boldston, William Tuder, Raphe Dawson and Chr: fauell Scrivener.

19 September 1657 letters of administration issued to Martha, sister of said Mary Williamson, wife of deceased.

Twisse, 189.

SAMUEL FILMER, of East Sutton, County Kent, gent. Will 17 July 1667; proved 28 May 1670. To my mother Lady Anne Filmer, my Brothers Edward Filmer, Knight, and Robert Filmer, Esq., and my sister Lady Anne Godstall, widow, mourning rings of 10s. To my friends and cousins Mrs. Frances Stephens, wife of Mr. Samuell Stephens of Virginia, Mr. Archibald Clinkard, of Lynton, County Kent, gent., Mr. Warham Horsemanden and Susan his wife, and Mr. Anthony Horsemanden, a mourning ring each. My friend and cousin Mrs. Mary Horsemanden, eldest daughter of aforesaid Warham and Susan Horsemanden of Ham in the parish of Lenham, County Kent (between whom and myself there is an agreement of marriage), to be sole executrix and legatee of all my estates real and personal. If I live to marry her and have any children, she to have half and the other to our children. Overseers: Mr. Warham Horsemanden, father of said Mary, and Mr. Anthony Horsemanden, his brother. Witnesses: Anne Godstall, Ursula Horsemanden, Susanna Chapman, Warham Horsemanden. Proven by Warham Horsemanden, father of said Mary Filmer als Horsemanden, now in Virginia.

Penn, 58.

[Samuel Filmer was 3d son of Sir Robert Filmer, of East Sutton, Kent, the once famous Tory author. Sir Robert was a strong cavalier and suffered much during the civil wars, during which, it is said, his house at East Sutton was plundered ten times, and he imprisoned in Leed's Castle, in 1644. Berry, in his Kentish Genealogies, states incorrectly, that Samuel married Maria, daughter of Maurice Horsmanden, of Lenham, Kent. He married (and appears to have survived the marriage only a short time), Mary, daughter of Worham Horsmanden.

Warham Horsmanden was the son of Rev. Daniel Horsmanden, rector of Ulcomb, Kent, and his wife, Ursula, daughter of Sir Warham St. Leger, of Ulcombe. Rev. Mr. Horsmanden was a loyalist and was expelled from his charge, and his son Warham removed to Virginia, where he was member of the House of Burgesses for Charles City county, 1657-'8, and 1658-'9, and appointed to the council in 1657. After the restoration, Warham Horsmanden returned to England. Mary, daughter of Warham Horsmanden, married secondly, Col. Wm. Byrd, of Westover, Charles City county, Va. Her tomb, which states that she died Nov. 9th, 1699, in her 47th year, remains at Westover.

There were a large number of Kentish people of this connection who came to Virginia, Diggeses, Codds, and Fleets. Henry Filmer, who settled in Virginia at an earlier date appears to have been an uncle of Samuel Filmer. He was member of the House of Burgesses for James City county, 1642-3, and a justice of Warwick where he finally made his home in 1647.

He obtained the following grants: (1) Henry Filmore, 1,000 acres in the county of James City, on Chickahominy River, near Warren's landing, adjoining the land of John White, 350 acres thereof formerly granted to John Orchard, Aug. 15, 1637; 350 acres granted to John White, April 29, 1639, and 300 acres granted to Thos. Stout, April 10, 1639, and by the said Filmore purchased from them, now granted to him Feb. 6, 1653. (2) Mr. Henry Filmore, 360 acres in Warwick formerly granted to Anthony Barham and lately found to escheat Oct. 27, 1673.

In Isle of Wight county is recorded a bill of exchange dated June 16, 1668, on "Mr. Robert Filmer, Esq., living near ye Talbott, at ye sign of ye Goat, London," 'and signed "Your Loving Uncle, Henry Filmer."

The brother Edward, named in the will, was a gentleman of the bed chamber to Charles I and II, and died unmarried in 1669. The brother Robert was created a baronet in 1675. These Filmers descended from a sister of Sir Samuel Argall, governor of Virginia.]

RAPHAEL THROCKMORTON. Will 10 September 1669; proved 3 May 1670.

Penn, 68.

[Abstract printed in *Virginia Historical Magazine*, Vol. X, p. 320.]

ROBERT ROSE, of Rochester, County Kent, being engaged in Maritime affirs. Will 7 October 1666; proved 5 October 1670. To my Brother Edward Rose 5s. To my Brother Christopher Rose 1s., and to each of his children 1s., but to his son Robert I give 20s. To my Brother Thomas Rose, now in Barbadoes, 5s. All the rest to my wife Mary Rose, my sole executrix, but in case it should be otherwise I appoint My Brother Chris: Rose and my Brother Henry West, dwelling at Warwicksqueare in James River in Virginia, to be by them equally divided and enjoyed. Witnesses: Marmaduke Bladder, William Pearson.

Penn, 149.

[Henry West with John Portis patented 900 acres on the branches of Blackwater, Isle of Wight county, 1673. He took part in Bacon's Rebellion, and by court martial held Jan. 24th, 1676-7, was found guilty of treason and rebellion, was banished from Virginia for seven years and all of his estate except £5, forfeited. It is possible that his sentence was not carried out.]

ANTHONY BACON, of Cyfartha, county Glamorgan. Will 14 June 1785, written 13 May last: proved 25 February 1786 and 27 March 1787. All my estates etc. to my executors to be disposed of as follows: To my wife Elizabeth Bacon an annuity of £700, my coach, and two of the best horses. To my neice Elizabeth Bacon £5000. To my relation the Reverend Thomas Richardson an annuity of £200 to be paid out of the profits from Herwin Furnace. To my relation Anthony Richardson all the debt which may be due to me at my decease from Gilbert Franklyn, Esquire, of the Island of Tobago. To my half brother William Bacon £500 and all my estate in the Province of Virginia which I hold in partnership with Sundry Gentlemen, called the Dismal Swamp, containing I suppose 30,000 acres, and all debts due to me in the several provinces of North America, desiring him to pay to the two daughters of my late brother the Reverend Thomas Bacon, now living in Maryland, one fourth part. My Executors to spend what money they think fit for the education and maintenance of the children hereafter mentioned which I acknowledge to be my own: The Reverend Doctor Samuel Glasse, Mr. William Stevens of Broad Street, London, Mr. Thomas Harrison of Whitehaven, and my agent Mr. Richard Hill at Cyforthe, Dr. Glasse £1000, Mr. Stevens £500, Mr. Harrison £500. To my godson Anthony Bacon Richardson £100. Godson Anthony Speeding £50. Goddaughter Elizabeth Hill £50. Cousin Ann Younger £100 and Cousin Mary Brownrigg £100. To Mary Bushby £1000, and she is to receive for the maintenance of her 4 younger children, viz: Thomas, Elizabeth, Robert and William £50 a year for each till they are taken away to go to school. To Anthony the eldest son of the said Mary Bushby, who is at the time of writing this will at school at Gloucester, under the care of the Reverend Mr. Stocke, by the Name of William Addison, May the 13th, 1785, all lands I hold under Earl Talbot and the late Michael Richards, Esquire, of Cardiff, in the parish of Merther Tidville, county Glamorgan, also the blast furnace called

Cyfartha Furnace, and the forge now let to Francis Homfray. To Thomas son of Mary Bushby and brother to above named Anthony, Leases held from Earl of Plymouth and the freehold estate bought of Mr. Philips. To Robert, 3d son of said Mary, my furnace called Herwin bought from Maberry & Wilkins of Brecon. To Mr. Harrison of Whitehaven my estate in Cumberland for the following purposes: To Elizabeth, daughter of said Mary Bushby, an Annuity of £300. This is the best way to provide for her as it has pleased God to afflict her with lameness. To William, the youngest son of said Mary, who was born at Gloucester in the month of March 1785, the remainder up to £10,000. If any of my said children and the children of said Mary Bushby die their share to remainder. If all my sons, the children of Mary Bushby die, my estate between my neice Elizabeth Bacon and my cousins Thomas and Anthony Richardson. Witnesses: Richard Crawshay, John Cocksfrutt, James Sutton.

Norfolk, 70.

[The first Dismal Swamp Company was chartered by the General Assembly in 1764. Rev. Thomas Bacon was rector of St. Peter's church, Talbot county, Maryland, and collected the laws of that colony. In 1751 he started a scheme for a charity school in Talbot county. Many Virginians contributed. See *William and Mary Quarterly*, VII, 142, 143.]

SIR NATHANIEL HERNE, Knight and Alderman of London. Will 12 April 1677; proved 28 August 1679. Estate of Nathaniel's brother Nicholas left to disposal of Nathaniel, valued at £10,868 10s. 6d. Two thousand, one hundred pounds laid out in purchase of lands called Broomfeilds parish of Stepney, county Middlesex, which I purchased of Captain Arnold Browne. Said lands to such of my sons as shall be my eldest at my Death. The rest of my brother's estate to be equally divided amongst my children. My house in Cheapside, parish of St. Vedast, called the three Cockes, in possession of James Lapley, and the back house in possession of John Garrett, to my son Nathaniell. To Dame Judith, my wife, apparel, jewels, £8500, my coach and horses, and the lease of my house. If all my children die before 21 years, then their portions to my brother Joseph Herne and his children. The interest of £600 to my sister Sarah Hall, the wife of Joseph Hall, Merchaunt, during her life, and after to her two daughters Sarah and Susannah Hall. To Alice Ostler, sister of the whole Bloud of said brother Nicholas, £30 per annum. The leases of my houses in Purse Court and Old Change which I purchased of William Townes, citizen and Draper, to my son Thomas. To Sir John Frederick, Alderman, £100, and Dame Mary, his wife, £20. To my brother Joseph £500 and saddle horses; to Elizabeth his wife £25. To my brother Thomas Fredericke £20. To Leonora his wife £50. To my Sister Rebecca Fredericke £5. To my cousin William Wheately £100. To his wife £20. To John Banckes of London, merchant, £100., To Rebecca his wife £20. To Mary Boys of the city of Norwich £20. To Isac Tillard of Plimouth, merchant, £20. To Prudence, his wife, £10. To Ephraim Skinner of London, merchant, £20. To Anne his wife £10. To John Gunstone of London, merchant, £10. To William Moses of Grayes Inn, Esq., £10. To all my servants 40s. apeece. To my brother Joseph's children that shall be living £20 apeece. To my apprentices £10 apeece. Executors and guardians of my children: Sir John Fredericke, Joseph Herne, William Wheatley and John Banckes. "Item: I give 20 shillings to ——— Whitlock, wife ——— Whitlock of Virginia, daughter of my brother John Herne, deceased." Witnesses: Nathaniel Whitwell, Daniel Short, Wi: Wyndham, Will: Yeo. (Administration 29 December, 1694, to son and heir Nathaniel Herne of estate left unadministered by Sir Joseph Herne, one of the executors, Sir John Frederick and William Wheatley being deceased, and John Banks not appearing when cited.—Probate Act Book 1699, folio 229.)

King, 107.

VIRGINIA GLEANINGS IN ENGLAND.

Communicated by Mr. LOTHROP WITHINGTON, 30 Little Russell street, W. C., London (including " Gleanings " by Mr. H. F. WATERS, not before printed).

EDWARD KINGSWELL of London, Esquior. Will 30 January 1635–6; proved 6 April 1636. My body to be buried in the Parish Church of Sainct Pulchers in London neere my late wife (the Lady Jane Clifton) as conveniently as may be. To the said church 40s., and to the poor £3. To Mrs. Elizabeth Wilson (my sister's daughter), £100 when 21 or married. To my Cosens William Ridgway, Mackwilliam Ridgway, and Thomas Brocas, Esqrs., 50s. rings. To my Cozen Robert Brocas (son of my said cozen Thomas Brocas) my Bible in folio of the Geneva Translation bound in Crimson Plush; and to Barnard Brocas (one other of his sons and my godson) a silver Bason and Ewer. To Mr. William Bradshaw £20 and my cloth suite and cloake, the Doublet whereof is lyned with Orange tawney taffety, together with the orange tawney silke stockings, and executors to recompense him well for paynes in business betweene mee and Mr. Vassall. To my friend John Guy, gent £10. Executors to recompense ditto. To my servent James Cooke, now in virginia, £5 and to be free of Indentures in making Accompt, &c. To my servant William Twitchell £5, bedd, etc. The results of a suit depening before the Lords Commissioners for Plantations in my name against Samuell Vassall, merchant, and Peter Andrewes (his brother in lawe) amounting to £611. 1s. 4d. and £2099. 15s. 8d. (whereof the £611 1s. 4d. had been paid, and the Referees are considering the other part) to my Brother and Sister Mr. Roger Wingate and Dorothie his wife, and also to them all my servants, money, Tobaccoe, Beaver, and other goods belonging to me, beyond the seas and in England, and do make them executors. Overseers: Mr. Edward Ridgway, Mr. Mackwilliam Ridgway, Mr. Thomas Brocas, and Mr. John Guy. Witnesses: John Guy, William Twitchell.

Pile, 34.

From Vol. XV, No. 3 (Jan. 1908), p. 297.

[Edward Kingswell was probably the first person, after the Raleigh failure, to attempt to plant a colony within the present limits of North Carolina. After the dissolution of the Virginia Company, when the territory of Virginia again became subject to grant by the King, Sir Robert Heath was, in 1629, granted the country embraced in the present North Carolina, and the district granted was to be known as Carolana or Carolina. No active attempt at settlement under the Heath appears to have been made except that by Edward Kingswell, and his attempt failed. The exact nature of Kingswell's rights does not appear, though no doubt it was derived from Heath or some of his assignees.

In October, 1633, Edward Kingswell with his partner Roger Wingate and their families and forty other persons arrived at Jamestown on their way to make a settlement in Caroiina. As no other vessel appeared to carry them to their destination, they waited in Virginia until the next spring when the proposed colony appears to have been abandoned. In March, 1734, Mr. Wingate with his wife and family left Virginia for England, and after making complaint to the Governor of Virginia, Kingswell followed him in June. On his arrival in England he immediately brought suit before the Privy Council against Samuel Vassall and Peter Andrews, who had contracted to carry his party to Carolina. They were arrested and when brought before the Council claimed that they had done all in their power to carry out their contract, and that it was Kingswell's fault that the settlers did not reach Carolina. The defendants were ordered to pay £611, 1, 4; but Kingswell continued to sue for the remainder of what he estimated to be his losses, amounting to above £2,000. The final result is not known; but it is certain that the colonists did not reach Carolina. Most of them, probably, remained in Virginia. (See *Calendar of State Papers, Colonial*, I, 190, 194, 197, 198. 207.)

Roger Wingate, Kingswell's partner, brother-in-law and residuary legatee, returned to Virginia and was, in 1639, appointed Treasurer of the Colony and member of the Council. He held both offices until his death in 1641. He married Dorothy, daughter of William Bedell of Catworth, county Huntingdon, and widow of Edward Burwell, of Harlington, county Bedford. His wife was the mother of Lewis Burwell, the emigrant member of that Virginia family.

As Kingswell's rights were devised to Wingate, it seems probable that from the latter they passed to his widow. There is on record in York county, Va., a deed dated July 28, 1648, from Dorothy Wingate, widow of Roger Wingate, Treasurer of Virginia, conveying to her "well-beloved son Lewis Burwell," all rents due at said Roger's decease, and confirmed to her by the King.

On account of this inheritance it is almost certain that a full list of Kingswell's colonists has been preserved. On April 18, 1648, a patent was granted to Mr. Lewis Burwell and Thomas Vause for 2,300 acres on the south side of York River, "about seven miles above the Narrows, and adjoining the river, "tanks Queen's Creek," and the lands of Mr. Francis Fludd, Mr. Thomas Broughton and William Black. The land was due for the importation of forty-six persons. As several persons among the head rights under this patent certainly came with the Kingwell colony, there is good reason to believe that the list represents that colony in its entirety. The head rights are :

Edward Kingswell.	Jno. Hastang.
Roger Wingatt.	Jno. Herman.
the minister his son.	Wm. Burtenwood.
Anthony Kingswell.	Fra. Barrington.
William Bradshaw.	Rich. Hewitt.
John Bell.	Vyas [or Virgas] Smith.
Eugene Burdett.	Antho. Waddy.
William Spry.	Elias Taylor.
Antho Wilson.	Thos. Lee.
Samuel Mayne.	Richard Smith.
James Cooke.	Elvas Clay his wife,
Eliz'a Letts.	his daughter, Fra. Walker.
Wm. Taylor.	Eliz'a Bennison.
John Tolson.	Dorothy Tillingta.
Wm. Harman.	her Daughter.
Jno. Macreall.	Sarah Dera: Coz.
Alex. Reynald.	John Davis.
ye Lady Clifton.	Wm. Burwell.
Eliz'a Booth. ⎱ Maids.	Fra. Harman.
Mary Daton. ⎰	his wife.
Thos. Adams.	

Several of the persons named in this list are known to have been later residents of Virginia. It should be remarked that the names are not printed as they are arranged in the Land Book. Frances Walker was evidently the daughter of Elias Clay. Edward Kingswell's wife retained, according to the English custom, her higher title. Another nxample of this in Virginia, is when the wife of Philip Ludwell was always called Lady Berkeley. Edward Kingswell, the testator, was probably the same as Edward Kingswell, of Southants, *arm. fil. nat. max.*, who matriculated at Brasenose College, Oxford, May 7, 1602, aged 15 ; B. A. Oct. 26, 1602, student of the Middle Temple 1603 as son an heir of Sir William Kingswell, of Shalden, Hants., Knight.]

EDMUND FABIAN of the parish of St. Andrews Holborne, county Middlesex, Citizen and Merchant Taylor. Will 3 July 1668; proved 8 August 1668. To be buried in St. Gregories, London. Whereas I and my sister Alice Haselfoote are possessed of the

Manor of Chigwell Grange, parish of Chigwell, county Essex, by Indenture 3 November 1662, from the Schoolemaster and Guardians of the Grammer Schoole att Brentwood in Essex for 21 years, I give to my son Symon Fabian, who is now beyond seas at Yorke River in Virginia, the moiety of rents of said Manor. To my said son Symon and heirs for ever my land at Great Parringdon, county Essex, now in occupacion of John Ingham. To my said son Symon £200, provided that if said Symon die before he shall returne to England then bequest to him to my four children, John, Susan, Katherine, and Sara Fabian. To my son John £700. To my daughter Elizabeth Brett, wife of Francis Brett, the yearly sum of £30. If said Elizabeth should marry a second time, then £15 yearly to my grandson Edmund, son of said Francis and Elizabeth. To my daughter Dame Vrsula Cremer £20. To my daughter Susan Fabian £500. To my daughters Katherine and Sara Fabian £500 apiece. To said grandson Edmund £20. To Mary Crompton £50 at 21 or marriage. Executors to sell wares in shop and warehouse also. To my sister Mirriam Playdwell, widowe, 20s, releasing her and her daughter Susan Memry of all they owe. To the poore of St. Gregories 40s. To the poor of St. Andrews Holborne Tenn dozen of bread. To my servant Edward Hercy £20. To my friend Mr. Beale 10s. To my maid servent Elizabeth Gibson 10s. Executors: my son Symon Fabian and Mr. Theophilus Smith and Mr. Christopher Pitt. Residue to my said children Symon, John, Susan, Katherine, and Sarah Fabine [sic]. Witnesses: Nicho: Seale, Ralph Tourney, Tho: Lea, scr.

Hene, 105.

[There is a pedigree of a family of Fabian in the early 17th Century *Visitation of London*, published by the *Harleian Society*.]

HENRY GERRARD, [late of Martin Brandon, Charles City County, Virginia—Probate Act]. Will 20 July 1689; proved 11 March 1692-3. To my daughter Elizabeth Bayley 20s. for a gold ring. To William and Elizabeth Bayley, my grandchildren, a mare filly. To Thomas Peters, son of John Peters deceased, a cow and a calf to be put into the hands of Mr. Henery Harman, provided he keeps the boy. To George Peters a heifer. To

Margaret Osborne the 250 lbs. of Tobacco she was indebted to me for a gowne and six hundred pounds of Tobacco which is her full wages. To Ferdinando and Nicholas Gerrard, my two sons, all the rest of my Estate and what money may be recovered in England. To Jacob Bayley, my son in law, two Barroes four years old each. Overseers: Captain Nicholas Gerrard and Jno. Tirrey. Witnesses: Mathew Adams, Will. Jennings. After signing I give to my Godson Francis Wrey a cow calf. Charles City county in Virginia, Oct. 3, 1689. William Jennings is sworn as evidence to this will in Cha. City County Courte, Hugh Davis, D. Cl. Cur. Entered in Records of said County pr. Hugh Davis, supradict. Hugh Davis. Administration to Micajah Perry, attorney for Ferdinando and Nicholas Gerrard, now in Virginia, sons and residuary legatees, no executors being named.

Coker, 51.

[The testator lived within the present Prince George county. It may be mentioned here that the parish written " Martimber," in the will of John Westhropp, published in the last Magazine, was intended for Martin Brandon. The tomb of John Tirrey, one of the " overseers " named in this will, is at the site of the old Martin Brandon Church, now known as "Church Pasture," on the Brandon estate. See this Magazine, VII, 211.]

JOHN EDWARDS. Will 3 February 1667-8; proved 24 November 1668. Mr. William Ball shall take into his custody all my estate in Virginia and make sale of my lands, houses, servants, cattle, for good bills of Exchange payable in London or good Tobaccoe, and the whole produce to my friend Mr. Spencer Piggott in Duke's Place, London. And what estate of Servants and goods abord the Ship Susan, William Goodlade, Master, I commend to the management of said William Goodlad, to give true account to said Spencer Piggott. And since I left behind me in England my dear wife and three children, what I left with them, as also the produce of my Virginia Estate and the produce of the Ship Susan, be divided into four parts to them equally, and if any depart this life (which God forbid) before the whole be divided, then among the rest. Executor Mr. Spencer Piggott of Duke's Place in London. Witnesses: Rich. Perrott, John Page, William Petherbridge, Henry Allen, Rich. Perrott, Junr.

Hene, 138.

[John Edwards was a resident of Lancaster county, Virginia. In May, 1657, Lancaster Court gave John Edwards a certificate of the importation of his children, John and Mary, and of other persons. On Nov. 30, 1659, there is mention that he had married Frances, daughter of Francis Cole, of Lancaster county, deceased. In November, 1664, Mrs. Bathsea Pee sued John Edwards, her "brother-in-law." There is a deed dated December 7, 1658, to John Edwards, surgeon. His original will is on file at Lancaster Court House. It was proved in Lancaster March 1667, and bears a seal with a *fesse indented between three heartlets*. The crest is mutilated, but represents an animal.]

THOMAS MATHEW, some years Maior of a Regt. now Millenor in Grais In Lane in Holburn, London. Will — November, 1665; proved 27 March 1667. I make my wife Mary executrix. To my son Matthias Mathew Lt. £5 and my Sord and hedpiece. To my daughter Elizabeth yt is married at Colchester to Dr. Elkins Sunn now living at Shergate £5 and the brass pott yt was brought from Wekham. To my daughter Mary living in Vergene in Mary Land with one Mr. Cames £3. To my daughter Hestir living with Alis Mundy 50s. and two fether beds. To my Sunne Nathaniell Mathew living at Burnett near Wekham 5 miles from Portsmouth where his aforesaid sister lives with one Mr. Millen Carpenter 50s. To my daughter Elizabeth, Child to my wife Mary aforesaid, £20 besides her Scholing and bred by my Executrix to the age of Twenty. Witnesses: Joseph Lansley, William Burton, bornner Sherley, Mary Balding.

Carr, 39.

ANN JONES of St. Clement Danes, county Middlesex, Widow. Will 20 February 1676-7; proved 6 February 1678-9.

King, 19.

[Sentence for above will (95 King) in case between Charles Stephen and Richard Southey, overseers, on one part, and Thomas Daniell, executor, residing in Virginia, on other part.]
[Printed in Waters' Gleanings.]

WILLIAM WINCH of London, Virginia Merchant. Will 22 Jan. 1739-40; proved 4 Feb. 1739-40. Whereas I intermarried with my present wife Fanny Parke Winch, the daughter of John Custis of Virginia, Esq., and was to have received from him £1000 for her marriage portion, said sum to be laid out in pur-

chase of Lands in Virginia, said John Custis has absolutely refused so to do, and having not received any portion at all, it is
my Will to barr said wife of all benefit in my Estates Real and
Personal, and I give all Lands, Tenements, Stock, Cattle, Negroes, Plantation, Implements, whether in London, Virginia, or
elsewhere to my cousen Mr. Francis William Massey of the
parish of Christchurch, in London, Apothecary, to him and his
assigns for ever. Executors: Said Francis William and Samuel
Haswell, Thomas Brooks, and William Hunt. Witnesses: James
Martin, Mary Martin, Jas. Hen. Kent.

Browne, 56.

[*The Virginia Gazette* of January 29, 1739, has the following notice:
"On Wednesday Evening Mr. William Winch, a very considerable Merchant in New Kent County, was married to Miss Fanny Parke Custis,
only Daughter of the Honorable John Custis, Esq., one of His Majesty's Council of this Colony, a very deserving well accomplish'd Young
Lady, with a good Fortune." At the time that this poor lady was being
so unceremoniously cut off by her husband, she was in Virginia writing
affectionate letters in regard to the business he had left behind. Several of these are in the manuscript collections of this Society.]

GILES PALMER, Bridgenorth. Will 17 May 1637; proved 15
June 1637. To the poor of Bridgenorth £5. To Mr. Samuell
Sambrooke £150 due from my brother Richard Palmer, Esquire;
and all writings in my possession that apperteyne to the lands in
Mapperlie, county Derby, to my brother Richard Palmer. To
my neece Bridgett Palmer all my lands in Virginia; if she die
without issue, the said lands to go to my sister's children, Margaret Elton's and Jone Charleton's. To my brother Richard
Palmer a ring valued at 40s. To my kinswoman Bridgett Palmer one gould ring set with Diamonds of Tenne pounds price.
To my Brother Richard Palmer £90 he has owed me for 14
years. To my sister Mary Palmer the use of £100 for life; after
her decease, to my goddaughters Anne Hammer and Elizabeth
Charleton. To my near Kinsman Edward Elton £50. To Mu-
riell, the daughter of John Elton, £10, and to my Cosen Cray-
crofte's wife £20. To my neece Margarett Charleton £50. To
my neeces Anne Charleton and Elizabeth Charleton £50 each.
To my brother Jno. Charleton all money due to me by Bills. To my
neece Anne Hammer £150. To my friend and brother Laurence

Spyke £5. To my friend Richard Lane £5. To Robert Newman 50s. To Winfeild Blakemore and Ralphe Saracould 40s.
each. To Robert Hayman 50s. To Ralph Woodward £5 for
his care of me. To Samuell Sambrooke money due from him
to me. To Mr. Samuel Sambrooke's eldest daughter a diamond
ring. To my friend Henry Pinson the elder £10; to Henry
Pinson the younger £5. To Elizabeth Pynson a fetherbed. To
Jane, Humphrey, William, and Mary Pynson £5 each. To my
nephew Giles Gilbey 20 Latine Bookes. To five of my nephews,
brothers of my neere kinsman Edward Palmer of Compton
£10 to be laid out in diamond rings for them. My rapier
to my kinsman Rouse Palmer. To my brother Rutter 40s.
To my sister Rutter £10. To Mr. George Savage of Bridgenorth £5, and to Mistress Elinor, his wife, my silver
watch. To Mistress Elinor, their daughter, £5. Residuary
Legatee and Executor: Edward Palmer of Compton, county
Warwick, to bestow some part of residue upon John Charleton's
daughters. Witnesses: Willm. Asplin, William Cresswell.

Goare, 92.

[Giles Palmer was son of Edward Palmer, who, by will dated 1624,
endeavored to establish on Palmer's Island in the Susquehanna river, a
Virginia University to be styled *Academia Virginiensis et Oxoniensis*.
As is well known nothing came of this attempt. See Neill's *Virginia
Vetusta*, 182-3. Edward Palmer's will is in Water's Gleanings.]

FRANCIS SAUNDER, Ewell, Surrey, gent. Will 17 August 1613;
proved 25 August 1613. "A miserable and sinful caytiffe." To
reparations of church of Ewell 10s. and to parson for tythes forgotten 2s. To poore of Ewell £3. To reparation of church of
St. Andrews Congham, Norfolk, 10s. To Mr. Edward Mvnford,
parson of said church, for tythes neglected, 5s. To poore of
Congham £3. To Sister[s], Marye Lusher, Frances Spellman, and
Elizabeth Garnishe, 1 angel each. To neeces Dame Jone Clyf-
ford, Dame Elizabeth Sanders and Dame Elynor Spellman, ditto.
To Neeces Jane Mynne, Anne Whitney, and Elizabeth Bays-
poole, ditto. To Nephew Sir Nicholas Sander, Knight, £10
and forgive debts. To Nephew Henry Sander, senior, £5, ditto.
To Nephew Henry Sander, son of Sir Nicholas Sander my stone
bowe. To Neece Mary Beavill £5. To Neece Fraunces Saunder

20s. To Neece Elizabeth Sander 20s. To Neece Isabell Sander £3 to buy Jewelles. To Nephew Nicholas Sander one Double Ryall. To Nephew Phillipp Sander ditto. To Nephew Henry Sander, son of Mr. Erasmus Sander, £3 yearly for life out of lands in Clyff, Kent. To neece Jane Foulefford £3. To Neece Anne Sander £20 yf unmarried and if married but 20s. To Nephew John Spellman my Crosse bowe inlayde the stocke with mother of perle. To Nephew Henry Spellman £3. To Nephew Clement Spellman £3. To Nephewe Francis Spellman, sonne of Nephew Sir Henry Spellman, Knight, £3. To Neece Dorathy Spellman, daughter of ditto, 1 Tablett of gould with a morion's face therein and a pendant knott of perles with the Spellman's Armes in the same. To Neece Katheryne Spellman £3. To Neece Alce Spellman £3. "Item, I geve and bequeath to the seaven Yongest Children of my Nephewe Erasmus Spellman Three Pounds a peece, my said Nephewe Sir Henrye Spellman shall receyve it for their good and not their Mother, whe'rof Henry Spellman in Virginia to be exemted." To Mr. Richard Saunderson and his wife £4. Forgive Sister Marye Lusher debts and arrearages of £5 rent due since the death of our good Father William Saunder, Esquior, out of lands in Surrey, and acquitting all questions between us and my brother Erasmus Sander, deceased, and hir. To servant Davye Ketchmaye yf in service 40s. and hosen and doublett so he direct scattered thinges of myne in his custodie at Congham, Norfolk, London, Ewell, Clyffe, Kent, Surrey, etc. To Nephewe Richard Sander, son of brother Erasmus Sander aforesaid, Coppyehould in Congham, Norfolk, houlden of Mr. Edward Yelverton, etc. and ditto held of Sir Henrye Spellman, Knight, also rectory of All Saints in Congham, etc, etc. alsoe landes in Clyffe, Kent, and Ewell, Surrey, and all other goodes, etc. etc. Executor said Nephewe Richard Sander. Overseers: nephewes Sir Henry Spellman and Sir William Mynne, Knightes, and to said Sir William 2 spurr royals and to Sir Henry Spellman best gelding and saddle etc. Mem. Whereas have by grant of my sister Elizabeth Garnyshe hir kindnes Annuitie of £10 out of her manor of Hornyngetofte, Norfolk, which shee gave me when shee was sole the wydowe of William Forde, Esquior, deceased,

which deed is in custodye of Gregorye Pagrave, countie Norfolke, gent., the same to be equally divided amongst sons and
daughters of brother Erasmus Sander, deceased, his son and
heir Executor.   Witnesses: Richard Bendysh, Edward Moundeford, James Munsers, scr., Symone Sillett of Congham, gent.
[Sentence (108 Capell) confirming will of Francis Saunder,
of Congham, Norfolk, gentleman, in case between Richard
Saunder, executor, on one part, and next of kin, Sir Nicholas
Saunder, knight, Henry Saunder and Nicholas Saunder, Esquires, and Philip Saunder and William Saunder, gentlemen,
read the 2d of the Feast of St. Edmund the King, viz., 23 November, 1613.]

Capell, 76.

[Brown, Arber and other writers state that Henry Spelman, well
known in the early history of Virginia, was third son of Sir Henry Spelman, the antiquary. Their authority is not known. This will, however,
shows that he was a son of Erasmus Spelman, and nephew of Sir Henry.]

VIRGINIA GLEANINGS IN ENGLAND.

Communicated by Mr. LOTHROP WITHINGTON, 30 Little Russell street,
W. C., London (including " Gleanings " by Mr. H. F. WATERS,
not before printed).

GEORGE CARTER [late of the Middle Temple, Esquire.—
Probate Act Book].   Will 2 January 1741-2; proved 13 January, 1741-2.   By the will of my deceased father Robert Carter,
Esq. of the Colony in Virginia, certain lands therein are given
to me as more particularly described with remainders to several
of my brothers in different Orders.   There are upon the lands,
sets of Slaves, stocks, etc. for the management of Virginian
estates.   Such of my brothers as become entitled at my decease
shall have no benefit in any other part of my real and personal
Estate.   As for certaine parts of my real and personal I leave to
my brother John in trust.   Such of my brothers as are entitled

by my father's Will shall have no share from the sale of lands or the residue of my estate unless they bring into Hotch Potch, the lands to which they succeed on my death, and all the Slaves, Stock, etc. To Edward Athawes, merchant of St. Martins lane, Cannon Street, £100. To my laundress, Anne Miller, £10 after my debts and demands are paid. To Anne, eldest daughter of said laundress, £10 and all my linnen. To Ralph Boot, who has waited upon me, my cast off clothing. To Charles Erskine, Esq., of Lincoln's Inn my MS. notes taken in the Courts of Westminster, and my Common place Book, 8 fol. vols. To Matthew Robinson Morris, Esq., of Kent my Milton's Works. To his brother Thomas, Clarendon's History, and to Morris Robinson of the Inner Temple the Abridgement of Cases. To Charles Pratt of the Inner Temple such of my Law Books that he has not of his own. To my friend John Mann of the hand in hand fire Office on Snow Hill £100, and nominate said John my executor as to all my effects here in England. Witnesses: Robert Livesey, Tho: Gamull, John Evans.

Trenley, 8.

[George Carter, a younger son of Robert Carter, of "Corotoman," was of the Middle Temple, and died unmarried. There are several acts in Hening in regard to his estate.]

HERBERT HAYNES of Virginia, county Gloucester, parish of Abingdon, Merchant. Will 20 January 1736–7; proved 15 December 1737. Commission issued St. Peter Cornhill, London. I empower Mr. Job Wilkes of London, Merchant, to receive my rents in and about the City and suburbs of London. Remainder to my wife Sarah Haynes and heirs forever. She and my father Thomas Haynes joint executors. Said Job Wilkes trustee for said wife. Witnesses: Thomas Shickle, Thos. Thompson, Geo. Fox. [A commission issued to Job Wilkes to administer in absence of Sarah Haynes the relict, and to Thomas Haynes, the father, now respectively residing in Virginia.]

Wake, 275.

[In 1738, the Assembly ordered the establishment of a warehouse, upon the old plantation of Thomas Haynes, gentleman, deceased, on Eastermost River, Gloucester county, this was probably the father named in the will. He must have died soon after his son. There is on record in York county, a deed dated August 18, 1746, from John Thruston, "of the town and county of Gloucester, merchant," in behalf of Martha Haynes, an infant daughter of Herbert Haynes, deceased, by Sarah, formerly wife of said Herbert Haynes, and now wife of said Thruston. Mrs. Sarah Thruston, died May 12, 1786 aged 69. She was the daughter of Captain Robert and Sarah Mynne, of Abingdon Parish, Gloucester county; was born September 15, 1716, Married (1) March 19, 1730, William Dalton, (2) Herbert Haynes, (3) Col. John Thruston. It is believed that members of this family removed to Prince George and Amelia counties, and thence to North Carolina, where the name has been prominent.]

HUGH HEYES [Hayes in Probate Act, and described as of Presbury, Cheshire]. Will 17 April 1637; proved 12 May 1637. To my mother Alice Heyes £20 by £4 a year, any residue to James Heyes als Mackrin her grandchild. To my brother James Heyes my horse and saddle. To his son John, my godson 50s, and to each other child of his 20s. apeece. To my sister Margerie £10 by 50s. yearly, any residue to Ellin Bacchus, daughter to my sister Mary, deceased. To James Heyes als Mackrin 20s. To the son of my Cozen William Stone in Virginia, my godson, a cow and her increase which I left in his ffather's hands. Residue in England and Virginia to the children of my sister Margarett Bannaster, the wife of Benjamin Bannaster, and to the forenamed Ellen Bacchus equally. Executors: My brother in law, Benjamin Bannester. Witnesses: Tobias Parnell, Robte. Bulkeley.

Goare, 79.

[William Stone, referred to was probably the person who was later Governor of Maryland.]

JOSEPH INGRAM, bound for Virginia. Will 6 October 1651; proved 22 September 1653. To my sister Anne Smith £5. To my brother Robert Ingram and Mary his wife £7. To my brother John Ingram £4. To my sister Hester £4. To my brother William Ingram £3. To the poor of my native town of St. Iues [Ives] 40s. Residue to Anne Smith, daughter to my Sister, Anne Smith. Executor: My Father Robert Ingram. Witnesses: Robert Ingram, Jun., John Ingram, John Blyhton. [Note: This is one of the four years (1650, 1653, 1654 and 1662) in which the Probate Acts books of the Prerogative Court of Canterbury are still missing—L. W.]

Brent, 367.

WILLIAM HARDICH, late of Nominy in the County of Westmoreland in Virginia, gent, and now of the Citty of Bristoll, in England. Will 24 October 1668; proved 8 January 1668–9. Estate in England, debts due from my brother in lawe Mr. Augustin Hull, and Adventures and Merchandizes all or vpon the Seas; and to wife Margarett £150, if she perform other will of this date relating to estate in Virginia. To sister Alice Foster £3, and to her three children Jane, Margarett, and John 10s. each. To sister Elizabeth Boyce 20s. To Dorothy Gyle and Mary Penyman 5s a Peece. To brother Thomas Hardich best Hatt. To executors 20s. a peece to buy Gold Rings with Deathes heads. To sonn William Hardich my Gelding and two Saddles and bridles, and my Gold Ring, all apparell, except best Hatt to brother Thomas Hardich, one Featherbedd with new Ticke, boulster, Two Pillowes, Rugg, Three paires newest sheets, bedstead, Matt, Seabedd, boulster, Rug and Pillow, Sea Chest, Case of great Screw bottles, new Trunke, little Trunke, Two Gunnes, little Brasse pott and Potthookes, and conferme vnto him great Silver Flaggon and Bowle I formerly gaue him, and caused his name to be putt upon them to witness that they were his. To daughter Elizabeth Wynston 2500 pounds of Tobacco and Caske, Two hogsheads whereof is sweete scented, all due from Robert Streete of Virginia, Planter, all sent for this voyage to be delivered to Mr. Hull for my vse, and Tobacco to be delivered vnto her vpon arrival, to buy Plate with, she freeing all Dutyes. Rest to said son William at 21, to be employed by executors during minority, he to continue in England in some Civill and Honest house, his schooling and Education according to his quality, and before 21 undertake a voyage for Virginia, executor to send an Adventure of £50 with him for my Executors in Virginia, and also provisions to be made for second voyage during his nonage, etc. If he die, then to daughter Elizabeth Wynston. Will touching estate in Virginia and Maryland of even date, of which Brother in law Mr. Augustin Hull and Cosen Thomas Youle are executors, to be observed as executors of will of estate in England.

216

Overseers: Thomas Burges of Citty of Bristoll, Chirurgeon, and sonne in law Robert Wynston. Witnesses: Frances Bell, James Bell, Thomas Boyce, Ja: Fulwood.

Coke, 6.

[This name is spelled in the Virginia records, variously Hardidge and Hardich. The testator, who was born about 1618, came early to Maryland, where he received pay as a soldier in 1642 and bore an active part in the disturbances of Richard Ingle, in 1645, and was evidently of the Puritan party. He is then described as a tailor. He shortly after removed to Virginia and settled in Westmoreland county. He accumulated a large estate. He married (1) Elizabeth, daughter of Thomas Sturman, formerly of Maryland and afterwards of Westmoreland, and (2) before May 16, 1659, Margaret, daughter of Col. Nathaniel Pope, of Westmoreland county. He probably had no issue by second marriage. William and Elizabeth (Sturman) Hardidge had a son William Hardidge, of Westmoreland county, who was member of the House of Burgesses 1685, 1686, 1688, 1691, 1692 and 1693. He married Frances—it seems probable that she was the daughter of Dr. Thomas Gerrard, and that she had previously married (1) Col. Thomas Speke, (2) Col. Valentine Peyton, (3) Captain John Appleton. They had one child and heiress, Elizabeth Hardidge, born 1678, died February 25, 1722, who married Col. Henry Ashton. Her tomb remains at "Booth's," originally an Hardidge estate in Westmoreland county.]

FRANCIS DANDRIDGE, lodging at Sant Benwell's, Stafford Row near Buckingham Gate, St. George the Martyr, gent. Will 21 February 1763; proved 19 November 1765. To my wife Elizabeth household goods. To my nephew William, son of my late brother William Dandridge, my gold watch. To my said wife £200. To James Nares, Doctor of Musick, and George Nares, Serjeant at Law, £50 each. To my neece Mary, daughter of my late Sister Mary Langbourne, £20. To Ralph, son of late brother Bartholomew Dandridge, £20. To Ellinor, daughter of late tenant John West of King Street, Covent Garden £10. Residue to said James Nares and George Nares in Trust and pay profits to my said wife during her life and after as follows. To Mrs. Frances Dandridge, widow of my late brother John Dandridge, £600 in 4% Bank Stock. To Mary Langbourne, daughter of my late sister Mary Langbourne, £500, and if she die before Stock becomes assignable, then to transfer to William,

son of my brother William Dandridge, Bartholomew and William,
and sons of my sister Mary Langborne. To ——— Danzey,
daughter of my late brother William, £100, To Ralph, son of
my late brother John, £100. To William Dandridge, son of my
late brother Bartholomew, now living with William Langborne
in York River, Virginia, as his clerk, £300. If said William
happen to die before he attains the age of 21, then to said ———
Danzey, Bartholomew, son of John, and William, son of Bartholomew, equally. Remainder of Government Securities to Nephew
William Langbourne, son of late sister Mary, and said William,
son of my brother William Dandridge, equally. Executors:
Said James and George Nares and my wife. Witness: John
Claridge, Symonds Inn. Mary Holmes of Chelsea, spinster, and
Elizabeth Nicholson, spinster, attest the signature before Arthur
Collier, Surrogate, 16 November, 1765.

Rushworth, 408.

[The testator's two brothers, John Dandridge, father of Mrs. Washington, and William Dandridge, were well known residents of Virginia. The existence of a fourth brother, Bartholomew, who probably
did not come to Virginia, has not before been noted. Mary, a sister of these brothers, married Robert Langborne, of Fetter Lane,
London. The tomb of their son William Langborne (who was born
October 2, 1723, died March 19, 1796, and married Susannah, daughter
of Augustine Smith, of "Shooters Hill," Middlesex county, Virginia),
is in King William county, Virginia. The tomb bears *two chevrons* for
Langborne, impaling a *lion's head between three mascles,* for Dandridge. They had issue: 1, Mary, married Warner Throckmorton;
11, William, entered the Revolutionary army, April 27, 1777. On
October 6, 1783, by a complimentary resolution, Congress gave William Langborne the brevet commission of Lieutenant Colonel
He married Elizabeth Dandridge, daughter of William Dandridge
Claiborne, and had two children, who died without issue. Col Wm.
Dandridge, brother of the testator, had a daughter Ann, who married Thomas Dansie or Dancie, and died without issue. Her will was
proved March 21, 1782, in Spotsylvania county.]

218

VIRGINIA GLEANINGS IN ENGLAND.

Communicated by Mr. LOTHROP WITHINGTON, 30 Little Russell street,
W. C., London (including "Gleanings" by Mr. H. F. WATERS,
not before printed).

ELIZABETH GRONOUS of St. Clement Danes, county Middlesex, Spinster, surviving daughter and Heir at Law of James
Gronous, late of same parish and county, and sole surviving
executrix of his Will. Will 14 August 1749; proved 6 June
1750. To be buried in Bunhill Fields by my said father, and
that his name and name of second wife Theodosia Gronous be
inscribed. All freeholds in county Radnor, my farm at Norton
excepted, in occupation of Thomas Partridge, to my brother in law
Edward Branston of London, Sugar Refiner, and Edward Lewis
of Copthal Court, gent, in Trust for sale. To my cousin Sir
Charles Peyton, Bart., £100. To my cousin Mary Peyton
£3000. To my cousin Elizabeth Peyton £100. To my cousin
William Probert of Potome River, county Worcester in Virginia,
£300. If said William die before me, then to his children. To
my cousin Richard Barnet £100. To cousin John Barnet £150.
To cousin Margaret Rogers of Kington, county Hereford, £250.
To cousin Ann Gronous and to Mrs. Mary Davis, neice to said
Edward Lewis, £50 apeece. To cousin Anne Roberts £20.
To John and Mary Taylor, son and daughter of John Taylor, late

From Vol. XVI, No. 1 (July 1908), p. 63.

Button Seller, £10 apeece. To all the children of said Anna Roberts sums hereafter mentioned, viz: To Philip Bodham Roberts, her eldest son, £100. To Charles, Elizabeth, Anna, and Martha Roberts £200 apeece. To William Smallwood, St. Clement Danes, Button seller, £10. To each of my servants £10. To my aunt Frances Probart £18 yearly. To Mary Pritchard of Clyro, county Radnor, annuity of one guinea. Whereas Edward Gronous, first cousin to my said father, claims some right to said farm at Norton, I direct my executors to lay the Writings before two eminent Counsel, and, if said Counsel be of opinion that said Edward has good right, to put him into immediate possession. If said Counsel are against his right, I give said Edward an annuity of £6, and I give said farm to my right heirs. To Samuel and Martha Collins, son and daughter of my late cousin Mary Smith, £500 apeece. To my cousins Margaret, wife of William Gregory, Mary, wife of Francis Tett, and to Ann, wife of Richard Purnell, £500 apeece. To Howell Thomas, son of said Margaret Gregory, £500. To Mrs. Mary Wilson of St. Clement Danes her sister's pictures. To Mr. John Lowe of Park Hall, county Derby, his brother's picture. To said Howell Thomas my father's picture. To Edward Barnston and Edward Lewis, executors, £100 apeece, and to them in trust £1600 to make good any breach of Trust my father, as a Trustee named in Will of my Uncle Philip Bodham, may have been guilty of. After settlement of claims, residue of said £1600 to Robert Crowe and Francis Dalton, executors of Edward Bodham, executor of said Philip Bodham. Residue of my estate to said William Probart or to his children, and to said Elizabeth Peyton, Richard Barnet, John Barnet, and Margaret Rogers equally, provided that my estate does not fall short, to pay all debts, annuities, and legacies. Witnesses: Thomas Tyrrill, Thomas Marth, Paul Porter, all of Richmond, Surrey.

Greenly, 198.

[The testator was probably of a Welsh family. A Thomas Gronows, of London, Esquire, was sheriff of Radnorshire in 1733. Sir Charles Peyton, who is referred to, succeeded to the baronetcy (held under a mistaken claim) on the death, in 1748, of his uncle Sir Yelverton Peyton, a naval officer, who was long in service on the Virginia station. Sir Charles died in 1760. He was a son of Bladwell Peyton, who married Mary, daughter of William Probart, Esq., of Cant Evengewenge, Radnorshire. Baldwell Peyton was a son of Charles Peyton, a younger brother of Major Robert Peyton, of Virginia. When the elder line failed, the baronetcy was assumed, in the belief that Robert Peyton had left no issue, by the descendants of this younger brother Charles.

There is of course, no county of Worcester, in Virginia, and the Maryland county of the name is not on the Potomac, so it is uncertain whether the testator has mistaken in writing "Potomac," or intended to say Westmoreland county, Virginia. The family of Probert seems to have been of some consequence. Among the sheriffs of Radnorshire, were William Probert, of Llanddwei, 1675; Henry Probert, Esq., of Llowes, 1680, and William Probert, Esq., of Llanddwei, 1691. Marshall states that there is a pedigree of Probert in Dwinn's Visitations of Wales, I, 267]

THOMAS BROOKS of Plaistow, county Essex, gent. Will 10 September 1744; proved 27 January 1745-6. The lease of house on Stepney Causeway, furniture, plate, coach, chariot, horses, to my wife. All the rest of property to be sold, and the money invested in some public stock, and of the produce two thirds to my wife during widowhood, the other third to education of my daughter Elizabeth, paid to my wife for that purpose. If said daughter should marry, then wife to have whole Estate, paying to daughter £1000 for Portion. If said daughter survives said wife, then whole estate to said daughter, and after her decease to her children, share and share as they arrive at the age of 21. If daughter dies without issue, then to my cousin Thomas Brooks of Ratcliff, Ship Chandler, £500. To each of my executors £21. To said executors £600 in trust to remit the produce thereof to my sister Ann Dawson, wife of Ben Dawson in Virginia, in such goods as she shall require or order (notwithstanding her Coverture). After her decease Stock of £600 to be sold and divided between children of said Ann Dawson. To the children of my cousin Dorothy, eldest daughter of my late sister Johanna Edwards, which children she had by her late husband Joseph Gregory, £150 equally between them. To the children of my cousin Anna, second daughter of my late sister Johanna, £150 to be divided between them. To the children of my cousin Elizabeth, third daughter of my late sister Johanna, which she had by her late husband Joseph Brookes, £150. To Mildred, daughter of my late brother Joseph Brookes, £20. To the children of my half brother Jonathan Brookes £400. To the children of my half sister Elizabeth Dawson £250. To my said half sister Elizabeth Dawson the interest of £100 to be remitted to her in such goods as she shall desire. After her death, said sum to be divided amongst her children. To the Brethren of the Corporation of the Trinity House £100 for the use of their poor. To my executors £100 in trust to pay the interest to the Society of Masters of Ships held at the Bell Tavern in Eastcheap, London, for benefit of their widows, so long as said Society shall pay at least £6 per annum to each widow and no longer. Residue to my brother in law Sir Robert Willmott, Knight and Alderman of London, and heirs for ever, and appoint him sole executor and guardian to my daughter Elizabeth. [Signed Thomas Brookes, and unwitnessed.] [On the 25th of January, 1745-6, James Spear and Thomas Anderson make oath that they are well acquainted with the Testator's handwriting and that they declare their belief in the authenticity of the signiture.]

Edmonds, 3.

ALLAN GOODFELLOW of London, Yeoman, now bound to Virginia. Will 22 Sept. 1636; proved 21 May 1638. To my mother Anne Goodfellow £10. To my brother Chris: Goodfellow £50. To my Brother William Goodfellow £20. To my Brother John Goodfellow £5. To my sister Mary Goodfellow £5. To my Brother Edward Goodfellowe 12d. To my sister Anne Rainscroft, wife of Mr. Rainscroft Upholder, 20s. To my sister Elizabeth Goodfellow 20s. To my friend Joane Newman, wife of John Newman, 50s. Residuary legatee and Executor: Chrisopher Goodfellow my Brother. Witnesses: Hen: King Scr: Thomas Burton, John Walker.

Lee, 61.

ROBERT ROANE of Chaldon, Surrey, Gent. Will 10 May, 1672; proved 5 May, 1676. Laus Anima mea Dominum. To son Charles Roane and to his Child or Children, if any, £600, and discharge him and them of all sums paid for his vse since his transport to Virginia. To his Wife Mrs. Frances Roane £20. To his Sonn Robert Roane £100 if his father be lyving and

Robert likewise. To son Thomas Roan and heirs, and in default to son Charles, my Mannor of Tollesworth in Parishes of Chaldon and Mestham, Surrey, and Moiety of Plate, goods, etc at Tollesworth, and all Books, Bedding, etc in my Chambers at Whitehall, and ditto of Lynnen and Plate there, also the Fee Farme rent of the Rectory of Oundle, County Northampton, lately purchased of his Maties trustees. To Mrs. Elizabeth Worseley Lease of Mannor of Freyrens. paying £30 yearly to my daughter Susan Gatton and Grandchildren Robert and Sarah Davy, also rents, etc. To daughter Elizabeth Askew £150, two flaxen sheetes, and keeping of my fine large holland sheete for her own and her sisters use. To daughter Susan Gatton £20 and £10 yearly out of Freyrens. To Daughter Lucy Roane, all lands in Northshowbery and Southshowbery, Essex, with Rectory, glebe, and tithes of Northshowbery and all Quitrents and Fee farme rents in Essex, also £300 on day of marriage. If she marry without consent of my executors, and of my cousin Thos. Roane Esq. the lands to be vested in my executors, and the proceeds to be distributed among my grandchildren then living. To my grandchildren, viz: Sarah Davy £200 also £10 yearly from manor of Freyrens; to Robert Davy £100 and £10 from said manor, to Thomas and Robert Askew, sons of my daughter Elizabeth, £150; and to each other grandchild £40. To nephew Thomas Roane of Southwark his two children and his niece Jane Turner, £5 apeece. To Robert and Katherin Daniell, children of nephew John Daniells £5 apeece. To Anne Burtock £5, Robert Meares £5, John Meares £5, and my kindred in and about Fodringhay in Northamptonshire, £5. To Elizabeth Burtock, wife of Thomas Carr, £6 yearly. To poor of Fodringhay 40s. yearly for ever out of Rectory of Oundle on 1st of January. To Marguret Gibson £5 out of said Reading. To poore of Chaldon 20s. yearly forever out of mannor to Tollesworth. To Minister of Chaldon 40s., and to the Clerke 10s. To Kinswoman Mrs. Mary May £5. To Patience and Richard, children of Richard Bowman, and to his sister Katherin Judrey, £5 each. To Kinsman Thomas·Roane of Wellingborow, Esquire, my little clock in my chamber at Whitehall, and to his daughter the China bason was my aunt Piggotts. To my daughter in law Mrs. Hall and Mrs. Upington a gold ring each. To Mrs. Anne Ginse, £10. To Patience Upington my silver watch. To goddaughter Mary Upington my silver candlestick. To friends Mr. George Perryer, Mr. Roger Lambert, and Mr. Thomas Landon the Elder, £10 each. To be buried at Chaldon. Residue five parts to my five children aforesaid and a sixth part divided betwixt my grandchildren Sarah and Robert Davy. Executors: George Perryer, Roger Lambert, and Thomas Landon aforesaid. Witnesses: William Harinston, Robert Mawer, Clem: Oxenbridg, Oliver Hering. Memorandum. Codicil dated 15 November 1675. Witnesses: Jacob Bosworth, Daniell Alford, servants to Geor. Perryer, Scr. Confirms the grant to Elizabeth Burlock, wife of Thomas Carr, of £6. To poor of Foddinghay 40s. yearly for ever. To Margaret Gibson £5 a year; also the lease of Freyrens to Mrs. Elizabeth Worsley. If daughter Lucy Roane marry without consent, Rectory of North Showberry to be sold for grandchildren. 2d. Codicil dated 26 February 1675–6. Witnesses: Thomas Roane, Henry Tillingham, James Short. All sums of money remaining of my estate after payment of legacies to my daughters Elizabeth Askew and Susan Gatton and grandchildren Robert and Sarah Davy. Robert Roane. Sarah Davy, to have the Sheets at Tolesworth and in the cheste in Thames Streete, rest to daughters Elizabeth Askew and daughter Gatton except fine holland sheete to Elizabeth Worsely and two shells to Elizabeth Buttock.

Bence, 55.

[Charles Roane, the son of the testator, came to Virginia as early as 1664, and Settled in Gloucester county, where some of his descendants still remain. The following grants to him appear in the Land Books:

(1) Charles Roane, 200 acres in Gloucester, adjoining Col. Lee's land, Pianketank Swamp, Rappahannock Road, &c., Sept. 13, 1664.

(2) Charles Roane, 100 acres in Gloucester on the branches of Pianketank River, adjoining Col. Warner's land, Dec. 6, 1665.

(3) Mr. Charles Roane, 401 acres in Charles City county on Kittewan Creek (north side). The "Oystershell landing on Mapsco Creek," mentioned as one of the boundary marks, August 7, 1667.

(4) Mr. Charles Roane, 50 acres of marsh land on the south side of Kittewan Creek, beginning at the lowermost end of Weyanock on James River, August 7, 1667.

(5) Charles Roane, 100 acres in Gloucester on the branches of Dragon Swamp, adjoining John Whittmore's land, "then along a line supposed be that of Col. Lee's children," Oct. 20, 1673.

(6) Charles Roane, 700 acres in Gloucester, on Dragon Swamp, adjoining the lands of James Reynolds, Thomas Dawkins and Richard Holloway, and those of Roger Shackleford and Mr. John Carver (formerly Samuel Partridge's). Dawkin's land formerly belonged to Edward Ross. John Whittmore's land also adjoined, April 23, 1681.

(7) Mr. Charles Roane of Gloucester county, 797 acres, part in New Kent [new King and Queen] and part in Gloucester. Five hundred acres thereof was bought by Mr. Roane from Edward Ross and Samuel Partridge, being part of a patent of 5,380 acres granted to Col. Cuthbert Potter, June 20, 1659 and by said Potter sold to said Ross and Partridge. The remainder, 297 acres, now first taken up. Beginning at a branch called Hanks Folly in sight of Charles Roane and Hanks, his old plantation; adjoining George Martin's and John Kelly's plantations and Dragon Swamp. Oct. 20, 1688.

(8) Charles Roane, 164 acres in Gloucester adjoining his own old dividend, and the land of William Brooking, Oct. 20, 1691.

(9) Mr. Charles Roane, 278 acres in Petsoe [Petsworth] Gloucester, adjoining Cole's branch, the swamp of Poropotanck Creek, the land of Col. Richard Lee, the main road to the Dragon Swamp, and "Mr. Brooking's land, Oct. 20, 1908.

In the report made of the loyalist sufferers in Bacon's Rebellion it is stated that one of them was "Mr. Charles Roane one that had his dwelling House and other Houses Burnt downe to the ground, and most part of his goods and provisions destroyed and carried away by a party of the Rebells Commanded [by] Gregory Walkate after Bacon's death."

On account of the destruction of the records of Gloucester county, and of the register of Petsworh parish,there is at present no positive information as to the children of Charles Roane; but there can be no doubt that William Roane, "of Petsworth Parish, Gloucester County," who in June, 1726, bought land in Essex county, was one of his sons. A short time after this purchase, William Roane removed to Essex and was ancestor of Judge Spencer Roane, and other prominent men of the name.

From Manning & Bray's *History of Surrey County, England*, vol. 2, p. 445 (Psh. of Chaldon). In the Parish Church, "on a stone in the middle aisle: 'Here lieth the body of Mr. Thomas Roane, of this Parish, gentleman, who departed this life the 28th of July, 1689, aged 39 years. *Arms:* 3 bucks horned trippant, impaling 3 gloves.'"

On another stone: "Here lieth the body of Mrs. Elizabeth, wife of Mr. Robert Roane, citteson of London, and daughter of Henry Bartelot, Esqr., who departed this life the 10th of August, 1701, in the 30th year of her age. Arms same as before."

Vol. 2, page 446, states that "Robert Roane, Gent, of the Parish of Chaldon, by will decimo die mensis Maii, ammo Dom. Millesimo sexcentessimo Septuagesimo secundo" vested one pound in money in the Minister of parish for the relief of the poor of the parish.

(The above is all that is given about people named *Roane* under Chaldon psh. which is treated in Vol. 2, pp–440–447 incl).

Thomas and Robert Roane, named in these epitaphs were sons of the testator and brothers of the emigrant to Virginia.

The psh. of Merstham adjoins Chaldon on the West, and is treated in this work on pp. 252–265, incl. There is no reference whatever to the name *Roane* under this parish, nor elsewhere in the 3 vols. of Manning & Bray's History of Surrey, except what has been given above from the parish. of Chaldon.]

WILLIAM LOCKLEY [not William Locksley] of Prince George County, Virginia, merchant. Will 4 February 1738; proved 8 June 1745, To my two children Elizabeth and Ann Lockley, and their heirs, my freehold and Meeting House with ground and appurtenances in poor Jury Lane als Crutched Fryars, parish St. Katherine Cree Church and Christ Church in London, in occupation of Solomon Gosfright, Philip Sanderson, and John Glover, expectant on the death of my mother Elizabeth Studley, wife of Joseph Studley of Nicholas Lane, London, gentleman. To my two dear children Henrietta and Emilia Lockley all my real and personal estate in the Colony of Virginia or these American parts at the age of 21. I appoint my wife Margaret Fraunces Lockley, sole executor. Witnesses: Law'r Biggins, Arthur Biggins, William Biggins.

Seymer, 173.

NICHOLAS DICKSON, York town, Virginia, but late of Bristoll. Administration 20 April 1770 to Charlotte, the relict.

Admon Act Book, 1770.

PAUL GUTTERIDGE, belonging to King's ship "Benjamin." Administration 18 August 1702 to Thomas Goodrich Barnes, guardian of Richard Gutteridge, the son of deceased, a minor, now in Virginia.

Admon Act Book, 1702.

EDWARD MARIA WINGFIELD, ESQUIRE [prisoner in the Fleet and the ex-governor of Virginia]. Mense Julii 1661. Decimo quinto die emanavit commissio Dorotheæ Wingfeild Relictæ Edwardi Mariæ Wingfeild nuper de Keyston in Comitatu Huntington Armigeri sed in Carcere vocat. The Fleete decedentis etc. habentis etc. Ad Administranda bona iura et credita dicti defuncti de bene etc. vigore Commissionis Jurat.

Admon Act Book, 1661, Folio 72.

[Edward Maria Wingfield, sometime President of Virginia, was born about 1560, and could hardly have been the man who died in the Fleet in 1661. Neill in his *Virginia Vetusta*, p. 9, quotes an order of Parliament authorizing the sale by Edward Maria Wingfield of Keston in the county of Huntingdon, of part of his estate. Mr. Brown, (*Genesis*, II, 1054), thinks that this was one of the Kimbolton branch of the family and not the Virginian. No doubt the man who died in the Fleet was the same person referred to by Neill].

TOBIAS HANDFORD, late of Parish of Ware in the Countie of Gloucester in Virginia, gent, nowe of London, gent. Will 14 April, 1677; proved 22 December, 1677. One third of estate in Virginia to wife Elizabeth Handford for life, and other two thirds to sonn Tobias Handford and daughters Elizabeth and Mary Handford. To son Tobias wife's third at her decease. Goods in Virginia to wife Elizabeth Handford, son Tobias Handford, and daughters Elizabeth and Mary Handford. If son Tobias become possessed of Manor of Shobden, County Hereford, in England, his legacy of personal estate in Virginia to be void, and he to maintain wife Elizabeth Handford and two daughters, Elizabeth and Mary till 21 or marriage. If children all die before 21, then estate in Virginia to wife for life, then to Brother John Handford, and at his decease to his Son Richard Handford. Executors: Wife, Brother John Handford, and Captain William Smith of Cittie of Bristoll. Witnesses: John Chambers, Pub. No'ry, Jon Smith, his Servant, Jno Robinson, servant to John Handford. [St. George Botolph Lane, Probate Act Book.]

Hale, 128.

[See this Magazine, VIII, 199–200, for will of John Handford, Esq., father of this testator.]

VIRGINIA GLEANINGS IN ENGLAND.

Communicated by Mr. LOTHROP WITHINGTON, 30 Little Russell street,
W. C., London (including "Gleanings" by Mr. H. F. WATERS,
not before printed).

ROBERT TERRELL of the City of London, Merchant.   Will
20 October 1677; proved 23 November 1677.   To Cosen William
Terrell, sonn of brother William Terrell, £10.   To Cosen ——
Terrell, daughter of ditto, £5.   To Cosen Mary Alpen £10.
To Cosen John Alpen £5.   To friend Mr. Robert Vaulx,
Merchant, £10.   To brother Richmond Terrell 10s for ring.
To friend Mrs. Elizabeth Wickens the elder £10.   Executor
not to be charged with legacies till accounts with Mr. Johnson
and others in Virginia shall be settled.   To sister Mary Mew
bigger silver Cupp.   Executor to deliver to brother Richmond
Terrell small silver Cupp and Three silver spoones I now have

of his.   Overseer: Mr. Robert Vaulx, merchant, to be assisting to executor in stating Virginia and other accounts.   Rest to Cosen Robert Alpen, Citizen and Cooke of London, executor. Lands in county of Hampshire or elsewhere to said Cosen Robert Alpen.   Witnesses: Antho: Horsmanden, Richard Wicking, John Wicking, Elizabeth Wicking.   [St. Nicholas Cole Abbey, Probate Act Book.]

Hale, 120.

[Though the testator was a member of the Fishmonger's Company, it is evident that his business was that of Virginia merchant.   Many years before the date of the will he appears to have resided in Virginia.   Robert Terrell was a witness to a deed in York Co., January 24, 1647.   There is on record in York a power of attorney from John Wiskers (or Wiskens) and John Robinson, merchants of London, to Robert Terrell, citizen and fishmonger of London, authorizing him to collect all debts due them in Virginia.   In the same county is a power of attorney from Robert Terrell, citizen and fishmonger of London, intending to take a voyage to England, appointing Thomas Williamson his attorney in Virginia.

Although the will does not specifically say so there can be no doubt that the brothers William and Richmond Terrell lived in Virginia. There is among the manuscripts of this Society a deed dated April 29, 1670, from Richmond Terrell of New Kent county to Henry Wyatt, conveying 600 acres.   The deed reserves "100 acres formerly given unto my brother William Terrell and since by him sold to Francis Waring."

On account of the destruction of the records of New Kent, King and Queen, King William and in part of Hanover, it has never been possible to prepare more than a fragmentary account of the Terrells.   The descendants of Richmond Terrell lived in Louisa, Hanover, &c., and some notices of them are given in the *William and Mary Quarterly* XIII, 263-265.   The register of St. Peters parish, New Kent, contains only two early Terrell entries; the baptisms of two sons of Timothy Terrell, viz: Robert on December 25, 1697 and Joseph December 31, 1699.   Timothy Terrell was probably a son of Richmond.   The name Timothy suggests a possible relationship to the family of Tyrrell of Thornton and Oakley, Bucks, England.

The descendants of William Terrell are much more numerous than those of Richmond and more has been published in regard to them ; but the early generations which have been given are not supported by any reference to authorities and are evidently entirely traditional. Most of the members of this branch of the family became Quakers, and from the admirable records kept by the Society of Friends, much information can be obtained in regard to these Terrells from a date as early as 1735.   See Bell's *Our Quaker Friends.*

Following are abstracts of early land grants to the Terrrells: (1) " Mr.

229

Richmond Terrell" 640 acres in New Kent on the S. W. side of York River, November 28, 1658; (2) Richmond Tirrell 600 acres on Chickahominy River in New Kent, February 8, 1670; (3) Robert Tirrell 170 acres in St. Stephens parish, New Kent, on the north side of Mattapony River, April 20, 1682; (4) Mrs. Elizabeth Terrell and Thomas Correll 720 acres in New Kent on the south side of York River, November 20, 1683; (5) Robert Terrell 63 acres in Middlesex on a branch of Parrott's Creek, October 24, 1701; (6) William Terrell 300 acres on the S. E. side of Pole Cat Swamp, King William county June 16, 1714; (7) William Terrell 100 acres on the north side of Pamunkey in King William county, March 22, 1715; (8) William Terrell 400 acres on a fork of Pole Cat Swamp, October 31, 1716; (9) William Terrell and Robert Chandler 300 acres on a fork of Pole Cat Swamp, April 1, 1717; (10) William Terrell and his son William Terrell, 400 acres on Pole Cat Swamp, King William Co., March 18, 1718; (11) William Tyrrell, Jr., 174 acres on Pole Cat Swamp, King William, July 12, 1718; (12) William Terrell of New Kent Co., 400 acres on Pole Cat Swamp, King William Co., January 22, 1718; (13) Joel Terrell of King William, 400 acres in St. Margaret's parish, King William, July 9, 1724; (14) William Terrell, Sr., of New Kent, 220 acres on Pole Cat Swamp, King William Co., January 22, 1718; (15) William Terrell of King William, 237 acres on Pole Cat Swamp, St. Margaret's parish, King William, February 22, 1724; (16) Joseph Terrell of New Kent, 400 acres in Hanover county, September 7, 1729; (17) John Terrell of Caroline county, 400 acres in Spotsylvania county, on the north side of Rapidan River, September 28, 1730; (18) Richmond Terrell 450 acres in Hanover, April 12, 1732.

Robert Vaulx the "overseer" was a prominent merchant of London and Virginia, and Anthony Horsmanden, one of the witnesses, was brother of Warham Horsmanden of Virginia.]

SILVESTER ALLIN of the Tower Liberty, London. Will 26 August 1635; proved 22 March 1635-6. Being bound on a voyage to Virginia, doe make my wife attorney. Witness 3rd July 1635 Edward Anivey, Fra: Lacy. Mem. That the sd Silvester Allin dying at sea in the ship Transport being bound for Virginia. Leave all to my wife and ordain her executrix. Witnesses: Francis Clarke, John Turway.

Pile, 26.

JOHN BEAUCHAMP, Saint Giles without Cripplegate, London, Merchant. Will 30 November 1668; proved 17 September 1668. To friend Gilbert Platt, my three brothers and sister and her husband, my Vncle Mr. James Jauncy, and Samuel Fisher, and Mr. Jennings, and John Taylor and his wife, mourning rings, and ditto to Mr. William Fisher in Virginia, and ditto also to friends Mr. Thomas Walton, Mr. Crewes, Collonell Stagge, and Mr. George Jorden. Rest of estate, goods, lands, in Virginia and England, in fower parts, three parts to brother Richard, and Abell Beauchamp, and sister Mary Sampson, wife of John Sampson, and of other part £100 to uncle Mr. James Jauncy, and residue to brother William Beauchamp, and said brother William in regard to being named as an executor, not to take advantage of satisfying himself before brother Richard, and Abell, and sister Mary. Executors: Vncle Mr. James Jauncy and brother William Beauchamp. Witnesses: Vincent Phillipps, Elizabeth Proudman, Widd, Tho. Pounsett, scr.

Hene, 152.

[John Beauchamp, a London merchant trading with Virginia, lived for a time in the colony in Henrico county. By deed recorded in Henrico in February, 1681, William Beauchamp, citizen and vintner of London, heir to his brother John Beauchamp, late of James River, deceased, sold to John Pleasants the plantation in Henrico, formerly owned by John Beauchamp, named Borrow and containing 630 acres.

Gilbert Platt, who is styled "gentleman" in a deed of 1679, died in Henrico where his will was proved in June, 1692. James Crews also lived in Henrico, and was executed for taking part in Bacon's Rebellion, (see this Magazine, IV, 122, 123). Thomas Walton lived, it is believed, in Isle of Wight county. Col. Thomas Stagge was Auditor-General of Virginia, and George Jordan at one time Attorney General.

This is another of the numerous instances in which London merchants whose trade was with Virginia, owned land and occasionally lived in the colony. This was, of course, bound to strengthen the tie between Virginia and her mother city.]

MARY ROBINSON of Marke Lane, London, widdowe, parish Saincte Olaves, Hartstreete, London. Will 13 February 1617–18; proved 26 September 1618. To be buried in church of St. Olaves without Pompe, etc. To poore children of Christes Hospitall £100. To Hospitall in Smithfield for poore sick folkes £50. To Hospitall of Southwarke called Saint Thomas for poore and sicke people there £50. To poor prisoners of New-gate, Ludgate, the two counters in London, the Marshalsey, the Kinges Bench, the white Lyonne, the counter in Southwarke £10 each place. To the poore of St. Olaves £20. To poor of Stepney parishe £20. To 80 poor women 3 yards of good cloth of 3 shillings per yard. To my maide servants black gowns of

13s 4d the yard and 40s. To Godaye Howell ditto. To brother Nicholas Wanton of York £100. To John Leare, Mathewe Joyner, Elizabeth Deakon, Anne Edwardes, all children of my sister Leare, deceased, £50 each. To Edward Wanton £20. For sermon in St. Olaves every Sabbath afternoon for two yeares £100, 20s each preacher. To said church guilte cupp I did lende to the Communion. To Mr. Sampson our Parson £50 and to be present at Buriall and have no Ringing but the bell to the Sermon and the knell. To Mayor and Bayliffs of Towne of Monmouth £150 for a stocke, for £12 a year to poore. To reparation of church of Monmouth and pewes and seates £50. To reparation of Wye bridge in Monmouth towne £50. To William Fortune the elder £200, and to his sister Anne Symes £100, and forgive her and her husband all debts. To Morris Fortune, late of Oxford, £40, and to his brother Walter Fortune £20, and to Morris Fortune, son of John Fortune, deceased, £20, and to his sisters Anne and Blanch Fortune £10 each. To Mary Fortune, widow of John Fortune of Monmouth, £20. To John Higgens als. Pemberton, Armorer, £40. To my sister Ramsey, widow, £50. To her son John Ramsey £100 to be delivered to Master and Wardens of Company of Grocers. To Cosen Margaret Binne, wife of William Binne, £200, and forgive debts of William Binne, and £50 each to Margaret's children. To Mary Barnes, daughter of my brother Powle Barnes, £100 at marriage of 21. To every one of Israell Owen's children married or unmarried £50. To Cosen Sir John Wolstoneholme, Master Nicholas Farrer and wife, my sonn Smith and wife, Mr. Sympson our Parsonn, and wife, Mrs. Taylor late wife of Mr. Doctor Taylor, old Mr. Highlord, Mr. George Tucker of Gravesend and wife, my son John Robinson and his wife, my sister Ramsey, my cosin Eme Thayer, widdowe, my sister Owen, my sister Farrington, and my cosin Goddard and his wife, my cosin John Farrer and his wife, my cosin John Highlord and wife, my brother Yeomans and wife, Cozen John Ramsey, Cozen Bonner and wife, Cozen Butler and wife, Cozen Symes and wife, Cosen Fortune and wife, Anthony Thayer and wife, Lady Hambden my kinswoman, brother Nicholas Warton (38 persons) £5 each for mourning. To Company of Mercers £30 for a Dynner and £200 to be lente to younge men at

£50 apeece. Also to Grocers Company £200 to be lent young men Grocers. To my good frende Mr. Nicholas Farrer, Skynner, £200 in trust for such poore people as have neade. To my goddaughter Dame Joane Knowles guilte cupp of £13 13s 4d and to her sister Catherine, ditto of £6, and to their brethren John and Henry Wolstoneholm, each ditto of £5. To Cosen Blanche Jackson of Southwarke and her sister Elizabeth Cliff £10 each. To Marie Mounte, Mary Morley, Marie Marcie, Mary Belfeilde, Mary Nicholson, and Mary Simpson (goddaughters) £10 each. To daughter of Mr. George Tucker of Gravesend, my goddaughter, ditto. To my sonne John Robinson's daughter Mary and my son Smith's daughter Mary (both goddaughters) £20 each at Marriage. To Mrs. Nicholson, widdow, £20. To kinswoman Lady Hambden £100. To my cozen Sir John Wolstonholme, Knight, two best spout potts all guilte. To Company of Grocers highest standing Cupp and cover on a Turk all guilt. To Mr. Nicholas Farrer Nutt Cupp and cover on a Turk ditto. To sonn John Robinson my longe fyne Tapistrie Carpett lyned with blewe and frynged with grene silke, and a picture of Charatie with two children, and a guilte salte and Cover with pillars. To my daughter Smith one large and two square cushions of tapestrie and gould and my other best carpet of tapestrie of the twelve signes of the yeares. To my sister Yomans one large and two square cushions of Crymson satten Trymed with gold. To old Mrs. Farrer one large and two square cushions of the Story of Abraham offering his sonne Isaack. To Mrs. Taylor, wyddowe, late wife of Mr. Doctor Taylor, best gold bracelett worth £18. To my cosen Eme Thayer, widdow, ring with large Table Dyamond worth £10. To the Worshipfull Company of Mercers in this Cittie of London £500 to purchase bonds at not more than £25 expenses for 4 poor divinitie students at Cambridge, Executors with Mr. Simpson, Parson of St. Olaves Hart Street, and Sir John Wolstonholm, to dispose £500 if Mercers refuse. To Company of Grocers £500 to purchase bonds of £25 annual value for 4 poor divinitie students of St. Johns College, Oxford, etc. If Grocers refuse, the Company of Skynners to dispose of £500, etc. To Towne of Tiverton in Devon to and amongst the poore sorte of people as have latelie had their houses and goods burnte with fyer £100. To Mr. Drannte, Mr. Shepparde, Mr. Holbroke, Mr. Wotton, and Mr. Edgworth, all preachers of God's worde, £10 apeece. To Mr. Hall, Minister, that did belong to the Lady Skynner, £5. To the poore of the parishes of Buttolphes within Algate and Buttolphes without Bishopsgate, Shorditch parish, White Chappell parish, Sainct Pulchres without Newgate, Sainct Georges in Southwarke, £20 apeece for poor householders. To John Graye of Combe, my husbandes Robinsons rent gatherer, £10 to be bestowed by Executors with help of Mr. Simpson our parson etc. "Item I give and bequeath towards the helpe of the poore people in Virginia towardes the buildinge of a Church and reduceing them to the knowledge of Gode's worde the sum of two hundred poundes to be bestowed at the discretion of my cozen Sir John Wolstonholme, Knight, with the advice and consent of four others of the cheifest of Virginia Company within two yeares nexte after my decease." To Cozen Israell Owen, not to molest executor, £600. To Cozen John Weedon £50 and £50 worth of househole stuff so he staye and remain here in the house, etc. To my goddaughter and now servante Mary Nicholson £20. To servant Edmund £18. To my good friends Mr. Nicholson Farrar and his wife lease of my house at Mylend with household stuff therein, paying to my cozen William Fortune the elder £50, and request Mr. Farrar, his wife, and son John, to hold residue of lease and for my sake to permit gooddy Howell to dwell therein and to bestow victualling and fyringe unto her as heretofore for looking vnto the house in my absence. To said Cozen William Fortune the elder £150 and forgive all debts he oweth. To his sister Anne Symes for her own use £200. To Cozen John Weedon £300 more. To my brother Israell Owen £600 in discharge of legacies. To Chelsey College neare London for maintenance of god's true religion £100. To my executors, Mr. Nicholas Farrar and Mr. Thomas Smith, my sonne in lawe, being one of the Skynners, £300 each. To my tennante Henry Cooke of Fleet Street for recompense of what I had of him for Syne of a new lease. Forgive Cozen John Weedon all debts. Residue one half to Nephew John Ramsey, and one half to Cozen Margaret Binnes' children. Executors: Mr. Nicholson Farrar and Mr. Thomas Smith. Overseers: Cozen Sir John Wolston-

holme, Knighte, and Mr. John Simpson, minister.   Sealed the
16 April 1618.   Witnesses: John High Lord, junior, Zacharie
Highlord, George Nash, William Frithe.

Meade, 88.

[Mrs. Mary Robinson was the widow of John Robinson, chief searcher
of the customs at London and a member of the Virginia Company,
who died in December, 1609.   He had children by a former marriage.
She was the daughter of William Ramsey of London, grocer.   Her first
husband, John Wanton of London, gentleman, died August, 1592, and
she married John Robinson on February 26, 1593.   She was buried by
her two husbands in St. Olaves, Hart Street, London, October 13, 1618.
She was a niece of Sir William Ramsey, Lord Mayor of London, who,
with his wife Mary, daughter of William Dale, merchant of Bristol, was
a great benefactor to many charities.   Mrs. Robinson's bequest was
used to found a church in Smith's (afterwards known as Southampton)
Hundred in Virginia, a great tract of land along the Chickahominy.
When the Smith's Hundred Company was dissolved, "Mrs. Mary Robinson's Church" was probably abandoned.   In 1619 a person unknown
gave to the Virginia Company a communion cup for this church.   At
some unknown time the cup passed to Hampton (or Elizabeth City)
parish and is now the property of St. John's Church, Hampton, Va.
This cup and a small paten (also owned by St. John's) bear the date
mark 1618-19.   The cup is enscribed "The Communion Cupp For S'nt
Mary's Church in Smith's Hundred in Virginia," and the paten: "If any
man eats of this Bread he shall live for ever. Jno. VIth."   These pieces
were used at the opening service of the General Convention of the
Protestant Episcopal Church at the Church of the Holy Trinity, Richmond, Va., in 1907.   They are the oldest pieces of communion silver
which have come down from the colonial period in the United States.

Mrs. Robinson's will gives a fine example of the broad and wise liber-
ality of the old citizens of London.   Nicholas Farrer was the well known
member of the Virginia Company and the father of Nicholas and John,
who were still more prominent in its affairs.   Sir John Wolstenholme
was also long and actively interested in Virginia.   For all of these see
Brown's *Genesis*.   George Tucker of Gravesend, also a member of
the Virginia Company, was a brother of Daniel Tucker, who lived some
years in Virginia, and was afterwards Governor of Bermuda, and father
of Henry Tucker, who emigrated to Bermuda and has many descendants there, in the United States and in England.]

HENRY DERICK of the Parish of St. Stephen in the City of
Bristol, now Resident in Virginia.   Will 14 May 1677; proved
6 October 1677.   All my debts to be paid.   All my estate to be

divided between my mother Mary Derick and my wife Sarah Derick, but if my wife have a child, it is to have one third. To my Cosen Thomas Derick all my wearing Apparell. Executrix: Wife Sarah. Overseers: Mr. Phillip Hanger, Mr. Samuel Pilsworth. Witnesses: Robert Hutchinson, Thomas Cock.

[Henry Derick, late of the Parish of St. Stephen in Bristol, but deceased in Virginia, on the oath of Sarah Derrick, relict.— Probate Act Book.]

Hale, 98.

ELIZABETH VANSOLDT of Whitegate Alley in the parish of Buttolphs, Bishopsgate, London, widow. Will 7 September 1665; proved 12 October 1665. To be laid out in buriall £5. To sonn Abraham Vansoldt, in Virginia or elsewhere, £20, also my feather bed in my Lodging Chamber and Bedstead of Walnott Tree thereunto belonging and one other featherbed and bedstead in said Lodging Chamber, also my oune Picture and my husbandes picture, greate Long drawing table and fower Joynt stools, my Daiper Table Cloth, and half a dozen Daiper napkins. To my daughter Mary Wills great Dansick Chest and woollen apparell, and hatts and fower holland shifts, halfe douzen Daiper napkins, the spice box with Drawers, my Court Cupbord in kitchen with one drawer, and two Cubbardes, rest of small wearing lynnen, and 50s. and small looking Glasse in kitchen. To my Cousin Mrs. Judith Bonnell of the old Jury, my Cabinet full of drawers. To my daughter Ann White £5, also Walnutt Tree Court Cubbard with six drawers, looking glass in my Chamber, two greene Cushions with silke frenge, six Holland shifts and greene Cubbord cloth with silke frenge, white Daiper Cubbord cloth, and all white Holland Aprons, one being laced, also two Pictures made and Draun for my brother Stripe and his wife, alsoe great long white Cubbord in kitchen and napkin presse, also pewter and Tynne, Iron potts and spitts, and all household goods made of Iron. To daughters Mary Wills and Anne White all earthen goods and things made of earth. To friend Mr. Thomas Parker of Walbrooke, London, and his wife 10s apiece. Executor: sonne James White. Overseer: sonne Richard Wills. Witnesses: Susanna Slater, Margaret Smith. If sonn Abraham Vansoldt doth not live to enjoy legacy, then to Mary Wills and Anne White. [Administration to daughter Ann White, executor James White, being deceased.]

Hyde, 126.

WILLIAM STURDEY of Stafford County in Virginia. Will 23 May 1698; proved 12 May 1705. All to wife Margaret Sturdey and son Robert Sturdey. Executrix: wife Margaret Sturdey. Witnesses: Rott Weight, Margaret Wright, John Jackson. Administration in Prerogative Court of Canterbury of said William Sturdey, late of Stafford County in Virginia over seas, deceased, to Robert Sturday, paternal uncle of Robert Sturdey only issue and universal legatee of said William Sturdey deceased, Margaret Sturdey the relict dying before administaation and said Robert Sturdy the son surviving his mother.

Fagg. 101.

VIRGINIA GLEANINGS IN ENGLAND.

Communicated by Mr. Lothrop Withington, 30 Little Russell street, W. C., London (including "Gleanings" by Mr. H. F. Waters, not before printed).

Robert Parker. Will 13 November 1671; proved 4 April 1673. To my wife and fellow traveller Jane Parker the rents of free land in Bosham during her life according to lease granted by she and mee to my son George Parker and by him to be paid to his mother Termina vite. To said wife in free land or Burgage Tenure in Meadhurst during her life or the minority of her and my sone John. To said wife the third part of free land in Southampton during her life. To said wife the third part of profits de claro from land in Virginia. As my wife has desired to have only left her Twenty five pounds per annum during her life with a room or two furnished. To the which is she so pleases she acquitting her former bequests above mentioned charging my son George who is of best ability and all the rest of her and my children to have speciall care of their dear mother. To my son John Parker £100 at 21 years besides his living at Medhurst. To my ingrateful son John Martin 13 pence which with £120 which he have already with my eldest daughter Abigaill is too much. To my daughter Margaret £60 at 21 years. To youngest daughter Constance Parker £60 at 21 years. If any of my daughters are willing to renounce their legacies in England and go to Virginia that daughter shall have for her portion rights due to me, with Plantation, housing and stocks to her and her heirs for ever with Patent in the hands of Mr. John Wise at Oenacot in Northampton County in Accomake the plantation in Anduen River. To Margaret Sherlock my apprentice 20s. To each of my servants 5s. To 8 poor men 8 pence apeece in the parish of Bosham. My grandfather John Parker did give 13s. 4d. to St. Laurence in Southampton ever out of demise in tenure of Mr. Petter Clarke where he and my father both lye buryed to be further continued as it hath been before. My son George Parker executor. Mr. William Peas-

---

From Vol. XVII, No. 1 (Jan. 1909), p. 65.

cod of Bosham and John Rawlings of Southampton take my
son John Parker into their tuition and shall be overseers. Witnesses: William Silverlock Henry Payell and William Pescodd.

Pye, 49

[Though the records, which have been examined, do not specifically
state that Robert Parker was brother of George Parker, ancestor of a
well known Eastern Shore family, there seems no doubt that he was so.
The testator was an example, of which there are many, of a resident of
Virginia· who owned land in England.   It is evident that Robert Parker
ʹwas of a Hampshire family, as his father and grandfather were buried in
the Church of St. Lawrence, Southampton. This English town seems
also to have been his own home. In the records of Northampton
county, Va., is a certificate, dated December 29, 1650, to Mr. Robert
Parker, proving that he might obtain a land grant, the importation of
certain persons.   Among these, in addition to himself, were Jane
Parker, John Waler [Waller?], Henry Etheridge, &c. This date doubtless indicates the time of his removal from England to Northampton
county.   In the same county is recorded a deposition, dated January 30,
1653, of Robert Parker, aged thirty-two years. On December 8, 1654,
Rober Parker made a deed of gift of a heifer to John Elzey, George
Parker a witness, and on the next day John Elzey conveyed the same
heifer to George Parker, Jr., son of Robert Parker, and, if he died, to
his sister Abigail Parker, George Parker being again a witness. On
March 21, 1656, Robert Parker, of Northampton county, Va., gave a
power of attorney to Mr. Richard Cornelius, of the town and county of
Southampton, England, merchant, authorizing him to ask and receive
all such rents " as shall be due me " from William Shawcroft [or Chaw-
croft] for a tenement or farm called Copers Hall [or Sopers Hall] now
in his tenure by lease from me, and also unto me from one Mendhurst
from rents " for lands in his tenure and occupation of my Lord Montague's holding," and also to dispose of said lands for tearme or time, and
to make absolute deeds of conveyance and sale.   Robert Parker's wife,
Jane Jones, John Elsye and George Parker witnesses. On January 28,
1658, Mr. John Parker, attorney of Mr. Robert Parker, by power of
attorney from Jane Elzey of Old England, petitioned Northampton
Court that Mr. John Elzey, executor of Mr. Ralph Barlow, be ordered
to pay to said Jane Elzey 500 lbs. tobacco given her by the will of said
Barlow. Robert Parker probably returned to England at the Restoration, as on November 12, 1660, there was a suit by the wife of John
Hould for her freedom from being a servant to Mr. Robert Parker. The
suit was brought in his absence, and he proved by evidence taken before
Mayor of Southampton, &c., that her service was not yet completed.
He was, however, apparently in Virginia at a later date, as there is recorded in Isle of Wight county a power of attorney, dated January 27,

239

1661, from Robert Parker, of Northampton county, to his friends, Mr. George and Mr. John Norsworthey, authorizing them to demand of Thomas Parker, of Isle of Wight county, any papers concerning the said Robert Parker which might be in his hands.

There is in Northampton county a deposition, dated April 25, 1654, of Mr. George Parker, aged 28, or thereabouts. Also two depositions of Mr. John Parker, dated in 1663, in one of which he states that he is 28, and in the other 29. George Parker, in his will dated 1674, names his brother John.]

RICHARD DAVYES, now of St. Leonards, Shoreditch, county Middlesex, late of Peankatanke River in Virginia, Planter. Will 25 August 1660; proved 5 July 1661. All debts to be paid. To my wife Joane Davyes, my plantation of 220 acres in Peankatanke River in Virginia, all my stock of Tobacco by crop and due unto me be specialtyes and my stock of cattle and hogs, all household goods and make her my executrix. Witnesses: Edward Boswell, Edward Tudman, William Davis, Adam Eve, Serp.

May, 107.

WILLIAM FILLETER of Southampton. Will 15 December 1657; proved 23 February 1658-9. To my son Edward Filleter £5 and my best cloak, and to his son William 20s. To my daughter Anne who liveth in Virginia £10. To my daughter Joyce Crooke 40s. To my godson Beniamin Crooke 40s. To my son Peter Filleter £15. Son Isaak Filleter £15. Son George Filleter £15. Daughter Susanna Filleter £40. To Anne Filleter, daughter by my third wife £60. To a protestant Minister for a funeral sermon 20s. Residuary Legatee and Executrix: Anne Filleter my wife. Overseers: Mr. John Holloway of Winton, Mr. John Clerke of St. Crosses and William Harvey of Whitewell Isle of Wight. Witnesses: John Holloway, John Clarke, William Harvey.

Pell, 106

WALTER IRBYE of the parish of Akeemacke, County of Northampton, County of Virginia, Planter. Will 24 September 1651; proved 30 July 1652. To my mother Olive Irbye als Cooper, widow, all my goods and chattels in Virginia, my lands and tenements in Hoggstrapp County Lincoln, now in tenure of Ann

240

Dobbett, widdow, for life and at her decease to the heirs of my late Aunt Anne Irbye. Risiduary Legatee and Executrix: Mother, Olive Irbye. Witnesses: Rebecka May, Thomas Welson, scrivener.

Bowyer, 149

ELIZABETH WINCH of the parish of Great Alhallowes, London, Spinster being now bound for Virginia in the parts beyond the Seas in the good ship the "Recovery." Will 9 January 1659–60; proved 9 May 1661. My grandmother Martha Rowse of Whitewaltham, county Berks, deceased left me a house now in possession of John Brooks tenant thereof, the said house in White Waltham having paid all legacies execpt £3 to Thomas Winch, my Brother I leave to my Brother Richard Winch and Brother John Winch. Executors: Brothers Richard and John. Witnesses: William Trigge: Francis Bartlett, Scrivener at Holborne Conduite.

May, 83

HENRY ROACH, mariner of parish of Abbots Ley. Will 16 April 1677; proved 24 March 1678. To poor housekeepers of Bristol £20 at discretion of Mr. Ed: Fielding and Mr. Wm. Scrynimer. Poor housekeepers of Abbots Ley £30 the interest to be distributed for ever. To Dorothy wife of John Sanders, Shipwright, 20s. per annum. To each of her children £5. To the children of Thomas Fry deceased £5 each. To Joane Stone wife of John Stone £10. To Hester wife of George Cable £10. To each of the children of Henry Roach formerly of Wapping, London £15. To Ann daughter of Richard Towne £10. To the Minister of Abbots Ley £20, the profits to be used therefor for a sermon in the Parish Church every year on 27 December. To the Poor £5. To each of my godchildren £5. To my cousin Samuel son of my Brother John Roach £500 when 21. To Ann daughter of my Brother Jm. Roach £300 when 18 and if she marry with her father's and mother's consent on the day of her marriage. To my sister Martha wife of John Roach £20. All my lands and goods, parts of ships, cargoes, etc in Kings dominions, Jamaica or Virginia or any other place to my residuary Legatee and Executor: my Brother John Roach. Over-

241

seers: Mr. Edward Feilding, and Mr. Wm. Scryminer. Witnesses: Robert Kirke, Sarah Wilsham.

King, 36

ROBERT THURSTON the younger, late resident in St. Pulckars parish, London, Armourer, but now bound forth on a voyage to Virginia where I am to remaine. Will 17 August 1669; proved 7 January 1677–8. Sole legatee and Executor: My Brother in Law: Thomas Wilde of Milend, parish of Stepney, county Middlesex, Armourer. Witnesses: Thomas Draycott, John Carvuer, William Deane, William Waterman.

Reeve, 9

SIR HENRY HYDE, Knight. Will 1 March 1650–1; proved 23 June 1660. To be buried in the Cathedral Church of Salisbury near my deceased parents and when the times bee safe with an inscription that I suffered temporal death for loyaltie, my debts viz: £100 to Dr. Thomas, £100 to Dr. James Hyde, £20 to Mrs. Frauncis Vivian, widow and £15, 10 groats to Dr. Hyde to be paid out my estate due from the Turkey Company and others "at hower of my execution." My lands in the Somer Islands and Virginia to my godson William Hyde and my houses and vineyards (and all Turkish papers) etc in Greece to him after decease of my Brother Dr. Thomas, in case he be a merchant and live there and in defect to the heirs male of my father's family, but never to bee alienated from Christs Church. To Godson Henry Crow £10. A mourning ring to every Brother and to my sister Gounter and her husband and my executors and overseers. Executors: Dr. Thomas and Dr. James Hyde. Overseer: Dr. Edward Hyde. Subscribed at the Tower 25 February 1650 in presence of John Browne, John Ward, William Edwards. I desire my executors to preserve the Tyn case left with the French consull of Singrua and ordered to be sent to Doctor Thomas at zant and to take out his Majesties Royal Instructions and Commissions and present theme to the King or princepall Secretary of estate humbly thanking his Majesty for his good opinion of and graces done vnto me who most contentedly suffers what his enemies enflicts for his loyaltie and praies for his felicitie, hee is the best master in all

242

the world.   Mr. Abbotts commission for Egypt may bee given him gratis if hee bee aliue and bee a good subiect, my red covered booke in 4° I desire may remaine in my Executors hands only that account thereby may bee given to the King or whom he shall comand of my faithfull endeavours to his service however iniured by the Turkish company and Sir Thomas Bendysh for whom I humbly begg his Majesties pardon in what relates to my particular.   mourning rings for my Lord Treasurer, Lord Jermyn, Sir Sack: Crow, his Lady and my Godson Harry Collonell Edwards, Mr. Maurice Abbotts, Mr. James Franes, Sir Edward Hyde and his sister Mrs. Susan Hyde, my cousin Mr. Richard and the two Laurence Hydes.   The Master of St. Cross and Resident of Pavina, Cousen Edward and William Hyde, Mr. Woodarfe, Mrs. Andrews, Mrs. Vivian, Mrs. Saintloe, all my Brothers their wives and my godduaghter Margarett, Sister Gounter, and her husband, Brother Humphries, and godson Will, Brother Radford, Widow Hyde of Heale and her Brother Dr. Thomas Hyde.

Nabbs, 95

[Sir Laurence Hyde, of Salisbury (uncle to Edward, Earl of Clarendon,) had many sons, one of whom was Sir Henry Hyde, Ambassador to Constantinople, who was beheaded on Cornhill, London, March 4, 1650-1, and was buried at Salisbury.   He was condemned by the new High Court of Justice of having accepted an embassy from the King.   It is possible that there may have been some relationship between Sir Henry Hyde and Robert Hyde, a prominent lawyer in York county, Va., about the beginning of the 18th century.]

CHRISTOPHER PERKINS late of the Borough of Norfolk in the Colony of Virginia, now of London (St. Annrew Holborn-Probate Act), Merchant.   Will 27 July 1765; proved 5 December 1765.   To Brother Thomas Perkins my little Close in the Crook adjoining on the Garth of Mr. William Hall on the South side, also fiue Pasture Gates and two Days works, parcel of eight Days works in the Low Field, which. I am entitled to as Heir at Law of late Brother William Perkins, deceased, under will of late dear Father deceased, also two other Days work (parcel of ditto) devised me under said will, all for his life, then to my Brother Hutton Perkins.   To friend John Langdale, late of Norfolk in Virginia, now of Haddon Field in West New Jersey

£20 Virginia currency to buy a piece of plate, to be paid by friend Colcnel Robert Tucker of Norfolk in Virginia. To Brother Thomas Perkins and Sister Hannah Perkins £200 sterling each as soon as effects recovered from Virginia. To Nephew William |Perkins and Neice Elizabeth Perkins each ditto. To Neices Ann and Mary Perkins, ditto. Plate, Jewels, Linne, etc to Nephew William Perkins and Neices Elizabeth Anne and Mary. Residue to Brother Hutton Perkins of Barnard Castle, County Durham, executor. Witnesses: Joseph Bambridge, Ann Bambridge, George Perkins.

Rushworth, 462

ANDREW CADE of East Betchworth, county Surrey, Esq. Will 30 September 1662; proved 23 October 1662. To my wife Magdalen Cade the interest I have in a Brewhouse in Rigate. To my cosen Andrew Cade son of my nephew Walter Cade, deceased, after decease of my wife the house I now dwell in called the Manor of Wonham late bought of William Wanham of this parish and all the lands I bought of Arnold the butcher of this parish, and after his decease to Henry Cade, Brother of aforesaid Andrew Cade now dwelling in Virginia to his heirs for ever. To my Brother Simon Cade £10 yearly for life and yearly to Henry and Peter Cade Brothers to said Andrew £10 each. To |poor of Betchworth for a stock £20. Poor of Reigate likewise £20, and to the poor of Betchworth yearly £5 and forever. Poor of St. Thomas the Apostle £10, St. Laurence Poultney £10, St. Martins le Ongar £10, all these last named parishes are in London city. To the poor|of the Company of Drapers of which I am a member 20 marks. To a poor child born in Betchworth called Anne Vernon when she shall be 18 £20. To my servants William Bishopp, Roger Lincock, Stephen Burrell, Richard Namdred, and Ralph Friday 20s. apiece. To my Sister Mary Hopgood, Brother Simon Cade, Cozen William Chilcott, Cozen Robert Chilcott 40s.|each. Residue and debts owing, vizt: Richard Savadge deceased of Reigate William Otway, and Jane his wife in Astred, Giles Thornton of Reigate to my wife and executrix. Witnesses: Charles Hoodman, Francis Bryant, John Friday, Peter Monck.

Laud, 124

THOMAS MATHER, Commander of the Ship Pitt of London, now bound out on a voyage from London to Virginia. Will 29 March 1766; proved 16 February 1767. To my wife Margaret Mather all my household goods and £40 and all the produce of my whole estate for one year. To my mother Mrs. Frances Mather of Newcastle on Tyne £20. To my 4 sisters Jenny Grundy of Newcastle, Becky Watson of Plymouth, Nancy and Francis Mather of London £1 each. Residuary Legatees: my children. Executor: Mr. James Mather of London, Merchant. Witnesses: Daniel Frazier, Thomas Briant.

Commissary of London (Town) Register No. 83, no folios.

WILLIAM WATSON of the ship Ratchell now bound to Virginia, Captain John Armstrong. Will 24 September 1750; proved 22 April 1756. All to wife Katherine of Dover, county Kent, Executrix. Witnesses: George Green, Robert Richardson.

127 Glazier.

GEORGE DOBBIE, Mariner of London, now living in Well Close Square. Will 27 January 1776; proved 13 April 1776. Executors: Mr. John Hyndman, Mr. Thomas Main, Mr. Edward Staple, and Mr. Robert Howden of London, and Mr. Robert Shedden and Mr. John Brockenburgh of Virginia. To my wife Sarah Dobbie £100 and my house No. 44 Well Close Square, two tracts of land in Halifax County, Virginia, one on Sandy Creek and the other on Buffalo Creek. My wife to educate and apprentice my children and my estate to be divided among them at her death viz. George Dobbie and William Hugh Dobbie or any others I may have. If they die, half at her own disposal, the other half to my neece Elizabeth Morton, Mantua maker, if she die to my granddaughter Sarah Susannah Dobie, daughter to Rev. Mr. John Dobie of the Magdalen, and Elizabeth Sussanna Robinson, daughter to Samuel Robinson of St. George in the East, Coal Merchant. Witnesses: Elizabeth Martin, Ann Reid.

Bellas, 171

VIRGINIA GLEANINGS IN ENGLAND.

Communicated by Mr. LOTHROP WITHINGTON, 30 Little Russell street, W. C., London (including " Gleanings " by Mr. H. F. WATERS, not before printed).

WILLIAM NELSON of Penrith, county Cumberland, Mercer. Will 24 October 1670; proved 8 November 1670. To Bridgett Nelson, my loueing wife, the house I dwell in Rowkeley Lane, and a tenement in Penreth I have in Morgage from my Brother Christopher Ramney. To Hugh Nelson, my son and heir, the house in Rowkely layne I usually let, 10 acres, etc., being on high wetherigg, a close called Gamblinge close, 3 roods on New-lands (which 3 roods Hugh Nelson my father is to have for life), a barne in Castle gate called Hall and Smithes Barne, he to pay to my father Hugh Nelson 6s. yearly for life. To John Nelson, my 2nd son, houses in Morgage from by Brother Christopher Rumney, 1 acre bought of Arthur Robinson, 1 rood of Mathew Smith, 1 rood of William Bowerbank, 1 acre on Brackenberry lands had in exchange from John Sanderson. To wife Bridgett £60. To Brother Christopher Rumney £5. To Anne Meason, my god-daughter, one of the children of my Brother in law Anthony Mason, 20s, and to Marion, Margarett, and Katherine Meason, other 3 children, 10s. apiece. To poor of Penrith 40s. Executors and joint legatees: Wife Bridgett, sons Hugh and John, my wife to have control till sons are 21; if she die before I make my Brothers John Nelson and Thomas Nelson, Brother in law Anthony Meason, and my friend James Collinson guardians. Witnesses: Heugh Nellson, Christopher Rumney, John Nelson, James Collinson, Anthony Meason, John Patteson.

Consistory of Carlisle, will filed 1670.

JOHN NELSON of Penrith, County Cumberland, Batchelor. Will 6 July 1724; proved 25 January 1725–6 [?]. To my sister Mrs. Sarah Nelson a guinea. To my neice Mrs. Dorothy Wilkinson a guinea. To my nephew Mr. William Nelson, late of Barbados, but now of Virginia, one guinea to be paid by my executor when he shall demand the same. To Sarah, Dorothy, Bridget, George, Mary, and Hugh Wilkinson, sons and daughters of Mrs. Dorothy Wilkinson, my aforesaid neice, £10 each when 21. To my nephew Mr. Hugh Nelson, mercer, my house in Nether End in Penreth, and he to be Residuary Legatee and Executor. An appprizement of goods and chattels 24 January 1725–6 [?] £11. 6s. od. Apprizers, Thomas Winter and William Richardson. Exhibited 25 January 1725–6 [?] a Bond of Hugh Nelson, Executor, and W. Richardson, Tho: Winter. Witnesses to will: Thomas Nelson, Ralph Vazie, Sam Denney.

Consistory of Carlisle, will filed 1725.

[In this Magazine, XIII, 402, 403, were printed abstracts of the wills of Hugh Nelson, of Penrith (pro. 1709), father of Thomas Nelson, the emigrant to Virginia, and of Hugh Nelson, of Penrith, brother of the emigrant. In the text are now printed the wills of William Nelson, grandfather of the emigrant, and of John Nelson, another of the emigrant's brothers. Thomas Nelson, who settled at Yorktown, Va., was born in 1677, and, therefore, by the ordinary computation of generations his father, Hugh Nelson, was born about 1647, grandfather, William Nelson, about 1607, and great-grandfather, Hugh Nelson, about 1587. Mr. Withington has compiled from the Consistory Court of Carlisle abstracts of a considerable number of wills and grants of administration, and copies of inventories, beginning with the will of George Nelson, of Penrith, proved 1556. These wills, administrations and inventories are thirty-four in number; but except the two here printed, none of them show any connection with the immediate ancestry of the Virginia Nelsons. None of them mention Hugh Nelson the elder, and there is likewise no mention of him in the numerous extracts from the transcripts of the Penrith parish registers which Mr. Withington has also made. The only entries referring to the immediate line of the emigrant are those of the marriage on April 3d, 1662, of Anthony Meason and Elizabeth Nelson; of the birth, February 20, 1663-4, of Hugh, son of Thomas Nelson; of the marriage of Hugh Nelson and Sarah Nelson, both of Penrith, in February, 1673-4 (the parents of the emigrant), and of the baptism of William, son of Hugh and Sarah Nelson, on October 15, 1674 (an elder brother of the emigrant).

The Nelsons were very numerous in and about Penrith, and, indeed, appear to have been almost a small clan, comprising people of various trades and occupations, though none of them large property owners.]

ADDENDA.

Mr. Withington returned from the United States to England

last year too late for his corrections of the "Gleanings," published in January, 1909, to be used. The most essential were as follows:

Robert Parker. The probate act styles him of "Bosham, Sussex." He gives to his "kind daughter Anne Parker £60 sterling." Sir Henry Hyde is "of London," in the probate act. His executors are his beloved brothers, Dr. Thomas and Dr. James Hyde.

VIRGINIA GLEANINGS IN ENGLAND.

Communicated by Mr. LOTHROP WITHINGTON, 30 Little Russell street,
W. C., London (including "Gleanings" by Mr. H. F. WATERS,
not before printed).

(CONTINUED.)

DANIEL GORSUCH of Walkerne, county Hertford, gent., late citizen and mercer of London. Will October 6, 1638; proved 24 November 1638. Laudable custon of City of London where I was born one third to wife one third to children, and one third disposed by testator. My wife Alice shall receive during her life all my rents in Southwarke which I hold by lease of dean and Chapter of Canterbury. After her death to John Gorsuch my son his executors and assigns, said wife to pay yearly and half yearly £34. 3s. 6d. at Dr. Warners house in Lyme Street. To said Alice my wife the rent of my three houses in Bishopsgate which I hold in fee simple now let at £37 per annum, two years hence £56. The quit rent of 3s. 6d. my wife shall pay to St. Bart's Hospital. To said wife out of a lease I hold of the City of London the rent which shall be due from William Hedgies and from Christopher Bond and from George Mourton. To said wife all my plate and household stuff which I value at £200 for her use during life. After to son John, if said John die before my wife then to Anne his wife, otherwise to such of their children who may be living. To my son my apparel. He shall receive all my rents in Thames Street, £88 yearly, and part of my rents in Bishopsgate of George Mullet, Innkeeper at the Angell £50 per annum, of William Herdmeate £42 and of John Burton £16. Said son shall pay £11. 13s. 4d. yearly to City of London. To said son all horses, cattle about parsonage grounds. I, wish that he leave the same to his wife Anne if she survives. To my daughter Katherine Haines in lieu of 6th part, £500 out of monies in East India Co's hands. To her husband Thomas Haynes £20 for mourning. To Daniel Haynes my godson £5. To my daughter Ann Gorsuch £20. To my grandchild John son of my son John and his heirs all those freeholds in Weston, county Hertford which I purchased of Robert Rumbold. Whereas I have lately contracted with Mr. Kimpton of Weston aforesaid to pay him for lands freehold and copyhold £1626. 16s. od. of which he has received 20s earnest. My will is that these lands shall be settled to the use of five of my grandchildren, my son John's children, viz : Daniell, William, Katherine, Robert, and Richard Gorsuch. And also to other children of said son John to be begotten, said estate to remain to survivors and their heirs. My brother in law Jonathan Browne Doctor of Civil Law will with my son John and Mr. Berisford of Munden my brother shall be trustees. If said Kimpton shall not confirme said estate, then said trustees shall disburse like sum of £1626. 16s. in land to be settled on said grandchildren, which sum is now ready to be paid by my executrix in case I depart this life before settlement. If all my grandchildren do depart this life before 21 years of age then to the heirs of me the said Daniell Gorsuch for ever. To my godchildren 40s. apiece. I forgive my cousin Edward Gorsuch in Lancs. the sum of £11 odd. To my Cosen Ferdinando Morecrosse £3 in remembrance. To my cosen Margarett Browne in lieu of £5 left by Mother Hall deceased, and of £12 left her by her father I add thereto so much to make up £100 to be paid at her marriage or otherwise. To poor of Walkerne where I now live £20. If my cosen Barnard or his wife be living either of them shall have 12d. paid them every week. To my said brother Joanthan Browne D. C. L. £10 for mourning entreating him to be overseer of my will. To said Richard Berisford £10. To William Gorsuch my gold ring with W. G. engraved on it. Lastly I ordeine my wife Alice Gorsuch together with my dutiful son John Gorsuch Joynt executors to whom the residue of all my goods. My desire is that my said brother Dr. Browne, said son John, and my brother Mr. Berisford shall provide for my daughter Anne Gorsuch if she shall outlive her husband. My executors shall weekly pay 12d. to Mary Brand during her life. Witnesses: John Beale, Francis Backwith, Joanthan Waller, and Nicole Clarke.

Lee, 165.

[John Gorsuch, the son named in the will was rector of Walkern, 1633, &c., and came during the Civil Wars to Virginia where he died about 1657. See this number of this Magazine, under title "Francis Lovelace," and also Vol. III, 81–83. There is a pedigree of this family in the visitation of London, 1633–35 (*Harleian Society*, p. 327). It begins with William Gorsuch, merchant, of London, "descended out of Lancashire from Gorsuch nigh Ormschurch," who married Amice, daughter of ———— Hillson, and neice of Robert Hillson, merchant, of London. They had a son, the testator, Daniel Gorsuch, merchant, of London, and Alderman's deputy for Bishopsgate Ward, who married Alice, daughter of John Hall, of London, merchant, and sometime one of the Bridgemasters. Daniel Gorsuch had two children, Rev. John (above) and Katherine, wife of Thomas Haynes, of Auborne, Wiltshire.]

JOHN STEELE, Marchand of London. Will 16 August 1638; proved 21 December 1638. Lately arrived from Virginia w'th god shipp Anna and Sara. To poor of English Church of this city tenn gouldens. To Mary Gos for service tenn gouldens. To Hester Desmeker, Mary Tielroos and John ystele amongst them twenty guldens. Residue to Amye Chatfield his loved wife. Whereas he hath store of tobacco to sell that belongeth to Mr. Joseph Hase, Marchand in London and others same shall be sold by John Desmeccker and reckon to the owners. Executrix his said wife and heire. Adam Borcel and James Gage appeared before Adrian Pulinge Notarius Publicus at Middelbourg as witnesses who together with said testator and me said Notarius publicus have signed and subscribed. Probate to Anne (sic) Steele relict at London.

Lee, 169.

VIRGINIA GLEANINGS IN ENGLAND.

Communicated by Mr. LOTHROP WITHINGTON, 30 Little Russell street, W. C., London (including "Gleanings" by Mr. H. F. WATERS, not before printed).

(CONTINUED.)

ARTHUR HORWOOD of the Island of Virginia in the partes beyond the seas and now resident in the parish of St. Peter the advuncle neere the Tower of London, Marchant. Will 3 November 1642; proved 12 December 1642. To Mris Elizabeth Harwood my Rubee Ring. To Mr. William Richbell my Turkee Ringe. To every one of his 3 children 10s. To Mris Sarah

From Vol. XVII, No. 4 (Oct. 1909), p. 393.

Symondes my great peice of gould w'th German impression of value of £4 or thereabouts. To Mris Sarah Lagee 40s. To Helen Pitchforke, wife of Henry Pitchforke, 40s. of legacies of £4 bequeathed to me by one George Horwood deceased now in hands of said Henry Pitchforke. To Leonard Harwood the other 40s. To Edmund Richbell 40s. To Andrew Richbell 40s. To Susan Harwood and Barbara Harwood, daughters of John Harwood, 10s. apiece. To Ruth Harwood, daughter of Christopher Harwood, 10s. To Mris Dorothie Harwood one of my Cowes that one in Virginia. To her Sonn Augustine Harwood a Cow Calfe. "Item I give vnto Mr. Richard Anderson a Cow Calfe. To Arthur Lawrence a Cow Calfe, which two last Calves my will and minde is shal be delivered within one yeare after they said Richard' Anderson and Arthur Lawrence have newes of my death from England." Rest to Alexander Harwood, Citizen and Mercer of London Executor. Witnesses: Arthur Lawrence, Amie Smith, Robert Yarway and others.

Cambell, 126.

[The names Horwood and Harwood are identical. Though several persons named Harwood were prominently connected with the early history of Virginia, only one of the persons named in the will appears in our records. From the bequest of a cow in Virginia it is evident that Mrs. Dorothie Harwood lived in the colony, and it appears from Hotten's *Emigrants* that Augustine Harwood, aged 25, left London for Virginia in the ship *Paul* in July, 1635.]

GEORGE TUCKER of Milton next Gravesend, county Kent, Esqr. Will 11 November 1622; proved 14 January 1625–6. To be buried in Milton under my stone. To Mary my wife all corn and grain and household stuff. To Son Robert Tucker £300 to be paid him when 24 at or in the porch door on south side of Gravesend parish church. To sons Henry and Daniell £500 marks each. To daughter Marie Tucker £500 when 21. Daughter Ann Tucker already provided for in marriage. To daughters Sarah, Martha, and Hester Tucker £500 apiece when 19: this money is given in performance of an indenture made 16 February 41 Eliz between me George Tucker, John Darell Esq, deceased, my wife's father, and Sir Robert Darell, Knt, her Brother. Residuary Legatees: Wife Mary and my eldest son George Tucker. Executrix: Wife Mary. Overseers: Brothers, Sir

Robert Darell, knight, and John Darell Esq. To Mary my wife my dwelling mansion in Milton called Sir Thomas Wyatt's place for one year and then to son George Tucker. To son George my manor of Milton and land purchased from John Childe and James Crispe, Sir William Page, Knight, and Henry Stacie, executors of will of Stephen Colt, and lands bought of —— Peers and Bradbent, and of one Anne Barnes widow at Dorkenstile with remainder to sons John, Robert, Henry, and Daniell successively. My son John to have the lands settled for my heirs males, and my annuity from the manor of Mallgraves, county Essex, and other lands in Hornedon on the Hill, and my tenn parts and shares in the Summer Islands als Barmother purchased of Sir Robert Mansfeild, Knt, and two shares purchased of John Watts Esqr, and 4 shares purchased of Sir Thomas Smith, knt. Lands bought of Earl of Salisbury in county Kent to my wife for life and then to son John. Witnesses: Lawrence Loulase, Francis Jackson, William Pepper, and Thomas Bolke. Codicil 14 December 1625. As I have given to son John lands purchased of George and Thomas Morris, and lands purchased of Roger Gardiner in Lower Sherne which cost me near £800, the 16 shares of the Summer Islands to go to my son George, he giving my wife half profits, and my son to do the best for his brother Daniell in those shares lately given him by his uncle Captain Daniell Tucker. To poor of Gravesend £10 and to poor of Milton £10. To poor of Hoo, Chalke, and Norfleet, each parish, 40s. Witnesses: Martin Stower, minister, Edward Tenche. Administration 1 July 1630 to Sir Nicholas Salter, crediter, executors being dead.

Hele, 5.

[George Tucker, of Milton, near Gravesend, Kent, was son and heir of George Tucker, of Milton, and grandson of William Tucker, of Thornley, in the county of Devon, Esq., by his wife Iota, daughter of William Ashe, of Devon. George Tucker, the testator, was a member of the Virginia Company. He married first, Elizabeth, daughter of Francis Staughton, of Crayford, Kent, and secondly, Mary, daughter of John Darrell, of Caleshill, Kent. By the first marriage he had a son, George, who was 25 years of age, at the Visitation of Kent in 1619, and by the second marriage, John, aged 19; Robert, aged 14, and Henry, aged 3. The son, Daniel, named in the will, was no doubt born after 1619. Captain Daniel Tucker, brother of the testator, was a member of the Virginia Company, sailed for North Virginia with Chaloner in 16c6, was a leading man in Virginia 1608-1613, was commissioned governor of the Bermudas February 15, 1615 6, and was in that island from May, 1616, to about January, 1618-19. He purchased lands in Virginia in 1621 and died at Port Royal, Bermuda, February 10, 1624-5. Henry Tucker, son of the testator, and probably other of his sons settled in Bermuda and left many descendants.

The history of the Tucker family is in some respects unique. Tracing its origin to the great colonizing and seafaring counties of Kent and Devon, fate seems to have given its members work to do in all quarters of the world.

Descendants of George and Daniel Tucker have played useful and frequently distinguished parts in Bermuda, Barbadoes, the United States, India, Japan, Africa and South America. Several of these Tuckers were members of the Virginia Company, and two or three settled in Bermuda, one of them being a very early governor. Their descendants held many positions of honor and trust in that island and in Barbadoes, whither a branch of the family migrated at an early period. From these two islands there have been several emigrations to the continent of North America, and one member of the family came directly from Kent to New England. A Tucker from Barbadoes founded in the eighteenth century a family of noted merchants in Norfolk, Virginia. In later migration from Bermuda came to South Carolina one member of the family who became treasurer of the United States, and to Virginia another who became an able judge and writer on legal and constitutional subjects and was ancestor of a very distinguished Virginia family, which now includes a Bishop, a president of a college in Japan, the president of the Jamestown Ter-Centennial Exposition, and one of the first American Rhodes scholars. Still later removals from Bermuda to Virginia gave the latter a noted professor of its State university and an admiral in the Confederate States Navy. While some of the Tuckers were leaving the over-crowded Bermudas for North America, others remained steadfast to England and entered her service in various parts of the world. One who settled in England was the author of "The Bermudian" and other poems of some note at the time. Another was a distinguished naval officer who was severely wounded in the fight in which the U. S. Frigate *Essex* was captured and rose to be rear admiral. Still another, a brother of the last, was eminent in the Indian Civil Service and returned to England to become a director and chairman of the East India Company. Several later members of the family have been prominent as civil officials in India, while an old obituary notices the death at Delhi in 1859 of a young lieutenant in the 58th Bengal Infantry, who bore a familiar Tucker name. Tuckers who were soldiers followed the family habit of scattering widely over the face of the earth. During the great war following the French Revolution, two of the Tuckers, brothers and lieutenants in the army, arrived in London the same day. One had been sent to announce the capture of the Cape of Good Hope and the other that of Buenos Ayres.

Another family trait which, appears in widely separated quarters is interest in moral and religious work. This, as has been stated has given to the American branch ministers, a president of a missionary college, and a Bishop, and to that in England the well known author of childrens books, A. L. O. E., and the gentleman who, as son-in-law of General Booth, is a leader in the Salvation Army.]

DANIEL PARKE, Citizen and Merchant tailor of London. Will 18 August 1649; proved 11 September 1649. Executrix to bestow £10 on burial. Item I give and bequeath unto my kinsman Daniel Parke, sonne of my nephew Gabriell Parke messuage in Islington als Isledon, County of Middlesex within the Manor of Newington Barrow, connonly known by the signe of the redd Bull, in occupation of Edmund Cradocke, etc. To Thomas Moore, Robert Betavehompe, and Edward Castleton, parishioners of Islington, messuage adjoyning in tenure of Thomas Johnson, upon trust for churchwardens, to take rents and pay 10s. to godly minister for sermons each year on 25 December and balance in bread to poore on last Sabboth day in year etc. Out of lease for 12 years near Charterhouse lane in parish of sepulchres 52s. annually for 12d. a week in bread to poore of precinct of Charterhouse lane. To Mrs. Rebecca Coleby of Kensington my booke called Gerrardes Herball. To Mrs. Mary Richardson 40s. for ring. To Margaret the servant mayd where I lodge 20s. for paynes in sickness. To brother in law Mr. Oliver Browne and John Bryan, as overseers, 20s. apeece for rings. Rest to sister Mary Parke, executrix. Witnesses: Mary Richardson, John Bryan, scrivener. Proved by sister Mary Sparke [sic] executrix.

Fairfax, 132.

[Probably one of the family in Virginia in which the name Daniel appeared several times.]

ALICE WOODHOUSE, Collingtree als Collingtrough, county Northampton, gentl[ewoman]. Will 14 June 1647; proved 11 November 1647. To deare Mother Mris Judith Woodhouse £5 per annum, executors to secure for ditto in some trustie hands as said mother like £70 in handes of Mr. Augustin Hall of Hayham, county of Norfolk, Esquire. To brothers Mr. Henry Woodhouse and Sir Michaell Woodhouse, knight, brother Webb and brother Jost Hane, each rings of 20s. out of money in hands of said Augustin Hall. To brother Mr. Horatio Woodhouse £100 out of said money. To Aunt Mris Veare Godfrey £10. neice Miss Judith Woodhouse £30 ditto. To cozen Mris Veare Danborne and nephew and neice James and Luce Woodhouse rings of 20s. ditto. To my daughter [sic, evidently goddaughter] Rebecca Cotton and Goddaughter Sara Haridene 40s. each, ditto. To poore of Parish where I dye 40s. ditto. Also to said brother Horatio Woodhouse £200 due to me out of Ireland by the last will of my deceased Father, also £200 on bond in hands of brother Webb, also all linen given me by my Aunt, the Lady Stonor. To neece Judith Woodhouse all wearing Clothes and wearing linen. Rest to brother Horatio, executor. Witnesses: Thomas Hensman, Anne Blancko, and Arthur Marriott.

Fines, 229.

[The testator was a daughter of Captain Henry Woodhouse, Governor of Bermuda, and sister of Henry Woodhouse, who settled in Virginia. See this Magazine, XIII, 202, 203, and references there given. The will of her brother, Horatio Woodhouse, rector of Collingtree, dated March 19, 1676, and proved June 16, 1679, was published in the *William and Mary Quarterly*, V, 41-42.]

MARGARET THORPE of Wanswell, county. Gloucester, widow, late wife of George Thorpe, Esq, deceased. Will 29 June 1629; proved 15 February 1629–30. To be buried in my seat in Barkley Church. If son William marries with consent of Overseers he'is to have the benefit of his wardship granted by King James. To son John Thorpe a pasture called Woòdcroft in Thornburg and my lands in Possett in Somersetsnire. Mr. John Gininge of Bristoll, Alderman, and his son John Guninge to convey to my son John the lands they purchased for me. To my daughter Margaret Thorpe £400 and my apparell and jewels and plate. To Doctor Chetwyne 20s. to preach at my funerall. To Mr. Yeomans at Bristol, preacher, 10s. To Mr. Marshall, Lecturer at Barkley, 10s. To Margaret Gonne, daughter of William Gonne, Clarke, 10s. To poore of Barkley £3 as Dr. Chetwyne and John Hurne of Pockington think fit. Residuary Legatee and Executor: Son John. Overseers: Sir George Crooke, Knight, Henry Roles, Esqr, John Doughtie of Bristol, Alderman, and William Edwards of Thornbury, gent, and guardians to my son John. Witnesses: Thomas Puleston, Francis Carpenter, George Strode. Administration to William Edwards during minority of executor. Proved by John Thorpe, son and executor, 30 April, 1638.

Scroope, 14.

[Margaret Thorpe was the widow of George Thorpe, member of the Virginia Council, who was killed in the Massacre of 1622.]

THOMAS BLAND, Citizen and Ironmonger of London. Will 28 July 1631; proved 6 September 1631. All my estate in goods, chattels, shipping, leases, to be divided into three parts. One to my wife Rebecca, one to my son John when 21. The other as follows: To Brother John Bland £10. To Mother Mary Bland £10. To neice Abigail, daughter of my sister Joane, £10. To Esdras Bland my kinsman 40s. To Robert Wakeland my apprentice £10. To my mayd servant 40s. To the reverend minister Mr. Shute our Lecturer 40s. for a sermon. To Mr. James our curate 20s. To my friend Robert Gosnoll in Abchurch Lane 40s. To poor of All Saints Barking where I was borne £5. Residuary Legatees: Wife and Son. Executor: Brother John Bland. Overseer: Robert Gosnoll. If son John die, his share as follows: To my mother £20 To my wife £50, and to my sisters children, namely Emanuell, Samuell, Hester, and Robert Demetrius, £5 each, and the residue to my Brother John Bland. Witnesses: Richard Haten, Robert Waklinn, John Heath, scrivener.

St. John, 101.

GEORGE GOWER of Christ Churche in the University of Oxon, Master of Arts. Will 24 November 1624; proved 7 February 1624–5. To my brother William Gower my lease hold of the Dean and Chapter of Worcester called Pittensaries Farm, the profit to be divided between my sisters Barbara Etkens and Amie Gower until my brother shall be 27, then he is to have full possession. To my friend Mr. Gilbert Jones of All

Souls College, Sir Walter Rawleyes Historie, the Florentine History written by Match avell, and my sanguine rapier. To John Chanse I forgive £10 out of the debts he owes me ot £22. To my Aunt Mary Gower 11s. To the poor of St. Johns in Bedwardine 20s. To James Crouch a hatt, too pair ot cuffs, and doublet and hose. Residuary Legatee and Executor: My Uncle Mr. Abell Gower. Overseers: Mr. Gilberte Jones, Mr. Edwarde Meetekerke, and Mr. Thomas Davis, City of Oxon. Witnesses: James Crouche, Anne Caney[?] Administration 1 November 1634 to Barbara Etkyn als Gower, sister of deceased.

Clarke, 24.

ABELL GOWER of Boulton, parish of St. Johns Bedwaedine, county Gloucester Esquire. Will 30 July 1632; proved 16 November 1632. To new building the Chancel of St. Johns £10. To poor of parish £5. To my wife the profits of my land in Sawfold untill Abell Gower my eldest son shall be 24, and all my lands in Napton, county Warwick, in occupancy of Nicholas Horrod, until my youngest son William Gower is 24. To my daughter Elizabeth Gower £500. To my wife my lands in Kington, county Worcester, and one salt Phate or Bullerie of Salt Water in Droitwich Colvores now in tenure of —— Davies and two houses in St. Johns Bedwardine purchased from Hughe Cotton. To my son in law Timothy Stampe of the Inner Temple, London, a cup of silver. To the said Timothy, William, John, and Marie Stampe, and Anne the wife of Thomas Clent of Martley, county Worcester, Clarke, my wife's children by her former husband, £10 each. Residuary Legatee and Executrix: Wife Marie Gower. Overseers: Son in law Timothie Stampe and my Brother in law John Gunner of Whitney, county Oxon, gent. Witnesses: William Stampe, John Burlie, John Chance, John Combey.

Audley, 111.

[The maker of the first will above appears in Foster's *Alumni Oxonienses*, as George Gower of the county of Worcester, gent., who matriculated at Oriel College, December 15, 1609, aged 15; B. A., June 17, 1613; M. A., June 20, 1616. Three Abel Gowers, of Worcestershire, were at Oxford, matriculating in 1581, 1650 and 1691. An Abell Gower, who was doubtless of this family, came to Virginia and settled in Henrico county. He was a justice of the county from 1677 until his death in 1689, sheriff in 1681, and a member of the House of Burgesses in 1679. He married Jane, daughter of Edward Hatcher of Henrico county, and widow of —— Branch of the same county. He seems to have but one child, a daughter Tabitha. His will was dated December 25, 1688, and proved in Henrico, June, 1689. He gave his wife Jane the plantation he lived on for her life, with reversion to his daughter Tabitha, and if she died without issue, to Priscilla and Obedience Branch. His personal property was to be divided between his wife and daughter. The inventory shows a comfortable estate and included 1 silver tankard, 2 silver porringers, 6 small silver salt cellars, 12 silver spoons, a gold ring, a bible in quorto and two or three old books.

The will of Mrs. Jane Gower was proved in Henrico in October, 1699. She gave lands to her grandson Wm. Cox and daughter Mary Cox; land she lived on called Great Stone, to her granddaughters Obedience Turpin and Priscilla Wilkinson; personal property to grandson Wm. Farrar, granddaughter Mary Womack, Priscilla Farrar, John Spike, Wm. Womack, her daughter Mary Cox, granddaughter Priscilla Farrar (a silver porringer), sister Hatcher (a damask gown and petticoat), and grandchildren Abell and William Farrar and Judith Womack. Rest of estate to Mrs. Mary Cox. Through a child of her first marriage, Mrs. Jane Gower was an ancestress of Thomas Jefferson.]

GEORGE NEWTON. Will 25 July 1633; proved 8 October 1634. Last will of George Newton, deceased 29 July 1633. To Michael Young, Surratt Calico. To my wife Mary Newton all wages and debts due to me from the Honouable East India Company or in the Ship Jonah. Executrix: Wife Mary. My clothes among the following: William Tice, Michael Flute, Owen Kibble, Michael Wilde, and William Fowler. Witnesses: Godfrey Boleyne, Pursers Mate, Michael Flute.

Seager, 94.

GEORGE HARRISON. Will 17 November 1630; proved 3 April 1634. To William Alleson and Richard Trippet my clothes. To Gerrald Pinson, Robert Coulson, Peter Holloway, and William Alleson a piece of Salpicadoe each. Residuary Legatee for wages etc due from East India Company: Brother Richard Harrison. Witnesses: Gerrald Pinson, purser, Hugh Bradle.

Seager, 34.

THOMAS CORBYN of Hall End, county of Warwick, esq. Will 5 June 1637; proved 1 June 1638. Whereas have by deed 3rd of this present month of June, 13th year of our Lord the King

that nowe is, settled vpon my truly and welbeloved friends Sir
John Repingham, William Purefry, esquire, John Dawkins, gent,
and James Prescott, gent, for forescore and nynteen yeares to
raise the portions of my younger sons and daughters, to
Thomas my son and heir my lands in Hallensfeilde purchased
from Sir Henry Goodacre in occupancy of Thomas Twelves and
Francis Atkins and lands purchased of Thomas Orme of Fresley
and Francis Nethersole of Pollesworth.   My father George
Corbin, deceased, requested me to give 10 of his grandchildren
£5 apiece and to 5 other Grandchildren £20 apiece when 21.
I give to Phillip Dawkins, Anne, Elizabeth, Susan, and Mary
Dawkins, his grandchildren and children of said John Dawkins,
£5 each.   To Jeffery, George, Thomas, Katherine, and Elizabeth,
5 of children of said James Prescott and his grandchildren, £5
apiece.   To my 5 children, George, Henry, Gawin, Charles, and
Lettice Corbyn, £20 each.   To my 4 younger sons when 24,
George, Henry, Gawin, and Charles, £400 each, and to daughter
Lettice £800 when 21.   Executors: Wife Winifrede, William
Purefoy, James Prescott, and Anketill Willington.   To cousin
Purefoy's wife £2.   To servant Drakote and his wife the house
they live for their lives and Old Mary his wife their house.   To
poor of Pollesworth £3.   To sister Dawkins 5 marks.   To poor
of Willingcott £2.   To brother James Prescott a bay nag.   To
brother Dawkins a ring.   To Katherine Newman's son 20s.
To Mrs. Neale her mare.   To Jone Lewis £2.   To Apprentice
Moll £2.   Son Thomas to deal well with cousin Hudson's wife.
Witnesses: Thomas Lewinge, Gowen Grosvenor, Gregory
Drakeford.

74 Lee.

[The pedigree of the family of Corbyn or Corbin as recorded in the
College of Arms, and given in Shaw's *Staffordshire*, &c., begins with
Robert Corbion or Corbin, whose son Robert Corbin gave lands to the
Abbey of Talesworth between 1154 and 1161.   This pedigree is rather
unusual from the fact that through successive entries in the College
of Arms some lines of the American branch have been brought down
to the present day.   The testator, Thomas Corbyn or Corbin, was
son of George Corbin of Hall End, and his wife Mary, daughter of
William Faunt, and was born May 24, 1594.   He married in 1620,
Winifred, daughter of Gawin Grosvenor of Sutton Coldfield, in the
county of Warwick, and dying in 1638, was buried at Kings Swinford,

in Staffordshire, the ancient seat of the family. He had several sons and daughters, but the male lines of all of his sons, except Henry, are extinct. Thomas Corbin, the eldest son, had an only daughter and heiress, Margaret (1658-1699), who married William Lygon, Esq., and carried the estate to that family, since become Earls Beauchamp. Henry Corbin, third son of Thomas and Winifred Corbin, was born in 1629, came to Virginia in 1654, and died in Middlesex county, June 8, 1675. He was a member of the Virginia Council, married Alice, daughter of Richard Eltonhead of Eltonhead, Lancashire, and was ancester of the well known Virginia family of the name.]

EDWARD PERRIN, City of Bristol, Merchant. Will 8 June 1702, proved 23 December 1709. To be buried near my last wife in the Quaker's burial ground. Sole executor: son Thomas Perrin, to whom I give all my land in Virginia, Mary land, Pennsilvania, or elsewhere in America, also the house Isaac Noble lives in in Castle Street in Bristol, and another in Castle Street where William Nicholas lives, he to pay my two daughters Susanna and Anne Perrin £300 each when 21 or married. To my three younger children, Edward, Susanna, and Anne, my messuage in which I now live. To son Edward two messuages in Broadmead, St. James Parish, adjoining the house of widow Skinner, both now in possession of Widow Evans and John Baker, and three messuages in Chapell Street in St Philip and Jacob in possession of Robert Rookes, and my silver watch when of age. Overseers: Robert Ruddle, my brother-in-law, and Cornelius Sarjant of Bristol, sopemaker, and Benjamin Morse, Hosier. Witnesses: Sam'l Fox, Thos. Hayne, John Brinsden.

Lane, 295.

[Possibly ancester of the Perrins of Gloucester county, Virginia. The births of several children of Thomas and Elizabeth Perrin appear in the register of Abingdon parish, Gloucester, between 1686 and 1702. See *William and Mary Quarterly*, V, 174.]

VIRGINIA GLEANINGS IN ENGLAND.

Communicated by Mr. LATHROP WITHINGTON, 30 Little Russell street,
W. C., London (including " Gleanings " by Mr. H. F. WATERS,
not before printed).

FRANCIS NEWTON of London, Grocer, now bound out vpon
a voyage to Virginia. Will 24 August 1660; proved 11 January
1661–2. To my wife Mary Newton £600. Residuary Legatees:
my sisters Elizabeth Newton and Susan Newton and my Brother
Joseph Newton. Executors: John Berry, Anthony Stanford,
Joseph Wilson, and to them 30s. each. Witnesses: Theo: Ixem,
Wm. Scorey. Proved by Anthony Stanford. [The probate act
book in the Prerogative Court at Canterbury has long been
missing.—L. W.]

8 Laud.

JOHN HALL of London, intending a voyage to Virginia. Will
5 December 1695; proved 5 December 1705. To my mother
Prudence Hall, widow, of West Ham in Essex, £300, and to be
sole legatee and executrix. Witnesses: Sam: Mansfield, Joseph
Pask.

Gee, 243.

EDWARD ABBES. Will 24 August 1636–7; proved 23 May
1637 To Sarah Browne, daughter of Nicholas Browne, as
much as will buy her a cow, and to Thomas Abbes my nephew
ditto. To William Goulder, my man, one year and a half of
his time in case my wife and child be dead. Residuary Legatees: my wife and child, but in case they both be dead my
nephew Thomas Abbes. Executrix: my wife. Overseers:
Friends Nicholas Browne and Robert Todd. Witnesses: Henry
Batt, William Batt. [Will of Edward Abbes, late in Virginia,
in parts, beyond the sea deceased, proved by Sarah, his relict.—
Probate Act Book.] Goare, 75.

[Robert Todd was living in York county in 1642, and patented land
in Gloucester in 1652. Two brothers, William and Henry Batte, sons of
Robert Batte, Vice-Master of Oriel College, Oxford, were living in Virginia as early as 1653. If these were the witnesses to the will they came
to the Colony much earlier than has been supposed.]

From Vol. XVIII, No. 1 (Jan. 1910), p. 80.

WILLIAM STRACHEY of St. Giles in the Fields, County Middlesex, gentleman. Will 1 February, 1634-5; proved 13 June 1635-6. To sonne John Strachey and his heirs, whom I had by my now wife Elizabeth, my houses in King Street, Cittie of Westminster, by indenture 30 December 1631-2, between me and my now wife by name of Elizabeth Jepp, widow, Robert Westcomb, and John Cockshuto, gentlemen. The rest of the houses in or near King Street to my son Edmond Strachey. To son William Strachey, when 21, houses on Fish streete Hill, London, the rent to educate and maintain him and the three other children I had by my first two wives. Residue to my three daughters, Katherine, Frances, and Elizabeth. If son Edmund marry, of money had with his wife £600 to daughters Frances and Katherine, etc., etc. Executors: my wife Elizabeth and Uncle Howard Strachey. Witnesses: Tho: Lloyd, Willm. Strackey, Will: Goode, John Hallywell, Jun., Scr., Mary Strachey. [Codicil.] If lands in Grinstead, in parish of Chipping Onger, Essex, late John Borne's, Gent., deceased, conferred on his son Richard and his heirs, failing them to Francis Strachey, daughter and heire to Andrew Borne, deceased, late wife of William Strachey the deceased come to a legacy of £300 is to be paid daughter Katherine. Witnesses: Tho: Lloyd, Will: Strachey, William Goode, John Hallywell, Jun., Scr.

Sadler, 69.

[A William Strachey, who was of Gray's Inn, came to Virginia in May, 1610, was Secretary of State and Recorder, returned to England about October, 1611, and about 1612 wrote the valuable *History of Travaile into Virginia, Britania*, which, however, was not printed until 1849. Sir Edward Strachey, of Sutton Court, the representative of the family, thought that the testator above was the author, while Alexander Brown (*Genesis*) believed that he was another William Strachey (father of the testator), who married Frances Foster in 1588, and " was living in 1620."

In the *William and Mary Quarterly*, IV, 192-194, V, 6-10, is an interesting account of the Stracheys. William Strachey, the testator, had a son William who went to Virginia and died in 1686, leaving an only child, Arabella, who was twice married. By a later marriage, William Strachey, of the text, was great-grandfather of John Strachey, M. D. (1709-1756), who settled in King and Queen county, Va., and of Henry Strachey, of Sutton Court, ancestor of the present baronets of that place.]

263

GEORGE HEALE of City of Lancaster in Rappa hanock. Will 30 December 1697; proved 10 March 1708–9. Land and Plantation wherein I now live bounding upon South east side of the main road which leads from Mr. Ball's Mill to a Mill which was formerly Josias Draper's, between the said Roads and Thomas Davises, containing about 1300 acres to my son George Heale. Remainder of dividend Land upon North West of said Main Road, then up along the white Marsh to Timothy Stamp's, then to aforesaid Main Road, 500 acres, to my son John Heale. Main Road to be dividing line between George and John, and if either are without heirs, to longest liver whole 1800 acres. My land in the Forrest at the head of Corotom' on west side of the Main Swamp, bounding on land formerly Nathaniel Browne's then along the Head line that divides this land from the land of Giles Robinson and Randolph Miller, so far along said head line that a direct course to Main Swamp shall include 400 Acres, to my son Joseph Heale, if he die, then to John. My land in Cherry Point, bounding on land of Mr. Keen and Mr. Crawley, 100 acres, to my daughter Ellen Heale, if she die to daughter Elizabeth Heale, then to daughter Sarah Heale. My Land down at Corotoman, 350 acres adjoining lands of William Clarke, Mathew White, Mr. Arms, Mr. Harrison, and the main road, to my two daughters Elizabeth and Sarah Hele. My quarter Plantation in the Forrest at the head of Corotoman to son George Heale for use of son Nicholas Heale, but if he die, to child, be male or female, my wife is now with, and if he to die Son George Heale is to have the quarter. Executor: Son George Heale. Overseers: Mr. Robert Carter and my son-in-law Mr. William Ball. Witnesses: Jas. [sic. Query "Jos." in original] Ball, James Innis, Wm. Ball. Administration to Arthur Bailey, Esquire, attorney for son George Heale, now in Virginia, executor, as to effects in Great Britain and Ireland.

Lane, 58.

[This name is more generally spelt Heale. This will was also proved in Lancaster county, Va. For a genealogy of the family see *William and Mary Quarterly*, XVII, 202–204, 296–299.]

WARRIN SMITH. Will 24 February 1613-4; proved 5 May 1615. By my father Robert Smith's will he gave to Wm. Smith

Brockatt Smith, and Robert Smith (Robert being at the making of the will still unborn) my brethren a rent of £10 yearly during their lives out of lands at Hitchin in Countie of Hartford, and then revoked because the Hitchin lands were entayled by my grandfather Symon Warren. I give to them as follows: To Brother William £150. To Brother Brockett £100. To Brother Robert £100, to be paid from debt of John Mynn of Ewsham, County Surrey, Esq. To Brockett and Robert, my youngest brothers, my benefit of my Adventures to Somers Islands otherwise called the Barmodies and Virginia wherein I paid in £137. 10. To John Hollifax £10 and my twoe suites and Cloake lyned w'th velvett left in custody of Mr. Dennys Bretton. To Dennis Bretton £50. Residuary Legatee and Executor: Dennis Breton. Witnesses: He: Bretton, James Goodman, Willian Robotham.

Rudd, 47.

[In 1615 Warren Smith was one of the charter members of the Somers Islands Company.]

[THE HON'BLE] BENJAMIN TASKER of the City of Annapoles, Esq. Will 15 February 1766; proved 30 December 1768. To my wife Ann the dwelling house and lots adjoining and all plate and personal estate, she to be executrix, Land and negroes, to be sold and produce divided between her and my children. To my daughter Anna Ogle £2500. To daughter Rebecca Dulany £2500. To daughter Elizabeth Lowndes, wife of Mr. Christopher Lowndes, £2500 to be used in trust for her during her husband's lifetime. To daughter Frances Carter, wife of Robert Carter in Virginia, £2500. Whereas the late Governor Ogle left me one of his executors, and each of his daughters £1000, already paid his eldest daughter, to his youngest daughter to be paid as on my Book of Accounts, marked S. O. fol. 40. To my four grandsons which are my godsons, viz: Benjamin Ogle, son of the late Governor Ogle, Daniel, son of Daniel Dulany Esq., Benjamin son of Christopher Lowndes, and Benjamin, son of Robert Carter of Virginia, £1000 each. To my daughter Anne Ogle, Mr. Christopher Lowndes, and Robert Carter £1000 in Bank of England for use of Benjamin Benson when 21, meanwhile the interest for his education in some public school in Great

Britain. As my son Benjamin Tasker, deceased, by his will desired me to sell his real estate, I make the aforesaid three his executors or any two of them. As two tracts of land in Frederick County one called Vine containing ——, the other the Will, containing 100 acres, belonging to late Governor Ogle were patented to Mr. William Steuart and by him conveyed to me I give them to Benjamin Ogle heir at law to the said Governor. Witnesses: Joseph Galloway, Sam'l Galloway, And'w Buchanan. Before Walter Dulany, Commlssary General, 4 July 1768 Ann the widow swears to above will. Administration with will annexed to Osgood Hanbury and William Anderson attorneys for Anne Tasker, relict, in Prerogative Court of Canterbury for receiving dues and transferring £10,000 in Capital Stock of Bank of England, except £1000 thereof, etc. Second grant 20 November 1770 to James Anderson of Great Tower Hill in parish of St. Olave Hart Street London, Merchant, as one of attorneys for Ann Tasker, widow, residing in Annapolis, on transferring £5000, part of £9,950 in Bank of England to Anne Ogle of Annapolis, widow and Benjamin Ogle of ditto gentleman, also £3950 to said Benjamin Ogle, also £1000 to said Ann Ogle of said Annapolis, Royal and Christopher Lownds and Robert Carter, Esquires. Administration of goods in Kingdom of England 3 November 1772 to said James Anderson of Great Tower Hill, St. Olave Hart Street, London, Merchant, attorney for Anne Tasker, relict and executrix.

Secker, 470.

[Benjamin Tasker was President of the Council of Maryland for thirty-two years, and acting Governor 1752–53. For notices of the family see *Dinwiddie Papers* I, 13, 14, and *Maryland Historical Magazine*, IV, 191, &c.]

JOHN CUSTIS of New Romney, County Kent, Gentleman. Will 21 August 1704; proved 27 October 1704. To my daughter Elizabeth, wife of John Mathews, living in Acamack in Virginia, £100. To Daughter Ann, wife of Richard King of New Romney, County Kent, Gentleman, £100. To each of her children £50. Residuary Legatee and Executor: My son in law Richard King. Trustee and guardian for my daughter King and her children: My loving kinsman Mr. Arnold King of

Bromly, County Kent, gentlemen.   Trustee for daughter Elizabeth: Mr. Arthur Bayly of Mile end, County Middlesex, Esq.
Witnesses: Walter Batson, John Yeates, Henry Darington.

Ash, 196.

[John Custis was, of course, a member of the Eastern Shore family of the name; but his exact place is unknown to the writer.]

THOMAS ISHAM of Middle Temple, of London, Gentleman. Will 13 June 1676; proved 20 July 1676.   To be buried in the Chancel of Hilsden Church, if convenient.   To cousin Francis Drake of Stretton Rudely £400 upon trust for the heir male apparent of my Cousin German Henry Isham of Virginia who shall come to live in England for one whole year after he is 21. If no heir, I give £100 to my said cousin Henry Isham.   To my uncle Denton, Doctor of Phisick, £100.   To Cousen Alexander Denton, Barrister of Middle Temple, £20.   To cousin George Nicholas of Covent Garden £10.   To cozen Anne his wife £10.   To cousin Robert Dormer of Lincoln's Inn, Barrester, £10.   All lands and Residue of estate to my dear friend Francis Drake, of Stretton Rudely, whom I appoint executor. Witnesses: Paul Perrott, Nich: Page.   Codocil 17 July 1676. To Uncle Dr. Denton £50.   To Mrs. Mary Gape, widow, £10. To my Lady Tippen my bed and furniture at Wheatfield.   To my cousin Ann Woodward, my dear Franck Drake's mother, the best piece of plate I have.   Rest of plate to deare Cousin Francis Drake's wife.   To Nicholas Page, Cooke upon Littleton, Cooke's Reports and Trotman's Abridgements Authorized to all law Books and law noates.   One of the greatest reasons of this guift to my Cozen Isham was to encourage Sir Edward Brett to be very kind to him when he comes over into England and therefore I begg his kindnesse to his kinsman and mine aforesaid. Witnesses: Jane Fowke, Richard Parker, Tabitha Parker.

Bence, 92.

HENRY ISHAM of Henrico County in Virginia.   Will 13 November 1678; proved 5 June 1680.   To Joseph Ryall, my half brother, £40 in goods.   2. To Richard Perrin his wife, John Wilkinson his wife, and William Byrd, and his wife, to each a gold ring about 12s. price. 3. To my Hono'le Mother Mrs. Katherine Isham one full third of my personal estate in Virginia and England. 4. To my sister Mrs. Anne Isham. Ditto 5ly. My plantation in Charles City County in Virginia commonly known as Doggams to my sisters Mrs. Mary Randolph and Mrs. Anne Isham. 6thly. All the rest of my estate in Virginia and England to my executor, Mr. Wm. Randolph. Witnesses: Ja: Tubb, John Wynn, Wilbert Daniel, Hugh Davis.

Bath, 81.

[Henry Isham, Sr., came to Virginia about 1656, where he had a grant of land. As the records of Henrico county, where he lived at Bermuda Hundred, previous to 1677 have been destroyed, no copy of his will remains; but the records show that he died about 1675. He married Katherine, widow of Joseph Royall, of Henrico county (stated in the Isham pedigree to be a daughter of —— Banks, of Canterbury, Eng.,) and had issue (1) Henry, died 1679, unmarried. His will is given above; (2) Mary, married William Randolph, of "Turkey Island," Henrico county; (3) Anne, married Frances Eppes, of Henrico county. For notice of the Ishams, with abstracts of wills, of Henry Isham, Jr., and his mother, Mrs. Katherine Isham, see this Magazine IV, 123, 124.

The wish of Thomas Isham was granted, for Sir Edward Brett in his will, dated in 1652 and proved in 1683 (*Waters*, 447,) gave Mary and Anne Isham £200 apiece. Their brother Henry was then dead.

The genealogical volume for Northamptonshire, of the *Victorian County History of England*, contains the latest and most authentic Isham pedigree.]

Robert Isham [of Pytchley?]
b. ——
d. 1424, March 13.
m. —— —— ——

|

Robert Isham [of Pitchley ?]
b. 1402.
d.
m. Elizabeth, daughter Aston of Knuston, near Irchester,
Co. Northampton.

William Isham of Pytchley.
b.
d. June 13, 1510 [16?].
m. Elizabeth Bramspeth, d. Thomas of Glooston, Co. Leicester.

|

Thomas Isham of Pytchley.
b.
d. 1547 +?
m. Elena Vere, dau. { Richard Vere of Addington, Co. Northampton.
(Eleanor)   { Isabella Green, d. John of Drayton, same Co.
        Descended fr. Robert de Vere, 2nd son of Aubrey de Vere,

Euseby Isham of Ringstead.
    He never inherited Pytchley; his father's long life and his mother's
"joynter" prevented.
b.
d. will Aug., 1546; proved Dec. 11, 1546.
m. Anne Poulton, dau. Giles, of Besborough, Co. Northampton.

Gyles Isham of Pitchley.	Robert.	Gregory Isham	John of	Henry.
b.	A	of Braunston.	Lamport.		
d. Aug. 31, 1559.	Priest.	b.		Gregory of
m. ——		d. Sept. 4, 1558.	Lamport	Barby.
No sons.		m. Elizabeth	Line.	
		Dale of Bristol.	Present	Barby
			Bart's.	Line.
		Sir Euseby Isham		
		of Pytchley.		
		b. Feb. 26, 1552.		
		d. June 11, 1626.		
		m Anne Borlase, dau. of John		
		of Marlowe, Co. Bucks.		

John.	Euseby.	William.	Gregory.	Thomas.	Anthony.
d. Dec. 9, 1616.		bp. March 20, 1587–8.			
		d. bef. 1631.			
Anne.		m. Aug. 15, 1625, Mary Brett, d. William,			
		of Toddington, Co. Bedford.			

Henry Isham of Virginia.
b. c. 1628.
d. c. 1676.
m. Katherine Banks, wid. Joseph Royall.

Henry Isham.	Mary.	Anne.

JOHN TEMPLE of Bishipstrowe, County Wilts, gentleman. Will 4 March 1635-6; proved 23 January 1637-8. To be buried in the Chancel of Bishopstrowe Church. To the church 40s. To poor 20s. To my wife and executrix Mary Temple all household stuff, Plate, etc., in my house at Bishopstrowe. To my wife until my son William Temple shall be 22 my lands in Hachbury, Parish of Warminster, and my mills, he to pay her £1000 when he reaches 22 to enable her to pay the legacies. To my daughters Mary, Elizabeth, and Hester Temple £500 each. Overseers: My brothers in lawe William Seaman, Clearke, and Samuell Seaman, gentlemen. Witnesses: Tho. Seaman, Samuell Seaman. Commissary for oath, William Seaman, rector of Upton Skidmore.

Lee, 4.

[Burke's *Landed Gentry* (edition of 1886) begins the account of the Temples, of Bishopstrowe House, near Warminster, Wiltshire, with the statement that William Temple, of Bishopstrowe (son of John Temple, of Kingston Deverell,) had, with other issue, Peter, born 1661, ancestor of the present Temples of Bishopstrowe, and Joseph, born 1666, "whose descendants are settled in Virginia, U. S. A."

The will in the text is that of John, called by Burke, "of Kingston Deverell."

The "Marriage Licenses at Salisbury," now in course of publication in the *Genealogist*, gives the license, dated January 3, 1616–17, of John Temple, of Bishopstrowe, gent., to Marie, daughter of William Seame, of Upton Scudamore. The will gives this name as Seaman. John Temple's will refers to property in Hachbury. The Salisbury licenses give, also that of Philip Temple, Mercer, of Hachbury (Heytsbury), and Mary Maton, of Stockton. Probably Philip Temple was of the same family.

It is not certain whether Joseph Temple (born 1666) came to Virginia, or whether it was his son. Destruction of county records prevents certainty. By deed dated October 22, 1722, recorded in Essex county, certain Bristol merchants, who had established an iron works in Virginia, appointed, as their attorney, Joseph Temple, of Bristol, merchant, &c., "now resident at said iron works."

The following are the earliest grants of land to Joseph Temple :

(1) Joseph Temple, of King William county, Merchant, 1,000 acres on the north side of Northanna River, in Spotsylvania county, September 14, 1728.

(2) Joseph Temple, of King William, gent., 250 acres on the north side of Northanna, in Spotsylvania county, September 1, 1728. On January 31, 1732, he had a regrant of these two tracts.

270

(3) Joseph Temple, of King William, gent., 1,390 acres in Hanover county. adjoining the lands of John Harris, Thomas Wash, Major Thomas Carr, Richard Bullock, Jr., and Mr. Benjamin Brown, August 5, 1731.

Joseph Temple bought other land in Spotsylvania in 1744, but was dead before 1760, as in that year and in 1762 Joseph Temple (and Mary his wife), and Benjamin Temple, of King William, sold lands in Spotsylvania which had formerly been granted to their father, Joseph Temple, deceased, and by him, in his will, devised to them. Joseph Temple, the elder, was a justice of King William in 1732, and sheriff in 1738.

The following account of the family was contained in a letter written in 1831 from Mrs. Polly Williamson, daughter of Col. Benjamin Temple, to Dr. William Gwathmey, of King William county:

Mr. Joseph Temple came to this country a wealthy merchant. He was born in England, and was a descendant of Sir William Temple [of course untrue], British Resident at Brussels in the reign of Charles II. He married Ann, daughter of Benjamin Arnal [Arnold]. He was first a merchant at Ayletts, King William county; after marriage he lived at the place now called Presqueisle. Joseph and Ann Temple had ten children—five sons and five daughters.

Joseph, the eldest, married Molly, daughter of Col. Humphrey Hill. [Joseph Temple was a member of the King and Queen Committee of Safety, 1774-75.]

Liston Temple married Agnes, daughter of Dr. Elliott. [Liston Temple was captain of King William county militia in the Revolution. See this Magazine XV, 90.]

William Temple married Miss Cowne from the place called Cownes, in King William county.

Benjamin Temple married Mollie, daughter of Robert Baylor and Mollie Brooke, his wife. [Benjamin Temple served as a lieutenant in the French and Indian War, and in the Revolution was commissioned Captain Virginia Dragoons, June 15, 1776; lieutenant colonel First Continental Dragoons, March 31, 1777, transferred to Fourth Dragoons, December 10, 1779, and served to the close of the war. He was a member of the Virginia House of Delegates and Senate and the Convention of 1788. His wife died August 7, 1820, aged 72.]

Samuel Temple married Fannie Redd, of Caroline county. [Samuel Temple was lieutenant in the Caroline county militia in the Revolution. See this Magazine XV, 90.]

Hannah married Mr. Owen Gwathmey, of "Burlington," King William county.

Sally married Mr. John Tunstall, son of Col. Richard Tunstall, of King and Queen county.

Molly married Col. Thomas Elliott, son of Dr. Elliott.

Martha married Benjamin Elliott.

Nancy married Mr. John Fleet, of King and Queen county. [She died May 7, 1754.]

JOHN POPE of Bristoll, Mariner, about to go to sea. Will 4 February 1700-1; proved 19 August 1702. To my mother Joane Pope of the City of Bristol, widow, all that Plantation commonly called the Clifts in County Westmoreland in Potomake River in Virginia. Witnesses: William Scott, Abraham Alyes, [Quakers].

Herne, 138.

THOMAS OPIE of the City of Bristoll, Mariner, now in Virginia. Will 16 November 1702; proved 26 July 1703. To be buried in the grave of my Grandfather Mr. David Lindsay. To my Brother John Opie my second best bed, etc., likewise my large silver cup to my brother Lindsay Opie. To my three sisters, Hellen, Susannah, and Sarah Opie, remainder of bedding or lynen, &c. To my Sister Hellen my Silver Tankard, Sister Susannah Opie my gold chaine, Sister Sarah Opie my Dyamond ring and other rings (my signett ring excepted). To Susannah my silver papdish and spoone. To my three sisters my eighth part of the ship Adventure and Cargoe. If my Brother John hath my Fathers Signet ring, then I give mine to my Brother Lindsay Opie, otherwise to John. To my brothers and sisters what my father left me, only the Plantation will fall to my Brother John. To Uncle Edward Opie 20s. mourning ring my hat and gloves. To Mr. Francis Thruppe the same. To Mrs. Anne Keen, widow, and Mrs. Sarah Keen, both of Cherry point in Potomak in Virginia, mourning rings of like value to be sent them. To an old servant named Mary Edwards £3. To Brother Lindsay Opie the produce of my watch sent to Jamaica by Mr. William Williams, or if undisposed the watch. Executrix : my Sister Susannah Opie, first paying George Bartlett and all other debts with what bills of exchange I have drawn upon my own account since my being last in Virginia. "Item: I would have likewise have sent by my Executrix a Tombstone to Virginia to be put over my grave with my Grandfather's on top. Witnesses: Fra's Thruppe, William Burwood, Edward Evans.

Degg, 116.

[This will, recently discovered by Mr. Withington at Somerset

272

House, throws most interesting light on a mysterious and much debated question. In 1889 was published by the Munsells, of Albany, a work on "The Lindsays of America." by Miss Margaret Isabella Lindsay. In Chapter IV she gave an account of Rev. David Lindsay, an early minister of Northumberland county, Va. He is frequently mentioned in the county records, and by his will, dated and proved in April, 1667, gave his whole estate to his daugter, Helen Lindsay, apparently his only child. On page 49 the author says: "In 1849 my father commissioned a relative to visit the old homestead and burying place on it, and he took from the stone the following inscription, although even then it was difficult to discipher; it was surmounted by the engraved coat of arms of the family:

"Here lyeth interred ye body of That Holy and Reverent Devine, Mr. David Lindsay, late Minister of Yeocomico, born in ye Kingdom of Scotland, ye first and lawful sonne of ye Rt. Honerable Sir Hierome Lindsay, K'nt of ye Mount, Lord-Lyon-King-at-Arms, who departed this life in ye 64th year of his age ye 3d April, Anno Dom. 1667."

In the account given in the earlier portion of the book, relating to the Scottish Lindsays, it is shown that Sir Hierome Lindsay had a son, David, who was baptized January 3, 1603. It would not appear from her book that the author was ever in Northumberland county, or claimed to have seen the tomb herself.

Miss Lindsay also states (page 41) that in the same tomb with the epitaph of Rev. David Lindsay, quoted above, was the following:

"Here also lyeth the body of Captain Thomas Opie, Jr., of Bristol, grandson of Mr. David Lindsay, who departed this life 16 November, 1702."

In 1902 Rev. G. W. Bealy, D. D., the foremost antiquary of the Northern Neck of Virginia, visited the old Lindsay burying ground in Northumberland. He found one massive stone which bore, with a few verbal differences, the inscription in regard to Thomas Opie, Jr., which has been quoted, but which had in regard to Rev. David Lindsay only the following:

"Here Lyeth The Body Of Mr.
David Lindsay, Doctor of
Divinity, Who Departed This Life
The 3d Day Of April, 1667."

There was no question as to the authenticity of this description; so the only conclusion which could be drawn was that the copyist for Miss Lindsay's father had deceived him.

In 1906 Mrs. Juliet Opie Ayres, a descendant of the Opies, also visited the place and had excavations made in and about the graveyard. As the existence of two tombstones over one grave is a most unlikely thing to expect, it is not known what suggested that digging might result in discoveries ; but it did, and two fragments of a stone were found which had sufficient portions of an inscription left to show that it must have been the one quoted in " The Lindsays of America."

Immediately a warm discussion began in the press. Mrs. Ayers produced the evidence of several reputable citizens of Northumberland and of a geological expert, but many of those who did not know her were unconvinced. That there should be two stones over one grave, erected in memory of the same people, seemed most improbable, and the doubt was heightened by the fact that Miss Lindsay's copy quoted correctly the Opie epitaph, which was stated by the copyist to be on the same stone with the Lindsay epitaph quoted by her.

The will in the text, coming to light after an interval of more than two hundred years, settles the question in a most remarkable manner. Thomas Opie says : " I would have likewise sent by my Executrix a Tombstone to Virginia to be put over my grave with my grandfather's on top." So the unprecedented did happen, and here was a grave with two tombstones upon it—one above the other. And the copyist quoted in " The Lindsays of America," Mrs. Ayers and Dr. Beale were all absolutely correct in their statements of what they found.

VIRGINIA GLEANINGS IN ENGLAND.

Communicated by Mr. LOTHROP WITHINGTON, 30 Little Russell street, W. C., London (including "Gleanings" by Mr. H. F. WATERS, not before printed).

EDWARD FIELDING, ESQ., one of the Aldermen of the City of Bristol. Will 9 February 1690–1; proved March 1690–1.

Vere, 53.

[Printed from an old copy preserved in Virginia, in this Magazine, XII, 99, &c.]

JNO. BAYNTON bound on a voyage to Virginia intending to return. Will 17th of 7th month 1688; proved 11 January 1689–90. To Jane Brickhead £10. To sister in law Sarrah Gibbons £6 and one broad piece of gold. To sister Elizabeth Hardy of Hatch £20. To Mary Day £3. To the poor friends of this City £7 for men's meeting and 40s. for women's meeting. To poor friends of Gregory Stocke meeting in Somersershire £3. To Brother Daniell Gibbons £2 2. All else to my son Benjamin Baynton. I make Daniel Gibbons, Charles Hardford senior, and William Bathe, all of this City (Bristol?), to be his guardians. [Then follows a list of the above legacies and] the account of my Stok for this year 88.

	£	S	D
In my trunke			
100 guinyes ½ in a purse	108	00	09
In bro. goulde in a booke and ½ guiny	12	18	3
In a leather Purse	40	00	00
In a Wallet	23	10	00
In a Bagg	13	00	00
I carried with me in the Bristoll Merchant	145	10	00
Due from Daniel Gibbons	22	3	00
3 bonds which come to	490	10	00
	898	12	00
	54	8	00
	844	4	00

From Vol. XVIII, No. 2 (April 1910), p. 177.

To my Brother James Baynton as much as will pay Daniel Gibbons booke debt and £5 to his son Jno. Baynton. Administration to Charles Harford and William Bathe two of the guardians nominated in the will of John Baynton late of City of Bristol deceased to administer during minority of his son Benjamin Baynton.

Dyke, 1.

[The testator was evidently a Quaker.]

HOPKIN PRICE, now residing in London, otherways of Rappahannock River in County Middlesex in Virginia. Will 8 December 1677; proved 28 November 1679. To Henry Atherton, now apprentice to my good Friend Mr. Thurston Withnell, £10 one year after certain notice of my death. Residuary Legatee and Executor: Mr. Thurston Withnell, now of St. Giles Cripplegate, Distiller. Witnesses: Francis Banister, Tho: Trowell.

King, 147.

Late of Stepney, Middlesex.—Probate Act Book.

THOMAS CROOKE, junior, Citizen and Plaisterer of London. Will 14 Januarie 1679–80; proved 16 June 1681. I the said Thomas Crooke being now by God's grace outward bound for Virginia or parts adjacent upon the Continent of America, aboard the Merchant's Delight, Captain Joseph Eton commander. My goods on this side, beyond the seas, and on board ship as follows, one half to my daughter Elizabeth Crooke, the other to my father Thomas Crooke, senior, citizen and plaisterer of London. Executor: Father Thomas Crooke. Overseers: Samuel Smith, Citizen and Plaisterer of London, and Jeremiah Howes, Citizen and Stationer of London. Witnesses: Elizabeth Slamaker [?], Charles Wright, Sam. Smith, Edward Thistlewheate, Jeremiah Howes.

North, 88.

JOHN GWIN of James City County, Merchant. Will 6 July 1682; proved 25 November 1684. Sole Legatee and Executor: friend and loving kinsman Mr. Henry Jenkins. Witnesses: John Heyward, Robt. Higginson, David Arthur. Virginia, James City County. Hen. Hartwell C'k Cur., certifies that above is a true copy of will which was proved there 7 August 1682. Proved in Prerogative Court of Canterbury by Thomas Starke, deputy for Henry Jenkins, executor of will of John Gwin, late of James City, Virginia, deceased.

146 Hare.

[John Gwin no doubt lived at Jamestown. No other notice of him appears. He was, of course, a different person from Rev. John Gwyn, minister of Ware parish, in 1672, and of Abingdon, in 1674 and 1680, both parishes being in Gloucester county.

Captain Henry Jenkins was, in 1695, "a justice of the quorum and commander-in-chief for ye County of Elizabeth City." His will was proved in Elizabeth City on September 24, 1698. See *William and Mary Quarterly*, IX, 129, 130. He had a brother, "Daniel Jenkins, Gent.," living in the city of Dublin.]

ROBERT LANCASTER of Bristol, Chirurgeon, dated at sea, aboard the ship Unicorne. Will 3 January 1684–5; proved 13 August 1685. My body to sea or earth. To my wife Anne Lancaster the estate I had with her and my house joining unto William Thurnston upon the Key in Bristol and the Star Taverne on the other side wherein liveth one Samuel Bandrum a cooper. Also my part of a cargo between me and Mr. John Dudleston, to pay off debt contracted by her mother to one Freeman a lawyer, and all my goods in England or Virginia. To my two widowed sisters Anne Cooper and Rachel Parret the house the widow Hedge now lives in, they to pay my cozen Baker £10. To Brother Edward my silver cup. To Sister Mary Lewis three gold rings now on my finger. Executrix: My mother Anna Lancaster, widow.

Cann, 111.

[The earliest appearance of the name Lancaster in the Virginia Land Books is a grant to Gawen Lancaster, on March 1, 1652, 75 acres in the county of Charles River (New York), adjoining Captain West's Creek and Thomas Moreland and William Reynolds.

On October 8, 1672, Rowland Horsley and Robert Lancaster were granted 473 acres on Mattadequon Creek, New Kent county, adjoining the land of Charles Bryan.

There were other Lancasters, seafaring men, who had relations with Virginia. In Northumberland county, February 23, 1704–5, was a suit by Cuthbert Sharpless, Richard Gildert and Thomas Mason, merchants of Liverpool, and John Lancaster, mariner, *vs.* William Mason, shipwright, late of Liverpool, but then of Northumberland county, Va. John Lancaster was probably master of a merchant ship.

Elizabeth Nelms of Northumberland county, in her will dated July 23, 1779, left all of her land and 20 slaves to Joseph Lancaster, son of her nephew William Lancaster, deceased.]

SAMUEL SANDFORD sometimes of Accomack County in Virginia and now being in the City of London. Will 27 March 1710; proved 20 April 1710. To be privately buried in the Parish Burial place at Avening in County Gloucester. To sister Mary Freeman, widow, 25s. a month for life out of my money in the Bank of England and to her daughter Mary Freeman whose name is mentioned in my base granted by Phillip Sheppard, Esq., for my tenement at Avening, the said tenement, she paying her sister Jane Freeman 30s. a quarter while unmarried. To my sister's son Thomas £20. To Sandford Green, son of Mordicay and Thomazen, £50. To Susannah Sandford, my neice and daughter of my Brother John Sandford, sometime of Princess Anne County in Virginia, £500. To his daughter Mary Sandford £500. For learning of six poor male children of Avening £200. Each child to have brown coloured cloth coat, buttons of Horn, a Hatt, one pair of shoes, and one pair of stockings. Mr. Samuel Sheppeard Senior and Junior to be trustees. For education of poor children in Accomack County, from Guildford Creek to Sea side, and to Maryland, 2500 acres, according to survey of Edmond Harborough made April 1700, which lands I bought of Coll. John West and adjoining to Lixess Island, Mosongoe Creek, and Pocomack Bay, and a piece of land near Crooked creek which I bought of Nathaniell Rackliffe. To John, son of Thomas Pary, my kinsman, now in Maryland, the two corn mills bought for my account of Ralph Foster of St. Mary's County in Maryland. To my kinsman Thomas Sandford, living in Fenchurch Street in London, the remainder of a debt due me by his subscription. If my servant Will, a Mallagascoe man, desires to go to Virginia, his fare and necessarys are to be paid. Residuary Legatee and Executrix: neice Katherine Sandford, daughter of my Brother Giles Sandford.

Overseers: Mr. Thomas Sheppard, late of Avening, but now of London, and John Pary aforenamed. Witnesses: John Powell, Lewis Smith, Tho: Sheppard, Tho: Witheby.

Smith, 98.

[Samuel Sandford was a member of the House of Burgesses for Accomac in March, 1692-3. Meade (*Old Churches and Families of Virginia*, I, 264, 265) states that the school founded by Samuel Sandford in Accomac was in existence in 1857. He states that the will was recorded in Accomac and gives an extract. The total amount of the land left to the school was 3,420 acres, and the testator asked the Governor and Council of Virginia to see that his purposes in regard to the school were carried out.

John Sandford, the brother, was a considerable land owner in (Old) Norfolk-Princess Anne county and was J. P. at the formation of the latter county in 1691. Administration on his estate was granted March 1, 1692-3, to his widow, Sarah. See this Magazine, XI, 144.]

VIRGINIA GLEANINGS IN ENGLAND.

———

Communicated by Mr. LOTHROP WITHINGTON, 30 Little Russell street, W. C., London (including " Gleanings " by Mr. H. F. WATERS, not before printed).

———

JOHN COLLYER of London, merchant and Clothworker. Will 18 December 1649; proved 8 January 1649-50 To be buried at Beddington in Surrey. One third of my goodes to Regina my wife, one third to my heir Charles Collyer, the remainder as follows: To my Brother Isaack Collyer I forgive £500 he owes me, to my nephew Isaacke Collyer Junr. £150. To my mother in law Mrs. Anna Semiliano £50. To her daughter my sister in law Mrs. Anna Maria £200. To my Brother in law Vincentio Malo £200 from which is to be deducted what he owes me for pictures. To Brother John Knight my interest in the house he now inhabits in Mark Lane and to my sister Mary his wife £20. To my couzins William and Mary Jurner £25. To

From Vol. XVIII, No. 3 (July 1910), p. 303.

279

Henry Swift £15. To poor of Bedington £10. To Mr. Job Throgmorton £50. To Poor of London £20. To William Jolliffe I restore of what I had with him £100. Executors: my deare friend Mr. Job Throgmorton, brother Isaacke Collyer, wife Regina. If my wife leaves England at any time my son Charles is not to go with her, he is to be brought up in English learning and Protestant faith. Sealed at Wallington in Surrey. Witnesses: John Heather, William Blacke.

Pembroke, 3.

[Edward Lockey, of York county, Va., brother of John Lockey, grocer, of London, died without issue in the parish of St. Catherine Cree Church, London, in 1667. In his will, dated in that year, he bequeathed that "Morgan's Plantation," in York county, to his "cousin" Isaac Collier, Jr., son of Isaac Collier, Sr., and the reversion of two other plantations. Isaac Collier, Jr., was dead in 1671. In 1675 was recorded in York county the inventory of the estate of Isaac Collier. The will of Isaac Collier, Sr., was proved in York May 24, 1688, and names his children Charles, Abraham, Thomas and Sarah. In 1693, Thomas Collier (who was dead in 1704), sold Morgan's Plantation, styling himself "brother and heir of Isaac Collier, dec'd." For account of the Colliers see *William and Mary Quarterly*, III, 278; VIII, 202; IX, 183, 184.]

EDMOND CLEBORNE of Killerbye, county York, Esquire. Will 17 May 1648; proved 14 February 1649–50. To my son Thomas Cleborne an annuity of £20 out of manor of Killerbye in Yorkshire and my manor of Cleburne in Westmoreland. To my youngest son Mathew Cleburne a like annuity of £20. To my daughter Elizabeth Cleburne £100. To Frances and Ann Bennett my nieces £25 each. To my sons Thomas and Mathew £100 each. To poor of Cattericke £5. Residuary Legatee and Executrix: Wife Elizabeth. No witnesses.

Pembroke, 15.

[Edmond Cleborne was nephew of William Claiborne, of Virginia, son of his eldest brother, Thomas Cleburne.]

HUGH BULLOCKE of London, gent. All Hallows Barking 72 years of age and dim sighted. Will 22 October 1649; proved 2 November 1650. I have the half of Dungeonesse lights which I purchased from Sir Francis Howard. The half of which half I sold to Andrew Burrell which half was purchased from him by my son William Bullocke. My son William married

William Lamply's daughter and purchased William Bing's part in the other half and my son William at his goeing into Virginia let his part for £100 per annum. To my grandchild Francis, daughter of my said son William, £20 per annum during term of the patent which has 17 years to run. To Mary Bennett, now living in London, £4 per annum during the patent. To Ellinor, daughter of my sister Ann Mason, £3 per annum during patent. To Mary Rose, widow, living in Ratcliffe, 40s. per annum. To Barnard Smith, my deputy in the Custom House, £3 per annum during patent. My estate in Virginia amounting to £100 per annum left me there 10 years past to my son William and his son Robert. Executors: John Limbry Esq. and Barnard Smith. Overseer: Master of the Trinity House for the time being. To Mary Snow, wife of Nicholas Snow, 7s. yearly; to Elizabeth her sister 7s. yearly. Witnesses: William Walklett, James Turner, Beniamine Sheppard, Scr. Proved by Samuell Burrell, principal creditor.

Pembroke, 168.

[On March 12, 1634, Captain Hugh Bullock was granted 2,550 acres, probably in York county. By deed dated July 8, 1637, and recorded in York, Hugh Bullock, of London, gentleman, conveyed to his son William Bullock, of London, gentleman, his corn mill, saw mill and plantation in Virginia. Hugh Bullock had evidently lived in Virginia, as he was appointed member of the Council in 1631. His son William, whose will follows, was the author of the well-known tract.

In the Virginia General Court Records, April, 1672, is an entry of a suit by Robert Bullock, son and heir of William Bullock, who was son and heir of Hugh Bullock, vs. Col. Peter Jennings, guardian of John Mathews, orphan of Col. Mathews, deceased, in regard to a tract of land containing 5,500 acres in Warwick county.]

WILLIAM BULLOCKE, gent, of Essex. Will proved 10 May 1650. Being bound for Virginia in the partes beyond the seas. To my wife Elizabeth Bullocke, trusting that she will proportion to either of my children as well as my daughter Frances as my son Robert, childrens portions of my estate. Executrix: wife Elizabeth. Witnesses: Thomas Harrison, Richard Mills.

Pembroke, 61.

SIR JOHN HARVEY of London, Knight. Will 15 September 1646; proved 16 July 1650. I am now bound on a voyage to sea. The King owes me £5500 as appears under account of Mr. Orator Bingley and Sir Paul Pinder, and several persons in Virginia owe me £2000. I owe Tobias Dixon citizen and Haberdasher of London, £1000, and Mr. Nickolls of London, Ironmonger, £200. To Ursilla my eldest daughter £1000. To Anne my daughter £1000. If my daughters die without issue, £500 to my nephew Simon, son of my Brother the late Sir Simon Harvey of London, knt., and £400 to his two daughters and £400 to poor of St. Dunstans in the West. Executor: Tobias Dixon. Witnesses: Miles Arundell, Henry Wagstaffe, Thomas Smith, servant to Arthur Tirey Scr., Thomas Bland, Roger Escame.

Pembroke, 113.

[Sir John Harvey, so long associated with the government of Virginia, disappeared from view, as far as any records heretofore known were concerned, with his melancholy letter to Secretay Windebank of May 6, 1640 (this Magazine, XIII, 388). It has been conjectured that he died soon afterwards, but the will given above shows th t he did not die until 1650. What he did in the interval is unknown. Perhaps the English Domestic State Papers of the period may have references to him ; possibly he was in a debtor's prison.]

WILLIAM EWENS of Greenwich, county Kent, mariner. Will 2 April 1649; proved 12 August 1650. To Mary my wife £100 out of my lands and tenements in England. The Ballast wharfe and 4 tenements in Greenwich to my daughter Mary; if she die before 21, then to Thomas Ewens the elder during life and at his decease one half to William and Thomas Ewens his two sons and their issue, failing them or their issue to my kinsmen Ewen Johnson and Ewen Peters, the other half to Ewen Johnson, Margarett Johnson, Ewen Peters, Mary Noble, and her daughter. My executors to take a friendly care of my cousin Mary Noble and her daughter. To Mary my wife one third of all my shipping debts oweing by bill bond or from the Parliament in any wise, the other two thirds I give to my daughter Mary. To Mary my daughter the two shares of land I have in the Sommer Islands, being 60 acres now or late in the occupation of one William Farmer. To Thomas Ewens the elder the North Mill standing upon the Deanes at Yarmouth now in the occupation of John Broome. To William Stevens my son in law £100. To

Thomas Ewens the elder and to his four children William, Thomas, Thomazine, and Martha Ewens 20s. each. To Margaret Johnson, Ewen Johnson, Ewen Peters, Susan Pigott, Mary Noble, and her daughter 20s. each to be raised out of my shipping and the sale of my land in Virginia. Executors: Wife and Daughter, Thomas Stevens and Arnold Browne. Witnesses: Frances Cordwell, William Denmay, Paul Paine, John Weeks John Wardall. Codicil 30 April 1650. Mentions £30 in my hands for Ewen Peters when 21 given unto him by his grandfather John Ewen. Witnesses: William Ewen, Mathew Walker.

Pembroke, 132.

[In the records of Surry county, Va., is an entry stating that whereas Mrs. Mary Ewens, by power of attorney, June 30, 1659, had given authority to Mr. Francis Newton, or his substitutes, to take possession of a plantation, &c., in Virginia, belonging to her, and the said Francis Newton substituted his brother Nicholas Newton (now dead) and Richard Hopkins as his attorneys, by an instrument dated June 30, 1659. Mrs. Ewens owned in Virginia 7 negroes, 50 head of cattle, 15 hogs and other personal property. Francis Newton was a London merchant, trading to Virginia. See his will in this Magazine, XVIII, 80. The will in the text is one of not infrequent instances where masters of English merchant ships trading to Virginia owned plantations in the Colony. Most of these masters, however, like William Ewens, did not long live in the Colony. Greenwich was a more congenial place for a sailor than a plantation in Surry county.]

HENRY HOBSON of Citty of Bristoll, Innholder. Will 16 March 1634–5; proved 27 May 1636. To be buried in All Saints, Bristoll, where I now live, as near the place where my late wife Alice lieth buried as convenient. I confirm a deed made 10 March 5 Chas. I between me Henry Hobson of the one part and Myles Jackson of Bristol, Merchant, and Godfrey Creswicke of the same city, hardwareman, of the other part, except touching the lands called Beggerswell, Riglinges, and two closes near the same which I have settled otherwise by a deed 14 of this instant moneth of March. To my grandchildren Henry, Matthew, Richard, and Myles Cary, children of my daughter Alice, wife of John Cary, draper £5 each. To my grandchildren Thomas and Henry children of my daughter Anne Jackson, widow £5. To my grandchildren Alice, Honor and Mary Cary daughters of my daughter Alice Cary, £100 each, and to my grandchildren Mar-

garett and Ann Jacksonne £100 each. To my kinsman and
servant Richard Burrowes £20. To my kinsman Christopher
Reynoldes, son of George Reynoldes deceased, £5 and to his
sister Anne Reynolds £10. To Company of Inholders of Bristol 40s. To my kinsman Francis Creswicke, merchant, and
Thomas Hobson, pewterer, my messuage in St. Nicholas Street in
Bristol where Arthur Stert now dwelleth for the use of my
daughter Alice Cary. To my daughter Anne Jackson my wyne
license which I bought from Hugh Hart to drawe wyne by in
Bristol and also the tenement in St. Nicholas Street in which
Phillip Love, merchant, liveth. The residue among my three
children William Hobson, Alice Cary and Anne Jackson. Exec-
utor: son William Hobson. Overseers: Kinsman Francis Cres-
wicke and Thomas Hobson. I doe give to my old servant
Edward Drabble whom I had almost forgot 40s. Witnesses:
Roger Roydon, Richard Gregson, Bryan Ratcliffe, George
Hartwell, notary public.

Pile, 52.

[Henry Hobson was Mayor of Bristol. He was buried in the Church
of All Saints on March 29, 1635, and a funeral certificate was duly filed
in the College of Arms. His coat of arms was: *argent, on a chevron
azure between three pellets as many cinque—foils argent, with a chief
chequy or and azure.* His grandson, Miles Cary, was the emigrant to
Virginia. Keith's *Ancestry of Benjamin Harrison*, p. 39, and chart.]

JONAS STOCKTON of the City of London, gent. Will 2 February 1647–8; proved 22 February 1648–9. Taking into consideration the long and dangerous journey that I intend shortly
God willing to take into the Island of Barbados. The lands and
tenements in the Manors of Balsall and Berkeswell in county
Warwick which descended to me after the death of Thomas
Stockton my brother caused strife amongst my kindred upon
pretence that I was then dead in Barbados but of regard for the
kindness and affection which my aunt Debborah Savage and
John Savage gent her husband deceased and their children
showed to me in my minoritie and since I did on the last day of
January last past before the date of these presents surrender the
said lands to the use of my said Aunt Debborah and her son John
Savage. To my kinsman Clement Fisher £20. To my cozen
Ann Fisher his wife £20 and to their daughter Anne £20. To

my cozen Katherine Savage, late wife of William Savage, clerk, deceased, my kinsman, £10. To John her son and Anne her daughter £10 apiece. To Mr. Simond Kinge £10. To my cozen Priddie of London, vintner, 20s. and to his wife my kinswoman £10 To my cozen Elizabeth Silvester £10 and to my cozen Abigail Biddle £5. To my cozen John Jelliffe (Jolliffe ?) 20s. Executor: John Savage. Overseers: Clement Fisher, Simond Kinge. Witnesses: John Repington, Thomas Norton, Richard Nillin.

Fairfax, 25.

[Doubtless a kinsman of an early Virginia minister, Jonas Stockton, who was born 1584, came to Virginia in 1620, patented land in Elizabeth City September 8, 1627, and died before September 20, 1628. He was the author of a well-known letter in regard to the Indians. See this Magazine, II, 78, 179.]

JOHN BICKLEY, Citizen and Haberdasher of London. Will 12 August 1636; proved 26 January 1636-7. Goods in three ports as by landable custum of the Citty of London to my wife Sarah one third. To my Francis and John and the child my wife now goeth with the second third. The other third as follows: To sons Francis and John £500 when 21, etc. To my sister Barnett 20 Marks and to my sister Anne Love £10. To my neece Susan Barnett £40 at 21 or marriage. To my nephew Joseph Wise £30 and to my nephews John Love, Nicholas Love and Thomas Love £20 each at 21. To my daughter in law Jane Sarnell £10 when 21 or marriage. To my wife's mother 40s. for ring. To my apprentice Thomas Garrard £10 when 21. To my wife the messuage where I now dwell in St. Olave Southwarke till sonne Frances is 21, etc., etc. Residuary Legatees and Executors: Sons Francis and John. To poore of St. Olave £5, etc. Overseer: my wife. To be put in the Chamber's hand £600 to lone at interest to sister Anne Love &c., and if she die becomes John, then Francis, then to my sister Susan, &c. This will blotted out by my own hand in three places, viz one about buriall, one about sister Anne, and one about cousin Francis Bickley. Witnesses: Thomas Worseley, John Pickering and John Pyott. Proved by Sarah 26 January 1636-7, the relict of John Bickley late of St. Mary Aldermary during the minority of Francis and John executors. Administration 24 November 1642 to Laurence Brinley, husband of Sarah Brinley als. Bickley, deceased, and executor of her will during minority of Francis and John, executors.

Goare 8.

[This John Bickley was probably father of John Bickley, who married Anne Bell and had a son Francis Bickley, who was in Virginia in 1656. These people were probably related to, but not ancestors of, the family of Bickley, baronets, also in Virginia.]

FRANCIS BEDELL of Great Catworth in the Counties of Huntingdon and Northampton, gent. Will 2 August 1648; proved 24 August 1648 and 27 August 1650. To my wife Susanna all houses in Town of Great Catworth. To son Julius Bedell all lands in Worneditch and Newtowne in parish of Kimbolton and the house and lands in Great Catworth after decease of my wife, in default to my son William Bedell. Mr. Ironmonger of Leighton Buzzard, county Beds and Mr. John Chapman of Willing, county Bucks owe me £50. To my son William Bedell £200. If Mr. Barnardbe in this Countrey he is to make the bonds for the satisfaction of my will but if he be not in this Country then Mr. John Loftis of Lutton to hold the bonds. My Cosen Mr. Jasper Trice and my son Michaell to see the bonds sealed. To Brother John Bedell, Sister Pennell and Sister Hawys 10s. each. To my daughter Hastinges two sons £10 apiece when 16 years old. To my son Hastings and my daughter his wife, to son Mitchell and my daughter Francis his wife and my man and maid 10s. apiece. Executrix: my wife. Overseers: Cosen Mr. Jasper Trice, Sons in law Mr. Robert Hastings and John Mitchell. Witnesses: Thomas Foster, William Musgrave. Administration to eldest son William Bedell 27 January 1650-51 of goods not administered by relict Susan Bedell now deceased.

Essex 126.

[Dorothy, wife, first, of Edward Burwell, of Harlington, Bedfordshire, (and by this marriage mother of Lewis Burwell, the emigrant to Virginia), and secondly, of Roger Wingate, Treasurer of Virginia, was daughter of William Bedell, of Great Catworth, Huntingdonshire. The family is traced in Camden's *Visitation of Huntingdonshire* to John Bedell, of Wallaston, Northamptonshire, who died in 1485.]

VIRGINIA GLEANINGS IN ENGLAND.

Communicated by Mr. LOTHROP WITHINGTON, 30 Little Russell street, W. C., London (including " Gleanings " by Mr. H. F. WATERS, not before printed).

MORRYS BARKELEY of Bruton in Summerset, Knight. Will 10 February 1579-80; proved 16 November 1581. To wieffe Elizabeth Barkeley, daughter of Anthony Sandes of Threwleye, Kente, Esquier, for Dower All my Mannor house of Bruton where I dwell withe the Desmesnes commonlie knowen to be parte and parcell within fortie yeares with stocke of Cattell uppon the same and on departinge this life viz: 26 kine, 16 plough oxen, and 300 sheepe with her apparrells, jewells, and £100 also in Personages of Bruton, Bruham, Redlinche, Pitcombe, Colle, and Wike. Furder to my saide wieffe all furniture in the chamber at the toppe of the house called the gallerie chamber as well hanginges, beddes, bedstede, testers with A pallette and canopye and three pallettes in the gallerie, as the bedde in the little case, and Also to wieffe half of linnen and Vessells in the kitchene, as well pewter as brasse. Furder to wief her Coche with the two horses and a good geldinge. To seconde sonne Edward Berkeley my Farme in Datchett in Buckingham sherre commonlie called Redinge courte. Also to Edward Annuitie of £10 owte of the Priory of sainte Jermine as by conveyance between his brother in lawe Henrie Champernon and me. Furder to Edwarde Combe Fearme in Bruton w'ch he hath for 80 years at stock paying rent of £4 5s od. To third sonne Francis Barkley my Fearme of Horsley in sowthe Bruham lett out at present with a stock of 12 kine for £50 a yeare. Furder to Francis Annuitie of £10 w'ch Richard Fitz James Esquire is bounde to paye him for life and then to my fyfte sonn John Barkeleye. To fowthe son Roberte my Mannor of Patnedon in Kent called Patendon place let out at present for £67 10s yearlie. Furder to Robert lease of Fearme at Wilkenthorpe that William Harman houldeth 60 years in Reversion of Hannom's estate.

From Vol. XVIII, No. 4 (Oct. 1910), p. 435.

Further Robert to have a lease of little Deane and Parsons Close with a stocke 10 kyn and a Mare what nowe Gastarde and Bartlette houldeth for £16, paying Lords rente of 20s. To youngest sonn John Barkeley lease of Wanstrowe with stocke. Furder to John reversion of Fearme in North Bryham that Hugh Batt holdeth called Batts Fearme. Whereas I bought a lease of Sir James Fitz James in sowthe Bruham commonly called Gallys Fearm for Ten hundred yeares and did lette it owt with stock of 10 kyne for £22 a year w'ch Lease my wief his mother hath solde for £240 and will answer for rent during his lieff w'ch I bequeath to sonn John. To two daughters Ann and Margarett Barkeley £600 each in marriage and 20 markes apece yearly out of my Fearme of Smaldon towards theire feedinge. To servants years wages. Overseers: Nephews Sir George Speake, Sir Richard Barkeley Knightes and Nephew John Frauncis Esqre. Rest to eldest sonne Henrie Barkeley, Executor. No witnesses. "Item I will that my executor shall geve twentie poundes to the poore at the daie of my buriall by shillinges, halfe shillinges, or groates at his discretion and thoughe I knowe it wyll doe me no good, yet I am perswaded it will doe them no harme. Item I will that my three youngest sonnes Frances Barkley, Robert and John Barkley shall have my cheyne equally devided betweene them w'ch weigheth fortie two ounces of fyne goulde. Also I will that my fower daughters Gartrude, Besse, Anne and Margaret shall have twentie poundes apeece to buye them chaynes with all."   Darcy, 40.

[Sir Richard Berkeley, of Stoke Gifford, Gloucestershire (who died 1514), a descendant of the Lords Berkeley, of Berkeley Castle, married Elizabeth, daughter of Sir Humphrey Conningsby, and had Sir John, of Stoke Gifford, ancestor of Lord Botetourt, and Sir Maurice, whose will is given in the text. Sir Maurice Berkeley, K. B., of Bruton, Somerset, standard bearer to Henry VIII, married, first, Catherine, daughter of William, Lord Mountjoy, and secondly, Elizabeth, daughter of Anthony Sands, Esq., and sister of Sir Thomas Sands, of Kent. The will of the second wife is given next below. The Visitation of 1623 gives no children of the second marriage, but Burke's *Extinct Peerage* says there were two sons and a daughter. However this may be, Sir Maurice Berkeley had by his first marriage (1) Sir Henry of Bruton, who married

Margaret, daughter of —— Ligon of Madresfield, county Worcester;
(2) Sir Francis, whose son Maurice was living in Ireland in 1623. Sir
Maurice Berkeley also had four daughters: (1) Gertrude, married Edward Horne, Esq.; (2) Elizabeth, married James Percival, Esq., of Weston Gordon, Somerset; (3) Anne, married Nicholas Poynings, Esq., of
Adderly; (4) Frances, died unmarried.

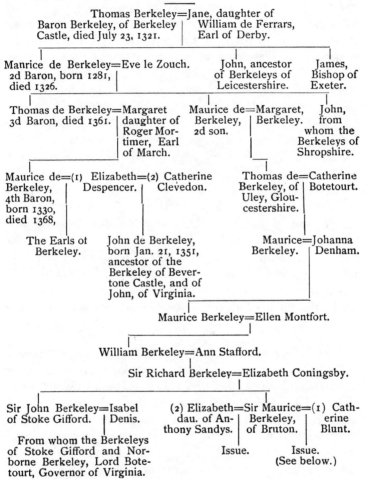

Thomas Berkeley=Jane, daughter of
Baron Berkeley, of Berkeley | William de Ferrars,
Castle, died July 23, 1321. | Earl of Derby.

Maurice de Berkeley=Eve le Zouch.   John, ancestor   James,
2d Baron, born 1281, | of Berkeleys of   Bishop of
died 1326. | Leicestershire.   Exeter.

Thomas de Berkeley=Margaret   Maurice de=Margaret,   John,
3d Baron, died 1361. | daughter of   Berkeley, | Berkeley.   from
| Roger Mor-   2d son. | whom the
| timer, Earl | Berkeleys of
| of March. | Shropshire.

Maurice de=(1) Elizabeth=(2) Catherine   Thomas de=Catherine
Berkeley, | Despencer. | Clevedon.   Berkeley, of | Botetourt.
4th Baron, | | Uley, Glou- |
born 1330, | | cestershire. |
died 1368, | |

The Earls of   John de Berkeley,   Maurice=Johanna
Berkeley.   born Jan. 21, 1351,   Berkeley. | Denham.
  ancestor of the
  Berkeley of Bever-
  tone Castle, and of
  John, of Virginia.

Maurice Berkeley=Ellen Montfort.

William Berkeley=Ann Stafford.

Sir Richard Berkeley=Elizabeth Coningsby.

Sir John Berkeley=Isabel   (2) Elizabeth=Sir Maurice=(1) Cath-
of Stoke Gifford. | Denis.   dau. of An- | Berkeley, | erine
From whom the Berkeleys   thony Sandys. | of Bruton. | Blunt.
of Stoke Gifford and Nor-   Issue.   Issue.
borne Berkeley, Lord Bote-   (See below.)
tourt, Governor of Virginia.

The Berkeleys have the (almost unique) honor of an unbroken male
descent from a Saxon ancestor living before the Conquest. Modern
genealogical investigation has made it practically certain that the family
descends from Eadnoth "the staller," (equivalent to master of the horse)
a high official at the court of Edward the Confessor.]

Dame Elizabeth Barkeley, of Clarktonwell, County of Middlesex, Widowe, late wyff of Sr. Morris Barkley of Bruton, countie Somersett, Knight. Will 11 November 1584; proved 6 June 1585. To poore of parish where buried £20. To poore of town of Bruton, Somerset sheire, £10 to be discharged by chiefe Governor of the Towne and the £20 by my two brothers or one of them. To 12 poore men 12 black gowns and to 24 poore women 24 ditto to be nominated by said two brothers so many as nominated by mee. To my daughter Margaret 3 Coffres or Chestes one called my Jewells Coffre one other with a black lether cover and the thirde a cipress coffer with Jewells, plate, money, lynnen, silke, etc and these without prisement or looking into by any other, charging her if any writinges there which concern her brothers lands to deliver them, etc. To servants a years wages except Rachaell my mayd and to her £5. Also to her Jewells to be delivered by two brothers to value of £100 and £40 to buy her wedding apparell at marriage. To my two brothers Mr. Thomas Sondes and Mr. Michaell Sondes my two best ringes, they to see me buried, and bestow on my burial 200 markes over somes already appointed, and two brothers, executors, to pay debts, etc., and remainder to my son Robert. To my nephew Cheyney and his wief fetherbed, etc., I had of my brother by my Father's bequeth. No witnesses.

Brudenell, 33.

Henry Barckley, Bruton, Countie Somersett, Knighte. Will 30 May 1600; proved 21 October 1601. To be buried in my parish church of Bruton in the vault which I made for my Father yf I depart within 100 myles thereof. To wife Dame Margaret Barkley manor house of Bruton where I dwell with demesnes and in as ample maner as Dame Elizabeth Barkley my mother in lawe held the same. To wife for life my milles in Bruton known by name of Wynes myll. Also to wife use of household stuffe and my personages of Bruton, Bruham, Redling, Weeke, Cole, Pitcombe, and Hatchpine with all tithes and Also all her Apparell and Jewells and also plate she bought also £100 out of my parte of Norwood yearlie. To my second sonn Henry Barkley my mannor of Yerlington Somerset. Also to said Harry Barkley for 9 acres of meade in Cave Moore brougte of Mr. Sedborowe soulde in Lue 10 acres bought in North Cadburie Allso to Harry household stuff at Yerlington but to take no benefit lest he put estate in Mannor Foxcock to such person I promise yt in my life time and as shall be past not my overseers etc debts. To third sonn Edward Berkley mannor of Pill als Pull Somerset. till death etc. younger sons Harry and Edward to have £40 yearlie out of Yerlington. Son Edwarde Barkeley to have £20 out of my uncle Brodrips estate in Pill Farm, the extinguished Leases of Norwood to remain in hands of cozen Mr. George Speak and Morris Gilberte, Mr. Robert Woodford, and Mr. John Barnerd. If elder son Morris Barkelie die under age younger sons Henry and Edward to have benefit of Norwood. To son Morris Barklie lease of Smallden also and all my armour and furniture for warres. Also my Tentes and such other things as in my Armoury at Bruton. To two younger sons each a geldinge nagge. To eldest son best horse after his mother hath chosen. To poore of Bruton £20. To servants a year's wages. Overseers: kinsmen Mr. George Speake, Mr. Morris Gilberte, Mr. Robert Woodford, and friend Mr. John Barnerd, and to them £10 each. Stocks of cattell at Norwood, Bruton, Yerlington, and Smalldon to be sold. To third son Edward Barkley £500 yf redeem not Pill Farm. Executrix: Wife Dame Margaret Barkley. No witnesses. Woodhall, 68.

[The wills of Sir Henry Berkeley, of Bruton, and of his wife, Margaret Ligon, are given in the text. They had issue: (1) Sir Maurice; (2) Sir Henry, of Yarlington, married Elizabeth, daughter of Sir Henry Nevill, of Berkshire; (3) Edward, of Pull, Somerset, married a daughter of ——— Holland, of Somerset.

Margaret Berkeley makes a bequest to a Ligon, nephew. Thomas Folliot, of Pirton, married Katherine, daughter of Sir William Lygon, of Madresfield, and had a son, Sir John Folliot, who married Elizabeth, daughter of John Aylmer, Bishop of London. They were the parents of Rev. Edward Folliot, loyalist rector of Alderton, Northamptonshire, who was evicted by the Parliamentary Commissioners, and came to Virginia, becoming minister of York parish from 1652 to 1690. Governor

Berkeley's grandmother and Edward Folliot's grandmother were sisters—another instance of the influence of kinship in Virginia. Rev. Justinian Aylmer, also a Virginia minister, was of the family of Bishop Aylmer, of London.]

DAME MARGARET BARKLEY OF BRUTON, SOMERSET, WIDDOWE. Will 9 February 1616-17; proved 28 June 1617. To be buried in the vaulte within the church of Bruton the next day after my decease yf I depart this life at Wells in said Countie. if not then where yt please God etc. To my Soon Sr Maurice Barkley Knight my wedding Ringe which I had of his father my late husband Sir Henry Barkley Knight, deceased w'ch Ringe he hath alreadie and all household stuffe in my house at Bruton at the hour of my death. To my said soon all household stuffe in the Lodge at Norwood Parke Countie Somerset, praysed at £40 in his Father's Inventory which is in his possession alreadie. To daughter in Lawe the Ladie Elizabeth Barkley wife to Sonn Sir Maurice my best border she hath alreadie and best lardge Damaske table cloth. To my sonn Thomas Russell of Rushooke, Countie Wigor, esquire, one bason and Ewer of silver which was his Fathers Sir Thomas Russell. To my sonn Sir Henry Barkley, Knight, £100 in his hands. To my son Edward Barkley, Esquire, best skarlett bedd in best Chamber at Wells with furniture that belongs to him that is the bedstead, the Curtaines and Double Vallence of skarlett caste with Crimson silke and frindge with Crimson silke, etc. To daughter Margaret Pollard, wife of Lewis Pollard of Kinges Nimpton, Devon, esq., £100 worth of plate and greate gould chayne and greate Pearle in her keeping, also a Coach, Coach horses, my leading gelding with furniture, etc. To my sister Catherine Folliott, wife of Thomas Folliott of Pirton Wigor esq best gorwne To said daughter Pollard. To neece Catherine Jerrard wife of Robert Jarrard of Sandfourd Countie Somerset gent my third best gowne. To grandchild Elizabeth Pollard daughter of said Lewis and Margaret Pollard £200. To neice Catherine Jarrard wife of Robert Jarrard of Sandfourd, Somerset gent my third best gown. To grandchild Elizabeth Pollard daughter of Lewis and Mar-

garet Pollard £200 at marriage or 21 etc also greene Mucka-
doe Cheste at end of my Cobbard in drawinge chamber at
Wells. To nephewe Hugh Lygon sonne of Hugh Lygon of
Hanley Castle Wigor. £60. To Mrs. Moore of Wells peece
of Stannell for petticote (2 yardes) To Doctor Bourne of
Wells, Doctor Wright—of Welles, Mr. Henry Southworth,
Mrs. Wright, wife of Dr. Wright 40s. each for rings. To
Mrs. Hughes of Wells, Mrs. James widdowe of Wells, Mrs.
Jane Southworth Mr. Henry Southworth and wife 10s. each
ditto. To servants William Cuffe £20, William Cole £20,
Thomas Tyce als Rigile £10, William Loomis £10, William
Gilbert £5, Humphrey Green £5, Edward Labram £5 Thomas
Bigges £5, Henry Shee an Irishman £3, Dorothy Cole wife of
William Cole £5 and little silver salte and four silver spoones
and a new pewter at Brewton all in their keeping. To rest of
men servants and maid servants years wages etc. To Towne
of Bruton for poore £20. To poore of Town of Welles £10.
to poore of town of Goe Willey county £10. My dwelling house
etc at Wells to be sould. Residue to two sons Sir Henry
Barkley Knight and Edward Barkley, executors. Witnesses:
Henry Southworth, Francis Cottington, William Cole.

Weldon, 26.

Sir Maurice Barkeley of Brewton in the Countie of Somerset Knight. Will 20 April 1617; proved 3 July 1617. To
be buried in christian buriall till body and soule united meete
my saviour in the cloudes etc. To Overseers of the poore and
Churchwardens of Brewton £20 for poore and poore tradesmen to remain a stock for ever. To repayringe of Brewton
church £8 to be paid to Godfrey for makinge battlemments for
the church which I bespoke. To Cathedral church of Wells
20s. To wife Lady Elizabeth Barkley use of all houzes with
Beddinges household stuff etc for life then to my sonn and
heire Charles Barkley to continue ympetualie with my Capital messuage of Brewton from heire to heire. To wife all
plate (except £200 worth already appointed to be sold for
debts) Jewells rest of personal goods and profitts of lease of

Smaledon to go for debts etc   To my fower younger sones
Henry Barkeley, Maurice Berkeley, William Barkeley and
John Barkeley my Closes and lands in Brewham Somerset
called Parkes and all other lands held by leases from Sir John
Carew Knight and John Fitzioms Esquire for severall greate
number of yeares each determined uppon Three lives etc also
dwelling house known by name of Staverdale in Staverdale
in parish of Wincanton Somerset held from William Wolla-
scot esquire for three lives etc wife to take rents till eldest son
Charles Barkley is 21 and for bringing up of said four youngest sons, then if son Charles desire to rent Brewham and
Staverdale to him before any other then to said four sons
Henry Berkley, Maurice Berkley, William Barkley, and John
Barkley Horsley Farm in Brewham for 99 years at £6. 13s 4d.
rent etc wife to take rent till Charles is 21 etc.   To daughter
Margaret Berkley £2000 for a marriage portion.   To daughter Jane Barkley £1500 ditto., both to be paid at 18 years of
age etc to marry with consent of wife and son Charles etc.
Whereas loving father in lawe Sir William Killigrew Knight
and William Norwood Esquire and Robert Woodford Esqr
stand possessed for divers years of the late disparked Parke of
Norwood called Norwood Parke within the parish of Glaston,
Somersett for use of son Sir Maurice Barkeley and myne
seirs.   I devise of first Rents £1000 to my debts and £2000 and
£1500 for daughters to be raised out of Rentes etc.   Whereas
there is only two lives in beinge of Capital Messuage and
Farme called Combe Farme in Brewton Executors to make
up estate for one life if I am prevented by death and son
Charles at age to make good etc.   To servants Arthur Upton
gent, Thomas Dale, Bartholomew Neale, John Maunder and
Henry Rixon 20s. each.   To Edward Labram, Maslyn Wal-
lys, Nurse Maunder, Nurse Lenmys, Naman Grym and Agnes
Allwater, and Agnes Elliott 10s. each.   Whereas friends
Henry Bainton gent and Toby Pearce gent are somewhat engaged for debts, wief Elizabeth Barkley and Henry Bainton ·
and Toby Pearce to be executors and administratiors till debts
are paid.   Sole Executrix wief Elizabeth Barkley.   To Henry

Bainton and Toby Pearce each a geldinge or nagge as wief think fit. Overseers: Sir Robert Killigrew knight, Sir John Horner, knight, and Robert Hopton Esquier and Edward Bysse esquire. Witnesses: Thomas Elson, Henrye Banninge, William Lewes, and William Powell. Codicil 28 April 1617: "Now for as much I would willinglie have a Reverend and learned Preacher provided for and brought to Bruton w'ch much desire for instructinge and Teachinge the people in the servise and fears of God And my will is that the said Preacher doe preache everie Saboth daye in the forenoone throughout the year as Farr forth as God shall enoble him And for and towards the maintenance of such a Reverend preacher I desire my lovinge wife and my sonn Charles Barkley to procure a convenient house and a garden thereunto for him and to give yearlie unto him for his zealous endeavour in his function a full some of Fortie poundes of lawfull money of England which maintenance I doe hereby apppointe to remaine for ever." To wief 90 acres in Norwood Parke for debts till son Charles is 21, part of 300 acres etc. To son Charles Barkley all my Armour and furniture for warres and also my Tewles and such other thinges as are in my Armourie at Bruton or elsewhere etc. Witnesses: Henry Bainton William Cole and Christian Lewes.

Weldon, 64.

[Sir Maurice Berkeley, of Bruton, was son of Sir Henry Berkeley. He married Elizabeth, daughter of Sir William Killegrew, of Hanworth, Middlesex. Sir Maurice was knighted by the Earl of Essex for gallantry at Cadiz in 1596, was M. P., 1597-98, 1601 and 1604-11, member of the Virginia Company, and of the Council for the Virginia Company in 1607 and 1609. In 1621 his widow was admitted to the Virginia Company. They had issue: (1) Sir Charles, a loyalist, M. P. and member of the Privy Council. He was father of Charles Berkeley, Earl of Falmouth, killed at sea in action with the Dutch, June 3, 1665, and of Vice Admiral Sir William Berkeley, killed also in action with the Dutch in 1666; (2) Sir Henry; (3) Sir Maurice; (4) John, Lord Berkeley, of Stratton, a distinguished cavalier officer, and a proprietor of Carolina and of the Northern Neck; (5) Sir William, baptized July 16, 1608, Governor of Virginia; (6) Margaret; (7) Jane married ———— Davies.]

VIRGINIA GLEANINGS IN ENGLAND.

Communicated by Mr. LOTHROP WITHINGTON, 30 Little Russell street,
W. C., London (including "Gleanings" by Mr. H. F. WATERS,
not before printed).

DAVID WAUGH. Will 27 December 1692; proved 20 February 1693–4. "A Board the Elizabeth of London Captaine George Hill Master this twenty Seaventh day of December one thousand six hundred and ninetie two yeares I David Wauch Planter in Staford County Virginia being sick and diseased in body but perfect and whole in mind, for the love favour and received obligations and for the consanguinity of blood betwixt Peter Wauch Sailor in New Castle upon Tyne and me I doe hereby by this my last will and Testament freely give and bequeath to the said Peter his heires and assigns Tobacco marked W and number from one to sixteen shipped by me in the Pittomock river aboard the Spencer of London Captaine Nicholas Goodridge Master and consigned by me to Thomas Stark part owner of the said vessell to be disposed upon to my best advantage and behoof in and to the which Tobacco in forty pounds English money as the Neate prize thereof dutty fraght all charges cleared I hereby devolve my full power in favour of the said Peter Wauch or his assigns," etc etc. [Signed] David Waugh. Witnesses: George Hill, Robert Young, Ar. Bleeck. Administration to Henry Bowen, attorney for Peter Waugh (now over seas), brother and universal legatee of David Waugh, late of ship Elizabeth, deceased, over seas.

Box 207.

[Possibly a kinsman of the strenuous parson, John Waugh, of Stafford county, whose speeches in 1688 aroused strong anti-Catholic feeling in that section.]

BENJAMIN BLANCHFLOWER of Fitzhead, County of Somersett, Gent. Will 17 August 1671; proved 19 May 1685. To Brother Alexander Blanchflower and heirs forever all Land in Parishes of Thurloxton and Michael Creech, Somersett, commonly called Bickhams Feilds, now in possession of Joane Heycock, Widow, or one of her Daughters. All goods to said Alex-

From Vol. XIX, No. 2 (April 1911), p. 186.

ander Blanchflower, executor. Witnesses: Jo. Hayley, William Hurchell, Walter Microoke. [Testator of Fitzhead, Somersett, but in Virginia over seas, deceased.—Probate Act Book.]

Cann, 54.

[The inventory of the estate of a Benjamin Blancheflower, deceased, (which included a parcel of old books) was recorded in Westmoreland county, November 26, 1701]

SIR HENRY PAYTON [signed Peyton, member of Virginia Company] of London, Knight. Will 18 Aprill 1618; proved 20 February 1623-4. Body to earth, sea, or other funerall. All goods to wife Lady Mary. To brother Thomas his children that are unmarried £20 each. Executor: brother Mr. Thomas Peyton. Witnesses: Edward Palauicin, John Lea, Peyton Cooke. Administration to Sir John Peyton junior, Knight, creditor and next of kin, the brother Thomas Peyton the executor having died before proof of will, said Sir Henry Peyton having died over seas, and grant issued on oath of Sir John Peyton, senior Knight.

Byrde, 18.

[Sir Henry Peyton was son of Thomas Peyton, Customer of London (and his wife Cecilia, daughter of John Bouchier, Earl of Bath), who was a descendant of the Peytons of Isleham. See Hayden's *Virginia Genealogies*, 464, &c. Sir Henry was a member of the Virginia Company in 1610, and an incorporator under the second charter. He married Mary, widow of Andrew Rogers, and daughter of Edward Seymour, Duke of Somerset. She died in 1620, without issue.]

MARY PEACHEY of parish of St. Stephens in King and Queen County in the Colony of Virginia. Will 6 August 1713; proved 18 January 1716-7. To my Neice Mary Peachey Walker, Daughter of Mr. Thomas Walker and Susannah his wife, my Negroe named Viall to she and her Heires for ever. Likewise my five Lottery Tickets as I took out of the Exchequer numbered 92567, 92568, 92569, 92570, and 92,573. Also to said Neece Mary Peachy Walker £200 sterling when she comes att age or marriage. 2d, To my Nephew John Walker, son of Mr. Thomas Walker my Negroe man called Consul and £100 out of my Mortgage of Mrs. Mary Drys, Haberdasher of Gracious Street, London. Rest to Nephew in Law Mr. Thomas Walker and Neece Susannah his wife, executors. Witnesses: John Waller, R. C. Walker, Joseph Hayle.   Proved by Thomas Walker, reserving to Susannah Walker.

Whitfield, 15.

[This Mary Peachey does not appear to have been a daughter of Samuel Peachey, of Mildenhall, Suffolk, who emigrated to Virginia in 1659, and settled in what was afterwards Richmond county.   Her will reads as if she was a Londoner who had not been very long in the Colony.   For the family of Samuel Peachey see *William and Mary Quarterly*, III, 111-115; V, 277.

The old Walker family Bible is still preserved.   One entry is "September ye 24, 1709, I went to St. Clemond's Church.   Thomas Walker " This has been taken to be the date of his marriage.   The births of his daughter Mary Peachey Walker, January 30, 1710 (old style); son John, April 29, 1711, and son Thomas, January 25, 1715, are recorded.   The last named was the well known Dr. Thomas Walker, of "Castle Hill," Albemarle county, the early explorer of Kentucky, &c.   For the Walker family see this Magazine, IV, 357-359.]

WILLIAM JENNINGS, St. Giles in the Fields, Middlesex, late of Swartha in the parish of Kildwicke, County of York, Gent. Will 21 August 1710; proved 29 August 1711.   Wife Elizabeth to have for life (if she so long keep my wife) all reall Estate at Swartha Morgaged and Unmortgaged.   "And also all the Estate both reall and personall which of right appertains and belongs to me on any wise lying in the Coll. of Virginia as Heir at Lawe to Colonell Pieter Jennings Yeares ago Deceased which I empowered my Cousin Edmond Jennings Gent son of Sir Edmond Jennings Knight of Ripon, Deceased by Letter of Attorney to receive for me which I am informed he hath."   Wife during her life to provide Meat, Drink, lodging and washing for my Daughters Jane Jennings and Agnes Jennings till 21, wife to put said Daughters out to trades she thinks agreeable to their severall inclinations, and if Daughters be dissatisfied at 21 wife to provide further allowance, etc., and at decease of wife then to them all reall estate, but if they die without issue to my brother Edmond Jennings.   Executrix: Wife Elizabeth, she to pay to my poor sister Mary Jennings 20 s a year or £5 as Mary approves and let Brother Edmond Jennings all apparell and a pair of mourning gloves.   Witnesses: John Green, Fran: Rook, and Tho: Metcalfe.

Young, 169.

[Peter Jeninngs, the first Attorney-General of Virginia, was born in
——, and died in 1671. He is spoken of as one who "faithfully served"
King Charles I, probably as an officer in the Civil War. In March, 1662,
he was "attorney for the King's most excellent majesty"; on September
16, 1670, was commissioned Attorney-General, and sworn a member
of the Council October 12, 1670. He married Catherine, daughter of
Sir Thomas Lunsford, and she married, secondly, Ralp Wormeley, Esq.
See *William and Mary Quarterly*, X, 31, 32. The cousin, Edmund Jennings, referred to in the will was Governor of Virginia. For the family
of Governor Edmund Jennings see this Magazine, XII, 306-310. The
relationship of the testator to Attorney-General Peter Jennings does
not appear.]

HUMFRIE COLE of Tillingham, Essex, Clarke. Will 4 November 1623; proved 17 May 1624. To be buried in Chancell of
Tillingham. To poore of Tillingham fower markes to be distributed by Overseers of the Poore. To sonne Robert Cole,
student of Emanuell Colledge in Cambridge, towardes his bringinge vp in learninge all bookes, my wearing apparell both Linen
and woollen, with sex yardes of broad cloth vpwardes wch
I bought of Mr. Purchase of Mauldon to make myselfe newe
clothes together with five yardes of blacke Kersey a halfe wch
I bought of a Widdowe at Malden to make myself a newe
suite. Also to Robert all Corne in house and hay in fieldes
except two quarters each of Corne, barley, or mault, and oates
for my beloved wife Hester Cole for housekeeping and Executor
or Executrix and Overseers to sell advowson of Rectorie or
Parsonage of Okeley magna, Essex, and money to sons etc., also
to sell (with consent of wife Hester two whom they are given for
life) my free lands in Tillingham commonly called Hodgewattes,
lately in tenure of John Bridge of Tillingham, husbandman, and
the use of £80 to wife Hester for life and rest of money and £80
when due to my sonns William, Thomas, Robert, and John.
"Item I do give vnto William Cole now in Virginia (if he be livinge) my three acres of free hold more or lease with a newe barne
built vpon it called sewders head in Tillingham & next adioyninge
to a Cottage & two acres of Coppihould land called Finches &
Doth belonge vnto his brother Robert Cole. And if my said
sonne William be not livinge at the time of my Death then I give
& bequeath the same land & Barne to my second sonne Thomas
Cole & his Heires forever." My plate, household stuffe & wch

299

wife Hester shall enioye for life by deed made by me to Sr John Sames, Knight, and Mr. Blunt, Gentlemen, and the other goodes to be divided to my sons at her death and my Keyne, horses, Sheep, lambes, Swine and debts due to be imployed for payment of my debts and except one spaid Mare colte of two yeares to wife Hester. Executrix: wife Hester Cole. If she refuse then son Thomas Cole. Overseers: my two sonnes in lawe Michaiah Wood, Person of much Okeley, and John George of Writtle, Essex, yeoman, giving to same Wood my clocke that hangeth in the Vikaredge Hall and to same John George three yeare ould coult to be sent to his house. Witnesses: John Traske, John Moody.

Dean and Chapter of St. Paul, Register D, (1608–1633), folio 233.

[The son William Cole, in Virginia, was born in 1597, came to Virginia in 1618 and was a member of the House of Burgesses for Nutmeg Quarter 1629.

Foster's *Alumni Oxonienses* gives " Robert Cole, created B. D. 1 or 2 November, 1642. perhaps rector of Great Oakley, Essex, 1628, and of Little Oakley, 1629, &c.," and also "Michael Wood, B. A. from Broadgates Hall, supd. 18 February, 1586-7; vicar of Great Thurneck (resigned) and perhaps rector of Great Oakley (both), Essex, 1617.]

JAMES FOWLER, Mile end, Stepney Parish, late an inhabitant of Nansem[on]d County on James River in Virginia, gentl. Will 27 April 1709; proved 13 May 1709. Debts in England to be paid and present stock for Trade in Virginia to be kept intact for purchasing of Moneys, Tobacco, and other Goods etc. as Executor or Executrix desire to Remitt and Ship for England, and my wife Elizabeth Fowler yearly consigne such Goods to my loveing Friend Mr. John Goodwin, Merchant in London, or as said John Goodwin shall order Elsewhere in England, etc. This my desire Mr. Robert Betty, who with my wife has the sole management of my concerns in Virginia during my absence be still continued and executor and executrix allow him yearly sallary I agreed to allow which was as much as he was to have from Capt. Richard Lovell, late of Norfolk County, Virginia, deceased. To wife Elizabeth Fowler my Mannor house and plantation in Upper Parish of Nansem[on]d County in Virginia for life, then to Brother Daniell Fowler's son called Roarry Fowler, being eldest son now living. Also to said Roarry Fowler Edy's Plantation. To God Daughter Margaret Sullivan, daughter of Mr. Daniell Sullivan, Land and Plantation at Summerton called Oadhams Plantations, now in tenure of one Mr. Crawford, and if she die to her brother Daniel Sullivan. To said Margaret Sullivan Two Cows and Two Calves and silver spoon marked J: S: To Mr. Robert Betty my black Rideing Horse and my own rideing Saddle and furniture and £6 for mourning. To Friend Richard Parker my Negro Boy called Cadger, but if wife not willing to part with him, she to buy a Negro boy of 14, healthy and sound in his Limbs, for said Richard Parker. To Hester Mackey 12,000 pounds of Tobacco with Six head of Cattle (three Cows and three Calves) and a feather bed, suit of Curtains and Vallence or Rugg, and pair of Blancketts at 21 or marriage to be paid to her in Nansemond County. To servant Boy John Tabor when he shall be free two suits of Clothes, Set of Mathematicall Instruments, with my long Boat, Sailes and other materials for sailing her. To my very good Acquaintance Mr. Daniel Sullivan my own wearing watch with a mourning Ring. To wife all Negroes and Household Goods, Linnen, Plate, and Stock of Cattle, Horses, Mares, Sheep, and Hoggs in Virginia, but if Kinsman Roarry Fowler goe to Virginia then wife to fitt up a handsom Lodging Room for him till otherwise provided. Executor and Executrix: Wife Elizabeth Fowler and Mr. John Goodwin. Witnesses: Adam Watson, Rich. Waplington, Phil. Traheron.

Lane 115.

[The testator had evidently bought lands in Nansemond, as his name does not appear in the land grants. Daniel Sullivan was clerk of Nansemond in 1702, &c., and Burgess for the county in that year. He owned the land on which Suffolk was afterwards built. The fifty acres on which the town was laid out belonged, in part, to Jethro Sumner in right of his wife Margaret, one of the two sisters and co-heirs of Daniel Sullivan, Jr., deceased, who was only son and heir of Daniel Sullivan, also of Nansemond, deceased. (*Hening*, V, 242, 243.)

"Mr. Richard Parker" patented 400 acres on the south branch of Nansemond River, October 5, 1654; 300 acres on the north side of James River in Henrico county, at the head of Four Mile Creek, October 28, 1669; 314 acres in Surry county on Blackwater Swamp, December 20, 1670 (due to him in part for coming twice to Virginia); 100 acres in Nansemond at Hood's Neck, February 24, 1675-6. On April 23, 1681, Thomas, Richard and Francis Parker, the three sons of Richard Parker, deceased, were granted 1,420 acres on the south branch of Nansemond River, at Parker's Creek, &c., left them by their father's will. At the end of the century these three sons were living in Nansemond county. See this Magazine, V, 444, 445. Some members of this family of Parker appear to have lived in Surry county. There is in Sussex county a deed reciting that Thomas Jarrell, of Isle of Wight county, by his will dated April 20, 1741, bequeathed a negro woman to Thomas Parker, son of Richard Parker and Sarah, his wife, who was daughter of said Jerrell, and said Richard Parker, by his will dated January 20, 1750, and recorded in Surry, bequeathed the negro to his daughter Martha Parker.

It seems certain that Richard Parker, the patentee of 1654, was a son of James Parker of Trangoe, Cornwall, who was descended from the ancient family of Parker of Browsholme. An account of this Cornish branch of the family was published in this Magazine, V, 442–443, and soon afterwards a descendant of the Nansemond Parkers wrote as follows:

I am the son of Dr. Richard Henry Parker, died in Portsmouth, Va., 1855, who was the son of Willis Parker of South Quay, Nansemond or Isle of Wight county, who was magistrate of Nansemond in 1800 and whose wife was a Miss —— Harrison, daughter of a Col. Henry Harrison of Surry or Isle of Wight, who was a relative in some degree of the ancestors of W. H. Harrison, who was President. Willis was the son of a Richard Parker who was the son of another Richard Parker and the same from father to son back to the Dr. Richard Parker who came from England.

Family tradition, as related by my mother and other older members of the family, was that our first Virginia ancestor was a Dr. Richard Parker, one of a very large family and whose wife was from London and that other members of same family also came to Virginia. There were three sons and three daughters. Some of the latter, or may be two of them, died. The sons were Thomas, Francis and Richard. This tradition is so well corroborated by the article of Maj. John Parker of Browsholme Hall, Yorkshire, published Vol. V, No. 4, of the Magazine, that I am inclined to accept it as proof of the ancestry of this branch of the Parkers.

The family tradition from my mother and aunt is to the effect that from the emigrant Dr. Richard Parker to my brother's son, Richard, that with the one exception of my grandfather, Willis, that it would be either nine generations of Richards from father to son or nine Richards with one instance of another name.

I do not think that Willis could have been old enough to have served in the Revolution, but his father, Richard, may have been. I figure him out as born about 1730 or 1735 and I will thank you to try and find record of this Richard or of the great-grandfather, Henry Harrison. I believe, from what I remember of tradition, that it is possible that this Richard, father of Willis, may have served in the Revolution and in the North Carolina troops.]

VIRGINIA GLEANINGS IN ENGLAND.

Communicated by Mr. LOTHROP WITHINGTON, 30 Little Russell street,
W. C., London (including "Gleanings" by Mr. H. F. WATERS,
not before printed).

ANDREW COX of Suffolk parish in Nansemond County. Will
20 September 1761; proved 16 February 1764. The land I now
live on and that by William Robert's be sold and the money I
give to my son Andrew Cox. The rest of my estate real and
personal between my sons Andrew and Chappell if they die before lawful age unmarried my three sisters, Charity, Sarah and
Prudence shall have it. My brother Chappell Cox to bring my
sons Andrew and Chappell up and he to have the management
of their estate in England and Virginia. Executors: James Holt
and William Sheppard. Witnesses: James Turner, William Ballard, and John Webb. [Administration with will annexed of
goods of Andrew Cox late of Suffolk parish in Nansemond
County in Virginia but in the Merchant Ship Happy Return deceased to Peter Hodgson, Attorney for William Shepherd and
James Holt, executors residing in Suffolk Parish aforesaid.]

Simpson, 42.

ROBERT DINWIDDIE late of the Colony of Virginia but now
of Saint Albans Street in the City of Westminster Esqr. Will
2 May 1769; proved 9 October 1770. To my sister Mrs. Sarah
Dinwiddie of Glasgow in North Britain the sum of £25. To
sister Mrs. Jannet McCullock £25. To her husband the Reverend Mr. McCullock £20. To his son Mr. Robert £50. To
such children as living of brother in law the Rev. Mr. Hamilton
by my sister Christian his late wife deceased besides his son Archibald Hamilton £200. To said Archibald £50. To Mrs. Dinwiddie, widow of my late Brother Lawrence Dinwiddie deceased,
£25. To nephew Robert, son of late Brother Lawrence, £100,
and to his other children £200. To Mrs. Elizabeth Hawker of
Bath £10. To Mrs. Elizabeth Parish, widow of Edward Clarke
Parish Esqr. deceased, and to her two daughters £10 each. To

University of Glasgow for books for their publick library £100. To the Merchants House at Glasgow for their poor £50. To Mrs. Buchanan, wife of James Buchanan Esquire deceased, £20. To Mr. John Pyland £50. To the Reverend Mr. Richard Hotchkiss and his wife £10 each. To each of my daughters Elizabeth and Rebecca Dinwiddie £10,000. If my nephews Robert Dinwiddie and Archibald Hamilton should survive my wife I give Robert £200 and Archibald £100. To my wife Rebecca the use of all my household goods for life. The messuage I have in Bermuda and which is now used as H. M. Custom House to my wife for life and at her decease to my two daughters. The residue of my estate I bequeath to Robert Scott, John Hyndman, and John Hunter, of London, Esquires, in trust to pay my wife Rebecca £350 per annum for life and £1000 unto such persons as she shall direct by her last will. Witnesses: Richd. Griffiths, Saml. Gradby, Richd. Ryland. [Proved by John Hyndman and John Hunter, Esquires, with power reserved to John Scott, the other executor.]

Jenner, 357.

[Robert Dinwiddie, son of Robert Dinwiddie, merchant, of Glasgow, was born in 1693, and died at Clifton, Bristol, July 27, 1770. He was Governor of Virginia 1751–1758. See *The Official Records of Robert Dinwiddie* (&c.), 2 vols., Virginia Historical Society, Richmond, Va., 1883. A biographical sketch and account of the Dinwiddie family appear in Vol. I, vii–xxviii. John Dinwiddie, the brother named in the will, emigrated to Virginia and became a merchant in King George county. He married a daughter of George Mason and has descendants in Virginia and elsewhere in the United States.]

JOHN DIXON of the City of Bristol Esquire. Will 28 April 1757; proved 5 December 1758. My intention being to divide my lands equally among my five sons, John, Roger, Cornelius, Lyonell, and Robert. First I give to my son the Reverend John Dixon, Minister of Kingston Parish in Gloster County in Virginia, the upper half of my land adjoining Town of Falmouth in the County of King George which I purchased of Mrs. Martha Todd including Vicaris's Island, the land to be divided in a line from the River back, Also one lot or half acre in the said Town whereon is the new Inspection called Dixons Warehouse. To my son Roger Dixon Clark of the County of Culpeper all my land about Pretty's Creek in Louisa County. To my son Cornelius Dixon all my land in Louisa County which I bought of Major John Lee and all the land which I bought of Henry Graves, John Saunders, John Milam, and John Howlett, which are near Taylers Creek, New-found River, and Little River, and all my land I bought of Richard Holland and Robert Estes on Beaver Creek near Louisa Court House. To my son Lyonel Dixon all my land in King William County, my two lots of land in Town of Newcastle in Hanover County, and the land in Hanover County near Newcastle which I bought of Charles Culquohene. To my son Robert Dixon the lower half of my land near Falmouth, County of King George, with my three lower lots in the Town and the Inspection thereon called Falmouth Warehouse. To my sons Cornelius and Lyonel all my land at the Rappidan River in Culpeper County. To my wife Ann Dixon £100 per annum to be paid her yearly in Bristol or London by my five sons John, Roger, Cornelius, Lyonel, and Robert and the use of all furniture and plate which I shall leave in England. To my son Thomas Dixon, now Captain of the ship Patriot, £500 after decease of my wife Ann if he have any lawful issue then living. To my daughter Susannah £500 when she is married or 21 and £500 after the decease of my wife. To five sons John, Roger, Cornelius, Lyonel, and Robert all stock of cattle and all other Real and Personal estate. To my wife Ann and son Lyonel my houses and land at Lateridge in parish of Iron Acton, county Gloucester, in trust to be sold for the benefit of my estate. To my sister Sarah Hume £10. Executors: Wife Ann Dixon and my two sons John and Lyonel Dixon. My wife to be guardian of her own children while a widow, if she marry again, I appoint my son Reverend John Dixon guardian. Witnesses: John Rogers, John Shadwall, Peter Gettoes. [Proved by Ann Dixon, with power reserved to John Dixon and Lyonel Dixon. Proved 27 April 1772 by John Dixon, surviving executor.]

Hutton, 361.

[John Dixon, of Bristol, came to Virginia during the early part of the eighteenth century, attained grant for 1,000 acres land in the fork of Rapidan river, 13th October, 1727, and on the 27th September, 1729, as "John Dixon, of King and Queen county," a grant for 135 acres on s. e.

side of Aracaico creek, adjoining lands of Howell McGregory and Gibson on n. side Mattapony river. Apparently he engaged extensively in merchandizing. He owned large tracts of land in Hanover, Louisa, Albemarle and Culpeper counties, a plantation on the Chickahominy, and lots in New Castle and Williamsburg. He was a vestryman of St. Paul's Parish, Hanover county, 1744–1748, when he " departed the parish." In the *Virginia Gazette* of the 19th of September, 1751, Dixon advertised for sale some of his Virginia property, "intending for England in the spring, with his family." He returned to England with his second wife and their children, and his will [abstract above] dated 8th April, 1757; probated 5th December, 1758.

John Dixon married, *first*, Lucy, daughter of Thomas Reade, of Gloucester county, Va., who died 22nd November, 1731, in the thirtieth year of her age, and is buried near Gloucester Courthouse, Va., [tombstone inscription in *William and Mary College Quarterly Historical Magazine*, III, p. 29.] Issue :

1. Reverend John Dixon ; 2. Roger Dixon; 3. Thomas Dixon, a sea captain.

John Dixon married, *secondly*, Ann ——, (probably a Lyde, of King William county, Va.) Issue :

4. Cornelius; 5. Lyonel ; 6. Robert (all of whom died unmarried); 7. Susannah Ann, m. —— Godwin.

1. Reverend John Dixon, b. ——; d. 1777; was educated at William and Mary College ; entered the ministry of the Church of England ; appointed Faculty usher of William and Mary, March 28, 1747 ; appointed Rector of Kingston Parish, Gloucester, now Matthews county, 1754; Professor of Divinity, William and Mary, 1770. During the Revolution he sympathized with England. He was prominent in Masonic circles. He was buried in the New Church of Kingston Parish, May 4, 1777.

John Dixon married Lucy ——, who died November, 1769, aged forty-one years [tombstone inscription in *William and Mary College Quarterly Historical Magazine*, Vol. III, p. 256] Issue :

8. John ; 9. William Dixon, b. 12 October, 1758 ; 10. Thomas Dixon, b. 26 December, 1760 ; 11. Lucy, b. 10 November, 1761 ; 12. Elizabeth (doubtless eldest child), married, 2 November, 1772, Lindsey Jervis.

2. Roger Dixon, of Fredericksburg, Va.; b. ——; d. 22nd May, 1772. Went from King and Queen county to Spotsylvania ; admitted to practice as an attorney in Spotsylvania Court, 7th February, 1748. He lived in Fredericksburg, where he purchased a large tract of land at the lower end of the town, which he later divided into lots and sold. Dixon street was named for him. He owned large tracts of land in Spotsylvania, Albemarle, Culpeper and Frederick counties, and engaged extensively

in merchandizing. He was a vestryman of St. George's Parish; Justice of the Peace for Spotsylvania county, 1760-1770; first clerk of Culpeper county, 1749-1772; trustee of the town of Falmouth; member of the House of Burgesses of Virginia, 1769-1771.

Roger Dixon married Lucy, daughter of Major Philip Rootes, of "Roswall," King and Queen county, Va., and Mildred his wife, daughter of Thomas Reade, of Gloucester county, and therefore his (Dixon's) first cousin. Issue:

13. Roger, b. 1763; d. 2 July, 1833. He removed to Mississippi in the last decade of the eighteenth century; m. Mildred ——; b. ——; d. Fayette county, Mississippi, 30 December, 1849. Issue: (a) Thomas Rootes, 1795-1855, m. 1st, Rebecca Stovers; 2d, Sarah Williams (nee Cole) Malone; 3d, Eliza Ann (nee Cole) Christian. (b) Philip, m. Rachel ——; (c) William; (d) Robert; (e) Lucy; (f) Eliza, m. —— Minor; (g) Priscilla, m. —— Strong; (h) Mary; (i) Nancy, m. —— Christmas. 14. John, who removed to Hampshire county, now West Virginia. Probably has descendants. 15. Philip Rootes, of whom all trace has been lost. 16. Mildred, b. 1754-5; d. Jefferson county, Ga., 17 October, 1799; married at Stephensburg, Frederick county, Va., 11 April, 1777, Philip Clayton [Samuel³, Samuel², Samuel¹], b. 1746-7; d. Richmond county, Ga., 13 September, 1807; member of Georgia Constitutianal Convention, 1795; treasurer of Georgia, 1794. Issue: (a) Lucy Reade Rootes, 1778-79. (b) George Rootes, 1779-1840, secretary of the Executive Department of Georgia, treasurer of the State and cashier of the State Bank; married, 17 January, 1804, Elizabeth Mildred, 1783-1829, daughter of John and Ann Hargrove. (c) Dixon, 1782-1790. (d) Augustine Smith, 1783-1839; student Richmond Academy; graduate University of Georgia; admitted to the bar, member of the Georgia House of Representatives, 1810-11; clerk of that body, 1813-15; State Senator, 1812, 1826-7; judge of the Western Circuit, 1819-25, 1828-31; Presidential elector 1829; member of Congress, 1831-35; member Board of Trustees University of Georgia, and secretary of the board; author; married, 20 December, 1807, Julia, 1787-1873, daughter of Hon. Peter Johnson Carnes, of Georgia. (e) Mildred Dixon, 1787-1790; (f) Ann Marbury, 1789-1791; (g) Philip. 1791-1791; (h) Lucinda, 1792-1823, married, 1817-18, Edward Cary, son of Dudley Cary and Lucy Tabb, of Gloucester county, Va. Hon. Philip Clayton removed to Georgia from Virginia in 1784; he married, secondly, 15 November, 1801, Elizabeth, widow of Peter Carnes, a distinguished lawyer, the daughter of Jacob Wirt, of Maryland, and sister of Hon. William Wirt, Attorney-General of the United States. No issue. 17. Eliza, married George Conway Taylor son f Col. George Taylor, of Orange county; no

issue. 18. Lucy, of whom nothing is known; 19. Susannah, of whom nothing is known; 20. Mary, b. ——; d. before 1819; married William Throckmorton, of Frederick county, Va. Issue: (*a*) William; (*b*) Warner; (*c*) Lucy Rootes, 1785-1821, married, 17 September, 1801, Dr. John Thomson, of Berryville, Va.; (*d*) Henrietta; (*e*) Mildred, married Dr. Cornelius Baldwin; (*f*) Edwayhue.

[8]John Dixon, of Mt. Pleasant, Gloucester county, Va., b. ——; d. ——; married, 6 February, 1773, Elizabeth, daughter of Sir John Peyton, of Isleham, Gloucester county. John Dixon was captain of the Gloucester county militia, appointed by the Committee of Safety, 13 September, 1775. Issue:

21. John Dixon, Sr., of Airville, Gloucester county, Va., only son, b. 1778; d. 5 September, 1830; buried at Mt. Pleasant; married Sarah, daughter of Warner and Julia (Langhorne) Throckmorton, and had issue:

(*a*) John Dixon, M. D., b. 1812; d. 24 June, 1835, unmarried;
(*b*) Harriet Peyton, m. Jacob Sheldon, and lived for many years in Williamsburg, Va.

Authorities—Spotsylvonia County (Va.) Records; tombstone inscriptions published in *William and Mary Quarterly; Virginia Gazette;* Kingstan Parish Register; legislative petitions in the Virginia State Library; Executive papers, Virginia State Library; family B.bles.

We are indebted to Mr. William Clayton Torrence, Curator of the Valentine Museum, for this note on the Dixons.]

EDWARD CHAMBERLAINE of Westhide, county Hereford, Yeoman. Will 27 December 1747; proved 11 February 1649-50. To poor of Westhide 20s. as a stock. To my sister's daughter Elizabeth Smith £5. To John Wellington, son of my Brother in law James Wellington 20s. To Thomas Chamberlaine, my servant, 5s. To my youngest son John Chamberlaine £300. To eldest son Edward Chamberlaine £200. Residuary Legatee and Executrix: Wife Margaret. Witnesses: James Willington, John Chamberlen, Edward Chamberlain, junior.

Pembroke 16.

[As younger sons are frequently styled yeomen, it is possible that this Edward Chamberlaine belonged to the Herefordshire family from which William Chamberlayne of Virginia came, and which descended from Richard Chamberlayne, Esq., of Astley, Warwickshire.]

PHILIP LUDWELL late of the Colony of Virginia, but now of
the City of Westminster, Esquire. Will 28 February 1767;
proved 6 May 1767. All my estate in Virginia not otherwise
bequeathed to Richard Corbin Esq., H. M. Receiver General of
Virginia, Robert Carter Nicholas Esq., Treasurer of Virginia,
John Wayles and Benjamin Waller Esqrs. Attorneys at Law in
Virginia, in Trust for my daughters Hannah Phillippa Ludwell,
Frances Ludwell, and Lucy Ludwell. All my land in Virginia
to be divided into three parts viz: all land in Green Spring part
i. e. in James City County on Western side of Pouhatan Swamp
with everything thereon as Slaves, Stock, Household Furniture
etc. in which I include Pouhatan Mill and the miller—The Rich
Neck part viz: on Eastern side of Pouhatan Swamp and at Archer's Hope and in Williamsburg—The Chipokes part viz: all
my land in County of Surry. The Green Spring part to daughter Hannah Phillippa Ludwell, the Rich Neck part to daughter
Frances Ludwell, The Chipokes part and all Surry estate to
daughter Lucy Ludwell, executors to sell all Household Furniture, China, Glass and Books in Virginia, excepting one large
Mahogany Escratore with glass doors and one large Mahogany
Dressing Table with a looking glass in a mahogany frame,
already the property of daughter Hannah Phillippa Ludwell.
To said daughter Hannah £100 to bring over to England and
put in a way of getting their living two of my slaves named Jane
and Sarah, daughters of Cress, to whom I promised their freedom for the faithful and unwearied care in nursing my dear little
Orphans from the death of their mother. Executors: My daughter Hannah now and Frances and Lucy when they come of age
with the four trustees joint executors in Virginia, and Peter Paradise Esq., John Paradise Esq., of the city of Westminster, and
William Dampier Esq., Master Apothecary of Saint George's
Hospital, Executors in England and guardians to my two daughters Frances and Lucy. If daughters Frances or Lucy go to
Virginia during minority or unmarried Executors in Virginia to
have power as guardians. To my friend Charles Carol Junr
Esq. of Maryland such of my books in my study in Virginia as
he shall choose. The tobacco and other annual produce between
my death and the partition of my estate to be shipped as usual
to my friends Messrs. Cary, Moorey, and Welch Merchants in

London and accounted for to Messrs. Paradise and Dampier.
Witnesses: Jos^a Sharfe of Lincolns Inn, Sam'l Lum of the Strand,
Thomas Trafford of Cecil Street. Codicil 2 March 1767. Witnesses: Jos^a Sharpe, Tho. Trafford, John Brown.

Legard, 183.

[Philip Ludwell, of "Greenspring," James City county, Va., son and
grandson of Philip Ludwells of the same place, each of whom held a
prominent place in the Virginia government, was born at " Greenspring"
December 28, 1716, died in England, March 25, 1767, and was buried in the
Church of Bow, near Stratford, Essex. Some years before his death he removed to England. He married at "Moratico," Richmond county, in
1737, Frances, daughter of Charles Grymes of that place and his wife
Frances, daughter of Governor Edmund Jenings, and had issue: 1. Hannah Phillippa, born at "Greenspring" December 21, 1737, married at
St. Clement's, Danes, Middlesex, England, William Lee, merchant, of
London, son of Governor Thomas Lee of Virginia, and died at Ostend,
Flanders, August 18, 1784. Her remains were buried in the Ludwell
vault in Bow churchyard. 2. Lucy, married, 1769, John Paradise, Esq.,
of Charles street, Berkeley Square, London. He was son of Peter Paradise (of Greek descent), a British consul in the Levant. John Paradise
was a friend of Dr. Johnson's, and he and his wife are several times
mentioned in Burney's Memoirs. After her husband's death, Mrs. Paradise returned to Virginia in 1805 and died in 1814. Her only child,
Lucy Paradise, married, in 1787, Count Barziza, a Venetian nobleman,
and also settled in Virginia. Their descendants live in the South.
3. Frances, born 1750, died unmarried, September 14, 1768.

Philip Ludwell, the testator, who was appointed member of the Virginia Council in 1752, was the last male member of the Virginia family
of the name, which almost since the middle of the seventeenth century
had been one of the most influential and wealthy in the Colony. Philip
Ludwell left a very large estate. This Society has many papers in regard to it.]

EDWARD CREFFIELD, JUNIOR, now of London, Merchant.
Will 24 November 1694; proved 9 December 1694. To honoured Father and Mother Mr. Edward Creffeild and Mrs. Dorothy Creffeild of Chappell, Essex, £40. If both dead then to
my three dear sisters hereafter particularly named. To brother
Mr. Henry Creffield of Colchester Essex £20. To sister Mary
Creffield spinster £5. To sister Elizabeth now wife of Mr.
John Keeble £5. To sister Ann wife of Mr. William Brewer
£50. To friend Mr. Francis Willis now of London, Mercer

£20 To Friend and Correspondent Mr. Phillip Richards of London, merchant £50 he to care for payment of legacies etc To my Daughter in Lawe Mrs. Lucy now or late wife of Mr. Thomas Reed of the County of Gloucester in Virginia one Diamond Ring, which my late wife (Mother of said Lucye) used to weare, one Gold Necklace consisting of six chains Fastened to a Locket of Massey gold, also £20. Rest of estate real and personal in Virginia unto loving Friend Mr. Benjamin Clements of Ware in said County Gloucester in Virginia paying legacies and to said Mr. Phillip Richard £260 sterling for Father, Mother, brother and three sisters. Executors: said Mr. Benjammin Clements of Virginia and Mr. Phillip Richards of London. Witnesses: John Warr, George Wilmshunt and Thomas Farnalls

Box, 244.

[Thomas Read, of Gloucester county, Va., married Lucy, daughter of Edmund Gwyn, of the same county. Therefore the widow of Edmund Gwyn, Mrs. Gwyn-Creffield, was Lucy, daughter of William Bernard, Esq., of the Virginia Council, who was a younger brother of Sir Robert Bernard, Bart.]

THOMAS PATTISHALL of Bombay, Merchant. Will 25 March 1715; proved 23 October 1717. Estate to be delivered to Trustee in India hereafter named and disposed as most beneficial for Executor hereafter named, having collected my estate in India said real estate to be paid by Trustee into Honourable Company's Treasury at Bombay and take Bills of Exchange payable to other Trustees in England, and trustee to be prudent etc., and if Executor happen to reside in England he to receive said Bills sent him for his proper use, but if he should happen to be in Virginia and other parts beyond sea Trustees to acquaint Executor, etc. Whereas I stand bound to my Honoured father Joseph Dampney of London in two obligations for £55 and £23, the £23 to be discharged and the £55 to be paid conditionally on my safe return to England and not if I die in India. To my Hon'ed friend and Benefactor the Honourable Willm. Aislabbe Esqr Gen'll of India and Governour of Bombay 200 Rupees to buy him a Ring. To good friends and shipmates Mark Anthony Crommelin, Blacket Midford, and John Hope each

100 Rupees for mourning rings. To John Hope my gold head Caine and silver hilted Sword and all silver plate, also a slave Thomas to whom I give his Freedom after seven yeares service to him. To my father Joseph Dampney aforesaid £25 sterling. To Edward Picket of London, Dyer, £10 for mourning. Trustee in India: John Hope of Bombay merchant. Trustees in England: father Joseph Dampney and Edward Picket aforesaid. Rest to brother William Pattishall, now or late in Virginia, executor. Witnesses: Richard Cobb, Ch. Dix, Jone Sarson. Memorandum 9 Aprill 1715 that this will of Thomas Pattishall of Bombay merchant deceased was produced before me the Generall of India for Affairs of the Honourable vnited East India Company and Governor of Her Majestys Castle and Island of Bombay for Affairs of the East India Company in Bombay Castle, where the Reverend Richard Cobbe, Chr. Dix, John Sarson being sworn, etc. [signed] Willm. Aislabie. Entered April the 10th 1717 in the Register Book of wills in Bombay Castle per John Hope, Sec'ry. Attestation 23 October 1717 of John Taylor of Gracechurch streete, London, gentleman, for upwards of seven yeares past one of the clerks of the Secretary's Office of the United East India Company of Merchants of England trading to the East Indies, and well knows Mr. John Hope, Merchant of Bombay, was for several years Secretary to the Counsell of said Company at Bombay and is now one of said Counsell and attests signature to Attestation before William Aislabie Esquire, late Governor of Bombay. Similar attestation for William Phillip of St. Mary Whitechapel, Esq., another of the clerks. Proved in Prerogative Court of Canterbury by brother William Pattishall, executor.

Whitfield 197.

[There is recorded in King George county a deed dated 1721 from John Grayson, of Spotsylvania county, conveying 900 acres, in King George, to William Pettishall, of Middlesex county.]

JOHN WEBSTER late of Meriland in Virginia in parts beyond the seas, a bachelor, deceased. Administration 16 November 1671 to Robert Webster brother of the above.

Admon Act Book, 1671.

VIRGINIA GLEANINGS IN ENGLAND.

Communicated by Mr. LOTHROP WITHINGTON, 30 Little Russell street,
W. C., London (including "Gleanings" by Mr. H. F. WATERS,
not before printed).

JOSEPH TORKINGTON of Virginia in the parts beyond the Seas,
Planter. Will 28 January 1652 [i. e. 1651–2]; proved 26 April
1652. The temporall estate whereof it hath pleased God to place
mee his Steward as well in Virginia as in this Commonwealth of
England I give it all to my brother Samueil Torkinton, citizen
and grocer of London, whom I make my executor. Witnesses:
Zach. Cropton, John Hothersall, Richard Hopkins, Harbert Ake-
hurst, Edward Bridgman.

Brent, 320.

[The only thing approaching a list of colonial emigrants to Virginia is the collection of land grants in the State Land Office, though
this does not contain very many names of persons who settled here.
The name Torkington does not appear among the grants. The will
of John Tarkington, of North Carolina, was proved there in 1716.]

JAQUES JONES of St. Catherine Colman, London, yeoman.
Will 7 June 1629; proved 20 April 1629. To my daughter
Marie Jones who (as I hope) now liveth in Virginia £5. To
daughter Anne Jones £10 and to daughter Elizabeth Jones £10
when 21 or married. Residuary Legatee and Executrix: Wife
Alice. Witnesses: Rich. Alsoper, Scr., Darby Younge, Robert
Wallis, servant to the said Scr.

Archdeaconry of London, Book 7, folio 45.

AYLIFFE WILLIAMS, lately of North Carolina in America,
planter, now residing in Westminster. Will 22 November 1734;
proved 2 May 1735. As to my body I do not think about it but
if it may be of service to others I care not what is done with it.
All moneys due from my attorneys Christopher and Edmund
Gale, Esqrs., of North Carolina, the receipt for which is in hands
of David O. Sheal of Nansimond County in Virginia according

From Vol. XIX, No. 4 (Oct. 1911), p. 396.

to my book B., to my executors. My land on New River to be
sold. Mr. Henry Nean of Compton Street, St. Ann's, West-
minster, to be paid what I owe him and £10. To Mr. James
Webb of Broad Street behind the Royal Exchange, perwig
maker, £10. To my mother Mrs. Esther Williams of Old
Gravel Lane, Wapping, the rest. If she dies, among my brother
John Williams and my sister Esther Taylor, who are to assist the
children of our unhappy brother Daniel as they see occasions.
Executors: Mr. Henry Nean and Mr. James Webb. Witnesses:
Oliver Farmer, Wm. Coumbe.

Ducie, 113.

[David O'Sheal, of Nansemond county, seems to have been a lawyer
of some prominence. In April, 1737, on the death of Sir John Randolph, he was chosen to succeed him as Recorder of Norfolk.]

ROBERT JOHNSTON of the Colony of Virginia, merchant, at
present in London. Will 5 March 1765; proved 5 April 1766.
All lands etc. in Virginia and elsewhere to Mr. James Russell of
London, merchant, and make him my executor. Witnesses:
Jno. Johnston, Joseph Wilkinson, George Hill.

Tyndall, 144.

JOHN MASSENBURGH of Elizabeth City County in Virginia,
Mariner, now lodging with Mr. Thomas Turner, Baker, in St.
Catherines near the Tower of London. Will 15 May 1749;
proved 6 July 1749. My plantations etc. in Elizabeth City
County to my four Brothers Nicholas, Josiah, Zachariah, and
Robert Massenburgh, they to pay £80 Virginia currency to my
three sisters Susannah, Barbora, and Elizabeth, to whom I give
all my stock and negroes and the residue of my goods. Exec-
utors: Brother Nicholas and Mr. Thomas Turner. Witnesses:
Chas. Turner, Elizabeth Chambers, Thos. Cotton, attorney in
Red Lyon Street, Wapping.

Lisle, 225.

[The name Massenburgh or Massingberd was of prominence in
Lincolnshire, England, but it is not known that any connection has
ever been traced between them and the Virginians of the name. There
is but little accessible information in regard to the family in Virginia.
Representatives of the name, doubtless from the same stock, lived in

Elizabeth City and Sussex counties. John Massenburgh patented seventy-five acres in Elizabeth City, adjoining his own land, August 20, 1741. There is a deed in Elizabeth City, dated December, 1761, to Josiah Massenburgh of that county. The will of Nicholas *Massenburg was dated April 4, 1772, and proved in Sussex, April 16, 1772, the legatees being his wife Lucy, son Nicholas, and children (whom he does not name). His wife, brother-in-law John Cargill and sons Nicholas and John Massenburg, executors. The will of Ann Cargill of Sussex, dated October 27, 1780, includes bequests to her daughter Elizabeth Massenburg and to John Massenburg. John and William Massenburg were justices of Sussex, 1798. William Massenburg justice of Sussex, 1804. William Massenburg, County Lieutenant of Sussex, resigned 1799. Died March 2, 1845, aged 47, Col. Thomas Massenburg of Greensville county, who was born and lived some time in Sussex, and was J. P., left a wife and six children (*Newspaper obituary*). Dr. W. A. Massenburg of Southampton county, alive 1843. Alexander Massenburg was a master in the Virginia Revolutionary Navy. Joseph Massenburg, member of the Warwick county Committee of Safety, 1774. John Massenburg, clerk of the Sussex county Committee of Safety, 1775. There was a later emigration from England. A newspaper obituary gives the death January 1, 1842, at his residence in Pocahontas county, Va., of George Massenberg, aged nearly ninety, a native of England "and one of the first families of that country," who came to Virginia about the close of the American Revolution.]

JOHN MICHELSON of Virginia, Merchant, now in London. Will 7 September 1749; proved 19 August 1750. All estate to father Mr. James Michelson, Jeweller, in Edinburgh in North Britain. Executors in London: My Brother Mr. James Michelson, Jeweller, and Mr. William Bowden, merchant, both of London. Executors in Virginia: The Honourable William Nelson, Esquire, and Richard Ambler, Esquire, both of York Town in Virginia. Witnesses: James Catwell, Jon. Blanshard, and Jon. Mackaners. Proved by Brother James, power reserved to other executors.

Glazier, 227.

BRETT RANDOLPH late of H. M. Colony in America called Virginia, but now of Dursley in County Gloucester in England, Esquire. Will 31 August 1759; proved 25 October 1759. To Wife Mary the rents and profits of my estate called Warwicke in Chesterfield County in Virginia. To Joseph Farrell of Bristol, merchant, James Murray of Prince George County in Virginia, Esq., John Markham of Chesterfield County in Virginia, Gent., and John Scott of Dursley County Gloucester, Peruke maker, all Tenements called Chester and Scotts in Virginia and my lands in the Great Patent in Luingberg and Bedford Counties in Virginia during the minority of my children and to sell them if they think to their advantage. To daughter Susannah, if my wife be not ensient at my decease, £2000 when 21; if my wife be ensient, then the £2000 equally between the two children, and I also give the profits of lands and negroes at Curls I am entitled to after decease of my mother by the will of my late father to my wife until my son Henry and other children are 21. If my children die I give the lands at Warwick to my Brother Ryland charged with payment of £1000 to my father in law the said John Scott of Dursley and Susannah his wife. To Brother John freehold lands at Fighting Creek in Cumberland County in Virginia charged with payment of £1000 to father in law John Scott and Susannah his wife. Residuary Legatees and Executors: Wife Mary, Joseph Farrell, James Murray, John Markham, and John Scott. Witnesses: E. Wallington, Chas. Whittard, Will Holbrow.

Arran, 337.

[Brett Randolph, son of Richard Randolph of "Curles," Henrico county, was born in 1732 and spent most of his life in England. He married in London, July 14, 1753, Mary Scott, and had issue: (1) Richard, born August 17, 1754, and died September 8, 1775, at "Chester," near Warwick, Chesterfield county; (2) Henry, born October 7, 1758, at Woodmancoate, Dursley, England, returned to Virginia and married Lucy, daughter of Seth Ward of Chesterfield county; (3) Brett, born 1760, returned to Virginia and married Anne, daughter of Richard Randolph, Jr., of "Curles"; (4) Susanna, married August 23, 1783, at the parish church of North Nobley, Glaucestershire, Charles Douglass of Standes, Mt. Fitchet, Essex, England (born October 11, 1752, at Sawbridge court, Herefordshire), stated to have been son and heir of Captain Charles Douglas of the British Army, second son of Col. Charles Douglas of the "Old Buffs," who was killed at Carthagena. Col. Douglas is said to have been second cousin and heir-presumptive of the Earl of Moreton. Charles Douglas and his wife came to Virginia, and her beautiful full-length portrait by Copley is one of his most noted works. For an account of the descendants of

Henry and Lucy (Ward) Randolph see Goode's "Virginia Cousins," page 111, &c., and for the children of Brett and Anne Randolph see Robertson's "Descendants of Pocahontas," page 47. There are several deeds in Chesterfield county in regard to Mrs. Mary (Scott) Randolph's interest in her husband's Virginia property.]

ERASMUS FELGATE. Memorandum that on or about 1st days of February Anno Dni 1621(2) Erasmus Felgate of Parish of St. Buttolphes withoute Aldersgate London Taylor said that his five children being four sons and one daughter should have £20 apiece out of his estate. Residuary Legatee and Executrix: Wife Margerie. Proved 5 March 1621(2).

Savile, 23.

[A London family of Felgate was actively interested in the settlement of Virginia. There were three brothers—Tobias, a merchant captain, who made many voyages to Virginia; William, of London, skinner, a member of the Virginia Company, and Robert. The last two settled in Virginia. As Robert Felgate had a son, Erasmus, there was probably relationship between the brothers and the testator above. Perhaps they were his sons.]

LAWRENCE BOHUNE of London, Doctor in Phisicke. Will 10 March 1620; proved 29 April 1622. My wife Alice to have all my estate, but if she marries only one half and the other half to be divided among our children, viz: Elizabeth Bohune, Edward Barnes, Anne Barnes, and Dorothy Barnes, my daughter Elizabeth to have £10 over and above my wife's children. Residuary Legatee and Executrix: Wife Alice. Witnesses: John . . . (sic) Thomas Nicolls, Nichol Gibson, Tho. Tailor, Ed. Constable. [Late of Lambeth in County Surrey but in parts beynd the seas deceased.—Probate Act Book.]

Savile, 30.

[Dr. Bohun, who was "a long time brought up amongst the most learned surgeons and physicians in the Netherlands," came to Virginia with Lord De la Warr in 1610. He was granted land in the colony, and on December 13, 1620, was appointed Physician-General to Virginia. He soon after sailed from England on the *Margaret and John*, Captain Chester. In the latter part of March, 1621, this vessel had a severe action with two Spanish men-of-war in the West Indies, and Dr. Bohun was killed. When he was mortally wounded, Captain

317

Chester embraced him, saying, "What a misfortune is this!" and Dr. Bohun replied: "Fight on, brave men, the cause is good, and Lord receive my soul." The Spaniards finally were driven off.]

JOHN LUDWELL of St. John's in Glaston, county Somerset, husbandman. Will 24 March 1650–1; proved 7 August 1651. To poor of St. John's £1. os. od. To Mr. Luffe to preach my funeral sermon 10s., for my grave in the Church 6s. 8d. To Amy daughter of Thomas Townsed of Pillton 1s. To Thomas Ludwell my brother 10s. To John son of said Thomas 1s. To Thomas son of said Thomas 1s. To my brother William Harris of Somerton 1s. Residuary Legatee and Executor: My brother William Stickler. Overseers: Richard Bytham of Glaston and Robert Stone of Northover. Witnesses: Richard Bayle and Richard Bitham.

Grey, 161.

[It is possible that this John Ludwell was a brother of Thomas Ludwell of Bruton, Somerset, who was father of Thomas and Philip Ludwell, emigrants to Virginia. The tradition in the family in Virginia is that the Ludwells were originally from the continent of Europe. Probably they were Protestant exiles. See for the Ludwells *William and Mary Quarterly*, XIX, 199, &c.]

VIRGINIA GLEANINGS IN ENGLAND.

Communicated by Mr. LOTHROP WITHINGTON, 30 Little Russell street, W. C., London (including "Gleanings" by Mr. H. F. WATERS, not before printed).

MATHEWE STONE, late of St. Pancrasse in Soaper Lane, London, Haberdasher, about 4 April 1629 last past made his will noncupative. To his cousin Mrs. Margaret Hall a piece of plate value £8. His brother Henry Stone owed him £180 and should only have to pay £80, and his brother John Stone owed him money for a long time and should only pay the principal. His wife's sister Margaret Cheshire, then dwelling with him, should be well dealt with. Amdinistration 21 April 1629 to Ellen Stone relict of deceased, Andrew Stone, John Warner, and Margaret, Cheshire witnessing the truth of above.

Ridley, 28.

[In an article on the ancestry of William Stone, of Accomac county, Va., and afterwards Governor of Maryland, in the *New England Historical and Genealogical Register*, XLIX, 314, 315, it is shown that he was a nephew of Thomas Stone, merchant and haberdasher of London, whose eldest brother was John Stone, Esq., of Carr House, in Much Hoole parish, Lancashire. The Visitation of London, 1633-5, shows that Thomas Stone also had brothers Henry, Andrew, Robert and Mathew. The will above is evidently that of the brother Mathew. Governor Stone must have been a son of one of the other brothers. The connection, if any, of "Mathey Stowne" (below) is unknown.]

MATHEY STOWNE [of Reach in Parish of Leighton Buzzard, Bed.—Probate Act Book. Stonn at foot of will and Stone in probate act]. Will 23 November 1629; proved 2 April 1630. To my mother £40. To Brother George £4. To Brother John Weles £8. To Vncle Sanderstone £3. To Sister Wells a sheep and to each of her children. To Brother Hendere children a sheep each. To Brother George rest of sheep. Wit-

nesses: William Lawley, Bennet Sharpe.   [Proved by his mother
Agnes Stone.]

Scroope, 37.

SAMUEL EACH of Lymehouse in County Middlesex, maryner.
Will 13 November 1618; proved 21 April 1623.   To Elizabeth
Shephard a Cottage in Ropemaker's feild in Limehouse now in
occupation of one Thomas Craften and if she die before expiration of lease then to my daughter Mary the wife of John Wiles
of Lymehouse Marryner.   To my wife Elizabeth Each the house
I now live in and after her death to said daughter Mary.   Residuary legatee and Executrix: Wife.   Witnesses: James Hall,
Scrivenor, Nicholas Hitson.   [Deceased in parts beyond the
seas.—Probate Act.]

Swann, 34.

[In a letter from the Virginia Company, June 10, 1622, to the Covernor
and Council of Virginia, it is stated tkat Captain Samuel Each, master
of the ship *Abigail*, had contracted, in consideration of 60,000 pounds
of tobacco, to erect a block house on the oyster banks at Blunt Point on
James River, as a fortification for the river.   On the voyage a desperate
"distemper" broke out on the ship, and the master, with most of his
men, died, so nothing was done on the proposed fortification.   See also
this Magazine, XIX, 118.   Captain Each owned land at Martin's Brandon.]

SIR RICHARD MORISON of Tooley Parke, county Leicester,
Knight.   Will proved 30 December 1625.   His estate has been
impaired because of the stopping of the entertainment by his
Majesty when serving him in England and Ireland, but he is con-
fident that when his services to Queen Elizabeth and nis present
Majesty are put before his Majesty by his noble friends, His
Majesty will recuperate him.   The manor of Bushopps fee conveyed to Sir Thomas Coventry and Sir Robert Heath, H. M.
Attorney General and Solicitor General, is to be redeemed, also
his office of Lieutenant of the ordinance which I have for my
own life and the life of Sir William Harrington to be sold.   My
wife to have any estate for the upbringing of my younger children.   I have already provided for my eldest son and propose
to turn over in company to him if I can obtain favour of his
Matie &c.   Executors: William, Earle of Pembrooke, Sir John

Jephson, and my brothers in law Sir Benjamin Rudyard, Sir William Harrington, and George Alington Esq., and my brother Fynes Morrison Esquire. No witnesses. Codicil dated 29 August 1625. Left a will made by Mr. Anthony Loe in a boxe in my study at the Minories to stand good. I desire Earle of Rutland and Sir Thomas Savadge to join with my good Lo: the Lo: Chamberlayne, in seeing it executed because they both are witnesses of what is agreed between my Lo: grace of Buckingham and me I shall have in respect of my surrender of the Presidency of Munster to Sir Edward Vyllyars now lo: president.

Clarke, 140.

[Sir Richard Moryson, or Morrison, of Tooley Park, Liecestershire, was a distinguished soldier. He married Elizabeth, daughter of Sir Henry Harrington, and had issue: (1) Sir Henry, d. sp., a friend of Ben Jonson; (2) Major Richard, emigrated to Virginia; (3) Col. Francis, Governor of Virginia 1661–62; (4) Captain Robert, emigrated to Virginia; (5) Letitia, who married the celebrated Lucius Cary, Viscount Falkland. Fynes Moryson was brother of Sir Richard and a noted traveller. He published an "Itinerary" in 1617. See this Magazine, II, 383–385, and lives in the *Dictionary of Natural Biography*. In a letter, 1665, from Francis Moryson to Lord Clarendon, he claims compensation for the office of lieutenantship of the Ordnance, purchased by his father from Sir Edward Villiers.]

MR. FINES MORISON. Will 15 September 1629; proved 18 March 1629–30. To Mrs. Elizabeth Dynne his pictures. To George Allington Esq. his best night cap. To Mr. Francis Dynne his books and cabinet. To Mr. William Ireland his guilded Halberd. To Mrs. Susan Ireland his wife all linen. To Sarah Ireland chairs. To Mr. Edward Waterhouse 20 s. To Servant Isaack Pywall wearing apparell. Executor: Mr. Francis Dynne. This is the effect of the will of Mr. Fynes Moryson who died the 12 February last. Fra: Dynne, Isack Pyevall, Susan Ireland.

Scroope, 27.

DOROTHY KEMPE of Flordon, county Norfolk, widdowe, late wife of Robert Kempe of Gissing, Esq., deceased. Will 30 March 1626; proved 29 November 1626. To be buried in the place called the Chapel belonging to Church of Gissing and near my said husband. To poor of Flordon 40s. To poor of Gissing £10 to be paid to Mr. Robert Proctor or his successor. To poore of Hapton sos. and of Braten Ash 20s. To Dorothie Kempe my daughter in lieu of bequests to her by her father, Alice Pooly her grandmother deceased, and Roger Payne, and Gressell Herbert of Gissing deceased, all lands purchased of John Thurston Esqr in Hoxen and Eye, County Suffolk, and all lands in Gissing which were surrendered in trust by John Cocke late of Gissing aforesaid and Thomas Morse of Twetshall, gent, unto my cosen Edward Rouse of Flordon. To daughter Elizabeth Kempe my lands late purchased of Charles Lovell Esqr., of John Tindall als Kendall the elder, and John Tindall als Kendall the younger in old Buckenham, County Norfolk, assnming land in Gissing to my daughter Dorothy Kempe and pay £100 of debt or else lands to be sold and 1000 markes to Elizabetb, etc. If Elizabeth die before she is 18 her said lands in old Buckingham called Harling wood and lands in Gissing to be sold and money to daughter Dorothy and Sonnes, Arthur, Edward, Edmond, and Thomas Kempe. To Sir Robert Kempe, my Sonne a peece of plate of £20 and to my Daughter Dame Jane Kempe a portugall piece of gold weighing £3.10s. To Jane Kempe my Grandchild £20. To Sonne Arthur Kempe £100 and six paire of sheets with letter A set above my ordinary marke etc. To Sonne Edmond Kempe £100 and six Tableclothes with letter E set in a corner by itself. To Sone Edward Kemp £100 in four years also linnen with letter E etc. To Sonne Thomas Kempe £100 in five years, linnen with letter T, etc. To Sonne Edward £60 and Sonne Thomas £30 each a year during minority. To Arthur son of my Cosin Thomas Kempe of Barrow Hapton and to Dorothy daughter of my Cozen Clere Talbot of Wymondham and to Prudence daughter of my Cozen Edward Rowse of Flordon, being my godchild £5 each. A commemoration service to be preached by Mr. Robert Proctor, my cosen Edward Rowse, and my cozen Thomas Kempe. Wheras Sonne Sir Robert mortgaged to his Sister Dorothy Kemp certain lands for £600,000, and said Dorothy passed same to me, if 2000 odd not paid, Executors to enter etc. To my chamber maid 10s. To other servants 30s. eace. To my executors lease which I had from Sir William Parkhurst, Knight, of a certain house in Finsbery. Executors: Cozen Cleere Talbot of Wimondham, Doctor of the Civill Law, and Henry Bing, Sergeant at law of Granchester, county Cambridge. Witnesses: Edward Rouse, Thomas Kemp. [Sentence (59 Skipmore) confirming will 15 May 1627, in case between Executors and Sons Sir Robert Kempe, Kt., Richard, Arthur, Edmund, Edward and Arthur Kempe and daughters Dorothy Kempe and Elizabeth Kempe.]

Hele, 120.

[While it seems practically certain that Richard Kemp, Secretary of State of Virginia, and his nephew Edmond Kemp, of Lancaster (afterwards Middlesex) county, were of the family Kemp, of Gissing or Gessing, absolute proof has not yet been produced. It is hoped that this may yet be done. Richard Kemp was Secretary of State of Virginia, 1635-1649 (in a letter he states that he obtained the office through the influence of the Duke of Lennox and the Earl of Pembroke), and was Governor of the colony from June, 1644, to June, 1645. He died in 1656. In his will, proved in London, December 6, 1656 (of which a copy was printed in this Magazine, II, 174-176), he makes bequests to his brother Edward Kemp and his nephew Edmond Kemp. The latter was evidently in Virginia. Edmond Kemp was J. P. for Lancaster county, Va., in 1655. In 1656 he recorded in that county a power of attorney to him from Sir Robert Kemp, Knight. Edmond Kemp died about 1660. For a notice of the family in Virginia see this Magazine, III, 40-42.

From Mr. F. H. Kemp's extensive work on the English Kemps it appears that Robert Kemp, Esq., of Gissing and Flordon, was baptized at Hampstead 1567, and buried at Gissing 1612. He married Dorothy, daughter of Arthur Harris, of Cricksea, Essex. Her will is given above. From another source was received, a number of years ago, an abstract of the will of Robert Kemp, Esq., just referred to.

"Will of Robert Kempe, of Gissinge, Norfolk, Esq., dated November 20, 1611; proved by Dorothy, his relict, May 5, 1613. To be buried in the chapel at Gissinge. Various gifts to the poor of Disse, Dulburth, Burston, East Ruston, Shelpager, and to the churchwardens of the town of Flordon £3.6.8 for a silver communion cup. To Robert Kemp, his eldest son, all lands, &c., in Gissinge, Tibuar, Tinotshall, Burston and Shemplinge and also all in Flordon, Broken and Hopton and all in East Ruston, namely the manor of Burrells and all in Shelpanger in the occupation of Fulter. To second son John Kempe, £40 a year out of John Fulter's farm in Shelpanger. To Richard Kemp, third son £40 a year issuing out of the manor of Burrells in East Ruston. To Arthur, fourth son £40 a year out of Burrells. To Edmond, fifth son, £40 a year out of the farm of William Tibrum in Gissinge. To Edward, sixth son, £40 a year out of the manor of Dallines. To Thomas, seventh son, £40 a year out of the manor of Dallines. Until the sons are 21 years of age his wife is to have the use of their annuities for their education and bringing up. To daughter Dorothy 1,000 marks at the age of 18. To daughter Elizabeth 1,000 marks at 18. To wife two-thirds of the land in until son Robert is 24. To son Robert the hangings in the great parlor, Norfolk the parlor chamber, and the hall chamber; the bason and ewes of silver gilt "which was my grandfather's," "my own armour and my library of books." To father-in-law [evidently stepfather] Edmond Polie, Esq., my best gelding. To mother, Mrs. Alice Poley, my gold ring "

Richard, third son of Robert Kemp, was baptized at Gissing in 1600, and Arthur, fourth son, in 1601.

Edmond Kemp, son of Robert Kemp, matriculated at Magdalen Hall, Oxford, April 16, 1624, aged eighteen years.

Mr. F. H. Kemp states that letters of administration on the estate of Edmund Kemp, of Middlesex, England, was granted in 1649. He believes that this was Edmund, son of Robert Kemp, and states that Edmund, eldest son of Edmund, and grandson of Robert, was the emigrant to Virginia.

An abstract of the will of Arthur Kemp, son of Robert, was received a number of years ago from the same person who kindly sent the will of the father. It is as follows:

Will of Arthur Kemp, of the parish of Michael at the Thorne, Norwich, dated January 15, 1644; proved at London May 12, 1645. To four eldest children of brother Edmond £8 each. Niece Dorothy Jackman £6. The wife of my cousin Robert Freeman, of Gissinge, 40 shillings. To poor of Gissinge. Niece Walgrave 10 shillings. Niece Elizabeth Kemp 40 shillings. Mr. Thomas Sair, of Bestreete, 40 shillings. Mr. Bayfield 20 shillings. Little George Bayfield 10 shillings. My sister the Lady Kempe, of Spain's Hall, Essex, whom I wish to be executrix, 40 shillings. My cousin Rowse. Cousin Thomas Rowse. Sister, the Lady Kemp of Finchingfield, Brother Sir Robert Kempe.

Unless the writer of the letter to be mentioned was in error, there was a third emigration of the Kemps of Gissing to Virginia. There is in existence a letter, dated 1730, from Dorothy Seaton, of Pianketank [Gloucester county], Va., addressed to the third Kemp baronet (Robert, brother of Richard, Arthur, &c., was the first), in a piteous manner, stating she was a widow with several children and in reduced circumstances. She claimed to be the eldest and only surviving daughter of Peter Kemp, a brother of the second baronet.

The will of Sir Robert Kemp, 2d baronet, was dated May 3, 1704, and proved in the Consistory Court of Suffolk, 1710. In it were legacies to

Thomas and Peter, sons of his deceased brother Mathew Kemp. The names Peter and Mathew appear repeatedly in the Gloucester county, Va., family, and it is possible that Mrs. Seaton's father, Peter, was not a brother of the second baronet, but his nephew. The whole connection requires, however, farther proofs, though there can be little or no doubt that Richard Kemp, of Virginia, was son of Robert Kemp, Esq., of Gissing, and Edmond Kemp of Virginia, a grandson of the same person.]

EDMUND KEMPE late of Stepney, Middlesex. Administration 25 September 1649 to widow Bridget Kemp.

P. C. C. Admon Act Book 1649, folio 101.

JONATHAN STOUGHTON, of the citte of London, gent. Will 27 January 1629-30; proved 5 March 1629-30. To Mrs. Venn my late Mris £20. To Mrs. Edes all her household stuff and £13.0s.6d. in money which was made of her plate. Mr. Tusely may be satisfied all due to him, his bills for which he hath sent me over money to be paid. Residuary Legatee and Executor: Brother Thomas Stoughton. Witnesses: Tho: Talbot, John Bateman, Agmondesham Pickaye. [At side it sayd, "Late in parts beyond the seas deceased." Probate Act Book says St. Vadest, Fish Lane, and "deceased over seas" erased.]

Scroope, 27.

MICHAEL SPARKE, Citizen and Stationer of London, Parish of Sepulchres without Newgate. Will 22 October 1653; proved 3 March 1653-4. To be buried in church of Sepulchre, if I dye in London, neare vnto my former wife without vain ostentation and without the Livery of the Company or any woman kind but only my wife, daughters, and grandchildren, and without funerall Sermon. Whereas have by writinge 19 December 1651 assured now wife Isabell and some frends of hers for her use Competent means on Conditions she revoakes two thirds in Custome of London and have alsoe purchased the house and ground at Hampstead, Middlesex, late bought of Robert Marsh, gentleman, for her use, etc., yet for naturall loue I bequeath vnto sayd Isabel all plate and money she had formerly of myne and furniture of Household bought by me and now at Hampstead, with Cowes, Hoggs, and Poultrey, etc., all messuages in Clamperds Court, als.

greene Arber in parish of Sepulchres to be enjoyed by Severall persons as in Indenture between me Michael Sparke of one partie and Humphrey Baskevile, Cittizen and Vintner, of thother partie, 12 February 22nd yeare of our late Soueraigne Lord King Charles: "Item. I giue and bequeath vnto my good frend William Prynn Esquire my Seale ring of gold." To frend Anthony Hudson best book he make choice of in my shoppe and to his son Nathaniell Hudson next best ditto. To Ellen Coles widdow ring her husband left me in his will. "Item. I giue and bequeath vnto my nephew Nathaniele Sparke in the Barmoodies and to his two Sisters Elizabeth Evans and Mary Sparke to ever of them tenn pounds a peece in money to be payd vnto them out of the money that Robert Sparke oweth me he to detayne Soe much out of the last money that shalbe in his hands of the Sayd debt to pay them." Forgive brother Thomas Sparke all debt. To grandchildren Elizabeth Baskerville and John Hutton £50 a peece out of money owing by kinsman Robert Parke. Remainder of Robert Park's debt to rest of grandchildren. "Item. I giue more unto the Sayd Elizabeth Baskervile my grandchild fyfty pounds out of the money oweing vnto me by Mr. Thomas Stegg of James Citty or James Towne in Verginia marchant and twenty pounds of his Sayd debt to my grandchild John Hutton. Item. I giue the remaynder of the debt of the Said Thomas Stegg with the monie oweing vnto me by Mr. Thomas Boler and Mr. Anderson of Yorketowne in Virginia to the rest of my grandchildren equally amongst them, And when the Sayd money oweing me in Verginia and Barbadoes shalbe payed I giue vnto each of those Countreys one huudred bookes on the Second part of the Crums of Comfort with groanes of the Spirite and handkerchiffe of wet eies ready bound to be distributed amongst the poore children there that can read." To my loveing frends and chapmen John Hamond, Henry Hamond, Thomas Thomas, William Newton, Walter Dight, Edward Dight, William Fugill, Richard Price, Richard Ireland, and John Jones 20s. apiece for rings mourning fashion to weare in remembrance of me. To John Cleaver, Brian Greenhill, —— Cotterell, and Parr Betty, booke binders, 5s. apeece. "Item. I giue and bequeath vnto the parish of Eyntham in the county of Oxon one hundred pounds out of the money oweing unto me from my cousin Richard Hions and

Mr. Thomas French towards the maintenance of a free Schoole in the Sayd parish to be payd so Soone as it shalbe gotten in of them And if the Sayd money shall not be gotten in of them Then I giue Fifty pounds in money to be payd by my Executor towards the maintenance of Such a free Schoole in the sayd parish or to be layd out towards the purchaseing of some howse or Land for that purpose and not otherwise nor for any other vse whatsoever at the discretion of my good frends Henry Eccleston, John Hampshewe, Richard Evans, John Oakes, Nicholas Hart, and James Caterman. And intreat them to be Careful to see the same done accordingly." To Brother Richard Sparke and Sister Elizabeth Macock 20s. each for mourning rings. To Sister's daughter Ann Macock 10s. To kinsman John Macock, kinsman George Sparke, and to William Sparke 1s. each. To my daughter in law Isabell Sparke, lieving in Scotland, £5, and her two children to have like part of my estate with my other grandchildren here in England. To Sorn in law Humphrey Baskervile £10. To two Sonns in law George Hutton and John Hutton 40s. each for rings. To servants Edward Thomas and Elizabeth Piggott 10s. each. To the poore in the old bailey quarter of the parish of St. Sepulchres 50s. in bread to be distributed by the Churchwardens, Sidemen, and Collector for the poor or that quarter. To Cousen Thomas Sparke in Gloucester some of my worser apparell. To Constance Jones, widdow, 5s. To Fifty Apprentices of the old Bailey fifty prentices practice of piety. To those invited to my buriall and doe come instead of biskett or plums to every of them a booke of the grievances of the Spirite. Rest to three daughters, Elizabeth Baskervile, Mary Hutton, and Sarah Hutton. Executor: said Sonn in lawe Humphrey Humphrey [sic i. e., Humphrey Baskervile.] Overseers: two sonns in law John Hutton and George Hutton. Witnesses: Anthony Hudson, scriven., Nathaniel Hudson. Nuncupative codicil of said Michael Sparke deceased on or about 26 December 1653. Wife Isabell to enjoy her Estate according to Agreement and to be paid £150 borrowed of her. Witnesses: Mr. Thomas Gonge and Mr. Charles Doyly.

Alchin, 158.

[The testator was evidently an ardent Puritan. Thomas Stegg, Jr., was afterwards Auditor-General of Virginia. Thomas Boler was, no doubt, Thomas Bowler, afterwards of Rappahannock county, who was appointed to the Council in 1675 and died in 1679. The reference to Yorktown is a very early appearance of the name. Probably the old " York Plantation " was now called Yorktown.]

ANDREW THOMPSON of London, mariner, son of Thomas Thompson of parish of Awter howse near Dundee in Scotland 1624–25 notary publique. Will 2 February 1624–25; proved 1 April 1625. Now bound on a voyage to Virginia in the good ship called the Jacob of London. My estate and goods, etc., in five equal parts, four to Brother Walter Thompson, and two to sisters Christian, Mary, Margaret, and Elizabeth, and the other part to Cousin Thomas Ireland of Dundee and my friend John Cannady of East Smithfield, gunnemaker. Executors: Thomas Ireland and John Cannady. Overseer: Henry Rouse, Scrivenor. Witnesses: Robert Chapman, John Darley, and Hehry Rouse, Scr. [Of Saint Botolph, Algate.]

Archdeaconry of London, Register 6, fo. 143.

VIRGINIA GLEANINGS IN ENGLAND.

Communicated by Mr. LOTHROP WITHINGTON, 30 Little Russell street, W. C., London including " Gleanings " by Mr. H. F. WATERS, not before printed.

[During the past winter Mr. Withington was for some time in the United States. This accounts for the present short instalment of "Gleanings."]

ROGER FARLEY of City of Worchester, gentleman. Will 29 March 1622; proved 25 September 1622. To my wife Jane the tenement my son Robert Farley now dwells in the broadstreete of Worcester and adjoining to the East side of now dwelling house and at her decease to my son Robert. To son Robert the house in my own occupation and the house in occupation of my sister Alice Kent. To wife Jane £300 and all the goods which were her own when I married her. To William Farley my son £120 and various articles of furniture and the lease of the house John Younger now dwelleth in. To son Elliot Farley £100. To Edward Farley my son £10 to buy him a cloak and his wife a gown. To son Thomas Farley £5. To son Humphrey Farley

£5. To Susanna Ceycill my daughter £5. To daughter Margaret Broadhurst £5. To Daughter Jane Rogers £5. To daughter Katherine Barnsley £5. To wife's son Robert Allen £40. To sister Alice Kent £3. To each of my apprentices and servant maids 10s. each. To Poor of Worcester £7. To Thomas and Edward Evans my wife's brethren 20s. each. Robert Farley my son to use my Clothmarke in any clothes he shall make. I forgive my brother Thomas Farley of all debts he owes me and also discharge Thomas Rogers my son in law of all moneys and also my son in law William Ceycill. Lands I hold from Corporation of Worcester to Jane my wife. The deeds of feoffment to some of my children of lands in Anbury als Avenbury in co. Hereford and of lands in City of Worcester to remain in safe custody of my executor. To John Clyman 22s. Residuary Legatee and Executor: son Robert Farley. Overseers: John Watts of City of Worcester gent, and John Breynton of same city, Dyer. If I die in the forenoon of any day my body to be buried in the afternoone of the same day, and if I die in the afternoone of one day to be buried in forenoon of next. Witnesses: Edward Waringe, William Allen, Richard Oswald, John Hill, Scr.

Savile, 83.

["Thomas Fairlay of Worcester in Worcestershire, gent," came to Virginia in 1623, and was a member of the House of Burgesses in 1629-30 and 1631-32. An examination of records at Worcester would doubtless show whether he was son or brother of the testator. See this Magazine, XIX, 131, 132.]

BENEDICT LLANDEN of the Middle Temple, London, Esquire. Will 14 January 1631-2; proved 14 March 1631-32. I being a younger brother and had nothing from my father but an allowance for maintenance at Innes of Court and then only till I had been two years an utter barrister. To Mary my wife 1000 marks and the house we now dwell in at Isleworth. To Edward my eldest son my law bookes. Residuary Legatees and Executors: my two sons Edward and William. My eldest Brother William Llanden of Dalby, county Lincoln hath forfeated a bond of £1500 unto me. Witnesses: Phi: Llanden, Ri: Legh, Ed: Pigott and Willm Myghtin.

Audley, 34.

[This is possibly the will of an ancestor of the Landons of Credenhill, Herefordshire, from whom came Thomas Landon of Virginia. Edward Llanden, born in Stafford, first son of Benedict, of London, England, matriculated at Magdalen Hall, Oxford, October 11, 1633, aged 18; student of the Middle Temple, 1628, his father was a barrister of the Middle Temple, 1610. (*Foster*).]

JOHN PEACHIE the elder of Mildenhall, county Suffolk, yeoman. Will last November 1626; proved 9 February 1627-8. To be buried in parish Church of Mildenhall. To Agnes my wife land bought of Nicholas and Henrie Willis for life and then to son Robert Peachie. To said Agnes land in the Beckfield in Mildenhall sometime the land of one John Childerstone which came to me by decent after the decease of my father Richard Peachie, and then at her decease to son Robert. To son Robert Peachie land late purchased from Robert Clarke, also £60 when 21. To son Peter Peachie my tenement in Wilde Streete in Mildenhall and land purchased from Joseph Heynes and also a piece of land which was late my Aunt's Alice Huske deceased and £20 to him when 21. To James Peachey my son a cottage called Brownes with land called Leaches and £20 when 21. To son Richard land bought of the widow Spalding, he to pay to the 4 daughters of my late daughter Anne Sheene deceased £10 when they are 21. To the four daughters of my daughter Alice Yaxeleye deceased 20s. each when 21. To Richard, John and Agnes sons and daughter of son Richard 10s. each when 21. Residuary Legatee and Executor: son John. Overseers: James Knight, George Loker. Witnesses: Henrie Peachie, William Dalleson, and And. Cropley.

Barrington 20.

[Samuel Peachey, emigrant ancestor of a well-known Virginia family, came to Virginia in 1659 with his uncle William Hodgskin, and was son of Robert Peachy, of Mildenhall, Suffolk. Though John Peachie, the testator, was evidently a prosperous yeoman, Samuel Peachey, as his will shows, owned silver plate and seal rings, bearing his arms. See *William and Mary Quarterly*, III, 111-115.]

VIRGINIA GLEANINGS IN ENGLAND.

Communicated by Mr. Lothrop Withington, 30 Little Russell street, W. C., London including " Gleanings " by Mr. H. F. Waters, not before printed.

Barbara Levermore of the Colony of Virginia. Will 28 July 1716; proved 25 September 1716. Debt appearing to be due to Capt. Thos. Richardson by orders under my hand and seal on Mr. Benj. Hatly and Cutbert Jones Merchant in London to be first paid and satisfyed. Unto John Bacon and John Turner, Geo: Wilkenson, James Turner, and Joice Turner, all money due in England (over and above 80 pounds due Executor and 5 pounds which I appoint be given to James Henderson), share and share alike. I give Eliz'a and Benj'a Wicker all due from them and the like to James Henderson. Executor: Capt. Thos. Richardson. Witnesses: Phi. Lightfoot, Tho: Crompton, Ja. Woolsey. [Died on the high seas on merchant ship Mary.—Probate Act Book.]

Fox, 180.

Roger Dixon, Citty of Bristol, Accomptant and Victualler. Will 19 November 1744; proved 16 March 1746-7. All estate Real and personal as well in Virginia as Great Britain or elsewhere to wife Ann Dixon, executrix. Witnesses: Sam'll Holbrook, John Taylor, Rachel Holloway, John Harding.

Potter, 68.

[Probably the testator was brother of John Dixon, of Bristol and Virginia, who had a son named Roger. See this Magazine, XIX, 283.]

Hesther Pritchard, St. Andrew Holborn, Middlesex, widdow. Will 20 April 1690; proved 8 July 1691. To Granddaughter Elizabeth Daughter of Robert Pritchard late of Virginia one shilling. To Mada, Sarah Clifton 10s. for ring. To

From Vol. XX, No. 3 (July 1912), p. 292.

Mr. Smith and wife ditto each. To Mr. Hinton an apothecary of St. Giles in the feelds all money due mee in Virginia vpon the papers I gave to him not long since. To Mr. Mathew Turner what he owes, except 40s. to be distributed for charitable uses. To Mrs. Mary Moone 10s. To Mr. Thomas Moone 10s. To Sarah Holtham one bed, one pillow three blankets, one rugg with a stuff gowne and petticoate and bodyes, a looking glass one little wayscot box one little long chest one little hayre trunke and all pictures (except Mr. Monteages) and 5 pounds (out of money Mr. Smith owes deducting charges in keeping a poore woman to attend mee dureing my sickness) also a black crape gowne to Sarah abouesaid. To Ellen Griffith one Askedhored petticoate, one long scarfe, two suits of Night Cloaths and one silke Hood. To Mrs. Grace Dudley 10s. To Mrs. Bridget Dudley 10s. To Richard Shute 10s. only being executor with Mrs. Anne Turner. Rest vnto loving friend Mrs. Ann Turner (wife of Mr. Mathew Turner) shee being chief executrix. To be buried in churchyard of St. Andrews Holborne. Witnesses: Mathew Turner, Thomas Metcalfe, Thomas Moone, Sarah Holtham. Vere 120.

OSMOND CRABBE, Brislington als Busselton, Somerset, gent. Will 8 December 1684; proved 3 April 1695. Burial in decent manner and debts to be paid out of legacies given to brother John Crabb hereinafter named at discretion of Executors ditto. To sister Anne Adlam, wife of Joseph Adlam messuage in Brislington als Busselton for life, then to my neece Ann Adlam, daughter of said sister Ann. Also for life, then to my brother John Crabb now in Virginia, Merchant, to him and his heirs forever. To said brother John Crabb all houses in Citty of Bristoll and parish of Bedminster, Somerset. To said sister Anne Adlam for life, then to niece Anne Adlam, all goods, etc, except apparel to brother John Crabb. To poore of the parish of Temple within the citty of Bristoll 10 pounds. To said brother John Crabb messuage in Temple Street Bristoll, wherein Samuell Whitehurst, Sope boyler, dwelleth, paying to my Sister Alice Vaughan 6s. weekly for her life etc. All debts owing me etc to William Hayman and William Swimmer of Citty of Bristoll, Merchant, Executors. Witnesses: Jno King, Abraham Menne Junr, Jno Hall, Nico. Pearson. Administration to sister Alice Vaughan, executors Sir William Hayman, knight and William Swimmer, renouncing.

Irby, 46.

[The brother, John Crabbe, settled in Westmoreland county, Va., and married, about August, 1675, Temperence, daughter of Dr. Thos. Gerrard, of Westmoreland, and widow of Daniel Hutt, of the same county. The family has been resident in Westmoreland to the present day. An examination of the records of the county would doubtless produce much information. The inventory of the personal estate of Osman Crabbe, deceased (no doubt a son of John), was recorded in Westmoreland February 24, 1719.]

JOHN HARRIS, Saint Stephens parish in the County of Northumberland and Collony of Virginia. Will 20 September 1718; proved 12 September 1723. Of Legacy left me by My Vncle William Harris Esqr of Hayne in parish of Stowford in County of Devon being 300 pounds Sterling in hands of Christ: Harris Esqr in parish of Padstow and County of Devon aforesaid (sic. i. e. error Cornwall) 100 pounds I spent in England and 106 pounds I have drawed upon the aforesaid Christopher Harris 3 Severall Setts of bills to three Several persons, and the remainder I give as followeth Xpher Harris, Brother William Harris, Sister Margaret Pergeny, Sister Jane Kitt 10s. each. If bills protested then to be paid to my wife Hannah Harris. Rest to Wife Hannah Harris executrix. Witnesses: Tho: Hobsen, Jarvas Ellistone. Proved by relict Hannah Crabbe als Harris wife of Thomas Crabbe.

Richmond, 190.

[This will was also proved in Northumberland county, Va., May 20, 1719. An abstract of the Northumberland copy, in possession of the writer, shows that the will also contains legacies to "my father Joseph Harris" and "my *brother* Christopher Harris." The Harrises of Hayne were an old and prominent Devonshire family. The uncle William referred to was William Harris, of Hayne, M. P. for St. Ives and Oakhampton in several parliaments in the reigns of William and Mary and Anne. Accounts of the family can be found in Burk's *Extinct Baronetage*, and *Commoners*.

THOMAS HORSEMANDEN, Doctor of Divinity and Rector of Purleigh, county Essex. Will 25 April 1630; proved 17 February 1632. To Poor of Purleigh 5 pounds. To Brother Daniell Horsemanden, Doctor of Divinity and to his wife and their son Warham and to my five sisters, Katherine Baldwyn (and to her son Richard Baldwin), Elizabeth Cobham, Martha, Anna, and Rebecca Horsmanden 20s. each. To my curate my gown. To John Streater of Gouthurst in Kent 20s. My perpetual advowson of Purleigh to be sold. Residuary legatees and executors: Wife Jane and son Richard. No witnesses.

Russell, 15.

[Thomas Horsmanden was fellow of St. John's College, Cambridge, March 18, 1596; incorporated D. D., Oxford, July 12, 1614; Canon of Lincoln, 1608; Vicar of Gondhurst, Kent, 1613; Canon of Canterbury, 1618, and Rector of Purleigh, Essex, 1624–1632. In 1632 his widow, Jane, presented Lawrence Washington to the benefice. At Purleigh his sons, John and Lawrence Washington, the emigrants to Virginia, spent their childhood.

Rev. Daniel Horsmanden, D. D., the brother of the testator, was rector of Ulcombe, Kent, 1627–1643, when he was evicted for his loyalty. He married Ursula, daughter of Sir Warham St. Leger of Ulcombe, and their son, Warham Horsmanden, named in the will, came to Virginia and has many descendants. See this Magazine, XV, 314–317.]

VIRGINIA GLEANINGS IN ENGLAND.

Communicated by Mr. Lothrop Withington, 30 Little Russell street,
W. C., London including "Gleanings" by Mr. H. F. Waters,
not before printed.

Daniel Parke Esq'r Captain Generall and Cheefe Governor
of all the Leeward Islands. Will 29 January 1709-10; proved
15 May 1711. All estate in these Islands both Lands Houses
Negroes Debts etc. to Thomas Long Esq'r and Mr. Caesar Rodney for use of Mrs. Lucy Chester being the Daughter of Mrs.
Katherine Chester tho she is not yet Christened. And if her
Mother thinks fitt to call her after any other name I still bequeath all my estate in the four Islands of my Government to
her. If she die before 21 then to her Mother Mrs. Katherine
Chester to remain in hands of friends Collonell Thomas Long
and Mr. Caesar Rodney and after her decease to my Godson
Julius Caesar Parke, but if said youngest Daughter of said
Mrs. Katherine Chester lives to Marry and have Childred (sic)
then to her Eldest son and Heirs Made provided he calls him-
self by name of Parke and said youngest daughter of Mrs.
Katherine Chester to alter her name and call herself Parke and
use my Coat of Armes etc. which is that of my Family of the
County of Essex, but if she refuse to godson Julius Caesar
Parke then to heirs of my Daughter Frances Custis then of my
Daughter Mrs. Lucy Bird always to call themselves Parke etc.
To daughter Francis Custis all estate in Virginia and England,
then to Daughter Lucy Bird, then to youngest daughter of Mrs.
Katherine Chester, then Julius Caesar Parke, and in case of
failure of heirs to poor of Whitchurch in Hampshire. Daughter Frances Custis to pay out of estate in Hampshire and Virginia. To Daughter Lucy Bird £1000, to godson Julius Caesar
£50 yearly for life, to each of my sisters and their children £50
for rings, to executors in England £20 each. Executors in
Leeward Islands Tho: Long Esq. Mr. Caesar Rodney and Major

From Vol. XX, No. 4 (Oct. 1912), p. 372.

Samuell Byam. Executors for England and Virginia Macajah
Perry Esq'r Mr. Tho: Lane and Mr. Richard Perry of London
Merchant. Sealed in St. Johns in Antigua. Witnesses: H.
Pember, John Bermingham, Will'm Martin. Codicil 7 Decem-
ber 1710 Appoint in Room of Collonel Long deceased Mr. Abra-
ham Redwood one of Executors. Antigua 20 December 1710.
Before Honourable Walter Hamilton Esq. Lieutenant Generall
and Commander in Cheife ouer all her Majesties Leeward Carribee Islands in America. Oath of Herbert Pember of said
Island Esq'r and William Martin of Town of St. Johns Vintner
Recorded 22 December 1710 vera Copea. Thos. Kerby Secr'y
15 May 1711. Oath of Michael Ayon of Island of Antigua
Esq'r that he hath been Provost Marshall of said Island and
other Carribee Island and well acquainted with Daniel Parke
Esq'r deceased late Captain Generall before his death in De-
cember last and saw last will in hands of Mr. Caesar Rodney of
said Island Merchant one of Executors and is acquainted with
Thomas Kerby Sec'y at said Island of Antigua etc. Proved in
Prerogative Court of Canterbury by Micajah Perry Esq. and
Richard Perry two of executors.

Young, 112.

[Daniel Parke, Jr. (1692), only son of Colonel Daniel Parke, who was
also a member of the Council, was born in 1669. He was probably educated in England, but was back in Virginia soon after reaching manhood,
and, in 1692, was appointed a member of the King's Council. He was
an intimate friend and favorite of Governor Andros, who, besides making
him a Councillor, gave him the places of collector and naval officer of
Lower James River, escheator for the district between the York and
James, and colonel of militia.

The accounts of Col. Parke's character which have come down to the
present day show him in a very unfavorable light, but as they are all
from sources hostile to him and to his friend, Governor Andros, they
should perhaps be accepted with a "grain of salt." The earliest notice
of him occurs in a memorial by Commissary Blair, attacking the administration of Andros. He says: "There is a handsome young man of that
Country [Virginia] one Mr. Daniel Parke, who to all the other accomplish-
ments that make a complete sparkish Gentleman has added one upon
which he infinitely values himself, that is, a quick resentment of every
the least thing that looks like an affront or Injury. He has learned, they
say, the art of fencing, and is as ready at giving a challenge, especially
before Company, as the greatest Hector in the Town." Dr. Blair adds

the charge that Parke is a tool of Andros, who has advanced him to the Council and made him a Colonel. He says that there was no way by which Parke could so readily win the Governor's good will as by opposing Governor Nicholson, of Maryland. He soon found an excuse to do this. A letter from him, which the Doctor says contained nothing that should not have been read, was shown by Nicholson to Dr. Blair. About September, 1695, Colonel Parke, having a sword much larger than the one with which he commonly travelled, came to Dr. Blair's house where Nicholson was visiting, and said to him: "Captain Nicholson, did you receive a letter which I sent you from New York?" "Yes, I received it," said the Governor of Maryland. "And was it done like a Gentleman," asked Col. Parke, "to send that letter by the hand of a common post, to be read by everybody in Virginia? I look upon it as an affront, and expect satisfaction." "You must go to Pennsylvania, then," replied Governor Nicholson; "my hands are tied up in Virginia, but if you go thither you shall have the satisfaction you desire." Said Parke, "Come out here;" and so putting his hand on his sword went towards the door. "What!" says the Governor of Maryland; "is this your way, Mr. Parke, of giving challenges before so much Company? If you have anything to say to me you know always where to find me. I am often in these parts, and you shall never find that I fly the road from you. I am going this very afternoon to Sir Edmund Andros's. But you shall not catch me making any appointments in Virginia." Upon this Colonel Parke began to insult at a strange rate, and told the Governor of Maryland how he used to huff and hector when he was Lord Governor of Virginia, but now, he had met his match, he had nothing to say. When he spoke of huffing and hectoring, "That's your part, Mr. Parke," says the Governor of Maryland. "But you would say no more if my hands were not tied here; half of these words should do." Then he proffered him, if he would go to Pennsylvania, to furnish him horses and to defray his charge thither. When Parke refused this he whispered him something in his ear which was not too low but that the Company overheard it. It was something to this purport, "that if he would let him know privately at any time he would meet him anywhere but in Virginia or Maryland." Thus ended the affair for a time. Dr. Blair goes on to say that Colonel Parke showed also a violent hatred towards him, and as his cloth prevented a challenge, the Colonel took another method of displaying this feeling. He had ceased to come to Bruton Church because the minister, Mr. Eburne, preached several times against adultery, and Parke, "at this time, and still, doth entertain a Gentleman's Lady, one Mistress Berry, whom he had conveyed away from her husband in London, in 1692, and carried her to Virginia along with him, calling her by the name of his cousin Brown." One Sunday morning, however, Parke came to church where Mrs. Blair was sitting (by invitation) in the pew of Colonel Ludwell, Parke's father-in-law, and violently dragged her out of the pew.

337

Sometime in 1696 a quarrel arose between Parke and Nicholson at a meeting of the Visitors of William and Mary College, and Parke struck the Governor of Maryland with a horsewhip. Nicholson rushed at him, but the bystanders separated them. Governor Nicholson then challenged his assailant to meet him in Carolina, but, according to Dr. Blair, Parke contrived by letting Governor Andros learn of the affair to have himself arrested. There is, doubtless, substantial truth in Dr. Blair's statements, but he was a man of very strong prejudices, and perhaps exaggerated and misconstrued Parke's conduct to some degree. A letter, written in 1698, from Parke to his daughter, conveys a message to her from her aunts and her "Cousin Brown." It is hardly probable that an affectionate father, as Parke seems to have been, would have insulted his daughter by mentioning her "Cousin Brown" if Dr. Blair's charges in regard to that lady had been true. There can be little doubt, however, that Colonel Parke, while a man of courage and energy, had the morals, or lack of morals, of the average man of fashion and pleasure of his day.

In 1697 or the year following Parke went to England, and is not known to have ever returned to Virginia. It would seem from some letters that have been preserved that he and his wife did not live happily together, and that may have had something to do with his long stay abroad. His wife and daughters remained in Virginia during his absence, and Mrs. Lee, in her Memoir of G. W. P. Custis, prefixed to the "Recollections," refers to the numerous letters to and from Parke preserved at "Arlington." "The mother," she tells us, "in many long and urgent letters, implored him to return, pleading the state of her health as rendering her unequal to the task of caring for the family and estate in Virginia." "She even wrote to his merchant and man of business, Micajah Perry, to use his influence in persuading him to return."

Mrs. Lee quotes in full several of the letters from Colonel Parke. One of them was to his daughter Fanny, afterwards Mrs. Custis, Here it is:

"St. James, October ye 20.

My Dear Fanny—

I Rec'vd y'r first letter, and be shure you be as good as y'r word and mind y'r writing and everything else you have learnt; and do not learn to Romp, but behave y'rselfe soberly and like a Gentlewoman. Mind Reading; and carry y'rself so yt Everyboddy may Respect you. Be Calm and Obligeing to all the servants, and when you speak doe it mildly, Even to the poorest slave; if any of the Servants committ small faults yt are of no consequence, doe you hide them. If you understand of any great faults they commit, acquaint y'r mother, but do not aggravate the fault.

I am well and have sent you everything you desired, and, please God I doe well, I shall see you ere long. Love y'r sister and y'r friends, be dutiful to y'r mother. This, with my blessing, is from y'r lo: father

DANIEL PARKE.

Give my Duty to y'r Grandfather, and my love to y'r Mother and Sister and serviss to all friends. My Cosen Brown gives you her serviss, and y'r Aunts and Cousins their love."

Mrs. Lee also prints a letter written by Daniel Parke to John Custis in response to an application from Custis in behalf of his son John, who was a suitor for the hand of Frances Parke.

"LONDON, August 25, 1705.

Sir: I received yours relating to your son's desire of marrying my daughter, and your consent if I thought well of it. You may easily inform yourself that my daughter Frances will be heiress of all the land my father left which is not a little nor the worst. My personal estate is not very small in that country, and I have but two daughters, and there is no likelihood of my having any more, as matters are, I being obliged to be on one side of the ocean and my wife on the other. I do not know your young gentleman, nor have you or he thought fit to send an account of his real and personal effects; however, if my daughter likes him, I will give her upon her marriage with him, half as much as he can make it appear he is worth.

I have no one else to give my estate to but my daughters. This is what I think convenient to write at present. My service to you and all friends in Virginia.

From your humble servant,

DANIEL PARKE.

To Colonel Custis."

Anderson, in his *History of the Colonial Church*, says that Col. Parke's offences compelled him to fly from Virginia to England, where he bought an estate in Hampshire and became a member of Parliament, but was expelled from the House for bribery. At that time as at later periods, both in England and America, political parties were but little scrupulous in turning out members of the opposition, so though Parke may have been guilty of bribery, the fact that he was expelled on this ground is no proof. Anderson's added statement that Col. Parke's offences compelled him to fly to Holland (where he was a volunteer in the army of the Duke of Marlborough), is almost certainly false. He served the campaign of 1701 in Flanders, with Lord Arran, and was again in England the next year, as the following letter to his daughter, formerly preserved at "Arlington," proves:

COL. DANIEL PARKE.
From a portrait at Washington-Lee University.

My Dear Fanny: I am going a volunteer under the Duke of Marlborough, to Flanders, where I served also the last campaign with my Lord Arran, the Duke of Ormond's brother, and was in every action. God knows if I may ever see you more, but if I do not, I shall take care to leave you and your sister in very happy circumstances, therefore do not throw yourself away on the first idle young man that offers, if you have a mind to marry. I know it is the desire of all young people to be married, and though few are so happy after marriage as before, yet every one is willing to make the experiment at their own expense. Consider who you marry as the greatest concern to you in the world. Be kind and good-natured to all of your servants. It is much better to have them love you than fear you. My heart is in Virginia, and the greatest pleasure I propose to myself is seeing you and your sister happy. That you may be ever so is the earnest desire of your affectionate father,

DANIEL PARKE.

I got some reputation last summer which I hope I shall not lose this; I am promised the first old regiment that shall fall, being now a Colonel."

Col. Parke served as an aide to the Duke of Marlborough, and with high distinction. At Blenheim he so particularly covered himself with glory, that the Duke accorded him the honor of carrying the first news of the great victory to England, and made him the bearer of the following note to the Duchess, written, in pencil, on a leaf torn from the Duke's notebook. It is still at Blenheim, and a facsimile is to be found in Coxe's *Life of Marlborough*:

"I have not time to say more, but to beg you will give my duty to the queen, and let her know her army has had a glorious victory. M. Tallard and two other generals are in my Coach and I am following the rest. The bearer, my aide-de-camp, Col. Parke, will give her an account of what has passed. I shall do it in a day or two by another more at large.

MARLBOROUGH.

August 13, 1704."

The report of the victory was heard with great enthusiasm throughout England and the English colonies. In the remotest settlements the great news was celebrated, proclamations were issued and addresses of congratulation sent to the Queen, while the number of places in the older colonies, called Blenheim, attest the general feeling of the people. In Virginia an especial pride was taken in the victory,

341

for Governor Nicholson (past quarrels now apparently forgotten) calls attention to the fact that the good tidings were brought to England by "Col. Parke, a gentleman and native of this colony."

It was at that time the custom in England to give the bearer of the first news of a victory a gratuity of £500, but Col. Parke begged that, instead, he might have the Queen's picture. His gallantry (in both senses of the word), fine appearance and handsome bearing pleased Queen Anne, and being patronized by the Churchills, he was, on April 25, 1704, appointed chief governor of the Leeward Islands. The government of these islands had been very lax, the settlers were inclined to be rebellious, and like those of the other West Indian Colonies had among them many desperate and lawless characters. The appointment of Parke was unpopular from the first, and the policy which he adopted in his administration, instead of wiping away the prejudice against him, wrought his complete undoing.

Having repelled the French who had plundered the islands of St. Christopher and Nevis, Governor Parke endeavored to carry out some much needed reforms, and being sure of support at home, he aroused the displeasure of the colonists by disregarding the articles of a formal complaint against him drawn up by them, and made a somewhat ostentatious display of the small military force placed at his command. At least this is the account given by Parke's friends, particularly by George French who published the whole story in England, while on the other hand, the colonists claimed that their Governor's oppressions drove them to revolt. The savage cruelty, however, with which they treated him, would incline us to give judgment against them. Whatever the cause, a violent insurrection broke out in 1710, at Antigua, the seat of government. Col. Parke made a gallant resistance, and with his own hand killed Captain John Piggott, one of the leaders of the insurrection, but finally overpowered by numbers, and made helpless by a shot in the thigh, he fell into the hands of the rioters. "They had now an opportunity of sending him away to what place and in what manner they think fit," says French's account, "but instead thereof they use him with the utmost contempt and inhumanity. They strip him of his clothes, kick, spurn at, and beat him with the buts of their muskets, by which means at last they break his back. They drag him into the streets by a leg and arm, and his head trails and beats from step to step of the stone stairs at the entrance of the house, and he is dragged on the coarse gravelly street, which raked the skin from his bones. These cruelties and tortures force tears from his eyes, and in this condition he is left expiring, exposed to the scorching sun, out of the heat of which he begs to be removed. The good-natured woman, who, at his request, brought him water to quench his thirst is threatened by one Samuel Watkins to have a sword passed through her for her humanity, and the water is dashed out of her hands. He is insulted and reviled by every scoundrel, in the agonies of death, but makes no other return but these mild expressions, 'Gentlemen, you have no sense of honor left, pray have some of humanity.' He gratefully owns the kindness of friends, and prays God to reward those who stood by him that day. At last he was removed to the house of one Mr. John Wright, near the place where he lay, and there, recommending his soul to God, with some pious ejaculations, he pays the great debt of nature, and death, less cruel than his enemies, put an end to his sufferings.

After they had surfeited themselves with cruelties, they plundered the General's house and broke open his store-houses, so that his estate must have suffered by that day in money, plate, jewels, clothes, and household goods, by the most moderate computation, five thousand pounds sterling, for which his executors have obtained no satisfaction to this day. Thus died Colonel Parke, whose brave end shows him sufficiently deserving of the commission he bore, and his death acquired an honor to his memory, which the base aspersions of his enemies could not overthrow."

The date of this shocking tragedy was December 7, 1710.

Mrs. Lee, in the memoir already quoted, says: "Colonel Parke's will, in which he devised all of his fortune in the Leeward Islands to an illegitimate daughter, on condition that she should take his name and coat-of-arms, naturally gave great offence to his children, and a tedious law-suit was the consequence. His legal descendents are still in possession of much of this property in Virginia, and part of the handsome service of plate presented to him by Queen Anne."

Among the old family papers at Arlington House, have been found many amusing and interesting letters written by Colonel William Byrd, of Westover, who, as we have observed, married a daughter of Colonel Parke, and was for a long time in London after the death of his father-in-law, attending to the settlement of that gentleman's estate. The following letter, in which reference is made of Colonel Parke, was written in Virginia two years before the tragedy occurred in Antigua:

"October, 1709.

I have lately been favored with an unusual pleasure from Antigua, in which I find we are not altogether forgotten. Father Parke says his time was very short and he could not write to you *then,* but is much in charity with us all. I give you joy of the blessing you have had of a daughter, and hope she will be an ornament to the sex and a happiness to her parents. Our son sends you his dutiful respects, and I may venture to say as much for Miss Evelyn, who has grown a great romp and enjoys very robust health. How is Madam

Dunn? for there goes a prophecy about, that in the eastern parts of Virginia a parson's wife will, in the year of our Lord 1710, have four children at a birth, one of which will be an admiral, and another Archbishop of Canterbury; what the other two will prove the sybil cannot positively say, but doubtless they all will be something extraordinary.

My choisest compliments to Mrs. Custis, and if Mrs. Dunn be not too demure a prude, now she is related to the Church, I would send her my salutes in the best form.

Your most affectionate humble servant,

W. Byrd,

To Colonel John Custis."

Col. Daniel Parke married Jane, daughter of Philip Ludwell, of "Richneck" and "Greenspring," James City county, Virginia, and left two daughters: Frances, who married Col. John Custis, of "Arlington," Northampton county, and Lucy, who married Col. William Byrd, of "Westover," Charles City county. On December 18, 1716, Col. Byrd wrote from London to Col. Custis, announcing the death of his wife, Mrs. Lucy Byrd, from smallpox, "the very same cruel distemper that destroyed her sister," adding, "Gracious God what pains did she take to make a voyage hither to seek a grave. No stranger ever met with more respect in a strange country than she had done here, from many persons of distinction, who all pronounced her an honor to Virginia. Also how proud I was of her and how severely I am punished for it."

There are two fine portraits of Col. Parke, by Kneller, preserved in Virginia; one at "Brandon," which was formerly at "Westover," and the other the property of General G. W. C. Lee, which was formerly at "Arlington," Fairfax county, and is now at Washington and Lee University. Each of these portraits shows on the breast the miniature of Queen Anne, which at Col. Parke's request, she presented to him after Blenheim, instead of the usual gratuity of money.

A letter from Micajah Perry, the London merchant, to Col. Byrd, with which was enclosed a copy of this will, expresses great astonishment, sorrow and disgust at the character of the bequests made by Col. Parke. Says Perry: "He drew from thence so much, and then placed (as we are told) 12,000£ to entaile it upon that which leaves a stain behind it, and tie all of his legacies and debts upon the estates in Virginia and England left to his heirs." The writer states that Lucy Chester and Julius Caesar Parke were illegitimate children of Col. Parke. He also gives an account of Parke's debts in England (and Col. Byrd adds that many more were afterwards brought to light) which were: to Messrs. Perry ("in dry money") £2,400, Ann

344

Humphreys, Rebecca Goodart and Mrs. Berry, £500 each; a mortgage on his estate at White Church, with interest, £2,230. According to Perry, the White Church estate could have been sold for £4,000.

So much for the eventful career, the wayward character and the unsavory memory of the handsome and dashing Col. Daniel Parke.

Authorities: Perry's *Colonial Church; Calendar of Virginia State Papers, I;* Sainsbury's *Abstracts;* Campbell's *History of Virginia;* Anderson's *Colonial Church; Memoir of G. W. P. Custis,* by Mrs. R. E. L., prefixed to *Custis' Recollections of Washington; Dictionary of National Biography;* Coxe's *Life of Marlborough;* Murray's *Letters and Dispatches of Marlborough;* Meade's *Old Churches and Families of Virginia.*]

VIRGINIA GLEANINGS IN ENGLAND.

Communicated by Mr. Lothrop Withington, 30 Little Russell Street, W. C. London, (including "Gleanings" by Mr. H. F. Waters, not before printed.).

DAME ELIZABETH FILMER widow, late the wife of Sir Edward Filmer of East Sutton, county Kent. Knight. Will 23 March 1635; proved 16 August 1638. Body to Church of East Sutton aforesaid beside the body of my late husband. To poor of Maidstone in Kent if I am dwelling there at my death 40s. To poor of East Sutton £5. To dame Anne Filmer wife to my son Sir Robert Filmer my jewel with diamonds and pearls. To Elizabeth Filmer their daughter and Sara Filmer my daughter my four ropes of pearls containing 600 in number equally between them. To Edward Filmer eldest son of my said son Sir Robert a Portugues piece of gold and a piece of gold of King Henry VII coinage both which were his great grandfathers. To the two younger sons of my son Robert viz; Robert and Samuel 40s. apiece. To Anne youngest daughter of said Sir Robert 40s. To my daughter Mary Knatchbull widow my boder of gold and pearl and £10. To her daughter Marie the wife of John Vnderwood, gent, my agate and pearl jewel. To her two sons Edward and John Knatchbull 40s. each. To my daughter Katherine Barham £10. To her eldest daughter Elizabeth Barham £300 at 21 years or marriage. If she die before then said £300 to Elizabeth and Anne Filmer daughter of my son Reginald Filmer. To Susan and Ann Barham two younger daughters of my said daughter Katherine 40s. apiece. To my daughter Elizabeth Falconer £10. Moreover to my aforesaid daughter Sarah Filmer £10. To my son in law Robert Barham my

From Vol. XXI, No. 2 (April 1913), p. 153.

346

biggest ring. To his son Thomas £10 at 24, and to each of his other sons Edward, Robert, Charles, Richard and John 40s. To his daughters Susan and Ann Barham 40s. each. To my daughter in law Jane wife to my son Reginald £10. To her daughters Elizabeth and Ann Filmer each 40s. To my said son Sir Robert Filmer my silver warming pans. To my son John £10. To my son Henry £10. To my son Reignold Filmer my lease of three tenements in Knightrider Street, London. To my son in law William Falconer Draper 40s. To my brother John Argoll esq a gold ring. To my sister Dame Jane Fleetwood a piece of Queen Elizabeths' coyne. To my sister Dame Sarah Jenkinson a like piece of gold of Queen Elizabeth's coyne. To Elizabeth Pierson widow 40s. To each of my manservants 10s. To Elizabeth Fryde my apprentice 40s. To my every other maid servants 10s. Residue of my goods to my son Edward Filmer sole executor. Published August 2, 1638. Wa: Retorick, Scrivener. Dame Elizabeth Filmer willeth that her three houses in Knighrider Street (now that her son Reginald Filmer is deceased) shall be disposed as follows; £30 of the first years rent to Jane late the wife of said Reginold and after decease of testatrix to the use of her executor he paying yearly to Elizabeth Faulkner daughter of Dame Elizabeth Filmer and wife of William Faulkner £10. Whereas said Dame Elizabeth had bequeathed to Elizabeth daughter of Robert Barham gentleman a competent porcion her will is that £50 of the said legacy in case said Elizabeth Barham depart this life before attaining 18 years shall be equally divided between the two daughters of said Reginald And lastly said Dame Elizabeth Filmer willeth to Susan Barham £50 apeece (sic). Memorandum the legacy of £50 apiece to Susan and Anne Barham were enterlyned before the signing hereof. Witnesses; R. Batchurst, Frances Batchurst, Edwd Batchurct, Wm. Wiseman, Thomas Walter. Lee, 95.

[The will of Samuel Filmer, the grandson, named in the will, was printed in this Magazine XV, 181. He was the first husband of Mary Horsmanden, who afterwards married William Byrd of "Westover," Virginia. The son, Henry Filmer, named in the will, came to Virginia about 1637. See this Magazine XV, 181, 182.]

VIRGINIA GLEANINGS IN ENGLAND

Communicated by Mr. Lothrop Withington, 30 Little Russell Street, W. C. London, (including "Gleanings" by Mr. H. F. Waters, not before printed.).

GEORGE MARTIN of Dublin Esquire, Doctor of Physicke. Will 29 July 1746; proved 3 February 1755. To my sister Mrs. Letitia Campbell £100 for herself and children. To John son of my nephew John Galt deceased and 3 daughters of deceased £200. To Mrs. Ann Tombe widow £5 and £1. 1s. 0d. each Christmas for life and to her sister Mrs. Sarah Tombe £5. To poor of Caple Street Meeting £5. To my relation and servant Alexander Stewart of Woodtowne county Meath my interest in lands of Kilcoskin and £40 to stock the same. To Andrew Stewart of Milltown £5. To neice Agnes Cunningham widow, household goods in house she holds from me in Mary Lane Dublin which I distrained for arrears of rent and all rent she owes me. To cousin Samuel Martin of London Esq and nephew Samuel Campbell Esq £10 each. Lands in Milltown county Meath, charged with £400 for children of my Brother James Martin as follows, nephew John Martin £100, neice Agnes Cunningham £200, niece Letitia Thomas £100, to be held in trust by Samuel Martin and Samuel Campbell for my Brother Colonel John Martin and his heirs. Executor: Brother John Martin. Witnesses: Tho: Pageitt, Richd Thwaites, Ben: Johnston, N. P.

Prerogative Court of Ireland
will book 1754–5 fo.

[Col. William Byrd describing his return from his "Progress to the Mines" (Governor Spotswood's iron-works at Germanna) tells of a night spent at the home of Col. John Martin, in Caroline County about eight miles from Caroline C. H. and four miles from the Mattapony River at Norman's Ford. During a long talk at night, says Byrd, "We were forced to go as far as the Kingdom of Ireland, to help out our conversation. There, it seems, the Colonel had an elder brother, a physician, who threatens him with an estate sometime or other." That the doctor kept his promise is shown by the will printed above. For a note on Col. John Martin, see this Magazine XIII, 197-199.]

From Vol. XXI, No. 3 (July 1913), p. 249.

RICHARD CHICHESTER [late of Virginia beyond seas, deceased—Probate Act]. Will 16 May, 1743; proved 15 March, 1745-6. To Wife Ellen Chichester my Negro Wench, Barbara and Molatto Girl Hannah, with their Increase, and my Negro Boy Prince, likewise my Chair and Sorrel Horses belonging to it, and my Horse Rover, and her Saddle and Furniture. Also to my wife £500 Sterling out of Estate in England, also use of Plantations where I live known by name of "Fairweathers" with Stocks, use of eight working Negroes during widowhood, and after her marriage or death, said Plantations, &c., to Son Richard Chichester. To Son John Chichester my Plantation in Lancaster County, known by the Name of "Newsoms" and six good Negroes, Stock, &c. To my four Daughters, Elizabeth, Ellen, Mary, and Hannah, each £500 sterling at marriage or age of 21, &c., also to each a Negroe to wait on them. To Son John Chichester Black Stone Horse called "Potomack" and my big Grey Colt "Jugler" (or Ingler), Household goods in England to Sons John and Richard. All Plate, Rings, Clocks, Jewells, &c. in England or Virginia to wife and children. If wife with child, and a son to him at 21 £1,000, and if a daughter £500, &c. To son Richard Chichester £500 sterling out of Estate in England, to Son John Chichester, all Estate, real and personal, in England. To Son Richard Chichester all Land, Negroes, &c. in Virginia not disposed of, &c. To son John Chichester his Estate at 21. Executtrix: Wife Ellen Chichester. Executor: Son John Chichester. Trustees: Joseph Carter, Robert Mitchell, and Joss. Ball, Gentlemen, to manage for sons John and Richard Chichester. Witnesses: Joseph Carter, Ann Carter, Gawen Lawry, Michael Dillon. Proved in Prerogative Court of Canterbury by John Tucker and Richard Tucker, Esqrs., Attorneys for Ellen Chichester, widow, mother of John Chichester, a minor, till of age. Administration 28 May 1763 to Richard Chichester brother and one of the executors of John Chichester, deceased, the son and executor of said Richard Chichester late of Virginia deceased, the wife Ellen Chichester having formerly renounced and said John surviving the testator but himself dying before taken as executor and the grant to Richard Tucker and John Tucker expiring by reason of John attaining 17 years. Administration 9 June, 1803 of Richard Chichester of Virginia, deceased, to William Murdock, as to administration (with will annexed) of the son John Chichester, deceased, as to goods left unadministered by his brother Richard Chichester, also deceased, for use of Sarah Chichester, Widow, relict and executrix of will of said Richard Chichester, now residing in the County of Fairfax in the Commonwealth of Virginia in the United States of America, Ellen Chichester, widow, having formerly deceased, and administration to Richard Tucker and John Tucker, Esqrs. having ceased by John Chichester having attained seventeen years, &c.

Edmunds, 79.

[The Virginia branch of the ancient and wide-spread English family of Chichester has been recently authoritatively traced to its English source. At Raleigh, Arlington, Hall and elsewhere in Devon, and in Ireland, the family was of note. A "History of the Chichester Family" by Sir A. P. B. Chichester, Bart. (London, 1871) is in the library of this Society, presented by Captain Arthur Mason Chichester of Leesburg, Va. An account of the Virginia Chichesters may be found in Hayden's "Virginia Genealogies," pp. 91-95, 106-109. An abstract of the will of Richard Chichester, the emigrant, (proved June 12, 1734, in Lancaster County, Va.) is given on page 93.

Following is an account of the Widworthy branch of the family from which the Virginia line came. It began with John Chichester, third son of John Chichester, of Raleigh.

John Chichester, son of John Chichester of Raleigh and Johanna Brett, inherited from his father the Manor of Widworthy. He married November 6, 1538, Katherine, daughter of Thomas Piard of Taustock, Devon.

John Chichester of Widworthy, eldest son of John Chichester and Katherine Piard, buried at Widworthy, February 19, 1609. Will proved Archdeacon's Court, 1609; married Dorothy, daughter of Hugh Daubeney of Waxford, Somerset. Buried at Widworthy the 18th of October, 1598.

Hugh Chichester of Widworthy, eldest son of John Chichester and Dorothy Daubeney, baptized at Widworthy June 7, 1573; buried February 22, 1641 at Widworthy; married Martha, daughter of Richard Duke, of Otterton, County Devon.

Richard Chichester, oldest son and heir of Hugh Chichester and Martha Duke, baptized at Widworthy, June 13, 1600, died in his father's life time, buried at Widworthy 17th of March, 1638; married Joan, daughter of John Smithes of Kington, County Somerset; married at Kington 22nd of May, 1625; buried at Widworthy 5th of August, 1643.

John Chichester of Widworthy, heir to his grand-father, Hugh, baptized at Widworthy 11th of October, 1626, buried June 11, 1661; will dated June 3, 1661; married Margaret, daughter of John Ware of Hallerton and Silverton, County Devon, and his wife Margaret, daughter of Thomas Dart of Silverton.

John Chichester of Widworthy, eldest son of John Chichester and Margaret Ware, born 1649, buried at Widworthy 25th of October, 1702. Will dated 29th of April, 1693; married Elizabeth, daughter of Edward Court of Lillisdon, buried at Widworthy, December 7, 1711. Had no issue.

Richard Chichester, second son of John Chichester of Widworthy and Margaret Ware, born at Silverton the 5th of March, baptized the 16th of March, 1657; married Anna —; came to Virginia in 1702, bringing with him his son John. He married a second wife in Virginia, Anna Chinn nee Fox; bought lands in Lancaster County. Will dated April 14, 1734.

John Chichester, son of Richard Chichester and Anna —, baptized at Widworthy, May 10, 1681, died in Virginia, 1728. Married Elizabeth Symes of Dorset, England, buried at Powerstock, Dorset, January, 1728.

Richard Chichester, son of John Chichester and Elizabeth Symes, died in England, December 30, 1743, buried at Powerstock, January 3rd. Married July 3, 1734, Ellen Ball, daughter of Col. William Ball and Hannah Beale, and lived at "Fairweathers," Lancaster County, Virginia.]

WILLIAM WILLIAMSON [of St. Mary, Whitechapel, Middlesex-Probate Act Book] of London, Merchant. Will 10 February 1722-3; proved 24 February 1722-3. To be buried with my parents in Foulford Church Yard, County of York, under a plaine Stone with only my name and age engraven, for such interment £100 to be laid out, and if not laid out residue to poore of Foulford. "Item. I order and Direct that all my just Debts be fully paid and Satisfied. Item. I give, devise, and bequeath unto William Welch, Natural Son of Susannah Welch, of Nancemond County in Virginia, widow, all my right, title, and Interest at, in, or to one Stone house, Situate and being in Hampton Town in Elizabeth Citty and County in Virginia, with land, &c., now supposed to be in possession of Edward Kearney, being recorded in said County Court and my Title in hands of said Edward Kearney. Also to said William Welch £100 to be put out at interest by my Executor in Great Britain and profits paid annually to Virginia till he is 21, &c., but if he die said legacy to my Sister Annoball Newhan of Foulfard, Widow, her son Jonas Annobell, her Daugthers Alice and Ellinor, Annaball, &c. To my god son Francis Robinson £10 to be paid to his father John Robinson of London, Gentlemen. To said John Robinson and his present wife Frances £10 apiece. To George Capper of London, Sadlier, and wife Ellen, ditto. To Elizabeth Newnham of London, Spinster, ditto. To my Nephew William Stavele, of Foulforth aforesaid, all my Garden and Tract in Lordship of Gate Foulforth known by name of Dilwod Croft, £100 at 21, &c. And if he dies to his brother, &c. To Sister Rebecca Patrick of City of York, Widow, £100. To my Niece Elizabeth Wade £100.

Richmond, 41.

PETER HOOKER of London, Tallow chandler intending to voyage to Virginia in the good shipp called the Globe of London. Will 6 August 1636; proved 22 November 1639. To the poor of Chilcombe county Southampton 20s. To my Aunt Stroud £5 out of my adventure. To my uncle Egers children 20s. a-piece out of my Adventure. To my Cosen Anne Hooker my uncle Richard's daughter £3 out of Adventure. To her brother Richard 40s. To Henry Hooker my uncle Peter's son 40s. at 21 years. To his brother Nicholas the like sum. To Sibell Hooker my uncle Peter's daughter 20s. To Richard Wood's children Hannah, John and Samuel 20s. apiece. I give to my brother John Hooker all my goods that I left in his hands and £30 to be paid out of my Adventure. If my brother John die before the legacy is due to be paid then to his son John Hooker. If both hap to dye then to my executor or his children. I constitute my beloved brother Edward Hooker my executor to whom I bequeath the residue of my Estate. I intreate my uncle Edward Hooker and my cosen John Wood to be my Overseers to them 10s apiece for to buye a paire of gloves.
Witnesses: Edwd Hooker, Richd Potter, George Stratton.

Harvey, 187.

ROBERT DINWIDDIE, Esq. formerly of Colony of Virginia in North America, but late of the City of Bristoll, Esq., deceased. Will proved 9 October 1770—Probate Act Book.

VIRGINIA GLEANINGS IN ENGLAND.

Communicated by Mr. Lothrop Withington, 30 Little Russell Street, W. C. London, (including "Gleanings" by Mr. H. F. Waters, not before printed.)

JOHN MARTIN of Dublin, Merchant. Will 30 April 1760; proved, Brother George Martin devised his lands in Milltown etc to trustees for my benefit. I have paid the sums to children of Brother James Martin. To daughter Agnes Martin £2000. To son Lewis Martin £500. To grandson George Barclay £200. To Andrew Stewart in full satisfaction out of my benefits under George Martins will £10 yearly out of my estate in Virginia. To Caple Street Meeting £5. Lands of Milltown to eldest son George Martin and at his death to Edmon Sexton Perry and James Ager the younger of Dublin Esqrs in trust for his male heirs failing whom to second son Samuel Martin and heirs male, in default third son Lewis Martin and heirs male, then Eldest daughter Lucy Agar and heirs male. To 2nd daughter Agnes Martin and heirs male and the right heirs Lands in Virginia to 2 youngest sons Samuel and Lewis with succession in default to daughter Lucy Agar and Agnes Martin. Daughter Alicia Martin otherwise Campbell wife of son George Martin entitled under Marriage settlement to rent charges on lands in Virginia of £150 a year Irish currency. Daughter Lucy Agar wife of James Agar Esq £2000 her portion to be paid. Executors: sons George, Samuel and Lewis Witnesses: Jas Shiel, Tho Leech, Thomas Fitzsimmons Codicil 15 October 1760. same witnesses. Lands in Kilcoskanl charged with payment of rents to Ann Stewart widow and Jane Benson widow.

Prerogative Court of Ireland
will Book 1761, fo. 215.

From Vol. XXI, No. 4 (Oct. 1913), p. 372.

[This John Martin, the testator of 1760, was certainly Col. John Martin of Virginia, to whom his brother, Dr. George Martin, of Dublin, bequeathed an estate in 1746, (see this Magazine XXI, 249). It is equally certain that he was the Col. John Martin who lived in Caroline Co. in 1732, when Col. Byrd visited his house, and who was a Burgess for that County. It will be seen from the will of Thomas Turner (This Magazine XX, 439,) that Turner states he bought a tract of land in Caroline from "Col. John Martin and his son George." This was the land sold in 1752 (see this Magazine XIII, 198) by "John and George Martin, of the City of Bristol, merchants," through "John Martin, gent., of Virginia," their attorney. Col. John Martin and his son George evidently removed from Virginia to Bristol, where they became merchants. John Martin of Virginia, their attorney, was no doubt another son of Col. Jno. Martin, and was the Burgess for King William County, who died during the session of 1756. It seems probable, as there is no mention of any children of his in Col. Martins will, that John Martin, Jr., died without issue. Of the daughters, Elizabeth married in 1742, Patrick Barclay, of Louisa Co., Va., Lucy, the eldest daughter, married first Henry Boyle, youngest son of Henry, first Earl of Shannon, and secondly, March 20, 1760, James Agar, of Co. Kilkenny, Ireland, who, in 1776 was created Baron, and in 1781, Viscount Clifden. Lady Clifden died July 26, 1802. The second surviving daughter, Agnes Martin, was unmarried at the date of her father's will. Patty youngest daughter, married in 1756, Edmond Sexton Perry, Speaker of the Irish House of Commons 1771-1785, and in 1785 created Viscount Perry. She had doubtless already been provided for. The will of Lucia, Viscountess Clifden (born Martin) was proved in 1802 in the Prerogative Court of Dublin. That of George Martin, of the City of Dublin, Esq., was proved in 1811. These would probably give additional information in regard to the family.]

LEONARD BAGGE of Killbree, county Waterford, Esquire. Will 1 August 1719; proved 8 December 1719. To my wife Cicilia for life £500 and a bond of Andrew Bagge for £100 now in hands of Matthew Jacob Esqr and Mr. Hercules Beer according to marriage settlement on 4 October 1708, also £250. My stock in Moned and Duftcarrick, Kilbree and New Aftane to my children subject to following legacies. To mother Mrs. Susanna Bagge £20 yearly. To William Connolly als McJames of Ardmore £1. 10s. yearly. I forgive Brother Luke Bagge all he owes me and give him my partnership with Mr. Barry Strongman of tithes in County Cork purchased from Mr. John Pembrock of Dungarvan. I forgive my nephew Joseph Conghlan what he owes me. To eldest daughter Mary Bagge £400 as a marriage portion. To second daughter Ann Bagge ditto. Wife now with child, if daughter ditto. Residue to sons William and John. To my dear Brother ye reverand Mr. John Bagge £500 provided he comes to Ireland and demands it. Executors and Trustees: My Brother Revd Mr.

Jo: Bagge of Virginia, Brother Jeremy Coughlan of Lismore Esq, Brother Luke Bagge of Clattahenny gen and nephew Joseph Coughlan Esq Witnesses: Fran: Flaherty, Edwd Butter, Jn Hely, Wm. Coughlan.

Prerogative Court of Ireland
Will Book 1718-20, fo. 225.

JOHN BAGGE, of Monea, county Waterford, gent. Will 14 April 1772; proved 11 December 1772. To be buried at Kilmolish near my father and mother. To Roger Green of Youghal county Cork merchant and Thomas Judge of Clerkstown, county Waterford gent lands of Grange held from Earl of Grandison and land of Monea held from Bishop of Waterford also my sixth part of Monegarroff in County Tipperary. In trust for my son John Bagge and heirs male. To daughter Anna Bagge £800 above money left by her grandfather William Cooke. To daughter Cecilia Judge wife of Thomas Judge £24 yearly. To John son of Roger Green £5 to his son James £5. House in Cork to son To sister Ann Greahicks £5 yearly. To Mary Cox £5. Witnesses Franc Ellis, John Walker, Edwd Smyth.

Prerogative Court of Ireland
Will Book 1772, fo. 12.

[Rev. John Bagge, brother of Leonard Bagge, was minister of St. Anne's Parish, Essex Co.., Va., 1771–1726, when he died. He had a nephew, Edmond Bagge, who also lived in Virginia, and died in Essex County in 1734, leaving a son Robert. See this Magazine XII, 299, 300. The will which follows is that of a later member of the Irish family. The will of Rev. John Bagge, of Virginia, which had first been recorded in the Colony, was proved in Dublin in 1726.]

JOHN COOKE of Youghall County Cork, Esq. Will 7 February 1712; proved 4 March 1713. To be buried either in my own burial place of Youghall Church or by my father in Church yard of Affame. To my mother Cecilia Cooke my farm of Graige county Waterford or £20 yearly. To wife Ann Cooke houses in Youghall also my estate of Kilbrush and Kippane. To son Thomas Cooke my dwelling house in Youghall and £1000 in hands of Mr. James Tynt als Worth for which estate of Dame Mabell Tynt and Harry Tynt Esq deceased stand liable, failing him and his heirs if my daughter Mabell Cooke als Harrison shall survive her now husband Henry Harrison clerk and marry again then the issue to have reversion. Bequests to son Thomas according to provisions of marriage settlement between me and his mother Margaret Tynt by deed of 5 August 1687. Servant John Moore £5. House that Mr. Welch and Mr. Robinson now live in to wife. Executors: Wife Ann Cooke and son Thomas Cooke. Overseers: John Walker of Youghall gent and Thomas Baker of Lismara gent. Witnesses: Francis Boyse, David Crafford, He. Crotty.

P. C. Ireland. Prerogative
Will Book, 1713-15, fo. 80.

THOMAS COOKE of Youghall, county Cork, gent. Will proved 27 November 1750. To cousin Thomas Cooke of Arnasack in the Liberties of Youghall one third of lands of Ballyhay Ardra in county Cork which belong to me by right of my mother Margret Cooke otherwise Tynte   To sister Mable Harrison otherwise Cooke £20 a year. Residuary Legatee and Executor: cousin Thomas Cooke. Witnesses: Samuel Luther, George Mannix, Thomas Gimlett.

Prerogative Court Ireland
will Book, 1750-51, fo. 196.

JOHN COOK of the parish of Over Wharton and County of Stafford in the Colony of Virginia gent. Will 26 December 1732; proved 11 April 1733. To be buried as his executrix thinks fit. To wife Elizabeth Cooke for life a plantation on Potomack river side of 462 acres and 40 acres adjoining and negroes Corkpegg and Charlott, at her decease to my son Traverse Cooke, in default of issue to my 3 daughters Ann, Hannah and Million Land on Cedar River 400 acres to son Traverse. 1664 acres to 3 daughters Ann, Hannah and Millian. Negro Slave Dublin to son Traverse. Slave Sarah to daughter Ann, slave will to daughter Hannah, Slave Tomboy to daughter Millian. Money in Ireland to wife and children. Land: 1500 acres on north side of the Bever dams to Samuel Timmions of Stafford

County on payment of 1261 lbs of tobacco due to my estate. Executrix: Wife Elizabeth. Overseers: Rev. Alexander Scott, Mr. Rawleigh Traverse. Witnesses: Wm. Allison, Rawleigh Travers, Nath. Smith, Robt Smith, Mary Row. Codicil 27 December 1732. Negro Slave Ann Versper to wife. Witnesses: Simon Pearson, Wm Brent, Benj Brent, Rawleigh Travers. Proved at Stafford County Thomas Claiborne, C. Cur. William Henry Terrett, clerk of Thomas Claiborne certifies copy. Witnesses: Henry Washington, Chandler Fowke, as justices according. witnesses: James Nicholson Jo. Gill junr, Robt. Jackson.

Prerogative Court of Ireland
Will Book 1735, filed will.

[Though neither the will of John Cooke, of Youghall, nor that of his son Thomas Cooke, of the same place, names the Virginia Cookes of Stafford Co., it is evident that they belonged to the same family. John Cooke, a native of Ireland, settled in Stafford County, Va., early in the Eighteenth Century, and married Elizabeth, daughter of Raleigh Travers of Stafford County, and his wife Hannah, daughter of Joseph Ball. She was half sister of Mary Ball, mother of George Washington. Mrs. Travers married secondly Simon Pearson, and in her will, proved December 13, 1748, names her daughter Elizabeth Cooke, and her grandchildren, Travers and Hannah Cooke. John Cooke, of Stafford, died in 1732 and his will was among the portions of the Stafford records destroyed by Federal Soldiers during the Civil War; but a copy of his will was proved in Dublin, from which the abstract given here was made. In this will he refers to his money in Ireland. Besides several daughters, one bearing the peculiar name, Million, which was derived from the Travers family, he had one son, Travers Cooke of Stafford County. The will of the latter, dated December 1759, and proved June 13, 1759, is of record in Stafford. His legatees were his wife Mary, and his sons John and Mott. He states there is "A large balance due me by my uncle Thomas Cooke, of Youghall in the Kingdom of Ireland for the rents and profits of my estate there." He directs that his sons should have as good an education as his estate would afford. The inventory of his personal property amounts to £947.14.4, and includes a set of Spectators at £1.8, Tattlers at 14 shillings, two Guardians at 5 shillings, 4 prayer books at £1.5, and a parcel of "old books" at 7 shillings 6 pence. Evidently the appraisers were fond of the essayists. As Thomas Cooke of Youghall died in 1750, without issue, it is probable that Travers Cooke's uncle Thomas, was the "Cousin Thomas Cooke" who was the residuary legatee of Thomas of Youghall. A proper examination of wills and other records in Ireland would doubtless furnish a satifactory pedigree. There is a notice of the Cookes of Stafford in Hayden's Virginia Genealogies, p. 300.]

VIRGINIA GLEANINGS IN ENGLAND.

Communicated by Mr. Lothrop Withington, 30 Little Russell Street, W. C. London, (including "Gleanings" by Mr. H. F. Waters, not before printed).

MAX(IMILIAN) ROBINSON, late of Rederiffe, Marriner bound out to Sea. Will 28 October 1694; proved 8 October 1695. Imprimis I bequeath my Soule to God etc. (2) To my Neece Anne Robinson the Daughter of James Robinson all Household goods and a Trunke of Goods in hands of Mr. Dealesly. Alsoe my 32 part of Ship Jeffery with proffitts from present Voyage (3) To Margarett Bridger my Goddaughter money left in Alderman Bristows hands which I presume may be about £70 to put out to Interest till her marriage (4) Whereas I have on Eighth of Ship Avarelia and near £200 Adventure in her if please God She safe arrive in England the part of the Shipp to brother Henneage Robinson and whatever else I have in her to be divided to brother James Robinson, Tho: Creeston, Ann Robinson and Elizabeth Haney daughters of my late wife and the Sonn of my brother John Robinson by his first wife (5) To Maximilian Haney sonn of my wife's Daughter Tract of Land lieing in New Kent alias King and Queene County which I bought of Mr. Breeding and one Negro woman named Pendot with what children she hath (6) To Nephewes William Robinson and James Robinson my Tract of Land lying in Rappa. river comonly Called Southings Ferry provided they or hee that live to 19 actually go and live on Land. Also to said nephews all Negroes English Servants Stocke and cattles—rest of Estate etc etc at age of 20 of eldest of eldest Three Nephewes a Division to be made and Eldest to have his part, the other to be in hands of Mr. Henry Awbrey

From Vol. XXII, No. 1 (Jan. 1914), p. 22.

and Mr. John Deane to be delivered at same age at first notices of my death, said Henry Awbrey and John Deane to take Custody of Estate and Improve it and Shipp the Croops yearly to Mr. Robert Bristow junior if living, otherwayes to Mr. Phillipp Richards (7) To Mr. Robert Bristow junior £10 for mourning, to Mr. Henry Awbrey and Mr. John Deane £5 each (8) Executors: Mr. Robert Bristow Junior and my brother Hen: Robinson. Witnesses: William Revil, Richard Sergant Jno Haselwood. (Proved by Robert Bristow junior reserving to Heneage Robinson. Probate Act Book describes testator as late of ship Aurelia dying on high seas.

Irby, 159.

[Maximilian Robinson, the testator had probably at one time lived in Virginia. An entry in the Richmond Co, Va. order book under date, October 7th 1696, states that the Henendge [Henneage] Robinson, one of the executors named in the will of Mr. Maximilian Robinson, deceased, by his attorney Mr. Arthur Spicer, presented an authentic copy of the will of said Maximilian Robinson, proved in the Ecclesiastical Court of the Diocese of London. Richmond Court "allowed" the will and appointed said Henneage Robinson administrator.

The *Richmond Critic*, of Aug 23, 1890 contains an account of this family evidently derived from authentic private records, as in almost every instance it is corroborated by the county records.

WILLIAM ROBINSON, the nephew, came to Virginia, (according to this account) "from Yorkshire" about 1695, and settled on an estate, later known as "Bunker Hill" in Richmond Co. The section in which this property is situated was first in Richmond Co, later when King George was formed, was in that county and still later was added to Westmoreland. He was high sheriff of Richmond County 1708, County Lieutenant 1718, and was a Burgess for that county at the sessions of March 1702-3, April 1704, April 1706, October 1710, November 1711, Oct. 1713, Nov 1714, and for Stafford Nov 1720, May 1722, May 1723, May 1726, & May 1730, and probably in intervening years

In 1701 Wm Robinson of Rappahannock Co gave bond for his wife Frances as administratrix of Captain Samuel Bloomfield. There is in Richmond Co. a deed, dated April 3, 1704, from Wm Robinson, of Richmond Co, gent., and his wife Frances, only daughter and heir of Samuel Bloomfield, of Rappahannock Co, gent, deceased. By deed, in King George Co, July 5, 1727, William Robinson of Sittenbourn parish, gent, gave to his son Maximilian Robinson, 600 acres of land, 15 negroes, the following plate, viz: 12 silver spoons, 1 gallon tankard, 2 porringers, 2 salts, 1 salver, 2 cans, 1 teapot and lamp, 1 milk pot, 2 castors, 6 tea spoons, a pair of tea tongs and a silver strainer, together with a considerable amount of handsome furniture, stock of cattle &c. William Robinson died Sept 20, 1742, and on Dec 3, of that year his will was proved in King George Co, by his executor Maximilian Robinson, gent. (The will-book for that period was carried off during the Civil War, and a few years ago was known to be in existance in the State of New York. It is hoped that it may yet be returned to the county)

William and Frances Robinson had issue: 2. *Maximilian*[2] (of whom later)

2. MAXAMILIAN[2] ROBINSON, lived at various times in King George and Westmoreland. He was a justice of King George 1722–1751 and perhaps later. There is on record in King George a deed, dated Sept 8, 1760, from Maxamilian Robinson, of Washington parish, Westmoreland, conveying land in King George, which had been purchased by his grandfather Samuel Bloomfield. He married twice. The name of his first wife is unknown, the second was a daughter of Wm Fauntleroy, who in his will, dated 1757, names his grandson Henry Robinson. The will of Maxamilian Robinson, of King George, was dated Jan 4, 1775, and proved in that County Feb 1777. Legatees: his son Henry his lands in King George, and if he d. s. p. to the testator's son William, and if he d. s. p., to the heir of testator's deceased daughter, Alice Ford, provided said heir took the name Maxamilian Robinson; wife. Appoints friends and neighbors Thos Jett, and "Mr Moore Fauntleroy the elder, my wife's brother, executors."

Issue of Maxamilian Robinson (by 1st marriage): 3. *William*[3] (of whom later), 4. Alice, married _____ Ford; (by 2d marriage) 5. Henry[3], d. s. p.

3. WILLAM[3] ROBINSON, of King George, was a vestryman of Hanover parish, a signer of the Northern Neck Declaration of 1766, and of the County Committee of Safety 1774–75. His wife was Ann, probably daughter of Richard Watts, of Westmoreland. A deed, 1770 (?) recites that Richard Watts, late of Westmoreland, possessed a tract of land in King George which, at his death, descended to Mary ("now dead") wife of John Ashton, and to Ann, wife of Wm Robinson, gent, of King George. The will of Wm Robinson Feb 17, [date of year missing from copy], bequeathed £750 to his daughter Alice and the rest of his estate to his son William.

William[3] Robinson had issue: 6. *William*[4] (of whom later), 7. Alice.

6. WILLIAM[4] ROBINSON, of King George, and Westmoreland, married Margaret (born Oct. 16, 1755, died Nov 18, 1837) daughter of Dr Walter Williamson, of King George, a native of Scotland, and his wife Mildred, daughter of John Washington, of King George, (Mrs. Robinson married secondly John Rose, and had Mildred and William Rose). Wm Robinson died in 1782 or 1783. His will, ("Wm. Robinson of Westmoreland") was dated Oct. 3, 1782, and proved in Westmoreland Feb 25, 1783. He gave his wife Margaret one third of his estate, to each of his daughters 20 negroes, and the rest of his estate to his son. The state assessment book shows that in 1782, Wm Robinson owned in Westmoreland 93 slaves.

William[4] and Margaret Robinson had issue: 8. Ann Washington, born 1778, married Dr Rose, of Alexandria, and had a son William, who died unmarried; 9. Margaret, born Nov. 30, 1780, died May 31, 1808, married (1st) Daniel McCarty, of "Pope's Creek," Westmoreland, who died Jan 31, 1801, and (2d) at "Montrose" July 28, 1802, Richard Stuart; 10. *William*[4] (of whom later)

10. WILLIAM[4] ROBINSON, of "Bunker Hill," was born June 1, 1782. He married (1st) Ann Aylett, daughter of Corbin Washington, of "Haywood," Westmoreland (and had three children who died in infancy); (2d) Ann Calvert, daughter of Dr David Stuart, of Fairfax Co (and had Edwin Wilberforce, and Claudius, who died young), (3d) Frances Hunt Peyton daughter of Samuel T. Turner, of Georgetown D. C. William[5] Robinson had issue by 3d marriage: 11. Henry[6]; 12. Gwynn[6]. 13. Margaret[6]; 14. Edwin Wilberforce[6]; 15. Samuel Augustine[6]; 16. William[6]; 17. Frances Vicessimus; 18. Walter William Hambleton.)

360

THOMAS WOTTON of London, Barber Cjirurgeon. Will 15 March 1635; proved 28 April 1638. Being now bound forth in Sir William Curteene's voyage in the good ship called the Planter of London. —— Hill, master. I have constituted John Cartwright, citizen and Salter of London my Attorney. If it shall please God to call me out of this life in or during my intended voyage I doe then give all my goods, wages, Adventures, substance and estate whatsoevver to my said loving friend John Cartwright this to stand for my last will and testament whereof I make said John Cartwright sole executor. Witnesses: Thos Symonds, John James, Humphrey Tomkyns, Ralph Fryth, scr.

Lee, 38.

[Possibly the testator was "Master Thomas Wotton," who came with the first settlers to Virginia in 1607 as surgeon general, and who was one of the expedition in May-June of that year, which ascended James River to the site of Richmond. Sir William Courteen's voyage was to the East Indies]

ANNE BARHAM of the city of Canterbury, widow, deceased. Nuncupative will 21 June 1640; proved 13 July 1640. "There is in the hands of Mr. William Somner of Canterbury £20 which was given by Mris Shrubsole her late mother and by herselfe to her son Graves his child and intrusted with said Somner he paying eight pounds % interest" There is remaining in the hands of Mr. Wraigh of Feversham county Kent, £30 one silver salt and one silver cup. In the hands of Mr. Charles Shrubsole £17. 10s. 0d. In the hands of Thomas Lyne £9. 10s. 0d. Out of which £30 aforesaid she willed to William Graves £10 to be paid to him at 21 years Until that time, said sum to Robert Graves father of said William he paying no interest but putting in security. To Mrs Lyne £5. To Mrs. Graves £5. £10 of said £30 to be expended for her funeral. Out of the moneys in hands of aforesaid Mr. Shrubsole and Thomas Lyne she gave to Anthony Barham now in Virginia £5. To Sibill and Anne Lyne £5 each. To Mrs. Bowling 20s. To Goodwife Aleberry 10s. To Goodman Gray 10s. To Goodman Warren 10s. To Mary Fusser 10s. Mr. Thomas

Lyne executor. Spoken in the presence of John Berry and Robert Graves, John Berry and Robert Graves.

Coventry, 102.

[Anthony Barham, referred to in the will, was a member of the House of Burgesses for Mulberry Island, March 1629-30. The will of Anthony Barham of Mulberry Island, in Virginia, gentleman, was proved Sept 13, 1641 in England. See Water's *Gleanings,* and this Magazine III, 228. He gives a legacy to his "loving friend Mr Edward Aldey, minister of St Andrews in Canterbury"]

NICHOLAS DOWNE, Cittie of London Esqre. Will 17 April 1653; proved 21 May 1653. To be buried in church of St. Margaretts Westminster. Executrix: Wife Ann Downe and to whom all estate in England, Virginia or elsewhere. Vnto my Neece Jane Downe if shee be living in Virginia 1000 waight of Tobacco which I desire my said wife to give order to Livet Coll. Bredge Freeman (in whose hands I left a farr greater quantitie) to deliver her in Virginia on notice from Executrix under hand and seal with Coppie of this my last will and Testament and in case she be dead then to revert to my wife. Witnesses: Joshua Mullard, Jo: Johnson.

Brent, 332.

[Nicholas Downes was a shareholder in the Virginia Company 1621-23. Possibly the niece Jane Downes of Virginia, was daughter of George Downe or Downes, who was living in Elizabeth City Co, as late as 1638 and who was a member of the House of Burgesses for that county Feb 1631-2, and Sept 1632.]

NICHOLAS HARRISON late of Virginia, Planter, but dying in the parish of St. Sepulchres, London. Nuncupative will undated; proved 28 September 1653. Hee did give and bequeath vnto his Mother Dorothy Harrison all his estate if hee should dye a Bachelor or vnmarried. Witnesses: Jane Parsons, Echlizabeth Lewis, widdow. Administration to mother Dorothy Harrison, no executrix being named.

Brent. 230.

[Nicholas Harrison lived in York County.]

RICHARD COLE, Salisbury Parke, County of Hertford Esquire. Will 15 September 1653; proved 28 September 1653.

To sonne William my Manor of Shruely (sic i.e. error for Shenley) hall als Salisbury parke, and heirs male and female, in default to sonn Richard, then Sonn Francis etc. To wife Dorothy Cole all lands vndisposed of by this will to dispose to other children etc. Also for wiefe annuitie lately purchased in Buckinghamsheire. Executor to distribute one years profits of lands in Gloucester, then to children of kinsman Thomas Cotton and said lands to Sonn William. Also to William all plowe harness Cartes harness houses Cowes higgs sheepe except those comonly reputed to be my wife's. To Sonn William halfe of plate in house. Other half to wife. To wife all money in house   To poore of Shenley £50 as Mr. Robert Pemberton, Alice Ewer, and George Sibley of ditto think fitt. Executrix: my Brother in law Mr. John Scargill of West Holland county of Darby and my wife. Witnesses: Robert Pemberton, John Beamond, John Holms.

Brent, 378.

A Richard Cole who lived on the Potomac River in Westmoreland Co Va, as early as 1659, and named his plantation "Salisbury Park," was very probably the son Richard named in the will. The Virginia Richard seems to have been a gentleman of vivid language and imagination, both probably frequently stimulated by drink. In 1665 he was brought before Westmoreland Court on the charge that in the presence of several gentlemen he said that, "Sir William Berkeley durst not show his face in England," that if the said Cole were in England he had better credit than "His Honour," that he was better born and better bred, that "he expected his brother to come in Governor, who should kick his Honour from his place, And he should be a Councelor at least, and then would Act knavery by Authority;" that "he had formerly a better man (than Berkeley) for his pimpe, for a Knight of Malta was his pimpe" &c. His neighbors "Hardwick and Hutt were rogues," and Washington "an ass-negroe-driver," whom he would have up before the Governor and Council, "as a Companie of Caterpillar fellows," who "live upon my bills of export." When Richard Cole died in 1674 he directed that his body be buried upon his plantation in a neat coffin of black walnut, and over it a gravestone of black marble to be sent for out of England "with my Coate Armour engraven in brasse & under it this Epitaph:
   Heere lies Dick Cole a grievious Sinner
   That died a Little before Dinner
   Yet hopes in Heaven to find a place
   To Satiate his soul with Grace."

The records show that he had a great quantity of merchandize and many servants. The provisions of his will in regard to his funeral were rescinded by a codicil.
He bequeathed his estate to Nicholas Spencer Jr, son of Nicholas Spencer, Secretary of State of the Colony. Anna, widow of Richard Cole, married (2d) Roger Malloch, and (3d) Thomas Kerton.

Richard Cole's idea that he was better born than a Berkeley is but little borne out by the pedigree of Cole of Salisbury Park in the Visitation of Hertfordshire. It was quite an inconspicuous family of gentry beginning in Tudor times]

THOMAS CHESLEY, Welford, County Gloucester, Shoomaker. Will 3 June 1653; proved 23 September 1653. To be buried in Welford Churchyard. To eldest sonne Phillip Chesley 12d. To youngest sonn Edward Chesley 12d. To Thomas Chesley youngest sonn of my sonn Edward 12d. Rest to wife Bridget Chesley, executrix. Overseer: Thomas Roberts, Witnesses: Thomas Robertes, William Porter.

Brent, 263.

[Philip Chesley of York Co Va mentions in his will his "relations at Welford in Gloucestershire," came to Virginia in or before 1650, acquired a comfortable estate. His will, proved 1675, was printed in this series of Gleanings (Vol XIII, 63, 64). He was very probably the son of the poor shoemaker, whose will is printed above. A reference to Philip Chesley's will will show how kindly he treated his relations at home. In comparison with the property of Thomas Chesley he must have seemed to them a very rich man. It is a concrete example of the opportunities which the Colonies gave to poor; but energetic men]

VIRGINIA GLEANINGS IN ENGLAND.

Communicated by Mr. Lothrop Withington, 30 Little Russell Street, W. C. London, (including "Gleanings" by the late H. F. Waters, not before printed.)

EDWARD BARKHAM of London, knight and Alderman. Will 14 January 1632; proved 17 January 1633. My body within the chapel in the church of southacre county Norfolk within the vaults on the North side of the chancel which I lately made. To Anne Barkham my wife all her apparel, jewels, chains and ornaments of gold, and all household stuff at my house at Tottenham High Cross, county Middlesex. To Sir Edward Barkham Knight and Bart my eldest son gilt bowl standing cups, tankards etc and best tapestry hangings. The said Jane (sic) my wife shall have the use of said plate and hangings during her life. To each of my grandchildren £20 at 21 years. To said wife Jane (sic) all my copyhold lands in Tottenham and.... all my tenements, lands etc. in Wainflete St. Maries Wainflete All Saints and Friskney in county Lincoln for her life., afterwards to my son Robert Barkham and heirs males. For want of issue then to my said son Sir Edward and for want of issue then to my right heirs. To my nephew Mr. Joshua Gallard silver bowl to be engraven with my arms. To my nephew Mr. Edward Barkham of East Walton a piece of plate with m arms. To the Mayor and Citizens of London yearly £6. 13s. 4d. issjing out of my tenement in Cheapside called the Flower de Luce near the Cross there for the benefit of the poor children in Christs Hospital after the decease of Elizabeth Mallory widow. To the Master Wardens Brethren and Sisters of the Misterie of Drapers of which Company I am free an annuity of £6. 13s. 4d. out of the Messuage aforesaid called the Flower de Luce for the poor and free of said Company and to said Company two silver Voyders much or better than Sir John Garrard gave to the Cittie. To the Leatherseller's Company a bason

---

Ewar of silver. To parson of new church in Dukes place called St. James 40s. yearly out of said Flower de Luce on condition that the parson preach a sermon on Maundey Thursday yearly. To the poor of that parish who shall have been at said sermon 2s. apeace out of the said Flower de Luce. To the poor of parish of St. Lawrence Jewry yearly 52s. out of said Flower de Luce. To poor of said parish of Tottenham High Cross 52s. yearly to be bestowed in bread weekly after divine service in the forenoon out of the said Flower de Luce. To poor of Tottenham aforesaid £3. 6s. 8d. To poor of St. Mary Bothawe (sic) in London where I now dwell £3. 6s. 8d. To poor of Stl Lawrence Jewry £5. To the four towns in Norfolk viz° East Walton, Southacre, Westacre and Aileswithorp £5 apeece to be distributed amond the poorest inhabitants. To the poor of Watton Market, county Norfolk £5. To my son in law Sir John Garrard for mourning £30. To my son in law Sir Charles Caesar and my daughter his wife £30 for mourning. To my son in law Sir Anthony Irby and my daughter his wife for mourning £30. To my son in law Robert Walpoole Esq for him and his children for mourning £30. To my son Robert Barkham and children for mourning £25. To my nephew Mr. John Gallard and his wife for mourning £15. To my man William Davy for a ring £5. To all my men servants 40s. apece. To those at Tottenham 20s. apeece. My well beloved wife Jane Barkham and the said Sir Edward Barkham Knight and Baronet my son and heir apparent executors. Witnesses° William Davy, Francis Windham, Nathaniel Fordham, *seager* 1.

[Edward Barkham, draper, of London, a member of the Virginia Company. He was son of Edward Barkham by his second wife Elizabeth Rolfe, of Norfolk; was a member of the East India Company; alderman of London, successively of Faringdon and Cheap wards, sheriff 1611; lord Mayor 1621-22; knighted June 16, 1622; readmitted into the Virginia Company July 3, 1622; died Jan. 5, 1633-4. His son Edward was created a baronet 1623 and was M. P. for Boston 1625 and 1626. Margaret, daughter of Sir Edward, the younger, married Sir Edmond Jenings of Ripon and was the mother of Edmond Jenings (acting governor of Virginia 1710), an ancestor of General R. E. Lee and others of prominenc. Sir Edward Barkham's (the testator's) daughtor Jane, married Sir Charles Caesar, Master of the Rolls, a nephew of Capt John Martin of Virginia. Another, Margeret, married Sir Anthony Irby, also a member of the Virginia Company, and a third, Susan (who died in 1622) married Robert Walpole, Esq. of Houghton, and was ancestress of Sir Robt Walpole.]

VIRGINIA GLEANINGS IN ENGLAND.

Communicated by Mr. Lothrop Withington, 30 Little Russell Street, W. C. London, (including "Gleanings" by the late Mr. H. F. Waters, not before printed.)

WILLIAM TUCKER, of the Cittie of London (endorsed St. Dunstans in the East) Esq. now bound for the Kingdom of Ireland. Will 12 October 1642; proved 17 February 164¾. To wife Frances Tucker £1000 p. Remainder of estate in three parts to three children viz: my sonne William Tucker, sonne Thomas Tucker, and daughter Mary Tucker (together with a Cabbinet of Mother of Pearle embossed with siluer gilt knobbes and one Standing Cupp with Cover of ditto with a siluer guilt handle and Couer to her owne use), but if daughter decease before 21 or marriage then her third the Cabbinett etc to sonnes William and Thomas. If sons or daughter die before 21 then to others etc etc. If all die to children of Brother Thomas Tucker then living. If wife die before my returne from Ireland then whole estate to my three children if alive etc etc. Overseers: Brother Edmund Smythe Esq., Brother Maurice Thomson, Merchant, Brother Elias Robertes, Merchant, and Cozen Mr. Thomas Dawney, Cittizen and Mercer of London. "For my Lande in Virginia I bequeathe unto my sonne William Tucker to enjoy to him and his his(sic) heires for euer, wch is for my Adventure of Fiftie Poundes as p billes of Adventure may appeare. I haue transported divers servantes thither wch for every servant I am to haue Fiftie Acres of land, for my first Dividend, wch will amount vnto 3000 acres for the first dividend, 3000 for the second dividend & 3000 acres for the third, wch land may prou^o beneficiall in time to my heire the record bookes in Virginia will produce the number of men I have transported thither." Witnesses: John Bodington, Letitia

From Vol. XXII, No. 3 (July 1914), p. 267.

Atkinson (Seal a griffin sejent)   (Proved by oath of relict, no mention of executor or executrix)

Peculiar of the Arches

File 1643.

[Captain William Tucker was born in 1589 (Hotten) and came to Virginia in 1610.   He was a member of the House of Burgesses 1623-4, appointed to the Council March 4, 1626, and was first justice in Elizabeth City in 1632.   He was one of the greatest Merchants of his time in Virginia.   In the census of 1625 his wife is given as Mary (born 1599) who came to Virginia in 1623 and they then had one child, Elizabeth, born in Virginia.   Maurice, George, Paul and Wm. Thompson were brothers of his wife Mary.   He had evidently married a second time, Frances.   For notes of Wm. Tucker and the Thompsons see this Maganize I, 188-190, 193.]

VIRGINIA GLEANINGS IN ENGLAND.

Communicated by Mr. Lothrop Withington, 30 Little Russell Street, W. C. London (including "Gleanings" by the late Mr. H. F. Waters, not before printed.)

WILLIAM BRETT of Hearne, Toddington, county Bedford, Esq. Will 4 June 1624; proved 20 September 1624. To Mary my wife all household stuff and plate. To my son Robert Brett my lease from my son William Brett of lands in Toddington aforesaid for 98 years a yearly rent of £80 to be paid to said son William, after my decease. Whereas I made a feofment to my brother Richard Brett of Quayton county Bucks, doctor of divinitie, John Thorpe of London Esq, and George Johnson of Brogboroughe Park, county Bedford gents and their heirs of premises therein mentioned which shall be sold and the money received employed according to my last will. I therefore bequeath to said Mary my wife £1000 in lieu of her joynture. Residue which shall be made of as such sale disposed of as follows—£100 to my son Richard Brett he to enjoy his mother's lands after her decease. The rest to my two daughters Mary and Elizabeth. And my sons Randall, Edward, John, Frances and Benjamin Brett equally. If either of my daughters marry contrary to their mothers liking then she or they shall have but £100. To my said three feoffees 40s. apeece for rings. To poor of Toddington 40s. My said wife Mary sole executrix. Witnesses: Robt Woodford, scr, Wyatt Fowler, Byrde, 82.

[This was an ancestor of the Virginia Ishams and Randolphs. William Isham, son of Sir Euseby Isham, of Pytchley, married, Aug. 13, 1625, Mary daughter of William Brett, of Toddington, Bedfordshire, and had a son Henry Isham, who emigrated to Virginia. Sir Edward Brett, one of the sons of Wm. Brett, the testator, in his will dated Dec. 22, 1682, and proved March 17, 1683 (printed in Waters' *Gleanings*) made bequests to his Isham relations in Virginia. See this Magazine IV, 123, 124; XVIII 85-87. The Visitation of London 1568

From Vol. XXII, No. 4 (Oct. 1914), p. 396.

(Harlean Society) gives the following pedigree: Alexander Brett, of Whitstanton in Devon, married a daughter of Rosemaderos, and had issue: 1 John, 2 Robert, of Lincolnshire, Gent., married Elizabeth, daughter of Edward Bush, of Sisson, 3d brother of the Bushes of Hoburn; 3, Symon. Robert and Elizabeth (Bush) Brett had issue: 1, Robert, Citizen and Merchant-Tailor, of London, married Elizabeth, daughter of Reginald Highgate;.2, Margaret, married ———— Veale, of Lincoln, shire. Robert and Elizabeth (Highgate) Brett had issue: 1, John-oldest son; 2, William, (the testator); 3, Robert; 4, Richard; 5, Elizabeth 6, Catherine.

Several of this family of Bretts appear in Foster's *Alumni Oxoinienses*. Alexander Brett, of Whitstanton, Somerset, matriculated at Exeter College Dec. 3, 1575, aged 17, was a student of the Inner Temple, 1575, and was knighted June 20, 1603.

Alexander Brett, of Somerset, Eng., matriculated at Hart Hall July 1, 1603 aged 15, and was perhaps the person of the name knighted Dec. 2, 1624. Arthur Brett, of Whitstanton was a student of the Inner Temple 1579, & was probably the Arthur Brett, of Devon, gent, who matriculated at Exeter College Dec. 20, 1577, aged 16. George Brett, of Whitstanton, gent, matriculated at Exeter College Dec. 3, 1575 aged 16, and was a student of the Inner Temple 1575. John Brett, of Somerset, Esq., matriculated at Magdalen College June 4, 1601, aged 12, student at Lincolns Inn 1604. Richard Brett, the brother mentioned in the will, matriculated at Hart Hall Feb. 8, 1582-3, aged 15, fellow of Lincoln College, B. A. 12 Oct. 1586; M. A. 9 July 1589, B. D. 6 June 1597, D. D. 13, June 1605, rector of Quanton, Bucks. 1595, one of the translaters of the Bible 1604, died 15 April 1637. Robert Brett, of Somerset Esq., matriculated at Hart Hall April 15, 1586. aged 20. Several of these persons no doubt descended from John, eldest son of the Alexander Brett of the pedigree given above.]

In the Church at Quainton, Buckinghamshire, is the tomb of Richard Brett D. Th. (the brother named in the will) rector of the parish and one of the translators of the Authorized Version of the Bible, erected by his wife Alicia in 1637. It has kneeling figures of man and woman, sons and daughters, of alabaster and black marble colored, in recess, with frieze, pediment and pilasters; inscription on frieze in Hebrew, Greek and Latin; tablet below recess with long inscription in Latin; shield with Brett Arms.

RICHARD BARHAM of Battell. Will June 10 1620; proved 28 November 1621. To poor of Battell 10s. To my sisters Hellen Bishopp, Mary Lake and Dorothie Seer 20s. each. Residue to Mary my wife with my house in Battell and all belonging to her and heirs for ever. She to pay to my sister Hellen Bishopp £10. To Mary Lake £10. To Dorothy Seer £10. To Micoll (sic) Barham 40s. To Arthur, Thomas and Jasper Barham my brothers 10s. each. To Ann Eagles and Elizab. Barham my sisters 10s. each, James Bachellor of Hastings and Abraham Bodle of Hailesham Overseers. Witnesses: Marmaduke Burton, Edward Otwaye, Bridgitt Otwaye, Dale,87.

[See will of Anthony Barham of Va. in **Waters Gleanings,** and that of Ann Barham in this Magazine XXI, 25.]

JOHN FARRAR the elder of London, Esquier. Will 24 April 1628; proved 28 May 1628. To poor of Mary Aldermanbury £6. 13s. 4d. To Henry Farrar my eldest son my messuages lands etc called Great Ewood, Little Ewood, Upper Whiteleigh and Stony Rode in parish of Hallifax county York, to him and heirs for ever. To Martha his wife £10. To my son John Farrar whom I have settled already 20 nobles. To his wife Susan £10. To my son William Farrar all my messuages la nds etc in Hodesdon Bloxbourne and Amwell in Hertford here tofore conveyed to Henry and John Ferrar my sons to my use, to my sonWilliam and heirsTo him also and his wife and children £20 annuity and the longest liver of them. To my son Humfry Farrar and heirs my leases and lands called Sandwith Hall, Neilsinge and all other parcel of the Manor of Stansted under Borgh, county York. To said Humphry also my lease in the parish in St. Mary in Aldermanbury London. To six children of my son Henry Farrar £4 to each. To Cicely Farrar daughter of my son John £40. To seven children of my son John £4 each. Overseers: my son John Farrar and my nephew Henry Wilkinson of Woodesdon, county Bucks B. D. To each of them £10 and charges. Residue to my son Henry Farrar sole executor. Witnesses: Marke Bradley, Senr, John Bulkeley, Saml Wilkinson, Edwd Wilkinson. John Farrar of London esquier make this addition. £200 was delivered to my son John Farrar of Fena, county York to stock lands at Sandwith Hall, the said £200 to be divided between my two sons John and Humphrey. My son William shall receive of my executor £50 at his return into England. My books and apparel equally between my sons Henry, John and Humphrey. Other goods between my sons Henry, John, William and Humphrey. William's part shall be reserved for him or the value, in case he be not living to be reserved for his wife and children. Twelve pence· a week for ever in bread upon the poor in Croxton in Lincolnshire out of my estate. Witnesses: Henry Cooke, Hen. Wilkinson, Barrington, 50.

[As it is evident that William Farrar, of Virginia, was not a son of Nicholas Farrar Sr, it looks as if his father has been placed by this will. Wm Farrar, came to Virginia in Aug. 1618, and at the census of 1624–5 was aged 31, making his birth about 1594. An examination of the wills of the other sons of Jno Farrar might settle the question.]

SIR THOMAS FARNEFOLD of Gatewicks, county Sussex, knight. Will 1 June 1639; proved 17 December 1644. I desire to be buried at Stayning in Sussex as neere my wife as conveniently may be in the same buriall place that doth belonge to my family in that churche. I give all my goods plate and household stuffe whatsoever in my house at Westminster and likewise in my house called Gatewickes in Sussex, and all other my chattles whatsoever, to my eldest sonne Heny Farnefold and my daughter Dorothie Farnefold, to be equally divided betwixt them. And my said daughter shall have in her custody all my personal estate till my said sonne accomplish his age of 21. I give to my said daughter £200 out of the sale of Wixkham lands; and the judgment, which I have for £1000 against the lands of Sir Edward Bellingham, I give to be equally divided among my daughter Dorothie and all my younger children. If my said daughter die before she be 21 or married all my personall estate shall be divided between my said sonne Henry and my sonne Thomas at their ages of 21. Item, I give to my sonnes Thomas, Richard, John, Raphe and Edward, £200 apeece at their severall ages of 21. To my sonne Thomas a house and land called Jarvis House now in the occupation of Laurence Davenport which my said sonne shall enter at his age of 21. My will is tha Wickham farme in Stayning now in the occupation of John Smithe the elder, for which he payeth me £50 per annum, shall be sould for the payment of my sonnes portions abovesaid, but if my sonne Henry shall pay his brother's portions, as before provided, he shall have the said farme. My executors shall receive the profits thereof during the minority of the said Henry towards the breeding and education of my sons. I make my daughter Dorothe and my very good friend Mr. Robert Marr of Westminster my executors till my son Henry be 22, when he shall be my sole executor. I give to the said Robert Marr £10 and my cast of hawkes, which are a mewing neare Colebrooke, also the best horse I shall have at the tyme of my death. I give to my wife all the household stuff I had by her, desiring her to be good to my children and not to take the thirds of my lands, as Mr. Hanchet and Mr. Siptharpe can justifie that shee promised before I married her, that shee would never claim any dower out of my landes, if so be that shee did outlive me. My desire, is, if it may be conveniently done, to be buried by my first wife at Stayning, and that Mr. Robert Marr may have the wardship of my eldest son and breeding of my younger children, and I hope his Majestie will be favourable to me for my sonnes wardeship, by reason I have lost my life in his Majesties warrs. Mr. Willis hath a note of mine for £50 for a ring. Mr. Pickhayes sawe me deliver the ring to him again, nothing due to him. Mr. Edward Watkins and Mr. Daniel Colwell have my statute for 5500. They were my bayle at Sir John Mitchells sute, I have not that statute and there is nothing due to them. I owe to Mr. Almery and Mr. Nocton my lease of mortgage, £530; to Mr. Churchman by bond £50; this is my brother's debt and I have his counterbond. To Mr. Anthony Myldmay £25, to my brewer £8, to my counsin Edward Culpepper £40. Proved 17 December 1644 by Dorothy Farnefold with power reserved for a like grant to the other executor named. 20 November 1655 administration with will annexed was granted to John Farnefold son of the deceased the executorship of the said Dorothy Farnefold having expired by reason that the said Henry had accomplished his age of 22, yet died before he took upon himself the execution of the said will. 13 February 1660-1 commission issued to Dorothy Mayer otherwise Farnefold daughter of the testator, to administer the goods left unadministered by the said John Farnefold then likewise deceased, Rivers, 11.

[Sir Thomas Farnefóld, the testator, was knighted Dec. 22, 1621, and was M. P. for Steyning 1624-26, April-May 1640, and 1640 until his death. His son Thomas matriculated at Christ Church, Oxford Dec. 20, 1641, aged 15. John Farnefold, another son, matriculated at New College Oct. 2, 1652, B. A. April 19, 1656. He (John) came to Virginia before Aug. 2, 1672, when he was minister of Fairfield parish, Northumberland Co., and was minister of St. Stephens in that county from 1680 until his death in 1702. In his will (printed in the *William & Mary Quarterly* XVII, 245) he gives the inscription to be placed on his tomb, and says he was the "son of Sir Thomas Farnefold of Gatwicks in Steyning in the County of Sussex Knight." Sir Thomas evidently did not die in "the Kings Wars," by which he probably meant the campaign against the Scots in 1639.]

VIRGINIA GLEANINGS IN ENGLAND.

Communicated by Mr. Lothrop Withington, 30 Little Russell Street, W. C. London (including "Gleanings" by the late Mr. H. F. Waters, not before printed).

DUDLEY DIGGS (late of the city of Oxford—P. A). The thousand poundes which was parte of my father's legacie, I bequeath after this manner following: To my brother Hammon and my sister I give £100 apiece. The remainder I give equally among the rest of my brothers and sisters. Concerning my personall estate now in my owne possession I bequeath it after this manner following: All my bookes I give unto the college of All Soules, except 20, which I bequeathe unto Master Warden, of which he please to make choise. The money in my possession and the averages of my annuitie in my brother's handes, being seaven quarters, amounting to £100 and more, I desire Master Warden to bestowe according to his discretion to some good and pious uses. To Doctor Edward Graves my physitian I give 50s. To Master Thomas Gorges, Mr. Thomas Darell, master Henry Barker, Master John Wainewright, Mr Thomas Smithe, Master John Watkins, Master Thomas Croft, Doctor Nicholas Graves, Master John Lloyd, Master Tymothie Baldwin, Master Francis Newman and Master William Bowman 20s. apiece. To my servant Richard Payne £5 and all my clothes which are useful for him. I desire that Thomas Flowre a tailor in London, to whom I owe about £20 may be paid out of the £1000 above mentioned I owe to Humphrey Boddicot about £9 or £10 for stable rent and other things. To the apothecaries (sic) These wordes the daie before he died September the thirthieth 1643 he spake in the presence of us, Thomas Gorges, Edward Graves.

From Vol. XXIII, No. 1 (Jan. 1915), p. 47.

27 March 1647 commission issued to Edward Diggs, brother of the deceased, to administer etc. etc. *Fines*, 53.

[Dudley Digges, son of Sir Dudley Digges, of Chilham, Kent, matriculated at University College, Oxford, June 18, 1630, aged 16, B. A. Jan. 17* 1631-2, fellow of All Souls 1632, M. A., Oct. 15. 1637, a member of Grays Inn, 1641, died at Oxford of camp fever Oct. 1, 1643, buried in All Souls Chapel. The brother Edward, named administrator, was afterwards Governor of Virginia and ancestor of the Virginia and Maryland families of the name.]

SAMUEL BUSHROD in the countie of Dorset, clothier. Will 13 Aprill 1647; proved 1 June 1647. I give unto the ministers herafter named viz; to Mr. William Bon £5, Mr. John White the elder £3, Mr. Hugh Thompson 40s., Mr. Peter Ince 40s, Mr. Gundry, clerke 40s, and Mr. John Barnard 40s. Also I give unto Mr. Frederick Losse £3, and to Mr. John Forward 40s. To my daughter Martha £200 to be employed for her education and maintenance, and to be paid over to her together with the increase and benefit thereof, at her age of 21 or marriage. If she die before I give £100 thereof to my wife Martha, £20 to the children of my brother John Bushrod living at the tyme of my decease, £5 to my sister Mary Allambridge, £10 to my cousen Mary Whitfield and the residue to the children of my sister Marshall living at the time of my decease Also I give to the three children of my cosin John Gilbert which are now living, and to the five children of my cosen Henry Bushrod now living, 20s. apiece. To Ann Squib 20s. To the poor of Trinity parish in Dorchester 40s. To the poor of St. Peters and All Saints there 20s. severally. To my brother John Bushrod to be recovered at his cost, all the debt due to me by Thomas Whitle, merchant, and the moiety of of all the judgements recovered by my father Mr. John Allambridge deceased, against the said Thomas Whitle given me under the last will of the said John Allambridge. To my brother Thomas Bushrod halfe the summes of money that he oweth me, the other halfe I give to my brother Richard Bushrod, for the recovery whereof the said Richard is to bear the cost and charge, To my brother Marshall's children equally among them, all debts due unto me from Joseph Cole and Nathaniel White, merchants, save only £20 thereof, which I give unto my cousin Mary Whitfield. To my three cosens John, Elizabeth, and Joseph Scovile, the money owing unto me by John Stansby, mariner, who was heretofore master of the barque called the George of Weymouth, whereof Mr. George Churchey was owner or part owner, which money is for the proceed and provenue of three serges, costing £12. 15s. delivered by me upon adventure unto the said John Stansbye. All the rest of my goods I give to my wife Martha, whom I make my executrix, and I desire my kinsman John Bushrod clothier, my friend George Cole, marchaunt and my brother Scovile to be overseers of this my will, and to take security of my executrix in behalf of my daughter. And as a·testimony of love and thankfulness to my overseers I bequeath unto them 20s. apeece to be bestowed in rings. Witnesses: Ri: Scovile, Richard Rapson of Dorcester, clothier, Mary Coke of Dorchester spinster. Proved by the executrix. *Fines*, 120.

[This will at least gives a clue to the English ancestry of the Virginia Bushrods and very probably is that of a brother of the emigrants. These emigrants were two brothers Thomas and Richard. Thomas came first to Mass. and afterwards to Virginia. He was long a prominent man in York County and was Burgess for the county 1658-60. His frequent clashes with the parish clergy and the direction in his will that there should be no "common prayer" at his burial would indicate that he was a Puritan. The numerous legacies made by Samuel Bushrod to ministers would indicate that he was of the same faith. Thomas Bushrod married twice but left no children. His will was probated in York Co. in 1677. Richard Bushrod, his brother, lived in Gloucester Co., and according to a deposition was born in 1626. He married Apphia—, and was ancestor of the Virginia family of the name. See *Wm. & Mary Quarterly*, XIV, 177.

George Scovel, born "infra the Isle of Purbeek, Dorset" about 1601, was a merchant in Virginia 1640.

VIRGINIA GLEANINGS IN ENGLAND.

DAME ANNE ARGALL of Higham Hill, Walthamstow, county Essex, widow. Will 30 December 1638; proved 26 March 1639. To every of my younger sons and to every of my daughters 10s. each for rings. To poor of Walthamstow 40s. It has pleased God to liberally provide for my younger children. I give all the rest and residue of my goods, chattels and estate to my eldest son Sir William Rowe of Walthamstowe aforesaid Knight, sole executor. Witnesses: John Herne, Wm Freeman, John Farmer. *Harvey*, 44.

[Anne Argall, daughter of John Cheyney, Esq., of Chesham Boys Buckinghamshire, married first, William Rowe, and secondly, in 1599, Reginald Argall, of Lincolns Inn, gent., brother of Sir Samuel Argall, Governor of Virginia.]

THOMAS BROADHURST of Clecton, county Salop. Will proved 26 February 1619. To poor of Broomsgrove £4. To my son Thomas Broadhurst one Phates walling (sic) in vpwich. To him also £100 if then living. If he be not then the Phate to my two daughters eldest sons if they have any. And for want of sons the eldest daughter of either and the £100 to my daughter Jane's children. To said daughter Jane £100. After her to her children. To her also half my household stuff, the rest to my daughter Elizabeth. Residue to John Pardoe saving the lease of this house and land in Clecton this I give to Thomas Pardoe my daughter's son and to Johane Pardoe my daughter's daughter. John Pardoe sole Executor. *Soame*, 10

[Thos Broadhurst, no doubt of the same family as Walter and Hugh Brodhurst, of Westmoreland Co., Va., who were sons of Wm. Brodhurst, gent., of Lilleshall, Shropshire.]

[EDWARD] BURWELL. Directions taken from my brother Burwell being upon his sick bed 18 October 1626. He desireth that his children may be educated in the fear of God "to which

From Vol. XXIII, No. 2 (April 1915), p. 156.

purpose I leave my estate to my wife to be disposed of as she shall think fit—so long as she doth kepe hereslf unmarried." My sister Sheafe to take my eldest daughter as her servant as she has promised. I commend my daughter Elizabeth to my sister Wingate in the same manner. I entreat my lord Bruce to consider my faithful service and manner of my death and be a good lord to my wife and children. My brother Wingate to be an Overseer and with him my Brother Henry Beadles, Mr. Edward Blofield, Ed. Burwell, John Orpin, Clerke, Edward Wingate. 9 November 1626 emt com to Dorothea Burwell. *Hele*, 126.

(The probate act styles him, Edward Burwell, Houghton Park, Arupthill, Bedfòrdshire.)

[He was the father of Lewis Burwell, the emigrant to Virginia. See Keith's *Ancestry* of *Bemiamin Harrison*, 34, 35.]

EDMOND CHAMBERLEYNE of Malgersbury, county Gloucester Esqre. Will 12 April 1634; proved 8 May 1634. To my daughter Grace £1200 to be paid out of the first moncys received by the Sale of my parsonage of Norton in the county of the City of Gloucester. Said parsonage to be forwith sold by executors. To Charles trinder £100. My son Edmond shall have out of the lease of the parsonage of Stow £20 per annum until the estate of Hannes tent shall come in possession. To Church of Stow £10. To poor of Stow £5 to be distributed by my wife. To Henry Chilmead £10. To Anne Hellinger £10. I make my wife my son John and Charles Trinder executors. My wife shall have the use of all my goods for her life and then the same shall come to my said son John. Witnesses: Jo: Chamberlayne, Henry Chiltmead, Robt. Keeble, Edmd Ockey. *Seager*, 40.

[The 1683 Visitation of Gloucestershire gives as second son of Edmund Chamberlayne of Maugersbury "Thomas, of Virginia, who married Mary, daughter of Abraham Wood of Virginia", This Thomas Chamberlayne settled in Henrico County, and as he was evidently a hard drinker and a man of violent temper he makes frequent appearance in the court records. He had married the daughter of one of the leading men in Virginia, and had the opportunity to acquire a prominent place in his county, which he failed to attain. He first appears in the year the extant records of Henrico begin, 1677, as an opponent of the Baconian party, who had been pillaged by some of Bacon's adherents and who were disposed to persecute the ex-"rebels." On

Dec. 1, 1677, Charles Roberts deposed that he heard the Thomas Chamberlayne (who in 1678 and perhaps earlier, was a justice of the county) threaten to disarm Mr. John Pygott because he had been one of Bacon's officers. On the same date Joseph Ekin deposed that Mr. Chamberlayne, about July last, desired his neighbors to come to his house and that the deponent saw Mr. Pygott give Mr. Chamberlayne two scabbards and two sword hilts; but he would not swear there were blades in the scabbards because he did not see them.

About the same time Judith Randolph testified that, at the house of John Sturdevant she heard John Pygott swear and wish God damn men that would not pledge the juice and quintessence of Bacon, and Mr. Chamberlayne said he could as soon pledge the Devil and left the room in a passion.

On Dec. 1st, 1677, was recorded a note of things taken from Mr. Thomas Chamberlayne "in the rebellious times," viz: a set of curtains, one large chest, two beds, two bolsters, one large feather pillow, one pair blankets, one rug, one pair sheets, one "fine canvis tester," three guns, one whole beef, four turkeys, one washing tub, one small shovel, two or three books, two men servants from the house and three from the landing; sworn to have been taken by William Clark and his company.

In April 1678, Thomas Chamberlayne was commissioned sheriff of Henrico, and in April 1679. he made an agreement to pay 1200 lbs tobacco for the erection of a frame house, forty feet long, twenty feet wide, two stories with outside chimneys. In June 1679, he began to get into trouble. In that month William Puckett deposed that Major Chamberlayne came to his and John Puckett's house, and in conversation in regard to some tobacco plants he had taken up and which they claimed, he said that John Puckett was a blockhead, and a son of a ——, and John Puckett said that his mother was no more a ————— than Chamberlayne's was, and then Chamberlayne asked him if he compared himself to him, and took up a hachett and said, if he said another word he would find his heart. About this time Thomas Chamberlayne was several times prosecuted by the grand Jury for being drunk and fighting. It should be stated however, that in that hard-drinking time an indictment for being drunk might have been a little mortifying; but evidently was not especially disgraceful. There were too many in the same box. Chamberlayne's behavior, however, became too offensive for the Governor and Council to stand, and on April 30, 1679, they suspended him from his place as one of the justices of the county court. "It having been shown by many witnesses that he had highly and contemptuously offended the said court."

There is on record a deed Feb. 1686-7 from Thomas Chamberlayne and Mary his wife, daughter of Major General Abraham Wood, conveying to George Archer and Joseph Royall land which had been devised them by General Wood. By deed dated July 18, 1675, recorded June 28, 1678, Major General Abraham Wood had conveyed land to Thos. Chamberlayne.

In Aug. 1687, is a deposition stating that Major Thomas Chamberlayne had abused Thomas Bott and called him a rogue.

In June 1685, Mr. Humphrey Chamberlayne (doubtless a brother of Thomas) was presented for stripping off his upper clothes, and standing in the road near the Court House with his sword drawn, and other misdemeanors, and attempting to break jail; and attempted to excuse himself as being a stranger and ignorant of the laws; but the Court imposed a fine, thinking no stranger could be so ignorant, expecially "an English gentleman." He appealed to the General Court, with Thos. Chamberlayne as security, but in Dec. 1685, probably not finding Virginia congenial, put up his name at the Court House door as "intending for England." About this time Thomas Chamberlayne was also tried for riotous behavior, resisting arrest and damaging the jail. The last mention of this roistering gentleman in the Henrico records is on May 16, 1692, when having been imprisoned, he violently broke jail, and was again arrested and tried.

Soon afterwards he removed to Charles City County, and under the sobering effect of years evidently subsided into a sedate and respectable citizen for he was a member of the House of Burgesses for that county in 1695. As the records of Charles City for that period have been destroyed, we know nothing of his will or children, but he was not the ancestor of the Chamberlaynes of New Kent, Richmond, etc., who descend from a later emigrant, William Chamberlayne of Herefordshire.

As stated above the Visitation of Gloucestershire, 1683, identified Thos. Chamberlayne of Virginia. This has been published with additions in the annual report of the "Chamberlain Association of America" 1806-1907, pp. 70-81. (Omitting earlier generations)—Sir Thomas Chamberlayne of Prestbury, Gloucestershire, Ambassador from Henry VIII, Edward VI, and Elizabeth to several courts, died in the latter end of Elizabeth's reign. By his second wife, Elizabeth, daughter of Sir John Ludington, he had (2d son) Edward Chamberlayne of Maugersbury, high sheriff of Gloucestershire in the 39th Elizabeth, who died April 29, 1634, and was the testator above. By his second wife Grace, daughter of John Strangeways, of Melbury, Dorset, he had Edmund Chamberlayne, of Maugersbury, who died 1676. A long abstract of the Catter's will is given in the Annual Report referred to. His tomb at Stow bears this epitaph "Here lyeth Interred the Body of Colonel Edmund Chamberlayne, who departed this life 11 day of April 1676." He married Eleanor daughter of Humphrey Colles, of Clotteslad, Gloucestershire, and had a number of children among them, Edmund, who succeeded, Thomas, of Virginia, and Humphrey (doubtless the one who appears in the Henrico records), who was left land at Abbots Leigh, Somerset, and who in 1676 had three children.]

JOHN CODRINGTON of the Inner Temple London Esquier. Will 19 November 1622; proved 23 May 1623. All my plate jewels household stuff, cattle and chattels whatsoever about my house at Codrington to my wife Jane. To her also all my right in the Manor of Codrington and Rectory of Wapley and all my lands and tenements in Erlingham county Glocester and unexpired term of lease granted to me by Christopher Stoakes gent. To poor of Wapley and Codrington 40s. My wife Jane sole executrix. My friend Vnton Croke Overseer. To him a gold ring To Mrs. Cheshire for pains taken in my sickness 20s. To her daughter Margaret 10s. To her daughter Silvester 10s. To Vnton Croke my best bar gowne. *Swann, 44*

Witness: V. Croke.

[From a branch of the ancient family of Codrington, of Codrington, descended the two Christopher Codringtons, who were governors of Barbadoes, and of Henningham Codrington who married about 1701, Dr. Paul Carrington of Barbadoes and died Jan. 28, 1744-5, aged 69 years, leaving a son, George Carrington, who emigrated to Virginia.]

MARY DIGGES of Chilham Castle, County Kent, virgin, youngest daughter of Sir Dudley Digges Knight, late Master of the Rolls, deceased. Will 4 May 1643; proved 23 May 1643. To be buried in vault in Chilham built by my father. To poor of Chilham £5. To Bridge 40s. To each of my brothers £100. To Brother in law Arnold Brayning Esqre £140. To kinsman Richard Thornchill Esqre £50. To Mr. Francis Lovelace £10. To Dame Frances ye Lady of Sir Thomas Baker Knight £10. To sister in law Mary Diggs wife of my Eldest Brother Thomas Digges £20. To sister Elizabeth Brayning wife of Arnold Brayning £20. To sister Ann wife of Anthony Hammond Esq my jewels. To Joan Lovell my maid servant £20. Executor: Anthony Hammond my Brother in law. Witnesses: Paull Stroud, John Stroud. Sentence. Parties Anthony Hammon and Thomas Diggs of Chilham, Edward Diggs gent, Leonard Diggs, gent and Herbert Diggs gent Brothers. *Archdeaconry of Canterbury Liber*, 1643, *No.* 35.

[Mary Digges. A sister of Edward Digges, Governor of Virginia.]

GAWEN GROSVENOR of Sutton Coldfield, county Warwick. Will 12 March 1625; proved 24 October 1626. To poor of Sutton Coldfield £10. To my daughter Katherine Grosvenor £333. 6s. 8d over and above the 1000 marks which I have appointed to be raised for her, so as she marry with the assent of Fowke Grosvenor her brother, Thomas Corbin her brother in law and with the assent of my kinsman Walter Grosvenor of Tetnall, Walter Payton, and Edward Newman gent, or any two or three of them (her brother Fowke being one of the two or three) To George Corbyn my godson £20. To my daughter Winifrid Corbyn my watch. To Judith Grosvenor my cosen Walter Grosvenor's wife £5 for a ring. To my cosen Judith Newman my table diamond ring. To either of my sisters Hester Thornebury and Uenys Francke £5 apeece. To William Newman £20. To Raphe Cooper my servant the house (now in occupation of Nicholas Evans) in Sutton for his life. To Barbara Lee £5. To the rest of my servants 20s. apeece. Residue to my said son Fowke Grosvenor sole executor. Thomas Corbyn, Walter Grosvenor, Walter Payton and Edward Newman Overseers.

To my said son Thomas Corbyn £10 for his pains and the rest of my Overseers £5 for their pains. "These being witnesses" (not any named) *Hele*, 140

[The testator, whose name Gawen or Gawin has been borne by many descendants in Virginia, was descended from a family of Gravenor in Shropshire. Full pedigrees of various branches of the family may be found in Vols. IV, V, and VI, of the *Herald and Genealogist*. Adam de Gravenor was living in Shropshire in the time of Edward I, and from him the line is traced to the testator. Pedigrees of the family are entered in the Staffordshire Visitation of 1583 and 1619. John Grosvenor of Bushbury, Staffordshire, married Rose, daughter and heiress of John Clayton, of Harwood Parva Lancashire, and had a son Walter Grosvenor, of Bushbury, who married Joyce, 3d daughter of Roger Fowke, of Gunston. They were the parents of the testator, Gawen Grosvenor, of Sutton Coldfield, who was aged 53 at the Visitation of 1619, and who married Dorothy, daughter of George Pudsey, of Langley, in the County of Warwick, Esq. Gawen and Dorothy Grosvenor had issue: (1) Fulke, (2) Job, "non compos mentis," (3) Gawen, (4) Winifred, eldest daughter, who married in 1620, Thomas Corbyn, of Corbyn's Hall, Kingswinford, Staffordshire, Eng., (4) Catherine. The will of Thomas Corbin, who married Winifred Grosvenor, and whose third son Henry came to Virginia, is printed in this Magazine XVII, 401. An old manuscript, quoted in the *Herald and Genealogist* gives these minute details of the birth of Winifred (Grosvenor) Corbin. "Winifrede Gravenour was born ye 29 of April being Monday between 7 & 8 of ye Clock in ye morning, 1605, in ye 3d year of King James."

The Pudseys of Warwickshire can be traced to the old Yorkshire family of that name, and, through intermarriages are descended from various other distinguished families of Yorkshire.]

VIRGINIA GLEANINGS IN ENGLAND.

Communicated by the late Lothrop Withington, London (including "Gleanings" by the late H. F. Waters, not before printed.)

ROBERT BATHURST of Lechlade, county Gloucester Esqre Will 11 September 1623; proved 20 November 1623. To poor of Lechlade, and poor of Horsmondine, county Kenty £5 apeece. The Lady Elizabeth my wife shall have my household goods. To the Lady laurance my said wife (sic) coach horses. To my servants one years wages. To Bridget Bathurst my servant £4 annuity and £40 at 18 years of age. For payment of my debts and legacies my executor to take profits of leases etc. According to deed dated 22nd June 6 Jas. I. and my executor to be in trust till Robert Bathurst my eldest son come to full age. To children of my late sister Heylin £100 viz: to Peter Heylyn £20, to Jane wife of Charles Trinder £15, Edward Heylyn, Mary Polhill widow, Mercy, Joyce Heylin and Elizabeth wife of John Gearinge £10 apeece. To Francis and Grace Heyling £15. 10s. 0d. apeece. To children of my sister Katherine Spencer £40 divided. The rest for use of my youngest son Edward Bathurst and Mary Bathurst my daughter. Furthermore from other leases said Edward and Mary £20 apeece yearly. My brother in law Mr. William Rainton sole executor. To him £100 and charges. Henry Laurance Esq owes me £300 which I give to my loving wife aforesaid Lady Laurence. Witnesses: Wm Phipes, John Hucks, Chas. Trinder, Wm Hall. **Swan, 118.**

[Robert Bathurst, an ancestor of Launcelot Bathurst of Virginia, married Elizabeth, daughter of Robert Waller, Esq. and widow of Sir John Lawrence, Lord Mayor of London. His second son Edward who was born 1615, was created a Baronet Dec. 4, 1643, and died 1674. Launcelot Bathurst, son of Sir Edward, emigrated to Virginia and has many descendants.]

From Vol. XXIII, No. 3 (July 1915), p. 294.

HUMPHREY BELL, of London, skinner, now dwelling at Deptford in the county of Kent. Will 24 September 1653; proved
10 June 1653. I devise my seven messuages in Wapping, county
Middlesex, on the south side of Wapping street, unto Ellen, my
wife, for her life. The remainder thereof, and all my tenements
lying in or near Budgrowe in London, to my trusty friends Evan
Seize and Henry Colborne, upon trust to pay to my daughter
Anne Bickley or to whom she shall appoint, for her maintenance
apart (and no part thereof to her husband, John Bickley) all
the rents thereof during the life of the said John Bickley; afterwards to reconvey and settle the premises on the said Anne
Bickley, and her beirs; and for default of issue to her, on the
heirs of my nephew Hollis, Thomas, and Humphrey Bell. And
I give full power to my daughter, if my trustees refuse so to do,
or she dislike them, at any time hereafter to nominate any person or persons whom she shall think fit in trust for her, in the
places of the said Evan Seize and Henry Colborne, whom I
hereby appoint my executors, giving them £10 apiece for their
pains. Item, I give to William Benson, £20. (signed) Humfrey Bell. Witnesses: Edward Higgins, John Higgins, William
Neale. Proved by Henry Colburn, one of the executors named
with power reserved for a like grant to the said Evan Seise.
7 July 1656 letters of administration issued to Robert Bell,
nephew of Humphrey Bell, deceased, to administer the goods
etc. left unadministered by Henry Colborn, now deceased, the
other executor and Anne Bickley, alias Bell, only child of the
testator, having judicially renounced execution. 10 June 1658
letters granted to Frauncis Burghill, one of the trustee appointed
on behalf of the said Anne Bickley alias Bell on the decease of
the above said Robert Bell. **Brent,** 163.

Francis Bickley, son of Anne Bickley named in this will, was in Virginia in 1656, though he was not the ancestor of the later family of the
name. See this Magazine XI 151, 152; XVIII, 309.]

HUGH CHICHESTER of Widworthie in the county of Devon,
esquire. Will 28 September 1640; proved 10 May 1642. I
give unto the poore of Widworthy 40s to remaine as a stocke
for ever to be employed for their best use and advantage. To
my sonnes, John, Robert and William 5s apeece, having already

otherwise provided for them. To my daughters Anne and Dorothie 5s apeece, they being allready married and haveing had their portions. To my grandchild John Chichester, all my table bordes formes and stooles in my dyening chamber, and hall, and all the seeling about my house, and one silver bason and ewer, which I had from my brother Smith. All the residue of my goodes I give to my daughter Mary, whom I make my executrix, desiring her to be frendly to my brother William Chichester her uncle. Witnesses: Edmond Clode, Thomas Francklyn, William Francklyn. Proved by Mary Chichester the executrix named. **Cambell,** 59.

[Hugh Chichester (1573-1641) was great grandfather of Richard Chichester, who emigrated to Virginia. See this Magazine XXI, 250-252.]

VIRGINIA GLEANINGS IN ENGLAND.

Communicated by the late Lothrop Withington, London, England.

WILLIAM CATTLETT of Sittingbourne, County Kent, gent. Will 15 March 1646-7; proved 2 November 1647. I give to the poor of Sittingbourne £5, to the poor of Cong, Baptheile [sic], and Radmersham, to each parish 40s. To Edward Garland of Sittingbourne, clerk, £5. To Mr. Lane of Bredcar, clerk, £5. To Mr. Wood of Lenham, clerk, £5. To Mr. Pidcard, clerk, of Bapchild, 40s. To my neece Dickenson of Feversham, widow, £20. To my neeces Kennet and Simpson £20 apiece. To my cosen John Dix of Bapchild, esq., and to his son William and daughter Katherine, £10 apiece. To my cousin Nicholas Adye £20. To Elizabeth Adye alias Smith, his sister, £40. To my cousins George Hickes, Adye Hickes, Jane Adye, alias Jeffery, and Elizabeth Frind, £10 apiece. To my cousin Anne Bradley alias Brockhull, £20. To my cousin Allen of Sittingbourne, taylor, £5. To my cousin Edward Tomlyn of Sittingbourne £10. To my cousin Thomas Allen of Bredger £10. To my cousin Thomas Currall of Rochester Boteson £20. To his sons Robert and Thomas £10 apiece, and to his daughter Elizabeth Currall £20. To John Pawson of Sittingbourne £30. To my servant Elizabeth Medler £20. To Henry Lawrence £10. To Solomon Bowell £10. To my cousin William Catlett of Cong £20. To his son Richard £20. To my cousin Susan Allen alias Lambert, £10. To John Lambert of Blackwall, husband of the said Susan, 40s. To my cousin George Catlett of Blackwalle £20. To my cousin Grace Catlett of Sittingbourne £20. To John Clench of Stafford £5. To Jane Burgis alias Sharpe £5. A declaration or codicil nuncupative to be added to the last will of the said William, spoken in

From Vol. XXIII, No. 4 (Oct. 1915), p. 381.

the time of his last sickness, about twelve of the clock in the night time of or after Tuesday the nyneteenth day of October 1647, he being then in good memory and understanding. The said William Catlett being putt in mind by Samuell Packer, one that that very night attended upon him, of some that had done him service, and that if he did not or had not remembered them the world would condemne him, whereto the said William answered that he had given something to the poor, but not much. And then demand being further made of him, who shall be his executor, he thereto (sic) and very readily and cheerfully answered that his cousin John Bix of Bapchild, esq. (sic). Witnesses: Samuell Packer and John Pawson, both of Sittingbourne. Proved by the executor names. *Fines*, 218.

[William Catlett, the testator, was probably a brother of John Catlett, the elder, of Sittingbourne, Kent, gent., who appears to have been grandfather of Jno. Catlett of Virginia. George Catlett, of Blackwall, named in the will, was a son of John Catlett, the elder. John Catlett, who emigrated to Virginia, owned lands at Sittingbourne and Radmersham, which were sold by his son John about 1701. Dr. and Mrs. W. C. Stubbs of New Orleans, have, it is understood, a genealogy of the Virginia Catletts nearly ready for publication.]

WILLIAM CODD, of Pellicans in the parish of Watringbury, county Kent, esquire. Will 16 December 1652; proved 25 July 1653. My body (my soul being thence departed) I commend to the earth, whereof it was made, desiring that the interring thereof may be in decent and Christian like manner, agreeable to the usage of the protestant church of England, in some convenient place in the body of the church or chancel of Waterbury aforesaid. I give to the poor of the parish 40s. To my sister Anne Ayhurst, 20s, to buy her a ring. I forgive my sister Elizabeth Polhill, widow, £20, parcel of a greater debt which she oweth unto me upon several bonds, upon condition she shall within 2 months after request made pay the remaining part thereof. I give to Mary, my beloved wife (she taking upon her the execution of this my will), one moiety of all my plate and household stuff. The rest of all my goods I bequeath to my six daughters, viz., Mary, Barbara, Deborah, Katherine, Elizabeth and Anne, and to such daughter as may hereafter be born to me, towards the raising and increasing their portions, their shares being paid to each at their several ages of 18 or days of marriage. I desire my loving kinsman William Dixon, esquire, to be overseer of this my will, and I set over to him all my interest in the lands or estate of James Perry, gentleman, my deceased kinsman, under the will of the same James Perry, and I commend unto the said William Dixon the education and bringing up of Katherine Perrey and Mary Perry, two of the daughters of the same James Perry, and of Katherine Perry, niece of the same James Perry. As touching the disposing and settling of all my lands and tenements, I give unto my said daughters all my messuages and lands in East Malling, and my messuage and lands at or a place called Redhill in Watringbury, aforesaid, and in Teston in the said county now in the tenure of Thomas Rolfe, to hold to them and the heirs of their bodies in equal parts and portions. I give to my eldest son Seintleger Codd all my lands called Parke Lands and Churchgate Feild alias East Feild [later called West Feild] in Watringbury, and my lands in Lenham and Witchling, commonly called Evells Landes, late the lands of John Parkhurst, gent., deceased, in tail; with remainder, in default of issue to him, to my sons Anthony and Rowland, and my right heirs for ever. To my second son Anthony, my messuage and lands, which I lately purchased of John Pattenden, in Nettlestead, county Kent. My wife and overseer aforenamed shall have the letting of the said lands, and take the profits thereof, till each of my daughters shall have received towards their portions two years' rent of the premises. In witness whereof I have written these with my own hand, and set my seal and subscribed my name unto each sheet hereof, being two in number. (signed)William Codd. Witnesses: Alexander Culpeper, Hen: Wood, John Leversidge. Proved by the executrix named. (In the margin is a receipt by Chr. Crispe for the original will to the use of the executrix, 10 August 1653.) *Brent*, 120.

[William Codd, the testator, was father of St. Leger Codd, who emigrated to Virginia and afterward to Maryland. St. Leger Codd, in his will proved in Lancaster Co., Va., April 18, 1708, bequeathes his lands in Watringbury, Lenham, and Witchling, Kent. William Codd, his father, married in 1632, Mary, daughter Sir Warham St. Leger, of Ulcombe, Kent. See this Magazine X, 373-376. The Londoners whose wills follow, were no doubt relations.]

SAMUEL CODD, Citizen and Grocer of London, St. Anne and Agnes parish Aldersgate. Will 9 March 1622; proved 26 May 1623. Body to parish church. To my brother Anthony Codd £40. To my daughter Anne Codd £300. If my daughter decease before 21 or marriage then said £300 to my wife Suzanna Codd, sole executrix. Witnesses: Martha Rand, Elizab. Bayllye, Peter Hughes. *Swann*, 104.

ANTHONY CODD, Citizen and haberdasher of London. Will 8 January 1635; proved 21 August 1637. To my son George Codd a house in Gainsburie county Lincoln for ever. To him also one tenement in St. Michaels Querne the sign of the Queen's Arms in occupation of ....Bullard. Mris Joane Tichborne my son's godmother shall take the rents or dispose of said tenement for said son's benefit. To said son George Codd £26. To my daughter Susan Harvye widow £155. 5s. 0d. in hands of Mris Ann Browne. To my daughter Ellen Codd £108 in hands of Mr. John Lidiate. To Mris Hill wife of Mr. Hill linendraper, apparrel. To my daughter Lidia 2s. 6d. To my daughter Button 2s. 6d. To Christian Adkinson 20s. for a ring. To Anne Gase my goddaughter £3. to buy her a Cowe. To the poore of St. Buttolph without Aldersgate 20s. My son George sole executor. Mr. Hill and Mr. John Browne of London, Merchants supervisors. All my household stuff to my daughters Susan and Ellen. Witness: Jacob Crowder, scrivener. *Goare*, 114.

VIRGINIA GLEANINGS IN ENGLAND.

(Contributed by the late Lothrop Withington, London, Eng.)

SIMON ASTON, Citizen and Grocer of London. Will 2 August 1638; proved 15 August 1638. To wife Elizabeth ½ of goods and executrix. Overseers: Brothers William Wheeler Esq. and Robert Aston, Citizen and Grocer of London. Richard Nelme £10 to make up accounts of Shopp. To poor of St. Peters Cheap £4. To Mother £20 per annum. To eldest son William Aston £50. Witnesses: James Smith, Thomas Lavender, John Hope. **Lee, 99.**

ELIZABETH ASTON of London, widow. Will 12 April 1647; proved 25 September 1647. I commit my body to the earth to be buried in decent manner in the parish church of All Saints Staining, London, as near to my later dear father, John Wheeler, esq., deceased, as conveniently may be, but not with pomp and solemnity or mourning, which I leave to the discretion of my brother and executor to do therein as I have to him declared. I give to my sisters Ann Wynn and Mary Anesworth 40s apiece to buy them rings. To my sister Lucilia Dodd £10 to remain in the hands of my executor to her proper use. To my brother John Wheeler 40s. for a ring to wear in remembrance of me. To my sisters Agneta Moone and Clara van de Welde the like sum apiece. To my sister Mrs. Elizabeth Wheeler a ring of 40s. price in testimony of my love and affection unto her. To my cousin Mrs. Elizabeth Aby 40s. To my cousin Mrs. Mary Ruddiard, widow, a ring of 40s. price to wear in remembrance of me. To my servant Elizabeth Cornwell £5. To Marie Butt, sometimes my servant, 20s. To eight poor widows, at the election of my executor, 10s. apiece. To the poor of St. Katherine Coleman, London, and of all Saints Steyning, 40s. to either parish. To Master William Engler 40s. To my three sons, William, Simon, and Robert Aston, £200 apiece at their several ages of 21. To my eldest daughter Anne Aston £300, and to my youngest daughter Sarah Aston £200, at their several ages of 18. I give also to my said daughters such of my plate, linen, and woolen things, as I have set apart for them, and parcelled out with my own hands and set their names thereon. To my three sons, £5 apiece in old gold. I give unto my executors, children, and servants mourning apparel only, and desire that the rest of my friends will be contented with the legacies only before mentioned and intended unto them. The residue of my goods I give equally among my said five children. I ordain my very loving brother William Wheeller, of Westburie county, Wilts, esq., and my son William Aston my overseers. And to my said brother Master William Wheeller, for his great care and pains to be taken therein, and for a remembrance of my love to him, I give £10 to buy him a piece of plate at his discretion and pleasure. Codicil 24 July 1647. I do further declare that, in regard my sister Dod has shown great love to me in the time of my long sickness, to the £10 formerly given to her £10 more be added; and likewise that £5 more be distributed to poor widows. The mark of Elizabeth Aston Witnesses: William Steedman, Thomas Coleman, servt. to Thomas Bostocke, scr. Proved by William Wheeller, with power reserved, etc. **Fines, 188.**

The *Visitation* of London, 1634, states that Walter Aston, of Longdon, Staffordshire (grandson of Sir Walter Aston of Tixall), had issue: 1 Thomas, living at Kilbary, Ireland; 2. Simon, of London, Grocer, who married Elizabeth, daughter of John Wheeler, of London; 3. Walter, "now in the West Indies;" 4. Robert, of London, grocer. As Virginia was then frequently referred to as in the West Indies, it is very probable that the Walter Aston referred to was the one whose tomb is at the site of the old church at Westover. The epitaph is as follows:
"Here Lyeth interred the body of leftenant
Colonell Walter Aston who died the 6th
Aprill 1656. He was Aged
49 years And
Lived in this country 28 yeares
Also here lyeth the Body of Walter Aston
the son of Leftenant Collonel Walter Aston
who departed this life ye 29th of Ianuari 1666
Aged 27 Yeares and 7 Monthes."
Walter Aston, Sr., came to Virginia in 1628, and settled in Charles City County. He was a member of the House of Burgesses for Shirley Hundred

Island 1629-30, Both Shirley Hundreds &c., 1631-32, Shirley Hundred Maine and "Cawseys Care" Sept. 1632, and Feb. 1632-3, and Charles City Co. 1642-3. He was also justice of the peace and lieutenant colonel of militia. His first wife was named Warboro, or Narbrow, and his second (who survived him and married Col. Edward Hill) was Hannah. On Aug. 2, 1646, Walter Aston patented 1040 acres in Charles City on Kymages Creek, including 200 more on "Cawseys Care." Lt. Col. Aston died in 1656 having issue: (1) Susannah, widow, in 1655, of Lieutenant Col. Edward Major; (2) Walter; (3) Mary, married Richard Cocke; (4) Elizabeth, married ——— Binns. The will of Walter Aston, Jr., was dated Dec. 21, 1666, and proved Feb. 4, 1666-67. Legatees: to his mother Hannah Hill, a parcel of land called "The Level;" to godson John Cocke, son of Richard Cocke, deceased, 4000 lbs. tobacco; to godson Edward Cocke, son of Richard Cocke, 6000 lbs. tobacco; the survivors to have the whole amount of 10,000 lbs. and if they were without issue it is to go to the other children, sisters Mary Cocke and Elizabeth Binns 20 shillings each for a ring: a gun called Pollard to servant John Mitten and a sow; to testators Irish boy Edward a sow, to Mr. George Harris, merchant, all the dividend of land at Cawseys Care, the land at Canting Point and rest of estate].

HENRY ELTONHEAD of London Merchant bound for a voyage to the East Indies in the good ship called the Hound of London. Will 23 November 1616; proved 12 February 1619-20. To my brother Nicholas Eltonhead of Greenwich county Kent, gent all my estate whatsoever and I make him sole executor. William Manley servant to Nicholas Reeve, scr., Edward Pierce servant to said scrivenor. **Soame, 22.**

The ancient family of Eltonhead, of Eltonhead, Lancashire, has many descendants in Virginia. See Hayden's *Virginia Genealogies* 228-230. Henry Eltonhead, whose will is given here was evidently the son of William Eltonhead. His name and that of his brother Nicholas appear on the chart pedigree. Henry Eltonhead. whose will was dated in 1665. was a brother of Richard Eltonhead, of Eltonhead, though not named in the chart. This is evident as he mentions his brother Thomas Meares].

HENRY ELTONHEAD late of London Esq deceased. Will 27 July 1665. These seuerall following I doe giue to my Brother R. Eltonhead if I dye a single man. Moneys due to me in Ireland by bond in Mr. John Doughty's hands in Dublin £100. Mr. Thomas Houghton is bound interest due 10 in hundred this bond·is in hands of Mr. Walter Scudamore. In hands of Mr. Timothy "Grolliers" in Dublin wherein Mr. James Butteele is bound at 10 in hundred. In my landlords hand Mr. Joseph Stokers in Dublin £100 at his house in Castle Street Dublin, interest to be paid by him by reason I lay two yeares in his house and paid nothing for my chamber which I ought to pay for after the rate of fiue pound ten shillings a year. In my brother Richard Barrys hands my salary due from the King as Commissary for Munster £97. Two bonds of Mr. Edwd Rands £90 some years ago. Two bonds of my brother Tho. Mearas £6 in hands of Mr. Nathaniell Foulkes he lives at the sign of the Horseshoe in Castle Street Dublin. I owe Mr. William Richardson £24. Mr. Clement Hog for two last terms Business £8. Due from Mr. Denton £100. Due to my proctor Mr. John Clements £10. Grant Book 1668-1675 fo. 54. Letters of Administration with will etc to Richard Eltonhead of Eltonhead in county Lancashire in England Esq of goods of Henry Eltonhead late of London Esq deceased on 23 August 1670. **Prerogative Court of Ireland, Will Book 1668-72, folio 166.**

WILLIAM BARLOWE. Will 21 February 1617; proved 15 June 1625. If I die at Easton my body to the Chancell. God having given me ability in my lifetime to provide for my wife and children, I will now be the shorter. My daughter Anne having as yet very little of certainty I make her estate worth £300. To my brother John Barlowe 100 marks. To my son Thomas all my Loadstones and Mathematical books and instruments. To the poor of Winchester 40s. To those of the seale 30s. To poor of Easton 40s. To poor of Avington 20s. To my men servants and maids half a years wages. My wife Julyan Barlowe and my son William Barlow joynt executors. My son William Barlow shall have £40 to assist his mother but all things to her direction. My daughters Mary and Katherine portions may amount to £300 apiece. All such reversions of the Church Coppihoulds as I shall have at my death unbargained for and unsold I give to my son Barnaby Barlowe. **Clarke, 67.**

About the middle of the Seventeenth century a Ralph Barlowe lived in Northampton Co., Va. Various references in the records there show that he was related to Robert Parker of that county, who, like William Barlowe, whose will is given above, was a Hampshire man. On Oct. 28, 1653, Mr. George Parker sued Mr. John Elsey, executor of Mr. Ralph Barlowe, and on June 28, 1658, Jone Elzey "of Old England" petitioned Northampton Court that Mr. John Elzey executor of Mr. Ralph Barlowe, should pay her 500 lbs. tobacco left her, in Ralph Barlowe's will].

VIRGINIA GLEANINGS IN ENGLAND.

(Contributed by Leo Culleton, 92 Piccadilly, London, W.,
and the late Lathrop Withington.)

(continued)

SIR SAMPSON DARELL, KNIGHT.   Will 21 May 1635;
proved 1 July 1635.   To each of my children £1000 each
except my eldest son.   Sir John Parsons to have the order-
ing of my part in the Cole farm for my wife.   Executors-
my wife and Sir John Parsons.   Witnesses: Buchan Robert
Lesley, Barth: Cressener.   Proved first by Elizabeth Darrell, relict. and 14 June 1642 by Marmaduke Darrell son of
deceased on death of Elizabeth.   *Sadler*, 84.

[Sir Sampson Darrell probably had descendants in Virginia as the name
Sampson was frequently borne by members of a Darrell family here.
See this Magazine XVII, 115.]

ROBERT FILMER of East Sutton, county Kent, gentleman.
Will 11 April 1629; proved 4 May 1629.   Body to upper
Chancel of Church of East Sutton.   To the poor 40s.   To
the lady Filmer my sister £10.   To my brother Henry Fil-
mer my gold ring and three suites of apparel two of cloth and
one of pink sattin.   Two hats and two pairs of silk stockings.
To my neece, Mrs. Mary Knatchbull, to Sir Robert Filmer,
Mr. Edward Filmer, Mr. John Filmer, Reynold Filmer and
Henry Filmer gent, my nephews 40s. apeece.   To my neeces
Mrs. Elizabeth Faulkner, Mrs. Katherine Barram and Mrs.
Sarah Filmer 40s. each for rings.   To Edward Filmer my
brother Anthonie's son £20 at 22 years.   To his brother
Henry £10 at 23.   To his sister Mrs. Francis Filmer my
neece £10.   To my daughter in law Penelope Bellinger
her mother's wedding ring.   To Mrs. Elizab. Faulkner
my neece a black taffeta gown.   To my Lady Filmer my
sister a pair of gloves wrought with pearls.   Residue to my
brother Sir Edward Filmer Knight, sole executor.   Witnesses: Laurence Foxe, Thos. Gateley.   *Ridley*, 49.

From Vol. XXIV, No. 2 (April 1916), p. 158.

Sir Edward Filmer of East Sutton, county Kent, Knight (aged 63, 17th January last.)   Will 20 October Vth Chas. I; proved 5 December 1629.   To my daughter Elizabeth wife of William Faulkner Citizen and Draper of London, if she survive her husband £500.   If said husband survive said Elizabeth then to her children £300 equally divided.   If she die without issue then to her husband £20.   Executors to find meat drink and apparel to said Elizabeth to the value of £40 yearly.   To my three sons Edward, John and Henry Filmer £10 each.   And because my son Reynald's estate consists in trading beyond the seas I forgive him all debts (£550).   To said Reynold £50.   To my son Henry if he commence M. A. in University of Cambridge £40 and furthur £100.   To my daughters Mary Knatchbull and Catherine Barham £20 each.   To Edward Knatchbull my godson £5.   To his sister Mary £20.   To his brother John £2. To Edward Barham my godson.   To Elizabeth Barham my wive's goddaughter £5.   To other grandchildren, Robert, Thomas, Charles, and Richard Barham 40s. each.   To Dame Ann wife of my son Sir Robert Filmer ℔20 for a ring. To my daughter Sara £1000 further £500 annuity of £10 to my brother Henry.   To Dorothy daughter of my brother Anthony Filmer £10.   To Dame Elizabeth my wife £120 and all her chains and jewels and all my household stuff in Colledghouse in Maidstone, a third part of linen and silver. My lease of Rectory of East Sutton towards payment of my debts.   The other two parts of linen, silver, etc., to my son Sir Robert Filmer.   My wife shall have the leases of certain houses in Knightrider Street lately given me by my brother Robert Filmer, esq., Dame Elizabeth and Sir Robert my son executors.   Witnesses: Wm Davy, Wm Gregory, Richd Clowgh.   For disposing my land in county Kent and elsewhere.   Lands called Nicholls in Chartham, my lands in Otterden and lands in Romney Marsh shall stand according to Indentures made.   To my son John £15 yearly out of houses in Darrant.   To said son John also my houses and lands in Yalding and to his heirs.   For default to my eldest son Sir Robert and heirs.   For default to Edward Filmer my second son and heirs.   For default to Reynold my fourth son and heirs.   For default to Henry my fifth son and heirs.   To my son Edward after my wife's decease all houses and lands in Darrant.   For default to Sir Robert my eldest son.   For default to John my third son.   For default to Reynold. For default to Henry.   To Henry my 5th son and heirs after my wife's decease tenement and land in Warren Street parish of Lenham and one in parish of Charing.   For default to Sir Robert.   For default to Edward.   For default to John.   For default to Reynold.   To my wife Dame Elizabeth for life all my houses and lands in Darrant, Lenham, Charing and Sutton Valence, one tenement in parish of Borden. After her decease the lands in Sutton Valence shall be sold by Sir Robert if need be.   If not needed lands to Sir Robert and heirs.   Witnesses: Wm. Gregory, Wm. Davy, Richd Clough.   *Ridley*, 110.

[Robert Filmer, whose will was proved in 1629, was a brother of Sir Edward Filmer, whose will (also proved in 1629) follows. Sir Edward was the father of Henry Filmer, who emigrated to Virginia. See this Magazine, XV, 181, 182; XXI, 153, 154. Edward Filmer, grocer, was no doubt a descendant of some younger son of the family. These wills add considerably to the pedigree in Berry.]

EDWARD FILLMER of Cittingborne, county Kent, grocer Will 3 March 1646 (-7); proved 1st July 1653.   I give unto the poor of the parish 40s., to be distributed among them at the discretion of the churchwardens.   To my cousin Thomas Fillmer, son of my brother Robert Fillmer, in recompense of the title which the said Thomas hath, or henceafter may claim, in certain land in Ottenden, county Kent, now in my occupation, £60 at his age of 21, provided he then release all such right or title to my daughter Elizabeth Fillmer.   To my cousin Jane Fillmer, daughter to my said brother Robert £5 at 21.   To my cousins John and Anne Fillmer, son and daughter of my brother William Fillmer, £20 apiece at 21.   To my brothers Henry and William Fillmer, 20s. apiece to buy them rings.   To my apprentice Thomas Leshington, all the wares in my shop and warehouse, and all debts due unto me by my books, on condition he discharge all such debts as I shall owe at the time of my decease in the city of London.

To my friend William Allen of Cittingborne, gent., £5.   I
will that the said Thomas Lessington shall during the term of
his life enjoy my shop, with the workhouse and warehouse,
and one half part of my dwelling house with the half of the
backside thereunto belonging, with the garden called the White
Heart garden, which is in my occupation, and also the house
and garden that Roger Pannell now dwelleth in in Cittingborne
aforesaid, on condition he pay to my daughter for rent of the
premises £20 a year.   My wife Eleanor shall, during her
life, hold the other part of my said dwelling-house rent free;
and if she be not minded to continue her dwelling there, the
said Thomas Leshington shall have the whole of the said house,
paying yearly to my wife for her half part £4.   I give to my
wife all the bed, bedding and furniture belonging to it, which
is in my best chamber; also (in lieu of her dower in all my freehold lands,) an annuity, of £20.   I bequeath all my freehold lands and tenements where soever to my daughter Elizabeth Fillmer and her heirs; for default of issue to her, I give
the house and land where Roger Pannell dwelleth to the said
Thomas Leshington, and my said cousins Thomas and John
Fillmer in bail successively, and for the rest, in case of my said
daughter dying without issue, I give them to the said Thomas
and John.   All the residue of my goods I give to my daughter; and I make the said William Allen and Thomas Leshington
my executors, earnestly entreating them to be careful of my
daughter.   (signed) Edward Fillmer.   Witnesses: John
Wheately, scr., Willm Goddard.   My will is that my executors shall deliver my estate to my daughter at her age of 21.
7 February 1651 (-2) I, the said Edward Fillmer, of Sittingborne, mercer, will that my former will and testament shall
stand in full force, except that whereas I appointed Mr. William Allen one of my executors, my mind now is that the said
William Allen shall not any ways intermeddle therein, but that
the other executor by me named shall by my sole executor;
and I give to the said William Allen 10s.   To my brother
William Fillmer, an annuity of £5.   My mind is that my
faithful servant Thomas Lushington shall have my cherry
garden commonly called Butts garden in Sittingborne, until

my daughter Elizabeth accomplish her age of 19 years, and for a term of 20 years after, if he will, at a rent of £20, payable half to my wife Ellen, half to my daughter.   And my wife, and daughter shall yearly have delivered to them 3 bushels of cherries of the choicest of the fruit, and shall have free liberty with their friends to walk in the said ground, and take and eat of the fruit upon the trees there growing at their will and pleasures.   I devise to my daughter my messuage or inn called The Adam and Eve in Sittingborne, immediately after she accomplishes her age of 19.   (signed) Edward Fillmer.   Witnesses: John Hurlstone his mark; Willm. Bowell.   Proved by Thomas Lesington the executor named. *Brent*, 216.

VIRGINIA GLEANING IN ENGLAND.

THOMAS ATKINS of Chard, county Somerset, being aged but of good and perfect memory. Will 10 August 1641; proved 20 July 1653. I give my body to be buried in the churchyard of Chard according to the discretion of my friends. All such implements and household stuff as my wife Elizabeth had before I married her, I wholly bequeath and redeliver to her again. Out of my own proper goods I bequeath unto Anna Sellwood, my daughter, my bedstead now standing in the parlour, with the truckle bedstead under him. To Mathew Sellwood, my grandchild and godson, my small square table board standing in the hall. To Sarah Sellwood, my grandchild, my small chest. All the rest of my own proper goods I bequeath to Thomas Sellwood and Abraham Sellwood, whom I ordain my executors, provided that all the goods and chattels that were bequeathed to me by Elizabeth Atkins, my aunt deceased, shall remain to the use of my wife, to use with her own, as formerly she hath done, without any voluntary spoil thereof, for such time as she doth remain my widow. I do appoint to be my overseers in trust for the benefit of my executors, my brother William Atkins and my cousin William Atkins the younger, desiring them of their loves, as much as in them lies, that this my will may be performed according to my true intent and meaning. Per me Thomas Atkins. Witnesses: John Boyle, Amfusten Walker. Proved by Thomas Sellwood one of the executors named, with power reserved to grant a like commission to the abovesaid Abraham Sellwood *Brent*, 166.

John Atkins, of Chard, Somerset, merchant, died in 1636. His will, published in this Magazine XI, 150, shows that he had a grandson, John Atkins, then living in Virginia. The will also names a brother Thomas Atkins, probably the testator above.]

From Vol. XXIV, No. 3 (July 1916), p. 261.

WILLIAM BEDELL, of greate Catworth in the Countie of Hunt., Gent., Dated 27 May 1612. Proved 6 July 1612. My bodie to bee buried in the Chauncell of great Catworth aforesaid And as concerninge the disposition of my landes, Tenements, and Hereditaments. I doe devise as followeth: All the Ferme called the Brooke end Ferme in Catsworth with all landes, Tenemts, and hereditamts. thereunto belonging, nowe in the tenure of Silvester Bedell my sonne, and all those twoe Cottages in the tenure of Michaell Smith and Edward Kinge, to my sonne George Bedell. To hold the same during the life of Elizabeth my wyfe And after her decease the same to Henry Bedell my sonne and to the heires males of his body, and for want of such issue to George Bedell my sonne and to the heires males of his body, and for want of such yssue to Francis Bedell my sonne and the heires males of his body, and for want of such yssue to Silvester Bedell, my eldest sonne and the heires males of his body, and for want of such yssue to the right heires of mee the said William Bedell for ever. All the residue of my messuages, houses, landes, and Hereditaments, in the Towne parish and Feildes of great Catworth aforesd. in the Counties of Hunt, and Northampton to my wife Elizabeth during her lyfe and after her decease the same to my said sonne George Bedell and to the heires males of his body. And for default of such yssue then to Henry Bedell my sonne, and to the heires males of his body And for default of such yssue then to Francis Bedell my sonne and to the heires males of his body. And for default of such yssue then to Silvester Bedell my sonne and to the heires males of his body. And for default of such yssue to the right heires of mee forever. All that my wood and woodgrounds in the parish of Ellington and my meadowe and meadowe grounde in Waybridge meadowe in the parish of Awconburye and my Closes in the parish of Brington in the Countie of Hunt, to my said wife Elizabeth during her lyfe, and after her decease to my said Sonne George Bedell and to the heires males of his body. And for want of such yssue to Henry Bedell my sonne and to the heires males of his body. And for want of such yssue to Francis Bedell my sonne and to the heires males of his body. And for want of such yssue then to Silvester Bedell my sonne and to the

400

heires males of his body. And for default of such yssue then to the use of the right heires of mee for ever. Also to my said wife Elizabeth, my two Cottages with the landes thereunto belonging in Bythorne in the said County of Hunt, during her lyfe, and after her decease to my grandchild Willm Bedell sonne of my said sonne Sylvester Bedell and to the heires males of his body.

And whereas I have reserved certain pastures and inclosed groundes called Moldesworth olde als Moldesworth wolde in Moldesworth in the County of Hunt. for the terme of my lyfe and twelve yeares after my decease, as appeareth in the conveyance betweene my brother in lawe Mr James Pickering and me, my will is that all my stocke of Cattell going upon the said groundes shalbe sould towards the payment of my debts. And that the groundes and Closes shalbe given to Elizabeth my wife.

To my daughters Dorothy and Jane Bedell, one hundred poundes a peece. I will that all my Writings concerninge my landes in Kymbolton shalbe kept by my wife unto the use of my Executors. . . . . And my said landes, Tenements, and Hereditaments, in the towne and parish of Kymbolton, aforesaid, in the County of Hunt. to my Executors and their heires to be sold by them for the payinge of my debtes, (except that Messuage wherein widdow Carter now dwelleth, which I give to said sonne Francis Bedell and to his heires for ever upon Condicon that hee paye the some of one hundred poundes towardes the payinge of my debtes). And to my said wife Elizabeth that Tenement in Moldesworth olde wherein–Petiver nowe dwelleth and the Close there called Petivers Yarde containing by estimacon eight acres and also that other Close there called Horse Close containing by estimacon xxiiij acres.

To my Cosen Bate and his wyfe, Tenn shillings apeece.

To such Children as my sonne in lawe Mr Henry Godfrey hath by my daughter Ann, deceased, twenty marks, to be equally devided amongst them. And to my said sonne in lawe Henry Godfrey his wife that nowe is, tenne shillings. And to their lytle sonne Henry Godfrey tenn shillings.

To my daughter Bedell, the wife of my sonne Silvester Bedell, Tenn shillings. "And to my grandchild Willm Bedell, twentie shillings and to the rest of their Children, tenne shillings apeece."

To my daughter Elizabeth Robinson twentie shillings.

To my sonne in lawe Richard Dixey and Bridgett his wyfe, my daughter Twenty shillings apeece, and to every one of their Children, tenne shillings apeece.

To my twoe sonnes Gabriell Bedell and John Bedell, Five poundes a peece.

"To Sr Thomas Bedell xxvs. and to my Nephew Capell Bedell his sonne, tenne shillings. And to every of the Children of my brother Sr John Bedell tenn shillings a peece other then to the said Sr Thomas Bedell."

My will is that George Bedell my sonne shall remaine with my wyfe and have his meate and drinke and lodgeinge free, "to the end hee may loke to her husbandry and bee a good husband for her profitt." I have in my yron Chest in great Cattworth thirty poundes and also a gold ringe having my seale of Armes uppon it, which was my fathers. I give thereof to my said wife one peece of gold beinge a "portigne," to my said sonne Silvester one other "portagne". and also the said gold ringe.

To my sonne Petitt and my daughter Petitt, twenty shillings apeece, And to every of the Children of my said daughter Petitt, tenne shillings a peece, And to every of the Children of my said daughter Pettitt tenne shillings a peece.

To my sonne Hawes and Mary my daughter his wife, twenty shillings apeece, and to my other Children George, Henry, Dorothy and Jane, twenty shillings apeece.

To my Cosen Mr Gabriell Clarke, tenn shillings. To Mr Mosley and his wyfe, Five shillings a peece. To the Towne of Hamton for the use of the poore, Five poundes. And to the towne of greate Catworth other Five poundes to the use of the poore. And to the towne of Moldesworth other Five poundes to the use of the poore. To the townes of Brington, Laighton, Stowe, Tilbroke, lytle Catworth and Covington to the uses of the poore, Five shillings apeece to every of the said townes. To my godchildren xijd a peece (other then to Willm Mosley) my godsonne to whom I give Twenty shillings. To every of my servants, Five shillings apeece. To the poore of great Catworth, Twenty shillings to be distributed amongst them on the daye of my buriall.

Executors. my said wife Elizabeth Bedell and my sonnes George Bedell and Francis Bedell.

Overseers. Sr John Bedell, my brother, and my brother in lawe, Mr Thomas Wightman and my said sonne in lawe Mr Henry Godfrey.

Residuary Legatees. my said Executors.

Thomas Whitman, Thomas Emery, Gabriell Clarke, Brudenell Mosley: Witnesses.

Proved 6 July 1612 by the Executors named. *64 Fenner.*

[Dorothy, daughter of William Bedell, the testator, who, in the Huntingtonshire Visitation of 1613, is styled "of Moldsworth," married first, Edward Burwell, of Harlington, Bedfordshire (and was mother of Lewis Burwell, emigrant to Virginia) and secondly Roger Wingate, Esq. of Bedfordshire, who was Treasurer of Virginia 1639-1641. The sons Gabriel and John were probably in Virginia. Gabriel and John Beadle (a frequently used spelling of Bedell) came in the Second Supply in 1608, and Captain Smith, who soon afterwards took Gabriel on an expedition, called him "a gallant" and "a proper gentleman." John and Gabriel Bedell were members of the Virginia Company. Sr John Bedell whose will follows, was brother of William Bedell, above, and Sir John was a son of Sir John. See also Keith's *Ancestry of Benjamin Harrison,* pp. 34, 35.]

SR JOHN BEDELL of Hamerton in the Countie of Hunt, knight. Dated 25 Feb. 1612-13. Proved 23 Apr. 1613. To my sonne Henry Bedell, All those my Messuages, Fermes, Cottages, Closes, landes, Tenements medowes and hereditaments in Steple Giddinge in the Countie of Hunt, to the said Henry Bedell and to his heires for ever. And upon Condicon that he shall not Convaie the same to any person or persons, one Annuytie of Twentie poundes to be taken out of my Mannor of Wolley wth thappurtenances in the Countie of Hunt.

To John Bedell, my sonne, All that my Mannor of Wolley, and all my messuages, Fermes, Cottages, laandes, tenements, and hereditaments in Wolley aforesaid, And all my meadowes, landes, Tenements, and hereditaments in Anconburie in the said Countie of Hunt, And the Donation, free disposicon and right of pronage of the Rectorie, pishe Churche, and psonage of Wolley. And the donation of the Rectorie, parish Church, and parsonage of Thurning in the said Countie of Hunt. The said Annuytie of Twentie poundes given to my said sonne Henry out of the Mannor. of Wolley accepted. To the said John Bedell and to his heires for ever.

And whereas I have purchased of my sonne Sr Thomas Bedell certen landes in Cottesbroke conteyninge fyftene acres more or lesse. In Condicon my said sonne be pleased to accept the same in satisfaccon of his porcon of my goods I doe give unto him all the said fiftene acres, to hold to him and his heires for ever. To Capell Bedell, sonne of my said sonne Sr Thomas Bedell, my Bason and Ewer of Silver

To my daughter Francis Bedell, the some of foure hundred poundes, and all my howsehold stuffe in my house in Hamerton aforesaid. And whereas there is Due to me by my sonne in lawe Mr George Catesbie upon a statute the some of Threescore poundes. I doe forgive the said Debt, and will that my Eexecutor shall deliver unto him the said statute to be cancelled. And upon Condicon that my saide sonne Catesbie doe not molest or troble my Executor I doe give unto everie of the Children of my said sonne and daughter Catesbie nowe livinge wch shall accomplish the age of one and Twentie yeres. Twentie poundes a peece, to be paid unto them as they accomplish their severall ages of one and Twentie yeares.

To every of the Children of my sonne in lawe Sr Seymor Knightley and my Daughter Dorothie his wife nowe livinge wch shall accomplish the age of one and twentie yeares, Twentie poundes a peece to be paide unto them severall when they shall accomplish the ages of one and Twentie yeares.

Towardes the repaire of the Church of Hamerton, Five poundes, To the poore people in Hamerton, aforesaid, fourtie shillings. To the poore people of Buckworth, Laighton, Old-weston, Steple Gidding and Coppingford, To each Townshipp, Twentie shillings a peece, to be distributed wth the adivce of my *"Tennt (sic), *[Tenant?] Phillipp Hustwhatt of Wolley aforesaid.

To every one of my yeoman servants, that have dwelt with me two yeares, Fortie shillings a peece And to everie one of my

maide servants wch have dwelt with me one yeare.   Five shillings a peece.

Residuary Legatee and Sole Executor, my said sonne John
Bedell.   Supervisor, my said sonne Henrie Bedell.

RO: STEVENS ·)   Witness.

Proved 23 April 1613 by the Sole Executor named.   28 *Capell.*

SIR THOMAS BEDELL, Knighte, *of Hammerton, Hunts.
Dated 5 July 1613.   Administration 21 July 1613.
*Pro Act Book.

To be interred in Hammerton in the Countie of Huntingdon
in the churche there at the feete of my Fathers Interment.

I commend the Tuition and guardianshipp of my sonne
Capell Bedell, during his minority to Sir Arthur Capell, Knighte,
his grandfather.   I will that all the debtes which I owe be dulye
payed: to Mr Woodrooffe at the Golden Bell in Cheapeside,
twelve poundes.

To my brother Henrye Beadle, threescore poundes.   "To
my brother John Bedell, the debts (sic) touching which I re-
ferre my selfe to my specialties sealed to hym."   I have in the
handes of my cosin William Smithe a bond for the satisfying
of twoe thousand poundes with the Interest which is due to me
from the Companye of the Adventurers to East India.

All my goods Cattells, moveable and unmoveable reall or
personall of what nature soever, to my said sonne Capell Bedell.
And for the ymploying and disposing of all my sayed goods to
the best benefitt of my sayd sonne during his minority, I doe
appointe Sir Arthur Capell to take the Chardge.   Out of which
sayd goods I doe except suche parte as I shall hereafter dispose
of vizt:

To my Cozen Silvester Bedell, one guilt bowle with a Cover.
To my brother Harry Bedell, one hundred poundes.   To my
brother John Bedell, twoe hundred poundes and twoe gueld-
inges which I nowe have in the Citie of London.   To my Sister
Bridget Catesbye, one hundred pounds.   To my Sister Dame
Dorothie Knighteley, one hundred poundes.   To my Sister
Francis Bedell, one hundred poundes.   To Sr Arthur Capell
Knighte, one Bason and an Ewer of Silver, twoe Salts of Silver,

405

three Silver Bolles, twelve silver spoones, and One hundred poundes. To my Cosin Mr Henry Smithe, Doctor of phisicke, Twelve peeces of gould of twentie and twoe shillings the peece. To Mr John Bignett, Minister at Hamerton, fyve poundes. To John Baker, tenne poundes. To Thomas Else, my servant, tenne poundes. To my servant John Hill, fower poundes. To John Tall, of Woolley in Huntingdonshire, a Sorrell nagg which I have at Hammerton. To Moncke and Woodall, my twoe Sheppards at Hammerton, fyve poundes a peece. To my servant Richard Allen, fortie shillings. To my servant, Thomas Brilston, fyve poundes, whome I doe entreate Sr Arthur Capell to receyve into his service. To John Frier, my servant, fortye shillings. To my servant, Thomas Pitman, fower poundes. To my servant, Solomon Johnson, tenne poundes. To every of Sr Arthur Capells Children a peece of gould of twoe and twentie shillings. To my brother in lawe Mr Arthur Capell, a blacke Cloathe cloake lyned with plush. To the poore Inhabitants of Hammerton, fyve poundes. And to the poore Inhabitants uppon my parte of the Land in Cottesbrooke, tenne poundes. To the Reparacon and use of the Parish Churche of Hammerton, fyve poundes. To the Reparacon of the parishe churche of Cottesbroke, fyve pound To the children of both my Sisters the Ladye Knighteley and my Sister Catesbye. to every of them a peece of gould of twoe and twentie shillings. To Sr Francis Canlton [Caulton], Knighte, fyve poundes.

Sole Executor, my said sonne Capell Bedell.

Thomas Cannon, Henry Smithe, Maurice Canon, Solomon Johnson, Johane Bayhe, Witnesses.

21 July 1613. Administration of the goods etc. of the late Sr Thomas Bedell Knight, granted to Sr Arthur Capell, Knight, during the minority of Capell Bedell the Exor named. **87** *Capell.*

JOHN BELFIELD of Paignton in the Countie of Devon. gent. Dated 24 Feb. 14 Jas. Proved 4 July 1617.

My bodie to be buried in the Church of Paington.

To the poore of the parish of Paington, the some of fower poundes, to bee disposed by the discreacon of David Davies, vicker of Paington and Allen Belfeilde my sonne.

To Allen Belfeild, my sonne and Amies Bickford, daughter of Gregory Bickford of Rattery whome the said Allen intendeth to take to wife, all those cloases of land called or knowne by the name of the North Kill parke. And alsoe one other Cloase of land called the plaine Close before Huckwill "Yeat" [?Yeat: that] with all and singuler thappurtenaunces "which before this tyme unto the said two Closes of land were allotted and laid out and were parcell of Goodrington parke" all wch premisses doe containe *[yt: it] by estimacon threescore and six acres of land be *yt more or lesse and are seituate within the parish of Paington aforesaid, to have and to hold unto the said Allen Belfeild and Ames Bickford and their assignes duringe the lives of John Belfeild the younger, Richard Belfeild and Suzan Belfeild Children of the said John Belfeild thelder and every of them longest livinge the said Allen Belfeild and Ames Bickford payeinge therefore all such Rentes and agreementes as the said John Belfeild and his assignes or any of them are bounde to pay and performe for the same during the said term.

I will that my sonne Allen Belfeild shall demise and lease unto John Belfeild the younger, my sonne, "Flatchers bargaine" and "Fosses Browne Parkes," for terme of two lives in revercon of the lives alreadie in possession by deed sufficiente in the lawe of which twoe lives the said John to be one. My sonne Allen shall lykewise lease unto Richard Belfield, my sonne, two lives in one Tenemente called Brownswill otherwise Browneswill lying in Holberton in revertion of the state alreadie in the same graunted by deede sufficiente in the lawe of which two lives the said Richard to be one.

To Catherin, my daughter, the some of five poundes.

To Margaret Belfeild, my daughter, one hundred poundes.

To my daughter Joane Belfeild, the some of one hundred poundes to be paide to each of them at their marriage daies.

To each of the Children of my daughters, vizt. Marie, Catherine, and Cicellie, fower Ewes and foure lambes.

To my daughter Suzan, her childe, yf she be with child, fower Ewes and fower lambes.

Residuary Legatee and Sole Executrix, Margarett my wife.

Davide Davies "Vicario de Paington," Edward Sweatland and Allen Belfeild, Jacob Emott, Witnesses.

Proved 4 July 1617 by the Sole Executrix named.   74 *Weldon*.

[In a note to Worthy's *Devonshire Wills*, there is reference to a Toby Belfield, clothier, who was a witness to the will of Wm Adam of Paignton, 1688. Worthy states that subsequently the Belfields acquired property at Paignton, known as "Primley" by marriage with Finney and the manor of Leworth in the parish of Heatherington. In Paignton Church is a memorial inscription to Allan Belfield, 1800. The latter endowed a school at Paignton with the sum of £1000. John Finney Belfield, son of Rev. Finney Belfield, succeeded to Primley and other property at Paignton in 1858. The will proved here gives much earlier information in regard to the family. The index to Devonshire wills, administrations and estate accounts in the Consistory Court of the Bishop of Exeter (Harlein Society, Vol. II) contains references to the following: Alane Belfield, of Mauldon, 1548; Allan Belfield, Paignton, 1715; Allen Belfield (reference to p. 23. but not there); Elizabeth Belfield, Paignton, 1640; John Belfield, Paignton, 1567; Margaret Belfield, Paignton, 1639; Richard Belfield, Paignton, 1589; Richard Belfield, Paignton, 1664; Thomas Belfield, Chardleigh, 1669; Tobias Belfield, Paignton, 1707; Tobias Belfield, Paignton, 1748; Tobye Belfield, Paignton, 1626; William Belfield, Paignton, 1593, and William Belfield, Paignton, 1666. The will of Thomas Belffylde or Belfield, Paignton, 1573 is also noted. Dr. Joseph Belfield emigrated from England and settled in Richmond County, Va., prior to 1707. His grandson John Belfield, born 1725, left a short account of the family in which he stated that Dr. Joseph Belfield was son of John Belfield of England. This John Belfield would have been born about 1635. Dr. Belfield was the ancestor of a well-known Virginia family. It would seem from the information here given that any one especially interested might with the aid of a competent English genealogist, probably trace the ancestry of the emigrant.]

VIRGINIA GLEANINGS IN ENGLAND.

(Contributed by Leo Culleton, 92 Piccadilly, London, W, and
the late Lothrop Withington.)
(Continued)

JOHN BENSKYN, Citizen and Vintener of London.

Dated 15 Nov. 1617   Proved 28 Nov. 1617.

My bodie to be buried within the parish Church of St. Magnus
the martir, London whereof I am a parishioner. To the poore
of the said parish of St Magnus the martir, neere London Bridge,
Forty shillings. To my Brother Thomas Benskyn of Sallowe
in the Countie of Nott, yeoman, Tenne poundes. To my
Brother Raph Benskyn, Fyfteene pounds. To my sister
Margaret Pick, wief of William Pick of great Dawlby in the
County of Leic, husbondman, Fyve pounds. To her daughter
Hanna, Forty shillings. To my sister Sara Wyatt, wief of
Thomas Wyatt of Thrummiston [? Thurmaston] in the said
County of Leic, husbondman, Tenne poundes. And to her
three Children Forty shillings a peece. To every one of the
Eight Children of my said Brother Thomas Benskyn, Forty
shillings a peece. To my sister Martha Hoden, wief of Robert
Hoden, Citizen and Dyer of London, Tenne poundes. To my
Father in lawe, Nicholas Oesley, Fyve pounds. To my sister
in lawe, Ellen Oesley, Tenne pounds. To Judith Smyth,
Widdowe, whoe nurseth my Child, Twenty shillings. To my
Cosen Sibbell Pye, wyfe of Henry Pye, Fortie shillings. To
my freinds Mr Richard Sleigh, Citizen and Vintner of London,
to Mr Frances Benbowe, to my Aunt Merrick, to my Cosen
Anne Poole and unto her mother Mary Overton, Forty shillings

From Vol. XXIV, No. 4 (Oct. 1916), p. 379.

a peece to make them Ringes. To my servants, Edward Johnson, John Mills and Alice Tewks, Fortie shillings a peece. To my Child Frances [Francis?] Benskyn, the sume of two hundred and Fiftie pounds. And unto the Child wherewith my wife nowe goeth, the like sume of two hundred and Fifty poundes. And if my said wife shall nowe goe with more than one Child then the same twoe porcons of two hundred and Fifty poundes shalbe and remayne equally amongst my said Children. And the said legacies to be paide unto them at the age or ages of one and twentie yeares of my sonne or sonnes, and at the age or ages of one and Twentie yeares or Dayes of marriages, first happening, of my Daughter or Daughters. And whereas I am seised of certen lands and hereditamts in Suyston als Seston als Sytheston, in the Countie of Leic. my will is that my Executrix and Overseers hereafter named shall make sale thereof to the most benefytt they can, For and towardes the payment of such Debts and summes of money as I owe.

Residuary Legatee and Sole Executrix. my wife, Katherin Benskyn. Overseers: my Unckle Sr Jno Merricke of London, Knight, and Jno Poole, Citizen and Mercer of London.

James Goodyer, Scr., John Bludworth and Christopher Fanell, (servt to the said James Goodyer, Scr.) Witnesses.

Proved 28 Nov. 1617 by Catherine Benskyn, the relict and Sole Executrix named.

P. C. C. 102 Weldon.

[The wills of Francis Benskin, Esq. of St. Martins in the Fields, proved Jan. 2, 1691, and of his son Henry Benskin, "lately arrived in England from the plantation of Virginia," proved Oct. 19, 1692, are in Waters' Gleanings. The latter had two daughters, Mary wife of William Harman of New Kent Co. and Frances wife of William Marston of James City County. Benskin appeared later as a Christian name among the Marstons and their descendants. It is possible that John Benskin, the testator above was father of Francis Benskin.]

HENRY BUSHRODE of Craford in the Countie of Dorset, yeoman.

Dated 10 Sept. 1612.   Proved 12 July 1614.

To be buried in the Churchyarde of this same parish. To the Churche of the same parish, sixe shillings eight pence. To the

410

poore of the same parish, Five poundes. To the poore of little Craford, Twentie shillings. To the poore of Keniston, Twentie shillings. To Henry Brushrode, the sonne of Robert Bushrode of Shireborne late deceased, Thirtie poundes, to be paid him at the age of one and Twentie Yeares. To his other two sonnes, Twentie pounds, a peece, to be paid at the age of one and twentie yeares. To the youngest of my brother John Bushrods daughters, of Tawnton, late deceased, Twentie poundes. To Mary Bushrode, my kinswoman, Ten poundes. To my Cosen William Bushrode, Tenne poundes. To the Children of Robert Rapsham of Shireborne, Fortie shillings a peece. To Henry Roberts, Fortie shillings. To George Schovell, the sonne of George Schovell, six poundes, and two heyfers which are nowe at pasture with William Hughes. To the Children of John Bushrode, late of Shireborne, Five poundes a peece, to be paid at the age of twentie and one yeares. Residuary Legatee and Sole Executor. Richard Bushrode* of Dorchester.

Thomas Frampton and George Batt, Witnesses.

To my brother William Bushrode, Five poundes. To my godchildren, two sheepe a peece.

Proved 12 July 1614, by the Sole Executor *named.

*[No relationship given].

[In Vol. XXIII, 48, this magazine, was printed the will of Samuel Bushrod, of the County of Dorset, clothier, proved June 1, 1647, who seems to have been brother of Richard and Thomas Bushrod the emigrants to Virginia. This Henry Bushrod was evidently nearly related to Samuel. In each will is mention of members of the Scovell family.]

Mr. Martin Jefferson an Enlish man merchant adventurer living in Rotterdam. Will 1 October 1650; proved 28 October 1651. Appears before John Froost notary public admitted by the Court of Holland and left all his property and the guardianship of his children to his wife Weyntge Jefferson. Witnesses: William Ende Jongh and Martine Alma my clerks. A. Sommetradt Not: Pub: 1651 & H. de Custer Not: Pub: 1651 swear that John Frost is a notary and that instruments affected before him are legal and attesting the translation appears Josua

Mainet not: pub: 1651. Proved by Wentgen Jefferson **the** relict. *Grey*, 188.

[This abstract and the one following have been printed to preserve possible clues for tracing the Jefferson family. The John Jefferson, whose will follows, may have been the one who was a member of the **Va.** House of Burgesses in 1619.,

---

JOHN JEFFERSON the elder of the parish of St. Peter ad Vincula within the Tower of London, citizen and bowyer of London. Will 26 December 1645; proved 30 October 1647. I give to my son John Jefferson my livery gown and all my wearing apparel whatsoever, and all my bows, bowstaves, working tools, and other implements of archery, together with my seal ring. To Mary Jefferson, my said son's daughter, my Cyprus desk. To my daughter Elizabeth Tyrer my ring set with a blue stone and other stones. To my daughter Dorothy Watkins my gold ring that was my Wife's wedding ring. All other my rings I give to my son Nathaniell Jefferson. To each of my aforesaid four children, a silver spoon apiece. I will that all my beds, bedding, and household stuff shall be duly and justly appraised, and indifferently shared into four equal parts, one part whereof I give to my said son John, one other part equally amongst my grandchildren, children of my said son Nathaniel, one other part amongst the children of my daughter Elizabeth, and the other amongst the children of my daughter Dorothy. The parts given to all the children shall remain in the custody of my son Nathaniel, and shalbe by him kept or sold to the best profit he can for the benefit of the said children at their respective ages of 21 or marriage. All the rest of my goods I give amongst all my said grandchildren, viz., the children of my said two sons and two daughters, to be divided amongst them at their ages of 21 or marriage. I appoint my son Nathaniel Jefferson to be my full executor. (signed) John Jefferson. Witnesses: Joseph Alfort scr., Johes Aurelius, not. pub., Oliver Obery, servant to the said scrivener. Proved by the executor named. *Fines.*

ELIZABETH BRAXTON of the parish of St. Gregory, London, widow. Will 8 April 1652; proved 30 April 1653. I give to my cousin Elizabeth Wilson, and to her brothers John Watson and William Watson, and to my cousins Elizabeth and John Watson, son and daughter of John Watson deceased, 12d. each. To Margaret Guy 10s. to make her a ring. To Mr. Thomas Bruise, junior, a little gold purse and an enammelled ring with a death's head on it. To my maidservant Christian Lucas my best wearing apparel, and to my maidservant Sara Underwood my ordinary wearing apparel. To my sister Joanne Dawson, my wedding ring. To John Dawson and Ellen, son and daughter of William and Joane Dawson, my two gilt bowls. I make my brother William Dawson, cook, my sole executor; and if any of my kindred (by me not now remembered) shall happen to disturb my executor in the performance of this my will, I give to each of them that shall come in 12d, which legacies I give not unto them to cut them off from what is their due, but to ascertain my executor (as in all conscience I am bound) that he shall not be endangered by any engagements that be upon him concerning me, and to enable him the better to pay my debts, he being very well known to, and better respected amongst my creditors than any other friend that at this time I could make use of. (Signed) Elizabeth Braxton. Witnesses: Richard Hodgekinson, Robt. Gebbins. Proved by the executor named. *Brent*, 298.

[As the name Braxton, or Brexton (the same name) appears so rarely in English records, and as absolutely nothing is known of the English ancestry of the Virginia family, it has been thought worth while to preserve these two wills as possible aids to investigation.]

WILLIAM BREXTON of St. Martin in the Fields, county Middlesex, gent. Will 1 August 1634; proved 28 August 1634. Body to Church of Holy Trinity in Winton. To repair of said church £10. To my brother Richard Brexton £1000 remaining in the custody of Sir Richard Titchbourne Baronett as by Bond in my Custody. Said £1000 to remain in the hands of said Sir Richard for three years after my death and in the meantime if mine executor be so minded to renew the same but not to call it in.

In token of my love to Sir Richard and for many curtesies I have received I give to him £30. To my Lord Weston £30 humbly desiring him to accept the same. To my father and mother and the longest liver of them the lease of a house in the city of Wiston which I bought of Mrs Savage together with the wine licence which I took from Mr. Diggens of the wine office. To my said brother Richard Brexton the sums of money which may accrue upon a Privy Seale made by assignment of Mr. Melvill with Captain Milwoode and Mr. Bedingfield of Gray's Inn. To my said brother the residue of the term of said howse as shall be unexpired after the death of said father and mother. To my sister Ellen Zouche a diamond ring of about £20. To my three brothers Thomas, Cornelius and Francis £40 apiece I release my cousin Mr. Thomas Travers of £13 and all arrears. My said brother Richard sole executor. Mr. Edward Bettes and Mr. William Longland the elder Overseers. To each of them 6s. 8d. Witnesses: Tho. Travers, Hen. Crosse, Thos. Stockton. *Seager, 78.*

WILLIAM CORDEROY of Chuet county Wilts esqre. Will 15 June 1621; proved 4 November 1623. Body to my Chappell in Chuet church. To Lady Church of Sarum 40s. To poor of Chuet 40s. and 10s. to church. To my daughter Annah £400. To my daughter Ellenor £400. My brother Edward Godderde esq my cosen William Sotwell esq and my cosen William Stanton esq to raise money for 12 years on my land, and pay to my son William Corderoy £50 yearly. To my said son all my lands in Chuet Conholt, Langley Mowse, Upham and Wilton for ever. In default then to my son Edward and for default to my son John. My son William sole executor. To my wife and her maid beds bedding etc. and their diet. To my three daughters £20 yearly, i. e. £6. 13s. 4d. apeece. Witnesses: Wm. Corderoy, Andrew Kingsmill, Jasper Mompesson, Edwd Flower. Memorandum. The legacy of £400 (there is no mention of it in body of Will) given by testator to said Bridget Corderoy was stricken out by testator in presence of witnesses 6th January 1622, Wm. Stanton, Ann Arnold, Kingesmill Long, Constance Browne. *Swann, 109.*

[Chester's *Marriage Licenses* shows that "Richard Bernard, of Petsoe, Bucks, widower, aged 26," was granted a license, Nov. 24, 1634, to marry "Anne Corderoy, aged 26, daughter of —— Corderoy Esq.," at St. Andrews-in-the Wardrobe, London. They came afterwards to Va., and in a grant of land to Mrs. Anna Bernard July 2, 1652, appear the names of Ellinor, William and Edward Corderoy, headrights. From the names in the will and the headrights it looks very much as if this William Corderoy was the father of Mrs. Bernard. There are other things which seem to prove that this was indeed the fact. Among the other headrights to the Bernard grant, which has been referred to, were William, Francis and Elizabeth Ironmonger (or Iremonger). In the Salisbury marriage licenses, now in course of publication in the (English) *Genealogist*, it appears that on July 23, 1628 a license was issued for the marriage of Samuel Iremonger of Dennington (Donnington?), Berks., gent., aged 21, and Bridget Corderoy of Chute, Wilts., aged 24. We have therefore the three daughters of William Corderoy, the testator, accounted for. Anna, who married Richard Bernard, Elinor, who came with her sister to Virginia, and Bridget, who married Samuel Iremonger. Evidently Mrs. Iremonger's children came with their aunt to Virginia. There were also others not included among these headrights. In this Magazine XI, 75, 76, are the administrations granted 1681 to Elizabeth (Iremonger) wife of Anthony Evenden, on the estates of her sisters Martha (Iremonger) wife of John Jones, and Ann (Iremonger) Rumney, and her brother Corderoy Ironmonger, all of whóm had died intestate in Virginia.]

From a pedigree printed in *The Genealogist*, XII, 22, and in the *Visitation of Wiltshire*, 1623, edited by Marshall, the following genealogy of the family of Cordray or Corderoy of Chute, Wiltshire, has been compiled.

"Arms: Sable, a chevron or between two mullets of the second in chief and a lion passant ducally crowned of the second in base within a bordure of the third."

THOMAS CORDRAY of Chute, Co. Wilts., gent., married Jane, daughter of —— Gray in Co. Somerset, and by her had issue: 1. Thomas[2], son and heir; 2. Richard; 3. Maude, married Lucas Linton, of Alsford, Co. Hants.

THOMAS[2] CORDRAY of Chute, marr. Jane, daughter and heiress of Roger Sennore of Andover, Co. Southampton (Seamor, according to the *Visitation* of 1623) and had issue: 1. Thomas[3], son and heir; 2. Alys, married first Thomas Bartholomew, of Salisbury, second Robert Elliott, of the same place; 3. Katherin, married William Poton of Colbarwick.

THOMAS[3] CORDRAY of Chute, gent., married Jane, daughter of Thomas Coxwell, of ——, Co. Berks (Thomas Morris, of Coxwell, in the Visitation) and had issue: 1. Edward[4], son and heir married a sister of James Merum, and d. s. p.; 2. William[4]; 3. John; 4. Thomas; 5. Robert; 6. Richard; 7. James; 8. Jeromy; 9. Elizabeth; 10. Jane; 11. Alys; 12. Mary; 13. Jane.

WILLIAM[4] CORDRAY, Esq., of Chute, brother and heir of Edward[4], married Bridget, daughter of Edward Goddard, of Woodhay, in Co. Southampton. Issue: 1. William, Esq., son and heir, aged 22, in 1623; 2. Edward aged 20; 3. John aged 16; 4. Bridget, aged 21; 5. Anna, aged 15; 6. Ellinor, aged 11.]

JOHN CULPEPER of Greenway Courte, county Kent, Esquire. Will 14 December 1635; proved 3 January 1635-6. To be buried in chancel of Hollingbourne Church where Sir Thomas Culpeper shall think fit or most convenient and in such manner as my son Thomas Culpeper shall think fit. To Anne Culpeper my wife all debts owing to her as administratrix to her late husband, except debt owing by the Lord and Lady Lambert which I give to my son Thomas Culpeper. To son John annuity for life of £30 payable by Sir John Culpeper. To daughter Sicely Culpeper £300. To James Medlicott my son in law and Frances Medlicote my daughter 20s. each. Residuary Legatee and Executor: son Thomas. Witnesses: Tho. Culpeper, Alexander Culpeper, John Culpeper, Willm Cragge. *Pile*, 4.

[The testator was evidently nearly related to the Lord Culpeper. A Francis Culpeper of Greenway Court, uncle to the first Lord, died in 1591, leaving a son Sir Thomas Culpeper of Hollingbourne. Lord Fairfax must have had some special cause for attachment to the place for he named his home in Frederick Co., Va. after it.]

ROGER FOWKE of Little Wisley, county Stafford Esq. Will last June 1627; proved 6 May 1630. To be buried in Norton church or if possible in Chancel. To poor of Norton 40s. To eldest son Thomas all evidences and charters and court rolls belonging unto him that concerns the lands in Brewood Norton little Wirley or Pelsall. To my 3 younger sons James, Roger, and Walter Fowke, all my goods and household stuff and make them my executors. *Scroope*, 45.

[Roger Fowke, of Little Wisley, was a kinsman of the Fowkes, of Gunston, and married, in 1570, Joan, daughter of Roger Fowke of Gunston. Her brother Francis was the great grandfather of Gerrard Fowke of Va. and Md.]

GEORGE HOPE of Dodleston, Chester, esquire. Will 4 January 1653-4; proved 15 March 1653-4. I give my body to be buried in the parish church of Hope. I bequeath to my grandchild Mary Hope, towards her preferment and maintenance, £400 within 3 years of my decease. To my grandchild Magdalen, now wife to Sqmuell Cawley Gwersvilt, gent., £200 within 2 years. To my daughter Magdalen, now wife to John Baskervile of Blagdin, £100. To my great grandchild Hugh Roberts the younger £20. To my grandchild Roger Hope an annuity of £20, and a like annuity to my grandchild John Hope, to commence immediately after the decease of their mother Anne Hope. All the rest of my estate, real and personal, I bequeath to my grandchild George Hope, whom I make my executor. (Signed) George Hope. Witnesses: Hugh Roberts, Thomas Rolland, Roger Decke. Proved by the executor. *Brent*, 395.

[Magdalen, daughter of George Hope, of Queens Hope, County Flint, and Dodlester, Co. Chester, Eng., married John Baskerville, of Old Withington, Cheshire, Eng. (1599-1661) and was the mother of John Baskerville, born 1635, who emigrated to York Co., Va., and was ancestor of the family here.]

VIRGINIA GLEANINGS IN ENGLAND.

(Contributed by Leo Culleton, 92 Piccadilly, London, W, and
the late Lothrop Withington.)
(Continued)

WILLIAM CODD of Watringbery in the Countie of Kent,
yeoman
and within the dioces of Rochester.
Dated 14 Nov. 1606   Proved 3 March 1607 [-8]

My bodye to be buryed in the churchyard of Watringbery.
To the poore people at my buryall Two bushells of wheate in
bread. And in money twentie shillinges. To some learned
man to give the people some good lesson at my buryall, sixe
shillinges eighte pence. To my mayd servantes two shillinges
a peece. And to all my men servantes twelve pence a peece.
To Hester, my wife, the best Bedstedle in my owne Chamber,
and the bedstedle in the porche lofte with all the Beddinge belonging. I will that William Codd my sonne when he cometh
to his landes shall pay unto his mother, yf she be then living,
three score poundes. To Hester & Elizabeth my daughters,
two hundred poundes a peece at twentie yeares of age or dayes
of marriage. I will that if Hester my wife happen to dye before
my sonne be one and twentye yeares of age Then Thomas Perri,
gent of Leneham do take my lyving and children till they be of
age or married. And if he be dead or will not take them. Then
my wives brother John Lampord to take them in manner aforesaid. To Hester my daughter & Elizabeth my daughter out
of my land in Nettlestead and East Peckham, sixteene poundes
a yere till my sonne William ys full one and twentie yeres of age
and appoynted by me to enter uppon his lande. To Hester, my
wife the profitt of all my houses and lande in Watryberye or els
where within the Countie of Kent, till my sonne is of age. To

William Codd my sonne, my dwelling house barnes, stables with all other buildings, Landes, meadowes pastures and woodes lying in Watringbery or any other place within the Countie of Kent upon Condition that yf Hester my wife be with childe, of a man childe, then I will him to be baptised by the name of Robert, & William my sonne shall pay unto Robert my sonne (yf any be) thirteene poundes six shillinges and eight pence a yeare for ever. And yf my wife be with Childe of a mayde childe Then I will her name to be Anne. And William, my sonne to pay unto Anne (yf any be) one hundred poundes at twentye yeares of age.

Residuary Legatee and Sole Executor: William Codd my sonne.

Supervisors: Thomas Perri, gent, John Lamport & Thomas Ayarste, gent of West Malynge.

John Brown his marke, Walter Brovoke his marke, William Panckas his marke, Witnesses.

3 March 1607 Administration granted to Hester Codd, relict of said deceased during the minority of William Codd the Executor named. 19 *Windebank.*

JAMES CODD of Watringburie in the Countie of Kent, gent.

Dated 14 Nov. 1611   Proved 18 Nov. 1611.

To WILLIAM CODD, my eldest sonne, All my landes Tenements and hereditaments scituate in Watringburie aforesaid. To have and to holde the same unto the saide William his heires and assignes for ever from and after the decease of Constance my nowe wife * * .   Also all my wood land in East mawlinge in Countie Kent, after he shall have come to the age of twentye one.

To Richard, my second sonne, All my Landes Tenements and hereditaments with the appurtennes thereto belonging scituate in Pemburye in the said County of Kent. * * unto the said Richard and to his heires and assignes for ever, after he shall have accomplished his age of Twentie one. To my youngest sonne Henrie Codd, all my landes tenements and hereditaments scituate in Towne Sutton als Sutton Valence in the said Countie of Kent.** to the said Henrie, his heires and assignes for ever from and after the decease of my wife Constance. Also all my landes and tenements scituate in Easte Farley in the said Countie of Kent.** from and after he shall have accomplished his age of twentye one. To my daughter Jane, One hundred and thirtie poundes, to be paide unto her when she shall accomplish her age of Twentie and one yeares or daie of marriage. To my daughter Anne, One hundred and thirtie poundes to be paide unto her when she shall accomplish her age of Twentie and one yeares or daie of marriage. To my daughter Bridgett, One hundred and thirtie poundes, to be paide likewise to her at the same age, or daie of marriage. Provided alwaies that if my wife Constance shall happen to be nowe with childe. Then fowerscore and tenne pounds shalbe deducted out of my said daughter's porcons, and paide to such childe or children as my said wife shall happen nowe to goe with. * all when he she or they shall accomplish their lawfull age of Twentie and one yeares or be married. To the poore of Watringburie, Twentie shillinges. To the poore of Easte Mawlinge, Tenne shillinges. To my Mother Agnes Codd, Thirtie shillinges to buye her a ringe. To my brother Thomas Codd, Twentie shillinges to buye him a Ringe. To my sister Katherine Perry, Twentie shillinges to buye her a ringe. To my cozen Julyan Charleton, sixteene shillinges to buye her twoe silver spoones. To my freindes Henry Wood, Judith his wife and Elizabeth Wood their daughter, Three poundes to buye each of them a Ringe of golde. To Katherine Fuller & Ellen Puplett, Tenne shillinges a peece.

Residuary Legatee and Sole Executrix: Constance my wife.

Overseers: my brothers Thomas Perry & "Shemaia" Selherst.

Lawrence Mansfeild, Henry Wood & John Ashenden, Scr., Witnesses.

Proved 18 Nov. 1611 by the Execturix named. 94 *Wood.*

[The mention of land at East Molling in the will of James Codd, above, and in the will of William Codd (1652), published in this Magazine XXIII, 382, makes it probable that the former was the father of the latter, who was father of St. Leger Codd of Virginia and Maryland. William Codd (1606) above may have been the brother of James.]

THOMAS CHICHELEY of Wimple in the Countie of Cambridge, Knight.

Dated 29 Oct. 1616   Proved 27 Nov. 1616.

First, my will is that my Executors shall soe soone as they maye convenientlie, take and renue the lease of the Mannor or farme of Malton in the Countie of Cambridge with the appurtenncs, of the Master and Fellowes of Christes Colledge in Cambridge in the proper names of my said Executors and to them their heires and assignes for and duringe the lives of the Lady Dorothy Kempe my Mother-in-lawe, Thomas Chicheley & Henry Chicheley my sonnes and for and duringe the life of the survivor of them for which I have alreddie contracted with the said Master and Fellowes of the said Collidge. And my will is that my Executors shall Keepe the lease in their handes untill my heir male shall accomplish his full age of one and twentie yeares to the uses and purposes hereafter expressed. Also my said Executors shall take in their names the lease of the parsonage of Arrington in the said Countie of Cambridge for which I have already contracted with the same Master, Fellowes and Schollers for soe longe tyme as they may grant. And my said Executors shall retayne the lease in their handes to the uses and purposes hereafter expressed untill my heir male shall come of age.*** To my said Executors, twoe partes of my mannor of Wimple in the said Countie of Cambridge and all my other Landes tenements leases and hereditaments whatsoever in the Realme of England into three partes to be devided untill my said heir male shall accomplish his full age. Also to my said Executors, all my plate, jewells household stuffe goods and Chattles whatsoever.*** to the uses and purposes that my said Executors with the aforesaid goodes and Chattles and with the rents and profitts of the aforesaid Mannor Landes Tenements hereditaments and leases shall pay and discharge all my debts, to distribute amonge the poore of Wimple, Tenne poundes and to the poore of Arrington, five pounds, and to the poore of Weady, five poundes and to mayntaine and bring up my younger Children And when my heir male shall attaine his full age my

421

will is that the aforesaid twoe parts of the Manor of Wymple and of all other my freehould Mannors landes tenements leases and hereditaments, Except the aforesaid leases of Malton and Arrington parsonage and all such land tenements and hereditaments as I latelie bought of Robert Hoods of Wendy, in the said Countie of Cambridge, shalbe and remayne to my said heire male and to his heires for ever.**** And if my Executors cannot, out of the meanes aforesaid provide sufficient portions for every of my said younger Children, then they shall keepe in theire handes the said leases of Malton and Arrington parsonage untill they shall have raysed sufficient portions.*** And afterwards my Executors shall assigne the Residue of their interest in the said leases to my heir male.

Executors: My Wife the Lady Dorothy Chicheley and my brother-in-lawe, William Harrington, Esquire and my Cosen John Piggott Esquire.

Thomas Chicheley, Edward Anngier, George Holder, Paule Kente, Witnesses.

Proved 27 Nov. 1616 by Dorothy Chicheley, one of the Exors name, power reserved to William Harrington and John Piggott. 115 *Cope*.

[Sir Thomas Chichley, of Wimple, or Wimpole, Cambridgeshire, was the father of Sir Thomas Chichley, Master of the Ordinance, and of Sir Henry Chichley, who served as an officer in the Royal Army during the Civil War, came to Virginia in 1649 and as Burgess, Councillor, Deputy-Governor and Governor, was long prominent in the Colony. He married Agatha (Eltonhead) widow of Ralph Wormeley, of "Rosegill," Va., and died Feb. 5, 1682. See this Magazine III, 39; XVII, 144. His mother was Dorothy, daughter of Sir Thomas Kempe, of Olantigh, Kent, and sister of Mary, wife of Sir Dudley Digges, of Chilham, —— two governors of Virginia, Sir Henry Chichley and Edward Digges were first cousins. Mary Chichley, whose will follows was a sister of Sir Thomas the elder.]

———————

MARY CHICHELEY, of Wymple in the Countie of Cambridge, Spinster.

Dated 1 March 1616 [-17]   Proved 3 June 1617.

To be buried in the Chappell to the Church in Wymple. To the poore Inhabitants in Wimple, Five poundes. To the poore in Arington, Fifty shillings and to the poore in Wendy, fifty shillings. To my mother Mris Anne St. John, one hundred

poundes.   To my sister the Lady Dorothie Chicheley, my sister
Elizabeth Pinchebacke, my brother William Harrington Esq.,
my sister Dorothie his wife and to my brother John Chicheley,
either and everie of them, Fourtie poundes.   To my brother
Devereux Chichley, one hundred poundes.   To my brother
Oliver St. John, and to my sister Anne St. John, either of them,
Twenty poundes.   To my Cosyns, Thomas Chichley, Dorothie
Chichley, Jane Chichley, Henrye Chichley & John Chichley,
the Children of my brother Sr Thomas Chichley, Knight late
deceased, everie of them, Twenty poundes.   And to my Cosyn
and Goddaughter Anne Chichley, fourtie poundes, to be payde
unto them as they shall accomplish theire age of one and twentye
yeares.   To my Cosin John Pigott, esquire, five poundes to buy
him a Ringe.   And to Mris. Frances Bowyer, three poundes to
buye her a Ringe.   To Mr Edwarde Marshall and to George
Holder either of them, Tenn poundes.   To my Nursse Pincke,
five poundes And to my Mayde Alice [space] three poundes.   I
bequeath Six poundes, to be distributed amongst my sister
Chichley's servants in her howse at the tyme of my death.

Residuary Legatees and Executors: my sister the Lady
Chichley & my brother Devoreux Chichley.

William Hinton, John Hinde, Timothie Atkinson, Witnesses.

Proved 3 June 1617 by Devoreux Chichley, one of the Executors named, power reserved to Dorothie Chichley, the other
Executor.   61 *Weldon*.

HENRY CHURCHILL of Steeple Claydon, county Bucks, gent.
Will 23 May 1651; proved 10 February 1653-4.   I bequeath
to my eldest son Tobias at his age of 24 my mansion house
wherein I now dwell, with my close adjoining called Sand Fur-
long; a parcel called Peartree Hill abutting on the land of Richard Doggett, with the meadow adjoining called the lower part
of Great Riffams; to remain, in default of issue to him, to my
sons Henry, John, Thomas, Joseph, and William successively.
And I charge whichever of my sons shall inherit the premises
to pay to my third daughter Phillis Churchill £.10 yearly for
her maintenance till her age of 21, and then a portion of £200.

I give £200 apiece in like manner to my eldest daughter Anne Churchill my second daughter Marie Churchill and my fourth and youngest daughter Frances Churchill. I give to my son Henry at his age of 24 my close in Steeple Cleydon called Gabrielle Ground. To my sons John and Thomas my pasture called Bushy Close and the meadow called Cowmeade. To my son Joseph, my moiety of the ground called Bournheades. To my son Tobias my freehold land in the common fields of Leighton Buzzard, county Bedford, called Midsomer Plott, and 11 acres of copyhold which I purchased, and my will is that my wife shall surrender to him and his heirs my messuage and land and one cottage wherein the Widow Doggett now dwelleth, all in Leighton Buzzard aforesaid, and I charge these premises with the payment of £300 to William Churchill, my youngest son, at his age of 21, with £10 yearly for his maintenance meanwhile. I bequeath to my godson Henry Churchill, son of my brother Thomas Churchill of Clifton in the parish of Deddington, county Oxon, yeoman, £5. To my godson Henry Churchill, son of John Churchill, late of Steeple Cleydon, deceased, 10s. To the poor of Leighton Buzzard, 40s. at the discretion of the minister, churchwardens, and overseers of the poor. To the poor of Steple Cleydon 40s., one half in bread, the other in money. All the rest of my goods to my wife Phillis Churchill, whom I make my executrix; and I appoint my said brother Thomas Churchill and his eldest son Thomas, my kinsman, Joseph Townesend, son of my brother in law William Townesend of Princes Risborow, county Bucks, and my eldest son Tobias, my overseers. (signed) Henry Churchill. Witnesses: William Fry, the mark of Henry Chamberlaine. Administration granted to the abovesaid Tobias Churchill, the executrix named being then also deceased. *Brent*, 367.

[The mention in this will of a brother living in Oxfordshire, makes it possible that the testator may have been of the same family as William Churchill of Va., who was born at North Aston, Oxfordshire.]

ROBERT CODRINGTON now within the precincts of the Cathedrall Churche of Bristoll, gentle.

Dated 11 Feb 1618.   Proved 7 May 1619.

To my eldest daughter Elizabeth Codrington, Two hundreth

poundes. To Anne Codrington my second daughter, Two hundredth poundes. To Francis, my third daughter, one hundredth poundes. To Susanne, my fourth daughter, Two hundreth poundes. To Dorothie, my fifth daughter, Two hundreth poundes. To Joyce, my sixt daughter, Two hundreth poundes. To Marye, my seaventh and youngest daughter nowe livinge, Three hundreth poundes to be paid within the space of one yeare nexte after the death of Mris Margaret Caple, wife of William Caple of Warrington in the County of Somersett, Esquire. To my sixe younger *sonnes, Tenne poundes a peece quarterly to be paid by my wiffe their mother "or to maintaine them with sufficient meate drinke and apparell, wth good education leavinge her my said wieff free libertie to take choice and at her pleasure to doe which of these she will," during the lyfe of my Father Symon Codrington, of Codrington in the County of Glouc., Esquire. To my eldest sonne John Codrington, a Lease of all woods, underwoods, Groves, and Tymber trees growinge in Chesecome Haynes grove, the Elm Hoye, and Winch haye adjoyninge to the aforesaid manner house, of Codrington granted, Lett and sett by lease unto mee, by and from my said Father Symon Codrington only upon this proviso and Condicon that he my said sonne John Codrington shall paye to my said* sonnes Twentie poundes a peece.

Residuary Legatee and Sole Executrix: Anne, my wyfe.

Overseers: my freinds Sr Thomas Estcoot Knighte, Mr Thomas Joye [Juye?], Gyles Codrington, and John Codrington my brothers.

Edward Greene, "Husey," Thomas Juye, nic: Hely, Witnesses
Proved 7 May 1619 by the Executrix named. [*Not named].
46 *Parker.*

[The testator, like John Codrington, whose will was printed in this Magazine XXIII, 159, was of the family from which came the Codringtons of Barbadoes, one of whom, Henningham Codrington, wife of Dr. Paul Codrington, has many descendants in Virginia.]

EDWARD FLEETE, citizen and —— of London. Will 8 March 1646; proved 12 January 1647-8. St Bennet Shirhog. [Probate Act]. As touching the disposing of all such goods and other estate as God hath lent me in this world, I give unto my daughter

425

Aurelia £400, and a ring with a table diamond, with other [sic] household stuff, which is in a note whereunto I have put my hand. To my daughter Jane, £400, a ring with eight small diamonds, and other household stuff, in the said note. To my loving sister Suzan Younge £100. All the rest of my goods to my four children, equally to be divided among them, to wit, my son Edward, and my three daughters, Judeth, Sarah, and Rachell. I give to my son my two seal rings of gold. To my daughter Judeth a small diamond ring. To my daughter Sarah a ring with a jacinth stone. To my daughter Rachell a ring with a white safier stone. To the poor of the parish where I now dwell, £5. I make my daughter Aurelia, and my friend Mr. Richard Holland my executors. Witnesses: Jonathan Tucke, John Speer. Codicil March the 9th, 1649. For Aurelia Fleete: A ring with a fair table diamond, a suit of table linen of damask, which she shall choose, a pair of childbed sheets, a pair of pillowbeeres to them, and of the small childbed linen a third part, a pillow of purple velvet embroidered with tentwork, a lesser cushion grounded with silver, a suit of hangings with tapistry containing five pieces, a bedstead, a furniture for it of crimson perpetuano, and a window curtain with crimson lace and fringe; a featherbed, boulster and pillows, a pair of blankets, a crimson rug [of] pintatho bordered with satin, a cupboard cloth of kersey, a great chair and six stools trimmed suitable to the bed, a pillow and two cushions of figured satin, and either the chest of drawers or the best trunk, which she pleaseth, a pair of brass andirons, fire shovel, and tongs. For Jane Fleet a ring, etc., and linen as above, the other suit of damask, a bedstead, a furniture of pintatho for a bed, a quilt of the same bordered with satin, a sideboard cloth, and a cupboard cloth, an inward furniture for the bed of white calico edged with bone lace, etc. [as above] (signed) Edward Fleete. Witnesses: Jonathan Tucke, John Speer. Proved by Aurelia Fleet, with power reserved, etc. *Essex*, 4.

[Henry Fleet, who emigrated to Virginia, had a brother Edward Fleet, who may have been the testator above. See this Magazine 11, 70-76, V, 253, 254. If so, this Edward Fleet had at one time lived in Maryland where he was a member of the Assembly in 1638]

VIRGINIA GLEANINGS IN ENGLAND.

(Contributed by Leo Culleton, 92 Picadilly, London, W., and the late Lothrop Withington.)

ROBERT HUNT of the parishe of Heathfield in the Countye of Sussex, Clerke, Vicar of the said parishe.
Dated 20 Nov. 1606.   Proved 14 July 1608.
To Grace Kyne, my nowe Servant and to Elizabeth Milles, my late Servant, 10s eatch.
To Elizabeth my daughter, £30, to be paide to her when she shall come to eighteene yeares.
Also one Tenement with five acres of lande, late being part of the waste or common called Highdoune in Heathfeilde, which I bought of Thomas Pankerst nowe or late of Retherfield.
To my Sonne Thomas, £10, to be paide him at the age of one and twenty years.   Also one tenement and twelve acres of land being in the parish of Warbleton and belonging unto Mr. Thomas Pellam his Mannor of Burwashe which Coppyhold Tenement and Landes I bought of William Stace of Heathfield.
Residuary Legatee and Sole Executrix:—Elizabeth my Wiffe.
Overseer: Mr. Tristram Siclemore.
Provided alwaies yf Elizabeth my said wiffe shall committ the act of incontinency or shalbe be defamed or suspected of anye suche acte, during my life or if after my death before the proving of my will she staie and abide in the same house or other place whatsoever together with John Taylor the eldest Sonne of John Taylor of the parish of Heathfeild.   Then she shall be exclude from being my Executrix and shall loose all other benefitt of this my will, and in her place I appoint Elizabeth my daughter to whom the residue of my Goods etc.   And I then make my

Brother Steven Hunt, now or late of Reculver, co. Kent, yeoman the onelie Overseer of trust.

Thomas Boreman, Roe? Noe Taylor, Witnesses.

Proved 14 July 1608 by Elizabeth the Relict and Executrix named.

[It seems almost certain that this is the will of Robert Hunt, the minister of the first settlement of Virginia. From 1594 to 1602, when he resigned, he was vicar of Reculver, Kent, a noble church torn down by a vandal Archbishop of Canterbury, early in the Nineteenth Century. From that date to 1606 we know nothing of his history; but, if this is his will, he became in 1602, vicar of Heathfield. John Smith says that while the Virginia fleet was lying in the Downs, Master Hunt was not more than 10 or 12 miles from his habitation. Heathfield is about that distance from the coast. It would be desirable to ascertain how long Robert Hunt was Vicar of Heathfield; but the only work accessible at this time, Dallaway's Sussex, does not cover the whole county nor include Heathfield. The will was dated Nov. 20, 1606, and the expedition for Virginia sailed from Blackwall exactly a month later. Mr. Hunt of Va. died sometime in 1608. The dates agree well; but the copy of the probate (which may not be a full one) does not say, as would be expected "died beyond seas." A year or two ago Mr. H. Dwelly of Herne Bay, Kent, kindly traced the signature of Robt. Hunt from the Reculver parish books. It is intended to compare this signature with that to the original of the will printed above. All the writers of all the factions in Virginia agree in praising Robert Hunt as a most godly and exemplary minister and man, and no doubt he was influenced by the highest motives in coming to the colony; but motives are often mixed. If this is the will of the Virginia minister we have again the old *cherchez la femme*. An unhappy home life made it easier for him to undertake the hardships of the settlement. The reference to a brother living at Reculver makes another point in favor of identification. It is hoped that this may ultimately be made positive, for no better man came to America than Robert Hunt.]

JOHN BEAUCHAMP of London, Gentleman.

Dated 15 June 1654.   Proved 9 Sept. 1654.

And whereas by an obligation bearing date 4 Aprill 1653 I stand bound unto John Harvey Cittizen and Merchant Taylor of London in £1600 for the true performance of severall promises and agreements I doe now confirme and ratify the same and charge my Executors to perform the said Obligation.

To Margarett my Wife, £100 also the household stuffe and other thinges which shall be remayning in my lodging Chamber and in the Closset att the further ende of the Parlour of my now dwelling house in the Parish of Buttolph without, Aldersgate, London.

To my Sonne John Beauchampe, £300.

To my Daughter Johane Wilkinson, the Wife of Edward Wilkinson, £200.

To my three Grandchildren, the daughters of my said Daughter Joahane [sic], £10 apeece, to be paid att the accomplishment of their ages of one and twentie yeares.

To the poore of the parish of Buttolph without Aldersgate, London, 50s.

To my freinde Master John Harvey aforesaid £5.

Residuary Legatee and Sole Executor. my said Sonne John Beauchamp.

For as much as my said sonne John Beauchamp is now remaining in Partes beyond the Seas I will that all my goods etc. which I shall leave at the time of my decease, if my said sonne shall not then be returned into England, shall remain in the Custodie of my said wife.

Proved 9 Sept. 1654 by the Sole Executor named.

[The mention by the testator of a son John "now beyond the seas," would seem to make it certain that he was father of John Beauchamp, merchant, of London and Virginia, who died in 1668, and whose will was printed in this Magazine XVI, 192. But the latter had three brothers, William, Abel, and Richard, and a sister Mrs. Mary Sampson, and these names do not agree at all with those in the will above. Possibly John, the son of the testator was the father of John, who died in 1668.]

GEORGE ARGENT of Hoxton, parish of St. Leonard, Shoreditch, co., Middx., Gentleman.

Dated 16 Aug. 1653   Codicil 27 Feb. 1653-4
                            Proved 23 April 1654.

To be buried in the Parish Church of St. Leonard, Shoreditch, as neere unto my late wife and Sonne William Argent as may be.

To my Daughter, Elizabeth Porter, that Messuage or Tenement, situate in Oxton, where I now dwell, to my said daughter and to the heires of her bodie, and for want of such issue, to my sonne George Argent and to his heires for ever.

To my Cousin William Argent my Watch and to my Cousin Mistris Mary Riggden, 40s.

To the poore of the Parish of St. Leonard, Shoreditch, £3.

To my servant Rebecha Coltman, my Trunck bound with yron.
To my daughter Mary Hodges, that Messuage or Tenement,
wherein Master Morrel Gouldsmith dwelleth, situate in Oxton,
during her life and after her decease, to my said sonne George
Argent and to his heires for ever.

To my daughter Mary Hodges, my great gylt standing Cupp.
All the rest of my plate I give as follows: to my Sonne George
Argent, Jane Steward & Elizabeth Porter, three fourth parts
thereof and the other fourth part to the Children of my late
daughter Anne Ivie, deceased, which were borne in Virginia
where she died, to be equally devided betweene them, according
to the Will of Jane Baker, deceased theire Grandmother.

To my Grandchild Anne Ivie, my Chest, that standeth in the
greate Chamber and the Sum of £200 upon Condition that she
doe not marrie without the Consent of my Executors. In Case
she marry without Consent, then the said bequest unto all the
rest of my Grandchildren whether they shall be in England or
out of England, equally amongst them.

To my freinde Thomazine Earle, 50s to buy her a Ringe.

The Residue of my Goods etc I bequeath as follows: two third
parts to my said sonne, George Argent and to my daughter
Jane Steward, to be devided between them and the remaining
third part to such of the Children of my late daughter Anne Ivey
as were borne in Virginia, to be devided amongst them, to be
paid unto them when they shall accomplish theire ages of one
and twenty yeares.

To my sonne in Lawe Henry Potter, my Yron Chest.

I forgive my sonne in Law Thomas Steward the thirty pounds he
owes me.

To my freinde Master Robert Earle, a suit of mourning.

Executors: my Cousins Master John Langley & Master John
Glascock.

Rebecha Coultman, her marke, Robert Earle, scrv., Thomas
Page, scrv., Witnesses.

Mem 27 Feb. 1653-4

To my Cousin Glascock one of my Exors, £10.

John Glascock, Anne Ivey, the marke of Rebeccha Coultman, Witnesses.

Proved 23 April 1654 by the Executors named.

[In 1663 the Court of Lower Norfolk County certified that Thomas and George Ivy were the sons of Thomas Ivy (who was aged 36 in 1640, and died 1663-4) and Ann his wife "who was the daughter of one George Argent Liveinge about London, England, as she often reported." Thomas Ivy the son, died in 1684, leaving a will. His legatees were his wife Alice, sons Thomas, Ludford and Anthony, and daughters, Katherine Taylor, Agnes, Frances and Elizabeth. The other son George died in 1689, leaving a will. His legatees were his wife Hannah, sons Alexander, George, Samuel, Thomas, John and Joseph, and daughter Elizabeth. The name has been numerously represented down to the present day.]

PETER ASHTON, of Grantham co., Lyncolne, Esqr.

Dated 27 Sept. 1653.   Proved: 9 June 1654.

And whereas I have formly given unto my Sonne John, all my Lands and Tenements in Fishkerton in Co. Lyncolne and the Lease of the lands I hold from the Deane and Chapter of Peterborough, I doe heerby Confirme the same.

To my Daughter Audley, £100.

To my Grandchild Elizabeth Audley, £20.

And whereas my Wife, deceased, did deliver unto the handes of my Mother in lawe, the Lady Ellis and my Sister Adams the Sum of £50 which since her decease they have given to my two daughters Jane Audley & Elizabeth Diamond £20 each I doe hereby Signify that I am Contented with the same.

Residuary Legatee and Sole Executor: my sonne James Ashton.

Margarett Adams, William Ellis, Thomas Adams, Jonas Martin, William Bellamy, Witnesses.

Proved 9 June 1654 by the Sole Executor named.

[Col. Peter Ashton emigrated to Virginia about the middle of the Seventeenth Century and was a Burgess for Charles City in 1656, and for Northumberland 1659 and 1660. In addition to other lands he owned an estate on the Potomac in the present King George County, which he named "Challerton." By will dated 1669 and proved 1671 he left his estate to his brothers James Ashton of Kirby-Underwood, and John Ashton of Louth, both in Lincolnshire, England. Both of these came to Virginia, where they died in Stafford County without issue, John in 1682, and James in 1686. A pedigree of the Lincolnshire Ashtons who descended from the Ashtons of Chaderton or Chatterton Lancashire (hence the name of Peter Ashton's Va. estate) shows that the testator above was of Long Sutton and Grantham, that he married Elizabeth daughter of Sir Thos. Ellis of Grantham and had four sons Thomas, James, John and Samuel. No Peter Ashton appears among his children, though the name was common in the family. The testator had a brother Walter Ashton, Vicar of Sutterton, Lincolnshire, who had a son Peter, living in 1629. This last named may have been the Virginian.]

THOMAS BAKER, Cittizen and Apothecary of London.
Dated 13 Dec. 1653.   Proved 9 May 1654.
All my Goods and Chattels to be devided into three equall
partes whereof one third part unto my Wife Sarah Baker, one
other third parte unto my five Children, Thomas Baker, William
Baker, Mary Baker, Francis Baker & Sarah Baker equally
amongst them. My Sonne Thomas being of full age his parte
p's'ntly payable, my Sonne William's parte to be paid when he
shall have accomplished the age of twenty one and all my daugh-
ters at same age or daye of marriage. And the other third parte
of my Estate I reserve to myself to pay my legacies etc.
To the Poore within the Parish of St. James Clarkenwell where
I am a Parishoner, 50s.
To my sister Abigail Fitzhugh, 20s. and to my Sister Frances
Hinde 40s. and to my Kinsman Master George Smyth, 20s. and
to my Ferinde Master Thomas Jenny, 20s. to buy them Ringes.
To my eldest Sonne Thomas, and my wife, my now dwelling
House in Clarken Well close. And to my sonne William my
other House next adjoining with the appurtenances thereunto
belonging as it is now in the Occupation of my said Kinsman
Mr. George Smyth.
Residuary Legatees: my Sonnes Thomas & William and my
Daughters Frances & Sarah.
Executors: my Sonne Thomas and my Wife Sarah.
Overseers: my said Kinsman, Master George Smyth and my
freinde Master Thomas Jenney.
Mem   before the sealing and publishing of these presents I doe
give unto my brother Richard Baker now in Virginia if he live
to come again into England, 30s to buie him a Ring.   To Heath,
"now grave maker" of this parish 10s.
    John Mathewes, Thomas Palmer, Edward Gregory, Scr.:
                                        Witnesses.
Proved 9 May 1654 by Sarah Baker the Relict and one of the
Executors named, Thomas Baker the sonne and the other
Exor renouncing.

[On March 18, 1662, Patrick Jackson and Richard Baker were granted
1500 acres of land in Charles City County (now Prince George) back of
and adjoining Merchants Hope, and adjoining the lands of Richard
Craven, and "the old town," now the property of Mr. Richard Tye.
This land was granted to Richard Jones March 10, 1655, and by him sold
to Jackson and Baker. Of course it is not certain that this is the
Richard Baker of '' ' —''']

VIRGINIA GLEANINGS IN ENGLAND.

(Contributed by Leo Culleton, 92 Piccadilly, London, W., and the late Lothrop Withington.)

THOMAS DANGERFIELD, of the parishe of Wickwarre, co. Gloucester, Clothier.

Dated 30 April 3 Jas.   Admon 30 May 1605.

My body to be buryed in the churchyarde of Wickwarre. To my eldest sonne, JOHN DANGERFIELD, £100.   To my eldest daughter, ELIZABETH, £100.   To my younger daughter, MARIE, £100.   To my sonne, EDWARDE, £120.   To my mayde servaunte EDITH ROCH, 20s.   To my sister ALICE, wife of RICHARD MABBET, £3.   To my sister JONE, £20.   To my sister MARIE CHAUNDLER, 40s.   To my brother in lawe ED-WARD CHAUNDLER, one suite of my apparrell.   And to his sonne RICHARD, one cowe, and to his two daughters, 20s. a peece. To my sister KATHERYNE, £4.   To my Journy-man, ANTHONY HOULDER, 20s.   To my apprentyce EDWARDE MERRET, 10s. To my brother JOHN TROTMAN, two suits of apparell, And to his sonne John, 40s.   To the poore of Wickwar, 20s.   And to the High wayes there 10s.   Residuary Legatee and Sole execu-cutor, my sonne THOMAS [sic.]

Overseers:—ROBERT HALE, of Alderley in the Co. of Glou-cester, esquire, my father in lawe EDWARDE TROTMAN of Haukesbury, and my brother in lawe THOMAS TROT-MAN of Cromwell and JOHN COOPER, Minister, of the Church of Alderly.

My will is that my eldest sonne JOHN and my eldest daughter ELIZABETH, be delivered to the tuition and keeping of Mr. HALE, my daughter MARIE to the keeping of my Father in lawe EDWARD TROTMAN and his daughter ELIZABETH, and my sonne THOMAS to the tuition of my brother in lawe CHRISTOPHER

From Vol. XXV, No. 3 (July 1917), p. 239.

TROTMAN, of Wynterborne, co. Gloucester, and my sonne EDWARD to be trayned up at the descretion of Mr. HALE and my father in lawe.

Money owing to me:

from JOHN CONNYNGAM, of Bristoll .... £11.
from THOMAS JEWELL, of Bristoll .... £5.
from ROBERTE WEBBE of Wickwarre .... £5.
from GEORGE CHAUNDLER, merchant at London .... £102.10.

EDWARD TROTMAN   —
THOMAS TROTMAN   —Witnesses
JOHN COOPER   —

Administration 30 May 1605 granted to CHRISTOPHER TROT-MAN, during the minority of THOMAS DANGERFIELD the Exor named.

P. C. C. 36 Hayes.

THOMAS DANGERFIELD, Citizen and Haberdasher, of London, intending very shortlie to travell over beyond the Seas abowte my affaires and buisynes.

Dated 29 March 1612.   Proved 17 Feb. 1618-19.

All my Goods chattells, readie money and Debtes whatso-ever to be divided into three equal partes. ELLEN, my wife shall have one third part, one other third part unto my Children, viz., THOMAS, WILLIAM, JOSEPH, ROBERT, REBECCA & ELIZA-BETH equally amongst them, to be paid unto my sonns at suche tyme as they shall atteyne to the age of twentie one yeares and to my daughters at like age or be severally marryed. And the other third part I reserve to my selfe. Out of which I bequeath the following.

To my mother a ringe of Golde of the valewe of 30-

To my freind HAUNCE [?HANNCE] Mus of Lubycke, a ringe of golde, of same valewe.

To my sister COWDALL and also to my sister ANNYON, 20- to each of them for a ringe.

To HANNCE PHILIPP STAMLER, Marchant straunger, my freind, a ringe of golde of 40- valewe.

434

To ANNE SYSOLL, of Lubyck, a ringe of golde, of the valewe of 30s.

The residue of my own third, to be divided amongst my Children.

"I entreate my wife to be good and kind to my brother WILLIAM DANGERFIELD yf he become a good husband."

Sole Executrix: ELLEN my wife.

Overseers:—my brothers, RICHARD COWDALL & RICHARD LEE, and my freind Mr. JOHN BRIDGES.

JOHN WAREN. Scr.   —
EDMOND JEFFERY   —Witnesses
GEORGE WATERS, Servant to the said Scrivenor   —

Proved 17 Feb. 1618-19 by the Sole Executrix named.

P. C. C. 24 Parker.

[It is evident that these Dangerfields were prosperous clothiers and merchants, probably coming originally from Gloucestershire. The Londoner evidently did business with Lubeck and other continental cities. The emigrant ancestor of the family of this name which has been of prominence from the first settlement, was William Dangerfield who patented land on the Rappahannock in 1667 and died before 1671. His son John was born in 1631 so the emigrant might well have been the son William named in the will of Thomas Dangerfield of London. Of course this would have to be proved by farther research. For an account of the Virginia family, see *Wm & Mary Quarterly, VIII, and IX*. Whatever the English descent of the Virginia family it can disclaim any connection with the notorious scoundrel, Thomas Dangerfield, the informer, of the time of Charles II. He was born at Waltham, Essex, about 1650, and was a considerably younger man than John Dangerfield, son of the emigrant to Virginia.]

WILLIAM DOWNEMAN, of Plymouth, co. Devon.
Merchant.

Dated 21 April 1607.   Proved 12 March 1609-10

To the poore of Plymouth, £5.

To JAMES DOWNEMAN, my sonne, two closes of Land conteyning five acres called Fryars Pricks within the borough of Plymouth, in the tenure of CHRISTOFER WILKINS as in the right of LEAR his now wife. Provided that, ALICE my wife injoye the same during her life.

To Christopher Downeman, my sonne, one tenement with two Closes of Land thereto belonging, now in the tenure of Roger Coomyn, within the town of Plimpton Morris, in the said Co. of Devon. And one other tenement lyeing in Mill-streete in Plimpton Mary also two Closes of land to the said Tenement belong in Plympton Underwood in the said Co. in the tenure of Francis Derrant.

To Zachary Downeman, my sonne, one Tenement, one Orchard and one Garden, now in the tenure of John Vosper lyeing within the borough of Liskeard, co. Cornwall.

To Robert Downeman, my sonne, one tenement wherein James Knapp now dwelleth, scytuate within the Burrough of Plymouth in Trevill streate, and also one Close of land conteyning by estimation, one Acre, now in the tenure of Christofer Wilkins as in the right of Loar his wife, scituate in the Burrough of Plymouth neere the Horsing poole. And also one parcell of land in Fursball, in Plymouth neere a place sometimes called Larry Milles now in the tenure of the said Christofer Wilkins.

To Prudence Downeman, my daughter, £100. To Judith Downeman, my daughter, £100. To John Downeman, my son £20. To Anne, my daughter, after the death of Alice my wife, my best sylver goblett. Residuary Legatee and Sole Executrix: the said Alice my wife.

Overseers: my freinds, John Philips and Thomas Payne, merchants.

Thomas Payne   —
George Jones   —Witnesses
Walter Glubb   —

Proved 12 March 1609 by the Sole Executrix named.

P. C. C. 27 Wingfield.

[In an old paper preserved by descendants of the Virginia Downman family it is stated "My father's great grand father Gave Great assistance to the building up of a Cathedral Church in plemouth (Plymouth) his name is set in the wall. William Downeman a Great rememberer of the poor * * my grandfather went to perbodus (Barbadoes) and lived at a place called Spiheres my father was left his Estate a youth," and is added in another part "Raleigh Downeman the young son * * * moved to Bermuda, thence to Lancaster County Va, 1653." This is a vague, crude tradition. The name Raleigh certainly does not appear in the family until after its arrival in Virginia, but the tradition may contain a clue as to the true line of descent. John Downeman was born in 1592 and came to Virginia in the *John & Frances*, 1614. His wife Elizabeth who was born in 1519, came in the *Warwick*, 1621. At the time of the census of 1624-5 they lived at Elizabeth City. John Downeman was appointed a Commissioner (justice) for that county March 1628-9, and was a Burgess October 1629. Another emigrant was "William Downeman, gent," who came in 1608. The first of the present Virginia family of the name was William Downman who lived in Lancaster County in 1652, and who died in 1659, leaving a widow Dorothy. They were no doubt parents of William Downman who married about 1679, Million, daughter of Raleigh Travers of Lancaster County, and died in 1712. See *Wm & Mary Quarterly, XVIII*, 138-141, and Hayden's *Virginia Genealogies*. Wm. Downman, who died in 1765, or his brother Raleigh who died, a very old man, in 1781, may have been the writer of the old paper referred to. They were grandsons of William and Million Downeman. It will be noted that the family tradition, as given in this paper, traces to a resident of Plymouth.]

JOHN DOWNES, Citizen and Merchanttaylor of London.

Dated 7 Feb. 1616-17.   Proved 20 May 1617.

My goods and chattels to be divided into three equall parts, to ANN my wife, one part, one other parte unto my three Children, JOHN, ANN and MARGARETT, to be divided and paid unto them at their ages of Twentie and one yeares or daye of marriage, the other third part as follows:

To my father and mother EDMOND & JOANE DOWNE, £20. To my brother GEORGE DOWNE and to my Sister his bedfellowe, to each 10s. to make them a Ring. To ROGER CLAXTON and to my sister ALICE his wife, 10s. to make them Rings. To HUGH VYOLL and to my sister ELLEN his wife 10s. to make them Rings. To my sister JOANE DOWNE, £5. To my brother NICHOLAS DOWNE, a peece of "brode" Clothe. To my three overseers, hereafter named 20- each, to make them Rings. To Mr. ANES Preacher, xxijs. To the poore of the parish, xxs.

Residuary Legatee and Sole Executrix: ANN my wife.

Overseers: JOHN MOTHE, and NICHOLAS HOOKER, Citizens and Goldsmiths of London and my brother NICHOLAS DOWNE and my freind GEORGE TURSEMAN mchanttaylor. And concerning my lands in Eastham neere Crewkerne in the Co. of Somerset I bequeath the same unto ANN my wife, her heires and assigns for ever.

EDWARD ROMENY, Scr.   —
THOMAS HOUGHTON, Scr.   —Witnesses.
              &   —
EDWARD COOKE.   —

Proved 20 May 1617 by the Sole Executrix named.

P. C. C. 48 Weldon.

[The Nicholas Downes named as brother, may have been Nicholas
Downes, of London, Esq., whose will was printed in this Magazine
XXII, 26, and who had a niece Jane Downes in Virginia. George
Downe or Downes was a Burgess for Elizabeth City Co., Va., 1631 and
1632, and may have been the brother George named in the will. In
this case, as in many others, the wills are printed, as affording good
clues for further work.]

DOROTHIE DUKE within the precinct of the Cathedrall Churche
   of the Holy Trinity of Norwiche, the widowe of Mr. ED-
   WARD DUKE of Benhall in the Countie of Suff. Esq.
Dated 20 Jan. 1611.   Proved 23 May 1614.
   My body to be buryed in Benhall Churche. To my sonne
in Lawe Sr. JOHN *BLUENERHASSET, Knighte, one guilte Cupp
of iiij£. To my daughter his wife, the best Bedd and Bedstead. To theire sonne and heire HENRY BLENERHASSET, £40,
to be paid him when he comes to the age of one and twentie
yeares. To my sonne SAMUEL BLUENERHASSET of Lowdham,
Esquire, one silver Cupp of iiij£. To my daughter, his wife,
one gould Rynge. To my goddaughter, DOROTHIE BLEUNER-
HASSET, £50. To my sonne in lawe, Mr. WILLIAM WEBB,
gent, One silver Cupp of iiij£. To my daughter, his wife, one
Golde Rynge. To her daughter, ANNE WEBB, one silver boll.
To my sonne SYDNOR, my silver Boll that is used every daye.
To my Brother Sr. ROBERT JERMYN, a golde rynge. To his
Ladye, a golde rynge. To my Brother, WILLIAM JERMYN, a
golde rynge. To Mrs. CORBET, one little square quishion. To
my brother SIDNOR, a golde rynge. To my god sonne WILLIAM
SIDNOR, twoe silver spoones. To my goddaughter DOROTHIE
SIDNOR, twoe silver spoones. To my Ladie ASHEFIELD, one
white taffata quishion. To my godsonne EDWARD DUKE, one
guilt Cupp and one Crimson velvet quishion "wroughte with

438

the DUKES & JERMYNS Armes." To my Cosin Mrs. JANE
TURRELL, twentie shillings. To my Cosin THEISTON [?THIRS-
TON] of Hexton, one gould rynge. And to his wife a golde
rynge. To my goddaughter Mrs. FRANNCYS ARCHDALE, my
Canopie. To her sonne, my godsonne, twoe silver spoones.
To WILLIAM FUGILL, CLARKE, 10s. To my Cosin NICHOLAS
EDGAR, one golde ringe. To my Cosin SMITHE his daughter,
my goddaughter DOROTHIE, one peece of plate, of 20s. price.
To my goddaughter, DOROTHIE, the daughter of Sr. JOHN
TARSBOROUGHE one peece of plate, of 20s. price. To Mr.
THOMAS CORBETTS sonne, my godsonne, one peece of plate of
20s. price. To my Neiphue, EDWARD ELMES, V£. To my
Cosin, EVEREDS sonne, my godsonne, one peece of plate, of
20s. price. To my Neece KATHERINE, the wife of WILLIAM
SNOWDYNE, V£. To my Neiphue PERCEY, one Teaster of a
Bedd of Tawney coulor Damaske. To my Servant, GEORGE
TOOGOOD, 10s. To my man, THOMAS ASHLIE, 10s. To ANNE
CREATEMORE, one featherbed. To the Cannons and Singing
men, 10s. to be devided amongst them. To the poore of Catton,
10s. To my servant, EMM, Vs.
Residuary Legatee and Sole Executor:—my sonne THOMAS
DUKE.
THEORDORE GOODWYN, & WILLIAM FUGILL, Clerke & MARY
GOODWYN wife of the said THEODORE, Witnesses.
Yt is my intent that whatsoever I have given unto my daughter
ELIZABETH WEBBE, yf she dye, then her daughter ANNE shall
"have them."
Proved 23 May 1614 by the Sole Executor named.

P. C. C. 33 Lawe.

AMBROS DUKE of Benhall, co. Suff., Esquire.
Dated 22 Oct. 1610.   Proved 2 Feb. 1610-11.
   To ELIZABETH, my wife, all my Mannors, Lands, tenements
and hereditaments whatsoever, scituate within the counties of
Suffolk and Norfolk   And also all the rentes, fines, profitts,
and Commodities whatsoever wch shall arise or be levied or
taken by calls or force of a grant and assignment made by JOHN
HOLLAND, esq. unto WILLIAM WEBBE & THOMAS GOODWYNE,

esq., of the Manor of Benhall, with the appurtenances which is made to them in truste unto my proper use and benefitt for divers years.

And I will that after all my debts are paid the profitts of my above said Mannors and Lands wch I late purchased of THOMAS ERLE of Arrundell THOMAS ERLE of Suffolk and WILLIAM Lord HOWARD, shalbe yearlie collected and taken by my wife untill my *sonne shall accomplish the age of six and twentie yeares, for and towards the benefitt of ANNE DUKE & ELIZABETH DUKE my daughters.

*Not named.

I will that THOMAS DUKE, my brother shall have his borde and lodginge at the charges of my wife for himself and his Man, and also pasture for his two geldings.

To my goddaughter JANE BLEUNERHASSET, one of the daughters of SAMUEL BLEUNERHASSET esqr, and MARIE his wife, my sister, £100. To my brother in lawe, WILLIAM WEBB, and to my sister his wife and to ANNE WEBB their daughter, £5 each. To my godsonne AMBROS BLEUNERHASSET, the sonne of Sr. JOHN BLEUNERHASSET Knight, £20. To DOROTHY DUKE, my mother, THOMAS DUKE, my brother **[WILLIAM SIDNOR, (sic) gent my brother in lawe and unto MARGARET his wife, my sister] and unto THOMAS GOODWYN, my brother in law, unto everie of them a peece of plate of the valew of £5.

To WILLIAM BARNES, of Benhall, my servant, 40s. yearlie. To JOHN JOHNSON, my Man, two suites of apparrel. To ROBERT CORBOULD and ROBERT FEVERYEERE, my servants, 40s. a peece. To JOHN BARNES, my servant, £3. To JOHN COZEN, my servant, 40s. To ELIZABETH FORMAN, 40s. To the poore of Benhall, 40s. and to the poore of Saxmondham, 20s. the poore of Snape 30s., the poore of Sweflinge, 20s., and to the poore of Farnham, 10s. To THOMAS EDGAR, gent of greate *Glemham my kinsman, a Sylver Cupp

Sole Executrix, the said ELIZABETH my wife.

Supervisor:—Sr. HENRY GLEMHAM, knight.

**[In the margin is the foll.]: "This legacy to Mr. SIDNER and his wife were revoked by the testator_____by reason that his said sister died before him." [The erased words have been printed here in brackets.]

Thomas Goodwin, John Sherwood, Edmond Coleman, Francis Coleman, & Robert Spacham Witnesses.
Proved 2 Feb. 1610-11 by the Executrix named.

P. C. C. 14 Wood.

*[Glemham in Suffk.]

Abstract of the WILL of
Elizabeth Duke, of Benhall, co., Suff., widdowe, the late wife
of Ambrose Duke, Esq., deceased.

Dated 22 Dec. 9 Jas.   Proved 21 Jan. 1611-12.

Whereas the foresaid Ambrose Duke did give all his Mannors, lands tenements, and hereditaments whatsoever scituate within the Counties of Suff. and Norff. And also all rents fines and profitts whatsoever which should in any wise be due or be levied or taken by Color or force of a grant or assignment made by John Holland Esqr. unto William Webb and Thomas Godwyn esquires, of the Mannor of Benhall. To have during my life, Provided that I paye all the debts of the said Ambrose and paie all his legacies and "keep upp" all his children. And after all his debts were paid, then the profitts which could be raysed should be yearly taken by me, my executors and assignes, during my life, or untill his sonne Edward should accomplish the age of six and twenty, for and towards the benefitt of the daughters of the said Ambrose. And for that I have taken uppon me the execution of the said will I doe stande bound and one Robert Sparham with me in fouer severall obligacons for the payment of £300 or thereabouts. And whereas I finde myself much subject to sickness * * * Therefore "I discharge of myself and the foresaid debts and of the said Robert Sparham," and for the preformance of my said husband's Will, doe hereby bequeath all the said Mannors etc to my Executors.

And whereas it has pleased our Sov. Lord the Kings Matie, with the advice of the master and Councell of his highnes Court of Wards and liveries, to commit and grant unto me the Custodie,

441

wardshipp and marriage of my said Sonne EDWARD DUKE, his highnes Ward and onlie sonne and heire of my said husband And also to grant unto me the third part of the said Mannor Lands To hold the same from the 29th Nov. in the "eight" yere of his Mats. reign during the minority of the said EDWARD. And whereas some of my friends have ingaged themselves for me in divers somes of money by their special bonds Therefore for the discharge of my conscience and their discharge which have soe ingaged themselves I desire the Master and Councell of the said Court to permitt my Executors to injoye the benefitt of the said grants * * * And after my said Executors have satisfied and paid my said freinds soe bound etc. then the overplus to my Sonne EDWARD to be paid him att his age of twentie yeares. And as for the benefitt to be raysed for the preferment of my daughters and their education and bringing upp I referr the same whollie unto the discretion of my executors.

To EME, the now wife of the said ROBERT SPARHAM, £5, and to EDWARD HOLMES, gent., my late husband's "Kendisman," £6.13.4. And to my sister WEBB her daughter ANNE, £10. And to the Widdowe SOYER, 20s to the Goodwife ARTIS, 40s. and unto Mris HARDIER, 40s. And to ELIZABETH my mayde servant, £3 to my mayde DIANA, 30s. to ROBERT FEAVERYEARE, my man servant, 20s. to ELIZABETH BEART, 10s. ROBERT CORBOULD 20s. JARMEYE BUTTOLF 20s. and JOHN MAN, 30s. all my servants. And to Mr. DAYVES, the preacher, 40s. And to EDMOND COLEMAN of *Hacheston gent., 40s. And to Mrs. DOROTHE DUKE my mother in lawe, 40s. to buy her a ringe. Also to Mr. THOMAS EDGAR gent., 40s. to buy him a Ring. Also to FRANCIS COLEMAN, the Sonne of EDMOND COLEMAN, gent., of Hacheston, 10s. Also to my two daughters ANNE & ELIZABETH, five payer of Sheets etc to either of these. And the residue of my thrid parte to be devided amongst the Children of EDWARD DOYLE, esquire by MARIE now his wife and RICHARD GOODRICK, esquire by MARGARETT nowe his wife.

Executors: the said THOMAS GOODWYN & THOMAS DUKE, gent my late husband's brother.

Supervisor: WILLIAM JERMYN, esquire.

EDMOND COLEMAN, FRANCYS COLEMAN, GEORGE HATFIELD, his
marke, JOHN ALDRICHE, WILLIAM GOULDES, his marke,
JOHIS ALDRICHE, Witnesses.
Proved 21 Jan. 1611-12 by the Executors named.

P. C. C. 5 Fenner.
*In Suffk.

[These wills are of the family of Duke, of Benhall, Suffolk, ancestors
of Elizabeth, wife of Nathaniel Bacon, "the Rebel." The pedigree
begins with Richard Duke who was sheriff of London in the reign of
Richard I. His descendants for a number of generations were people
of position in Suffolk. Edward Duke, Esq., of Brampton and Shading-
field, Suffolk, purchased Benhall, married Dorothy, daughter of Sir
Ambrose Jennings, of Rushbrook, Suffolk, and died 1598. His widow's
will is printed above. As Dorothy Duke makes no bequest to any
Duke children, it would seem that in this, as in other cases, the will
corrects the printed pedigree, and that she was step-mother to Ambrose
Duke, her husband's successor. Edward Duke was succeeded by his
son, Ambrose Duke, Esq., of Benhall, who married Elizabeth, daughter
and co-heiress of Bartholomew Calthrop, of Suffolk, and died in 1610.
His will and that of his wife are printed. It will be noted that he
calls Dorothy Duke "my mother." Ambrose Duke was succeeded by
his son Edward Duke of Benhall, who was first knighted and was created a Baronet in 1661. He married Ellen, daughter of John Panton,
of Brunslip, Derby, and among his numerous children was Elizabeth,
wife of Nathaniel Bacon.]

VIRGINIA GLEANINGS IN ENGLAND.

(Contributed by Leo Culleton, 92 Picadilly, London, W., and the late Lothrop Withington.)
(Continued.)

MARGRET BARNARD. Will proved 1 April 1623. My five shares in the Somer Islands to my brother Henry Barnard and heirs. Chests of linen and silver left at Mr. Caswell's to my two children Joane and Elizabeth equally. The suite of Tent Stick with Mr. Wilkinson with 40 lbs of pewter and a warming pan to said daughters. The book of Martirs with an Irish rugg to them also. My husband's cloak to Mr. Henry Waller. The Bible bequeathed to me by William Baispoole to Mrs. Wilkinson. My goods and stock of money in magazines of the Somer Islands to my daughter Elizabeth. My daughter Joan is provided in England Legacies of articles to servants and articles to said daughters. To Mary Baynain bedding and apparel To goodwife Michell apparel. To Henry Bould articles. The clothing my husband wore to Nathaniel Prudden. To George Duncombe, to Thomas Tanner, Daniel Deweese, Patrike Wingate articles of apparel. To my cosen Nicholas Barnard my books here in the Somer Islands. My scarfe to Margaret Barnard my goddaughter Standing cup with cover to Nathaniel Barnard my cosen. To Rebecca Barnard a beer bowl of silver. All the rest of my plate to my two daughters. To Church of St. Georges an Altar Cloth There is 48 pence and 12 halfpence in the little trunk these to be devided between the wives of my brothers William and Nicholas. To Mrs. Wood a gold ring. To Mr. Wood the girdle hangers and sword. My husband's Colours leading staff and Drumme. To Captain Felgate a sword. My husband's seal ring to my daughter Joane. My daughter Joanne Tanner to care of my brother Nicholas. Residue to my two daughters. My cosen Nathaniel and Mr. Wood executors. Witnesses: Nathl Barnard, Roger Wood. *Swann,* 35.

[Margaret Barnard was the widow of Capt. John Barnard or Bernard, who was appointed Governor of Bermuda in 1622. She was living there when the will was made. This must be one of the very earliest wills of a resident of the Island. Captain Felgate was Tobias Felgate, who, for a time, lived in Virginia.]

AMBROSE BENNETT of London Esquire. Will 18 December 1629; proved 28 March 1631. To be buried in St. Bennetts Finkes near the Exchange in London. To Sister Dame Marie Crooke now wife of Sir George Crooke knight one of his Maiesties Justices of his Court of Kings Bench £50. To godson Ambrose Bennett son of my Brother John Bennett £600 when 21, if he die before to his brother John Bennett. To my uncle John Taylor the elder £6. 13s. 4d. To cosen John Taylor the younger son of said John Taylor the elder £6. 13s. 4d. To Dorothie Taylor daughter of John the elder £6. 13s. 4d. To servants of my brother John Bennett, if I die in his house 20 marks. To cosen Richard Purke vintner £10. To cosin Marie Norton widow £5. To cosen Frances Freeman wife of Thomas Freeman now dwelling in Wallingford £10. To my cosen Arthur Burt carrier of Worcester £10. To Brother in law George Lowe Esq £50. To cosen George Lowe son of my brother George £50. To Mr. Thomas Hampson Esq £6. 13s. 4d. To Mr. Brownlow my kinsman £10. To cosen the Lady Marie Dutton wife of Sir Raphe Dutton knight £5. To servant Ambrose Hall £100 if dwelling with me at my decease. To my brother Sir Symon Bennett Knight and Barronet £50 and to his wife £50. To sister in law Joan now wife of my brother John Bennett £50 and to two of her sisters viz.——Muncke widow and Joan Heather 40s. each. To cosen Marie Woodward 40s. To Bridgett Masemore sometime servant to my father £10. To cosen Marie Turvyn wife to William Turvyn £20. To Mr. John Bancks mercer £6. 13s. 4d. To cosen

Dorothie Dun widow 40s. To my Barber Richard Hersey 40s. To loving friend Mr. Watson attorney 20s. To Edward Worsley my fathers servant 20s. To Poor of St. Olave Old Jury, St. Lawrence Old Jury, St. Stephen Coleman Street, St. Stephen Walbrook £10. To Cosen Marie Grimston one of the daughters of my Brother in law Sir George Crooke £5 and to Elizabeth and Fraunces Crooke two other of the daughters £80 each when 21. To Thomas son of Sir George Crooke £25. To widow Surby late wife of John Surby of Wapping, Mariner deceased £3. To Godson Ambrose Strugnell son of John Strugnell Citizen and Pewterer of London £5. Residuary Legatees and Executors: Brother Sir George Crooke and my sister Marie and Brother Bennett (Brother John to have half the residue) Witnesses: Hum: Dyson, notary Public, Jero: Smith, Will: Filtonn and Jos: Ferret servant vnto the said notary. An annuity of £350 out of the manors of Saulton, Braby, Estone, and Beach and other lands in county York to Brother Sir Symon Bennett. My half of lands in Redreth, county Surrey bequeathed me by my father Sir Thomas Bennett who owns the other half All my lands in Redriff county Surrey purchased of Mr. Gardener to the relief of the poor as follows £9 to parish of St. Bennett Fink Bread Street, Waterstocke, county Oxon £8, Redreth £9, Calverton county Bucks 20s. to be paid yearly to Churchwardens on demand at my Brother John Bennetts dwelling house in the Barge Court in Bucklesbury, St. Stephen Walbrook. dated 24 May 1630. Witnesses: Hum: Dyson, notary Publiq: Jero: Smith on 25th May this was ratified in Presence of Rich Smith, Hum:. Dyson notary publique and John Strugnell, Ambrose Hall, Tho. Dyson, William Filtonn and Jos Ferrett servants unto said notary. *St. John*, 29.

JOHN BENNETT of London gent. Will 26 November; proved 1631 11 May 1631. To my wife Jone Bennett £500 and the use of £1000 during her life and at her death to my daughter Mary Bennett if she die to such child as shall be born after the 20 November 1630, for want of such issue to my sons John and Ambrose. To daughter Mary Bennett £1000 when 21 or married. My dwelling house in Barge Yard to my wife Jone for life and then to son Ambrose. To eldest son John Bennett £500. To son Ambrose £2000 when they are 21. To parson of St. Stephen Walbrook for preaching my funeral sermon 20s. and £5 for the ground wherein my body shall be buried in the Chancel. To Brother Ambrose £20 if he be living in house with me. To sister Dame Mary Crooke wife of Sir George Crooke £10 for a ring. To cosens Mrs. Anne Hampson, Mris Elizabeth Brownlowe, and Dame Mary Dutton 40s. each for rings. To goddaughter Rebecca Hampson 20s. To wives sister Alice Monck £10. To Jane Heather another sister to my wife £10. To my uncle John Taylor 20s. To Cosen Mary Woodward 20s. To Margaret Jenkinson £5. To each of my servants 40s. Executrix: Wife Jone Bennett. Overseers: Brother in law Sir George Crooke and mt Brother Sir Symon Bennett Baronet £30 each The residue to such children as shall be born after 20 November 1630 Witnesses: Jero: Smith, Richard Warner, Walter Warson. Codicil dated 24 April 1631. £400 to be expended on funeral. To wife Joan Bennett coach and coach horses. Revokes legacy of £500 to son John Bennett and gives it to my wife. To Sir Heneadge Fynch, Knight, Recorder of the City of London £5. To servant Jerome Smith £5. Revokes bequest to Margaret Jenkinson and rest of servants and gives them £4 each. To poor by direction of wife Joan and Mr. Aaron Wilson is to be by direction of wife only. To such child wherewith my wife is now conceived and which she now goeth withall £1500. Witnesses: Hum: Dyson Notarie Publique., William Fittonn, John Bartram, Jos: Ferrett, servants vnto the said Notary, Ott: Meverell, Jero: Smith. A second proof 26 May 1636 to Richard Bennett and Thomas Hampson two of the executors named in will of Joan Wright als Bennett during minority of Ambrose, Mary and Elizabeth, the children of deceased. *St. John*, 54.

[Edward Bennett, merchant, of London, was a member of the Virginia Company and was for a time Deputy Governor of the English merchants at Delft, Holland. On Nov. 21, 1621, the Virginia Company granted to Edward, Richard and Robert Bennett and others a large tract of land in Virginia. This settlement was made within the present Isle of Wight County, and Edward Bennett for some years continued to carry on an extensive trade with the Colony. The date of his death is unknown nor has his will yet been found in England. The Council and General Court minutes show that he had a son Richard, who died in Virginia about 1625, while his father's agent in the Colony. In 1664, 1500 acres of land in Virginia was divided between Silvester, wife of Nicholas Hill of Isle of Wight County, and Mary, wife of Thomas Bland, heirs (probably daughters) of Edward Bennett. Stith says, doubtless quoting, as usual, old records, that Richard Bennett, Governor of Virginia, was a nephew of Edward Bennett. Thomas Ludwell, Secretary of State of Virginia, writing to Henry Bennett, Lord Arlington, in 1666, says that he believes Governor Richard Bennett "is of your lordship's family," and that his arms are the same. This, and other circumstances, make it almost certain that Edward Bennett was a member of the family of the name, several of whose members were eminent London merchants and from which came several families of baronets, the Earl of Arlington and the Earls of Tankerville. Other Bennetts in Virginia were Robert Bennett, said to be a brother of Edward Bennett, and his agent in 1623-4; Philip Bennett who in 1648 was administrator of Robert Bennett; Ambrose Bennett, who was a "head-right" in a patent to Richard Bennett, in 1635, and who, himself, patented land in Isle of Wight in 1638, and Thomas Bennett, aged 38 in 1624-5, who came to Virginia in 1618 and later lived near Edward Bennett's plantation.

The wills printed above will be of service in beginning an investigation of the family. Collins (under "Earl of Tankerville") has an account of the Bennetts of London, which is far from complete or correct. Thomas[1] Bennett, Esq., of Clapcot, Berkshire, had several sons, among them, Richard[2], the eldest, and Thomas[2], 3d son. Richard[2] Bennett was the father of Ralph[3] (who left male issue); Sir John[3], who died in 1627 and was the ancestor of the Earl of Arlington and of the Earls of Tankerville, and Thomas[3], Alderman of London, who is said by Collins to have had two sons, Richard[4] and Thomas[4], who was created a baronet in 1662. The will of Alderman Thomas[3] Bennett, proved 1620 (printed in J. H. Lea's Abstracts) names the two sons, Richard and Thomas, and also brothers Ralph and Edward (a son of Richard[2] Bennett not named by Collins, and who may have been the Edward Bennett of the Virginia Company). The will also names Sir Thomas Bennett (uncle of the testator), Ambrose, John, Richard and Symon, sons of Sir Thomas, and "cousin" David Bennett and his wife.

Thomas[2] Bennett, 3d son of Thomas[1], of Clapcot, was sheriff of London, 1594, Lord Mayor, 1603, and knighted in that year. He married Mary, daughter of Robert Taylor, sheriff of London, and had issue (according to Collins) 1. Symon[3], created a baronet, 1627; 2. Richard[3], an eminent merchant of London, who married Elizabeth Craddock and had at least one son Simon[4], of Beechampton, Bucks, Esq.; 3. John[3] (said by Collins to have died without issue—a statement which his will, printed above, shows to be incorrect); 4. Ann, married William Duncomb, of Brickhill, Bucks; 5. Margaret married Sir George Crooke, Justice of the Common Pleas. Collins omits a fourth son, Ambrose[3], whose will is printed above

John³ Bennett (will above) had, in 1631, two sons, John⁴ and Ambrose⁴, both minors. This last named Ambrose Bennett may have been the person of the name, who settled in Virginia. If so, he returned to England, as in 1649 Ambrose, son of John Bennett, Esq., of London, was appointed by the Parliamentary visitors a fellow of University College, Oxford, was A. M. 1652, and a barrister-at-law of Grays Inn 1661 (Foster's *Alumni Oxonienses*). Richard Bennett, of London, gent., son and heir of Richard Bennett, of London, gent, matriculated at Menton College, June 3, 1603, aged 16, and was a student at the Temple 1606. This Richard (born 1587) could not have been Richard² Bennett, as the latter's son Sir John was a student at Oxford 1573. Perhaps he was a son of Richard² Bennett, who like Edward, is not named by Collins.]

THOMAS BOWKER in the parish of St. Gregories, London. Will 15 May 1640; proved 2 March 1640/1. I commend my spirit into the handes of Jesus Christ my Saviour, faithfully beleeving he will, after this life ended make me partaker of his everlasting kingdome. As for the worldly riches wherewith yt hath pleased God of his goodness to enrich me, I devise in manner following: I will that my nephue John Bowker shall enjoy my tenement in Bickerton, wherein John Russell lately dwelled, for soe many yeares as he may live, with remainder during the terme, to his sonne John, to Thomas, my late brother William's sonne, and to his brother William, for soe longe as they shall live successively. To my nephew John Bowker's sonne John £100 when he cometh to the age of 16 yeares. To Thomas my brother William's sonne my lease which I hold of the Right Honourable Robert, Viscount Cholmely in Minshull, in the tenure of Arthur Warburton, and I will that the said Thomas shall pay 2s. yearly to the said Viscount besides the rent of 18s a yeare reserved in the said lease. To William Bowker, his brother £200. To my said nephues Thomas and William £220 to see it bestowed to the best proffitt of their sister Dorothie in respect of her marriage. I give £50 more to my said nephues, to bestowe on their sister Anne to her best benefitt. To their mother £10. To my nephue John Bowker's wife £20, and unto his mother £5. To my cosen Amy Bressy £6. 13s. 4d., and the like summe to her son Hugh Bressy. To every other of her foure sonnes Thomas Bressy, Richard, Hugh, and James, 40s. apiece to buy them ringes. To my cosen Randall Palyn of Eaton, £6. 13s. 4d. To his brother Thomas Nettles 50s. To my loving friend Edward Bosdon of the Middle Temple, London, esquire, £6. 13s. 4d. To my loving frendes Mr. John Povall and his sonne £6. 13s. 4d. half to the father and the other half to the sonne, to buy them ringes. To my cosen Thomas Buckly and to my cosen Randle Palyn of Bicker 50s. apeece to buy them ringes. To my cosen Robert Buckly and his brother William £6. 13s. 4d. to be devided betwixt them. To my cosen Richard Heath 50s. to buy him a ringe, and unto Anne his wife £5 to buy her a silver bolle. To my cosen William Dodd, my table diamond ring, and unto Anne his wife, 50s. to make her another ring, to his sonne John and his wife £20. To my cosen Thomas Cowper 40s and I remit the debts he oweth unto me. To my cosen Calcott of Calcott, 40s. to make him a ringe. To every childe of old John Maddocke of Agton, and of Thomas Maddocke, his brother which are nowe living 20s. To the poore of Malpas, Bickerton and Hartill, to each towne £3. 6s. 8d. To my loving frend John Minshill of Minshull, esquire, the Author uppon the five bookes of Moses and Doctor Case uppon Aristotles Phisickes and Ethickes. To the young Mr. Thomas Cholmely of Vale Royall my Alphonsus Testatus workes being thirteene volumes to begin a library at the place aforesaid. Item, I give unto Thomas Bowker of Buckley £5. To my nephue Thomas Bowker my seale ringe. To his brother William my rubie ringe. I hereby constitute my said three nephues John, Thomas and William Bowker my executors. To them I devise all my tenement in Wimbersley and Church Minshull, which I late purchased from Thomas Cotton of Cotton esquire, and Thomas Wilkinson and Elizabeth his wife, to be sould for the better performance of this my last will. All the rest of my goods to be divided equally among my executors, according to the likeing and allowance of John Minshull, Thomas Cholmely the father and Edward Bosden aforesaid esquires, whom I appoint overseers of this my last will. Published in the year abovesaid in the presence of us,

Gilbert Gayne, Willm Sommer, James Ely. 31st July. Proved by the executors named. *Evelyn*, 32.

[Rev. James Bowker, minister of St. Peters, New Kent, and Rev. Ralph Bowker, minister of St. Stephens' King and Queen, at the beginning of the 18th century, had a brother Edward Bowker, of London. The will of Rev. James Bowker was published in this Magazine XI, 313. Rev. Ralph Bowker left descendants. The family was apparently of Cheshire origin and the will printed above will give suggestions for farther research.]

RICHARD EVERARD of Much Waltham, co. Essex, Gent. Dated 10 June 1616.   Proved 1 Augt. 1617
                                                 Sentence 2 Dec. 1617
My bodie to be buried in the Church of Much Waltham as neere unto the lefte syde of my late wife as may be. To the reparacons of the stooles in the Church of Waltham 40s. Towards the mendinge of the highway leading from Waltham Burye to Pleshye, 5 marks. To HUGH EVERARD, my sonne, my Tenement called Caprons and one garden and two peells of pasture belonging and one Tenement called "Shrynes sometime of WILLIAM BARNARD" all scituate in Muche Waltham, upon Condicon that he pay xiijs. iiijd. to the poore of Much Waltham yerely, on Good Friday, in the Church of Much Waltham, for ever, accordinge to the WILL of RICHARD EVERARD, my grandfather, deceased. To JOHN EVERARD, my Sonne, £100. To MARY, my Daughter, £200. To RICHARD WISEMAN, THEOPHILUS WISEMAN, JOSEPH WISEMAN and to ELIZABETH WISEMAN, CLEMENCE WISEMAN and MARY WISEMAN, the children of the said MARY, my Daughter, Tenn pounds a peece. To my Cosyn ANNE Ladye MAYNARD, my silver Jugge. To MARY the wife of the said HUGH, my sonne and to URSULA the wife of JOHN my sonne, a Ringe of Golde, a peece. To RICHARD EVERARD and CLEMENCE EVERARD, the Children of the said HUGH my sonne and to RICHARD EVERARD the sonne of the said JOHN my sonne, Tenn pounds apeece. To my Brethren, ROGER GOODYAE and RICHARD GOODAYE, and to my Cosin THOMAS WISEMAN, a Ringe of golde apeece. To Mr.

GOFFE, 10s. To the poore of Muche Waltham, £xiij. viijd. To the poore of Chelmisford and Mowlsham,£v. To the poore of Rettendon, ls. To the poore of Bromefeild and little Waltham, xls. To the poore of Pleshye, £iij. To the poore of Goodster, xxs. To the poore of Mashbury, xxs. To the poore of Rayne, xls. To JOHN HOWELL, sometimes my servant, liijs. iiijd. To WILLIAM AYLARD and THOMASIN his wife, 20s. each. To WILLIAM SANDFORD, my kinsman, £10. To JOHN GLASCOCKE, my servant, £v. To JOHN SERICH, my servant, foure marks. To THOMAS BEVYSE, my servant, 20s. To WILLIAM BEVYSE, my servant, xxv. To AGNES DEWEDEN and CLEMENCE CARTER, my servants 40s. each. Residuary Legatee and Sole Executor, my said sonne HUGH EVERARD.

THOMAS SORELL ⎫
       & ⎬Witnesses.
THOMAS BYRD ⎭

Proved 1 Augt. 1617 by the Sole Executor named. 82 *Weldon* P. C. C. 124 Weldon.

RICHARD EVERARD, gent.
2 Dec. 1617.

Sentence promulgated in a suit between HUGH EVERARD, son and Executor of the Will of RICHARD EVERARD, late of Great Waltham, co. Essex, gent., deceased, of the one part and Dame ANN MAYNARD Als EVERARD, granddaughter, by the son and next of kin of deceased, being daughter of Sir ANTHONY EVERARD, late of Great Waltham deceased, son of said RICHARD of the other, pronouncing for the sanity of deceased and for the validity of the Will produced by the said HUGH, the rightful executor.

From the Latin.

ANTHONY EVERARD, of Much Waltham in the County of Essex, Knight.

Dated 1 Oct. 1614.   Proved 27 Jan. 1614-15.
                                Sentence 27 Jan. 1614-15.

My carkas I will to be disposed of accordinge to a direction under my owne hande left with my sister WISEMAN.

Touchinge all my Landes and Hereditaments. I leave them wholly to my daughter ANNE, and the heires of her body.

Sole Legatee and Executrix: the said ANNE EVERARD.

JOHN SMITH
               } Witnesses.

JUDITH SMITH

Proved 27 Jan. 1614-15 by the Sole Executrix named. 6 Rudd

Sir ANTHONY EVERARD, Knight.

27 Jan. 1614-15.

Sentence, promulgated in a suit between Lady ANNE EVERARD, widow, relict of deceased, of one part, and ANNE EVERARD, daughter of deceased, testatrix of the Will of Sir ANTHONY EVERARD, late of Waltham Holy Cross, County Essex, Knight, deceased, pronouncing for the Will produced by the said Executrix and for the sanity of deceased. 6 *Rudd*

[The family of Everard is traced, by Burke, to Ralph Everard, living in the reign of Henry III. Richard Everard, whose will is printed above, was of Langleys, Much Waltham, Essex. His grandfather, Richard Everard, Esq., of Langleys, Much Waltham, married first Elizabeth, daughter of Richard Stephens, gent. (and had Richard, father of the testator), and secondly Agnes Upcher or Upshur (Arthur Upshur, emigrant ancestor of the Virginia family of that name, was a native of Essex). Richard Everard died Dec. 29, 1561, and was succeeded by his grandson, Richard (the testator). The last named Richard married Clementia, daughter of John Wiseman, Esq., of Great Canfield. He and his wife lived together fifty-three years. She died September, 1611, and he July 25, 1617. They had issue: 1. Sir Anthony, knighted 1603, who left an only daughter and heiress, Anne, who married Sir Henry Maynard, afterwards Lord Maynard; 2. Mathew, a s. p.; 3. Hugh, who succeeded his brother Sir Anthony; 4. John; 5. Mary married John Wiseman, Esq. Hugh Everard died in 1637, and was succeeded by his son Richard, who was created a baronet in 1629, and who married Joan, daughter of Sir Francis Barrington, and a descendant of George, Duke of Clarence. Sir Richard's great-grandson, Sir Richard Everard, Bart., was Governor of North Carolina and was the father of Susanna Everard, who married David Meade, of Virginia.]

GEORGE FITZJEOFFERIE of Creakers in the parish of Barforde, in the Countie of Bedd., Knighte.

Dated 28 Nov. 1618.   Proved 7 May 1619.

To be buried in my "Pue or seate in Barforde." To KATHERINE FITZJEOFFERYE, my eldest daughter, £400. To

URSULA FITZJEOFFERIE, my *third daughter, £300. to be paid unto her by WILLIAM BEECHER Esq. £50. by Mr. MOORETON of Cranfeild, gent £150. And by one RICHARDS als RICHARDSON of Bedford, mercer, £50. by WALTER SPENCER, gent., and ROBERT SCOTT, £50. To JUDITH FITZJEOFFERIE, my fourth daughter, £300. To MARGARET FITZJEOFFRYE, my "fifte" daughter, £300. To JOANE FITZJEOFFERIE my "sixt" daughter, £200. And whereas I have reserved, to dispose of by this my Will, out of the Joynture of my wife Dame ANNE FITZ-JEOFFERIE, one annuity of £100 to be yssuinge of my Mannor Howse in Creakers, Now for the better mayntennce of my younger Sonnes THOMAS FITZJEOFFERYE and ST. JOHN FITZJEOFFERYE, my Will is that my wife shall have the use and occupation of all suche lands Tenements and Hereditaments whereupon the said Annuity shalbe yssuinge. To my †third sonne OLIVER FITZGEOFFRIE, £200 to remain in the hands of my executrix during his life in regards of his impotencie. To my Kinswoman FRANCIS TEARLE, my sister's daughter, £20. To my Kinsman GEORGE FITZJEOFFERY, in respect of his lamenes, an Annuitie of £3. To Mris. SCROGGS, 40s. To the poore of Barforde, £4.

To the poore of Wilden** and Rhenold, 40s. to either parishes.

Residuary Legatee and Sole Executrix: ANNE my wife.

Overseers:—my brethren, JOHN OSBORNE, Esq. and THOMAS ANSTELL, Esq and my Kinsman OLIVER HARVIE, Esq.

RICHARDE FRANCKE, ⎫
                      ⎬Witnesses.
GEORGE FITZJEOFFERIE ⎭

Proved 7 May 1619 by the Sole Executrix named. 37 *Parker*

[*a "second" daughter not mentioned.]
[†"elder" sons not mentioned.]
**Co. not given.
There is Wilden in Bedds.
There is Renhold in Bedds.

[George Fitzgeffrey, "of Howton Conquest in Bedfordshire, gent.," and William Fitzgeffrey, "of Staple Inn, gent.," came to Virginia in 1623.]

VIRGINIA GLEANINGS IN ENGLAND.

(Contributed by Leo Culleton, 92 Picadilly, London, W., and
the late Lothrop Withington.)
(Continued.)

MARGARET WALLER of Baconsfield, county Bucks, Mayden.
Will 3 March 1631; proved 11 May 1632. To be buried in the
little Chancel or chapel within the Church of Beconsfield which
belongeth to my cosin Waller. To Poor of Beconsfield £20.
To poor of Chalfont St. Giles 40s. To sister Elizabeth Fredway £100 and at her decease to be divided among her children.
To my sister Thomasin Ballenger £200 and her children.
To sister Suzan Widmer £20 and to his brother Thomas Widmer £10. To my sister Parsons 3 children Francis, Edward
and Ann £10 each. To said Mrs Scroope 20s. for a ring.
To Elizabeth Petty £10. To sister Whitton's two sons £15
apiece. To niece Ann Kirle £20. To Robert Tompkins
son of my niece Sicily £10. To Griffin and John Waller £20
each. To Edmond Scroope son of Mary Scroope £10. To all
my sister Ann Wallars daughters a ring each. To goddaughter
Elizabeth Eaton £15 and to Mary Gaynes daughter likewise.
To sister Lucie £15. To Henry Dells wife 20s. To Richard
Bentley's wife 40s. To Ann Wolman the elder and Ann
Wolman her daughter 40s. each. To Nurse Wyan 20s and to
Nurse Clarke 10s. To Sarah Plaiter 20s. To poor Leresera
of Burnham £4. To Thomas Holl minister of Cholsbury £5
Executor; William Widmer abovementioned. Witnesses:
Thomas Holl and Phillis Stuter. Audley, 60.

[As there is great probability that one family of Wallers in Virginia
descended from the Wallers of Buckinghamshire, and a possibility that
another of our Virginia families of the name is of the same descent, two
Waller wills are printed here. It is hoped that others may be obtained
which will furnish definite information.

Col. John Waller, ancestor of the family in Spotsylvania County,
Williamsburg, etc., is stated in old family accounts to have been born
about 1670. He died in 1754. His seal and a copper-plate of his arms

(with the crest showing the arms of France pendant from a walnut tree) are still owned by his descendants. He gave the name "Newport" to his plantation in Spotsylvania. He married Dorothy King (born 1675, died 1759) and had issue Mary, John, Edmund, William, Thomas and Benjamin. They have many descendants.

The register of Newport Pagnell, Bucks, England, contains the births of the following children of Doctor John Waller and Mary his wife: (1) William, born Sept. 24, 1671; (2) John, born Feb. 23, 1673; (3) Mary, born May 23, 1674; (4) Thomas, born Oct. 17, 1675; (5) Steven, born Nov. 24, 1676; (6) Benjamin, born March 18, 1678; (7) Edmund, born Feb. 3, 1680; (8) Jemima, born Aug. 31, 1684. (See *William & Mary Quart rly, IX.* 63). Of these sons, Edmund, M. D., was a senior fellow of St. Johns College, Cambridge, and John is supposed to have been the emigrant to Virginia. While this is a probability (the names in the families of Dr. John and John of Virginia being much alike) it has not yet been proved.

The published pedigrees state that the first of the Buckinghamshire Wallers, was John, second son of William Waller, of Groombridge, Kent, who, in turn, descended from Sir Richard Waller, of Groombridge who captured Charles, Duke of Orleans at the battle of Agincourt. This John Waller married Elizabeth Farnefold, and had a son Richard Waller of Beaconsfield, Bucks, who was the father of Robert Waller, of Beaconsfield, (died 1545) who married 1st Tryon, 2d Elizabeth, daughter of William Duncombe, and had (according to'one account, by the 1st marriage); 1. Anthony, died Mar. 29, 1558; 2. William of Abingdon, Berkshire, buried Feb. 5, 1558, who married Joan, daughter of Thomas Bowland of Abingdon (and had a son Thomas, who married Dorothy Garrard, and died Sept. 1626); 3. Ralph, married Sarah Saunders; 4. Thomas, married a daughter of George Hampden; 5. Edmund of Coleshill, Bucks; married in 1555, Cicely Bell, and was father of Robt Waller of Coleshill, who married Ann Hampden. G. C. Waters *Chest rs af Chichl y*, a much higher authority, says that Edmund Waller of Coleshill, who married Cicely Bell, and was buried April 10, 1603, was a son of Robt. Waller and Elizabeth Duncombe. Robt. Waller, son of Edmund, was buried at Beaconsfield Sept. 2, 1616. He married Anne daughter of Griffith Hampden of Great Hampden. She died April 9, 1653. Robt. Waller's will was dated Dec. 21, 1615, and proved Feb. 7, 1616-17. His legatees were his eldest son Edmund (the poet), his sons Griffith, Steven, and John, and various daughters. The son John was born between the date of the will, Dec. 21, 1615, and that of a codocil, Feb. 19, 1615-16, and may have been the Dr. John Waller of Newport Paganell. Margaret Waller, the testator, was a sister of Robert Waller and aunt of the poet.

Thomas Waller, of Beaconsfield, (above) who married Dorothy Garrard, and died in 1626, has issue: 1. Edmund, married Lucy, daughter of Sir Richard Grobham, and died 1661; 2. Henry, married Jane Ady Sorg; 3. Robert; 4. John (who also may, possibly, have been Dr. John Waller of Newport, Pagnell).

ANNE WALLER of Beconsfeild, county Bucks, widow. Will 8 November 1652; proved 2nd August 1653. I desire to be buried in the churchyard of Beconsfeild, as near unto my dear and loving husband as may be. I give unto the poor of Beconsfeild £10 to be distributed unto them at the time of my burial.

To my daughter Mary, wife of Edmond Waller, esquire, my son, my coach and two coach horses. To Cicelie Tompkins, my daughter, £100. To my daughter Ursula Dobbins, £100, to be placed in the hands of the said Edmond Waller, who shall pay her the interest and increase thereof, and pay the principal to such persons as the said Ursula by her will shall direct. But my meaning is that she shall have the sole benefit and dispose thereof, in such sort as her now husband may not have anything to do therewith. To my grandchild Robert Waller, the messuage or inn in Beconsfeild called the Ball, and all the lands and tenements which I bought of my cousin Edmond Waller of Gregoryes, esquire. To my grandchildren Robert and Anna Mary Waller, my two great diamond rings; the said Robert shall have which of them he chooseth, his sister the other. To my grandchild Margo Waller, one of the daughters of my said son Edmond £100 within one year after my decease, if she then be 14 years old, or else to her father to be by him employed to her use till she attain her age of 14. To my said son Edmond, all my linen, household stuff, furniture and implements of household whatsoever. To every one of my servants dwelling with me at the time of my decease, half a year's wages over and above what may be due to them. All the rest of my goods I give to my grandchildren Robert and Anna Mary, equally, between them; and I make my friend Mr. George Gosnould my executor, to whom I give £20 for his pains and care to be taken therein, further authorizing him to reimburse himself all such sums as he may spend by reason of taking upon him the execution of this my will. I give to my grandchild Edmond Patty, esq., £5. To Sir Orlando Bridgman's lady, £3 to buy her a ring. Whereas there is due to me £1100 and upwards from my son Edmond Waller, my will is that all my debts, legacies and funeral expenses shall be paid out of that money, and the residue thereof paid to the said Robert and Anna Mary equally between them. (signed) Anne Waller. Witnesses: Edw. Ermiston, Henry Axtill, the mark of Thomas Sagwell, George Randall and Steven

Grove. Proved by Gosnold, gent., the executor named.
Brent, 250.

[This lady was of illustrious kinship and connection. She was aunt of
John Hampden, mother of Edmund Waller, the poet, and her brother
married Oliver Cromwell's aunt. She was, as stated above, the wife of
Robert Waller, and was baptized Dec. 10, 1589, and died April 9, 1653.
Her daughter Cicely, the niece mentioned in Margaret Waller's will,
married Feb. 10, 1624-5, Nathaniel Tompkins, who was executed July 5,
1643, for taking part in what was called "Waller's Plot," against the
Parliament. Edmund Waller, the poet, was born March 3d,1605-6,
married Anne Bankes July 5, 1631, married secondly, Mary Breese or
Breaux, and died Oct. 21, 1687. By the first marriage there were no
sons to survive infancy; but by the second marriage he had (1) Benjamin
stated (according to a letter from Sir Wathen Phipps Waller, Bart. to
have died in Virginia; 2. Edmund of Beaconsfield, will dated 1699,
d. s. p. at Bath, and buried in the Quaker burying ground there; 3. Stephen
LL.D, died Feb. 1707; 4. William, merchant in London; 5. Charles "of
whom nothing is known". If Benjamin Waller, son of the Poet was ever
in Virginia, there is no trace of him in the records. He may however
have lived in some of the counties where the records have been destroyed.
There is on record in Essex County a deed dated 1713 from Charles
Waller, of Essex, to Edward Waller of King & Queen, and another, dated
April 1740, from Charles Waller, and his wife Elizabeth, sister of Lodowick Rowzee, of Essex.]

WILLIAM WALTHALL of Coats, county Leicester, gent.
Will 24 May 1632; proved 7 February 1632. At the instance
of Alise Noone my natural mother dwelling at Evington
county Leicester, I sold one tenement in the parish of St.
Martins in the Burgh of Leicester for £40 and in consideration
did promise me to assign one other tenement in the parish of
All Saints in Leicester now in possession of Mary Gifford.
I hereby make my said Mother Alise Noone sole executrix
of my will. I entreat my said Mother to sell said tenement
in All Saints and out of the money pay to my sister Vrsula £20
and to my sister Dorothy £13. 6s. 8d. with residue to said
Mother. My said Mother is indebted to me £20 out of my
fathers estate and £20 more for the rents of certain lands
since my coming to full age, I give to my Sister Elizabeth £10
thereof and to Mary Noone my half sister £5, to my cousin
John Orme 50s. To my uncle Richard Pope £4. To my
Master Sir Henry Skipwith's servants £5 divided as he thinks
fit. To poor of Prestwould and Coates and Evington 40s.
apiece. To Clement and Edward Noone my brothers in law
20s. apiece. To the young men of Evington of my familiar

acquaintance 40s. to be divided by my Mother. All my books to Sir Henry Skipwith my Master his sons and to his daughters 20s. apiece. To Donaugh Bryan his footman 10s. To every my godchildren 2s 6d. Residue to said Mother. Witnesses: Henry Skipwith, And. Burton. *Russell, 11.*

[Wm. Walthall was probably a steward or other agent for Sir Henry Skipwith, ancestor of the Virginia family of the name. This is one of numerous instances in which men and women of families of the gentry were in service in other families.]

JOHN WELDON of Westminster, gentleman. Will 14 October 1644; proved 20 November 1644. I give the mannor of Summers in Much Parendon in Essex, with the advowson of the parsonage there, and all other my landes in Parendon and elsewhere in the said countie, in tail successively to my eldest sonne John, my sonne George and my daughters Elizabeth and Johanna. The lands I purchased of my brother in law George Bell in Wexham and Upton, county Bucks, I give to my daughter Elizabeth and her heirs, failing whom to the said Johanna and George successively. A house in Shoe-lane in the parishe of St. Andrews Holborne, which I purchased of —— Rookes, and is now in the occupation of Richard Goodman, spectacle maker, I give to my daughter Johanna Two shares of fower shares of land lyeinge in Pagetts tribe in the Bannuthos [Bermudas] which was purchased by my father in law George Prynne and myself of one —— Woodhall, barber, chirurgion of London, I give to my son George My lease of a house in the parish of Creechurche, London, now in the occupation of Mr. Genny, a comfitt maker, to my daughter Johanna. My lease of lands in Wexham and Upton aforesaid which I hold of Mr. John Peters of Darny in countie Bucks, to my daughter Elizabeth. My lease of the house wherein I dwell in Pettie France in the parishe of Margarett in Westminster to my daughter Elizabeth. My land which I have by mortgage of one —— Kedge, lyeing in Burnam, county Bucks. to my daughter Joanna, I discharge the said Kedge of a bond wherein he stands bound with my brother Henrie Welden for payment of £20 upon condition that, if he redeeme the said land from mortgage, he shall settle the same by good

459

conveyance upon Elizabeth, the eldest daughter of the said Henrie Welden and her heires I give to my daughter Elizabeth £150 and to my daughter Joanna £100 at their marriage or age of 21. All other my moveable goodes to be divided by my executor into three parts, my said daughters to have two parts, and my two sonnes one part and noe more. I make Mr. George Prynne aforesaid my executor, and give him the profits of all the above bequeathed leases and lands for the maintenance and education of my sonnes till 21, and of my daughters till 21 or marriage. I give to the poore of Westminster £5. To my sister in law Sarah Weldon towards the relief of her and her children £20. Witnesses: James Halliwell, James Heath, Jonathan Brand. Proved by the executor. *Rivers, 5.*

[Peter Efford, of York Co., Va., died in 1666, leaving a daughter, Sarah to the care of Rev. John Weldon, minister of the parish of St. Mary, Newington, Surrey, England. She married Samuel Weldon of London, doubtless a kinsman of her guardian, who came to Virginia in in 1675, and was the ancestor of the family of the name here and North Carolina.]

RICHARD WILLIAMS, late of the parish of Catherine Creechurch, London, bachelor, being bound on a voyage to Virginia in the service of this Commonwealth of England in the ship called the John, did divers times before his death and more especially. Will about the month of August 1651; proved 11 May 1653, declare his will and mind to be as followeth: I give all my wages and other personal estate whatsoever to Walkter Hawkins of the said parish of Catherine Creechurch, seaman, who was at that time bound for the same voyage, but did go in another ship; and I do make him my executor. Which worde he did utter to the intent that the same should stand as his last will and testament. Witnesses: John Farrar, the mark of Jane French. Proved by Walter Hawkins, the executor named. *Brent, 242.*

[This was a member of the crew of one of the ships in the Parliamentary fleet sent to subdue Virginia and the other royalist Colonies. The John was lost at sea on the voyage.]

THOMAS WILLOUGHBY late of Ostham, county Kent, gentleman. Nuncupative will 23 April 1636 (Saturday); proved 17 June 1636. He did request Mr. William Brewer who then came to visit him to calln his wife Mrs Julian Willoughby and his brother Mr. Peter Willoughby, and she coming in, said to her ''Jill I make thee my whole Executrix and give you all the goods I have here or anywhere else for my children are yours and I know you will have a care of them'' which words were declared in the presence of said Mr. William Brewer, and said Mr. Peter Willoughby. Witnesses: Willm Brewer, Peter Willoughby. Proved by Juliana Willoughby relict and executrix. *Pile, 77*.

JOHN WILLOUGHBY of Eatonbridge, county Kent, gent. Will 18 July 1633; proved 24 August 1633. To poor 10s. To my 3 servants dwelling with me at time of my decease 5s. apiece. To daughter Anne Willoughby £100 when 21 and £50 out of legacy given me by my father Christopher Willoughby gent deceased. Residuary Legatee: my son William Willoughby when 21. My mother to have my children for education etc. Executors: Mr. Richard Jennett, Mr. William Seyliard. Witnesses: Tho: Seyliard, James Seyliard, Jo: Seyliard, Francis Seyliard. Debts owing my testator: To Mr. W. Seyliard £30, Sister Bridgett Willoughby £40, to Brother Alexander Randall £20, Henry Stanford £20, Executors of Margaret Carpenter deceased £10. *Russell, 22*.

[Thomas Willoughby, of Lower Norfolk, Va., the emigrant ancestor of that family, was born in 1601, and came to Virginia in 1610 (*Hott.n*). He was a merchant as well as planter and made several trips to England. In the British Public Record Office is a certificate, dated 1627, by Thomas Willoughby of Rochester, aged 27, in regard to a ship in which he was about to go to Virginia. The correspondence in age leaves no doubt that this was the Virginia settler. Thomas Willoughby, the testator, seems to have been a son of Thomas of Wateringbury, and brother of Peter of, Adlington, (*Berry's Kentish Genealogies*). It has been siggested that this Thomas was the emigrant to Virginia; but the finding of his will disposes of that. It seems probable, however, that Thomas Willoughby of Virginia was a native of Kent.]

THOMAS WOODHOUSE. Will 14 August 1623; proved 26 July 1624. Who departed this life the 16th August 1623.

To my mother Elizabeth Woodhouse dwelling in London all my wages due from the Hon. East India Company. To William Parke 20s. To John Edwards 15s. To William Prichard 15s. to be paid by my mother out of my wages. To George Newton and William Prichard all my apparel and bedding. To Peter Cullamore my hat and coat. To Malachie Marten my girdle and screetore. Elizabeth Woodhouse, sole executrix. Witnesses: Richard Travell Proved by Elizabeth Woodhouse, mother of deceased. *Byrde, 66.*

ROGER WOODHOWSE. Stonweek. Will 1 August 1610; proved 5 November 1625. To Rutgera Woodhowse my wife named afore Van Eck all goods and money whatsoever intreating all officers that they will ayde the said Rutgera. Witnesses: Thos Cribs, Daniell Studley. Proved by Rutgere van Eck als Woodhowse relict nuper in partibus ultramarinis etc. *Clarke, 125.*

CAPTAINE FRAUNCIS WOODHOUSE. Nuncupative will on or about 15 June 1627; proved 9 August 1627. Taking his leave of Mr. Robert Terrill and his wife at whose house he lodged when in London saying that he could not tell whether he should see them again whereupon Susanna wife of Robert Terrill asked him if he had made his Will who answered that his Will was sonn made for all that I have I do give to my mother except one looking glass which I give to you, all which word he uttered in the house of said Mr. Terrell at his last departure to go with the Duke of Buckingham, in the presence of said Mr. Terrell Susanna his wife and John Gostellowe their servant and others. Commission to Marie Woodhouse matri FRauncisci Woodhouse. *Skynner, 86.*

HENRY WOODHOUSE of Winterton, county Norfolk, gent. Will 26 August 1636; proved 11 June 1637. To Nicholas Bacon of Gillingham esq and Humfrey Bowing neere Beccles (*sic*) gent and their heirs all my lands called Flatgates in Winterton East Somerton, Horsey and Waxtonsham, county Norfolk to be sold by them and the money paid to Jose Hane my son in law. To said Nicholas Bacon and Humfrey Bowing all my lands called Great Guntons in the manor of Skarning, county Norfolk, to be sold by them and they shall pay £150 which I do owe out of the moneys received for lands last given and also £200 to Elizabeth my daughter. All moneys that shall remain overplus to Judith my wife sole executrix. And I give her all my goods. Codicil 17 February All moneys due from Capt. Thomas Shocks and Capt. John Harrison which is about £100 I give to my daughter Doll also my books that do not belong to my son. To my daughter Alice £200 owing to me in Ireland. The lease at the Parmodes [Bermudas] to my son Harryes two daughters Betsey and Juday. My Bibell to my daughter Bettey. Rere Godfrey. *Goare, 97.*

SIR WILLIAM WOODHOWSE OF WAXHAM, county Norfolk Knight. Will 1 May 1638; proved 26 November 1639 Touching such manors lands tenements etc as were anyways in my disposition I have already by several deeds disposed of the same. I give to Elizabeth Smith the girl in my house £100. My will is that my executrix shall provide meat drinke lodging and apparel for her. Touching my personal estate in ready money plate, jewels, household stuff etc I give and bequeath to my loving daughter Frances Woodhowse sole executrix. Witnesses: Roger Gooch, Thos. Doodes, Thos, Doodes, Junr. *Harvey, 175.*

[Henry Woodhouse, son of Captain Henry Woodhouse, Governor of Bermuda, and grandson of Sir Henry Woodhouse, of Waxam (who died 1624) emigrated to Virginia, where he died in 1655. He has many descendants. Only a detailed pedigree of the family would show whether Thomas, Roger and Capt. Francis Woodhouse were of this family (for there was another in Norfolk, England); but "Henry Woodhouse of Waterton" is evidently the Governor of Bermuda, and the father of the Virginia emigrant. He names a wife Judith, son Henry, daughters Elizabeth, Alice, and Judith, and son-in-law "Jose Hane". He also had a son Horatio and a daughter Lucy, who married Sir William Dutton Colt, and other sons and daughters. The daughter, Alice, died unmarried in 1647, and in her will named her mother Mrs. Judith Woodhouse, and brother "Jost Hane".
Sir William Woodhouse, of Waxam, was father of Sir Henry Woodhouse, (who died 1624) and grandfather of Governor Henry Woodhouse. See this Magazine XIII, 202, 203; XVII, 397, and references given.]

VIRGINIA GLEANINGS IN ENGLAND.

(Contributed by Leo Culleton, 92 Piccadilly, London, W., and
the late Lothrop Withington.)
(Continued.)

RICHARD CHAMBERLAINE of Astly, county Warwick, Esq.
Will 7 October 1629; proved 12 May 1630. To be buried in
the Church of Astley. By various grants and leases of Manor of
Astley and lands in Bentley,Ansley, Riton,Bedworth, Fellongley,
Arley and Corley, county Warwick for benefit of Jane Chamberlaine my daughter the wife of Richard Chamberlaine of Templehouse, county Warwick and for benefit of Richard, Thomas
and John the three sons of said daughter. Said Richard
Chamberlaine of Temple house and Jane his wife in Trinity
1624 filed a bill in Chancery against me said Richard and Edward Chamberlaine my son and Edward Chamberlaine my
grandson and against John Gobert and Steven Hales Esqre
deceased and Humfry Cole Esq. I charge my son in law
Richard Chamberlaine and my daughter Jane Chamberlain
to continue the said manor in name and blood of Chamberlaines.
I have already given marriage portions to two daughters of my
son John Chamberlaine deceased and now to Elizabeth and
Fraunces two other daughters £100 each and £5 yearly for
maintenance. To married daughters of John 40s. each. To
Humfrey Adderlye Esq £300 and Richard Baldwin gent
£100 which they have paid for my son John's debts. If my
son Edward and grandchild Edward Chamberlaine confirm the
grant of the Manor to son in law Richard Chamberlaine before
18 months then Edward my grandchild and Elizabeth his
wife and others their children shall have the Annuity of £200
mentioned in an indenture made by me, Richard Chamberlaine,
my son in law and Jane his wife, and Edward Chamberlaine
my grandchild dated 1 June 1625. My sons Edward and Robert

From Vol. XXVI, No. 2 (April 1918), p. 145.

Chamberliane not to molest my son in law. To my daughters Margaret and Elizabeth 40s. each. To servant Marie Field £10. To Poor of Astley 40s. Residuary Legatees and Executors: daughter Jane and her son Richard. Overseers: Son in law and Humphrey Colles of Bicknell, county Warwick. Witnesses: Humfrey Colles, Henry Monforte, Thomas Chamberlaine, Richard Westly, Alexander Lynde, Mary Feild and Ed: Wayste. Scroope 41.

[In the chancel of St. Peters Church, New Kent County, Virginia, is a mural tablet (now nearly hidden by a modern lath and plaster partition which should be removed) bearing the following inscription

"Near this place lyes interred the
Body of Mr. Wm. Chamberlayne
late of this Parish merch't
Descended of an Ancient and
worthy Family in The County of
Hereford.
He married Elizabeth ye eldest
Daughter of Richard Littlepage of
This County, by whom he has
left issue, three sons, Edward Pye,
Thomas & Richard, & Two daughters
Mary & Elizabeth.
Ob. 20th Aug't, 1736, Aetat 36.
Hoc marmor exiguum suum
Amoris monumentum Posuit
Conjunx Moestissimi
1737
Also Ann Kidly Born since
Her Fathers Decease"

William Chamberlayne has many descendants; but it is with the English ancestry that this note is concerned. The name of the son Edward Pye Chamberlayne gives the clue.

The registers of the parish of Dewchurch, Herefordshire, contain entries of the baptism, on Oct. 29, 1605, of Bridget, daughter of Sir Walter Pye, of The Mynde, in that parish; of her marriage, Sept. 26, 1627, to Richard Chamberlayne, Esq.; of the death, Oct. 2, 1699, of Magdalen, wife of Thomas Chamberlayne, and of the baptisms of the following children of Edward Pye Chamberlayne, Gent; and Ann his wife:
(1) Edward Pye, Aug. 4, 1691; (2) Thomas, April 18, 1693; (3) Richard, March 26, 1695; (4) George, Aug. 12, 1697; (5) William, Sept. 25, 1699; (6) Ann, Aug. 15, 1700; (7) Mary, Feb. 2, 1702. It will be noted that the birth of the William baptised at Dewchurch would correspond exactly with the age of William of Virginia.

Two other sons of E. P. Chamberlayne, the elder, can probably be accounted for. There are in Surry Co., Va., several powers of attorney, dated 1734 &c, from Thomas Chamberlayne, of Bristol, merchant, and the Va. Gazette, in 1736 or 1737, announced the loss of the ship "Pye", belonging to Mr. Thomas Chamberlayne of Bristol. In *Familiae Minorum Gentium* (Harleian Society) in a Clarke pedigree is given the marriage of Mary (born 1698, died July 17, 1747) daughter of Samuel Clarke, to Thomas Chamberlayne, of Bristol, merchant. They had issue: (1) Edward Pye, born May 2, 1733, died 1742; (2) Thomas Gunter, born Aug. 17, 1735, died Aug. 19; (3) Thomas, died young; (4) Ann, born Feb. 8, 1737-8.

Atkins History of Gloucestershire (1711) says, concerning the manor of Dymock: "Edward Pye Chamberlain is the present lord thereof, who hath a very good seat called the Bois, and a great estate." Fosbrooke, in "Abstracts of Records (&c) respecting the County of G loucester," says that Edward Seys, Esq., in 1680, "sold the manors of Dymock and Boyce, the mansion house called Boyce Place, and Sundr y estates, to Edw. Pye, merchant, who dying 1692, Edward Pye Chamberlayne became seized by devise to whose son of the same name they descended in 1729. In 1769 he sold to Mrs. Ann Cam."

In the church at Dymock are the following epitaphs:

"Here lyeth the Body of
Edward Pye, of Boyce, Esq.
who departed this Life,
in Hopes of a better,
the 31st of August, 1692
in the eightieth year of his Age."

Arms: Ermine, a Bend lozengy Gulés, for *Pye*. Crest, a Cross fitchy, between two Wings. ——————

"In Memory of
Edward Pye Chamberlain, Esq.
of the Boyce, in this Parish,
who died April 20, 1729,
aged 38 years.

Likewise of
Elizabeth his Wife,
who died Nov. 19, 1775,
aged 76.

And also of four of his Children
who died Infants.

This Monument was erected by
Edward Pye Chamberlayne, Esq.
in Duty to his worthy and deceased
Parents."

The age of Edward Pye Chamberlayne, of Dymock, corresponds exactly with the baptism of E. P. Chamberlayne at Dewchurch.

There are also at Dymock tombs of Thomas Wall Esq. (d-1694) and of "Mary Chamberlain, widow and Relict of Thomas Wall, of Lintridge in this Parish, Esq., of the Family of Edward Pye, Esq., Lord of the Manor of Great Dymock" who died in 1707. The Visitation of Gloucestershire 1682-3, states that Thomas Wall, aged 23, 1683, married Mary, daughter of Thomas Chamberlayne, of London, merchant"; and among the allegations for marriage license, (Vicar General of Canterbury)" is the following: "Thomas Wall, of Dymock, &c. Gloucester, Gent., about 22, and Mrs. Mary Chamberlayne, of St. Gyles, Cripplegate, London, spinster, about 17, with consent of her mother, Mrs. Elizabeth Chamberlain widow."

The identity of Richard Chamberlayne Esq., who in 1627, married Bridget Pye is shown by a tomb at Astley, Warwickshire.

"NVDVS EXIIT VT ADVENIT
RICARDVS CHAMBERLAYNE,
SOLA SPE RESTAT. QVI OBIIT
VI DIE NOVEMB. AN. DNI. 1654.
[A cheveron between three escollaps.]

QVEM STATIM SECVTA EST BRID-
GETTA EJVSDEM, DVM VIXERVNT,
ANIMI, CONJVX CHARISSIMA,
EODEM NVNC SVB MARMORE
EADEMQ. SPE RESTAT. OBIIT
VIII DIE MARTII, AN. DNI. 1655
[A bend Lozenge.]"

The Visitation of Warwickshire 1619, has the following pedigree of the Chamberlaynes of Astley:

Edward Chamberlayne, of Sherborne in the County of Oxford had two sons: (1) Sir Leonard, of Sherborne, eldest son, (2) Edward Chamberlayne of Astley, Warwickshire, 2d son. This Edward had a son Edward Chamberlayne of Astley, Esq., who married ——— Harecourt, and had a son Richard of Astley, 1619, tne name of whose wife is not given.

Richard had issue: (1) Elizabeth, married George, or Gerrard Gifford, of Chillington, Co., of Stafford; (2) Jane, married Richard Chamberlayne of the Court of Wards; (3) John, married ———Grevill (and had Edward son and heir, Elizabeth, Mary, Frances, Margaret and Jane); (4) Edward; (5) Robert; (6) Margaret.

Richard Chamberlayne, who was the head of the family in 1619, was the Richard whose will is given above. He had, evidently conveyed the Astley estate to his son-in-law Richard Chamberlayne. It is probable that it was Richard, son of the latter and named in his grandfathers will, who married Bridget Pye, and died in 1654.

The Visitation of Oxfordshire, 1634, shows that a daughter of Richard Chamberlayne (the son-in-law of the will) married into still another branch of the family. It states that Sir Thomas Chamberlayne of Wickham Castle, Oxfordshire, a Justice of the Court of Common Pleas, had a son Thomas, 22 years old 1635, who married Anne (Jane?) daughter of Richard Chamberlayne of Templehouse, Warwickshire, of the Court of Wards and Liveries, descended from the Chamberlaynes of Denford. The same pedigree shows that Sir Richard Chamberlayne of Sherborne, (great grandfather of the Sir Thomas Chamberlayne) had a younger son, Thomas of Denford.

It is evident that Wm. Chamberlayne of Virginia was of the Astley family, but a good deal of work would be required to fix the exact line.]

That there were other members of the family at Astley not named in the Visitation of 1619 is shown by the wills which follow.]

WALTER CHAUMBERLEYN of Astley in the Countie of Worcester. [Warwick?]

Dated 22 June 1611. Proved 18 Oct. 1611. Towardes the Reparacons of the parishe church of Astley, three shillinges fower pence.

To poor folkes, fortie shillinges, to be distributed at the Discretion of the Overseers for the poore of Astley and of Mr SHEPHEARD, parson of Astley.

To my sonne JAMES CHAMMBERLEYN, one hundred and fower poundes, And my will ys that XPIAN my Wife shall have the moytie or one halfe of the Interest of the same so long as she shalbe charged for the keeping of hym. Also to the said JAMES, my Lease of Mytton provided that XPIAN my said wife shall have the Rent of the same during her life.

To HUMFREY, my sonne, one hundred and three score poundes and all my "Lambes, Slayes and gears and ymplementes belonging to weaving."

CHRISTIAN, my said Wife shall enjoye my Lease of my house I hold of Mr. JAMES, during her life and after her decease to HUMFREY my said sonne and to JOHANE his wife and to theire heires and assignes.

To the children of THOMAS PALMER, fower poundes. And to the children of my Cosin WALTER COLLIER, sixe shillinges eight pence, a peece.

To my brother in lawe JOHN MARTEN his children, fyve shillinges a peece. And to the children of JOHN VICARIES of Shrawley, two shillings a peece.

Residuary Legatees and Executors:—ZPIAN my wife and HUMFREY my sonne

Supervisors:—my kynesman WALTER COLLIER and JOHN FARELEY of Astley.

JOHN SHEPHEARDE, Clerke parson of Asteley, ⎰ Witness.
who wrote the same. ⎱

Proved 18 Oct. 1611 by the Executors named. Wood 62.

JOHN CHAUMBERLEYN of Astley in the Countie of Warwicke, Esquire

Dated 11 May 1618   Proved 23 Oct. 1619.
Sentence 23 Oct. 1619.

First I ordayne and make Executors of this my will Sr RICHARD HUSSEY of Adbright Hussey in the Countie of Salop, Knighte, Sr THOMAS CHEYNEY of Sondon in the Countie of Bedford, Knighte and HUMFREY ATHERLEY of Weddington in the Countie of Warwicke, esquire.

And I do will that they first paye all suche Debtes as I owe unto ALICE DUDLEY, daughter of Sr ROBERT DUDLEY, knighte, for the payment whereof my said Executors stande joyntlie bound with me.

And the Remaynder (yf any shalbe) shalbe bestowed uppon my daughters equallie to be devided among them.

RICHARD THORNES, JOHN MILLFORD, LEONARD WILLIAMS, JOHN POWELL, THOMAS JAMES, Witnesses.

Proved 23 Oct. 1619 by the Executors named.   83 Parker.

SENTENCE given 23 Oct. 1619, in a Suit between Sir RICHARD HUSSEY, knight, and Sir THOMAS CHEYNEY, Knight and HUMFREY ATHERLEY Esq, executors of the WILL of JOHN CHAMBERLEYN late of Astley, in the Countie of Warwick, Esq. on the one part and ELIZABETH CHAMBERLEYN, relict of the said deceased of the other, pronouncing for the sanity of deceased and in favour of the Will exhibited by the executors.   83 Parker.

From the Latin.

ELIzABETH CHAMBERLAINE of Ashley late wife of John Chamberlaine of Ashley, county Warwick, Esq. Will 11 August 1620; proved 1 May 1621.   £10 for a stone to cover my husbands Mr. Halmer's grave.   To my neece Mary Trussell £140.   To Sir Henry Martin Knight standing cup and the refusal of my best bed, and bedding.   To my sister Lewes £10 and some clothing.   To my sister Bendsteed ring and £10.   To my nepgew William Trussell £3.   To my kinsman Richard Dalton £5.   To John Trussell £6.   To the poor £3.   To Mr. Newdigate a ring.   To my servant Edward Hinshaw 30s.   To Dorothie Higginson my maid 20s.   To my neece Amy Trussell £5.   Residue to my neece said Mary Trussell, Executors: Dr. Morton Lord Bishop of Lichfield, the Rt. HonLord Spencer and Sir Henry Marten.   To each of them £10.   Witnesses: W. Hunsdon, Tho: Boyland, John Temple.   Proved. by the three executors.   Dale, 37.

VIRGINIA GLEANINGS IN ENGLAND.

(Contributed by Leo Culleton, 92 Picadilly, London, W., and the late Lothrop Withington.)

THOMAS SMITHE of London, Knight.

Dated 30 Jan. 1621.   Codicil 4 Sept. 1624.
                                                              Proved 12 Oct.1625.

To the Master and Wardens of the mistery of Skinners of London, my houses, messuages, landes, tenements and hereditaments scituate neere Paulesgate at the West end of Watling streete in city of London which I purchased of Sir FRANCIS TRAPPS BYRNAND, and my messuage in Lyme streete in London wherein   DE LA NAYE now dwelleth adjoining the house wherein Mr. JOHN CLARKE, Doctor of Phisick now dwelleth, they to pay the profits of the same yearly, viz., to the parson and churchwardens of the parish of Bidborrough in co. Kent, for ever, one annuity of £5. 10. 0. they to provide weekly six loaves of bread worth 4d the loaf, and to give the same every Sabbath day to six poor householders of the said parish. The parson, Churchwardens and Parish Clark for their pains to retain yerely to the uses following, 6s; viz., to the parson, 2s. to the eldest churchwarden 2s. and to the parish clerk, 2s.

To the parson and churchwardens of the parish of Tunbridge, in co. Kent an annuity of £10. 8. 0, they to provide weekly 12 loaves, worth 4d and give the same every Sabbath to 12 householders.

Also. to Spelhurst in co. Kent an annuity of £5. 10 to be disposed of in bread as formerly set down for the parish of Bidborough.

If the said parishes do not faithfully discharge the trust, the annuities to cease and be given unto the parishes of Hadlower and Lee in co. Kent.

From Vol. XXVI, No. 3 (July 1918), p. 267.

[To be distributed as above to the following parishes]: Otfor, £5. 10. 0; Sutton at Hone, £5. 10. 0; Durrant, £4. 6. 8.

To the Schoolmaster of the Free School at Tunbridge, for ever, £10 yearly and to the Usher of the same, £5 yearly for ever. Also towards the maintenance of 6 poor scholars at the Universities elected out of the said schoole, threescore pounds.

As concerning my Manors, messuages, howses, lands, tenements and hereditaments, one moiety thereof to my wife Dame SARA SMITHE, during her life and after her decease to my sonne Sir JOHN SMITHE and to his heirs, the other moiety to my said sonne Sir JOHN SMITHE and his heirs, in default of issue then as follows: to my nephew, THOMAS SMITHE of Ostenhanger, in co. Kent, Esq. sonne and heire of Sir JOHN SMITHE, my late brother, deceased, my messuages and lands lying in Bidborough, Tunbridge Pentherst and Spelhurst (except my lands in Tunbridge which I purchased of Mr. DYKE); to my nephew THOMAS SMITHE, sonne to my brother Sir RICHARD SMITHE, Knt., to my nephew JOHN SMITH, sonne to my late brother ROBERT SMITH, deceased, and to my nephew THOMAS FANSHAWE, sonne to my Lady FANSHAWE, my lands and tenements called Otford Parke (now disparked) situate in Otford, Sevenoke and Seale, in co. Kent, which I lately purchased of the Earl of LEICESTER, to be equally divided amongst them, and their heirs. To ''my nephew Sir THOMAS BUTLER, OLIVER BUTLER sonnes to my sister URSULA BUTLER '' and to my nephew Sir ARTHUR HARRIS, sonne to my late sister ALICE HARRIS, deceased, my lands and tenements called Cottington, situate near Sandwich, co. Kent which I lately purchased of WILLIAM RICHARDSON, gentleman, to be equally divided amongst them, and their heirs.

To my nephews THOMAS FANSHAWE & WILLIAM FANSHAW, sonnes to my sister JOANE FANSHAW, my lands and tenements, known as Saltangh grange situate in Kingingham, in co. York, and those in Halstead, in co. Essex, and those in Lewsham, in co. Kent which I purchased of Sir NICHOLAS STODDARD, Knight, to be divided between and their heirs.

To St. Bartholomewes Hospital; £40, Christ's Hospital, £20; Bridewell Hospital, £20 and St. Thomas Hospital £20.

To the childern of my sister Mris. JOANE FANSHAWE, £5. each. To the Childern of my late sister URSULA BUTLER, £5 each. To my sister the Lady FANSHAWE, £20, and to each of her children, £5 except her sonne RICHARD to whom £10. To the Lady St. LEGER, my goddaughter, £20.

To the childern of my late sister Lady KATHERINE HAYWARD als SCOTT £5 each. To the childern of my late sister the Lady ALICE HARRIS, deceased, £5 each. To my two neices, KATHERINE the Lady BAKER and EILZABETH the Lady NEVELL, daughters of my late brother Sir JOHN SMITH, Knt., deceased £50 each. To each of the childern of my late brother HENRY SMITH, deceased £5. To my brother SIR RICHARD SMITH, £20 and to my sister his wife, the Lady SMITH, £10. To Sir JOHN SMITH, sonne of the said Sir RICHARD SMITH, £10. To my nephew JOHN SMITH, sonne of my late brother ROBERT SMITH, deceased, £5. To Sir DAVID WATKINS, £20. To Captain EDWARD CHISTIAN £10. To JOHN WOOD, doctor in Divinity, £5 and to his wife Mris. ALICE WOOD, £5. To my friend Sir HUMFREY HANFORD, '5. To my friend Mr. EDWARD COOKE, apothecary, 40s. To master VALENTINE MARKHAM, 40s. To Mr. RICHARD AUSTEN of Sutton, 40s and to his wife, 40s. To my friend Sir THOMAS ROE, £10. To Mr. ROBERT SYMONDS, dwelling in my house, at Bidborough, 40s. To Mr. HUGH WILCOCKE, 40s. To Mr. THOMAS HICKS, of London, Merchant, £5. To Mr. GEORGE STROWD, 40s. To each of the children of Mris. SARA CLARKE, deceased, 30s. To Mr. JOHN WOODHALL, £10. To the Governor of the Company of Merchants in London trading into East India, £5 and to the then Deputy of the said Company, £4 and to the Treasurer, £3, to buy them rings.

To Mr. ANDREW ELLAM, Mr. CHRISTOPHER LAMNAN, Mr. RICHARD MOUNTNEY, Mr. ROBERT FOTHERBIE and to Mr. JOHN ROBINSON, servants to the said Company and to Mris. WALDER, widow, the late wife of Mr. JOHN

WALDER deceased, also of the said Company, 30s. each for rings. To the Muscovia Company, £500, towards the payments of such debts as are due by the said company upon the old joynt stock wherein I appoint that the poorer sort of the debtors as ARTHUR PANTHUR may be first satisfied. To the Treasurer, Counsell and Companies for the Plantation in Virginia and Somer Islands called the Virginia Companie and the Bermudaes Company, £100, to be divided between the two Companies towards the buildings of two Churches vizt. for each plantacon one. Residuary Legatees: my wife, Dame SARA SMITH and my sonne Sir JOHN SMITH. Executors: my wife Dame SARA SMITH, my sonne Sir JOHN SMITH, my brother Sir RICHARD SMITH and my friends, Sir DAVID WATKINS & Mr. NICHOLAS CRISPE.

WILLIAM SKELLTON, HENRY WHIT-
    AKER, ROBERT HEATH
             AND
    HUMFREY DISON, Not Pub.   WITNESSES.
Codicil 4 Sept. 1624.

Mr. JOHN LEAVESTON, in plate, £20, Mris. LEAVESTON, the same, Sir JOHN MERRICK, Sir JOHN WORSTEN-HOLME, Sir WILLIAM RUSSELL, Sir NICHOLAS FORT-ESUE, Sir JOHN OSBORNE, Sir JOHN COOKE, Sir FRANCIS GOFTON, Sir RICHARD SUTTON, Mr. WILLIAM BURRELL, Mr. SAMUEL WROTE, Mr. RICH-ARD EDWARDS, Mr. NATHANIEL RICHE, SAMUEL ARGALL, Mr. JOSIAFFANT in rings 60s each. Mr. SCOTT a ring 30s. ARTHUR LEAVET, £20, JOHN CAPPER, £5. ADAM BOWEN, £5. FRANCIS REYNOLDES, £10, Mr. ELLIS CRISPE, Doctor DEE, Doctor MEDDUS, Mr. HASTEWOOD, ALDER JOHNSON, Mr. HENRY FOTH-ERBUY, Mr. LOTTPEARE in rings, 40s. each. Proved 12 Oct. 1625 by Dame SARA SMITH, Sir JOHN SMITH, Sir RICHARD SMITH and DAVID WATKINS, executors named power reserved to NICHOLAS CRISPE, executor also. **107 Clarke.**

[Sir Thomas Smith, son of Thomas Smith of Ostenhanger, Kent, was one of the greatest merchants of his day and a leader in exploration and the extension of English commerce. He was born about 1558, .was an incorporator of the Turkey Company in 1581, "a principal member of the Russia Company" 1587, one of Raleigh's assignees of his Virginia interests 1580; an incorporator and first governor of the East India Company, ambassador to Russia, 1604, M. P. for Dulwich 1604-1611. For the first twelve years of the Virginia Company he was at its head as treasurer. He died Sept, 4, 1625, and was buried at Hone Church, Kent, where a most elaborate tomb was erected over his remains. An admirable sketch of the life of Sir Thomas Smith appears in Brown's *Genesis of the United States*, II, 1012-1018. In considering Smith's career as a member of the Virginia Company, the predjudices of ancient and modern writers have to be considered, Alexander Brown as well as John Smith. The numerous charitable bequests contained in the will, are still administered by the "Skinners Company."

Many persons named in the will were associated with Virginia. Brown says that Capt. Nathaniel Butler, who excited so much indignation in Virginia, by his accounts of the colony, was a half-brother of Sir Oliver Butler. Sir Thos. Smiths sister Ursula, who married Simon Harding, must have married again and became the mother of Sir Oliver and the step-mother of Nathaniel. This connection with the Smith party in the Company is worth noting. Sir Arthur Harris, another nephew named, was a member of the Virginia Company. Thomas Fanshaw, and hi father Sir Henry Fanshaw (Smith's brother-in-law) were members of the Company. Lady Kathrine Hayward was wife of Sir Rowland Hayward, Lord Mayor of London. Her daughter, Mary, married Sir Warham St. Leger, of Ulcombe, Kent, and was the mother of Ursula St. Leger who married Rev. Daniel Horsmanden. She has many descendants in Virginia. Sir Humphrey Hanford or Hansford, was a member of the Company, as were Sir Thomas Roe, John Woodhall, Sir John Merrick, Sir John Wolstenholme, Sir William Russell, Sir Francis Gofton, William Burrell, Samuel Wrote, Richard Edwards, Nathaniel Rich, Samuel Argall, Alderman Johnson, and probably others named in the will. "Smith's Hundred" a tract of 100,000 acres near the Chickahominy River (in the present Charles City Co.), was named for Sir Thomas Smith, but in 1620, the name was changed to "Southampton Hundred," in honor of the Earl of that name. There is no record of how the money bequeathed for a church in Virginia was used.]

EDWARD PYE CHAMBERLAINE of the Newhouse in the County of Hereford, Esq., dated August 6, 1719. proved January 19, 1727. He held by copies of court roll under the Lord of the manor of Kilpeck, Herefordshire, two messuages known as Nookes Court *als.* Newhouse, and also four parcels of arable land and pasture in one of the copies of court roll for the remaining part of the term of years expressed. He had surrendered the said messuages and lands for his own use during his life, and after his death the remainder to such persons and for the payment of such sums of money as he should by deed or his last will prescribe. He therefore gives his wife Ann all the lands &c. and all her other customary and copyhold messuages &c. in the manor of Kilpeck for her life, and after her death to his trusty and well-beloved kinsmen, Willian Jones, of Ross, in the County of Hereford, Esq., and James Gomond, of Kilpeck the said County, gent, in trust that they should, within two years after his wife's death, pay to his daughter Mary £600, and the lawfull interest thereof, half yearly, in the mean time, and the rest of the rents and profifs for said unexpired term of years, with rights of renewal &c. to said Jones and Gomond, also in trust for the benefit of his son Thomas Chamberlaine and his heirs forever, with reversion to sons Richard and William. Bequeaths all forehold, leasehold &c. property in the parishes of St. Weonards, Wellsh Newton, Much Dewchurch, and St. Devereux, and in the Parish of Gismond in the County of Monmouth &c. to wife Anne for her life and at her death to his children Thomas, William, Richard and Mary, in such proportion as she shall by deed or will prescribe and failing such dirctions by his wife, to be equally divided between the childern named. After debts &c. paid, remainder of personal estate to wife Anne. Appoints William Gamons, of Trelough in the parish of St. Devereaux in the County of Hereford, Esq., and Thomas Witherstone of the parish of Bringhill, County of Hereford, gent., trustees of his will

Proved in the Comistory Court of the Diocese of Hereford, at Herford.

[The testator was, of course, the Edward Pye Chamberlayne whose children were baptized in the parish of Dewchurch, Herefordshire. (See this Magazine XXVI, 146). In the last Magazine some details were given in regard to three of his sons. The abstract given above is from a copy of the will obtained in England a few years ago by a member of the Virginia family, who has kindly allowed its use. This descendant visited "Newhouse", Herefordshire, which is now but an ordinary farm-house. The inventory made in 1727 of Edward Pye Chamberlayne's personal property at Newhouse, only amounted to £157.]

EDWARD PYE, of the Island of Barbadoes in the West Indies, Merchant, now of the Boyce, in the parish of Dymocke, co., Gloucester.

Dated 10 Feb. 1690-1.   Codicil 22 Sept. 1691.
                                       Proved 27 Oct. 1693.

475

To my kinsman, EDAWARD PYE CHAMERLAINE, late of the Island of Barbados, merchant and to ANNE his wife and to their heires, all my Estate and Interest I have in or to Pentvoyer, parish of St. Waynords co. Hereford, which I purchased of Mr. HALL, also the new house, Cooks Meadows, the Meadows I bought of Mr. HOSKINS, called the Eight acres, and my houses and lands in the parish of Grismont, in co. and my houses and lands in the parish of Grismont, in co. Monmouth, Provided that my niece, ELIZABETH CHAMBERLAINE, mother of the said EDWARD, shall have to her owne use the rent of Cookes Meadow yearlie. And whereas I granted the Mannor of Dymocke and the Mannor of Boyce and all other my lands and tenements within the parish of Dymocke, unto RICHARD HOWELL & RICHARD GUY, of the City of London, Esqrs.,for 20 years at the yearly rent of £140 as in the lease dated 27 Sept. 1688 doth appear. I give £60 to my said Niece ELIZABETH CHAMBERLAINE and the remainder of the said £140 to her granddaughters [not named]

And whereas I am blessed with an Estate in the West Indies, my will is that the said RICHARD GUY, late of the said Island, and his heirs, shall enjoy the same, he paying out of the first goods and profits the following: to the grand childern of EDWARD GUY, late of London, merchant, deceased, £120; to St. George's Church in Barbados, a piece of plate for Sacrament use, to the value of £20; to EDWARD SKEETE & ROBERTA HIS daughter, ten thousand pounds of sugar a peice; to the value of four thousand pounds of sugar in rings amongst my friends as the said RICHARD GUY shall think fit.

And whereas I have several Negroes in sorts in Barbados whome I called my Merchants I will that they and their children shall be dealt with according to the Instructions which I left with Mr. JOHN CROONE.

My Lorship of Dymocke and Mannor of Boyce with all the messuages, lands tenements and hereditaments thereunto belonging, after the expiration of the term before granted, to my said kinsman, EDWARD PYE CHAMBERLAINE, and to his heirs male, in default of such issue, to the daughters, and their heirs, in default of such issue to the said RICHARD GUY and his heirs. To JANE BUGG and her three childern, JOHN, RICHARD & JANE, £10 each. To JANE HOPKINS and her two children, CHARLES &JANE. £10 each. To JOHN TUCKEWELL, £10. To EDWARD FREEMAN and his two childern, EDWARD & MARY, £10 each. To FRANCIS FREEMAN and his daughter ANNE, £10. To MARGARET WORME and her five childern, THOMAS, CHRISTOPHER, RICHARD, ELIZABETH & MARTHA, £10 each. To HENRY WORME, WILLIAM WORME & ELIANOR WORME, £10 each. To MARGARET READ, £10. To THOMAS, FRANCIS & CHARLES TUCKEWELL, £10 each. To JOHN FREEMAN and his five children, JOHN, VALENTINE, THOMAS, ELIZABETH & SARAH, £10.

Residuary Legatee: RICHARD GUY, late of the Island of Barbados.

Executors:- RICHARD HOWELL, THOMAS BATSON & WALLENGER, merchants.

WILLIAM WINTOUR, RICHARD HILL, RICHARD HILL, junior; WITNESSES.

Codicil 22 Sept. 1691.

I inform my Executors, in case I should depart this life before the debts due from the Guinny Plantation and Ferdinando Gorges be paid it is my will that whereas I have an assignment from my Neice Mrs. ELIZABETH CHAMBERLAINE of Mr. FRANCIS SONES Mortgage of the Guinny Plantation in the Island of Barbados and a Stocke thereon for the payment of £1,000 as by the said assignment dated 30 March 1691 that the said £1,000 be paid unto my neice ELIZABETH CHAM-BERLAINE if then living, in case of her death to her granddaughter. And for what shall be due on the said mortgage for interest to pay the same unto the daughter or daughters of Mr. EDWARD SKEETE of Barbados. And whereas I have lent unto Captain FERDINANDO GORGES, £200. I appoint my Executors on receipt of the same to pay it unto Mrs. JANE POWELL, Mrs. LEWSANNA HOLLAND and

Mrs. JOANE WHEELER, which I give them for their kindness to me and my friends, COLLO. RICHARD GUY& Mr. RICHARD HOWELL.

RICHARD HILL, RICHARD; Witnesses

Proved 27 Oct. 1693 by the Executors named. 43 **Coker.**

[The more information we obtain in regard to the pedigree of this family of Chamberlayne, the more the difficulties seem to increase. In the first place this will shows that Edward Pye and Edward Pye Chamberlayne had both lived in Barbadoes before finally taking up residence in England. This makes their original English homes entirely uncertain. Edward Pye, born in 1616, could not well have been a native of Barbadoes; but it is possible that Edward Pye Chamberlayne was. The will also shows that the Edward Pye Chamberlayne, who became heir to Dymock about 1727 was not Edward Pye's legatee; but that his father, Edward Pye Chamberlayne, the elder, (whose will is printed above) was. The younger inherited the estate after his fathers death. The will also shows that Edward Pye Chamberlayne, the elder, was son of Elizabeth, Edward Pye's neice. This Elizabeth was living at the date of the will, Feb. 1690-91. A probable clue to the parentage of Edward Pye Chamberlayne, the elder, is Mrs. Mary Wall"of the family of Edward Pye, Esq." who was buried at Dymock in 1707. She was daughter of Thomas Chamberlayne, of London, Merchant, dead in 1682, and his wife Elizabeth (living in 1682); was born about 1665 and in 1682 when living in St. Giles, Cripplegate, London, married Thomas Wall. It seems probable that this Elizabeth, wife of Thomas Chamberlayne, of London, was the niece of Edward Pye's will and that in this way Mrs. Wall was "of the family" of Edward Pye. The will of Thomas Chamberlayne of London, and of his widow, Elizabeth, if they exist, would be very helpful in tracing the line.

As the name Pye came into this Chamberlayne family through Elizabeth, niece of Edward Pye, the testator,, the theory that this line must descend from Richard Chamberlayne of Astly and his wife Bridget Pye, is not atall necessarily a correct one. Settlement in Dewchurch, near the main seat of the Pye family would indicate relationship; but the pedigrees of Pye in Burke's "Commoners", and the "Herald & Genealogist," do not name this Edward Pye. It appears about the beginning of the seventeenth century to have been a very numerous family.

Edward Pye was a prominent man in Barbadoes. He was a member of the Assembly in 1666. In 1670 he was in London and in that and in several succeedihg years as one of the "principal planters" of Barbadoes, he was frequently consulted by government as to the affiairs of the island.]

Abstract of the Will of EDMUND WALLER, Doctor of Physic, Senior Fellow of St. John's College, in the University of Cambridge.

Dated 20 NOv. 1745.   Codicil 11 Dec. 1745.

                        Proved 8 Jan. 1745-6.

                        Adm. 29 Jan. 1746-7.

If I die in Cambridge I desire to be buried there, if at Newport;

then in the family Vault in the churchyard. To my nephew, Mr. WILLIAM WALLER, an apothecary, in London and second son of the Revd. Mr. WILLIAM WALLER, £300. To each of my late brother BENJAMIN'S daughters, MARY PERROTT & ELIZABETH PERROTT, £200. To my brother, JOHN WALLER, in Virginia, or if he be dead to be divided amongst his children, £100, excepting his eldest son JOHN, to whom, £50. £40 to be laid out by my executor so that the interest be yearly applied by way of augmentation to be a benefaction given some time ago for preaching a sermon on Good Friday by the Vicar of Newport Pagnel. To my sister ELIZABETH WALLER, relict of my late brother, BENJAMIN WALLER, £50. To St. John's College, £200, also to the said College Library the "Curiosties" of the Bones mentioned in Weevers Monuments, page 30 together with a very antient calendar. To Dr. PHILIP WILLIAMS and the Revd. Mr. THOMAS ROWE, 5 guineas each, and to ROBERT GREEN, Esq., of Cambridge, my silver cup.

Residuary Legatee and sole executor:-my nephew, the Revd. Mr. JOHN WALLER.

ANDREW WHITE, JOHN INGREY; Witness

Codicil 11 Dec. 1745.

My purse containing all my silverpieces, to my brother, the Revd. Mr. WILLIAM WALLER. To Mr. Alderman WHITE, a ring. To the Revd. Dr. PRIME, a ring. To Mr. LUNN, the Surgeon, a ring.

Proved 8 Jan. 1745-6, by the sole Executor named. 31 **Edmunds.** 29 Jan. 1746.

Administration granted to WILLIAM WALLER, one of the executors named in the WILL of [Rev.] JOHN WALLER, now also deceased, to administer etc.

[This will proves that John Waller, of "Newport", Spotsylvania county, Va. was a son of Dr. John Waller, of Newport Paganel, Bucks. See this Magazine XXVI, 32-35. The brother, Rev. William Waller, is given in **Alumni Oxonienses,** erroneously, as a son of "W. Waller of Newport Paganel, Bucks. pleb." It should be "J. Waller". William matriculated at Wadham College, April 5, 1688, B. A. 1691; M. A. from Corpus Christi College, Cambridge 1697, rector of Gressenhall 1700, and of Brisley, Norfolk 1704, and of Walton, Bucks, from 1711 to his death Feb. 18, 1750.]

EDMUND WALLER, of Beaconsfeild ,co. Bucks, Esq.,
Dated 30 Aug. 1699.   Proved 18 July 1700.
My executors to lay out £300 for the erecting a marble monument or tombe over the place where my father and mother now
lye in the churchyard of Beconsfeild.

To the poor of the parish of Beconsfeild, £100 and the same
to the poor of Amersham, both in co. Bucks.

Whereas I stand seized of an Estate of freehold and inheritance
in fee simple, in divers messuages, closes, lands, tenements and
hereditaments situate in Beconsfeild Morton Donington als
Dynton Kymbell West Wickham Marsh and Stone, in co.
Bucks.

Now I hereby give the same to my executors, in trust they to
pay out of the profits the following annuities: to my brother,
BENJAMIN WALLER, £50 yearly, to my sister, DOROTHIE
WALLER, £50 yearly, to my sister, ELIZABETH WALLER,
£50 yearly, to my sister ANN, the wife of GEORGE TIPPING
Esq., £50 yearly, to my sister OCTAVIA WALLER, £50
yearly, and to each of the children of my brother Dr. STEPHEN
WALLER £50, yearly and to JOHN FANSHAW, Esq., £50
yearly.

To THOMAS SMITH of Beconsfeild, £20

And whereas I own the principles of the people called Quakers
I desire my exors to pay £50 unto the Elders, where I shall
die, they to take care of my interrment which I desire may be
in the burying ground belonging to the said Meeting.

Executors: HENRY GOULD, of Iver, co. Bucks, Esq.,
JOHN FANSHAW, of the Inner Temple, London, Esq., and
my sister ELIZABETH WALLER.

THOMAS GALLOW, RICHARD POMEROY, URIAN
WISE, JAMES PRESTON; Witnesses.

Proved 18 July 1700 by the executors named.   108 **Noel.**

[As there is a tradition that one family of Wallers in Virginia descends
from a son of Edmund Waller, the poet, the will of Edmund Waller above
and adm. of Stephen Waller, which follows, two sons of Edmund the poet,
will help, by elimination. Edmund Waller, the testator, above, matriculated at Christ Church, Oxford, Dec. 17, 1666, age 15, barrister at law,
Middle Temple 1675, teacher 1697, M. P. for Saltash 1885i7, and Agmondesham 1689-95. He names in his will only two brothers, Benjamin and
Stephen. Stephen Waller, left children; but died intestate. He matriculated at New College, Oxford, Aug. 21, 1672, aged 18, B. C. L. 1679;
D. C. L. 1685, advocate of Doctors Commons, 1685, died Feb. 22, 1707.]

STEPEHN WALLER
10 March 1707.
Administration granted to JUDITH WALLER, relict of the
Venerable STEPEHN WALLER, Doctor of laws, one of the
Advocates General*, to administer, etc.
P. C. C. **Adn. Oct. Book 107.**

*[of the Court of Canterbury of the Arches London.]

———

RANDALL BASKERVILE, of Bowe, co. Middlesex, Esq.

Dated 20 Feb. 1653-6.   Proved 7 March 1654-5.
To my Mayds ELIZABETH, £4; JANE, £4, and ALICE,
£3. To my man, RICHARD PRATT, £4. To my maid,
LAUDLYN TOWSE, £35. To MARGARETT WARDE,
widow, my late servant, £15, and to her three daughters,
REBECCA, JANE and ANNE, £5, each. To my sister
BRIDGETT TREVETT, of Sproson in Cheshire, £100. To
the childern of my nephew, JOHN BASKERVILE, of Blackdeane, co. Cheshire, £300 each. To Master LEE, Clarke to
the Fishmongers Hall, £5. To THOMAS WHITING the
upper Beadle, £4. To THOMAS ALSWORTH the under
Beadle, £4. To JOHN NANSON, JOHN KETCHMORE,
          PARKER, Almsmen, 20s. each. To the Worshipful
Company of Fishmongers, whereof I am a member, £200.
also a bason and ewre. of the same weight price and marking
as Mr. ROBERT GEARES' was, my arms and crest ingraven
on it. To Master WILCOX of Bray, 20s. To the poor of
the parish of St. Buttolphs Billinsgate, £10. To ANTHONIE
RAYNOLDS, Clarke of the said parish, £4, and to RICHARD
SERRINGTON, Sexton, £3. To my cousin LAURANCE
BASKERVILE, sonne of my Nephew, JOHN BASKERVILE
of Blackdeane, in Cheshire, £200. To Master TYSRO,
Minister in Woodstreete, £3. To Master BELLOWES,
Minister of Bowe, £3. To GEORGE YOUNG, fishmonger
in Thames street, London, £3. To my grandchild RANDALL
WILLMORE, sonne of my daughter REBECCAH, all my

lands, houses and buildings whatsoever, situate in Over and Gate Helmsley, co. York, and his heirs for ever and for want of such issue to my grandchildern, RACHELL, MARY and REBECCAH WILMORE, equally between them.

To my aunt MIDDLETON, £10. To the Hospital of Christ Church, £100. To Master Glyde, the treasurer, £5. To Master WIGGETT, the steward, £3. To my daughter REBECCAH WILMORE, £2,000. To my sonne, GEORGE WILMORE, Esq., £1,000. To my cousin, JOHN BASKER-VILE, of Blackdeane, £1,000. To JOHN ATKINSON, my mother's man, £20. To ANNE HALL, my mother's maid, £4. To Mistris REEVE, £5. To my brother WILLIAM THURSTON, Esq. and my friend WILLIAM ASHWELL Esq. £50 each.

Residuary Legatees: my daughter REBECCA WILMORE "and grandchildren WILMORE".

Executors:- the said WILLIAM THURSTON, and WILLIAM ASHWELL, and my said daughter.

ROBERT REEVE, THOMAS MAYHEW: Witnesses.

Proved 7 March 1654-5 by REBECCA WILMORE one of the Exors named, WILLIAM THURSTON and WILLIAM ASHWELL, the other exors renouncing.   397 **Aylett.**

[Randall Baskerville the testator, was a brother of Thomas Basker-ville of Old Withington, Cheshire, who was grandfather of John Basker-vill, the emigrant to Virginia. See "Genealogy of the Baskerville Family,' (P. H. Baskervill), p. 9.]

———————

WILLIAM BRACKENBOR of Munthorpe in the parish of
Greate Steepinge, co. Lyncolne, yeoman.

Dated 16 Sept. 1654.   Proved 10 Feb. 1654-5.

All my Goods, unto MAGDALEN, my wife and to my four sons, RICHARD, WILLIAM, THOMAS & JOHN whom I joyntly make executors.

EDWARD BRACKSBOR, ELIZABETH FISHER,
HUMPHRY SMITH: Witnesses

Proved 10 Feb. 1654-5 by MAGDALEN, the relict and one of the Extxs. named, power reserved to RICHARD, WILLIAM, THOMAS & JOHN BRACKENBORO, the other executors named.   346 **Aylett.**

EDWARD BRAY, the elder of Biggleswade, co Bedford, yeoman.

Dated 2 Oct. 1655.   Proved 13 May 1656.

To be buried in Biggleswade Church''neere my seats end''.

To my sonne EDWARD BRAY, and his heirs for ever, all my land lying in the parish of Biggleswade with the appurtenances on Holmeside, and the crops now growing thereupon, he to pay unto WILLIAM GOODE what monies I owe. To my wife KATHERINE, the use of my parlour, called the white horse parlor and all the goods and chattels in the same. To my sonne JOHN BRAY, the ''Tilth'' and Crop now made and growing, of the land I hold of Mr. BROMSALL in Caldicott Field, and in the parish of Northill. To my daughter, JANE, the wife of Mr. JOHN HOLINSTED, £50. To my daughter, RUTH BRAY, £20. I leave my sonne ROBERT BARY, to his mother's disposing and give him £50 which was promised by my sonne EDWARD BRAY.

Residuary Legatee and executors:-my said wife KATHERINE and my sonne JOHN.

EDWARD SMITH, JOHN SEARLE: Witnesses.

Proved 13 May 1656 by JOHN BRAYE, one of the exors named, power reserved to KATHERINE BRAYE, the other exctx named.   194 **Berkeley.**

[Robert Bray, who died in 1681, and Plomer Bray, who survived him, were brothers, and settled in Lower Norfolk County, Va. In a document recorded in that county, Robert Bray is refered to in 1681, a son of Edward Bray, Gent., desceased, of Biggleswade, Bedfordshire. They were doubtless sons of the son Edward named in this will.]

NICHOLAS LUKE, of Woodende, Co. Bedford, Esq.

Dated 27 May 1613.   Proved 9 July 1614.

To THOMAS LUKE, my second sonne, my Rectorie parsonage or parsonages appropriate of St. Paule and all Sts. in the Towne of Bedford, and twenty acres of meadowe lyeinge in Trumping-ton meadowe in the said towne of Bedford, to the said THOMAS during his life. The remainder thereof to such wife as my said sonne THOMAS shall happen to marrye, during her life. And after their decease to the first sonne of my said sonne THOMAS and the heires males of the body of such first sonne. And for default of such sonne, to the second, third, fourth, fyfth, sixth and seventh sonnes of my said sonne THOMAS. And for default of such sonnes, the remainder, to Sr. OLIVER LUKE, my sonne and heire and his heires for ever.

My intent is that after the expiracon of a lease made of the Manor or farme called Butlers alias Ashefeild in Gillinge als Yellinge in the County of Huntingdon made by NICHOLAS LUKE my Grandfather one of the Barons of the Excheqr. unto WILLIAM BUGBY for divers yeres yet to come, NICHOLAS LUKE my grandchild, third sonne of my said eldest sonne Sr. OLIVER LUKE shall have the Mannor or farme aforesaid; the same being nowe occupied by one MORGAN.

To my sonne Sr. OLIVER LUKE, my Mannor or Lordshipp of Towsland, my Mannor of Abbottsby alias Abersley in Countie Huntingdon, my Mannor of Basmy, my Mannor of Revensdon, in Countie Bedford and all other my lands, Tenements and Hereditaments in Towsland Yellinge Hemyngford Paxton magna Paxton pva Paxworth St. Ives Abbottsley Eaton Socon Ravensdon Arlsey Carington Willshamsted and Shitlington in the said Countys of Bedford and Huntingdon, to the said Sr. OLIVER, his heires and assigns for ever.

To my eldest daughter dame ANNE FLEETWOOD, wife of Sr. MILES FEETWOOD, Receiver generall of his Majesties Court of Wards and Liveries, £20; to bestowe in plate.

To JOHN COOKE, Esquire and JUDETH my second Daughter (his wife), £250. To KATHERIN, my youngest Daughter, £800, when she shalbe married.

To JOHN COCKAYN, my servant, £4. To MARK WATTS, MATHEW WATTS, WILLIAM BARKER, JOHN HILLS als COOKE, WILLIAM DAVIE, ANNE TURPIN, my servants five marks appece. To the poore of the town of Copley, twenty nobles.

Sole Executor: my sonne Sr. OLIVER LUKE.

Overseers:- Sr. HUMFREY WINCHE, of Everton, Co. Hunt., Knight, one of the Justices of H.Mties Court of Common Pleas, my Brother Sr. JOHN LUKE, of Annables, Co. Hart., Knight, Sr. MILES FLEETWOOD, JOHN COOKE, my said sonnes in law and NICHOLAS SPENCER of Copley, Co. Bedf., Esq.

M. FLEETWOOD, JO. LUKE, JOHN COOKE, RICHARD TAYLER, RAPHE HEYWOOD, JOHN SPENCER, JOHN SYMOND, JOHN COKEYNE: Witnesses.

Proved 9 July 1614 by the Sole Executor named.   67 **Lawe.**

[Nicholas Luke, the testator, married ≥argaret, daughter of Oliver, Lord St. John of Bletshoe. His son Sir Oliver was the father of Sir Samuel, the hero of **Hudibras.** George Luke son of Oliver and grandson of Sir Samuel, emigrated to Virginia, wher e he married a sister of William Fitzhugh of Stafford County. He was collector of customs for the lower district of James River in 1702. See this Magazine III, 166-168.

JOHN SICKLEMORE als RATCLIFFE, Captain of the Diamond nowe bounde for Virginia.

Dated 1 June 1609.   Proved 25 April 1611.

All my goods and chattels whatsoever and wheresoever unto my wife DOTOTHIE.

Executors:- my said wife DOROTHIE and RICHARD PERCIVALL, esq., my friend.

RICHARD STREAMER of Plymouth, HENRY SMITH, RICHARD LUELL, (sic) RICHARD HILL: Witnesses.

Proved 25 April 1611 by DOROTHY SICKLEMORE alias RATCLIFFE, relict and one of the the Exors named, power reserved to RICHARD PERCIVALL the other Exor named. 35 **Wood.**

[John Sicklemore alias Ratcliffe, was a member of the Virginia Company, came to the colony and was its President September 1607 &c. Contemporary writers do not speak well of him; but Mr. Brown defends him. He was murdered by Powhatan in the winter of 1609-10.

VIRGINIA GLEANINGS IN ENGLAND.

WILLIAM PUREFEY of Drayton, county Leicester gent. Will 26 April 1634; proved 19 May 1634. To my wife Jane Purefey one half of my household stuff. To the poor 40s. To my servants so much as my executors think fit. Rest of my goods to be sold and the money employed as I appoint. For the land in Atterton which was purchased by William Purefey of Caldecoate and Henry Grey of Burbage, Esqrs, with part of the legacy of £400 which was bequeathed to my only son Michael Purefey by the will of his godfather Michael Purfey deceased, my will is that said land shall either be assured to my said son and his heirs by said William Purefey and Henry Grey or otherwise be sold by them, if it shall seem good, to my executors and the price thereof together with the money formerly mentioned to be employed in the purchase of lands of inheritance in the name of my said son and heirs. Two thirds of the rents of said lands so purchased shall be paid to my said wife Jane half yearly: if said two thirds exceed £40 per annum then the overplus shall go as in my will disposed. The third part of the rents shall go to the maintenance of my son and for his education. If said son shall die before 21 years of age then the whole profits to my said wife so long as she continues a widow. After such death of her second marriage my executors shall have £100 apiece towards their pains and the rest of the profits of said lands divided betwixt my brother Edward Purefey and my nephew Raphe Purefey of Shaldeston, Clerke. I appoint my nephews George Purefey of Wadley, county Berks and William Purefey of Cgldecoate, county Warwick, and Henry Grey of Burbage

From Vol. XXVI, No. 4 (Oct. 1918), p. 380.

county Leicester Esqure executors. Aforesaid nephews and executors to be guardians of said son. Witness: Edw. Purefey, Geo. Abbott, Robt Mason, J. Withers.

Geo. Abbott, Robt Mason, J. Withers. **Seager, 36**.

[Capt. Thomas Purefoy came to Virginia before 1628 and was for a number of years a man of prominence. He named a tract of land (1000 acres) for which he obtained a grant, "Drayton". The intricacies of the Purefoy pedigree in England are too great for a genealogist not specially equipped; but the testator was probably a son of William Purefoy of Caldecote, who married Katherine Wigston, This William, a grandson of Thos. Purefoy, of Daryton, had a brother Humphrey Purefoy of Baswell (died 1598), who married Alice Faunt. Some Americans have jumped to the conclusion that Thomas, a son of Humphrey was the emigrant to Virginia. He may have been but there is no proof of it.]

Abstract of the Nuncupative WILL of WILLIAM WEST, of Dedsham in the parish of Slinfold, co. Sussex, gent.

[No month] 1610. (sic)   Proved 21 June 1616.

That he then taking his voyage unto Virginia (where he died) did declare, that all his goods whatsoever, unto MARY BLUNT, the wife of RICHARD BLUNT, of Dedsham, Esq. and did then appoint the said MARY, Executrix.

WALTER HENLEY, JOHN IRETON, and others: Witnesses.

Proved June 21 1916 by the Sole Executrix named. **60 Cope**.

[In the fall of 1610 the Indians killed, near the Falls of James River, Capt. William West, nephew of Lord Delaware, then Governor of Virginia. Doubtless he was the testator.]

Mr. THOMAS ROPER [no place] [Parts beyond the Seas]

No date.   Proved 5 Feb. 1626-7

I desire that JOHN WEST my servant maie bee sett free and likewise ALEXANDER GILL Servant to Captain PIERCE or else if he refuse to release him then the said ALEXANDER GILL to receive 200lb of tobacco from Cagtain PIERCE.

All tobaccoes due to me in Virginia tl my brother JOHN ROPER in England and that Mr. GEORGE FITZ JEFFERYES receave it to the use of my said brother.

One payre of linnen Breeches to WILLIAM SMITH of James City.

To my brother JOHN ROPER, £300 in the hands of my father in law Mr. THOMAS SHEAPERD, of Mome [?Moine] in Bedfordshire

To Mr. HAUTE WYATT, Minister of James City, 50s.

Residuary Legatee: my brother JOHN ROPER

HAUT WYATT, WILLIAM SMITH, GEORG FITZ JEFFEREY: Witnesses.

5 Feb. 1626-7 Administration granted to JOHN ROPER, principal legatee no executors being named. May 1624 administration granted to THOMAS SHEPARD father of JOHN ELIZABETH & CONSTANCE SHEPARD brother and sister "ex materno" of said deceased, during minor estate. 11 **Skinner.**

[Thomas Roper, "of Milden in Bedfordshire, Gent.", came to Virginia in 1623. Capt. Pierce was Wiliiam Pierce, member of the Council. George Fitz Geffrey "of Howton Conquest; Bedfordshire, gent," came to Virginia in 1623. Haute Wyatt, minister of Jamestown, was brother of Governor Sir Francis Wyatt, and had two sons who settled in Virginia.] ————————

Abstrat of the WILL of JOHN STEPTOE, late of Ockingham, in co. Barks., scrivenor.

Dated 20 March 1610.   Proved 27 March 1611.

He gave all his goods and chattels, to his daughter RUTHE STEPTOE.

Sole executor: his brother ALEXANDER STEPTOE.

ELIZABETH CLEERE, MARY CHILDE, widowe; JOHN WATMORE; ROGER HAWTHORNE; Witnesses.

Proved 27 March 1611 by the Sole Executor named. 22 **Wood.**

[Several of the wills here given are those of persons of rather unusual names, and will serve as clues for further research. Great Britian and the United States are now closer together than at any time since 1775, and when the war is over many more Americans will be interested in tracing their ancesty to the old home. Anthony Steptoe, the first of the name in Va. was born 1653 and was living in Northumberland Co., Va. 1697. He came with Mr John Cossens from Cudridge [Goodrich?] near Bishops Walton, Hampshire.]

JAMES HAWLEY of Brainford, county Middlesex, Esquier Will 2 September 1622; proved 4 May 1624.
To my son William Hawley £150. To my daughters Katherine and Susan £200 apiece. To my three children which I had by my last (sic) wife, Henry, Valentine and Thomas to be paid at their ages of 14 years. Residue to my son Jerom Hawley sole executor. My cosen Valentine Saunders thelder and my brother William Hawley and Henry Hawley, Overseers. Witnesses: Arthur Mundye, John Barnard, 42 **Byrde.**

[James Hawley, the testator, was brother of Jerome Hawley who was a member of the Council of Maryland 1634, returned to England in 1635; but came back to Virginia early in 1638 as colonial treasurer, and died during the year. Henry Hawley, long Governor or Councillor of Barbadoes, and William Hawley, long a resident of Maryland were also brothers of James. See Neill's *Virginia Carolorum* 139-142]

———

RICHARD KENNOR of Shipton under Whichwood, county Oxon, yeoman. Woll 17 September 1627; proved 13 November 1627 To Cathedral Church of Christchurch in Oxon 12d. To parish church of Hollywell suburbs of Oxford 6s. 8d. To Church of Shipton 10s. To poor of Shipton £5. To my daughter Elizabeth Surman's two children £10 each. To my daughter Edith Richardson £40. To my daughter Katherin Willet £40. To Jane Millerd the daughter of my daughter Anne Millerd £10. To my daughter Susan Harris now wife of John Harris £40. To Richard Kennor son of my son John Kennor deceased my house and lands in Handborough, county Oxon. For want of heirs of said Richard then I give said house and lands to the heirs of my daughter Katherine Willett for ever. To said Richard also £30. To Richard Painter my daughter Edith's son £5. To my wife Joane Kennor £50. with bedding and furniyure Residue to my sons in law William Otwell als Stevens and Thomas Skay executors. William Hunt of Faringdon and Mr. Fryers Minister of Askot Overseers 20s. each. Witnesses; Stevens, John Tomes, Zach. Smith. 103 **Skynner.**

[This will and the following one may indicate the localty where search should be made for the ancestry of Richard Kenner, who settled in Northumberland County, Va., before 1664, married in that year Elizabeth, daughter of Matthew Rodham, and was a member of the House of Burgesses 1688, 1691, 1692.]

HENRY KENNER of St. Peters Baylie in the city of Oxford, Taylor. Will 20 November 1639; proved 28 February 1639. Body to parish churchyard neare unto my children. My house and lands at Ockingham county Berks which I bough of Mr. Henry Langley of Abingdon to my wife Marie for her life. afterwards to my son Benjamin Kenner and lawful heirs. If he die without issue then to my two daughters Marie and Martha Kenner and their heirs equally, for default to my right heirs. To my son Benjamin £10 at 21 years. To my daughters Marie and Martha £10 apece at 21 years or marriage. So soon as my son Benjamin shall be seized of said house and land he shall pay to his said two sisters £5 apiece. To my father William Kenner and my mother Winifred Kenner 2s. 6d. apeece for a pair of gloves. To my father and mother in law Francis and Ann Lath 2s. 6d. each for gloves as a token. Residue to my wife Mary sole executrix. My friends John Banister of the city of Oxford, Cordwainer, John Bolt of the University of Oxford, Cordwainer, John Bolt of the University of Oxford, cooke, Mr. John Fulckes of Oxford Taylor and Richard Phillipps of Oxford, Cordwainer, Overseers. To each of them a pair of gloves. Witnesses; Francis Lath, Anne Lath, Thomas Holloway. 29 **Coventry.**

EPAPHRODITUS LAWSON of Drunmin parish of Kill. county Cavan, gent. Will 12 July 1718; proved 11 May 1719. To wife Margret Lawson benefit of a lease I hold from Honble Thomas Coote Esq of part of Drunmin part of Corncarrow, and 3 tenements in Coothill and at her decease to my son Coote Lawson. To my 4 daughters Mary Lawson, Jane Lawson, Katheren Lawson, and Elizabeth Lawson £100 my Brother in law Mr. John Williams put out at interest for my use. To my daughter Joan Grace £10. Executors: Wife and Cousen Henry Young of Cootehill. Witnesses: Allen Johnston, John Williams, John Williams junr.
Prerogative Court Ireland. **Will Book 1718-20, no 119.**

[Two brothers, Epaphroditus and Rowland Lawson, settled in Isle of Wight County, Va., as early as 1636, and subsequently removed to Lancaster County, Va. The family has many descendants. See this Magazine IV, 202, 203, 313, 314. What the connection with the testator was does not appear

JOHN PINKARD, of Keynsham, county Somerset. Will 6 May 1653; proved 30 Septemger 1653. I bequeath my body to be buried in the church of Keynsham, where I am now visited with sickness. I give unto my eldest son John £9, which Sir Thomas Bridges oweth unto me for meat; also one brown nag, and 10 fat ewes now in the marsh. To my son William £10 at the end of 7 years. To my daughter in law Mary Mascall, £5 at her day of marriage; and the like to my daughters Joane, Mary and Jane Pinkard, always provided that these my daughters be dutiful and obedient unto their mother, and match with her consent and approbation, otherwise my will is that they should have but 12d. apiece. All the rest of my goods I bequeath to my well beloved wife Mary, whom I make my executrix. John Pinkard his mark Proved by the executrix named. **Brent** 167.

WILLIAM PINKERD of Thenford, county Northampton, yeoman. Will 17 June 1645; proved 21 June 1653. I make my son Henry sole executor of my will, giving him all my temporal substance, including all my interests in a certain tenement in Sulgrave in the said county, and all my arable land in the fields of Sulgrave, with all the evidences, deeds and writings con?erning the same. To my son Robert I give 20s. The mark of William Pinkerd. Witnesses: William Osborn, minister of Thenford. Proved by the executor named. 3 **Brent.**

[The counties represented in these two wills are too far apart for them to be of much value as genealogical suggestions. The first of the name in Virginia was Capt. John Pinkard, of Lancaster County, who was a member of the House of Burgesses in 1688, and died in 1689. See Wm. Mary Quartity XI, 262 &c.]

EDMOND POYTHRAS of Dymock, county Gloucester, yeoman. Will 20 February 1639; proved 23 May 1630. To Edmond Harper son of Richard Harper of Much Markle county Hereford 3s. To Marie Williams daughter of Richard Williams of Dymock aforesaid 3s. 4d. To Marie Barnett daughter of John Barnett late of Ledbury 3s. 4d. To Elizabeth daughter of Edward Griffiiths 3s. 4d. To Elizabeth Barnett wife of Francis Barnett my daughter in law 40s. To Sibill Greene wife of

Nicholas Greene of Llsoignton, county Wigorne 40s. To Joane and Anne Loveridge my daughters in law, singlewomen, all my free land arable and pasture lying in Much Marckle aforesaid and their heirs for ever paying to the chief lord of lords such rents as are of right custom. Residue to Jane my wife sole executrix. Witnesses: Hen. Hooper, Thos. Hooper, Wm. Gamon, Rich. Hooper, Hen. Hooper, Thos Whoper, Wm Gamon, Rich. Hooper. **Coventry** 62.

[This name, spelled Poythress in Virginia, is a very unusual one, and has now, it is believed, only one male representative in America. The first of the name in Virginia was Francis Poythress, who was a planter and also agent for Lawrence Evans, a London merchant. In 1639 Evans charged that Poythress had behaved very badly in the affairs of his agency. The Governor and Council appointed four of the ablest merchants in Virginia to examine the matter and they decided that Evans owed Poythress 13,876 lbs. tobacco as commissions. Later in the year Evans procured from the English Sub-Committee on Foriegn Plantations order for a new trial of the case; but nothing appears in regard to it. Francis Poythress was a Burgess for Charles City October 1644, Feb. 1644-5, Nov. 1647, for Northumberland Oct. 1649, and in March 1645-6 was appointed to command a force against the Indians. On acco unt of the destruction of most of the records of Charles City and Prince George it is impossible to prepare any full and sufficiently proved account of his descendants; but there is much infornation in regared to them in vols. VII; IX; and XIX, of this Magazine. Any investigation in England would do well to begin in Glaucestershire.]

ROBERT LUNSFORD, of the parishe of Hollington

Co. Sussex.

Dated 13 Oct. 1611.   Proved 24 Jan. 1611-12

To the poor of the parish of Hollington, 10s.

To ELIZABETH, my daughter, £100.

To ANNE LUNSFORD, my daughter, fowerscore pounds to be paid at the age of eighteen yeares.

To my daughter JOANE, fowerscore poundes, to be paid at like age.

To my sonne, WILLIAM LUNSFORD, £100, to be paid at the age of one and twenty yeres. And my will is that WILL-

IAM BATHERST, of the Castle parishe shall have the bring-inge of him upp.

To my sonne ROBERT LUNSFORD and to his heires for ever, the reversion of my landes called Channey after my fath-er's decease, lyinge in the parishe of Saint Mihilles, Also two St. Clements in Hasting. Also one annunity of £3 out of the lands of JOHN YOUNGE, deceased, late of Tisherst called Qnedlye.

To my sonne HARBERT LUNSFORD, my farm called Harely and Filsome, he payinge unto my wife ELIZABETH, 50s. a yeare.

Residuary Legatee and Sole Executrix: ELIZABETH my wife. If my wife marrye after my decease she shall enter into sufficient bonds to WILLIAM WOOD of Crowherst, gent., for the pay-inge of my Childrens portions.

WILLIAM GRENEFIELD, PHILLIP WILSONNE: Wit-nesses.

Proved 24 Jan. 1611-12 by the Sole Executrix named. 5 **Finne.**

[The tesator was the same family as Sir Thomas Lunsford, of Wylie, Sussex, who came to Virginia, and who had a brother, Sir Herbert Lunsford; but his name does not appear in the pedigree in Berry's Sussex Genealogies.]

VIRGINIA GLEANINGS IN ENGLAND.

(Contributed by Leo Culleton, 92 Picadilly, London, W., and
the late Lothrop Withington.)

WILLIAM SKIPWITH, of Coates, Co. Leicester, Knight.
Dated 15 May 2 Jas.   Codicil 29 Oct. 5 Jas.
                                              Admon 8 May 1611.
My Manor of Prestwold, in co. Leicester, which was purchased
of HENRY HALL, esq. and all my messuages lands tenements
and hereditaments in Prestwold, Hoton, Loughborough, Burton,
Coetes (except my manor of Coetes and the farme or grange in
Burton known as Burton Grange) shall descend to my heir,
being a third of my mannors, lands etc. The residue of my
lands etc in Leicester which I hold in fee farm of his Matie
known as Temple Walk, Stonye Lane, Calver Haye, Kirbye
pastures and Beamont leyes and all the messuages lands tenements and hereditaments which I purchased of MARY ERDES-
WICK and Sir EVERARD DIGBY in Prestwold, Hoton,
Burton and Wymeswold, unto my executors in trust, for the
satisfaction of my legacies and the maintenance of my younger
children.
The Rectory and parsonage of Prestwold, to HENRY SKIP-
WITH my sonne and heir apparent, during his life and at his
decease to GEORGE SKIPWITH my second sonne.
To my younger sonne GEORGE SKIPWITH, an annuity of
£30 to be taken out of my manor of Coates and Burton grange,
(before excepted.)
To my youngest sonne, THOMAS SKIPWITH an annuity of
£30 to be paid out of the said manor of Coates and Burton
Grange.
Executors: my wife Dame JANE SKIPWITH and my friends
and brothers in law, Sir WILLIAM SAMUELL, knight,
MATHEW SAUNDERS, esq., and my brother, HENRY
SKIPWITH, Esq.
Codicil 29 Oct. 5 Jas.

From Vol. XXVII, No. 1 (Jan. 1919), p. 50.

Whereas I have bargained with Lord HENRY, EARLE of Huntingdon for that messuage in the town of Leicester, now in his tenure, for £400 whereof I have received £150, my mind is that my Executors will on the payment of £250 by the said Earl, convey the same messuage to him.
To CASSANDRA BRADSHAWE, £200. To my daughter, JANE SKIPWITH, £1,500. To my daughter ANNE SKIP-WITH, £1,000. To my daughter ELIZABETH SKIP-WITH, £1,000. To my sister URSULA, £20.
Overseer:–my freind ROBERT NOONE, of Walton upon the Wolds, in co. Leicester, gent.

WALTER STRIMGER
THOMAS HENWORTH   } Witnesses.
RICHARD SPICKE

8 May 1611 Administration granted to HENRY SKIPWITH, Knt. son of said deceased; MATHEW SAUNDERS, HENRY SKIPWITH, WILLIAM SAMUELL, Knt. and Dame JANE SKIPWITH, the Executors, having renounced. **42 WOOD.**

[This Sir William Skipwith, of Coates, Leicestershire, who died in 1611, was the father of Sir Henry Skipwith, of Prestwould, created a baronet in 1622. Sir Grey Skipwith, Bart., son of Sir Henry, emigrated to Virginia during the English Civil War, and the bearer of the title remained here until, Grey Skipwith, eldest son of Sir Peyton, of "Prest-would", Mecklenburg Co., Va., (who died in 1805) was bequeathed an estate by a distant kinsman in England, and removed to that country.
The wills show that Henry Skipwith and Sir William were brothers.]

———————

HENRY SKIPWITH of Knight Thorpe, county Leicester, Esquire.
Will 20 November 1638; proved 24 March 1639. My body to chancel of Tugby church near to Sepulchre of my father and mother. To poor of Longborrow £6 according to discretion of Mr. John Browne, parson To poor of village of Knight Thorpe £3 whereof 10s. was appointed by last will of William Bennett my vooke [sic]. To poor of village of Thorpe Ansker £3 whereof 10s. by said William Bennett. To poor of Tugby in which parish I was born 40s. at discretion of Robert Hill vicar or Grace his wife. To my deerest Nephew Thomas Wood-ward Esq £100. To Lady Jane Harrington my neece and

sister to said Thomas Woodward £40. To my only sister Mrs. Brigett Asen of Marsh in the Fen £10. Whereas I am guardian of Nicholas Low son of Francis Low late of Thorpe Awker and have in my hands all his estate and whereas my son Thomas in his lifetime did owe unto Francis Low his late father £10 my will is that said Nicholas ge paid said £10 at his 21 year. I received 50s. of my nephew Arthur Samuell for the use of Mary Morrice daughter of Thomas Morrice, Taylor, deceased, to which sum I added £5 which hath remained in my hands since 8 May 1635 My will is that said £7 10s. be paid to said Mary Morrice with interest at 21 years. To her also a Bond of £6 entered into by her brother in law John Hill. To my kinsman Captain Francis Cane the best horse I am possessed of with best saddle and furniture To Robert Stanley my antient servant of 40 years £40. To him also 40 ewes to be drawn by him out of stock at Goadby. To him also my fourth best ram and my third best horse with saddle and furniture To him and my servant William Greene all my apparel that is not silk or velvet. To said William Greene the nagge with saddle he useth to ride and £10. To Henry Gilbert son and heir to Thomas Gilbert of Lockoe county Darby my heare of grounds called the Upper Launde with two meadows belonging which I hold of Mr. Mosley son and heir to Sir Edward Moseley lately deceased with all sheepe and beasts there at my decease. My mares geldings and colts there to the use of Jane Ridgley the wife of Symon Ridgley Esq my dear daughter. To my wife's daughter Mrs. Mary Handson £20 for her lifetime After to her son Henry Handson my godson. To Jeremy Wilkinson my son Ridgley's cook 40s. To my cousin Brian Fitzwilliams a suit of clothes and £5 Residue to Symon Ridglye Esq and Jane his wife joint executors. Witnesses: Neele Ithall, Henry Shaw, Barnaby Jackson. Executors to give rings to: Sir Hen. Skipwith, Brigett Ayson, Thos. Skipwith, Ann Pate, Henry Aysen, John Aysen, Edw. Aysen, Neece Smyth, Thos. Brudnell, Neece Morgaine, Sybella Eglianbye Sir Richd. Samuell, Lady Samuell, Anto Samuell, Jane Brough, Thos. Woodward, Lady Harrington, Nephew Fetherston, Thos. Harrington, John Hawford, Elizab.

Sanden, Mr. Browne pson, Mr. Hill pson, Geo. Ashbye, Hen, Ashbye, Tho. Gilbert, Hen. Gilbert, Capt. Cane, Lady Willan his wife, Sir Geo. Willan, Ursula Porter, Will. Skipwith, Rich. Samuell, Jane Samuell, Sir Hen. Barkclay, Lady Digby, Sir Kellam Digby, Sir John Digby, Chas. Dymocke, Cyrian Day, Roger Smyth, Sir John Beaumont, Lady Grantham, Henry Smythe, Thos. Brudnell junior, Will. Skipwith, Dr. Morgane, Dr. Ehianbye, Nephew Lockye, Mary Handson. Codicil 20 November 1638. Appointment of my trusty cosen Francis Cane of Broksbye as Supervisor. Rings to be enamel with a death's head, and the value of 10s. each. To every servan not espressed 10s. each. Whereas Mr. Neale Ithell owes me £500 or therabouts I am willing to accept £300 to be paid to me or my executors in the year 1641-1642 to have on the last payment a General Release. Witnesses: Jo. Davenport, Wm Greene, Coventry, 33.

WILLIAM TABORER. Will 9 February 1652 (–3); proved 4 June 1653. Desiring a friendly and loving agreement betwixt my wife and children, I have thought good to declare my mind concerning every of them severally in this my last will. I bequeath to my wife Anne the house I now live in, and the three tenements thereto belonging in the occupation of Gilborth Peere, Robert Cutburne and Robert Saxelby, for the term of her life; also my half close called the Parcel Cose, the half of all my arable land within the liberties of Derby, and the half of my barn upon Nungreene. To my son William, one house in the Frearegate betwixt the houses of John Wright and Robert Banker, and 4½ acres lying severally in the Wall field, Parke field and White Crosse field. To my son James, the house I now dwell in and the three tenements, after my wife's decease. If my son James die without children, the same to come to my son Nathaniell. To my son Joshua, L.50 if he come for it. If not, to ge divided betwixt my son Nathaniell and my son John equally. To my son Thomas, L.10. To my son Nathaniell. the reversion of the other premises given to my wife foe her life; and one farm at Marketon, with all the land and meadow thereto belonging.

To my son John, two houses in the market place, now in the occupation of William Bould and William Buntinge, and L.120 towards his maintenance to the university; what remains to be restored to him, when he shall have occasion to use it or or call for it. To my daughters Saria, Mary and Rebecka, L.200 apiece at their several ages of 20; the interest of their portions to be for their maintenance and keeping. I give to my sister Margaret living at Morley, 10s. a year during her life. To my sister Elizabeth 20s.; to her son William 10s. To the poor of St. Warbur's parish, 20s. I make my wife my executrix. Whatsoever shall be made of my estate above these legacies shall be divided equally betwixt my wife and my son Nathaniel, and I make my sons William and Nathaniel my overseere. The mark of William Taborer. Witnesses: Nathaniell Taborer, the mark of Edward Clarke and Thomas Heane. Proved by the executrix named. **Brent, 254.**

[Two sons of the testator came to Virginia about the middle to the Seventeenth Century and settled in Isle of Wight County. One of them Joshua Taberer, made a will, dated Nov. 24, 1656, and proved in Isle of Wight. It is printed in full Vol VI, 117,118, of this Magazine. In it he gives to his brother Thomas Taberer all the estate given him, or which he may inherit under the will of his father William Taberer, of the County of Duby, said brother Thomas to bestow, as a legacy to his brother William Taberer of the County of Derby and the rest of his fathers kindred ten pounds sterling. He gives the remainder of his estate in England and Virginia to Ruth Taberer, only daughter and heir of his brother Thomas and to his brother Thomas.

Major Thomas Taberer (as was his title in the militia) was in Virginia as early as 1653, was long a justice of Isle of Wight County and died possesed of a considible real and personal estate. After the date of his brother's will he had several other daughters, though no sons. In his will, dated Jan 14, 1692, and proved in Isle of Wight he names his grandson Joseph Copeland. grandson Thomas Numan (Newman) son of John Numan and his daughter Ruth, grandson Thomas Webb, son of William Webb and his daughter Mary, daughter Christian Jordan, wife of Robert Jordan, daughter Elizabeth Copeland's children, and also makes bequests to Elizabeth Wombwell's children, without stating how related.

Jno Taberer who is provided for at the university must have been at Cambridge. His name is not among the Oxford Matriculations.]

PETER THACKER, the younger of the parish of saint Peter's
Mancrofte in Norwich. Will 12 April 1652; proved 2 July 1653.
I gequeath my soul to God, and my body to be buried in decent
burial without any manner of state and pomp. I give to the
poor of the said parish 20s, to the poor of the parishes of
Swethens and Stephens, 10s apiece. To Mr. Carter, Mr. Rain-
ham and Mr. Collings, 10s. apiece. My will is that, within
one year after. my decease, my executrix shall pay L.10 into
the hands of the most able and substantial parishioners of the
parish wherein I live, to the use of the parishioners of the said
parish, which L.10 shall be lent by the major part of twelve of
the most able parishioners, upon Easter Monday next after
payment of the same, to some honest tradesman upon good
security for 2 years, paying 5s. a year for the same to the
churchwardens for the time being for the use of the poor of the
said parish, and so from three years to three years forever.
I bequeath to Mary, my loving wife, for her life, all my houses
and grounds, she keeping the same in good reparations; and
after her decease, I give to my son William the house wherein
I now dwell; to my son Peter, the house wherein John Crowe,
my tenant in St. Andrewes now dwelleth; to my son Thomas,
the tenement next thereunto wherein Daniel Mathews, gouldsmith, lately dwelt, and the back tenement wherein Goodman
Shepard the brazier now dwelleth. The two last mentioned
tenements shall enjoy the liberty of water as formerly, paying
3s. a year towards the maintaining of the pump there. As for
the tenements in St. Peter's parish, wherein Peter Dale and
Francis Wilson now dwell, in case my wife be delivered of a
man child, I will that the said man child shall have the same,
and desire her soon after her delivery to settle the same tenement accordingly. Otherwise I give the said two tenements
to Rose Thacker and Mary Thacker, my two daughters. If
my wife be delivered of daughters I give them L.50 apiece at
their age of 20, and to the said Rose and Mary L.50 apiece at
20, desiring their mother to increase it , as she shall see cause.
give to every of my children L10 worth of householdstuff atg
their several ages of 20. To my loving father, my gold ring
engraven with P and T, and I entreat his care of and love to

499

my wife and children. To my brother Thomas Thacker and my sisters Linge and Paine, to every of them a death's head gold ring of 15s. price apiece, which I desire they will wear and keep in remembrance of me. In matters of near concernment to my said wife, I desire she will advise with my father, Mr. Alderman Davy, Mr. Alderman Cory, and my brother Violett Benton, and conclude nothing without the advice of two of them. I desire that my wife may have a special care that all my children may be brought up in the fear of the Lord, and that she will have a great care in placing them, as they shall be fit to be put forth, into godly and religious houses, though they be the meaner places and the more inferior callings. In witness whereof to this my last will, being all written with my own hand, I have set my hand and seal. (signed) P. Thacker. Admon granted to Mary Thacker, relict of the deceased, to administer the goods etc. in accordance with the tenor of the above will, there being no executor named. **Brent, 10.**

[Henry Thacker, of Lancaster and Middlesx Counties, Va. **1656-1673** &c., was in England in 1656, and in making the statement required by law at the time stated that he "intended to go to Norwich and there remain among his friends," while in England. He married about 1662, Eltonhead, daughter of Edwin Conway, of Lancaster Co, and his wife, Martha, daughter of Richard Eltonhead, of Eltonhead, Lancashire, England. She married, secondly, about 1677, William Stanard of Middlesx County. See Hayden's **Virginia Genealogies**, 235,236 &c., and register of Christ Church Parish, Middlesx.]

HENRY TUCKER of Gravesend, county Kent, gent. Will 20 January 1640; proved 26 April ·1641. To Dorathie my wife £50 yearly, bed, bedding and other necessaries. To my brothers Robert, Thomas and Richard 20s. each. To my brother John Tucker £5. To my three sisters Ann, Ellen and Elizabeth 20s. each. To Henry Frie son of John Frie 20s. To my kinswomen Anne Tucker daughter of Thomas Tucker and to Thomas Tucker servant to John Tuker, of Gravesand, mercer £5 apeece. To my kinswoman Elizabeth Tucker servant to Mr. William Davies £4. To poor of Gravesend and Milton 20s. a parish. To my son in law Will Davies gent, fower children Jane, William, John and Marie £10 apiece to be paid to their father for their use. To my son in law William Davies gent my moiety out of the field called the church field, said field stt over to John Reddoll of Milton. To enter upon the lease at Our Lady Day. To Jane Davies daughter of said William Davies a bowl set in silver. Residue to John Tucker my son sole executor. Witnesses: Wm Davies, gent, John Vincent, scr. Administration to Dorthy Tucker **Evelyn, 42.**

[The place of the testator in the family of Tucker of Milton and Gravesend, Kent, cannot be exactly assigned. George Tucker of Milton, (whose will was printed in this Magazine XVII, 394 &c., had sons Henry, Robert and John; but no Richard and Thomas, are given in Dr. Thos. Addis Emmett's genealogy of the family. Nor are sons Thomas and Richard named in George Tucker's will. It is possible that he was a first cousin of George Tucker, and son of John Tucker, of London.]

ALEXANDER WOODSONNE, of the City of Bristol,

"Phesion"

Dated 11 April 1616.   Md. 12 April 1616
                              Md. 25 Dec. 1616.
                              Proved 8 May 1618.

To be buried in St. Michaells Churchyarde in Bristol.

To MARIE, my daughter, all such goods as my late deceased wife had when I was married to her.

All other my goods to be devided into four parts, to my daughter MARTHA, one part, to ALEXANDER, the sonne of my sonne, JOHN WOODSONNE, one part, to FRANCIS and GRACE, the children of my sonne FRANCIS WOODSONNE,"*both" deceased, one part and to my daughter ANNE WOODSOONE, one part. Provided also that my soone HENRY WOODSONNE of Wells shall have such bookes that I have and that nowe are abreade in the hands of Mr. ISRAEL GLESON and Mr. WILLIAM SWIFT.

Sole Executor: my sonne HENRY WOODSONNE.

Overseers:-Mr. WILLIAM SWIFT and Mr. RICHARD BOSWELL. ·

[No Witnesses]

Md. 12 Apr. 1616.

To my children of my sonne HENRY,-izt. PHILLIPPE and THOMAS, 5 Apostle spoones of silver.

[No Witnesses].

Md. 25 Dec. 1616.

I revoke the legaciesjlegacies to my daughter "in lawe", MARIE and give her the bed and bolster she lyeth on, etc.

RICHARD BOSWELL⎫
⎬ Witnesses.
WILLIAM WIGHTWICKE⎭

Proved 8 May 1618 by the sole Executor named.

*? Does this mean the two sons, JOHN & FRANCIS, deceased.

40 Meade.

[The designation of the testator is an abbreviation of "phesition," physician. John Woodson, who came to Virginia in 1619, with his wife Sarah, is said, by tradition, to have been a physician or surgeon. The dates would suit well enough for him to have been son of Alexander Woodson but the latter seems to say that, in 1616, his son John was dead. Bristol and the neighborhood would, however, be a good place to look for the Virginian.]

VIRGINIA GLEANINGS IN ENGLAND.

(Contributed by Leo Culleton, 92 Picadilly, London, W., and the late Lothrop Withington.)

FRANCIS TERRELL, citizen and grocer of Lond.

Dated 13 Aug. 1609.   Codicil 30 Aug. 1609.
                                        Proved 19 Sept. 1609.

To Christes Hospital, Lond, £5; To St. Thomas Hospital in Southwarke, £3; To the poor prisoners of Newgate, Ludgate, the Fleete, the two Conpters in Wood Streete and the Poultrye, the Kings benche and the Marshalsey, 40s. to each prisone house. To the poor of St. Olaves in Southwarke, £20, St. George's in Southwarke £5. St. Mary Overies, also St. Saviours in Southwarke, £5, St. Giles without Creeplegate, London, £20, St. Sepulchers without Newgate, £10, St. Buttolphs without Algate, £10, St. Buttolphs without Bishopsgate, £10. To the poor of the parish of Croydon, co. Surrey 40s. yerely to be paid out of the profits of my dwelling house there. To the parishioners of the town of Croydon, £200 to be paid unto WILLIAM MORTON, of Croydon, gentleman, to the intent that he with the advice of my friends EDWARD ARNOLD & THOMAS WOOD shall cause to be erected a new market house upon Markett-hill in Croydon, "where the cage now standeth." Also £40 to provide a new Sayntes-bell to be hanged up in the Church. To the poor in my Lord of Canterburie's Almeshouses in Croydon, £5 amongst them. To ANNE, my sister THAIRES mayd, 10s. To Mr. FINCH, vicar of Croydon, £4. To ELLEN GILBERT, 20s. To EDWARD SHANKES, of Croydon, £3. 6. 8. To goodman TWYNER, of Croydon, dwelling in the old town, 15s. To goodwife SHANKE, widow, 20s. To goodman CASSY, dwelling in butchers rowe,

From Vol. XXVII, No. 2 (April 1919), p. 150.

20s. I forgive the widow EVE, and JOHN EVE, clothier, of Suffolk, all they owe me. I forgive AMBROSE BRIGGES, sometimes Schoolmaster at the free school at Croydon, all he owes me. To each of my godchildren, vizt., FRANCIS SHUTE, Junior, sonne of FRANCIS SHUTE, goldsmith, SAMUELL PRICE, sonne of PETER PRICE, GILBERT, sonne of THOMAS GILBERT of blackwell hall, THOMAZINE ARNOLD, daughter of EDWARD ARNOLD, brewer, FRAUNCIS POTTERTON, daughter of JOHN POTTERTON of Woodmansterne, HENRY PERKINSON, sonne of HENRY PERKINSON, and to FRAUNCIS LOVEDAY, sonne of JOHN LOVEDAY, £3. 6. 8. To my sister EMME THAIRE, widow, £300. of which one bond wherein HENRY PARAMOUR & FRAUNCIS BUTLER stand bound to her for the the payment of £105, shalbe in part of the said £300, for that the said money is my own and the bond made in her name of trust. To ,her sonne, HUMFREY THAIRE, £50. To my cosen, SUZAN TAYLOR, widow, £50. To THOMAS WEEKS, my sister's sonne, £200, and to his wife a mourning gown, and to his two children £20 each. To ALICE WEEKES, my sister' daughter, £200. To my cousion, THOMAS TERRELL, £100 and a mourning gown to his wife To each of his two sisters, ELIZABETH & FRAUNCIS, £50. To my cozen, ROBINSON and his wife, a mourning gown ,each. To my cozen, ANNE RAMSEY, widow, a mourning gown ,and to her sonne JOHN RAMSEY, a mourn ing cloke. To th dayghter of the said ANNE RAMSEY and her husband, a mourning gown each. To Mr. WILLIAM WILLIAMSON, vintenor, and to his wife mourn ing gowns. To EDWARD ARNOLD, £3. 6. 8. and to his wife a pair of gloves, value 6s. To JOHN AUSTEN, haberdasher, £3. 6. 8. To EMANUELL DROME, leather seller, £10. To EDWARD JAMES, merchantta ilor, £3. 6. 8. To ANNE WHITEHEDD, sometime servant to Sir THOMAS RAMSEY, 40s. To WILLIAM HANCORNE, servant to JOHN DORINGTON a mourning cloke. To my mayd servant JUDITH JENKLY, £13. 6. 8. If I be buried in London I give to 100 Batchelers that shall attend my funeral, a pairs of gloves of 1s. 6d. the payre. To

ROGER MAYDEN, haberdasher, £13. 6. 8. To my cozen, WILLIAM EVANS, £3. 6. 8. To WILLIAM POTTERTON my servant, 40s. To my godsonne, ANTHONY HAWKINS, sonne of WILLIAM HAWKINS, of London, Merchant tailor, £3. 6. 8. To THOMAS HILL and his wife, mourning gowns. To EDWARD SMYTH and his wife, mourning gowns. To the daughter of THOMAS WEEKES, £20. To the Master and Wardens of the Company of Grocers, London, 1,000 markes, to remain as a stocke in the Grocer's Hall for ever, to the intent that they every year provide 40 chaldron of sea-coles, 26 chaldron thereof to be distributed at Christmas to the poor within the parishes of St. Giles without Creeplegate, St. Sepulchers without Newgate, St. Olave's in Southwarke and to the poor at the further ende of Barmondsey streete in Southwarke and St. Buttolphs without Aldgate. I forgive RICHARD DANE, grocer of London, the debt he owes me. Residuary Legatees: sister EMME THAIRE, THOMAS TERRELL "my brother's sonne," cosin THOMAS WEEKES, cozen ALICE WEEKES, and the three children of said cosin THOMAS WEEKES

Executors:-WILLIAM HAWKINS, Merchant tailor and EDWARD BATES, haberdasher, citizens of London.

To the said WILLIAM HAWKINS, a bond of £109 wherein he with one Mr. JEFFREYS standeth bound to me, and to the said EDWARD BATES, one other bond of £105 wherein with his cozin HENRY BATES standeth bound to me.

Overseers:-my friends, EDWARD SMITH & THOMAS HILL, THOMAS HILL, Scr; EDWARD SMITH;

THOMAS WOOD; EDWARD ARNOLD. WITNESSES.

Mem. 30 Aug. 1609.

My executors to deliver to Mr. EDWARD ARNOLD two bills of debt, one for £50 and the other £55, for the payment whereof I have taken a bond, and given him till 1 Sept. 1610.

THOMAS HILL; EDWARD SMYTH. WITNESSES.

Proved 19 Sept. 1609 by the Executors named. **86 Dorset.**

[Francis Terrell was a younger son of George Terrell, of Thornton Hall, and his wife, Eleanor or Elizabeth, daughter of Sir Edward Montague, Chief Justice of England. He (the testator) was great uncle of Richmond and William Terrell, who emigrated to Virginia.]

WILLIAM TODD. Will 11 November 1625; proved 4 January 1626. To my two children REBECCA and ANN all whatsoever, wages, adventure or anie else in said (sic) Ship. After debts paid the rest to be put out for my childrens use. One jar of grene ginger between my servant GILES WADSLEY and DRUE DOBSON and one jar of Racke to RICHARD WOOD chirurgion of said Ship All things in England to be divided between my wife REBECCA TODD and my two children above named. Witnesses: THO: GOLLEY, WM GIBSON, RICHD GILLSON, RICHD WOOD, Overseer **Skynner, 5.**

THOMAS TOD of Ratcliff in the county of Middlesex, mariner. Will 15 April 1649; proved 18 May 1653. I give to my wife JUDITH all my estate both real and personal, if she survive me and have no issue by me; but if she have issue by me, I give one half to her and one half to the issue. If she die before me, I give my estate to ROBERT BRIDGETT and SUSAN TODD, my brother and sisters, equally. And I make my wife my executrix. (signed) THOMAS TODD. Witnesses: HENRY COLBRON, JOHN ELLIS, JOHN PARREY. Proved by by JUDITH TODD, relict of the deceased. **Brent, 241.**

[Thomas Todd was probably the man of the name who appears in the early records of lower Norfolk. He was evidently a mariner and shipwright.]

SIR FRANCIS SWANN of Denton, county Kent, knight. Will 8 December 1622; proved 14 February 1622. Body near my wife in parish church of Nonnington. To my son FRAUNCES £100 at 24,years. To my son PETER £100 at 24 years. To my son WILLIAM £100 at 24 years. To my son JOHN annuity of £20 towards maintenance hoping he will become a scholar To him also presentattion of "avoydance" (sic) of Church of Denton. If he fails in scholarship then gift void and £100 to him at 24 years. To my son ROBERT £100 at 24 years. To PAUL my youngest son £100 at 24 years. To MARY my eldest daughter £300. To ANN my daughter £150 at 18 years. To DORTHY my daughter £100 at 18 years. To ELIZABETH my daughter £100 at 18 years. To ANNE my youngest daughter £100 at 18 years. Towards performace of my bill all my goods with the revenue of my lands at Lye, Mydley and Old Romney for ten years to be received by my executor and afterwards said lands to my son EDWARD and heirs. My younger childrens portions to go for maintenance and education, until placed by my executor. My son EDWARD SWANNE sole executor and all unbequeathed to said executor. My brother Mr. ROBERT BOYS, Overseer, to him 20s. in gold for a ring. Witnesses: THOS BLESSHENDEN, JOHN BUTCHER, WM DAVIS. **Swann, 10.**

MERRIELL SWAN late of Southfleete, county Kent, singlewoman. Nuncupative will 10 July 1633; proved 16 October 1633. "I have been very sick, and if I should have such another fit I sould not live and delivered her mind before credible witnesses. To my brother WILLIAM SWAN £100. To my brother GEORGE SWAN the accompts which grew due to her from her father in law Mr. ROBERT WTHSHERS (sic) thought would amount to near £100. To Mrs. MERRIALL HILL her cousin £40. To JANE STONE her servant £30, To WILLIAM HILL £10. To THOMAS BERKETT £10. To her sister in law the Lady SWAN all her plate. To her brother Sir THOMAS SWAN all the rest of her estate. Being asked by said JANE STONE whether she had given to her godson son to Sir Thomas anything she says that which I give to the father will come to the son, and that she did give it to buy him a farm of Sir JOHN SEDLEY which she did think would cost £900. Being further demanded wherefore she did give her brother WILLIAM no more replyed I give him the £100 for a remembrance and that he was sickly and that he had maintenance for she did verily belive that he would never marry. Witnesses: JANE STONE, MERRIEL HILLES. Proved Sir THOMAS SWAN fictri nat. et leg was granted administration **Russell, 91.**

THOMAS SWAN of Southfleete, county Kent, knight. Will 1 March 1638; proved 11 June, 1639. My Body to Church of Southflete. To poor of said parish 40s. To my youngest son

THOMAS SWAN and to my two daughters ELIZABETH and MERIELL SWAN as much yearly as will serve for their education to be allowed by my two brothers GEORGE SWAN and WILLIAM SWAN to whom I shall, for a term, bequeath my estate. To my said son THOMAS £200 to be invested by my said brothers for his benefit. To my eldest daughter ELIZABETH £200 to be invested for her benefit. To my youngest daughter MERIELL SWAN £200 to be invested for her benefit. To my dear wife I give my horses, coac hand furniture. To her the use of all my household stuff while she continues a widow. If my wife Marry then my eldest son WILLIAM SWAN shall have the goods for ever. If my wife prove to be with child at my decease then £100 to such, child to be invested. To my brothers GEORGE and WILLIAM SWAN all my lands until my eldest son WILLIAM SWAN come of age then all my lands tenements etc to said son WILLIAM and heirs. And for default to my youngest son THOMAS and heirs. And for default then to such issue male as my wife may happen to be in at tyme of my decease and heirs. And for default then to the use of my severaldaughters and at their marriages, they to have £500 apeece. After such sums paid then to my brother GEORGE SWAN and heirs males And for default to my brother WILLIAM SWAN and heirs males. And for default to my right heirs. To my said brothers for their paines in said Trust £10 apeece. My welbeloved wife sole executrix. I desire that Sir ANTHONY WELDON of Swanscombe county Kent, RALPH WELDON seq his son and heir will be assistant to my wife and brothers. I ordain them Overseers To each of then £5. Residue to my elsest son WILLIAM SWAN. Witnesses: WM LAY, ANTHO: DABITOTT. **Harvey, 105.**

[William Swann emigrated to Virginia, patented land in the present Surry County and and died in or shortly before, 1638. His son, Col. Thomas Swann, of "Swan's Point", Surry, was long a man of prominence and died Sept. 16, 1680. There are several things apparently connecting the family with Kent. The tomb of Col. Thos. Swann, and seals on old letters &c, bear crest: **a demi-talbot saliant, g** ; arms: **az., a chev. ermine, between three swans ar.** These are the arms and crest of Swann of Southfleet and Denton, Kent. In the will of Thomas Butcher, of Medhurst, Kent, dated July 22, 1646 (printed in this Magazine XV, 60), he makes a bequest to his first cousin, Margaret, daughter of William Delton, "wife of Mr. Thomas Swanne, now resident in Virginia."

A George Butcher married Ursula, sister of Sir Francis Swann (the testator). The pedigree of the Swanns of Denton, Court, in Berry's Kentish Genealogies, does not give the date of the birth of William Swann, 4th son of Sir Francis, but from other dates given it must have been about 1609 or 1610. Col. Thomas Swann, however, was a Burgess in 1645, and must have been, at least, 21 years old. He was born, at the latest, in 1624, could not have been the son of a man born in 1610. If William Swann, the brother of Sir Thomas, was unmarried in 1633, he could not have been the father of Col. Thomas. The pedigree in Berry does not give the branch to which belonged Sir Thomas and his sister Muriel Swann, whose wills follow; but Burke's **Extinct and Dormant Baronstage** states that Sir Thomas (who was knighted 1630) was a son of Sir William Swann, living in the time of James I, and that he had a son, Thomas, of Hook Place in Southfleet, Kent, who was created a baronet 1666. Sir Thomas also had a brother, William, who might have been the emigrant. It is not likely, however, that a man in England would put a man of Virginia in charge of his estate. William Swann, the emigrant to Virginia, may not have come to the colony at the date of Sir Thomas' will. His stay here was, evidently, very short. These wllls are published as clews and suggestions for further research. It should be added, as an additional indication of Kentish connection, that an old manuscript genealogy handed down in the American family, states that the second wife of Col. Thos. Swann was named Codd—a Kentish name.]

VIRGINIA GLEANINGS IN ENGLAND

(Contributed by Leo Culleton, 92 Picadilly, London, W., and the late Lothrop Withington.)

DANIEL HORSMANDEN, of Maidstone, co. Kent, Doctor in Divinity being aged and weak.

Dated 27 Jan. 1654-5.   Proved 24 June 1656.

To URSULA, my wife, over and above her joynture, all furniture, bedding etc., to furnishe her one chamber. Wheras I have a judgment against my brother Sir ANTHONY ST. LEGER my will is, that whatsoever may be received, my daughter CHAPMAN shall have three parts thereof and my sonne WARHAM the remainder. To my sonne WARHAM HORSMANDEN, and his heirs for ever, all my messages, lands and tenements whatsoever.

To my sonne, ANTHONY HORSMANDEN- £200. To my sonne, RICHARD HORSMANDEN, £10 a year. Residuary Legatees and Executors:—my two sonnes WARHAM & ANTHONY. To my sister ELIZABETH COBHAM, widow, ANNE SMITH, wife of BRYAN SMITH, Clarke, REBECCA ST. LEGER, wife of JOHN ST. LEGER, gent., my friend WILLIAM COOPER, Esqr. and NICHOLAS BEAVER, 20s. each to buy them rings.

WILLIAM COOPER & NICHOLAS BEAVER: Witnesses. Proved 24 June 1656 by the Executors named.

Berkley, 227.

[Daniel Horsmanden, M. A. Cambridge, incorporated D. D., Oxford, July 15, 1617, rector of Whipsnade, Bedfordshire, 1622, Vicar of Guddhurst, Kent, 1625, and rector of Ulcombe, Kent, 1627, until evicted for his loyalty, 1645. He married Ursula, daughter of Sir Warham St. Leger, of Ulcombe. She died 1672. John St. Leger, referred to in the will was her brother and married, in 1632, Rebecca, daughter of Rev. Richard

Horsmanden, late of Ulcombe, deceased, probably a sister of Daniel Horsmanden. Rev. Daniel Horsmanden was a brorher of Thomas Horsmanden, D. D., rector of Purleigh, Essex. Warham Horsmanden, son
of Daniel, came to Virginia during the Civil War, settled in Charles
City county, was a member of the House of Burgesses 1657-8 and 1658-9,
and elected member of the Council in 1657....At the Restoration he returned to England and lived at Purleigh. Warham Horsmanden's
daughter, Mary, married William Byrd of "Westover", first of the name.
Her tomb at the site of the Westover Church bears the following inscription: "Here Lyeth the Body of Mary Byrd, Late Wife of William
Byrd, Esq., and daughter of Warham Horsmanden, Esq. Who Dyed the
9th Day of November 1699 in the 47th Year of Her Age".
For notices of the Horsmandens see this MAGAZINE XV, 181, 314-317,
XX 25. Daniel Horsmanden, born at Goudhurst, Kent, 1691, who
emigrated to New York and became Chief Justice and President of the
Council, was probably a grandson of Rev. Daniel Horsmanden.]

JOHN BARHAM of Lamberherst, county Kent, yeoman. Wil
27 January 3 Chas, I.; proved 19 May 1628. Yo Annis my
wife 20s. for a ring. To Nicholas Barham my eldest don 10s.
To John Barham my son 10s. To William Barham my son £300.
To David Barham my son £50. To Elizabeth Mocomber 20s.
To Anne Baker my daughter relict of William Baker 10s.
To Alice Barham my youngest daughter £200. To John,
Marie and Thomas Mercer the children of Thomas Mercer
and Marie Mercer my daughter and to the child the said Marie
Marie my daughter now goeth with £5 apiece at full ages.
To said Thomas Mercer the use and prlfit of said portions.
Annis my wife slle exedutor. Residue to her. Witnnesses:
Alexr Thomas, John Llck, Thos Pullinge

Barrington, 41.

ROBERT BARHAM of Lamberhurst, county Sussex, yeoman.
Will 24 February 1650 (-1); proved 11 May 1653. I give to
my eldest son Robert my house wherein I now dwell, called
Wickers, with the land sufficiently stocked as it now is and
my household stuff (except as hereafter is excepted) at his age
of 21. If it please God to call him out of this life before that
age, I give the same to my son John. I give to my wife Margaret, the profit of my lands and stock till my children attain
their several ages of 21, towards their education and maintenance and the raising of their several portions, so long as she
shall keep herself unmarried. To my son Richard, my house
at Wateringbury in Kent, at 21. To my daughter Elizabeth and

and my son John, £100 apiece at 21, and £100 at 21 to other child that may be born to me. All of the rest of my goods to my wife Margaret, whom I ordain my executrix. I give to every other of my children one bed and bedding. I appoint my brother Steephen Barbour my overseer. Witnesses: the mark of John Estland and John Chamberlein. Proved by the executrix named. **Brent, 281.**

NICHOLAS BARHAM, of Wadhurst, county Sussex, gent. Will 14 November 1652; proved 21st May 1653. I commit my body to the earth, to be decently buried in the chancel of the church of Wadhurst. I give to the poor of the parish L5, to be distributed at the discretion of my executor. To Elizabeth, Anne and Constance Elliott, children of my daughter Elliott, L5 apiece at their several ages of 21 or marriage. To John and Elizabeth Barham, children of my daughter Barham, L5 apiece in like manner. To my loving wife Marie the one half of all my linen, and half of all my household stuff and plate whatsoever remaining in my mansion house called Buttes (excepting only such household stuff as is in the hall, parlour and parlour chamber), provided she takes but one half also of the goods, which were hers at the time of our intermarraige. All the rest of my goods, household stuff, utensils of husbandry whatsoever, I give to my son John Barham, whom I make my executor; and I request William Peckham of Salehurst and David Holland of Wadhurst, my sons in law, and my approved and faithful friends, to be overseers of this my will; to whom I give 20s. apiece. As touching my real estate, I bequeath the same to my son John Barham, and his heirs forever, on condition he discharge all my debts and the legacies above bequeathed. (signed) Nicholas Barham. Witnesses: Nicholas Saunders, William Hendley, George Courthop. Gre: Dyns. Proved by the executor named. **Brent, 281.**

WILLIAM BARHAM "subscribed in Madrid". (Beyond the Seas)
Dated 24 Sept. 1623. Proved 22 May 1624.
"Receaved of Mr. BARHAM: in one Pondite of silver six hun-

dred twenty Rs In a little purse more in fifteene Escudos
at thirteene Rs one hundred nynety five Rs more in the same
purse in plate Rs more in the same porse 3s, 6d. in English
coyne. In HUGHE CRESWICKS handes, £30 and ᵉ30 more
upon a note of Mr. JOHN MAYNARDS. Owing by RICH-
ARD BUCOCK, £ 00. 15. 0. by Mr. WALTER MONUT-
AGNE, £11. 0. 0. I owe, RICE POWELL, £11. 0. 0. To Mr.
ABBINGTON, £00. 16. 0. To JOHN COOKE, £01. 10.. 0.
To THOMAS COOKE, £01. 10. 2. To the woman of the
howse for the use of her bed, £00. 05. 0. To my eldest daughter, CATHERINE BARHAM, £05. 0. 0. To JOHN WELCH,
£05. 0. 0. To my youngedt daughter, SUSAN BARHAM,
£53. 0. 0. Residuary Legatee and Sole Executrix:- my young-
est daughter, SUSAN BARHAM.
(Space)   FREWEN
JOHN STONE   Witnesses.
VINCENT GODDARD.
Proved 22 May 1624 by the Sole Executrix named.   **46, Byrde.**

ᵗ ᵗ [These wills add to the information already given in regard to the family of Barham, of Kent and Sussex, to which Anthony Barham, Burgess
for Mulberry Island, Va., 1629-30, evidently belonged. See this MAGA-
ZINE, III, 278; XXII, 25, 397.]

THOMAS BREWSTER of olde Buckenham in the Countie
of Norff. gent.

Dated 8 April 17 Jas.   Proved 10 Nov. 1619.
Towardes the repayringe of the parishe Church of olde Buck-
enhxm, aforesaid, Fortie shillings.   My will is that my Executrix shall yearle, during the space of Five yeares bestow
the some of Fortie shillings in Cloth to be given unto Five of
the pooerst, lame, olde and impotent peoplr of olde Bucken-
ham aforesid. To MARYE BREWSTER, my dayghter,
the some of Three hundred pouhdes. To Mr. ISAACK
BENTLEY, minister of olde Buckenham, Forty shillings.
To THOMAZINE BOTYPHANT, my wives grandchilde,
Twentie pounds. To   my "wives daugh-
Twentie pounds. To   my "wives" daughter
Fortie shillings. To THOMAS BRYANT and JOSEPH BRY-
ANT, my ':wives" sonnes, to either of them a Ringe of gould.

To FRANCIS BREWSTER, my brother, a gould ringe of ye value of Forty six shillings and sight pence. All my messuages, landes Tenements and heriditamts unto ALICE mn wife, untill THOMAS my sonne shall accomplish his full age of One and twentie yeares.

Sole Executrix, the said ALICE my wife.

JACOB PRESTO SMITH, (W.W. S.)., IZAACKE BENTLEY, Clarke. Witnesses

':Surrender was given unto the handes of JACOB PRESTON of all his Copyhould lands of the Lays Castel, and Close Mannor in the presence of WILLIAM SMITH and FRANCIS BREWSTER"

Proved 10 Nov. 1619 by the Sole Executrix named. **104**

104 Parer.

SARA BROUSTER of Stansfield in the Countie of Suff. singlewoman.

Dated 14 Aug. 13 Jas.   Proved 13 Apr. 1616,

To ROBERT BROUSTER, my Father and MARTHA BROUSTER my sister, Tenn poundes, equally betweene them. To THOMAS BROUSTER his Children of Toulbury in the Countie of Essex, Five poundes. To my sister ANN REEVE, Five poundes. To my ':sister Children ROOSE HARDIE", five poundes. To my sister MARGERY HAWKINGES, Tenne poundes. To SARA ABBOTT of Sudbury "Mr MAYOR daughter" Tenn poundes. To my sister "MARYE DEDMAN Children", five poundes.

Residuary Legatee and Sole Executor, LEONARD DEDMAN, my brother in lawe.

ANN CHRISTOPHER HOWTON & CHARLES DERISLEY, scr. Witnesses.

Proved 13 April 1616 by the Sole Executor named. **30 Cope.**

HUMFREY BREWSTER, of the Middle Temple, gentleman. etc.

Dated 2⁷ Feb. 1612   Proved 10 June 1613

My bodie to be buried in the Church.

And first touchinge my wife whome I have coupled my selfe latlie and unto whome I have made no joynture of my landes and Tenements. I do therefore give unto my said wife all those houses landes and tenementes with thappurteymances whatsoever which I purchased of EDWARD HAVUCHETT (?Haunchett) of Hartfordshire, Esquire, as well free as copie landes, lyinge in Ditchingham in the County of Norfolk. ':latelie THURTONES landes once Dwellings in Browne nowe deceased and nowe or verie latlie in the tenure of one SAWYER.'' And further ,all those houses lansed and tenementes whatsoever which I purchased of NICHOLAS KEANE of South cove in Suff: gentleman lyinge in cove and mutford in the said County of Suff, which the said NICHOLAS KEANE amongest other thinges soulde unto me aswell the possession as the revercon which he hxd and was posseste of in the righte of one JOHN KEANE his brother, beinge worth in all fifty poundes a yeare.   unto GRISSELL BREWSTER my said wife for tearme of her life and after her death unto that child of mine which remayneth nowe in her Woombe unborne at my Deathe yf it shall live Then to remaine unto the said childe and to his or her heires for ever. Wheras I have but the revercon of the Manner of Weyfeilds als Witherfeilds with all those houses landes and Tenementes whatsoever lyinge in Ilford and Ham in the county of Essex which SIR NICHOLAS COOKE and DAME ELIZABETH his wife doe nowe occupie for tearme of their two lives and the longer liver of them and after their Deathes unto me and to my heires for ever. Whensoever the said Mannor shall come to me I likewise give the said mannor unto my said Childe which nowe my wife is greate withall when that it is borne after he or she shall accomplish the age of two and twenty yeares, and then to remaine unto him or her and to his or her heires for ever. And yf my said Child shall dye, then all my landes houses and tenementes beinge in Coove and Mutford in the County of Suff: unto HUM-FREY BREWSTER sonne unto FRANCIS BREWSTER my brother and to his heires for ever, after the decease of GRISSELL BRESTER my nowe wife. And all my houses tenementes and landes beinge in Ditchingham in said County of Norff. unto ROBERT BREWSTER sonne unto FRANCIS BREWSTER my brother and to his heires for ever. And

515

alstlie concerninge my Mannor of Weyfeildes als Wither-
feildes beinge in Ilford and Ham in the Countie of Essex,
unto JOHN BREWSTER, my godsonne, sonne unto mt aforesaid brother FFRAUNCS BREWSTER and to his heires
for ever.

Sole Executrix, the said GRISSELL, my wife.

ROBERT ROLFE, ISRAELL FFOURTH, JOHN COOKE
Witnesses

Proved 10 June 1613 by the Sole Executrix named.   **52 Capell.**

WILLIAM BREWSTER of Brandon, county Suffolk.
Will 8 November 1625; proved 8 December 1625.   To Martha
my wife the house where I now dwell for her life.   And also the
lands I purchased of Robert Molle for her life.   To her also and
her heirs my arable lands lately purchased of Edmond Eastgate in Fowlden.   To William Brewster my son and hid heirs
the aforesaid house and also the lands purchased of Molle.
To Thomas my son £120 at full age.   To John my son £120
at full age.   To Ambros my son £120 at full age.   To Elizabeth my daughter wife of William Parke £5.   To Amy my
daughter wife of Nathaniel Hlwoet £5   To Alice my daughter wife of John Bereway £5. To Martha my daughter £105
at full age.   To Thomas Brewster my apprentice £5.   To Elizabeth Pinner my sister in law £5.   To pour of Brandonferry
£5.   Residue to Martha my wife sole executrix.   Richxrd
Cronshay of Hartest supervisor to whom 40s.   Witnesses:
John Rous, Clerhe, Thos. Brewster, Robt Dockinge.
Clarke, 135.

[The family of Brewster in Suffolk and Norfolk, had several representatives in the American Colonies. Of course the most prominent
was Elder William Brewster. William Brewster, possibly the same,
was a member of the Virginia Company. Captain Edward Brewster,
"son of William Brewster", was a member of the Virginia Company
in 1609, came to Virginia with Lord Delaware in 1610 and returned
to England in 1619. Richard Brewster lived in Virginia before 1623 and
in 1626 owned 100 acres at Archers Hope. Sackford Brewster was a
member of an exploring party from James River, westward in 1650.
On April 25, 1655, in Surry County, a marriage license was issued to him
as "Thomas alias Sackford Brewster, of Sackford Hall, in the County
of Suffolk, gent." His descendants in the male line long lived in
Virginia. Marshall's *Genealogists Guide* gives reference to pedigrees
of Brewster and Sackford of Suffolk.

Hunphrey Brewster (above) was a younger son of Humphrey Brewster, Esq., of Wrentham Hall, Suffolk, and married Grizel, daughter of Robert Rolfe, Esq., of Hadleigh, Suffolk.]

WILLIAM BUCKNER, of the parish of St. Sepulcher, London, yeoman.

Dated 30 Dec. 1653.   Proved 18 Dec. 1654.

To ELIZABETH my wife, £40 also all my hosehold stuffe in my house at Kentish Town, co. Middlesex. To WILLIAM BUCKNER, £10. To my other six children, MARY, ELIZABETH, BARNARD, FRANCES, LAURENCE & ANNE BUCKNER, £20 each to be paid at their full ages of 21 years. To JOHN, my wife's sonne, only 1s. To my brother JOHN BUCKNER of the parish of St. Sepulcher, London and to my sister his wife, 10s. each to buy them gloves. To my my cousins Master INNOCENTIUS HARRIS and Master BARNARD HARTE, and their wives, and to my cousin Captain THOMAS BUCKNER and his wife and to my friend Master ANTHONIR BONNER, 5s. each. To my brother's servants, JOHN HENLEY, EDWARD JONES, WINIFR‡D his wife JOHN CHEW, THOMAS COOKE and THOMAS HUDSON, 2s. 6d. each.

Sole Executor: my said brother JOHN BUCKNER.

GEORGE DODSON MICHAELL HUNT HENRY TRAVERS, Scriv in Smithfield.   Witnesses

Proved 18 Dec. 1654 by the Sole Executor nxmed.

31 Alchin.

LEONARD BUCKNER, Cittizen and Apothecary of the parish of St. Ann Blackfryers, London.

Dated 6 Nov. 1656.   Proved 23 Dec. 1656.

To be interred in the Vault of the church of St. Anne, Blackfryers, wherein my wife lyeth. To my sonne, ANTHONIE, £5. and to his eldest sonne, £5. To my sonne, THOMAS, £10. To my sonne, LEONARD, £40. To MARY, my only daughter, £100 and a trunk of linnen marked N. P. To my sonne, JOHN, £10, and to my sonnes WILLIAM & EDWARD, £40 each. To my friend Doctor NURSE, 40s. and to his wife 40s. To my sister Mistris FRANCES NEED-

HAM, 40s. and to her two daughters ANNE & MARY NEED-
HAM, 20s. To my cousin JANE ALLEN, 40s. Residuary
Legatees:—my children (equally between them.)
Executors:—my friends JOGN WILDMAN, of Westminster,
Esq., and Master BARNABY OLEY.
To MARY JONES, my maid, 29s.
ADAM CANE RICHARD JEWELL, Witnesses.
Memorandum (not dated)
That JOHN WILDMAN of the City of Westminster, Esq.,
was desired to be Executor with the said Mr. OLEY instead
That JOHN WILDMAN of the City of Westminster, Esq.,
wns desired to undertake to be Executor with the said Mr.
OLEY instead of HENRY *ALDRICH, Gent and ROLAND
ALDRICH*, gent. and his name was inserted by the consent
of the Testator.
Proved 23 Dec. by JOHN WILDMAN one of the executors
named, power reserevd to BARNABY OLEY, the other executors named, power reserved to BARNABY OLEY, the
other executor named.   (*Not mentioned in the WILL)
439 Berkley.

[These wills may aid in tracing the ancestry of the brothers John and
Philip Buchner, who came to Virginia about 1665. An Anthony Buckner
had grants of land in Rappahannock and Stafford counties in 1672 and
1678.]

THOMAS CHYNNE of Newnham, co. Glouc., yeoman.
Dated 5 March 1655-6.   Proved 12 May 1656.
Having made and executed under my hand and seale to THOM-
AS HAWKINS of Newnham, gentleman and ELEXANDER
YOUNG of Westbury, in said co., yeoman, one Deed dated
24 Feb. last past, conveying my free messuage barn, stable
houses, buildings, the garden and two orchards, now in the
tenure of RICHARD CHYNN, situate in Newnham and also
my other free messuage which I and RICHARD JOANES now
dwelleth in, and 3 parcells of pasture, now in the tenure of
WILLIAM (?) WINCH, lying in the parish of Westbury;
the said THOMAS HAWKINS and ALEXANDER YOUNG
to be sized of the said premises for the use of such person and
persons as I shall nominate. To be interred in ye church of

Newnham. To RICHARD JOANES, part of the said messuage viz., the "Ciching" Buttery entry and chamber over the shop and part of the garden now in his occupation, and the messuage in which RIVHARD CHYNN dwells, to THOMAS CHYNN, the sonne of JOHN CHYNN my late sonne deceased. To ELIZABETH CHYNNE, daughter of my said sonne JOHN ,£100. To GRACE & MARY CHYNNE, daughters of my said sonne JOHN, £100 between them. I devise for the maintenance of my said sonnes 4 children, the life time of MARGERY COLLINS, the wife of DANIELL COLLINS, of the parish of Witborne, co. Hereford gentleman, the annual sum of £26   Residuary Legatees:—the said ELIZABETH, GRACE & MARY CHINN   Executors:— the said THOMAS HAWKINS & ALEXANDER YOUNG-WILLIAM CLOTTERBOOKE RICHARD JOANES THOMAS WATTS: Witnesses.

To JANE JONES, my kinswoman, £10 and to SILVERSTER JONES, my kinsman, 20s.

(RICHARD JOANES, THOMAS WATTS.) Witnesses

Proved 12 May 1656 by the Executors named.   **144 Berkeley·**

WALTER CHINN, of the parish of Rosse, co. Hereford, yeoman.

Dated 18 Oct. 1653.   Proved 9 Feb. 1654-5.

To be buried in the church yard of Rosse, near unto my grandfather's grave and my child, deceased. To the poor of the parish of Rosse, 20s. To my daughters, MARGARET & ELINOR one half of a meadow, called Byrefields and another meadow called Tybb, containing 2¼ acres, scituate in the parish in Rosse, also 4 acres of arable land called Rudegway, lying in Walford, co. Hereford. To my daughter, REBECCA, three score pounds. To my daughter, MARY, £10. Residuary Legatee and sole executrix⁸—ALICE my wife. Overseers:— my brother in lxw, WILLIAM MORCE, of Lanwarne, and my brother ,RICHARD. To SARA ALLEN, 5s and to THOMAS SMITH, my father's man, my second suit of apparel. THOMAS SMITH, HUMFREY MARRICKE: Witnesses.

Proved 9 Feb. 1654-5 by the sole executrix named.   **224 Aylett.**

519

RICHARD DANGERFIELD of the parish lf Rowde, (Wilts).
Dated 10 Oct. 1655.   Proved 18 Feb. 1655-6.
To my sister JANE CHAMBERLANE, 40s. who is dwelling
in Pewsey. To my brother, ROBERT DANGERFIELD,
20s. To my cozen, EDWARD DANGERFIELD, 20s. To
my sister's daughter, SARAH SMITH, dwelling in Pewsey
20s. To PETER SMITH, the younger, 20s. To SARAH
SMITH, the younger, 20s. To RICHARD HILPES, the sonne
of WILLIAM HILPES, £5. To RICHARD HESSETER,
the sonne of JAMES HESSETER, lf Pllshott, £5. To the
other five of WILLIAM HELPES children, one sheepe each.
To the poore of the parish lf Rowde, 5s. Residuary Legtee
and Sole Executrix: my wife SARAH. Overseers:—my friends
ROBERT STEVENS & JOHN HISCOKE. To JANE
WATERS, my servant, one ewe sheepe.
WILLIAM HILPES FRANCES STEVENS JOANE WAT-
ERS. Witnesses.
Proved 18 Feb. 1655-6 by the sole Executrix named.

39 Berkeley.

[Though indifferent counties, Ross and Newnham are only about ten
or twelve miles apart.. The wills indicate the part of England which
would best repay research into the ancestry of John Chinn, who settled
in Lancaster Co., Va., about 1662. The calendar of Gloucester Wills,
1660-1800 (British Record Society) referes to the following Chinn wills
and administrations 1668, Francis Chinn, Newnham; 1670, William
Chinn, Kings Stanley; 1672, Dorothy Chynne, Newnham; 1690, John
Chinn, Awce; 1694, John Chinn, Woodside, Awce; 1700, Thomas Chinn.
Newnham; 1706, John Chinn, King Stanley; 1708, Elizabeth Chinn,
King Stanley; 1720, Johnathan Chinn, Newnham; 1735, Richard Chinn,
Newnham; 1742, Hannah Chinn, Newnham; 1743, Edward Chinn, Newent;
1758, Nathaniel Chinn, King Stanley; 1758, Sarah Chinn, Newent;
1758, Martha Chinn, Gloucester; 1780, Anne Cenn, Tewksbury; 1781;
Isabell Chinn, Newn- nham. [Vol. I. Cal. Gloucester is not now access-
ible.]

WILLIAM DANGERFIELD of Stonehowse, co. Glouc.,
yeoman.
Dated 1 Jan. 1653-4.   Proved 20 Feb. 1654-5.
To WILLIAM my eldest sonne, the dwelling howse and shopp
with the paddock adjoining, in the tenure of WILLIAM
SEAVER, Also 3 closes of pasture, vizt., Peare ground, Eabridge
close and Hanmend, when he shall accomplish the age of 21

during his life, "according to a laese granted by WILLIAM SELWIN, of Mattson, Esq."

To SAMUEL, my second sonne, 4 acres of arrable land lying in Great Donowe feild, during his life, "If JOHN DAINGERFIELD and THOMAS DAINGARFIELD my brothers, or either of them shall soe long live." To THOMAS, "another sonne," £10. To EDWARD ,another sonne, £10. Residuary Legatee and Sole Executrix:—MARY my now wife. Overseers:—EDWARD DAINGERFIELD, my brother and SAMUELL COLLWELL, my brother in law.

EDWARD DAINGREFIELD, his marke, SAMUEL COLWELL, ABEL SANDFORD: Witnesses.

Proved 20 Feb. 1654-5 by the sole executrix named.

211 Aylett^e

[The Calendar of Gloucester Wills (British Record Society) 1660-1800 (the first Vol. is not accessible) contains the following references to wills and inventories of Dangerfield or Daingerfield: 1663, Francis, of Stroud; 1665, Stephen, of Stonehouse; 1671, William, of King Stanley; 1673, Joan; of Eastington; 1679, Richard, of Avening; 1684, Richard of King Stanley, 1684, Nicholas, of Stonehouse; 1694, Richard of Stroud; 1693, Edward, of Stonehouse; 1694, Richard, of Randwick; 1696, Richard, of King Stanley; 1700, John, of King Stanley; 1703, William. of Stonehouse; 1713, Mary, of King Stanley; 1714, George, of Stonehouse; 1714, Stephen, of King Stanley; 1728, Thomas, of Stroud; 1736, Stephen, of King Stanley; 1744, Mary, of Dursley; 1767, Joanna or Hannah, of Minchinhampton; 1800, Daniel, of Codley.]

See this MAGAZINE XXV, 239-241, for the Dangerfield wills.

ALLEN EPES, of the Cittye of Canterbury, Gentleman Dated 30 June 1653.   Proved 15 Feb. 1653-4,

Tl be buried in the parish church of Sainte John the Bapttiste in the Isle of Tennet, (Thanet), neare unto the place where my wife is interred. Wheras by deed, dated 12 Oct. 1650 I settled upon my daughter MARY EPES and her heirs, several parcells of marsh land, called Robbins land lying in the parish of Lidd, co. Kent, now or late in the occupation of the BATEMANS, under power of redemption upon payment of £550 to my said daughter. Now I declare my sonne PAUL EPES shall pay the said sum unto her and the land to remaine unto my sonne and his heires for ever.

To my daughter MARY, all such households goods given to her by the WILL of Mistris MARIE CLAYBROOKE, her grandmother, and the greate wainscotte chest given her by ANNE DANE, my servant before her death I charge my said daughter not to marry Master EDWARD HUSSAM, being a man whom I have often diswaded her from marrying To my grandchildren, CAROLINA NORWOOD & ALLIEN-ETTA NORWOOD, £10 a year each, to be paid out of my Lease of the Manor and parsonage of Seasalter, co. Kent. Residuary Legatee and Sole Executor: my sonne PAULE EPES.

EDWARD PYARDS, PETER PYARDS, Witnesses.

Prīved 15 Feb. 1653-4 by the Sole Executor named.

306 Alchin.

MARY EPS, of Crundall, co. Kent, widow.

Dated 4 April 1651. Proved 22 Feb. 1653-4. To my sonne, JOHN, 10s. To my sonne, GEORGE, 10s. To my sonne, THOMAS, 1s. To my sonne, EDWARD, 1s' To my daughter, MARY, 5s. Residuary Legatee and Sole Executrix: my daughter SUSANNA.

WILLIAM BAKER, JOHN WOODLAND, WILLIAM BRIT-TEN; Witnesses. -

Proved 22 Feb. 1653-4 by SUSANNA EPS, daughter and sole executrix named. **306 Alchin.**

[Francis Eppes or Epes was living in Virginia in 1625, was later a member of Council and was ancestor of a large and prominent family. His descendants, in the colonial period, bore the arms ascribed to Eps, or Epes of Canterbury, Capt. William Epes, who settled on the Eastern Shore of Virginia, was a prominent man, 1619-1626. His brother, Peter Eppes was also in Virginia.

So far as is known there is no published pedigree of the Kentish line, but it was certainly one of those large Kentish families, part landed gentry and part yeoman, so frequently represented in the colonies.]

WILLIAM FRY of Othill, Crewkerne county Somerset gent. Will 12 March 1624: proved 25 February 1625 My wife and son Tristam executors. William shall have his maintenance from executors till 21 years and after if he dislike his diet 20 marks per annum. Henry to have maintenance and be kept at school till he be fit for Oxford and then £20 annuity. My daughter at her marriage lr full age £200. Thomas Hutchins my uncle and Richard his son my Overseers. To poor of

Wayford and Crewkerne, 20s. each parish. To poor of Broad⁻
winson 6s. 8d "This is the some of my will to be brought in
form at tyme of leisure" Witnesses: Chas. Cheriton, Catherin Pinny, Elizab. Hutchins,
Proved by Sara Fry relict and Tristam Fry filii.   **Hele 20**

[Joshua Fry, professor of mathematics at William and Mary College,
and colonel of a Virginia regiment at the beginning of the French and
and Indian War, matriculated at Wadham College, Oxford March 31,
1718, aged 18, as son of Joshua Fry, of Crewkene, Somerset, pleb, (yeoman.) He was propaply the same family as William Fry, above.]

GEORGE GYLSON of London, Esquire. Will 26 June
1616; proved 26 March 1617. To Robert Marshe my nephew
all my lands in Cliffe county Kent and a pasture called Port-
thill in Could Newton, county Leicester, and my tenements
in Fleete Street, St. Brides near Fleet Bridge in London he
paying my neices Alice Bland, Elizabeth Catmer, and Martha
Banfield £10 each yearly for their lives, and to my neices
Jane Freeman, and Anne Edwards £100 each if they prove
widows. Lands in Kerton in Holland, County Lincoln to Sir
George Gill and his heirs. My rights to copyhold lands
called Sowthfield in parish of Sandon, county Herts to my uncle
Thomas Gilsons daughters. I forgave Sir Rice Griffin all he
owes me and the wrongs he hath done me and £100 and my
Lady Lucy Griffin all the wrongs she hath done me and £50.
To nephew Robert Marshes 3 young children, Neice Alice
Blands three children, nephew Edward Mershes 2 children,
Neice Barfields son £100 each. To John Hamonds eldest
son late of Newchippihg, county Herts £50. To Dudley
Hawkes of Bucklers Burye in London rights in certain houses
in Mawkyng, county Kent, he to pay £140 to Mr. Edmond
Herndon of Morcott, county Rutland, the Manor of Morcott and the Manor of Todworth, county Surrey, which I
had of him, he paying £500. Executors: Sir Francis Smythe
of Ashbie Solevyle, county Leicester, Knight, and John Randall of Preston Baggott, county Warwicke £20 each. Witnesses: Christlfer Garland, Henry Coxe, Richard Brome-
field, Mathewe Moncke. Money due.
Clement Carter £3, James Dugby £100, Anthony Fawke-

ner £6, Walter Gardland £20, Dudley Hawkes £140, Sir Richard Ogle £120, Sir Guye Palmer £50, Sir Robert Tarle? (Toole) £120, Mr. William Fitzwilliam £60, Sir John Fitz William £3, Thomas Phillipps with what he hath received of Mr. Randall and Mr. Shute £200, Edward Payne, £4 James Hamond £20, Sir George Hyde £400, Edmond Randolphe £8, William Smythe £30, Thomas Cave £6, Sir Edward Noell £140, Mr. Chisseldyne £10, Sir Leonard Hide £50, John Randall by accounr John Marrice £248, Sir Francis Ventrice £20, and Thomas Welles £10,   Proved by executors.   6 April 1630, administration to Thomas Cornell and Anne Cornell als Bland his wife, nephew and next of kin to deceased.   **Weldon, 27.**

[This name, which rarely appears in the indexes to the P. C. C. wills, was represented in Virginia by Andrew Gilson, who was J. P. for Lancaster Co., Aug. 1656, appointed one of the first justices of Rappahannock Co., and later lived in Stafford County. He married before 1667, Beheathland (Bernard) widow of Francis Dade. He had a daughter Beheathland Gilson, born 1666, (who married ———— Stork and died 1693) and, apparently, a son, Thomas Gilson.]

ANDREWE READE, of Faccombe, in co. Southon, Esqr.
Dated 17 Oct. 16 Jas.   Codicil 15 Nov. 1621.
                                         Proved 24 Oct. 1623.
Whereas the Rt. Hon. WILLIAM Lord SANDYS by Indenture bearing date, 6 Oct. 15 Eliz. did demise to HERCULES AMERIDETH, gent., the entire manor of Faccombe and all lands and tenements belonging ,with the Rectory of Faccombe, for fower score and nineteen years, and afterwards did convey the same to the late Rev. father in God, THOMAS, then Lord Bishop of Winchester, for three score and tenn years, which after several estates are come to me . . .   And whereas ROBERT KNIGHT of Gods feild in co. Southon, gent. by Indenture Sept. 20 Eliz. did demise to RICHARD BEACON-SAWE, of Cheriton, in said co. gent., now deceased, THOMAS WEBBE of Newe Inne, co. Middx., gent., now deceased and RICHARD COOKE, of Beeksborne, co. gent., the said mannor and lands, which lease was made by my direction before I purchased the inheritance of the said lands Now I have caused the same to be assigned over to my sonne GEORGE READE and lately from him to EDWARD TUTT, of Chilbolton,

gent., and Mr. ROBERT WESTE of Andever for the payment of my debts etc. in trust.

Whereas I, by Indenture dated 17 Jan. "11 Kings Mats reigne" have limited to Sir THOMAS STEWKELEY, Knt. and MICHAELL PINDOR, Esqr., now deceased, my freehold lands in Faccombe, for 30 years. Also by Indenture dated 6 Oct. last past, have demised to THOMAS LAMBERT the Elder, Esqr., WILLIAM SOTWELL, Esqr., and GEORGE READE my sonne, all the said lands for three score years. Now I declare that the issues and profits of the same shall be bestowed as follows: to my sonnes, GEORGE, the farm of Upstreete, all those arable grounds called Broadeway lands; that Coppice, called Pilewood, adjoining to Chaldowne; a wood, called, Galewood, the herbage whereof doth belong to RICHARD GOODALL'S copyehold; And 2 other coppices, called Galewood, the herbage whereof did lately belong to WILLIAM TALMAGE'S hold; a little meade, called Greenes butting on the West end upon the garden in the possession uf HERMAN SMITH, to my said sonne, he paying to my sonne, HENRY READE, £100 yearly,and to ANNE his wife, £10 yearly and to FRANCIS, ROBERT, MARGARET, MILDRED & ANNE READ, his sonnes and daughters, £50 yearly among them.

To my grandchild, ANDREW* READE, £20 yearly.

To my grandchild, THOMAS* READE, £100, to be paid to my friend, Mr. Dr. LOVE, now Warden of Winchester Colledge, and to Mr. ROBINSON, now schoolmaster there, for his maintenance. To my grandchild, ALICE DOWRE, now wife or JOHN AYRES, £50, and to MARGARET READE, the daughter of my sonne HENRY, £300, besides the £500 already in her father's hands of the moneys that were payable to me after the decease of Sir THOMAS WINDEBANCKE, Knt. And to my grandchildren, ANNE, the daughter of my sonne ROBERT, MILDRED & ANNE, the daughters of my sonne HENRY, £100 each. To my daughter, MARY, £100. And whereas my sonne in lawe THOMAS KEBELTHWAITE hath received £100 towards my daughters MARY'S marriage, I bequeath to my daughter £100 more which is to be delivered to my sonne GEORGE, for her sole use. To my daughter, WINIFRED DOWSE, my cuppe of silver. To ALICE HELLIER & MARY herdaughter, my nest of Tunnes salt seller. To my daughter MILDRED, wife of my sonne ROBERT READE, a peece of plate. To ANDREW HANWELL, my grandchild, a peece of plate. To CHRISTOFER BISHOP, during his life, meate, drinke and apparell. And whereas I have already made a lease of the far,m of Upstreete to my sonne GEORGE, Nevertheless if my sonne HENRY, upon the request of my sonne GEORGE, execute such further devises for the better and more sure conveying of the said farme to him And also if the said HENRY shall enter into such sufficient securiry and with sufficient sureties unto my said sonne GEORGE for the quiet enjoying of the said farm, without any disturbance by my sonne HENRY, FRANCIS READE his sonne and of WILLIAM BLAKE, my sonne in law, or of the executors of WILLIAM BLAKE, deceased, father of the said WILLIAM BLAKE, Then my sonne GEORGE shall not take any benefit of an annuity given him of £50, but it shall be employed by my executors towards the payment of my legacies.

Residuary Legatees:—FRANCIS READE, sonne of my sonne HENRY and his children, my sonne GEORGE READE and his children, and ROBERT READE, THOMAS READE & GEORGE READE, sonnes of my sonne ROBERT.

Executors:—my friends, THOMAS LAMBERTE, the elder of Laverstock, Esq., WILLIAM SOTWELL, Esq., my counsellor in lawe matters and GEORGE READE, my sonne.

To ROBERT TALMAGE, my servant the revercion of the tenement which THOMAS MOODY now holdeth and to my servant FRANCIS BANISTER, £10.

Codicil Dated 15 Nov. 1621.

Since the making of my last Will by reason of a suite in law with great losses I am greatly decayed and brought in debt to Mr. (space) THURMAN, £100, to my sonne WILLIAM

BLAKE, £140, to Mr. (space) LOOKER, £$00 and small sums to Mr. BONHAM and the Mercers. The same to be paid.

Proved 24 Oct. 1623 by GEORGE READE, one of the Executors named, power reserved to WILLIAM SOTWELL, one other of the Executors THOMAS LAMBERT the other Exor being also deceased.   **100 Swan.**

*Sonnes of ROBERT READE.

[Andrew Reade bought the manor of Linkenholt, Hampshire, in 1585. His second son, Robert, lived at Linkenholt and married three times. By his third wife, Mildred, daughter of Sir Thomas Windebanke, of Haines Hall, Berkshire(and his wife, Frances, daughter of Sir Edward Dymocke, of Scrivelsby, hereditary champion of England) he was the father of George Reade, who settled in Virginia. See this MAGAZINE IV, 264-5. George Reade was an ancestor of George Washington.]

THOMAS WALLER, of Beaconsfeild, co. Bucks., Esqr.
Dated 8 Dec. 1621.   Codicil 16 Dec. 1626.
                              Proved 9 May 1627.

Being desirous of peace between my wife and EDMUND WALLER my eldest sonne I have laid out for payment of my sonnes debts and about the purchase of the wardship of his wife and of certain leases made to Mr. ADY SARE, Daq. of his said wifes lands, £1200. Whereas by Indenture dated 14 May Jas., made upon mysaid sonnes marriage, between me and the said ADY SARE, I have agreed that part of the lands and tenements, mentioned should be conveyed to mee and DOROTHY my wife, during our lives and after our decease to my said son Edmund & Mary his wife during their lives, with remainders over to their heirs succesively. Now I hereby confirm the same.

Whereas I have jointly, with my wife purchased one messuage and divers land in the occupation of AMBROSE ALDRIDGE, and lands and wood grounds in the occupation of CHDISTOFER READING, all which are in the parish of Beaconsfeild in co. Hertf. I do hereby give the same to my wife requesting her to convey the same to my sonnes in lawe, JOHN ADY, JOHN GODBOLD & HUMFREY [space] in trust that they convey the same to HENRY WALLER, my sonne. To my youngest sonne, THOMAS WALLER, one messuage and lands ,in the occupation of GEORGE LANE and the little tenement and lands in the occupation of GOODMAN, situate in Pennac and Beaconsfeild, cos. Bucks, and Hertf. which I lately purchased of [space] CRAWLEY Esq.

Whereas I have bought one messuage and divers lands and tenements in Beaconfeild, of ELIZABETH TREDWAYE, one of the daughters and co heirs of Sir WALTER TREEWAYE, Knight, deceased in the names of my sonnes in law, JOHN ADY & JOHN GODBOLD, upon trust, I devise they permit my wife to receive the profits, during her life and after her decease, to EDMOND WALLER my sonne and MARY his wife. To my sister ALICE PLATT, £40. My wife shall bear the charges of my three younger sonnes, viz., HENRY, ROBERT & THOMAS. To my grandchild, DOROTHY ADY, £200. If she happens to die then to her father JOHN ADY, to the use of her three sisters ELIZABETH, MARIE & FRAUNCIS equally between them. TO JOHN GODBOLD my sonne in lawe, £100 towards the charges of his reading in Grayes Inn. To ROBERT GOLD, my ancient servant, 20 marks and to WILLIAM GROVE, my butler, £5. (Bequests to various other servanfs, named.) To the poore of Beaconsfeild, £30. (In the margin): To my cozen, ELIZA: HODGES, wife of (space) HODGES; "to his cosen BOSWELL; to his sonne ADYE and to everye of the testators 3 daughters*, a ringee" value 4 marks, each. "to ZAC ADYE, the younger, £10."

Residuary Legatee and Sole Executrix:—DOROTHY my wife. WILLIAM SMITHER, JOGN MAYER, JA: FOYLE, EDWARD HUISH, Witnesses.

Codicil 16 Dec. 1626.

My wife being dead I make EDMOND WALLER, my sonne, Sole Executor.

EDWARD HUISH, THOMAS GERARD, RICHARD ATKINSON, Witnesses.

Proved 9 May 1627 by the Sole Executor named.

*Not mentioned in the WILL previously.

67 Skinner.

[Several Waller wills with notes, have been published in previous numbers of this Magazine (XXVI, 32-35, 275-278). One of these, the will of Edmund Waller (1747), proves that Col. John Waller, of Newport, Spotsylvania Co., Va., was the son of Dr. John Waller, of Newport-Pagnell, Bucks, England. Mr. Leo Culleton, of London, has kindly sent an extract from the Waller pedigree in Berry's BUCKINGHAMSHIRE GENEALOGIES, which gives the ancestry of Dr. John Waller. It is as follows: (1) John Waller, of Leigh, in the County of Kent, 2nd son died 1567 (younger brother of Sir William Waller, of Groombridge, Kent, who died during his father's lifetime in 1527, and was ancestor of Sir William and Sir Hardres Waller, the Parlimentary generals) married Elizabeth, daughter of William Farnifold, or Feanfold, of Sussex, and had a son (2) Richard Waller, of Beaconsfield, Bucks, who married Anne, daughter of John Symmons, of London, M. D., and had a son (3), Robert Waller, of Agmondesham, and Beaconsfield, died 1545, married 1st Elizabeth Fryer, 2nd Elixabeth Duncomb, and had (besides a son, Edmund Waller, grandfather of the poet), a son (4) William Waller, of Hartley, Hants, and Abingdon, Berks, (buried Feb. 5, 1558,) who married Jane, daughter of Thomas Bowland, of Abingdon, and had a son: (5) Thomas Waller, prothonotary of the Kings Bench, J. P. for Bucks, died 1627, buried at Beaconsfield (his will given above), who married Dorothy, daughter of William Gerrard, of Harrow, (she buried at Beaconsfield), and had a son; (6) Edmund Waller, of Gregories, Bucks, died 1619, buried at Beaconsfield, married (1st wife) Mary, daughter and heiress of William Smith, of Pauls Cray, Kent. (Another account says he married Lucy, daughter of Sir Richard Grobham. Probabbly she was his second wife), and had a son: (7) Thomas Waller, of Gregories, who married Ann, daughter of John Keat, of Stoke, Oxfordshire, and had a son: (8) John Waller, of Newport, Paganell, 5th son, who presented his son William to the rectory of Walton in 1711. The name of the wife of John Waller, of Newport Paganell is not given, but her children are stated to have been: (a) Rev. William Waller, 3rd son, M. A. ,Rector of Walton, died Feb. 18, 1750, buried in the church under the east window. Will dated Oct. 26, 1747, proved March 28, 1751 (*100 Busby*), (b) Edmund Waller, of Cambridge, B. A., 1701, Fellow of St. Johns College, M. D., 1712, died at Cambridge 1754. (See his will, this Magazine XXVI, 275. (c) John Waller, "settled in Virginia": (d) "Several sons and daughters, some of whom settled in Virginia and Pennsylvania" Berry is incorrect in stating that Edmund Waller died in 1619. His father's will shows that he was alive in 1626. Burke's Landed Gentry states that he died in 1667.) It also seems that may be errors in other dates. John Waller is said to have died 1567 and his grandson in 1545.]

529

VIRGINIA GLEANINGS IN ENGLAND.

(Contributed by Reginald M. Glencross, 176 Worple Road,
Wimbledon, S. W. 19, London, England.

(Continued.)

SAMUELL SWONE, of Brasted, co. Kent, gent.

Dated 1 Jan. 1603.   Codicil 29 June 1604.
                                  Proved 15 Jan, 1604-5.
To the poor of Brasted, 20s.
To my wife, MARTHA, all my goods and chattels for the
bringing up of, MARTIN, SAMUELL, WILLIAM, ELIZ-
ABETH, ANNE, MARTHA & MARIE, my children.
And touching the disposition of all that part of my lands
and woods in the parish of Sondrish, co. Kent, which I late
purchased of my nephew, WILLIAM SMITH, called Shut-
well Bothome and 3 acres of land, called Longe croft, which
I purchased of WILLIAM MYDLETON, lying in Brasted,
and one acre of meadow, which I purchased of HENRY
CROW, also in Brasted, I bequeath to my kinsmen and
friends, WILLIAM CROW, gent., THOMAS MARSHAM,
citizen and merchant tailor of London and EDWARD
DUCKET, cittizen and mercer of London, they to sell the
same, and the money arising by such sale to be paid to my
daughters, ELIZABETH, ANNE, MARTHA & MARIE.
Sole Executrix:—my wife MARTHA.
GILES CROWE; ROBERT MELLERSH; BRYAN
WILTON: Witnesses.
Codicil dated 29 June 1604.
Whereas THOMAS OVERY mortgaged unto me one acre
of meadow in Brasted which is now forfeited unto me,
never-theless I bequeath the same unto him again, upon
condition he pay such debt as is owing to my Executrix.

From Vol. XXVIII, No. 1 (Jan. 1920), p. 26.

530

EDWARD DUCKETS; ROBERT MELLERSH;
THOMAS MARSHAM: Witnesses.
Proved 15 Jan. 1604-5 by the Sole Executrix named. **Hayes 5**

RICHARD SWANN, of Charing in co. Kent, gent.

Dated 5 May 1609.   Proed 17 June 1609.
To the poor of Charing, 10s. and Lydd, 10s.
To my brother, JOHN SWANN, gent., an annuity of £20.
to be paid out of my part viz., the moyety of those lands
lying in Lydd which I hold together with one Sir FRAN-
CIS SWANN, Knight, of the parish of Denton, in said co.,
also the yerely rent which is due unto me by Sir FRANCIS,
viz., £3. 6. 8. being the moiety of a legacy unto me by the
Will of FRANCIS SWANN, my father, which ever since
the death of WILLIAM SWANN my brother remayneth
yet unpaid. To my brother, CHRISTOPHER DEERING,
of Charing, gent. 40s. and to my sister his wife, £5. To my
cosin, JOHN DEERING, sonne of my said brother, all the
goods and chattels in his hands jointly used between him
and me. To my cosen, THOMAS DEERING, one other
sonne of my brother, £10. To my cosen, FRANCIS
DEERING, one other of my brother's sonnes, £10. To my
cosens, JANE & MARTHA DEERING, the daughters of
my brother £5 each. To my cosen, CATHERINE HUD-
SON, the wife of my cosen, GEORGE HUDSON 20s. To
the children of my cosen BOULE, late of Warhorne, in said
co., deceased £5. To my cosen, FRANCIS BRING-
BORNE, 26s. 8d. and to my cosen JOHN BRINGBORNE,
10s. To my cosen BETTES, his wife, 10s. To my cosen,
MANNERING, his wife, 10s. To Mr. FRANCIS STON-
ARD, 10s. To STEPHEN PEMBLE, late of Egerton, 20s.
To the poor silenced ministers in London £10. To ROB-
ERT VIRGINE, 2s. To ROBERT PORTER, 2s. To
HENRY OLIVER, 2s. To THOMAS OLIVER, 2s. To
HENRY PROSSER, 2s. To COATS, 12d. To THOMAS

RAYNES, 12d. To PRISCILLA OLIVER, 2s. 6d. To
PHINE BATCHELER, 2s. 6d.
Residuary Legatee and Sole Executor:—my brother, AN-
DREW SWAN. Overseer:—my brother, CHRISTO-
PHER DEERING.
JOHN HUDSON; THOMAS OLIVER, senior; JOHN
BUSSON: Witnesses.
Proved 17 June 1609 by the Sole Executor named. **Dorset 55.**

WILLIAM SWAN, of Southfleete, in co. Kent, Knight.

Dated 10 Feb. 1618.   Proved 15 March 1618-19.
To be buried in my chappell in the churche of Southfleete
amongst myne ancestors. To the poore of Southfleete, an
annuity of 20s. to be paid out of one tenement and land
therto belonging, lying in a village neere Stonwood, in the
parish of Stone, in said co., in the tenure of one
PRICE. To the poore of the parish of Swanscombe, £5.
To my daughter, MERIELL SWAN, £1,000. To my second sonne, GEORGE SWAN, £1,000. And whereas I have
made him joynt purchaser with his elder brother, THOMAS
SWAN, of a farm, called Boteshams, and the land belonging in Southfleete, my will is that at his age of 21 he is to
surrender his estate therein to his brother THOMAS, on
payment of £500. To my third sonne, WILLIAM SWAN,
£1,000. To my sonne, THOMAS SWAN, all my plate and
household stuffe whatsoever. Residuary Legatee and Sole
Executrix:—my wife, Dame MERIELL.
Overseers:—The Revd. father in God JOHN, now Lord
Bishop of Rochester, Sir GEORGE WRIGHT, Knt. and
Sir HUMFREY MAYE, Knt., Chancellor of the Dutchey
of Lancaster.
All my lands tenements and hereditaments, to my eldest
son, THOMAS SWANN, and his heirs males. For default
of such issue, to my sonne GEORGE aand his heirs males.
For default of such issue, to my sonne WILLIAM

SWANN, and his heirs males. For default of such issue to the heirs males of JOHN SWANN, of Higham, co. Kent. gent. To my kinsman, THOMAS BIRKETT, that now serveth me £10.

WILLIAM BLAND; JOHN BACKHOWSE; JOHN HUNT; CHARLES GRYMES: Witnesses.

Proved 15 March 1618-19 by the Sole Executrix named. Parker 29.

CHARLES SWANN, of Southfleete, co. Kent, gentleman, lying sick in the house of one Mr. William Platers in Ditchlingham, co. Suffolk, gent., and fearing death he desired to see and speak with his brother in law, Paule Hill.

[No date] ["a little before his death"] Proved 11 Aug. 1618.

He declared as follows:

To my sister Hilles children, all my estate whatsoever, to be equally divided among them.

Executor:- my brother in lawe, Paule Hill.

"My brother Sir William Swann, is not to have twoepence of my estate."

Richard Baispoole; William Smythe; and others: Witnesses.

Proved 11 August 1618 by the Sole Executor named.

81 Meade.

[Samuel Swan or Swonne, whose will appears just above, does not appear in the pedigree of Swan of Denton, in *Berry's Kent*. He was probably of the Southfleet branch, and his Christian name would indicate a possible ancestry of the Virginia and North Carolina family. William Swann, the emigrant to Virginia, was born in 1585, so might have been the son of that name mentioned in Samuel Swan's will. Richard Swan, whose will has the second place, was a son of Francis Swan, of Wye, Kent. Richard Swan was a half-uncle of Sir Francis Swan of Denton.

Sir William Swan (will proved 1619) was the father of Sir Thomas Swan, whose will was printed in this Magazine XXVII, 154, and Charles Swan was a nephew of Sir William.

Several Swan wills and a note were printed in this Magazine, XXVII, 153-156.

We are indebted to Captain T. A. Ashe, of Raleigh, N. C. for the following copy of a family record prepared by Samuel Swann (son of Col. Thomas Swann of Virginia) who removed to North Carolina.

"The following is a copy of a paper compiled by Samuel Swann who died in 1707, (in Perquimans Co.—Albemarle, N. C.)

"My Grandmother, Judith Swann, was born on the 5th day of February 1589, being Wednesday and died on the 16th, day of March 1636 in the 47th year of her age and was buried at Swann's Point.

My Grandfather William Swann married again the 1st day of May 1637, and died the last of February following in the 52nd year of his age and was buried at Swann's Point.

My father, Col. Thomas Swann was born in May 1616,—was married to his first wife Margaret Debton the 13th of January 1639, by whom he had two sons and one daughter, to wit: Susannah Swann who was born the 26 October, 1640—and died the 25th of November 1660, without issue—having been married to Maj. William Marriot eight months and 22 days—and was buried at Swann's Point. William Swann—who was born 30th October 1644 and died young in London, England and was buried there. And Thomas Swann who was born the 23rd of March 1645 and died without issue at St. Edmunds Bury in Suffolk England the 19th of February 1666, and was there interred.

My said father's first wife died the 5th of April 1646 and was was buried at Swann's Point.

My father was married to his second wife, my dear mother, Sarah Cod, the 13th of January 1649, by whom he had issue, likewise, two sons and one daughter— Sarah; who was born the 15th of October 1651 and died the 9th of August 1652, and was buried at Swann's Point. Samuel who was born the 11th May 1653, and Sampson who was born the 28th May 1654, and died the 1st of November 1668, and was interred at Swann's Point.

My said mother departed this life to a better, the 13th of January 1654, having been married that day, just five years and was buried at Swann's Point.

My father was married to his third wife, Sarah Chandler, the 30th of July 1655, by whom he had two sons and two daughters, viz, Judith, who was born the 22nd April 1656 and died the 30th March 1668 and was buried at Swann's Point. Anne, who was born the 9th, of July 1657 and died the 21st of August 1659 and was buried at Swann's Point. A son—not baptized, who was born the 11th of December 1658 and died the 20th of the same month—and another son born 1st November 1662 and died at the birth.

My said father's third wife died 10th November 1662—and was buried at Swann's Point.

My father was married to his fourth wife, Ann Brown, widow and relict of Henry Brown, one of the Council of State, the 23rd day of * * * * *—who died the 12th of August 1668, without issue and was buried at the Four Mile Tree.

My father married his fifth wife. Mary Mansfield the 20th of December 1668, by whom he had issue one son and three daughters— Mary who was born the 5th of October 1669, who married Mr. .Richard Bland, Thomas and Frances, at one birth, who were born the 14th December 1670.

Frances died 14th April 1676 and was buried at Swann's Point.

Thomas married Eliza Thompson, daughter of William Thompson.

Sarah who was born the 8th of   and was first married to Mr. Henry Randolph and after his death to Mr. Giles Webb.

My honored and dear father, Col. Thomas Swann departed this life for a better the 16th of September 1680, being 64 years and was buried at Swann's Point at my Grandfather's feet.''

Extracts from a paper drawn up by Hon. Samuel Swann, Collector of His Majesty's Customs at Roanoke.''

My dearly and most entirely beloved wife Sarah, daughter of William Drummond Esq., was born the 2nd day of March 1654, being Friday, about 2 of the clock in the morning, and was married to me the 24th March 1673 being Tuesday,—by whom I had seven sons and two daughters.

My dear and most entirely beloved wife Sarah Swann departed this life to a better on Saturday the 18th of April 1696 about 8 o'clock in the morning in North Carolina, and was buried at Swann's Point in Surry County at her own mother's feet on Friday the 28th of the same month, being 41 years one month and 16 days old, having been married to me 22 years and as much more as from the 24th of March to the 18 of April aforesaid.

My dear and entirely beloved wife Elizabeth daughter of Alexander Lillington of North Carolina, was born the 17th of June 1679, married to me the 19th of May 1698, being Thursday, the widow of John Tandall, by whom I had issue as follows—viz:

1 Elizabeth who was born the 26th of June 1699, being Monday, about 12 o'clock at noon; baptized the 9th October following, being Monday. 2 Sarah who was born the 29th of December 1701, being Monday about a quarter of an hour before sunset—was baptized the 2nd of February, following, being Monday. Samuel who was born the 31st of October 1704 being Tuesday at 1 o'clock in the afternoon. The Moon being full at 12 o'clock, was baptized on Thursday the 23rd of August 1705. 4 John Swann, who was born the 25th of April 1707 being Friday about half an hour before Sundown and was baptized by William Gordon.

Addendum of Col. Edward Moseley.

Some of his children by his first wife were ''buried at my plantation at Lawns Creek''—so there he probably resided before coming to Albemarle, only William, Thomas and Henry, issue of his first marriage, seem to have survived—to attain manhood. One of that branch was John Swann, Member of Congress. The District Attorney in New York (1919) descends from Sarah, No. 2 who married a Jones—one of her sons returning to the name of Swann, about 1790.

The Honorable Samuel Swann Esq., Collector of His Majesty's Customs in Roanoke departed this life the 14th of September 1707 just at daybreak at his dwelling plantation in Perquimans and lies interred there, at whose death and funeral, I the subscriber was present.

EDWARD MOSELEY.

WILLIAM TURBERVILE of Winifrith Newborough, county Dorset, gent. Will 30 April 1630; proved 15 February 1630/1. To repairing Winifrith Church 20s., and to the poor 20s. To grandchild Elizabeth Clavell daughter of Edward Clavell gent, a lease of lands in common fields of Winifrith. To Marie, Richard, Grace, Edward, and Fraunces 5 other children of said Edward £20 apiece at 21. To William and John Smeddmore my grandchildren £5 each when 21. To my grandchild John Turbervile £100 which his father in law Mr. William Harbin borrowed of me. To be employed by my brother George Turbervile in advancing John. My wife to give bonds to my grandchild and heir John Turbervile, or if he die to his brother Thomas. Residuary Legatee and Executrix: Wife Elizabeth for life. Overseers: Brother George Turbervile and Robert Stricklande. Witnesses: George Turbervile, Thomas Hayte, Willm Edwards, Robert Strickland.

St. John, 20.

JOHN TURBERVILE of Wolbridge, county Dorset, Esquire. Will 5 December 1633; proved 30 April 1634. My body to Ile of Beere church where my dear Lady and wife, my father and other of my ancestors lie. To poor of Beere aforesaid £10 as stock. To repaire of Beere church 40s. To church of Stoake 40s. To poor of Stoake 10s. To churches of Woll and Winfrith 40s. apeece. To poor of Woll and Winfrith 20s. To my serving men (except Thomas Trew) £5 apeece. To Thomas Trew £6. 13s. 4d. To Mary Trew his wife £5. To every of my covenant servants 20s. apeece. To my brother George Turbervile two closes in East Burton, county aforesaid, for 20 years paying to my heir 4s. yearly. To my cosen Mathew Turbervile £10. To Grace and Mary his daughters £10 apeece. To the sons of my nephew William Turbervile deceased viz: John and Thomas Turbervile £5 apiece to be paid to my sister Elizabeth Turbervile their grandmother to their use. To my cosin Mrs. Elizabeth Rainger £50 to the use of her and her three sons George, Richard, and Samuel Reinger equally. To my cosin Margaret Streete and to her children by Poore and Streete £40. To my cousin Edward Clavells wife Bridgett and her children £30. To Elner and Mary daughters of my nephew Thomas Turbervile gent deceased £40, And to his sons Thomas and George Turbervile £40. To Margery Reade widow £5. To Mary Watkins £5. To Widow Steventon als Burgan £3. To my cosin Margery Loope as a token 40s. To Thomas Christophers the Keeper and his wife 40s. apiece. To my son in law Mr. Thomas Thornhurst £10. To my cosin Dorothy Turbervile widow, relict of my nephew Thomas Turbervile £10 token of my love. To the poor at my funeral £6. To said Dorothy Turbervile, widow, my farm of Wolbridge and my lands in East Burton to have and to hold until her son and my heir John Turbervile shall be 22 years, paying therefore £13. 6s. 8d. yearly. My two closes at West Burton, Winfrith, county Dorset to my nephew Mathew Turbervile gent untill such time as my heir John Turbervile shall be of 22 years paying during said term 10s. yearly. Concerning my plate, household stuff etc. at Wolbridge, Beere, West Burton or elsewhere I bequeath the same to my heir John Turbervile, said John Turbervile and his mother Dorothy executors. John Fussell of Blandford, county Dorset gent and my well beloved brother George Turbervile gentlemen, Overseers. For their love 40s. apiece.

Witnesses: John Gallton, Clarke, Mathew Turberville, Thos. Trew. Probate was also granted 15 September 1638 to John Turbervile.

Seager, 27.

[The first of the Turberville family in Virginia, was John Turberville, who, as is shown by a deed made by him in 1726, bought land in Lancaster County from Henry Fleet on Nov. 9, 1680. He was J. P. for Northumberland in 1692 and for Lancaster 1699 or, and a member of the House of Burgesses for the last named county in 1703 and 1704. He appears to have made no will but the inventory of his personal estate was recorded in Lancaster Oct. 9, 1728. Various deeds show that he had an only son and heir, George Turberville, of Westmoreland county. The Virginia Turbervilles, as shown on various book plates and tombs, bore the same arms as Turberville of Dorset: Ermin a lion rampant gules crowned or. Crest: A castle argent, portcullis or.]

WILLIAM WALTHALL, citizen and Alderman of London.

[P. A. B. St. Peter's Cornhill.]

Dated 16 July 1608.   Adm. 3 Sept. 1608·

To be buried in the parish churche of St. Peter, in Cornhill in the vault where my late wife Ciceley was buried, being in the chauncell and in the upper end of the South Ile.

To the poore of the parish, £20.

All my goods and chattels to be valued and devided into three parts. But forasmuch that before the marriage with my wife Dame Margaret Goddart there was an agreement made as will appear by her deed made to my brother Thomas Walthall and my sonne in law, Arthur Robinson that she will accept £8,000 in lieu of her full thirdes. Also she hath agreed, and I have entered into covenant to Sir Thomas Bennett and Sir William Romney to pay £1,900 to her 4

538

children, Giles Garton, Simon Garton, Elizabeth Dent & Alice Greene that so much of the said £1,900 as shall happen to be unpaid shal be defaulted out of the said £8,000. Provided also that she pay out of the same all that I have disbursed for her sonne Giles Garton for the procuring his pardon to save his life and living from the danger of the Lawe, "for the surplus and charges of Billinghurst land more then the rentes, with the money to John Quarles which amounts to £750." not doubting but my wife will give allowance thereof to my executors as she promised me before her sonne in law, Mr. Francis Dent in the litle parloure in my house in Fenchurch streete, 20 March 1607.

One third part, unto my three children, Thomas, Luke & Elizabeth, equally amongst them. And the other third part, I reserve to myself towards the performance of my legacies.

To St. Thomas Hospitall in Sowthwarke, whereof I am a governor, £40. To the Hospitall of St. Bartholmewes, and the poor house of Bridewell £20 each.

To the poor of Bedlam, 6£. 13s. 4d. To the two Compters in the Poultrey and in Wood streete and to Ludgate. £100 between them.

To the prisoners at Newgate, the Marshallsea, Kynges benche, and the White Lyon in Sowthwarke, £30 between them. To all householders in the ward of Bishopsgate 2s each so far as £20 will perform. (Numerous bequests to various other charitable institutions etc, etc.) To William Batte, my godsonne, £10. To Mr. Batt's two daughters, that were godchildren to my wife and daughter Margaret, £3. 6. 8. each. To Anne Payne, my goddaughter, £10. To Elizabeth Bainbrig, my goddaughter, £6. 13. 4. All my other godchildren 10s. each. To "that olde woman my cosen Flower", £6. 13. 4. To the children of Robert Bristowe, 40s. each. To my brother Paynes, three daughters, Margaret, Mary & Johane, fyve markes each. To my brother Banbriggs children, 40s. each. "To two kinsmen I have abowte Dover in Kent of my mother's side, to witt,

Roert & Stephen Vincent," £10 each. To my sister, Johane Dutton, 100 markes. To Margaret Fisher, and her husband, £200. £100 of which her husband oweth me by his bond and Richard Walthall's. To their eldest daughter who hath married one Burne of Darbie, £30. To Johane Stables, my sister Dutton's daughter, £50 and £25 each to the children she had by her husband Higgins. To Anne Hubberde, mayde when my children were young, £6. 13. 4. To Ciceley, our mayde that dwells at Darbye, 40s. To Nanne and Alice that were maydes and married Feltmakers, 40s. each. To Jane Elsworthe, a poor woman, 40s. To Emme, mayde, now with me, £30. To Richard Walthall, my brother Anthony Walthall his sonne, £200. To his sonne William Walthall, my godsonne, £50. To my brother Thomas Walthall, his children, viz., John & Thomas Walthall, £100 each. To my sister Anne Walthall, my brother's wife, £20. To Godfrey Reyner, £5. To my brother Sylvester,. £10. To Mrs. Crockstone & Mrs Lewse £5. To olde John Howland, £5. To Dr. Ashpoole, a ring of golde, of 40s. To Shelley and his wife that keepeth my house at Hackney, £4. To Mr. Johnson, the preacher at Hackney, 40s. To my three children, Thomas, Luke and my daughter Elizabeth Robinson, all my plate and household stuffe, equally divided. To the Worshipful Company of Mercers, £500. To my sonne Thomas Walthall, the house and land that I lately bought of John Bowyer, gent., that lyeth in Hackney. To Lambert Osbaston, on the Bridge, £5. To his wife and Mrs. Eaton her sister, each of them rings of golde 40s. value, "and to Mrs. Thomas." To Mrs, Varder, nowe the Matron of St. Thomas Hospital in Sowthwarke, £3. 6. 8. To Mrs. Dixon in St. Peter's Parish, £3. 6. 8.

To my friends rings of gold, (the womens rings to be of 40s. value and the mens 50s.) vizt. Sir Thomas Bennet and his Ladye, Sir William Rumney and his Ladye, Sir Stephen Soames and his Ladye, Sir William Craven and his Ladye, Mr. Robert Sandye and his wife, Mr. Vernon, my

540

brother and sister Stampforde, my sister Dutton, my cosen
Richard Walthall and his wife, my sonne Dent and his wife
my sonne Cowley and his wife, my sonne Poole, my brother Bambrig and his wife, Thomas Fisher and his wife, my
sonne Moore, Giles Garbin, Simon Garbin, George Green and
his wife, Godfrey Reyner and his wife, my two deputies
and their wives, in Farrington without, Mr. Cawdwell and
Mr. Hudson, my cousin Richard Walthall of the Manpt-
wiche, Mr. Humphrey Walcott and his wife, Edmund
Sleighes and Gervis Sleighes of Derbye, William Batts, on
the Bridge, Richard Chambers and his mother Dorothy
Chambers, Mrs. Awdley of Hackney, Mr. Humphrey Bashe
and his wife, Sir John Manners of Haddon in Darbieshire,
and Mr. Alderman Lemman.

Whereas my late brother Anthony Walthall deceased,
"fell into decay and brake", about 1581, at which time his
creditors "sewed out the statute of banckrupts," and by
virtue thereof did seise certeyne household stuffe in his
dwelling house in St. Margaretts parish in Lothbury, to
the value of £100, which the said creditors left in trust
with me, but owing to long keeping the same is perished
and spoiled with "moathes, rattes and vermyn and ruste
and wormes," Therefore I leave £200 in trust with the
Mercers Company in London, in place of the said household stuff. "What is not perished" is in the hands of Sir
Thomas Middleton, Knt. who marryed the widow of John
Olmested. Md. Mr. William Walthall dyed 3 Sept. 1608 and
this will was found lying upon a table in his compting
house, being present at the fynding of the same, Ladye
Margaret Goddart his wife, Mr. Thomas Walthall his
brother, Mr. Arthure Robinson his sonne in lawe and his
wife, his two sonnes Thomas Walthall & Luke Walthall
and his cosen Mr. Richard Walthall.

3 Sept. 1608.   Administration granted to Elizabeth Robinson als Walthall, daughter of said deceased, no Executor
being named.

85 Windebanke.

LUKE WALTHALL, citizen and Mercer of London.*
Dated 30 May 1617.   Adm. 16 Dec. 1617

To the poor of the parish of Westham, co. Essex, £4.
and to the poor of the parish of St. Peters in Cornhill, London, £4·

Residuary Legatee and sole Executor: my eldest sonne,
William Walthall.

Overseers: Charles Pressey, Esq., Humfrey Browne of
London, merchant Edward Panton, gentleman and Thomas
Hobson, merchant.

Robert Jenyngs, vicar of Westham, Raphe Turner &
John Thomas, Scrivener, Witnesses..

16 Dec. 1617. Administration granted to Mary Walthall
relict of said deceased, to administer, during the minority
of William Walthall, the son and sole executor named.

                                        120 Weldon.

THOMAS WALTHALL, thelder, citizen and mercer of
London.

[P. A. B. of St. Peters Cornhill·]
Dated 14 May 1611.   Proved 11 May 1613.
[at top of Will]
Dated 23 April 1613. [at end of Will]

To be buried in the parish church of St. Peter's on Cornhill in London, near unto the place where my brother Alderman Walthall, was buried.

My executors to provide for 50 poore men, mourning
gownes of black, six of them to be of the chief porters of
the Mercers Company, and they to carry my corpse to the
ground.

To the poore of St. Peter's, on Cornhill, 5 marks. To
James Buffeilde, a poor water bearer, 20s. To the "Wandringe and Roagish poore", 5 markes to be distributed
amongst them by two pence each. To Christs Hospitall,
£5. My goods and chattels and things whatsoever, to be
divided into three parts. One third to my wife, another
third to my two sonnes and another third to perform my

legacies etc. I owe certain legacies given by my late brother William Walthall, deceased which are not yet due, but as they become so, my executors are to see them paid. The house wherein I dwell, "being a lease belonging unto the worshipful Company of Mercers", my Wife to enjoy the same, and after her decease my two sonnes John & Thomas Walthall. To some learned man to preach at my funeral, 20s. To my godsonne Humfrey Walcott, the younger, a guilte cupp, of 5 markes value. To my sonne, John Walthall, my seale ring, with my Armes ingraven on it. To my second sonne Thomas Walthall, another golde ring, with my usual mark ingraven in the same. To Mr. Godfrey Reynor, a golde ringe, prayeing him to be helpful unto my sonne John in getting in my small estate which is abroad. To my friend Mr. Thomas Chapman, scrivenor, a cupp of guilte of 5 markes value. To my friend Mr. John Vernor, a ring of golde, of 40s. value. To John Walcott, the sonne of Mr. Humfrey Walcott, of London, grocer being now Student in Trinity Colledge, Cambridge, 40s. To my sonnes Tutor, Mr. Cearle, 40s. To my sonne John the tenement, at the old Jurie ende, now in the occupation of Francis Childe, a Chandler.

Executors: My wife Anne Walthall and my sonne John Walthall.

Overseers: Mr. Humfrey Walcott, thelder, grocer, and my brother in lawe Mr. Humfrey Robinson, grocer and my friend Mr. Thomas Dalbye.

Proved 11 May 1613 by the Executors named.

[No Witnesses.]

47 Capell.

[William Walthall, merchant, lived in Henrico County, Va., as early as 1656. He probably came from London. In his will, dated Aug 2. 1669, Raphael Throckmorton, of London, bequeathed £10 to "my dear wives brother Mr. William Walthall, now living in Virginia". If the marriage of Raphael Throckmorton could be found in some London register, William Walthall of Virginia, might be connected with the testators above.]

HENRY WOODHOUSE of Waxtonsham alias Waxham, in co. Norfolk, Knight.

Dated 18 Sept. 1624.   Admon 4 Feb, 1624-5

Whereas by Indenture made between me, of the one part and Nicholas Bacon, of Redgrave, in co. Suff, Esqr. now Knight Baronet, of the other, bearing date 2 June 17 Eliz. It was covenanted by me to convey the mannor of Waxham alias Waxtonsham, with all the lands and tenements belonging, to William Woodhouse, my eldest sonne, nowe knight, and to his heirs males. And whereas I afterwards did by fine and recovery convey the said mannor and lands to the intent of the said Indenture as by the records of the Court of Common Pleas it doth more plainly appear. Now I. being indebted to John Dee, citizen and goldsmith, of London for £400 and to William Engham of London, gent. for £100, I appoint unto them for the payment of the same, the profits of one close called the hundred acre close, concontaining by estimation 103 acres and one other close, called the midle Deanes, containing 50 acres, and another piece of ground called Lower Deanes, containing fower score acres, now in the tenure of Richard Cubit &John Lesingham, for 5 years. Residuary Legatee and Sole Executrix: my now wife, Dame Cicely.

James Sherringham, Samuel Walpoole, scriv. Witnesses. 4 Feb. 1624-25. Administration granted unto Thomas Elwin, one of the creditors of deceased, the Executrix, Dame Cecile Woodhouse, renouncing.

15 Clarke.

[Sir Henry Woodhouse, whose will is given above, was the father of Sir William Woodhouse, and of Captain Henry Woodhouse, Governor of Bermuda. Henry, son of the latter settled in Virginia. It is probable that the Sir William Woodhouse, who died 1639, and whose will has been printed XXVI, 40, was not father of Capt. Henry, as there stated, but his brother.

See this Magazine XXVI, 38-40, and references there given.]

VIRGINIA GLEANINGS IN ENGLAND.

(Contributed by Reginald M. Glencross, 176 Worple Road, Wimfleden, S. W., 19, London, England.)

JOHN BANNISTER, the younger [no place]*
*[no Act bk for 1650]

Dated 4 May 1650.   Proved 24 Oct. 1650.
                           Admon. 19 Dec. 1655.

"Deare Uncle I shall desire you to give these freindes of mine, these small legacies:" To my Cozens, your daughters, 20s. each. To Mr. ARCHBOLD and his wife, 20s. each. To Mr. DEE and his wife, 20s. each. To my cosen, PEASE, 10s. To my cosen BANISTER, 10s. more. To my friend Mr. DELAWNE, the apothecary, 10s. To my friend Mr. SMITH, Haberdasher, 10s. To my friend MATHEW WOOD at my Uncle STAN-LYES, 10s. To my fellow servant JOANE KIDDER, 10s. To the Pensions of this parish, 40s. To my cozen THOMAS BROCKETT, 10s.

All the residue, unto my uncle desyring him to see that my mother doth not want and that she may continue with my friend Mrs. ARCHBOLD, till her senses be restored again.

I declare this to be my will of I dye before I return into England again.

To my Uncle fowrescore two hundred acres of my land in the Barbadoes, to return to my uncle BANISTER or his heires after his decease.

JERIMIE BUSHER, FRANCIS WHEATELY: Witnesses.

Memorandum that the Testator after the sealing of his will appointed his Uncle JOHN BANISTER his executor.

FRANCIS WHEATLY, JERIMY BUSHER: Witnesses.

Proved 24 Dec. 1650 by the sole executor named.

From Vol. XXVIII, No. 2 (April 1920), p. 128.

19 Dec. 1655.

Administration granted to MARY CROSSMAN als BANIS-
TER and MARGARET BANISTER, daughters and execu-
trixes of JOHN BANNISTER, the elder, sole Executor named
in this will, to administer the goods etc., of JOHN BANISTER,
the younger, deceased, the said JOHN BANNISTER the elder
having died. **153 PEMBROKE.**

[John Banister, the naturalist, had travelled in the West Indies before
coming to Virginia. He was in Virginia as early as 1678 and died in 1692.
A John Banister patented land in Gloucester County in 1653 and Mrs.
Elizabeth Banister had grant in the same county in 1679. In the grant a
reference is made to her son John Banister, and her deceased husband
John Banister. In the fragmentary records of Charles City County,
under date, April 9, 1661, in a statement that James Wallis had married
the widow of Lieut. John Banister. The testator above may have come
from the same English family.]

THOMAS BROADNIX of Ospringe, co. Kent. Gentleman.
Dated 6 Dec. 1650.   Adm. 8 Dec. 1654.
To MARY, the now wife of JAMES HAYLES, and to his heirs
for ever, my lands called Newes, lying in Burshmosh Parish,
near Dym Church, co. Kent, containing, 40 acres, now in the
occupation of WILLIAM BRETT of Brensent.
To MARY BRADNIXE, my lands lying in Stirry, co. Kent,
and to hir heires for ever, now in the occupation of THOMAS
JENNINGS.
To THOMAS BRADNEXE, my kinsman, brother to the said
MARY BRADNEXE, my lands lying in Snave Parish in Rush-
idg Parish and Alstone in Romney Marsh, and to his heirs forever.
To HENRY BRADNEX, my brother in law, £5.
To THOMAS BRADNIXE, the sonne of ANTHONIE BRAD-
NEXE, deceased, £10.
To the poor of the several parishes where my lands lie, £20.
To EDWARD HALES of Faversham, gentleman, brtoher to
the said JAMES HAYLES, £20.
To JAMES HALES, and to his heirs for ever, my house and
land lying on the parish of Rushidg also one other house with
44 acres of land lying in Bethersden, co. Kent in the occupation
of JOHN FARMER.
Sole Executor:—the said JAMES HALES.
EDWARD HALES, SAMPSON KENNETT: Witnesses.
8 Dec. 1654.

Administration to THOMAS BRADNAXE the nephew and legatarie named, JAMES HALES, the executor named being renounced. **410 ALCHIN.**

[This Thomas Brodnix does not appear in the Brodnax pedigree in Berry's **Kentish Genealogies**. Many of the lines are, however, not fully carried down. As is we,l known, the Virginia line traces to John and Dorothy Brodnax, who appear in Berry's pedigree.]

JOHN COLLYER of Lendon, marchant and Cloathworker. Will 18 December 1649; proved 8 January 1649-50. To be buried in Church or Churchyard of Beddington in Surrey. One third of estate to wife Regina Collyer, one third to my heire Charles Collyer and other third as follows: I forgive my brother Isaack Collyer £500 lent him. To my nephew Isaack Collyer Junior £250, part to set him apprentice. To my mother in law Mrs Anna Senuliano £50. To her daughter my sister in law Mrs Anna Maria £200. To Brother in law Vincentio Malo £200 and what he owes mee upon accompt for charges pictures bought or otherwise only for diet I reckon nothing. To Brother John Knight my interest in the house he now inhabits in Marklane and to my sister Mary his wife £20. To my couzens William and Mary Jurner I forgive twenty five. pounds of what they owe me. To Henry Swift £15. To Mr. Job Throgmorton £50. To poor of Beddington £10. To poor of London £20. To Edward Denny £20. To William Jolliffe I restore of what I had with him £100. Executors: Mr. Job Throgmorton, Brother Isaac Collyer, Wife Regina. My son to be brought up in the English learning and Protestant faith, if my wife leaves England he is not to go with her except with consent of my other two executors. Made in the Hamlet of Wallington in Surrey 18 December 1649 in presence of John Heather, William Blacke. Proved by all executors. **3 PEMBROKE.**

[Edward Lockey, formerly of Virginia, died, without issue, in the parish of St. Catherine Cree Church, London, in 1667. He left a considerable part of his estate in Virginia to his "cousin" Isaac Collier, Jr., son of Isaac Collier. In 1671, Isaac Collier, Jr. was deceased. The inventory of Isaac Collier was recorded in Elizabeth City county in 1675, and the will of Isaac Collier, Sr., proved in York, May 24, 1688. He named his wife Mary and children Charles, Abraham, Thomas and Sarah It would seem from the names that the York county Colliers were of the same family as the testator was. The clue is sufficiently good to deserve further investigation. See **William & Mary Quarterly,** Vols. VII and VIII for notices of the Colliers.]

WILLIAM FARNFOLDE, in the parish of Steaning, in the

Countie of Sussex, gent.

Dated 7 Aug. 1610.   Proved 8 Nov. 1610.
To the poore of the parish of Steaninge, 40s.   To the Churche
of Steaninge, 10s.   To, the Churche of Chichester, iijs. iiijd.
To Mr. WILLIAM FARNFOLD, my godsonne, £20.   To
ANTHONY FARNFOLD, my kynsman, £10.   To DOR-
OTHIE FARNFOLD, my brother ANTHONYES daughter,
£5.   *To SUZAN FANRFOLD, £5.   *To MAGDALENE
FARNFOLD, £5.   *To JOHN FARNFOLD, £5.   "Children
of Mr. ANTHONY FARNFOLD."   To everie one of my
sister HARPENYES Children £4 a peece.   To ' the sixe of the
Youngest" of my brother RICHARDE FARNFOLDS Children, 40s. a peece.   To my brother BYNWYNS five daughters,
40s. a peece.   To all Sir EDWARDE COLPEPERS Children,
20s. a peece.   To my foure sisters a peece of goulde of 20s. a
peece.   To my "sister ANTHONYES wief [sic], a peece of 20s.
To Sir EDWARDE COLPEPER, my baye Gueldinge.   To
my brother BYNWYN, two Corsletts and Halberds.   To
ANTHONY FARNFOLD and his heires, one house and barn
and all my Lands called Wollies lyeing in the parish of Ash-
hurst.   Residuary Legatee and Sole Executor, my brother
ANTHONY FARNFOLD.
WILLIAM FAGGER, WILLIAM BYNWYN: Witnesses.
*All given as separate Items.
Mem of Debts due to me:
of THOMAS TAILO of Steanynge, £7., of HENRY COXE,
als Greeneslade, 45s., of Sir EDWARDE BELLINHAM, £20.
"Witness of it": JOHN FORDE, PETER SHELLEY and,
RICHARD FARNFOLD.
of Mr. Doctor TYCHBOURNE, 53s. 4d., of WILLIAM
HEATH of Petworthe, £4.
Proved 8 Nov. 1610 by the Sole Executor named.   **93 WING-
FIELD.**

[In Vol. XXII, p. 399 &c., of this Magazine, was published the will of
Sir Thomas Farnefold, of Gatewicks in Steyning, Sussex, whose son, Rev.
John Farnefold, came to Virginia.]

JOHN GRYME of Ightham, county Kent, clearke. Will 21 August 1643; proved 22 March 1644-5. I give my body to be buried in the chancell of Ightham, as neere as possible may be to the body of my late deare wife. I give to the poore of Ightham and of Raynham 20s to each parish, to be distributed among them on the day of my buriall or within one month after my decease. To Mrs. Jane James of Ightham, widdowe, the same ring which was given my be her late husband and my very good patron as the best token I am able to leave her of that thankfulness and dutifull respect which I owe to her and hers. In case she shall depart this life before me, I give the same ringe to Mrs. Anne James, her daughter in law, the wife of Mr. William James, esquire. I bequeath to the said William James Sa;azar one the proverbes, or any other booke (not hereby bequeathed) which he pleaseth to make choyse of out of my library To each of my servantes that hath remained with me the space of one whole yeare and shall remaine soe at the tyme of my decease 10s. To my son Charles Gryme £10 and my tenement called Tibbs, houlden of the manor of Ightham. To my daughter Elizabeth Gryme £50 and Cooper's workes. To my daughter Sara Dawlinge, Smythes workes in two volumes, and my lease taken of Mr. Gossage planted with young trees, adjoining to my tenement bought of Henrie Shoebridge, during her life. After her decease the same shall be annexed to m said tenement. I give her more the use of all the goods, plate and household stuff that were her husband's during her life, she paying 40s. yearly to my executrix towards the education of her daughter Sarah Dawlinge. To my neece Sarah Dawling £10 at 21, and all the said goods that were her father's (by him made over to me by deed of gift) after the decease of her mother. To every of my three daughters (Elizabeth, Anne and Sarah) one bedstead, feather bed and boulster, with all the bedding thereto belonging, the eldest chosing her bed first, the second next and the third last, as they are in age. All the rest of my goods I give to my daughter Ann Gryme, whom I ordain my executrix. And I entreat my loveing cosens William Duckett of Grayes Inne, esquire, Henry Gryme of Charterhouse lane, London, and Richard Bowles, clearke, to be overseers of this my will, to each of whom I bequeath a ringe of 20s price to be bought by mine executrix. As touching my landes, I give to my said daughter Anne two parcells called Downes, containing by estimation 18 acres, with two salt marshes to the same adjoyninge sometimes called Cockell Marsh and Snares Marsh and Downes Marsh all in the parish of Stooke in the Hundred of Hood, county Lent lately purchased by me of George Wilkins late of Stooke aforesaid, gentleman, to hold to the said Anne and the heirs of her body, failing whom to my son Clarke [Charles?] Gryme. To my said overseers I bequeath all that messuage and 3 parcels of land (containing by estimation 7 acres) lying in Igtham aforesaid and lately purchased of Henry Shoebridge deceased, and two parcels of land enclosed called Brownes and Dynes in Ightham aforesaid heretofore purchased by me of William Ferry deceased and others, during the joint lives of Ralph Dawlinge gentleman, and Sarah his wife, my daughter, in trust to bestow the issues thereof at the appointment of my said daughter Sarah and in case she survive her husband I give the premises to my said daughter for her life, with remaynder to my said neece Sarah Dawlinge, except as to Brownes and Dynes which shall remain to my daughters Elizabeth and Anne. But fi my daughter Sarah leave other lawful issue then her said daughter Sarah I give the said tenement and the land called Dynes. to such her other issue and Brownes to mv said neece Sarah. Witnesses: Thomas Collyer, R. Bowles, Richard Johnson. Proved by the executrix named. **Rivers 56.**

[It is highly probable that Charles, the son of John Gryme or Grymes, the testator, was Rev. Charles Grymes, who was minister of York parish, York Co. Va., as early as 1644. That the son of a country parson should become one in the colonies seems likely. The compiler of these notes thought he had seen, somewhere in **Archaeologia Cantiana,** a reference to the testator, and extracts from the Ightam register, giving the births, of some of his children; but a careful search of the indexes of all the volumes fails to discover the reference. A genealogy of the descendants of Charles Grymes was begun in the April 1919 number of this Magazine.]

EL ZABETH HAM, wife of HIEROM HAM of the Cittie of Bristoll, gent., late wife and Executrix of JOHN OLYVER, of the said Cittie, merchant.

Dated 24 Dec. 1619.   Admon. 30 Oct. 1628.

To my daughter, MARY GRYFFITH, one sixteenth part of

the Prysadge lease and to my sonne HENRY OLLYVER the other sixteenth part. To my grandchild, WILLIAM GRYF-FITH, the great spruce chest, etc. To MARY GRIFFITH 'my grandchild, my dozen of apostles spoones. To my husband 'JEROM" HAM, £10 yearly.

To my sonne, THOMAS ROWLAND, £10, yearly. If he die then to his children that have no portions left them by their grandmother REDWOOD.

To MARY OLIVER, the daughter of my sonne JAMES OLIVER, £10.

If my sonne HENRY OLIVER, whatsoever is given byt his Will shall remain to his children, JOHN, THOMAS, and HIEROM.

Residuary Legatee: my husband, HIEROM HAM, he to pay, the £100 due to the Chamber for ROBERT ROWLAND.

Executors:—my husband HIEROM HAM and my sonne in lawe, JOHN GRIFFITH.

JOHN SMYTH   ) Witness.

30 Oct. 1628. Administration granted to WILLIAM GRIF-FITH, grandchild, and next of kin, of said deceased, to ad-minister, JOHN GRIFFITH, one of the Executors named, having also deceased and JEROMIE HAM, the other Execu-tor "deferring execution." **92 BARRINGTON.**

[Hierome or Jerome Ham is a name occurring several times in a family of Bristol merchants. A Jerome Ham lived in York Co., Va., and represented it in the House of Burgesses at the session of March 1657-8, and was J. P. 1656. His widow, Sibella, married 2d Mathew Hubard, and 3d William Aylett. On Dec. 7, 1603, Jerome Ham and John Barker were granted reversion of price wine in the port of Bristol for 38 years.]

THOMAS HOTHERSALL of City of London, Surgeon. Will 11 February 1617-18; proved last October 1620. Being bound for East Indies in the good ship Sampson as a master surgeon. A Deed of gift to his uncle Robert Shuttleworth, citizen and merchant taylor of London. Witnesses: Da: Phillipps servant to George Rickner thelder, scrivenor, deceased, Edward Cotton. **SOAME, 92.**

[Thomas Hothersall, of Pashbehav, gent., patented 200 acres at Blunt Point, (Warwick County) 1623. The head rights were himself, his wife Frances, and Richard and Mary his children. He came to Virginia in 1621, in the **Margaret & John,** took part in a great fight with two Spanish ships, and wrote an account of it, in which he describes himself as "late zytisone and grocer of London."]

ANTHONY KEMP, then of Flordon in the Co. of Norff., gent.
Dated 9 April 1613.   Admon. 26. May 1614.
ANTHONIE KEMP did declare his Will Nuncupative:
"I am heere at board with my Nephew ROUS, (meaning ED-
WARD ROUS of Flordon, in Co. Norff., Clerk) and am in his
debt, and I can not ride myself, for I am an ould man, and there-
fore I am faine to trowble him to ride for my money to CAM-
BRIDGE and other places, and now I am going to sojourne at
Norwitch where he must be bound to pay for my diett", and
therefore, whatsoever that I have shoulde be his.
No Witnesses.
26 May 1614.   Administration granted to EDWARD ROUS,
         of Flordon, Co. Norfolk, Clerk, and principal
         creditor of ANTHONY KEMP, late of Flordon,
         aforesaid, Bachelor to administer, no Executor
         being named.   **37 LAW.**

[As has been before stated in this Magazine, it is practically certain
(though positive proof has not yet been obtained) that Richard Kemp
Secretary of State of Virginia, was the Richard, baptized 1600, son of
Robert Kemp, Esq., of Gissing, Norfolk. Secretary Kemp in his will
names his brother Edward Kemp, and his nephew Edmund Kemp (the
latter then in Virginia). This Edmund Kemp was probably son of Edmund, and grandson of Robert of Gissing. Anthony Kemp, whose will
is given above, was probably a brother of Robt. Kemp, of Gissing. A
very brief abstract of the will of Arthur Kemp, son of Robert, of Gissing,
has been printed in this Magazine, but the one given above is much fuller
and more satisfactory. For other notices of this family of Kemps, see
this Magazine II, 174-176; III, 40-42; XX, 71-75.]

ARTHUR KEMPE of the parrish of Michael at the Thorne in
the city of Norwich, being now (I thanke God) in convenient
health. Will 15 January 1644-5 proved 17 May 1645. Not
knowing when or how soone some great and dangerous sickness
and disease may sease upon me, made as above. I give my
body to be decently intered in the same parish where I shall dye,
and doe appoint £5 towardes the necessary charges thereof. I
give unto the poor of the parish of Flordon 10s, to the poor
of the two parishes in Antingham 20s, to the poor of the said
parish of Michael 10s. All these sums to be paid into the hand
of the churchwardens and overseers of the said parish within
three weeks after my decease. Item, I give to four of the eldest

children of my brother Edmond £8 apeece, but soe that my executor dispose of it some way for their good. To my neece Dorothy Jackman £6. To my cosen Robert Freeman's wife of Gissing 40s. To the poor of Gissing 10s. To my neece Walgrave 10s. To my neece Elizabeth Kemp 40s. To Mr. Thomas Sair of Bestreete for his great love and respect 40s. To M'ris Bayfeild besides what I owe her 20s. for a ring. To little George Bayfield 10s more. To the servants in Mr. BayfeildIs house 40s. To the woman that keeps me 10s. besides her wages. To my sister the Lady Kempe of Spaines Hall in Eessex whom I desire to be one of my executors 40s, and to my cosen Rowse, whom I desire to be another of my executors 40s. And I desire my said cosen Rowse to see that my cosen Porter, the widdow at Dover, have 40s, which I have owed her this 20 years for her father's library. I give to my cosen Thomas Rowse of Flordon 20s. To every of my elder brother's sonnes 20s for a token of love, and my silver seale to the fowrth sonne. To my cosen Tom Kempe the minister 20s. To Mrs. Elizabeth Sair the elder 10s for a ringe, and to her two daughters 10s apiece. For the overplus of my moneys not disposed, I will that my sister the Lady Kempe of Finchingfeild shall have the dispositng of it where the most need shall be, among my brothers and their children. Item, I will that Doctor Browne shall have the booke in my chamber called Toloseness. I give unto my brother Sir Robert Kempe, all my bookes in my chamber, and those at London I will that my sister Kemp of Finchingfeild shall dispose of to my kindred that are schollers. I will that my clothes shall be given to poore people. Witnesses: Thomas Browne, Geo. Bayfield, Eliz: Fowlsham. Proved by Lady —— Kempe one of the executors, with power reserved for the like commission to —— Rowse. **RIVERS, 68.**

DOROTHIE KEMPE, widow. Will 14 November 1626; proved May 1629. Body to parish church of Wye, Kent., by the shes of my dear husband Sir Thomas Kempe. For all charges £100 and out of which £10 to Dr. Jackson. To my daughter Lady Ann Cutts £150. To my daughter Lady Dorothy Chichely £100. To my daughter Lady Mary Diggs £100

To my daughter Lady Ann Skipwith £100. To Marie Chernock £100. To my son Sir John Cutts £100. To my grandchild Mrs Dorothie Chichely £50. To my grandchild Mr. Thomas Diggs £50. To my grandchild Mr. Wm Skipwith £50. To my son Sir Dudley Diggs £40. To my sister Tompson and Lady Tompson £10 each. To Lady Bowles and Mary Charnock £10 for mourning. To Sir John Cutts Sir Dudley Diggs, Sir Henrie Skipwith and Sir John Tompson my brother Mr Tompson and Sir Charles Boles £4 each for cloaks. To my chambermaid £3. Small legacies to servants for cloaks etc. To my daughter Cutts my wedding ring and my great jewel. To daughter Chichely diamond border, many other jewels given. To Mrs Mary Charnock all my wearing apparel and my Cabinet where my writings lye at Childerley____Gifts to children and grandchildren already referred to____linen at Olentey in Kent at Shelford. To Sir John Cutts the great standard at Shelford. To poor of Olentey £20. To ppoor of Lollworth £3. To poor of Little Shelford £3. To poor of Swansey £3. Sir John Cutts and Sir Dudley Diggs, executors. Witnesses: Jacob Bridgman, Tho: Ady, John Macarnesse, John Collier. Addition—I give £5 to the Steward of my Courts and £4.10s. for a cloake. And £4 to Grisell. All money that remains to my daughter Cutts "This Codicil was annexed to my Lady Kemps last Will—12th March 1626 And was read to her as she appointed and signed with her own hand. Witnesses: James Bridgman, Mary Charnocke, Roda Packe. **RIDLEY, 49.**

[This is quite a notable will as it illustrates the manner in which groups of kinsfolk emigrated from England. Dorothy (Thompson), the testator, married Sir Thomas Kemp, of Ollantigh, Kent, and had issue four children, daughters. They were: (1) Mary, married Sir Dudley Digges, Kt., of Chliham, Kent, and was mother of Edward Digges, Governor of Virginia; (2) Ann, married Sir John Cutts; (3) Dorothy, married Sir John Chichley, of Wimpole, Cambridgeshire, and was mother of Sir Henry Chichley, Kt., Governor of Virginia; (4) Amy, married Sir Henry Skipwith, Bart., of Prestwould, Leicestershire, and was mother of Sir Grey Skipwith, Bart., who emigrated to Virginia. The family of Kemp, of Ollantigh, was one of distinction, and to it belonged John Kemp, Archbishop of York, of Canterbury, and Cardinal, and Thomas Kemp, Bishop of London.]

STEPHEN KENDALL, of Hempstedd cum Eccles, in
Co. Norfolk, singleman.
Dated 12 March 1605-6.   Proved 9 Dec. 1611
To the poore of the parish of Hempstedd cum Eccles, xxs.
To every of the Children of my late Sister MARGARETT, the
late wife of JOHN LEAME, to either of them, 40s.
Residuary Legatee and Sole Executrix: my Mother DOR-
OTHIE, the now wife of ROBERT RYALL, of Hempstedd
cum Eccles.
JOHN SKYNNER, Clarke, STEPHEN KENDALL: Witnesses
Proved 9 Dec. 1611 by the Sole Executrix named.   **103 WOOD.**

THOMAS KENDALL of Great Yarmouth, county Norff, marriner. Will 12 March 1618; proved 14 February 1621. To
John Kendall my son £20 at 16 years. To Hellen my daughter
£5 at 16 years. Residue to be divided among Rose my wife
and my four children i. e. John my son to have his part at 16
years as also every of my daughters. To Henry Read and John
Lessingham of Great Yarmouth 40s. each and I make them
executors. To Alice Stevenson my goddaughter 20s. To
Elizabeth Lessingham my goddaughter 20s. Witnesses: James
Sheppard, Ri: Mighells, Scr. **SAVILE, 17.**

HENRY KENDALL als Tyndall of Bressingham, county Norfolk gentleman. Will 28 July 1637; proved 24 April 1638 to
be buried in church of new Buckenham Norfolk. To poor of
New Buckenham £10. To poor of Bressingham and Shelfangeo
40s. each. To 2nd son John Kendall als Tyndall messuage
in Shelfanger and Wynfarthinge, lands in occupation of Gylre
Banham lands in occupation of William Bagley and Widow
Awgar, John West. To eldest son William Kendall als Tyndall
£20 per annum and at her decease to his son Richard. To son
Edward £200. To 4 daughters Judith, Frances, Mary and
Jane £200 each when 20. To sister Katherine Hauers, widow

40s. yearly. Overseer: Loye Aggas gent. Witnesses: Willm Luke, Sam Brigges, John Blumfield, Gregy Wood, John Smith. **LEE, 71.**

[William Kendall, who came from England to Northampton County, Virginia, about the middle of the Seventeenth Century, and became Speaker of the House of Burgesses, in his will, dated Dec 29, 1685, makes bequests to a niece living at North Yarmouth, a nephew, son of his brother, John "living about Brinton," and a brother, Thomas, living in Norwich, all in Norfolk, England. It seems very probable that the testators in the three wills above, were related to him.]

Anthony Langston of South Littleton, county Worceister Esqre. Will 16 November 1633; proved 28 December 1633. It has pleased God to bless and enrich me with many children. And that no one son shall have preminence I make my wife Judith sole executris. To every of my sons £5 each not as a portion but as a token of my love to them. To my son Francis Langston and heirs the house and land now in occupation ol Henry Farmer the younger. To Anne Langston my daughter £800 hoping she will be ruled in marriage by her mother and brethren who love her most. I leave all charitable actions to my executrix not doubting she will have a godly zeal in disposing to the glory of God and to myne and her credit. Residue to my said wife Judith. Witnesses: Henry Langston, Russ Andrews, Fra. Harewell, John Gravison. **RUSSELL, 111.**

[It is possible that the testator was the father of Anthony Langston, who, according to a document in the English Public Record Office, was an ensign in Prince Maurice's regiment, went to Virginia about 1648, returned to England in 1662, and soon afterwards killed a man in a brawl. He was pardoned and became a captain in the navy. He prepared a letter on the condition of Virginia and especially on the need of iron-works, which is among the Egerton MSS., British Museum. Anthony Langston obtained two grants of land in Virginia. The first, to "Mr. Anthony Langston" Sept. 6, 1653, was for 1303 acres on the north side of York River in Gloucester County, adjoinging Mr. Hammond's land. Due for the transportation of 20 persons (names not given.) The other, April 26, 1653, was to "Mr. Anthony Langston" for 1000 acres in New Kent County on the south side of the freshes of York River, adjoining the land of Col. Man. [Mainwaring] Hamond. Due for the transportation of Daniel Rever, Hem. Chiversal,, Elizabeth Andrews, Mary Smith, Elizabeth Kent, William Feild, Mary Creeton, William Davis, Richard Clarke, Richard Crouch, Mary Puckerell, Elizabeth Thompson, Hoell Thomas, Richard Johnson, Mary Clerke, Runberen Davis, Roger Jones, and Robert Bridley.

A little later a John Langston was resident in the same county, New Kent. He took the side of Bacon in his Rebellion, and by act of Assembly June 1680, was disqualified from ever holding office. He had been elected a Burgess for New Kent in this Assembly, but was not allowed to take his seat. In 1704 the name does not appear among the landholders of New Kent or the counties formed from it, but it is possible that John Langston had a daughter or daughters, as Langston appears later as a baptismal name in several New Kent families. John Langston had two grants of land. The first, 1681, to "John Langston" for 1300 acres in New Kent, being the land formerly granted to Hannah Clarke, found to escheat by Marke Workman, Deputy Escheator, and now granted to John Langston. The other, to "Mr. John Langston," Sept. 28, 1681, for 1316 acres in New Kent, adjoining the lands of Sir Philip Honeywood, the river, land patented by Moses Davis, and of John Fleming, Thomas Glass, and James Turner, being the land formerly granted to Mrs. Hannah Clark and found to escheat.

There was a group of loyalists in this section. Sir Philip Honeywood, Col. Mainwaring Hammond and Anthony Langston had been loyalist officers, as had been William Bassett of the same county. Mrs. Hannah Clarke was widow of John Clarke, of York County, who was a son of Sir John Clarke, of Wrotham, Kent, England. She was also the executrix of Sir Dudley Wyatt, a Royalist officer, who died in Virginia in 1651, and was, no doubt, either his daughter or widow.]

WILLIAM OPRIE of Penkergard, in p'ish. of Helland, Cornwall, gent., will dated 17 June 1641. To my son John O. 12d. To my son Edward O. 12d. To my son Richard O. 12d. To my dau. Mary O. 12d. To my dau'r. Jane 12d. To my dau'r Philipp 12d. To my dau'r Emlin 12d. My wife Mary to have use of furniture in my house at P. for her life, remainder to my heirs. My son Thomas O. to have ploughs etc. To my dau'r Elizabeth wife of William Webbs of Landulp(h), gent. 12d. To my son Nicholas O. 12d. To my son Thomas Ol books etc. To my friends Anthony Gregory of Petrockstowe Devon, Clerk, Petherick Jenkin of Lanivet, Cornwall, gent., William Webbe, of Lardulp, gent. & John Courtier of Bridgerule, Cornwall, gent., in fee, my manor of Parke als the Parke p'shes of Egleshayle, Bodmin & St. Kew, Cornwall, messuages etc. in borough of Bodmin, lands in Bodiniell & Cobbleshorne, in p'sh of Bodmin, on trust to raise legacies for sd. four dau'rs M. J. P. & E. & then for son Thomas. Care of sons J. E. & R. & sd four dau'rs to sd. wife, she being their natural mother. Rest of goods to sd. wife & she to be ext'rix. Sd. Trustees to be overseers. Witnesses: Edward Opie, William Lobb, Hugh Bauden, Edward Littleton.

Prob. 23 Oct. 1656 by Marie Opie, relict & ext'rix.

[Thomas Opie, probably from Bristol, came to Virginia and married Helen, daughter of Rev. David Lindsay, of Northumberland County. The will of one of his sons, Thomas Opie, Jr., mariner, of Bristol, was printed in this Magazine, XVIII, 90. One of the descendants of the emigrant Thomas Opie, was the gallant Major Hierome Lindsay Opie (of Staunton, Va.), 116th Infantry, 29th Division, who so highly distinguished himself in the World War. As the chief commerical city of the West, Bristol attracted many people of Cornwall and other western counties.]

VIRGINIA GLEANINGS IN ENGLAND

Contributed by Reginald M. Glencross, 176 Worple Road, Wimbledon, London, S. D. 19, England.

Extracted from the Consistory Court Records of the Diocese of Gloucester.

CHAMBERLAYNE, EDWARD PYE.

Abstract of Will of Edward Pye Chamberlayne of the Boyce in the parish of Dimock Co Gloucester Esquire
I give unto my Son Thomas the sum of two hundred pounds An the rest of my personal estate & money of my Grove I have lately sold I give &c to be equally divided between my younger children namely my said Son Thomas, Deborah, Anne Elizabeth and Mary I give to my said younger children, Thomas Deborah Anne Elizabeth and Mary the sum of one thousand two hundred pounds to be equally divided between them charged and payable out of all my manors messuages lands tenements and hereditaments within the said parish of Dimock to be paid as soon as my elder son shall come to the age of 21 years for non payment of which said sum as aforesaid my Will is my Son Thomas & daughters Deborah Anne Elizabeth & Mary or survivors shall enter in & upon all said manors &c until sum of £1200 shall be paid & satisfied
I appoint my Mother Yem & my Wife Executors
    Will dated 14 April 1729
                                    E Pye Chamberlayne
Witnesses
    James Wingod   Peter Thomas   John Cam
    Proved 12 May 1729 by Dorothy Yem & Elizabeth Chamberlayne the Executrixes

From Vol. XXVIII, No. 3 (July 1920), p. 235.

THOMAS CHAMBERLAYNE OF CITY OF BRISTOL (*sic P. A. B.*) merchant

Will dat. 2 Mar. 1748 £1,000 which Ann my daur. will be entitled to after my death by virtue of settlemt on marre. with my late wife dec.; to sd daur. her late mother's watch etc. To my brother Richard C., grocer, Stephen Nash, woollen draper, John Harmer, merchant, all of Bristol, George Roberts of Leiston co. Hereford, gent., & George Smith of Kentchurch, co. Hereford, yeom., all my lands & two copyhold messuages called Nokes Court *als.* Newhouse & Cookes meadow part of the manor of Killpeck, Heref., which I have surrendered to uses of Will, in fee, in trust for sd. daur. at 21 or marriage, for life, remr. to her sons successively, in tail, in default to her daurs. equally, in tail, in default, one quarter to my nephew Edward Pye C. son of my sd. brother Richard C. in fee; the other three quarters to my nephews & neices Edward Pye, Thomas, Ann, Elizabeth & Mary C. sons & daurs. of my late brother Edward Pye C. dec., in fee. To sd. trustees £10 each for mourning. Rest of personal este to sd. trustees in trust to pay to my sister Mary C. so long as she live unmarried £10 a year, rest for sd. daur. for life & then among her children, but if none, to pay £3,000 as my daur. may appoint, £500 to my sd. sister, £300 a piece to my neices Mary & Elizabeth C. (daurs. of my late brother William C. dec), one quarter of residue to sd. Edward Pie C. son of the sd. Richard C., & the other three quarters to sd. Edward Pie, Thomas, Ann, Elizabeth & Mary C. sons & daurs. of sd. Edward Pie C. dec. sd. Trustees to be exors. in trust & guardians of my daur. till she be 21 or married. Witnesses: James Duffet, Geo. Adderley, Thos. Blackwell.

Prob. 13 June 1749 by Richard Chamberlayne, Stephen Nash, John Harmer & George Roberts, e. the exors. Power reserved to Geo. Smith the other exor. *Lisle 76.*

[Following a suggestion by the annotator of these "Gleanings", that Elizabeth Chamberlayne, niece of Edward Pye, and mother of Edward Pye Chamberlayne the elder, was the same Elizabeth, widow of Thomas Chamberlayne, of London, merchant, who was dead in 1682 (see wills and notes in Vol. XXVI of the Magazine), members of the family authorized a brief investigation in England. No will of this Thomas Chamberlayne was found; but he was probably the Thos. Chamberlayne, of Stepney, Middlesex, whose widow, Elizabeth, qualified as his administratrix, Sept. 16, 1674.

Mr. Glencross found the following in a chancery suit; Chamberlaynes *vs.* Kidley. The plaintiff was Edward Pye Chamberlayne, the elder. His son, William Chamberlayne of Virginia, had a posthumous daughter, Ann Kidley Chamberlayne, named for his mother.

Chanc. Proc. B. & A. bef. 1714 Ham. 265, 20

Dec. 1693

Answer of Thos. Batoon & Anthony Wallinger 2 of the Defts. to Bill of Edward Pye Chamberlayne.

They believe Compl. was Edward Pye's nephew & godson, that sd. E. Pye was a planter in Barbadoes & that he placed Compl. with Richard Howell & Richard Guy, 2 other Defts. in Bill, in Barbados. Do not know if sd. E. Pye advised Compl. to marry Anne Kidley (now Compl's wife) nor that Richard Kidley made proposal mentioned. Sd. E. Pye was owner of Lordship of Dymock & of manor of Boyce. Never heard sd. E. Pye say that Mrs. Whitaker had a writing to sd. other Defts. in trust for Compl.

Chanc. Proc. B. & A. before 1714. Ham. 265, 46.

29 May 1693

Edward Pye Chamberlayne of the Newhowse co. Heref. gent. son & heir app. of Elizabeth C. widow the only daur. & heir of Margaret Somors dec. who was sister & heir of Edward Pye heretofore of Barbadoes & late of the Boyce in prsh. of Dymock, Gloucs. merchant dec., orator. Sd. E. Pye, orators great uncle was for many years a merchant in Barbadoes & acquired much estate & having no child he bore affection to orator, his godson & provided for his education. He told Richard Howell esq & Richard Guy esq. both now of London & late of Barbadoes that he intended to make orator his heir but kept it private from fear of orator becoming extravagant. Orator sent to Barbados under sd. Howell & Guy. Sd. E. Pye procured orator to marry one Anne Kidley spr. one of the daurs. of Richard K. of Bromley, Herefs. esq. Sd. E. Pye proposed that the Newhowse &c. (£20 a year), Cookes meadow (£8 a year) etc, etc, in Herefs. lands in Gusmound, Monm. shd. be settled on orator. Sd. Mr. Kidley promised to settle on his daur. Anne an estate at St. Waynards called Reddican worth £40 a year. Orator on 29 Oct. 1689 married the sd. daur. of Mr. Kidley & sd. orator has had by her several children, 2 sons being alive. Sd. E. Pye was owner of manor of Dymock, Gloucs. & capital messe. there called Boyce which he had purchd. from Mr. Sergt. Leyes dec. value £300 a year. Sd. E. Pye made a lease of his property to sd. Howell & Guy in trust for orator & sd. Mrs. Whitaker who lived at the Boyce with sd. E. Pye had the writing. Sd. E. Pye on 10 Feb 1690 signed his will in presence of William Winteer esq. Richard Hill the elder & younger gentlemen all of Dymock viz. I. Edward Pye late of Barbados, merchant, now of Boyce in prsh. of Dymock Gloucs. to my kinsman Edward Edward Pye Chamberlaine of the Boyce in prsh. of Dymock Gloucs. esq.; orator, sheweth that Edward Pye esq. late of the Boyce afsd. dec. orator's uncle having no children of his own & having an estate of £600, having bred & educated orator, about Aug. 1689 proposed a marre. betw. sd. orator & Anne, daur. of Richard Kidley of Brom-

ley, co. Heref. gent. who had no other children but 2 daurs., it was
agreed that if marre. took place he would settle on orator, his wife
& issue his farm called Penvoirs, Herefs. & sd. R. Kidley should
similarly settle his farm called Reddicar in prsh. of 8 Waynards,
Herefs. As latter farm was more valuable sd. E. Pye was to deliver
goods to sd. R. Kidley to use of sd. orator etc. also £107 10s & this
was done & a schedule made. Orator then very young. Some time
after marre took effect sd. E. Pye about 168 [—] made his will &
(pursuant to an unwritten agreemt.) devised to orator in fee the
rest of his estate & orator hoped sd. R. Kidley would have paid sd.
£107 but he delayed & orator having expectations did not press him.
Orator now has discovered that sd. R. Kidley has settled all his
real estate on his other daur. or one of her children after his decease. Orator now asks for sd. £170 with intt.

Chamberlain vs. Kidley, Chan. Proc. Ham. 270|59.

The following pedigree is derived from the papers in this suit.
At the time the said suit was brought several of Edward Pye
Chamberlayne's children had not been born. It is hoped that same
member of the family will have farther investigation made in
England.

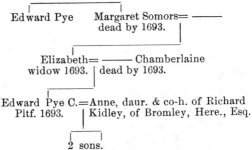

The wills given above are those of two of the brothers of William
Chamberlayne of Virginia.

WILLIAM CLOPTON thelder of Groton, county Suffolk, gent
Will 1 November 1640; proved 27 November 1640. To my
wife all customary lands in Groton holden of William Hobart
Esq as of his Manor of Lynsey. And all customary lands
holden of John Sampson Esq as of his Manor of Lillesey cum
Sampsons Hall in Carsey And all my Customary lands holden
of Isaac Appleton Esq in Groton aforesaid in tenure of Henry
Samford and Jerom Lamberde to her for 18 years, and after
expiration to my son William and heirs for ever. Whereas
I and my said son William by indenture 27 October last granted

to John Sampson the younger and Robert Sampson gentlemen my manors of Chastlynes Chipley and Saundefords my
freeholds in county Suffolk to hold for 18 years at a certain
rent set forth in said Indenture which said lease was made
for raising portions for my younger sons and daughters The
said leases shall in convenient time set over to my said wife
the said premises. My wife possessed in Trust shall raise
portions for my younger children. For every one of them
(except my youngest son) £200 apeece. I am seized of one
copyhold tenement and lands in Lynsey now in tenure of
Robert Pinson the custom of which Manor is that it descends
to the youngest son. My executor shall pay to my youngest
son £160 and if my son William observe obligations then the
said premises to my said son William and heirs. I desire that
my executrix continue my son Walter at the University of
Cambridge until one year after he shall have taken his degree
of Master of Arts. My loving wife Alice Clopton sole executrix. Witnesses: Richard Doggett, Henry Sanford, Ro:
Simpson. *Coventry, 146.*

[The emigrant of the Clopton family of Virginia was William
Clopton, who was born about 1655, and was living in York County,
Va., in 1682. Later he removed to New Kent County. His sons
were Robert, William and Walter, and he had a grandson Walde-
grave Clopton. William Hammond, Gent., of Ratcliffe, England, by
will July, 1732, left lands in Essex, England, to his uncle William
Clopton, of Virginia.
  William Clopton, of Castleton in Groton, Suffolk, 1636, married
Margaret Waldegrave, and had three sons, William, Walter and
Waldegrave, and several daughters, one of whom was Thomasine,
who married John Winthrop, Governor of Mass. This William
Clopton, of Groton, is probably the testator above, though he must
have married a second time, as he names his wife Alice. It is
probable that William Clopton, of Va., was a grandson of the tes-
tator. A genealogy of the Virginia Cloptons was published in Dr.
Lyon G. Tyler's *William and Mary Quarterly*, Vols. IX and X.]

JOHAN FOOTE of Tedbourne St. Mary, county Devon.,
widow. Will 27 December 1647; proved 2 September 1653.
I bequeath unto Agnis Westcott, daughter of Anthony Westcott, £20. To Anthony, son of said Anthony Westcott of
Tedbourne aforesaid, £1. To Peter Ware, my son in law, one
shilling. To Mary Ware, daughter of the said Peter, 10s.

To Jane Ware, her sister, 1s. To Margarett Foote, daughter of Humfrey Foote, my son, 1s. All the residue of my goods not bequeathed I give unto Anthony Westcott, my son in law, whom I make my executor; and I desire Robert Poope of Holcombe Bornell and Giles Westcott of Whitston to be my overseers, to whom I give 1s. apiece for their pans. The mark of Johan Foote. Witnesses: the mark of Thomas Ponsford; Will. Squier. Proved by the executor named. *Brent,* 181.

WILLIAM FOOTE of the parish of Pinnock, county Cornwall, gent. Will 1 August 1652; proved 19 July 1653. I bequeath to my wife Margaret two of my best chests, a dozen of pewter dishes of the best sort, my brewing kettle, my best riding nag or mare, the side saddle with its furniture, half a dozen of silver spoons, my little silver cup gilded, two of my best cows, etc. and £10, on condition she give security for the payment of £70 to my brother Mr. Simon Foot and our cousin Mr. William Symons (whom I make my executors) within 3 months after her marriage with any other person. I give her more one bedstead which now standeth over the hall at Boturnell. I give to the poor of the parish of Veryan 20s., to the poor of Pinnick 6s. 8d. To my daughter Elizabeth £300 at her age of 21 or marriage. To Margery Robbins, my mother, one gold ring. To my brother one birding gun. To my uncle Sumons, in token of my love, my best silver spoon. To my cousin William Symons my small gold ring with a signet on it. To John Clarke the younger my best serge suit. To each of my servants 5s. All the rest of my goods to my son William Foot at his age of 21. If both my children die under age, I give all my goods, to my said brother Symon, he paying my wife £100 if she be then alive. (signed) William Foote. Witnesses: William Cothler, the mark of Christopher Luke. Proved by the executors named. *Brent,* 347.

[Richard Foote, the emigrant to Virginia, was son of John Foote, Gent., and was born at Cardenham, Cornwall, August 10th, 1632. A pedigree of the Virginia family was published in Numbers 1 and 2, Vol. VII, of this Magazine. The testators, especially William Foote, of Pinnock, were doubtless relations.]

VIRGINIA GLEANINGS IN ENGLAND

Contributed by Reginald M. Glencross, 176 Worple Road, Wimbledon, London, S. D. 19, England.

(Continued)

JOHN LANIER

Will dat. 27 Jan 1649   My wife Ellinor Lanier to be ex'trix in whatsoever is due to me either in the Exchequer or the Great Wardrobe or the Treasury Chamber.   She to have disposing of my children.   Witnesses: Edw. Maylard, John Roberts.   Prob. 28 Aug. 1650 by Eleanor L. relict & extrix.

Pembroke, 135.

ELINOR LANIERE relict or widow of John L., of London, late dec.

Will dat. 23 Apr 1652.   To be bur'd in St Giles' churchyard where my late husband was.   To my son John L. ring etc., his father's picture & all his books.   To my dau'r. Frances, silver porringer etc., moneys at my present chambers.   To my dau'r. Elizabeth, Spanish silver dish etc.   Whereas there is due to me from Mr. Thomas Harris for so much goods of mine as he hath now in his hands, £70, same to my dau'r. Frances for maintenance of my younger dau'r. Elizabeth.   To my mother my deathshead ring.   Whereas there is an estate fallen to me by death of my kinsman Mr. John Woodburne, which is yet in dispute, what is due to go between my three children John, Frances & Elizabeth, And whereas my late husband Jo. L. left me his executrix & bequeathed me his whole estate & several sums still due, same to sd. three children equally, John & Elizabeth being under 18 & unmarried.   My son in law

From Vol. XXVIII, No. 4 (Oct. 1920), p. 340.

Thomas Hubbard to be ex'or & Mr. Ambrose Jennings, of
London, merchant, to be overseer. Witnesses: Will. Lulling-
den, Richard Seaman   Prob. 22 July 1652 by Thomas Hubbard, the ex'or. *Bowyer,* 150.

[In this Magazine XXV, 407 &c, XXVI, 321 &c, a kinship was
traced between Thomas Jefferson and John Lilburne, the ardent
defender of popular rights in England in the Seventeenth century.
It would be as interesting a study in heredity if the descent of
Sydney Lanier could be traced from the family of the name who,
as composers, musicians and artists, were in the service of the
English court from the time of Henry VIII through the reign of
Charles II.

The emigrant ancestor of the Virginia family (Sydney Lanier's
ancestor) was John Lanier, who lived in what is now Prince
George County in 1676. He died in 1717 leaving four sons, Nicholas, Sampson, John and Robert. It will be seen that Nicholas was
a favorite name among the English Laniers. There is a short
account of the Virginia family in the *William & Mary Quarterly*
XV, 77-79.

The Laniers in England are stated in the *Dictionary of National
Biography*, to have been of French origin. John Lanier, who died
in 1572 is referred to, in 1577, as having been a musician and a
native of Rouen, France. He owned property in Crutched Friars,
parish of St. Olave, Hart Street, London. He was probably father
of "John Lanyer, musician to her Matie". This John Lanyer or
Lanier, married, Oct. 12, 1585, at the Church of the Holy Minories,
London, Frances, daughter of Marc Anthony Galliardo, who had
served as musician to Henry VIII and his three successors.

The most distinguished of the family, Nicholas, son of John
Lanier just referred to, was baptized at the Holy Minories, London,
Sept. 10, 1588. He became a musician in the royal household and
in 1604 was "musician of the flutes". He held, subsequently, a high
position among the royal musicians, both as a composer and per-
former. Among other music he composed that for Ben Jonson's
masques; "Lovers Made Men" (1617), and "The Vision of De-
lights", as well as painting the scenery for the latter. At the accession of James I he was made Master of the Music, with a pension
of £200 a year. He was also a painter and skilled amateur of
works of art. In 1625 he was sent abroad by Charles I, to purchase
pictures and statues, and is considered to have been the first, with
the exception of Thomas, Earl of Arundel, to appreciate the worth
of drawings and sketches by the great masters. With the outbreak
of the Civil War the fortunes of the family declined, and Nicholas
Lanier followed the Stuarts into exile. At the Restoration he was
restored to his office and died Feb. 1665-6.

Another Nicholas Lanier, probably uncle to the preceding, was
musician to Queen Elizabeth in 1581 &c. He owned considerable
property in East Greenwich, Blackheath and the neighborhood. He
had four daughters and six sons, John (died 1650), Alphonso (d.
1613), Innocent (d. 1615), Jerome (d. 1657), Clement (d. 1661) and
Andrea (d. 1659). All of these were musicians in the service of
the crown and some of their children succeeded to their posts.

The will of Nicholas Lanyer, gent., gave his lands &c. to his wife Lucrece, and 12 d. apiece to his sons named. Mrs. Lucretia Lanier was buried at Greenwich, May 31, 1634.

Another Nicholas Lanier, probably a cousin of the musician and painter, was born in 1568 and published two volumes of etchings. He was probably the person of the name buried at St. Martins-in-the-Fields, Nov. 4, 1646.

It is possible that the John Lanier, named in the wills above, was the emigrant to Virginia.]

DEBORA FLEETE, of Westminster, widow.

Will dat. 27 Mar. 1651. All goods to my cousins Sir Robert Filmer & Sir Edward Filmer, both of East Sutton, Kent, knights, & they to be ex'ors, towards payment of such sums as sd. Sir R. Filmer lent me & my son Henry Fleete towards the recovering of my sd. son of a great sickness & for furnishing him with provisions & necessaries for his last voyage to Virginia. Witnesses: Henry Frenoham, Thomas Davy. Prob. 23 Jan. 1651[-2] by Sir Robert Filmer, knight, one of the ex'ors. Power reserved for Sir Edward Filmer, knight etc other ex'or. *Bowyer, 5.*

DOROTHIE SCOTT of London, spinster.

Will dat. 5 Mar. 1632(-3) 8 Car. I. To my brother Thomas S. esq. a silver spoon. To my friend Mrs Elizabeth Grovenor, widow, with whom I now sojourn, £5. To her dau'r. Elizabeth G. £3. Rest of goods to my sister Deborah Fleete (and she to be) ex'trix. My friend Sir Robert Phillmer, knight, to be overseer. Witnes: Thomas Dutton, Scrivener.

Prob. 29 June 1650 by Deborah Fleete, the ex'trix.

Pembroke, 100.

[Debora Fleete and Dorothie Scott were daughters of Charles Scott, of Egerton, Kent, (and his wife Jane, daughter of Sir Thomas Wyatt, of Allington Castle) and granddaughters of Sir Reginald Scott, of Scotts Hall, Kent. Debora married William Fleet, gent., of Chartham, Kent, a member of the Virginia Company, and had (with several other sons and daughters, some of whom emigrated to Maryland) a son Henry, born 1595-1600, died about 1661, who emigrated to Virginia and became a very prominent man in that colony and in Maryland. For notices of him and his descendants, see this Magazine II, 70-76, and V, 253-254.

The people to whom the Fleets were related form another of those groups of Kentish kinsfolk so closely associated with the colony of Virginia. Charles Scott, of Egerton, had a sister, Mary, who married Richard Argall, of East Sutton, Kent, and was the mother of Captain (afterwards Sir) Samuel Argall, Governor of Virginia, and of Elizabeth Argall, who married Sir Edward Filmer, of East Sutton. Lady Filmer was, in turn, the mother of Henry Filmer, who emigrated to Virginia, and of Sir Robert and Sir Edward Filmer, named in Debora Fleet's will. Jane Wyatt, wife of Charles Scott, was aunt of Sir Francis Wyatt, Governor of Virginia, and of Rev. Hawte Wyatt, minister at Jamestown. George Wyatt, brother of Jane (Wyatt) Scott married Jane Finch, who was aunt of Henry Finch, who emigrated to Virginia, and was member of the Council, 1630 &c. The paternal grandmother of Henry Fleet, the emigrant, Katherine (Honeywood) Fleet, was aunt of Col. (afterwards Sir) Philip Honeywood, one of the Royalist officers, who took refuge in Virginia in 1649.]

SIR EUSEBY ISHAM. "A note of such debts as I require my wife to pay". To my brother Tipping £5. To my cosin William Downall 42s. To Robert Lade of Cransby £10. To my son John Isham my sorrel mare. To Mr. (sic) Barbon so much money as she will say I ought to pay her. To Saxby the man that dwelled in my grounds £10. 4s. od. To my son Euseby Isham "as you can" £66. 13s. 4d. To my sons William and Thomas I refer them to yourself. To the servants with you a year's wages. To Richard Berry 60s. To Steynes for a horse £4. 10s. od. To my man Barber if he go away 40s. To poor of Picheley £5. Small debts which I cannot call to mind I pray you see paid. Witnesses: Feargod Barbon, Ha. Kinnesman. Memorandum that I Harold Kymesman of Picheley gent wished by Sir Euseby Isham, knight, on 7th June last to write the particulars specified as he spoke it which I did in his presence. He desired that his wife should see legacies paid . . . his sickness being such and he so short taken he could not do more neither was he desirous to the articles on Feargod Barbon subscribed as a witness, And to this I will depose Sir Euseby said he could not live long and his wife should have all. Anne should have all. 27 July 1626 emat com' to Lady Ann Isham, relict of Sir Euseby Isham, Militis. 1st

January 1627 em't com' to Thomas Isham fil. nat. et ltmo. etc. *Hele,* 100.

DAME ANNE ISHAM, late wife of Sir Euseby Isham of Pitchley county Northampton, Knight. Will 3 December 1627; proved 1st January 1627. Body to chancel at Pitchley. To my son Euseby Isham £150. To my son William Isham £200. To Euseby Isham son of said William £100. To said son Euseby Isham my Cabbinett. To Susan his wife my gilt cups. My border of Goldsmiths work to Mary wife of my son William. To my daughter Mary wife of Sir Fleetwood Dormer knight, two geldings. To my daughter Susan wife of Thomas Threlfall pearl chain and 20 marks. £100 which I owe to Euseby Glover my grandchild to be paid to him. To Susan Isham my gentlewoman £10. To each of my servants 4 marks. To poor of Pitchley £5. Residue of my goods to my youngest son Thomas Isham sole executor. I not meddling with goods left by my late husband Sir Euseby Isham to my eldest son John Isham deceased. Witnesses: Ri: Houselepp, Saml Garthwaite. *Barrington,* 4.

JOHN ISHAM of Braunston, county Northampton, Esquier. Will 29 September 1624; proved 4 May 1627. Sir Eusebie Isham my father and Thomas Isham my brother executors. To Thomas Isham said brother lease of the parsonage in Braunston and tithes belonging. To Ann Lane my daughter £10. To Blaise Adams for his pains £10 and all my wearing apparel. To William Eare my servant £20. To Robert Tymes £10. To John Allen my servant £6. 13s. 4d. To poor of Braunston £10. To poor of Vichley [Pitchley?] £5. Residue of my goods to my executors. Witnesses: Wm. Southam, Thos. Makepease, Richd Cooke, John Clarke, Blaise Adams. Codicil 8 December 1626. As the said Sir Eusebie my late father is deceased I now appoint my said brother Thomas sole executor to whom all benefit of my goods. I have given into the hands of Thomas Makepeace, William Southam, Robert Foster and Henry Bree four ancient copyholders of my Manor of Braunston £20 to be lent from year to year to three of the poorest copyholders of my said Manor at 8% said profit and increase to be distributed amongst six poor widows of the town of Braunston. My executor shall provide one treble bell tunable to the four bells already in the Church. To my cosen Gregory Isham 4 milk beasts. To my brother in law Thomas Threlfall 30 hoggerells, my stone horse and 7 cows. To Hanna my maid a cow. To Robert Tymes my sorrell mare and apparel. To my servant John Allen my grey Nagg and apparel. To Isaac Moule 20s. To Zephania Southam 2 ewes and my horse Geers. To Martha Burrowes one ewe for watching with me. Witnesses: Gregory Isham, This Threlfall, John Allen, Robt Tymmes. *Skynner, 52.*

[The wills given above are those of Sir Euseby Isham, of Pytchley, (b. Feb. 26, 1552, d. June 11, 1626), grandfather of Henry Isham, the emigrant to Virginia; of Anne, daughter of John Borlase, of Marlowe, Co. Bucks., wife of Sir Euseby, and of their son John, an uncle of the emigrant. It will be noted that the famous Praisegod Barbon or Barebones, was a witness to Sir Euseby's will. For other Isham wills and notes on the family, see this Magazine IV, 123-124 and XVIII, 85-87.]

VIRGINIA GLEANINGS IN ENGLAND

Contributed by Reginald M. Glencross, 176 Worple Road,
Wimbledon, London, S. D. 19, England.

(Continued)

*JOHN HARMAR, (Pro. Act Book says: "D. D. of City of Win-
chester") Dated 8 Oct. 1613. Proved 25 Jan. 1613-14.
My body to rest in the chambers of the earth, to bee enterred
in the Queere of the College (if I dye there warden), against
the Common Table on the South syde.
To the Churche of Winchester, xxs. To the library of the
Deane and Chapter, the greatest testament in the Greek and
Syrian sett forth by Tremelius. To the poore of the towne
of Newberye, the place of my nativitie, x£. To the poore of
my parish of Drokensford, v£. To the poore of my parish
of Compton, iij£. vjs. viijd. To the poore of the citie of
Winchester v£. To the poore of the Soake and Kingsgate
street, v£. To the Almesmen of St. Crosse, xls. To the
Almesmen of Magdalens, xiijs. iiijd. To New College, St.
Mary College of Winchester in Oxford, my Greeke books, and
to my brother, warden there xxxi. Towards the erecting of
the new Schooles in Oxford, x£. (Numerous bequests of
books, authors etc. given to the library and fellows of Winchester College.) To my brother ARTHUR HARMAR, c.
£. and my seale ring, sometime my father's, also the leases of
two houses buylt by me neere the College, after his decease to
his eldest son, one of them and the other to his daughter
BRIDGETT HARMAR. To my neece GRAY, my brother's
daughter, the Mazer bound about with silver and gylt. To
my nephew GRAY, St. Augustines works, six volumes in folio.

---

* We are indebted to Mr. Leo Culleton for the Harmar, Yeo and Bacon
wills.

From Vol. XXIX, No. 1 (Jan. 1921), p. 36.

To JOHN HARMAR, my brother ARTHUR'S eldest sonne xl£., also the revercon of the copyhold of the Church in Wymiall. To ROBERT HARMAR, of New College, the revercon of my copyhold at Westwood in Somersetshire. To my sister JOANE BATH, a gilt standing cupp, and to her sonne JOHN, a small gilt cupp. To her daughter DORCAS, xls, for a ring and as much to my brother ROGER BATH. To my sister ANN GINNER, a standing gilt cupp, also the lease of the house in Milk streete, London, provided she pays £4 yearly to her daughter, ELIZABETH GINNER, my wyves god daughter. To ANN GINNER her daughter, my house in Colbrooke streete, whereof the moyetie hold in socage the other by a long lease from the town and citie of Winchester. To my sister GINNER'S other 5 children, 1£. To my sister TRUSSELL, vj£. To AMY TRUSSELL, iiij£. To JOHN TRUSSELL, my nephew, v£. To WILLIAM TRUSSELL, his brother, v£. To my brother, WILLIAM TRUSSELL, x£. To MARY TRUSSELL, his daughter, the revercon of my copyhold of the Church at Ovington. To my brother, HARE-COURT, v£. To ELIZABETH, his daughter, the revercon of one of my copyholds at Chilbolton, held now by MAR-GERY LEWYS, widow, which I have to dispose of by a grant from the Dean and Chapter of the Holy and Indivisible Trin-itie of Winchester. To her sister, URSULA, my neece, v£. To my sister, BENSTED, xls. and as much to my sister, HARMAR. To my sister, LEWYS, xls. To the most Rev. the now Lo: Archbp. of Cant. for a token of my last dutie, a portague. To the Rt. Rev. my friend, Doctor KINGE, now Bishop of London, xxxs. To Dr. MORTON, the Dean of Winchester, xxs. To NATHANIEL ANGUR, vj£. To HIEROME HILLING, x£. To THOMAS WIGHT, xxxs. To THOMAS TURY, xxxs. To ROBERT HARDY, xxxs. To WILLIAM HOLBROOKE, xxxs. To ANTHONY HARMAR, my nephew, x£. To Mr. THOMAS CHILD, late mayor of Winchester, xls. My leases of Allington Farm, passed in trust to HIEROME HILLING & THOMAS WIGHT, and that of my house at Eastgate, that of Valebarne in Fullflud and

Weeke and that of my house in the close, late buylded, to my wife, ELIZABETH HARMAR.

Residuary Legatee and Sole Executrix:—my wife ELIZABETH HARMAR.

"I entreat and as far as I may charge my brother ARTHUR HARMAR to take that order that his sonne NICHOLAS take no right in that my copyhold of Hursley, which I will hee dispose of to any other of his children which shall please him."

Overseers:—my friends Doctor MORETON, Deane of Winchester, and Dr. HENRY MARTYNY, his Mats now Advocate.

Debtes due unto me:

From my cosen RICHARD HARMAR x£.

From my cosen BATE..............xls.

THOMAS SINGLETON Viceca Oxon., ⎱ Witnesses.
ROGER JONES, Not. Pub. ⎰

Proved 25 Jan. 1613 by the Sole Executrix named.

P. C. C.   1 Lawe.

[John Harmar, or Harmer (1555?-1613), Greek Professor at Oxford, was born, probably of humble parentage, at Newberry in Berkshire. He matriculated at New College, Oxford as *"plebei filius"* in 1575, was B. A., and M. A. (in 1582.) He was reckoned a "subtile Aristotelian", was well read in patristic and scholastic theology, and was "a most noted Latinist and Grecian". In 1585 he was appointed Greek Professor at Oxford, was head-master of Winchester 1588-1595, and in 1569 became Warden of St. Mary's College. He was rector of Draxford, Hampshire, and a prebendary of Winchester. In 1604 he was appointed one of the translators of the New Testament and had "a prime hand" in that work. He died Oct. 11, 1613, and was buried in the chapel of New College. He was author of various works.

John Harmer (1594?-1670) Professor of Greek at Oxford, was nephew of the preceding. He was born at Churchdown, Gloucestershire, educated at Winchester, and was M. A., Magdalen College, Oxford, 1617. He was a good philologist, an excellent Grecian and a "tolerable Latin poet". In 1650 he was appointed Professor of Greek at Oxford and in 1659 presented to the rectory of Ewhurst, was deprived at the Restoration and died at Steventon, Berkshire, Nov. 1, 1670. He was the author of a number of books. (These notices are derived from the *Dictionary of National Biography*).

It is probable that John Harmer, the younger, was son of Arthur Harmer, named in the will above. On July 4, 1635, Charles Harmar, or Harmer, was granted 1050 acres on the Eastern Shore of Virginia, in right of himself, his wife Ann Harmer, and nineteen servants—including eight negroes. Charles Harmer had come to Virginia in 1622 when he was twenty-four and became a prominent planter at Magothy Bay on the Eastern Shore. He died in or before 1644, leaving an only child Elizabeth, who died in childhood, and a widow Ann, daughter of Henry Southey, who married secondly Nathaniel Littleton, also of the Eastern Shore. There is recorded in Northampton County, Va., a power of attorney, dated March 1, 1652, and recorded Jan. 12, 1654, from '"Doctor John Harmer ye Greeke reader to ye Universitie of Oxford, heir of Charles Harmer, late of Accomacke in ye Dominion of Virginia, to his (John Harmar's) son Thomas Harmar now or late of Jamestown in ye Dominion aforesaid", authorizing him to demand possession of his (John Harmar's) brother's property, saving to his widow and her husband, Captain Littleton, Governor of Accomacke aforesaid, her dower and third.]

GEORGE YEO, of Fyeshleighe, in co. Devon, Esqr. Dated 26 June 1605. Proved 16 June 1607.

To the poor of the parish of Hatherleighe, 30s. To my second sonne, JOHN YEO, £200. To JHEROME YEO, my third sonne, £200. To my "fyfte" sonne, GEORG YEO, £100. To my fowerth sonne, NICHOLAS YEO, £100. My desire is that my Executor will keepe and maintain my daughter ARMILNELL YEO, during her life, if he refuse, then my will is, that such other of my children as will take her shall have £50. To GEORG NEELE, the sonne of my daughter MARGARET, £3. 6. 8. To MARIE NEELE, the sister of the said GEORGE NEELE, £10. To ELIZABETH YEO, the daughter of LEONARD, my sonne, £10. To MARIE COTTLE, my daughter, my gilte salte, which was given to my wife, by her grandmother, Mrs. KATHERINE MOUNCKE at the birth of the said MARIE. To MARGARETT ROBINS, my daughter, my black standing nutt cupp. To LEONARD YEO, my sonne, my great silver salt seller and cover, during his life, and after his decease, to my grandchild "and nephew", GEORGE YEO, his sonne. To my servant, ANN HOOPER, 40s. To JOAN GORFORD, 40s. To GILBERT MOORE, my servant, 20s. To ANTHONY NENOW, my servant 10s. To my sister, MILLICENT WALLER, a mourninge gowne.

Residuary Legatee and Sole Executor: my sonne, LEONARD YEO.

Overseers:—my brother GYFFORD and my sonne in law,
MARK COTTLE.

WILLIAM HELE ⎱
ROGER SELLY Clirico. ⎰ Witnesses.
LEONARD NORTHLEIGH ⎰

Proved 16 June 1607 by the Sole Exor named.

60 Huddlestone.

[George Yeo, the testator ,may be found in Col. Vivian's Visitation
Pedigrees of Devonshire, p. 835.

Leonard Yeo had, on Aug. 9, 1637, a grant of 850 acres in Elizabeth
City County, Va. In 1652, he and his wife Claire Yeo, appear in a
grant. He was long a man of prominence there, and was a member
of the House of Burgesses at the sessions of Feb. 1644-5, Sept. 1663
and June and October 1666. In 1666 he was commander in chief of
Elizabeth City, and the next year held the same command while a
hostile Dutch fleet was in Hampton Roads. He died in or before June
1670, as by that time his widow, Rebecca, (a second wife) had married
Charles Moryson. She again married Col. John Lear, of the Virginia
Council. In 1690, Leonard Yeo, of Back River, Elizabeth City County,
died and left all his estate to his wife Mary. The will of George Yeo
(probably a descendant of Col. Leonard Yeo) was proved in Elizabeth
City County in 1743. In addition to other bequests he gave his cousin,
George Arnold, merchant, of London, certain tenements in the borough
of Hatherley, Devon, commonly called Wadlands and Finch Park.

It seems possible that Leonard Yeo of Virginia, was a grandson of
the testator.

On Oct. 11, 1656, Leonard Yeo, of Elizabeth City Co., brother and
administrator of Robert Yeo, assigned 650 acres in Westmoreland Co.,
whic had been granted to said Robert Yeo, on Sept. 6, 1654. George
Yeo (above) and Elenor his wife, lived in Elizabeth City, 1727.

Hugh and Justinian Yeo, brothers, from Hartland, Devon, lived on the
Eastern Shore of Virginia in the latter part of the Seventeenth century.
The Visitation pedigree is not accessible here.]

———————

SIR JAMES BACON, of Finsburie neere London, in co. Middx.
Knight. Dated 6 Feb. 1618-19. Proved 23 Feb. 1618-19.

To JAMES BACON, my younger sonne, my manor house and
manor of Verlies, with all their appurtenances, and my lands,
tenements and hereditaments whatsoever lying in Starnefeild
Benhall Saxmondham and Kershall.

To my sonne NATHANIEL, the lease of the "manor of
howse Earle in Alderton", also one other lease of the manor
of Reymes in Alderton. Whereas my sonne JAMES hath an
estate for terme of yeares yet to come in the manors of Snape

Tastardes and Scotts with the late dissolved Monasterie of Snape and the demeasne lands thereunto belonging by vertue of a lease or grant made by the Rt. Hon. the Earl of Arundell and JOHN HOLLAND Esqr., deceased, bearing date 26 Nov. 1611. Now my will is that my son NATHANIEL suffer my sonne JAMES to enjoy the same peaceably.

All my controversies concerning my manors, lands etc. shall be compromitted and decided to and by Sir THOMAS BELLOYE, of Fleete streete nere London, Knt. and WILLIAM WALL, of Hoxton, in co. Middx. and EDWARD COTTON of Finsburye Esqrs.

Sole Executor: my sonne JAMES BACON.

EDMOND COTTON
STEPHEN ALCOCKE } Witnesses.
BENJAMIN BEARD

Proved 23 Feb. 1618/19 by the Sole Executors named.

15 *Parker.*

[James Bacon, Alderman of London, who died June 15, 1573, was a brother of Sir Nicholas Bacon, Lord Keeper and uncle of Francis Bacon, Lord Verulam, and had a son, Sir James Bacon, described in a pedigree as "Friston Hall, Suffolk", the testator above. This James Bacon was knighted at White Hall, in 1604 and died at Finsbury, Jan. 17, 1618. He married Elizabeth, daughter of Francis Bacon of Hesset, and had two sons: (1) Nathaniel, (1593-1644) of Friston Hall, grandfather of Nathaniel Bacon, the "Rebel", of Virginia; (2) James Bacon, rector of Burgate, Suffolk, who died 1670. He was the father of President Nathaniel Bacon of Virginia, and of Martha, who married Anthony Smith, of Colchester, tanner, and had a daughter Abigail Smith, brought to Virginia by her uncle President Bacon, who married Lewis Burwell, of "Carter's Creek", Gloucester County and has very many descendants. See this Magazine II, 125-129, and references there given.]

NATHANIELL ATHEROLD of Hasketon, co. Suffolk, Gent. Will date 12 Sep 1653. To my wife Martha, water mill in H. afs'd. & Tunmans meadow or Mill meadow adjoining, Thorphall meadow & Basseacre, also in H., for her life, also all freehold & copyhold lands in Bealings & Grundisbyrgh Suffolk which I purch'd of John Hayte, for life. To my dau'r. Mary, tenm't. in Grundisburgh wh'rin Nich's Curdye dwells & sd. N's occupation called Hyefeild, Thurstonfeild, Waylons

Plaggs & Poreltons (24 acres), two pieces of land held of
manor of Kingston in Burches feild in Halston, all in fee.
To my daur's. Anne & Susan tenm'ts, wherein Geo. Simpson
lately dwelt, with hopyard adjoining (14 acres), in fee equally.
To my dau'r. Rebecca tenm't. wherein Joseph Hall lately dwelt
in Grundisburgh & other tenm'ts adjoining, two pieces of
arrable land in Grundisburge feild (2½ acres), in fee. To
my dau'r. Sarah, two pieces of land in Grundisburgh called
(?S) wiland wood (12 acres), one tenm't. wherein Richard
Checkerell dwells, in fee. To my daur's Mary, Anne, Susan,
Rebecca & Sarah mill & lands formerly given to my wife for
life, in fee equally from sd. wifes death. To sd. daur's. my
messuage & tenm't. wherein I now dwell called Thorpehall &
all other lands in fee equally. If any overplus of personal estate to dau. Rebecca £50 to daur's Anne & Susan £50 between
them. Rest between my wife & five daur's. To poor of Hasketon & Grundisburgh 20/ a piece. To dau'r. Martha, wife
of George Goodwyn, gent. £5. To my dau'r. Elizabeth wife of
John Garners, gent. £5. My wife Martha & dau'r. Mary to
be ex'trixes. *Witnesses* Thomas Atherold, John Garners
Prob. 18 Sep. 1654 by Martha A. the relict & Mary the dau'r.
ex'tri'es. *Alchin,* 500.

[Col. William Ball (1615?-1680) emigrant ancestor of the Virginia
family of the name, is stated in an old record, to have married, on
July 2, 1638, Hannah Atherold.
Nathaniel Atherold, of Burgh, Suffolk, living 1660, may probably have
been the testator, in spite of the differences in statement. This Nathaniel Atherold of Burgh, was a son of Thomas Atherold, Barrister at Law,
who in turn was a son of Thomas Atherold, who was baptized at
Burgh, Aug. 16, 1590, died May 6, 1658, and was buried there, will
dated May 10, 1656. It is possible that Mrs. Ball was a daughter of
the last named. See Hayden's *Virginia Genealogies,* 51. 52.]

THOMAS BAYTUP of Parish of Tenterden, Kent. clothier.
Will dat. 14 May 1651. House & lands in p'rsh of Smarden,
Kent to my wife Mary for life & then between my two sons
Daniel & Thomas. To Thomas the house & some fields (spe-
cified) & to Daniel rest of fields—to both in fee. To wife
Mary £40. To eldest son Daniel £130 at 21. To son Thomas

B. £130 at 21. To son James B. £230 at 21. To my dau'r.
Mary B. £160 at 18 or marriage. To my dau'r. Susan B.
£150 at 18 or marriage. My wife Mary to be ex'trise. James
Baytup & William Boyse my brothers to be overseers & to each
40s., & if my wife marry again they to take children's portions.
Sons to be apprenticed when of suitable age. If all my children die, to my brother James B. & his children £160, to my
bro. Daniel B. £100 & to my sister Susan and her children
£100. Witnesses: James Fithenden X, John Grigsbee X,
Thomas Ramsden.
Prob. 19 Jan 1651[-2] by Mary B. relict & ex'trix.

Bowyer, 2.

[Thomas Baytup, or Baytop, came to Virginia in 1679 and settled in
Gloucester County, where he died in 1691, his brother Daniel Baytop,
of Maidstone, Kent, becoming his administrator. In the records of
York County, 1691, is the following, "Daniel Baytopp, of Maidstone, in
ye County of Kent, grocer, brother of Thomas Baytop, and guardian
and administrator of Thomas Baytop, the minor, constitutes Capt.
Francis Page in Virginia his attorney to take possession of ye plantations, stock, &c., of ye sid Baytopp in ye parts of America in right of
ye minor, Jan. 20, 1691. The said Thomas Baytop, merchant, deceased,
came over to Virginia twelve years before the above date, and came
from Staplehurst, where he lived for several years in the lawful estate
of matrimony with Hannah, his wife, and where was born his son,
Thomas Baytopp, May 9, 1676, as appears by the register of Staplehurst and the testimony of his godfather, Peter Burren, of the same
place, clockmaker, aged 58 years, and John Stanter, clerk and register
of the aforesaid parish of Staplehurst, aged 69 years". Thos. Baytop
who came to Virginia in 1679, was the son named in the will. For an
account of the family in Virginia see "A History of Two Virginia
Families Translated from County Kent, England", by Dr. and Mrs.
W. C. Stubbs.]

WILLIAM CODD, the elder, of Wateringburie, Kent, gent.
eldest son of James C. of W. afs'd., gent., dec.
Will dat. 11 Apr. 1652. I confirm writing of jointure made
by my late aunt Katherine Pery to use of Debora my wife &,
in addition, to sd. wife, my capital messuage wh'rin I now
dwell in W. afs'd. which was heretofore my sd. father's, during
widowhood, also all lands in West Farleigh, East Farleigh &
Maidstone, Kent, for life. To my son James C. in fee, manors
etc. in Kent. If sd. wife be with child at my death, to such
issue, in tail, my manor of Hall *als.* Wingmore in Sheham &

Barham, Kent. If sd. son James C. die under 21, s. p. all messuages etc to such issue of my wife, in tail, in default, to my neice Elizabeth Wood, dau'r. of my sister Anne late wife of Robert W., citizen & haberdasher of London, both dec., & her issue male, in tail, in default, to my godson St. Leger Codd, eldest son of my kinsman William C., of Pellicans in Wateringburie afs'd. eq., in tail male, in default to my right heirs. If either sd. E. Wood or St. L. Codd succeed they to pay my wife Debora £40 a year for life & to my sister Jane Codd *als* (Ower?) £40 a year while she remains sole & unmarried. Succeeders to manors to pay to Johane (the new wife of Mark Howland & formerly the wife of John Henman dec.) £4. 16s. half yearly as I have paid in discharge of my verbal engagement on my purchase of those lands from sd. John Herman & Johane. I forgive sd. neice E. Wood money due from her about estate of her father, she to release my estate from claims. To her £200 & all shopbooks etc which were her father's, now in my hands. To sd. wife & son James C. rest of goods equally. To be buried in the Common place of the church of Watringburie near my first son, if I die at W. If priest (*sic*) do bury me according as was proscribed in book of Common Prayer, to him 10s. Sd. son James C. to be ex'or. during his minority, Adm. c. t. a. to sd. wife. To sd. kinsman William Codd 40s. To sd. godson St. Leger Codd £10 at 21. To my godson William Crofts son of my old servant Robert Crofts at 21. Witnesses: John Leversedge, Robert Crofts, William Mitchell X.

Adm. c. t. a. 25 July 1652 to Deborah C. relict, during minority of James C. son & executor.

Bowyer, 203.

[The testator was eldest son of James Codd, of Wateringbury, gent. (d. 1611) whose will was printed in this Magazine XXV, 53. William Codd, Esq., of Pelicans, Kent., father of St. Leger Codd, of Virginia and Maryland, was the "kinsman" named in the will above. His will was published in this Magazine XXIII, 382. William Codd, of Pelicans, married in 1632, Mary daughter of Sir Warham St. Leger, of Ulcombe.]

VIRGINIA GLEANINGS IN ENGLAND

Contributed by Reginald M. Glencross, 176 Worple Road, Wimbleton, London, S. W. 20, England

(Continued)

DOROTHE COKE of Trowell, co. Nottinghamshire. Will dat 20 May 1651. To be buried at Kirkeby, co. Nottin. near my late husband William C. of Trulsley, co. Derby, Esq. To my sister Gilbert, ring & £5. To my nephew Henry Gilbert £20. To my nephews Philip Gilbert & John Gilbert £10 each. To my nephew Thomas Gilbert £5. To my nephew Henry Gilbert's eldest son Henry 5 marks & to his four younger sons, Thos., William, John & Charles G. 40s. a piece. To my sister Butler £40. To her son my nephew Sir Francis B. £20. To her daur's., my neice Susanna Aykeroyd £5. To my bro. Thos. Paramore £10. To my sister his wife 40s. To my sister Saunders of Siresham £10. To my neice Jane Ensor £10 etc. To my neice Mary Cartewright £10. To my neice Dorothy Saunders another of my sd. sister Saunders' dau'rs border of pearl & gold. To my nephew Francis Saunders son of my sd. sister 5 marks. To my nephew Francis Saunders & late of Shanketon £10. To my neice Jane Holford his sister £10. To my neice Elizabeth Saunders their sister, featherbed etc. at Trowell & 40s. To my sons & daurs in law Richard Coke, Elizabeth his wife, Timothy Coke, Elizabeth Sherman, Mary Fitzherbert & Alice Harper £5 a piece. To my bro. Gilbert Coke & his son Charles C. & his dau'r. Frances Coke 5 marks a piece. To my bro. Francis Coke & his wife £5 each. To my sister Elizabeth Willoughby 40s. To her son my godson Percivall W. 40s. To my son in law Thos. Thorneton's two sons by his first wife £5 each. To his two sisters my dau'rs. in

---

From Vol. XXIX, No. 3 (July 1921), p. 344.

law Margaret & Mary their children £40 between them. To my neice Ann Haeker, her husband & their son John £10 a piece of £5 which my cousin her sd. husband owes me. To Master Denham, minister of Trowell, if I die there, 20s. To minister of Kirkeby afr'd. 40s, if he preach at my funeral & afford me Christian burial after the ancient rites of the Church of England, otherwise 40s. to Master Scargill, minister of West Hallam. To my cousin Mary Barford & to Bell Cocker £5 each, if resident with me. To Mris. Morrice late of Trowell, 5 marks. To my neice, Hacker's maid servants & men servants in her service at Trowell if I die there 10s. each. To poor of Trowell 40s. To my nephew Henry Gilbert my coach. To my sister Butler, gown etc. To her dau'r. my neice Susanna Aikeroyd coat etc. To my neice Anne Hacker, gown, etc. To her, pewter for life & then to her son John H. To my cousin Jane Cooper, coat etc. To little John Hacker son of my sd. neice H. bed etc. To my nephews Philip, Thomas & John Gilbert, sheets etc. To my nephew Thos. Gilbert, table cloth etc. To my nephew Philip Gilbert, table cloth etc. To my nephew John Gilbert, table cloths etc. To my neice Anne Hacker, table cloth etc. for her life & then for her son John H. To my nephew Henry Gilbert, cushions. My two nephews Henry Gilbert & Tho. Gilbert to be exo'rs. Witnesses: William Hacker, Anne Hacker.

Prob. 1 May 1654 by Henry Gilbert, one of the exor's. Power reserved for Thomas Gilbert, the other exor. *Alchin,* 477.

[Dorothy Coke, was the second wife of William Coke (died 1641), of Trusley, Derbyshire, Esqr., and daughter of Francis Saunders, of Shankton, Northamptonshire, Esq. She died, s. p. Nov. 12, 1653. Her husband was the eldest son of Sir Francis Coke, of Trusley, and nephew of Sir John Coke, Secretary of State to Charles I. By his first marriage with Maud, daughter of Henry Beresford of Alsop-in-the-Dale, William Coke, was father of Richard Coke, of Trusley, whose grandson, John Coke (born Aug. 3rd, 1708), emigrated to Virginia, and was ancestor of the family here. See Coke's *Coke of Trusley* (London, 1880).]

JOHN ELLZEY of town & county of Southampton, merchant. Will dat. 23 Sep 1633. To be buried in chancel of church of

Holy Cross. Personal estate amounts to £1,642, 11s. My grandchild John E. now the younger, to be my ex'or. If he die during his minority then his father Arnold E. & Arnold E. his son to be ex'ors. To my wife Joan £66-13-4 & maintenance for life & about £280 worth of household stuff. To my son Thomas E., who allthough he hath been disobedient & many other distates in marrying without my consent & since framing of this will by a peremptory letter of threatening especially of a certain house which I sold & justly paid for the same paeing it in a legal manner by fine & recovery before Sir Thomas Hemying, knight & Richard Pigeon, gent. nominated for that purpose, yet I give him £40 & a licence for keeping a Tavern in town of Southampton. To my undutiful & ungracious son Henry £10. To my son Arnold E. £100 & to his son the child Arnold £50 if neither are ex'ors. To Elizabeth Bennett daur. of my daur. Elizabeth B. a ring. To my son Thomas E. a ring. To my wife a pair of bracelets. To poor of Hollirood p'ish. 40s. To p'ish of St. Laurence where I was born 20s. to the four ministers within this town 20s. a piece. To preacher of my funeral sermon 20s. If I die in this my languishing disease, merchandise now in warehouse & cellars to be sold. My poor family viz. my wife, if she live unmarried, my son Arnold, his wife & two children with a servant or two to keep together. Mr. George Gallop & Mr. Edward Exton to be ex'ors in trust & to each 20s. for a ring. Witnesses: Ja. Courtney, Peregr. King.

Adm. c. t. a. 12 Nov. 1633 to Arnold E. son during min. of John E. (his son *erased*) ex'or of Will. Geo. Gallop & Edw. Exton ex'ors in trust, having renounced. *Russell, 97.*

[About the middle of the Seventeenth century Ralph Barlow, probably from Hampshire, Eng., lived in Northampton Co., Va. In Oct. 163, Mr. George Parker (son of Robert Parker, a native of Hampshire) sued Mr. John Elsey, executor of Ralph Barlow, and on June 28, 1658, Jane Elzey, "of Old England", petitioned Northampton Court that Mr. John Elzey, executor of Mr. Ralph Barlowe, should pay her 300 lbs. tobacco left her by Barlowe. In Dec., 1660, Northampton Court certified certain "head rights", for Robert Windley, among them John Elzey. Later John Elzey removed to Calvert County, Md., where his will, dated March 3, 1699, was proved June 5, 1700. He left his whole estate to his wife Anne. He doubtless left sons who carried on the family. An Arnold Elzey lived in Maryland, 1717, &c. Major General

Arnold Elzey, C. S. A., (who changed his name from Arnold Elzey Jones) was born in Somerset Co., Md., 1816, an ddied in 1871. He served with great distinction in the Mexican War and the War between the States, and was severely wounded at Port Republic and Cold Harbor.]

SIR ROBERT FILMER of East Sutton, co. Kent, Knight. Will dat. 16 Nov. 1651. To my wife Dame Anne F. for life my manor of Wiltralinge (?Wikalinge) & lands called Langhams in E. S. afs'd. & all lands there purchased of Robert Bills & George Bills & lands in Newchurch in Romney Marsh. To her, in fee, my house of the Porters Lodge in Westminster. To my dau'r. Anne F. £2,500 at 18 or marriage with consent of her mother, to be raised by sale of my manors of Hoateley in Lamberhurst & Herst in Ottrindon & of lands in Chart next Sutton, Hetcorne, Ulcombe, Sutton Vallents, all in Kent & Sussex, unless my son Sir Thomas F. by other ways pay sd. portion. To my two sons Robert F. & Samuel F. £40 Annuitees for life each out of lands in Chart next Sutton, Hetcorne, Ulcombe, Sutton Vallents & Whandon afs'd., from death of my wife to each £10 more a year. To sd two sons £250 each. To my son Sir Edward F. Knight, in fee, all my lands in cos. Kent & Sussex. Sd. wife Dame Anne & sd. son Sir Edward F. to be ex'ors. Sd. son to pay £80 a year to my dau'r Anne until her portion be paid. To poor of E. S. £3. Witnesses: Thomas Culliver, Mathew Hernon, X, Thomas Davy, Thomas May, Nicholas Raith X.

Prob. 13 Jan. 1653[-4] by Anne F. the relict & Sir Edward F. the son, the ex'ors. *Alchin,* 409.

[The testator was the eldest son of Sir Edward Filmer, of East Sutton, and Elizabeth Argall his wife. Sir Robert, whose will is given here, was brother of Henry Filmer of Virginia, and father of Samuel Filmer, the first husband of Mary Horsmanden, who married William Byrd. Sir Robert married Anne, daughter of Martin Heton, Bishop of Ely. For Filmer wills and notes see this Magazine XV, 181, 182; XXI, 153, 154; XXIV, 158-160; XXV, 327, 328; XXVII, 288; XXVIII, 242, 243. The testator was the once famous Tory author.]

ROGER FOWKE of Gunston, co. Stafford & p'ish of Brewood, esq. Will dat. 23 June 1649. Whereas my father John F.

in his lifetime let to me, his son & heir apparent, his lands called Hattons co. Staff. p'ish of Brewood afs'd. with hall called Gunstone House, for seven years from death of Dorothy then wife of sd. J. F. I give same to my son Gerrard F. for residue of sd. seven years. He to be ex'or. & to him all my lands in Gunstone, Brewood, Codsall, Chillington, Hattons & Bintbrooke for use of himself, his mother my wife & Robert & Thomas & Judith, Mary & Susanna, his brothers & sisters, tii end of sd. seven years, remainder to Mary, my now wife as jointure & dower & to sd. son Gerrard F. & R. T. J. M. & S. my children for their portions at discretion of sd. Mary & sd. G. & R. my sons, all in fee. Witnesses: John Hope, Jane Hope, Judith Fowke, Robert Fowke, John Marten X.

Prob. 30 Nov. 1649 by Gerrard F., son & ex'or. *Fairfax,* 162.

[Roger Fowke, of Gunston Hall, Staffordshire, the testator, was son of John Fowke, of Gunston, and Dorothy Cupper or Cowper, his wife. Roger Fowke married Mary Bailey, of Lee Hall, Staffordshire. A family chart, preserved by his descendants in Virginia, gives this Roger Fowke a considerable number of children. Whether it is entirely correct is not known. His issue was: 1, John; 2, Roger; 3, Francisco; 4, Anthony; 5, William (the last four all Turkey merchants, who d. s. p.) ; 6, Gerrard, who emigrated to Virginia; 7, Thomas, emigrated to Virginia, was a member of the House of Burgesses for James City at the session of March, 1658-9, and for Westmoreland, March 1659-60. He patented 3500 acres in Westmoreland in 1654. The will of Thomas Fowke, gent., was dated May 11, 1660, and proved in Westmoreland June 24, 1663. His legatees were his wife Susanna and brother Gerrard Fowke; 8, Dorothy, married ——— Brown, merchant, of London; 9, Jane, married Richard Hope, of Neithills, Warwickshire (it will be noted that John and Jane Hope were witnesses to Roger Fowke's will) ; 10, Margery, d. s. p.; 11, Mary, d. s. p.; 12, Susanna, married ——— Smith, of Chillington, Staffordshire; 13, Judith.

Col. Gerrard Fowke, son of Roger Fowke, the testator, emigrated to Virginia. On Dec. 21, 1657, he bought 100 acres on Potomac Creek. In 1661, with three other men, he patented 2000 acres in Westmoreland, and in 1662, alone, patented 2650 acres in the same county. Gerrard Fowke was a Burgess for Westmoreland Sept., 1663, and soon afterwards removed to Maryland, probably on account of his marriage. He was elected a Burgess in Maryland in 1667 and died before Oct. 30, 1669, when his widow, Ann, became administratrix of his estate. He married Ann, daughter of Adam Thoroughgood of Virginia, and widow of Job Chandler, Councillor and Receiver General of Maryland. On March 11, 1672, Mrs. Ann Fowke made a deed of gift to her children, Richard Chandler, and Gerrard, Mary and Elizabeth Fowke. On Sept. 7, 1664, Gerrard Fowke had conveyed to his "beloved kinsman", Richard Hope, 400 acres in Virginia. On Sept. 18, 1672, Richard Hope, gent., of Neithills, Warwickshire, conveyed to Mrs. Ann Fowke, his land called Machapungo in Virginia.

Gerrard and Ann Fowke had issue: (according to the pedigree in Hayden); 1, Adam, died in infancy; 2, Gerrard, born 1662, died 1734, married Sarah Burdett; 3, Anne, married Major William Dent, of Charles County, Md.; 4, Mary, married George Mason. Miss Rowland in her *Life of George Mason,* states, probably correctly, that Mary Fowke, who married George Mason, was daughter of the second Gerrard Fowke.

The Fowkes trace to William Fowke, of Brewood, Staffordshire, *temp.* Edward IV, Gunston is a hamlet in the parish of Brewood. In 1865 there were two farm houses, the older of which was the former Gunston Hall. Brewood Hall, also an old Fowke house, is still standing. In the church are a number of monuments including some to the Fowkes. See Hayden's *Virginia Genealogies,* 154-161, 743-745; *Virginia Magazine of History and Biography,* III, 321-324.]

PETER JENINGS of Silsden Yorkshire, gent. Will dat. 15 July, 1651. If I die at Silsden, to be buried in Kildwick church near my son Edmond, if in York, in St. Crux church near my son Peter, if at Ripon, then in Rippon Minster, near my son Jonathan. All messuages & lands in 'pish of Ripon, Yorks., which I purchased of Geo. Dawson esq. & all other lands in townships of Gilsden & Waddington, Yorks. to my grandchild, Edmond Jennings in tail as by deed of feofment made by me to him dat. 5 July inst. Also my lease of title barn & to the corn of Silsden held of Christ Church Coll., Oxford & other leases in S. afs'd. Whereas I have by indenture of lease dat. 1 Feb. 15 Car. I 1639 leased to my grandchild Jonathan Jennings lands which I heretofore purchased of Wm. Stephenson, Lewis Sheffeild, Robt. Franke, Wm. Mitchell, Robt. Denbye, Wm. Smith, Laurence & Thos. Briggs, John Laycock, Walter Butterfeild & others for 1,000 years term; Edmond Jennings his brother to seal him a release of same. To sd. grandson J. debts due from John Stephenson & John Illingworth, also from Sir Bryan Palmes the bond for payment thereof being taken in name of my dau'r. Eliz. J., she to assign same to her son the sd. Jonathan, also debts from William Markinfeild the elder & the younger & Marmaduke Markinfeild, from Christopher Musgrave & Lyon Bampford, the bond for payment being in name of Peter Barrett of Silsden, debts due from Thos. & Fras. Warde of Plumtreebankes, Henry Goodgyon, Rob. Goodgyon, John Preston & Thos. Johnson, whereof bond is taken in name of Eliz. Jenings (now wife of Mr. Christopher Hodgson) sister of the sd. Jonathan, debts from Sir Ralph Blakeston, Sir Rob. & Sir Thos. Strickland. To sd. Jonathan, mare bought of Edmond Gell, also judgments etc. assigned him by Richard Nelson of Marton, gent., due by Wm. Sampson & Thos. Staveley & Arthur Grayson. Whereas my dau'r. Elizabeth J., late wife of my dec. son Jonathan, is seised of lands in Waddington, her son Edmond during her widowhood to pay her £60 a year out of lands at Gilsden as her jointure. She admi'x of her late husband. To poor of Kildwick £50. at discretion of my grandchild Edmund Jennings, Henry Currer of Kildwick, Roger Coates of Kildwick Grange, Wm. Watson the elder of Silsden Moor & my cousin Edmond Jenings of Silsden. To poor of Ripon £10. To Jonathan Mitchell £10 he to help my (grand) sons in management of estate. To Eliz. Frith £5. To Margaret Caterall £5, at 18. To Grace Claxton £5. Rest of personal estate to sd. grandson Edmond Jenings, & he to be ex'or. "I Elizabeth Jenings natural mother of sd. Edmond & Jonathan promise to perform this will" *Signs. Testator signs.* Witnesses: Jonath. Mitchell, Matth. Greene, Geo. Nayler. Prob. 13 Oct. 1651, by Edmond Jenings the ex'or. *Grey,* 188.

[Peter Jenings, of Silsden, the testator, died Sept. 1, 1651. His sons were Peter Jenings, A. M., died 1623, Edmund Jenings, A. M., died 1624, both unmarried; and Sir Jonathan, barrister-at-law, who died 1649. The latter's son, Sir Edmund Jenings, M. P. for Ripon, died in 1687, leaving (with others) two sons, Sir Jonathan, M. P. for Ripon, and Edmund, of "Ripon Hall", York County, Va., Governor of that Colony. See *Virginia Magazine of History and Biography,* XIII, 308, &c.]

JANE LUDLOW of Baycliffe co. Wilts., widow. Will dat. 10 Dec. 1646. To church of Mayden Bradley 10s. To poor of same p'ish 20s. To poor of Warminster 20s. To my son Roger L. one of my wedding rings. To my son George L. my other wedding ring. To Thomas Ludlow one of the sons of my son Gabriell L. £5. To Francis L. another of the sons of my son G., my nag colt etc. To John Ludlow another of the sons of my son G. £10. To Ann, Elizabeth & Sara the

dau's. of my son Gabriel £10 each. To my kinsman Capt.
Robert Langridge 20s. for ring. Rest of goods to my dau'r.
in law Phillis Ludlow & she to be extrix. To sd. Francis
Ludlow £10. Witnesses: Edw. Rickards, George Mech
(? Melt).

Prob. 6 July 1650 by Phillis Ludlow, the extrix. *Pembroke,*
115.

[The Ludlows were an ancient and distinguished Wiltshire family.
Some years ago a carefully prepared pedigree was published in the
New England Historical and Genealogical Register. A portion of it,
with additions from other sources, is given here.

Thomas Ludlow, of Dinton and Baycliffe (son of George Ludlow,
sheriff of Wiltshire, 1567, will proved 1580, and his wife Edith, 3d
daughter of Lord Windsor) was buried at Dinton, Nov. 25, 1607.
His will was proved June, 1608. He married Jane (the testator)
daughter of Thomas, and sister of Sir Gabriel Pyle of Bapton. They
had issue:

  I. George, baptized at Dinton, Sept. 7, 1583, died young.
  II. Gabriel, baptized at Dinton, Feb. 10, 1587, called to the bar
     Oct. 15, 1620, barrister, Nov. 3, 1657, married Phillis ———.
     Issue:

      (1) Gabriel, baptized at Warminster, Aug. 13, 1622, ad-
          mitted to the Middle Temple June 13, 1638, killed at
          the battle of Newberry, 1644.
      (2) Thomas, baptized at Warminster Nov. 1, 1624, emi-
          grated to Virginia and settled in York County, where
          he became Lieutenant Colonel of militia. He inher-
          ited the estate of his uncle George Ludlow. Thomas
          Ludlow died in 1660 and his brother John Ludlow,
          then in Virginia, qualified as his administrator in
          York Court Dec. 20, 1660. His inventory was re-
          corded the same day. His personality was appraised
          at 113686 lbs. tobacco and there was also £449.6.5 in
          money. Among the items were "a picture of Judge
          Richardson to ye waste", books valued at 250 lbs.
          tobacco, a rapier and a hanger and a black belt, a
          new silver hat-band, one wedding ring, one seal ring,
          one small silver tankard, 4 pr. gloves, 12 white ser-
          vants, 10 negroes, 43 cattle, 54 sheep, 4 horses, &c.
          Mary, widow of Lt. Col. Thomas Ludlow married
          Rev. Peter Temple, of York parish, and later re-
          moved to England. Her son George and daughter
          Mary Ludlow, died unmarried, and her daughter,
          Elizabeth Ludlow, married Rev. John Willes. There
          is on record in York County, a deed, dated Nov. 6,
          1686, from John Willes, of Culford, Suffolk, clerk,
          and Elizabeth his wife, and Peter Temple, of Sible
          Heningham, Essex, clerk, and Mary his wife, con-
          veying to Lawrence Smith of York County, Va., the
          land in York County which Thomas Ludlow had in-
          herited from his uncle, George Ludlow.

(3) Francis, baptized at Warminster Sept. 10, 1626, living at Maiden Bradley 1666, married and had issue. In Lancaster County, Va. Court Minutes ("Order Book") May 11, 1670, is the following entry: "Probate of the will of Mr. Francis Ludlow, deceased, and administration thereon granted to Capt. John Carter and an inventory, together with the accounts under the hands of the said Ludlow and Capt. John Carter, deceased, between them two", and also an order that the accounts between Col. John Carter, deceased, and Mr. John Ludlow, deceased, brother to the said Francis Ludlow, deceased, be recorded. Unfortunately the record book containing the will and the account is missing.

(4) Ann, baptized at Warminster, Dec. 4, 1628.

(5) Elizabeth, baptized at Maiden Bradley, Oct. 18, 1632.

(6) John, in Virginia 1660. In P. C. C. Admon. book is administration on the goods, &c., of John Ludlow, late of Virginia, bachelor, deceased, granted to his brother Francis Ludlow, Sept. 15, 1664.

(7) Sarah, married Col. John Carter, of "Corotoman", Lancaster County, Va. On his tomb at Christ Church, Lancaster, it is stated that one of his wives was "Sarah ye daughter of Mr. Gabriel Ludlow".

III. Roger, baptized at Dinton, March 7, 1590, matriculated at Baliol College Jan. 10, 1610. He was appointed an assistant by the General Court of Mass. in 1630, removed to Boston and held that office for four years. He became Deputy Governor in 1634, but removed to Windsor, Conn., where for many years he held public office. He was long prominent as a lawyer. In 1654 he is stated to have left Connecticut and gone to Virginia, but there appears to be no record of him here and the will of his brother George shows that he was living in Ireland in 1656. He had at least three sons and three daughters.

IV. Anne, baptized at Dinton July 5, 1591, buried at Dinton.

V. Thomas, baptized at Riverstock March 3, 1593. Inventory dated June 16, 1646. He married Jane Bennett and had several children, one of whom, Gabriel, is said to have been the ancestor of the New York Ludlows.

VI. George, baptized at Dinton Sept. 15, 1596. He emigrated to York Co., Va., about 1641, was J. P. for that county, Colonel of Militia, Burgess for that county 1641, and a member of the Council 1642-1656. In 1644 he bought the former estate of Governor Harvey, "York Plantation" (now Temple Farm) near Yorktown, and, adding other lands, took July 20, 1646, a patent for 1452 acres. He was influential in inducing the Virginia government not to make a useless resistance to the Parliamentary fleet. General Ludlow says in his *Memoirs*, "This news [that of the surrender of Barbadoes to the Parliament] being brought to Virginia, they submitted also, when one, Mr. George Ludlow, a relation of mine, served the Parliament in the like manner as Col. Middeford had done at the Barbadoes". Col. Ludlow died in 1656, and his will was proved on August 1st of that year. It was proved both in Virginia and England. Following is an abstract given in Waters' *Gleanings:*

"George Ludlowe of the County and Parish of York in Virginia, Esqr., 8 September, 1653. To my nephew Thomas Ludlow, eldest son of my brother Gabriel Ludlow, Esq., deceased, all my whole estate of lands and servants &c. that I have now in possession in Virginia [he had patented about 17000 acres], to him and his lawful heirs forever; also my sixteenth part of the ship Mayflower, whereof Capt. William White is commander, which part I bought of Mr. Samuel Harwar, of London, merchant, only this years "fraught", excepted, which I have reserved for my tobacco &c. My executor, yearly and every year during the natural life of my wife Elizabeth Ludlowe, to pay unto her fifty pounds sterling in London. My crop wholly this year to be consigned to Mr. William Allen of London, merchant, and one Mr. John Cray that lives at the Green man on Ludgate Hill, whom I make my overseer of my estate in England. Moneys due from Mr. Samuel Harwar at the Sun and Harp in Milk Street, London. To my brother Gabriel all his children now in England one hundred pounds apiece and the remainder of the money (in England) to my brother Roger Ludlowe's children equally, and to Mr. Thomas Bushrode to be paid seventy-five pounds.

Whereas my brother Roger Ludlowe hath consigned divers goods to me as per my books appears, as debts in England and in Virginia as by his letters and other writings appear &c. To my cousin Samuel Langrish three thousand of tobacco &c. To George Bernard, son to Col. William Bernard, my great tankard with my arms on it, &c. To George Webster, son to Capt. Richard Webster, of Jamestown, the silver tankard that Mr. Bowler brought in the year 1655. To Col. William Bernard, Major William Gooch and Capt. Augustine Warner ten pounds apiece, and I desire and nominate them to be overseers here in Virginia. To Doctor Henry Waldron all the debt he owes me by a book and the physic I have sent for him. To Mr. Bushrode five pounds. To my man Archyball a cloth suit, &c. To Jane Gresham my servant one year of her time. To Mrs. Rebecca Hurst all the clothes that I have sent for her in full of her time being with me in my house.
Wit: Nicholas Trott, Augustine Hodges.
Codicil—I Colonel George Ludlowe &c. My nephew Thomas Ludlowe intends to intermarry with one Rebecca Hurst that is at this present living in my house. In that case my will is and my desire that my overseers here in Virginia take into their custody all my whole estate and dispose of the same until they can send into Ireland to my nephew Jonathan Ludlowe, eldest son of my brother Roger, who lives in Ireland at Dublin. Now in case my aforesaid nephew Thomas shall marry with the said Rebecca then it is my will that I give and bequeath unto my said nephew Jonathan all the estate that I did formerly give unto my nephew Thomas Ludlowe and constitute him the said Jonathan my full and sole executor. Otherwise my former bequest to stand valid and the said Thomas shall enjoy that I have formerly given him to his use and his heirs as my executor and heir. 23 Oct. 1655. Witness: James Biddlecombe."

On the first day of August in the year of our Lord God 1656, there issued forth letters of administration to Roger Ludlow, Esq., the father of and curator lawfully assigned of Jonathan, Roger, Ann, Mary and Sarah Ludlow, minors, the nephews and nieces and residuary legatees in the will during the minority of the said minors—for that no executor is therein named as touching the said deceased's estate in England. *Berkeley,* 256.

Sir Edmund Ludlow, eldest brother of Thomas Ludlow of Dinton (above) was the grandfather of Edmund Ludlow, Regicide and Parliamentary General, and of Henry Ludlow, ancestor of the, now extinct, Earls Ludlow.]

GEORGE TUCKER of Dartford, Kent, gent. Will dat. 23 Aug. 1639. To my eldest son George T. my manor of Milton next Gravsend & lands in p'shes of M. next G., Gravesend & Denton (except one field in Milton called the Stonsfeild & one inn in Milton now in occupation of John Francis, called the Crown & in Gravesend one inn called the White Heart bought of my father in law Richard Sedley esq. not yet conveyed) in tail male, in default; to my second son Francis in tail male, in default, to my third son Robert in tail male, in default to any other son I may have of my now wife Elizabeth, in tail male. The sd. 'Crown' to my sd. wife E. for life in addition to her present maintaining, remains as my wife appoint among sons in tail, in default of appointment, to sd. son George T. in tail. To sd. son George T. all lands in the somer Islands otherwise called the Barbados (except shares which came to me from my uncle Daniel Tucker's will, the one in occupation of John Young planter, the other called the timber share, which shares I give to my son Francis T. in fee & also two other shares in occupation of the widow Perinchef in Warwick tribe & purchased of Sir Robert Marvell, knight, which shares I give to my son Robert T. in fee) in tail male remaindes as manor afs'd. To my wife during minority of my son George T. all profits of manors etc. My adventures upon the seas for payment of my debts etc. To my second son Francis T. & to my youngest son Robert T. £400 a piece at 24. If my wife be with child to it, £400. To my daur. Elizabeth T. 1,000 marks at 21 or marriage with her mother's consent. If all my sons die s. p. m. lands etc. in p'ishes of Bexley, Crayford, Dartford & also the 'Crown' Inn, the Stoncefeild in Milton, the White Hart inn Gravesend & lands in borough of Southwark to my dau'r. Elizabeth & any other dau'r. I may have in fee. My friend Sir John Wolstenholme the younger, knight, & my brother in law Mr. John Sedly to sell such of my ment'd land at their discretion. Rest of lands & money in case all my sons die s. p. m. To my brother John T. in fee provided my brother Robert T. be maintained like a gentleman in decent apparel & that my brother Henry T. have £20 a year for life. Sd. wife Elizabeth to be ex'trix & to her all goods. Sd. Sir J. Wolstenholme Jun., knight & my brother in law John Sedly gent & my brother John T. gent to be overseers & to each 5 marks. To p'ish of Digswell for poor 40s. To poor of Milton 40s. & to Gravesend poor 40s. Witnesses: John Sedley, George Tucker, John Darrell, Ann Stoughton, Elizabeth Tucker. Adm. c. t. a. 2 May 1648 to George T. eldest son. Elizabeth, the relict & ex'trix having died before taking execution of Will. *Essex,* 68.

[George Tucker, the testator, was aged about 25 in 1619. The will of his father, George Tucker, of Milton, Kent, was printed in this Magazine XVII, 394, &c. George Tucker, the younger, went to Bermuda but returned to England. He married Elizabeth, daughter of Richard Sidley, of Digewell, Kent. His eldest son George went to Bermuda, where his will was proved Sept. 16, 1662. This George Tucker (died 1662) married Frances, daughter of Sir Henry St. George, and was ancestor of St. George Tucker, the emigrant to Virginia.]

VIRGINIA GLEANINGS IN ENGLAND

Contributed by Reginald M. Glencross, 176 Worplee Road, Wimbledon, London, S. D. 20, England.

(Continued)

DAME JANE SKIPWITH of Cotes co. Leic. widow

Will dat. 20 Oct. 1629. Whereas heretofore I purchased of my brother John Welby, 9 acres in Luttongate, in p'rsh. of St Edmunds in Sutton Lincolnshire, now in occupation of Michael Fisher, 12 acres in p'rsh. of Godney, Lincs. called Swanpitt Dole, manor of Minnforth (?Mumforth) in Sutton, Lincs., also £4.1.9 payable to sd. manor, all same to my sd. brother John Welby in fee, paying to my nephew Vincent Welby £50 & to Richard Roberts 40s. a year for life and to Margery Smith 40s. a year for life. To my brother Sir William Welby, knight, £40 etc. To my nephew William W., son of my sd. brother Sir W. W. £20. To my nephew William Welby's wife £10. To my nephew Vincent Welby £60 above the £50 my brother John is to pay him. To my nephew Philip Welby £10. To my cousin John Gamble £20. Ty my cousin William Gamble £10. To my cousin Matthew Gamble £10. To my cousin Margaret Browne £30 Etc. To my neice Susan Joslyn £20 etc., the picture of Sir William Werby her father. To my cousin Susan Locke her dau'r. £20. To my cousin Francis Locke £10. To my nephew Wimberley 40s. To my neice Elizabeth Wimberley £10. To my nepehew John Wimberley 40s. To my neice Frances Wimberley £20 etc. To my neice Martha Welby £20. To my neice Anne Welby £20. To my brother Richard Welby £50. To my nephew Adlord Welby £5. To my nephew Richard Welby £13.6.8. To my nephew John Welby £13.6.8. To my nephew Edward Welby

£13.6.8. To my neice Susan West £20. To my neice Jane Welby £200 etc. To my neice Dorothy Welby £10. To my neice Elizabeth Welby £10. To my brother John Welby's wife £13.6.8. To my nephew William Welby, son of my sd. brother John W. £10. To my nephew William Welby's wife, silver & £10. To my neice Cassandra Welby £10. To my neice Elizabeth' Welby dau'r. of my sd. brother John W. £10. To my neice Jane Welby, dau'r. of my sd. brother John W. £10. To my nephew Peter Ashton £50 & cushions & couch he gave me. To my nephew Peter Ashton's wife £10 etc. To my cousin Thomas Ashton £20. To my cousin Peter Ashton £10. To my cousin James Ashton £10. To my cousin John Ashton £10. To my cousin Jane Ashton £10. To my nephew Edmund Ashton £20 etc. To his wife, two kine, etc. To my cousin Peter Ashton son of my sd. nephew Edmund A. £10. To my nephew Walter Ashton £10 & to his wife £10 etc. To my cousin Peter Ashton son of my sd. nephew Walter A. £5. To my sister Bradshawe £40 etc., my book of gold which was my mother's. To my nephew John Bradshawe £10 if he pay me the £50 he owes me. To his wife £5 etc. To all of my nephew John Bradshawe's children £5. To my nephew Robbert Bradshawe's two children £5 a piece. To my neice Elizabeth Bradshawe, 200 marks etc., a wrought waistcoat, my dau'r. Elizabeth Pate gave me. To my neice Margery Townley £20 etc. To my neice Mary Hixon £40 etc. & to her children £5 a piece. To my neice Anne Barnard £20 etc. To children of sd. A. Bernard £5. To my neice Alice Tickle £20 etc. To my brother Blewitt £20. To my sister Blewitt £20 etc. To my nephew John Blewitt £10. To my neice Elizabeth Marrowe £10. To my nephew Ives £5. To my neice Bridget Ives £20 etc. & to her children £5 each. To my neice Isabel Garsye £20. To my neice Susan Blewitt £20. To my neice Katherine Blewitt £20. To my neice Jane Blewitt £20. To my nephew Henry Ashhurst £30. To my neice Cassandra Ashhurst £30 etc. To my cousin William Ashhurst £20. To my cousin John Ashhurst £13.6.8. To my cousin Henry Ashhurst £10. To my cousin Anne Ashhurst £15. To my cousin Margaret Ashhurst £15. To my cousin Mary Ashhurst

593

£15. To my cousin Francis Ashhurst £10. To my cousin Ricard Aprice £10 & to his wife, weatherbed etc. To my cousin Jerome Aprice 40s. & to his wife 40s. To my cousin Symon Aprice £10. To the children of my uncle Edmund Aprice (except Priscilla) £5. To sd. Priscilla 40s. To Margaret Butler £10. Whereas my son Sir Henry Skipwith owes me £200, he to have same. To him meadow I took of the Earl of Huntingdon, except parcel of same in possession of Clement Thompson. To my dau'r. the Lady Skipwith £20 etc. To William Skipwith son of sd. Sir Henry S. £5. To Henry Skipwith, son of sd. Sir Henry S. £20. To Thomas Skipwith son of sd. Sir Henry £10. To Grey Skipwith £10. To Elizabeth Skipwith dau'r. of sd. Sir Henry, £10 etc. To Diana Skipwith £10, etc. To Anne Skipwith £10. To my son Thomas Skipwith, house & meadow in Loughborow which I bought of Mr. Lacock, with lease thereof. To sd. son Thomas's wife £40 etc. To Henry Skipwith, son of sd. Thomas S. £20. To John Skipwith son of sd. Thomas S. £20. To Susan Skipwith £20. To my son Edward Pate 40s. To my dau'r. Anne Pate £20 & her father's picture. To my son John Pate £5. To my godson Henry Pate £10. To Edward Pate £5. To Charles Pate £5. To Elizabeth Pate £5. To Amy Pate £5. To my brother Henry Skipwith 40s. To Jane Ridgley 40s. To my sister Bridget Askewe £5. To my son Charles Markham 40s. To my godson Thomas Saunders £5. To Partridge Ridgen £10. To Mr. John Porter, sometime my chaplain, £5. To Mr. Richard Palmer, now my chaplain, £3. To my servant Thomas Somerfeild, cart, plough, etc. & £6. To his wife £5. To my servant Richard Haley £10 etc. To his wife 40s. etc. To Thomas White's wife 40s. etc. To Judith White 40s. etc. To my servant Clement Thompson £20, money he owes me, etc. To my goddau'r. Jane Thompson £5 etc. To my servant Edward Renolles £10 etc. To John Fansley, money he owes me etc. To my servant William Aaron £10. To my servant Bryan Medcalf £20 etc. To my servant William Browne £10 etc. To my servant Austin Mawe £5. To my servant William Shelington 40s. To my servant Richard Pollard £3.6.8. To my ser-

vant William Greene 40s. To my servant Dorothy Nicholls
£100 etc. To Alice Lee 40s. To my servant Anne Clyffe £5
etc. To my servant Anne Chrashawe 40s. To inhabitants of
town of Whaplud £10, if they build again their market house.
To poor of sd. town £13.6.8 & of town of horbridge £5, &
of town of Floote 40s., of town of Moulton 20s. of town of
Weston 20s., of town f Coates, £10, of town of Houghton £6,
of town of Prestwold £6, of town of Burton £6, of town
of Loughborough £6. £100 for tomb for my late husband
Sir William S. & myself in Prestwold Church. £20 for tomb
for John Walpole es. my first husband in Sleford Church.
Rest of goods to ex'ors. My brother Sir William Welby,
knight, my brother Richard Welby, my nephew Peter Ashton & my nephew Henry Ashhurst to be ex'ors. My son Sir
Henry Skipwith & my nephews Bevill Wimberley to be supervisors. Witnesses: Edmond Ashton, Vincent Welby, Par-
tridge Ridgon
Proved & confirmed by Sentence 2 Dec 1630 by Sir William
Welby knight, Richard Welby, Peter Ashton & Henry Ash-
hurst the ex'ors.
   Action between Richard Welby, Henry Ashhurst & Peter
Ashton ex'ors. pltf's. & John Welby, brother of dec., William
Welby son of a brother of dec., Richard Apprice & Joan Cat-
lyn al's. Apprice, cousins of dec. defts.
   Sentence refers to Sir William Welby the brother & coex'or.
as "modo defunet ante testricem" but see Probate above.
R. M. G.   *Scroope, 115.*

[The gentleman who made the abstract of this will said, with some
justification, that when he finished he felt that Dame Jane was the Aunt
of the world. It is an interesting will to Virginians. Not only was
her husband ancestor of the Virginia Skipwiths, but it is possible, if
her various relations could be studied, (they only could be in England) it would be found that she was the connecting link of a number
of other Virginia families.
   We omit the earlier generations of the family, as easily found in
books of English pedigrees, and begin (Nicholl's *History of Leicestershire*, III, 368 &c.) with Sir John Skipwith, Knight, who married Katherine, daughter of Richward Fitzwilliams, and had issue:
   Sir William Skipwith, Knight, of Ormesby; who married, 1st, Elizabeth, daughter of Sir William Trewhit, Knight, and 2nd, Alice, daughter of Sir Lionel Dimock, Knight. By his first marriage he had Sir
William Skipwith, of Ormesby, Knight.

By his second marriage he had: 2. Lionel, of Coulthorp; 3. John; 4. George of Cotsham; 5. Henry, of Keythorp, Esq., M. P. for Leicester 1588, died 1588; married Jane, daughter of Francis Hall, of Grantham, co. Lincoln, and relict of Francis Neale, of Prestwould and Cotes, Leicestershire. She died 1598.

Henry and Jane (Hall) Skipwith had a son, Sir William Skipwith, of Cotes, Knight, M. P. for Leicester 1604, died 1610. He married, 1st, Margaret, daughter of Roger Cave, of Stamford, co. Northants., who died 1594, and 2nd, Jane, daughter of John Roberts, and relict of John Markham. She was buried April 4, 1630. She was the testator above. The will shows she was married three times, the first to John Walpole, Esq.

Sir William Skipwith had by his first marriage with Margaret Cave, a son;

Sir Henry Skipwith, of Prestwould and Cotes, Knight and Baronet, who was born in 1589 and was living in 1652. On May 28, 1645, Sir Henry entertained Charles I at Cotes, and later he was fined £1114 by the Parliamentary Sequestrators. He married first, Amy, daughter and co-heiress of Sir Thomas Kemp, of Kent, who died 1631, and second, Blandina, widow of John Acton, Citizen of London.

Sir Henry and Amy (Kemp) Skipwith had issue: 1. William, died unmarried before his father; 2. Sir Henry, Bart. died unmarried soon after his father; 3. Thomas, died without issue; 4. Sir Grey, Bart. went to Virginia; 5. Elizabeth; 6. Diana; 7. Ann.

Diana Skipwith married Major Edward Dale, of Lancaster county, Virginia. There are in that county deeds signed by Edward Dale and Diana his wife. There is also on record in the same county, a note, dated Feb. 1, 1664, from Sir Grey Skipwith to Major Edward Dale, beginning "Brother Dale", giving "our love presented to y^{r}selfe and my sister" and signed "your lo. brother". Edward Dale was clerk of Lancaster county 1655-1674, and a member of the House of Burgesses 1677 and 1682. His will was dated Aug. 4, 1694, and proved March 11, 1695. To be interred decently without any wine drinking. Legacies to grandsons Peter and Joseph Carter. "Imp'mis, if it shall please God that my now wife shall happen to outlive me, I give unto her for her maintenance during her life the whole profitt of my estate whatsoever, some respect being alwaies had to her as an honest woman and gentlewoman and many years my wife" and after her death, estate to his grandchildren aforesaid, to granddaughters Elizabeth and Katherine Carter, grandson Edward Carter, and daughter Elizabeth now wife of William Rogers. His other daughter, Katherine Dale married Thomas Carter. Their descendants are given at length in the work of Dr. J. L. Miller.

To return to Nicholls. He states that Sir Grey Skipwith had a son Sir William Skipwith, Bart., who resided in Virginia and died there in 1730, aged about 60 years. Sir William had a son Sir Grey, who had a son Sir Peyton, living in Virginia in 1771. Sir Grey Skipwith settled in that part of Lancaster county which was afterwards Middlesex. No thorough examination of the records of these counties has been made to obtain all existing details in regard to the family, but some notes have been made.

At December Court 1657, Grey Skipwith, gent., qualified as administrator of Mr. Richard Payte (a reference to this will be made later). In Lancaster Sept. 12, 1660, it was ordered that Sir Grey Skipwith be paid 150 lbs. of tobacco for a gun "lost in the Accomac expedition, belonging to his late predecessor Edmund Kemple, gent., deceased." Sir Grey had married Ann, widow of Edmund Kemp,. of Lancaster county. In Middlesex county, July 6, 1674, an order of Court was made in favor of Dame Anne Skipwith in behalf of her son Sir William Skipwith, on her petition to the Court, Feb. 1672, *vs.* Mr. Wm. Dudley for a parcel of land. In 1680 another order was issued concerning Dame Anne Skipwith, mother and guardian of Sir William Skipwith. On Apr. 26, 1698, Sir William Skipwith was appointed first in the commission of the peace (presiding justice) of Middlesex and on June 1, 1704, and May 27, 1725, he qualified as high sheriff of the county. On Feb. 6, 1732 "Grey Skipwith, gent." qualified as clerk of Middlesex.

The Christ Church, Middlesex, parish register has the following entries: "The Lady Ann Skipwith of the parish" died March 5, 1685. The following entries of births of children of Sir William Sikpwith and "Lady Sarah Skipwith his wife" are entered; Ann, born July 31, 1703; Gray, born Aug. 25, 1705; William, baptized Sept. 15, 1707; Henry, born Oct. 22, 1714; Sarah, born April 11, 1717; Fuller (Fulwer) born March 19, 1719; Elizabeth, born March 27, 1723, died, May 11, 1725. Lady Sarah Skipwith died Dec. 26, 1727.

The will of Sir William Skipwith, dated July 19, 1734, and proved in Middlesex June 1, 1736, is printed in full in the *William and Mary Quarterly*, VII, 89-91. A genealogy of the family, though not a complete one, is in Slaughter's *History of Bristol Parish*.

It will be noted that, in her will, Dame Jane makes bequests to Grey Skipwith, the emigrant to Virginia, and to his sister Diana.

The will of Sir William Skipwith, of Coates (proved May 8, 1611) was printed in this Magazine XXVII, 50.

Dame Jane names in the will her daughter Elizabeth Pate, sons Edward and John Pate, and Henry, Edward, Charles, Elizabeth and Amy Pate. As noted above, in Dec. 1657, Grey Skipwith, qualified in Lancaster County, Va., as administrator of Richard Pate. This makes it strongly probable that this Richard Pate of Virginia, was of the same family as those named in Dame Jane Skipwith's will. Richard Pate was a member of the House of Burgesses for Gloucester county, July 1653. On Dec. 12, 1650, he was granted 1141 acres in Gloucester county. He died in 1657 and his nephew John Pate qualified as administrator. This nephew was the heir. For what little is known of the family, see this Magazine XIX, 255 &c.

The testator names her nephew Peter Ashton and his wife, her "cousin" Thomas Ashton, "cousins" Peter, Jane, John and James Ashton, nephew Edmund Ashton and his wife, cousin Peter Ashton, son of Edmund, nephew Walter Ashton and wife, Cousin Peter Ashton son of Walter. "Cousin" evidently meant child of a nephew.

A Peter Ashton came to Virginia and named his estate on the Potomac, Chatterton. By his will, dated 1669, he bequeathed his property to his brother, James Ashton, of Kirby-Underwood, and John Ashton, of Louth, both in Lincolnshire. Each of those brothers came to Virginia and died here.

The pedigree of the Ashtons of Spalding, Lincolnshire, descended from the Ashtons of Chaderton or Chatterton, Lancashire (*Harleian* 2086, a 1549) explains some of the ramifications of Dame Jane's kinsfolk. Cassandra, daughter of William Apreece, of Washingley in Lutton, co. Huntingdon, married 1st John Roberts, of Wallaston, co. Northampton, Esq., (and was doubtless the mother of Dame Jane); 2nd, Adlard Welby, of Gedney, Esq.; 3rd, Peter Ashton, of Holmear

Grange, in Spalding, co. Lincoln; 4th, Robert Carr, of Aswarby, co. Lincoln, Esq. Dame Jane had, half brothers and sisters, Walter Ashton, of Spalding, Mary Ashton, married Hawes Apreece, and Isabella Ashton married John Bradshaw, of Bradshaw, co. Derby. Walter Ashton had three sons, the nephews named in the will, Peter, Edmund and Walter. Each had sons, the "cousins" named in the will. It is possible that a little investigation in England might identify the three brothers who came to Virginia. This detailed note has been given, in part, to show what information a single English will sometimes contains.]

WILLIAM LANGHORN of Barnards Inn in Holburn, London, gent.

Will dat. 19 Aug. 1631. My leases (except lease of a little parcel of pasture lying next a little lane leading out of a street at Westend in Stevington *als* Stephenton, Beds. to a gate belonging to Alice Allen's close of the one part & a little Pightle belonging to my messuage or farm in S. afsd. next to a lane leading also out of sd. street to my sd. messuage on the other part) to be sold. To my dau'r. Ann L. £500. To my dau'r. Barbara L. £500. Whereas my son William in bound to pay my sd. dau'r. B. £100, this to be included. To my brother in law Mr. Jasper Yeardley & to my son in law Mr. William Barker a £20 Ann'y out of lands in Stevington afsd., to pay rest of legacies. To my son John L. my farm in Stevington afsd. for life, remainder to his sons successively in tail male, in default to his right heirs. Sd. excepted lease to him. I surrendered by Copyholds of manor of Stevington to Thomas Baringer, then the Elder, now dec. to use of Will, same to sd. son John L. to son William L. bason & ewer. To my dau'r. Elizabeth, piece of plate. To Susan dau'r. of my sister Elizabeth £5. To my grandson William Barker £10. To his sister Elizabeth my granddau'r. £10. My Precedent Books to my son John when admitted a Clerk in King's Bench Office. To my nephew William Langhorne, my brother Robert's eldest son, 30s. for ring. I forgive my nephew John Langhorne what he owes me except £10. To poor of p'ish. of St. Mary Aldermary 40s, of Cheshunt 40s. Rest of personal estate equally among all my children, William, Elizabeth, Anne, John & Barbara. Son William L. to be ex'or & sd. brother in law & son in law to be overseers. Dat. at end 8

Jan. 1630. Cod. 17 Dec. 1631. To Margaret Taylor now
wife of one Austed *als.* Austey 20s. Witnesses: Ro. Den-
hurst, Will. Barker, Tho. Phippes. Prob. 10 Jan. 1631[-2]
by William L. son & ex'or.   *Audley, 9.*

[William Langhorne, the testator, was evidently of the family to
which belonged Mary, daughter of Needham Langhorne, of Newton
Brownshall, Northamptonshire, who married Col. Robt. Townshend,
of Stafford Co., Va. (He died 1675.) After her husband's death she
lived for a time at Newton Brownshall, and there is recorded in Virginia, a power of attorney from her dated at that place. In her administration (1694) she is called "Maria Townshead, late of Newton or
Higham Ferrars, co. Northampton, widow, late at Virginia, deceased."
In the Visitation of Hertfordshire (Harleian Society) 1634 is a
pedigree of "Langhorne of Bedford", which begins with William
Langhorne of Bedford (born about 1560) whose eldest son was Robert
—marriage and descendants not given—and whose second son was
William, father of William Langhorne, of the Middle Temple, 1634,
who married Lettice, daughter of Eustace Needham, of Little Wymondley, Hertfordshire. In the same Visitation is the pedigree of Needham, of Little Wymondley and Wilwyn, from which it appears that
John Needham, of Wymondley (of the 3rd generation in the pedigree)
had a daughter Margaret, who married Robert Langhorne, of Bedford, and a granddaughter, Lettice, as above, who married William
Langhorne. Doubtless Needham Langhorne was a descendant of one
of these two.]

VIRGINIA GLEANINGS IN ENGLAND

Contributed by Reginald M. Glencross, 176 Worplee Road, Wimbledon, London, S. D. 20, England.

(CONTINUED)

THOMAS BOLITHOE of Lanceston, co. Cornwall.
Will dat. 9 June 1654. To my brother William & my sister Mary B. & to my sister in law Mary Nicholls 10/ ring each. Whereas I have at present one daur. Mary & my wife now goeth with one other child, & whereas my lands in Tettridge is conveyed to my wife for jointure, after her death, if such child be a son the same lands will descend to him, but if a daur. sd. lands will go to both my daurs. I have made provision for sd. daur. Mary by surrendering some parcels of Townland to her use. House wherein I now dwell to wife for life if my estate last so long. Rest of goods to my wife Mary B & she to be extrix. *Witns.* Jo. Treise, Phillipp Peare, John Hickes
Proved 27 Oct. 1654 by Mary B. relict & extrix.

Alchin, 448

WILLIAM BOLETHOW gent., of parish of Gwendron (*Wendron*) Cornwall.
Will dat. 18 Nov. 1654. To my wife Elizabeth £120 the 2 chambers over the kitchen etc during my estate therein if she live so long. To my daur. Mary Flamanke £60. To my granddaur. Elizabeth Bolithow £30 at her marriage. To my granddaur. Sarah Kempthorne £5 at 7. To my sister Jane Flamanke the wife of Roger F. £6.6.8. To Mr. Robert Jagoe my pastor 20/. To poor of Gwendron 20/., of Helston 20/.

To my servants William Anthony 10/., John Thomas 10/., Tho. Joseph 5/. Ann Polcribbow 5/. & Blanch Thomas 5/. To Anne Boddy of town of Truro 10/. Rest of goods to my son Alexander B. & he to be exor. *Witns.* Roger Flamanke, Mr. Charll Manly.

Proved 9 June 1655 by Alexander B. son & exor.

Aylett, 284

[John Bolitoe came from Cornwall to Virginia and settled in Princess Anne County. He was a vestryman of Lynhaven Parish, 1725, 1728, &c. He married Yates ———, who subsequently married John Nicholas. There is on record in Princess Anne, a mutilated deed from Thomas Bolithoe, of Cornwall, heir-at-law of John Bolithoe, late of Virginia, dated 173—, conveying certain property to John Nicholas and Yates his wife, in consideration of her dower.]

———

JOHN FOXALL, late of Hardwicke in p'ish. of Lattingham, co. Stafford, bachelor.

Noncupative. Will made 2 May 1655 oratio recta. For my funeral £10 owing to me from Edward Jordan of Alveley, co. Salop., overplus to poor of p'ish of Worfeild in sd. co. To my sister Margaret Devie all my goods in her possession. To my brother William F. £10 in hands of Richard Wilkes & £3 in hands of Thomas Hatton, bed etc in his custody, & all rest of my estate. Witnesses: Humfry Steward (x), Ursula Foxall (x). Adm. c. t. a. 15 May 1655 to William F. brother & principal legatary, no ex'or. being app'ted.

Aylett, 149

———

WILLIAM FOXALL, of borough of Stafford.

Will dat. 6 Oct. 1653. To poor of S. £4. To my wife Elizabeth for life, cottage or dwelling house in Birmingham, co. Warw., in tenure of William Fisher & messuage & cottage in Durliston & land there in tenture of one Keelinge, my other house in borough of Stafford, which joins my house where I now dwell, lately in tenture of Mr. John Wilson my brother in law & barn standing in lower end thereof towards the Town

Wall, my 3 barns nigh to Broodeigh in Stafford, moiety of house adjoining St. Chad's Churchyard which is jointly between me & Mr. Walter Adeny. To my son John F. my land in p'ish. of Bushbury, Staffordshire, which was given to me by my father John F., house in Stafford wherein I now dwell, with tanhouse, all in fee & remainder of (much of) devises to sd. wife, also in fee, £100. To my son William F. house & tanhouse in Stafford in fee (which I bought of George Lees now deceased) messe in Darliston afs'd from decease of my s'd. wife, also in fee & £100 also Fisher's cottage. S'd. wife to maintain s'd. 2 sons till 21 if she remain widow. To my dau'rs. Elizabeth, Anne, Bridget, Sara & May F. £200 a piece. If any die under 21 unmar. survivors' clause to my own brothers & sisters children 10s. a piece & household servants 10s. a piece. S'd. wife E. to be ex'trix. My brother Ambrose F. & brother in law John Britton to be overseers & to them 20s. a piece. To my mother 20s. for a ring. Witnesses: Ambrose Foxall, Anthony Dewyste, Ambrose Foxall the younger. Proved 21 Nov. 1655 by Elizabeth F., relict & ex'trix.

Aylett, 432

["Mr. John Foxhall" was living in Westmoreland County, Va., in 1670. There is recorded in that county, a deed, dated 1673, from the wife and attorney of John Foxhall, of Popes Creek, Westmoreland, to her daughter Martha Foxhall. Wife and daughter apparently died before the date of John Foxhall's will. The will of John Foxhall was dated Feb. 10, 1697-8, proved in Westmoreland March 27, 1698, and in P. C. C. (*Ash.* 162) Aug. 31, 1704. He left to Robert Volkes (Vaulx) and Sarah Elliott, all his estate real and personal in the Kingdom of England in Bromingham (Birmingham) in Warwickshire. His water mill to James Volkes and John Elliott, Jr.; his plantation at the head of Popes Creek to Susan Cornock; to Elizabeth Volkes his plantation in Essex; to James Volkes, horse, &c.; to Mary and Martha Elliott, horses.—"Loving Brother Caleb Butler", executor.
The will of Caleb Butler dated Feb. 16, 1708-9 would make it appear that Butler married a sister of Foxhall. It is possible that Mrs. Butler was previously Mrs. Vaulx. The name Foxhall frequently appears as a Christian name in the Parker family, formerly of Westmoreland.]

SIR FRANCES BICKLEY, of Langford, co. Norfolk, Baronet.
Will dat. 23 Sep. 1740. To be buried in church of L. All estate real & personal to my friend Henry Cocksedge of Thet-

ford, Norfolk, gent. in fee in consideration of the favours
friendships & services by him done & performed for me. He
to be ex'or. Witnesses: Thos. Caton, Abra. Clerke, Jnº Roope.
Prob. 8 July 1746 by Henry Cocksedge the ex'or.

Edmunds, 199

[Sir Francis Bickley, 4th Bart., of Attleborough Hall, died, without
issue, July 4, 1746. He had several brothers, one of whom, Joseph
Bickley, emigrated to Virginia, and eventually, inherited the title. See
Wm. & Mary Quarterly, vol. V.]

WILLIAM HAMMOND, of Ratcliff in the p'ish of Stebenheath
als. Stepney, co. Middx., gent.
    Will dated 9 July 1732. My freehold farm in posession of
———— Pritchard at Thundersley, co. Essex, & my 2 copyhold
farms now in posson. of [*blank*] King & [*blank*] in p'ish of
Eastwood, co. Essex. To my uncle William Clopton of Virginia for life, remainder to his children equally in fee. My 2
freeholds messuages in possession of John Thompson, watch-
maker, & Joseph Scrafton, peruke maker, in Clements Lane
near Lombard Street, London. To my friends Samuel Skinner of Ratcliff, aforesaid esq. & Josiah Cole of same, apothecary, in fee upon trust for sale. They to pay £500 to my
servant Christian Waters now living with me. £500 to Mary
Hamond als. Mary Hamond Waters at 21 or marre. if she
die before, s'd £500 to her mother the s'd. Christian Waters.
Household goods at my now dwelling house on Stepney Causeway to s'd. C. Waters, & to her s'd dwelling house for rest
of term, all my plate & jewels. Rest of estate to my s'd. uncle
William Clopton & his children. S'd. S. Skinner & J. Cole to
be ex'ors. & guardians to sd. M. Hamond als. M. H. Waters.
Witnesses: Tho. Taylor, Hannah Norman, Wrudd (or Mudd)
Fuller ser.
Prob. 17 July 1732 to Samuel Skinner & Josias Cole ex'ors.

Bedford, 188

[William Clopton (born 1655, died before 1733) emigrated to Virginia
and settled in York County, removing later to New Kent. He married

Anne, daughter of Robert Booth of York County and had three sons, Robert, William and Walter, and two daughters, Anne, married Nicholas Mills and Elizabeth, married (1st), in 1713, William Walker, and (2nd), Alexander Moss.

The son William married Jan. 27, 1718-19, Joyce Wilkerson. Among other children they had a son, Waldegrave, whose name probably gives a clue to the English ancestry of the Cloptons.

It is probable that William Hammond was a nephew of the emigrant and did not know of his death.]

FRANCISCUS LUDLOW.

Octavo die [July 1671] emenavit Commissio Willelmo Rickard Avunculo et Curatori legitime Assignato Francisco Ludlow et Willelmo Ludlow Minoribus filiis naturalibus et legitimis Francisci Ludlow nuper de Horneingham in Comitatu Wilts sed in Virginia in partbus Transmarinis defuncti Habentis etc. Administrandum bona Jura et Credita dicti defuncti in usum et durante Minori ætate dictorum minoris (sic) etc.

$$P. A. B. \text{ 1671 fa. 80}$$

[Francis Ludlow, a brother of Sarah Ludlow, wife of Col. John Carter, of Corotoman, had evidently lived in Lancaster County, Va. See this Magazine XXIX, 350-354, and especially p. 352, where, an extract from the Lancaster County records shows that Francis Ludlow's will was proved there May 11, 1670. It is curious that in the Prerogative Court of Canterbury only an administration was granted and no notice taken of the will.]

WILLIAM TABB, of Thurlstone, Devon, yeoman.

Will dat. 10 Jan. 1648. To poor of T. 3s. 4d. To my dau'r. Joan Square 20s. To my son in law Ellis Square, suit. To my dau'r. Amy Scobble 20s. To my dau'r. Mary Nealde 20s. etc. To my wife Alice all my wool. To William T. & Alice T. children of my son John T., Andrew Square & Thomas Square sons of Ellis S. my son in law & to Agnes Scobble dau'r. of my dau'r. Agnes (sic) S., my grandchildren a ewe & lamb each. To each of my godchildren 12d. Whereas I have an estate in tenement & farthing of land in Buckland in p'ish of T. afs'd for years determinable on death of me & my

Alice & my son John T. I give same to my wife Alice for life 40 years if she so long live, but my son John T. to hold same during life of my sd. wife at £10 rent. Sd. wife to have househarbour with my son John for her life. To John Marten pair of breeches. To John Bridgman, pair of breeches. Rest of goods to my son John T. & he to be ex'or. Witnesses: Tho. Cornish, Thomas Square X.

Adm. c. b. a. 12 [*blank*] 1654 to Rebecca Tabb, relict & ex'trix of John T., whilst he lived, son & ex'or of W. T. late of T. Because that J. T. the son & ex'or. also died before he had taken upon him execution of same Will.

Alchin, 36

JOHN TABB, of Thurlestone, co. Devon, yeoman.

Will dat. 25 Dec. 1653. To poor of p'ish of T. 3s. 4d. To my son William T. & my two dau'rs. Alice T. & Prudence T. £30 each at 21. Whereas I have an estate in one tenement & one farthing of lands in Buckland in p'ish of Thurlstone afsd. determinable on deaths of me & my mother Alice T. out of which I am to pay to sd. mother £10 a year for life, by will of my father William T. dec., I give same to my wife Rebecca, she paying the sd. £10 yearly. Sd. Mother to have house harbour with my wife for life. Estate in two houses & close of land (4 acres) at Coton in p'ish of Sherford for years determinable upon Anne? Amy Nicholls for payment of £25 to Agnes Scobble da'ur. of sd. A. Nicholls, to my brother in law Ellis Square on trust for sd. A. Scobble. Rest of goods to sd. wife R. & she to be ex'trix. My uncle John Randoll to be overseer. *Testator made his mark.* Witnesses: Tho. Cornish, John Randoll, John Lakeman X, Thomas Squeare X.

Prob. 22 June 1654 by Rebecca T., relict & ex'trix.

Alchin, 36

[Humphrey Tabb, the ancestor of the Virginia family, came to Virginia in or before 1637 and settled in Elizabeth City County. Vol. I, Dwelly's *Parish Records,* shows that in the register of Firehead, Somersetshire, is an entry of the christening, Sept. 17, 1609, of Humphrey, son of John Tabb.]

FRANCIS SYDNOR, of Grays Inn, Middx., esq.

Will dat. —— —— 1653. Having long languished in body by reason of old age & infirmities. To poor of p'ish of St. Andrew Holborn 40s. To my kinsman Fortunatus Sydnor of Greenwich, Kent, aged about 15 years, £40 at 21, if he die before, same to my neice Judith Goldsmith of Purpoole Lane. St. Andr. Holborn afsd. & to Charles & Mathias Goldsmith, sons of my nephew Charles G. physician, equally whereas I lent to my nephew Henry Sydnor of Norwich, grocer, £20 by Bond, I release him of same & to him £10 more. To sd. Charles Gouldsmith & Mathias G. sons of my sd. nephew C. G. £60 between them, at 21. To sd. nephew C. G. the physician, my watch, same to be delivered to my sd. neice Judith G. to be kept for my sd. nephew until his return into England. Whereas Humphrey Wigan of Grays Inn Lane, St. Andr. Holborn, Middx. Chandler is bound to sd. neice Judith G. in £100 bond to pay £51. 10 s. to her at a day yet to come, which £50 (sic) was my property & £1. 10. in consideration of forbearance, sd. bond being in my custody, same to be delivered to sd. neice. Rest of personal estate to my sd. neice Judith Goldsmith. Sd. H. Wigan to be ex'or. & to him £10.

Prob. 19 June 1656 by Humphrey Wigan the ex'or.

Berkley, 215

[A Fortunatus Sydnor lived in Lancaster County, Va., 1670, &c. There is in existance an old Bible containing many entries of the children of this Fortunatus Sydnor and their descendants. Dr. Lyon G. Tyler proposes to publish this record, with additional information, in his *Quarterly.* The Sydnors were long associated with Kent. Paul Sydnour, of Brenchley, gent., contributed to a loan to the King in 1542. This Paul Sydnor in 31st year of Henry VIII was granted the advowson and vicarage of Brenchley. His son William Sydnor succeeded him about 1563 and shortly afterwards alienated them to William Waller. On April 13, 1573, "Mr. William Sydnor, of Blundeston in Suffolk, Esq.", sold the manor of Cryels in Brenchley to William Lambarde.]

VIRGINIA GLEANINGS IN ENGLAND

Contributed by Reginald M. Glencross, 176 Worple Road,
Wimbledon, London, S. W. 20, England.

(Continued from XXX, 44)

RICHARD CROSHAWE of London, Esq.
    Will dat. 26 Apr. 1631.   To be buried in p'ish. church of St
Bartholomew where I have long been a parishioner & now
dwell, in the vaults.   To 66 poor labouring men 8 s. a piece
for pair of new woollen stockings, a new cap & pair of new
shoes & a black coat at 12 s.   Of these, six to be of Almsmen of
Goldsmiths Hall, they to go before the Company of the Gold-
smith's at my funeral.   To the seven prsh's. of this Ward, viz.
St Margaret Lothbury, St Christophers, St Mildred, St Benet-
Fink, St Martin Outwich, St Peter le Poor & All Hallows in
the Wall £50 a piece.   To Christ's Hospital £100.   To St
Bartholomews Hospital £100.   To St Thomas' Hospital £50.
To Bridewell £50.   To poor p'rsoners in Ludgate £10 a piece.
To poor of this p'ish £50.   For church stock there £50.   To
prs'oners of Compter in Woodstreet £100, of Compter in the
Poultry £100.   For 20 poor boys born in Marton & Mackworth
co. Derby, for apprenticeing £5 each.   To 20 poor ministers,
10 in London whereof Mr. Freake of St Barthews to be one, &
10 in co. Derby within 15 miles of Derby, £10 each.   To my
kinsman Robert Carter of Osmaston Derbyshire, after death of
his mother, lands I bought of Mr. Cregson & his wife, in fee.
To Richard Carter & Thomas Carter sons of my sister Frances
C. of Osmaston, widow, & to the children of her dau'r. Alice
Leeper dec., £500.   To my cousin Carter, of Ashborne, & his
children £500.   £100 to my poor kindred in Derbyshire.   To
my kinswoman Ellen Carter now E. Hemsley £500 & forgive all
my [her?] husband owes me.   To my neice Judeth Haddon

From Vol. XXX, No. 3 (July 1922), p. 274.

lease of my house in Lothbury wherein she dwells, great debts her husband Francis H. owed me. To sd. Judith £1,000 or to her children. To Marie Haddon £500. To Richard Haddon, Elizabeth Haddon £500 to be paid to them the sd. children at their marriages or 21. To my neice Alice Child, ring & to her two sons £10 a piece. To my neice Ann Marshe £500, her husband Henry M. to pay his now dau'r. Ann M. £500 at marriage. I forgive my nephew Sir Thomas Metham £500 he owes me. To him & to his Lady my neice £1,000 more, he to leave her £500 besides furniture which is in my keeping. To Mrs. Smith & to her uncle Mr. Jordan Mecham, a ring each. To Mrs. Elizabeth Osborne wife of Mr. Henry O. a ring. To my ancient friend Capt. Jewes, a ring. To my cousin Daniel Darnelly £50 & to Stephen Darnelly £20 (& to Edward Darnelly £20) & to the two children my late cousin Darnelly had by Mrs Crooley £10 a piece. To Mrs Tompson £10. I forgive Stephen Darnelly all he owes me. To my ancient & unfortunate friend & brother Isaacke Woder & his wife, £200 & forgave them what they owe me. To them, in fee, lands I bought of them in Cornwall, & deeds concerning copper works, sd. Isaac to leave all to his sd. wife. If she die without issue sd. lands in Cornhill (sic) to my next heirs. To my cousin Mr. John Milward 50 pieces in gold & of my cousin his now wife, the same. To my cousin Elizabeth Milward £500. To my cousin Thomas Milward £40 & to his three brothers, John, Henry & Raphe £20 each & to nurse to continue her care of them £5. To George Taylor a ring, he never to forget respect to his good master, mistress & their children. To my friend Mr Richard Davies & his wife, 30 pieces of gold for them & his dau'r., much rejoicing in friendship between him & my cousin John Milward. To my ancient friend Mr. Charles Bostocke 50 pieces of gold, he to leave it to his five children. To Andrew Willingham, glover, £5 & forgive him all he owes me. To Henry Hawke, embroiderer, the same. To George Charles, my tailor £10. To the son of Osmand Pulcher, a glover, £5. To my old fellow Roger Spencer 12d. a week for life. Among my nephew Methams servants, £20. To Sir Francis Harris of Essex, Knight, £5. To my ancient friend

Lady Isabel Sames £50 of debt to me of her son Sir Gerrard S., she to leave it to my godson Richard Sames. To Sir James Palmer, Knight, 10 pieces of gold. To my ancient friend Mr. Simon Chambers which was servant to the Lord John Harrington & his Lady, £10, you shall hear of him at Sir Robert Heathe's, the King's Attorney. To the children of John Coles whose mother was my ancient servant £40. Old Mrs. Westcombe, widow, to be remembered in my gift to p'ish of St. Margaret Lothbury. Mrs. Johnson, widow & Hassard or his wife or children to be remembered in gift to St. Bartholomews. To my kinswoman Awdrey Carter, in fee, my great capital messuage in St. Martin Outwich, London, which I bought of Sir Robert Napier, wh'rin Mr. Bateman now dwells. To her house wherein I now dwell etc. To town of Derby £1,250 for a preacher to read a weekly lecture every Friday in forenoon in p'ish church of All Hallows there at £20 a year. £15 a year for seven poor inhabitants of sd. town, £28 a year for poor of Marton & Mackworth. To my two servants George Elkinton & Robert Davies £50 a piece & remit the time the latter has to serve me by his indenture. To my chief servant John Robinson who hath long dwelt with me £500. To my friend Mr Richard Holdsworth, parson of St. Peter the poor £10 etc., he to preach at my funeral. To Mr. Grant, parson of St Bartholomews £5 & remit him £12 he owes me. To my nephew Sir Thomas Metham, black nag, he to be well cared for when old. To Mr Shute of the Poultry, Mr Shute in Lombard Street & Mr Beamond, blacks. To Mr Melborne in the exchange towards better maintenance of his great charge of children £5. Diamond hat band etc., to my neice the Lady Metham. Turkey ring to my friends Mrs. South & her dau'r. To my kinswomen Judith Haddon, Ellen Hemsley, Anne Marshe & Alice Childe a diamond ring each. £100 for good cheese for pensioners of this p'ish. To my surgeon Mr. Browne £10. To my apothecary Mr. Buckner £10. To my nephew John Croshawe £200. To my old friend Mr. Buckner £5. To Company of Goldsmiths of London £400 for their poor. To my sd. kinswoman Awdrey Carter, for preferment in marriage £2,000. If she marry without consent, all her legacies to my

609

neice Judith Haddon & her children. To my friend Daniel
Benefild £30. To my friend Mr. Leake in Fleet Street £10 &
to Charles Bragg & Geo. Allcotry £5 each. To the Companies
of the Artillery Garden in London, two silver pots. To my
godson Richard Croshawe son of William C., late of Whitechapel, preacher, house etc. without Bishopsgate against the
Spital & my house at Basingshall in London & house at Mort-
lake, Surry, all in fee, for his education in learning, also £20.
To Robert Crashawe who dwells with me [Mr.?] John Wat-
kins of London, merchant, £20. To my nephew Sir Thomas
Metham, coat etc. To my kinsman Mr. Child, livery gown.
Ty my kinsman Mr. Maroke, the like. To my friends Sir
Paul Pinder & Mr. Robert Bateman, Chamberlain of London,
blacks, etc., also to my friend Mr. Barnard Hide & to Mr. Richard Bishopp, John Cooper & Francis Hordman my friends Sir
Thomas Metham, my nephew & my nephew John Croshawe of
Henor, Derbyshire, & Mr John Milward to be ex'ors. Friends
Richard Davies, Daniel Benefild & Charles Bostocke to be overseers. Rest of estate amongst my kindred. As to my little
fenements in St. Martin Outwich & elsewhere, these to ex'ors
for same purposes. I forgive my nephew Doctor Same & his
wife my neice, the world of offences & unkindnesses done to
me & desire to be forgiven. £20 a year for weekly lecture in
St. Bartholomew's Church every Wednesday morning. To sd.
town of Derby £100 for householders of Marton & Mackworth
[25 sheets of paper]. Witnesses: Hughy Perry, John Graunt,
Ric. Woodward, Ca: Bostocke Scr(ivener), Geo. Allcotrie,
Tho. Bostocke.
Cod. given by word to Henry Hutchins £5. To Bostocke £2.
To Mordica Keydon £5. To Cha. Bostocke's two sons £10
a piece. To his three dau'rs. £5 each. To his godson Rogers
£5. To Ales Child (to make up £100,) £90. To her two chil-
dren to make up £50 each £80. To Kate More (to make up
£40) £20. To Robert & Geo. More £20 each £40. To Mr.
Bostocke for my Will £5 To Humphreys of the Exchange £5.
To Mr. Beamond £5 & at another time £10. Sum £307. To
Baldwyne of the Exchange £5. To Company of Goldsmiths
two voiders of silver of £50.

Prob. 3 June 1631 by Sir Thomas Metham, knight & John Milward, ex'ors. Power reserved for John Crashawe the other ex'or.

Prob. 4 July 1662 [1632?] by J. C. the other ex'or.

Confirmed by Sentence 2 Johannis 1632. [25 June].

[Persons of the name Crashaw or Croshaw were associated with the settlement of Virginia both as members of the Virginia Company and as colonists.

This will of one of the great London merchants is one of numerous examples showing an open-handed charity and a loving remembrance of friends, which might be a model to modern testators.

Richard Croshaw was evidently from Derbyshire, and was related, though he does not state how, to Rev. William Croshaw.

The first of the name in Virginia was "Captain Rawleigh Crashaw, of Kequotan, gent., and ancient planter", "who has dwelt in this colony fifteen years and rendered many worthy services." He is so described in a grant of 500 acres at "Old Poynt Comfort" made to him in 1623. He was a member of the London Company, came to Virginia in 1608 and was a member of the House of Burgesses in 1623. When the Massacre of 1622 occurred he was on a trading cruise in the Potomac and challenged Opechancanough or any of his men to fight him naked; but the offer was not accepted. Crashaw spent much time amongst the Indians and was intimately acquainted with their habits and customs. From his first arrival, when he became a friend of John Smith, he took an active part in the business and defence of the Colony. Smith seems to have had a high opinion of his knowledge of Indians and Indian warfare and Crashaw was one of the authors of complimentary verses prefixed to the *Description of New England* (1616).

> "In the deserued honour of my honest
> *and worthie Captaine John Smith*
> and his Worke.
> *Captaine and friend; when I peruse thy booke*
> *(With* Iudgements *eyes) into thy* heart *I looke*:
> *And there I finde (what sometimes* Albyon *knew)*
> A *Souldier, to his* Countries-honour, *true.*
> *Some fight for* wealth; *and some for* emptie praise;
> *But thou alone thy* Countries Fame *to raise.*
> *With due* discretion, *and* unda[u]nted heart,
> *I (oft) so well haue seen thee act thy Part*
> *In deepest plunge of hard extreamitie,*
> *As forc't the troups of proudest foes to flie,*
> *Though men of greater* Ranke *and lesse* desert
> *Would* Pish—*away thy Praise, it can not strait*
> *From the true* Owner: *for, all good-mens tongues*
> *Shall keepe the same. To others that Part belongs.*
> If, *then,* Wit, Courage, *and* Successe *should get*
> *Thee* Fame, *the Muse for that is in thy debt:*
> *A part wheof (least able though I bee)*
> *Thus heare I doe disburse, to honor Thee.*
> RAWLY CRASHAW"

(Could the person "of greater rank" have been Percy?)

Raleigh Crashaw probably died early in 1625 (present style) as on March 13, 1625, there is in the General Court records an order referring to Capt. Francis West as administrator of "Capt. Crashaw".

He was married and may have been the father of Joseph and Richard Croshaw who for many years lived in the adjoining county of York.

Capt. Richard Croshaw and Major Joseph Croshaw are stated, in the records of York county to be brothers. Capt. Richard Croshaw (born 1621, died April 1669), had a son Benjamin, who died without issue, and daughters who have descendants. Major Joseph Croshaw was a Burgess for York 1659 and 1660, and died April 10, 1667. He had sons Benjamin and Joseph, who died without issue, and daughters who have descendants.

William Croshaw, Puritan divine and poet, who is named in the will, was son of Richard Croshaw, of Handsworth, near Sheffield, Yorkshire, was born in 1572 and died in 1626. He was educated at St. Johns College, Cambridge, where he entered as a sizar May 1, 1591. He was B. A. 1591-2, was ordained and became a preacher at Bridlington and Beverley, Yorkshire; became M. A. 1595 and B. D. 1603. In 1601 he was made a Prebend of Rippon, appointed preacher at the Inner Temple, and rector of Burton-Agnes, Yorkshire. In 1617 he became rector of St. Mary's Matfellon or Whitechapel, London. His will was proved Oct. 16, 1626. He was married three times, his first wife being the mother of the poet Richard Crashaw. William Crashaw was a good scholar, and eloquent preacher and a strong Protestant. He was the author of various works. He was a member of the Virginia Company. On Feb. 21, 1609-10, he preached a sermon before Lord Delaware and the Virginia Company on the eve of Delaware's departure for Virginia. Extended extracts are printed in Brown's *Genesis* 360-374. At the conclusion the preacher addressed Lord Delaware: "And thou most noble Lord, whom God hath stirred up to neglect the pleasures of England, and with Abraham to go from thy country, and forsake thy kindred and thy father's house, to go to a land which God will show thee, give me leave to speak the truth. Thy ancestor many hundred years ago gained great honor to thy house, but by this action thou augmented it. * * * Remember thou art a general of Englishmen, nay a general of Christian men; therefor principally look to religion. You go to commend it to the Heathen, then practice it yourselves; make the name of Christ honorable, not hateful unto them".

William Crashaw also wrote a long "Epistle Dedicatoire" to "Good Newes from Virginia" (1613). See Brown's *Genesis*, 611-620.

Richard Crashaw, the poet (1613-1649) was the only child of Rev. William Crawshaw by his first wife. He was educated at the Charterhouse, and at Penbroke and Peterhouse, Cambridge, and had the degree of M. A. 1638. His epigrams, published when he was barely 21 show marvelous capacity. He was intimate with Nicholas Ferrar. He went to Paris in 1641, was living there in great distress in 1646, went to Italy in 1648 or 1649 and died there August 25, 1649. He became a devout Catholic. He was author of "Steps to the Temple"—poems, mainly sacred. "His sacred poems breathe a passionate fervor of devotion which finds its outlet in imagery of a richness seldom surpassed in our language". It is hoped that farther investigation may connect the Va. Crashaws with the merchant, the divine and the poet.]

VIRGINIA GLEANINGS IN ENGLAND

Contributed by Reginald M. Glencross, 176 Worplee Road,
Wimbledon, London, S. W. 20, England.

(Continued)

ANNE DYGGES widow.

Will dat. 9 Aug. 1509. To be buried in p'ish church of
All Hallows, Canterbury before the Holy Rood next to the
choir door. To high altar there for tithes etc 6s. 8d. To the
Cross light there 6s. 8d. To church of St. John Baptist at
Swynkefeld, Berks., & a portucris written. For my soul in
Sd church at my burial 30 masses, also at my months day 30
masses, at Twelve months day 30 masses. To Dame Margaret
my dau'r. my heart's blessing & best standing cup & my great
book of prayers. All debts she owes me of my lands in Berkshire. Sir Richard Worthington to sing for my soul unto
the year be come up that he hath begon'. To each of the orders
of Friars in Canterbury 3s. 4d. To house of nuns at St.
Sepulchres 5s. To house of Canons at Leeds 6s. 4d. To our
Lady of Walsingham my best hoop of gold. Out of debts
owing me by Mr. James Digges, to Isabel D., his dau'r toward
marriage £4. To Anne Exherst 12 pairs of sheets. To Anne
Beell 6s. 8d. To Anne Saltyn & Anne Lambebart 20d. each.
Ex'ors to sell my lands at Asche which I have in fee except
place called Brookes which I give to Ric. Exherst in fee Rest
of Goods. Sd. Ric. Exherst & Thomas Beell to be ex'ors
(*Witnesses*) Henry of Rog. Squyer p'son of sd. Alhalows,
Thomas Halybell Mr. of the East Brigge in Cant. Rog.
Worthington Chaplyn, William Saltyn and other.
Proved 5 Nov. 1509 by Thomas Beell exor.

Bennett 21.

From Vol. XXX, No. 4 (Oct. 1922), p. 362.

[The wills printed here are those of members of the family from which Edward Digges, Governor of Virginia, descended. Anne Digges does not appear in the only pedigree now accessible—that in Berry's *Kent*. She was probably the widow of some member of the family in the generation preceding James Digges. She evidently left no sons and was not an ancestress of any of the branches of the family. Her will is of interest as that of a devout lady of the old faith.

James Digges, of Barham, whose will is printed below, was a son of John Digges of Barham and his wife Joan, daughter of Sir Gervas Clifton, Knight. John Digges had also a son William, doubtless the person to whose son Thomas, James Digges gave the reversion of much of his estate. James Digges married first, Mildred, daughter of John Fineux, Chief Justice of England and had a son John, who had a son William, both mentioned in the will. Barham descended in this, the elder line. James Digges married secondly, Phillipa, daughter of John Engham, of Cliart, and had a son Leonard Digges, of Wootton Court, who married Sarah Wilsford. Leonard and Sarah Digges were the parents of Thomas Digges (died 1595 and buried at St. Mary, Aldermanbury, London) who married Anne, daughter of St. Warham St. Leger, of Ulcomb. She died in 1636 aged 61. Their eldest son was Sir Dudley Digges, of Chilham (died March 18, 1836) who married Mary, daughter and co-heiress of Sir Thomas Kemp, of Olantigh. Edward Digges, Governor of Virginia, and ancestor of the Virginia and Maryland families, was son of the last named. Though James Digges does not seem to have been as ardent a Catholic as his kinswoman, he provides in his will for obits &c.]

JAMES DIGGES, of p'ish of Derham [Berham?] co. Kent, esq.

Testament dat. 20 Feb. 1535[-6] 27 Hen. VIII. To be buried in church of D. a'fs'd in North Chancel where my mother & my wife lie. Pious legacies to D., Kyngston next Darham a'fs'd., — & p'risoners at Canterbury. To my wife Philip a vestment of green. To William D., son of my eldest son John D., apparel & ornaments of my chapel in my mansion house that I now dwell in, at 24. To s'd wife & Leonard D., my son half of residue of goods & other half to s'd. William D. at 24. My wife Philip, John Sakevyle esq. Robert Brente my nephew gent & my son Leonard D., to be ex'ors. Sir William Hawte knight to be overseer. If my ex'ors be vexed for taking issues of my manor of Outelmynton which I now dwell in unto time s'd. William D. & Francis D., his brother be 24, half of goods bequeathed to s'd Wm. to go to ex'ors.

Will of same date as to lands in Kent, Canterbury & suburbs & town of Sandwich, all now held by feoffees to my use. My manor of Outelmyston charged with legacies etc., also lands thereto in Kyngston, Bishopsbourne & Pinyotede, Kent.

614

My wife Philip to have rents thereof till William D., son of
John D., my eldest son dec., be 24, (paying to my son Leonard
£5 a year during her (Philip's) life & to Francis D., brother
of sd. William D. 5 marks yearly for his life). Lands etc.,
to sd. William at 24 for life & to his heirs male charged with
obit in Darham church & 3s. 4d. To Master of Maidstone
College towards payment of obit under will of my cousin
Richard D. in Maidstone church. S'd. W. to pay to his brother
Francis at 15, 5 marks yearly for life. If s'd W. die s. p.
under 24, s'd manor etc. to s'd Francis at 24 similarly in default to next heir male of body of Thomas Digges son of
William D. late of Newington bende Sittingbourne in default
to my next heirs. Lands in Canterbury etc. to s'd grandchildren W. & F. D. in default to sd. son Leonard D. & his
heirs male in default to sd. Thomas Digges etc. *as before.*
Feoffees of my cousin Richard Digges to stand seised of my
lands in Maidstone, manor of Mayton to uses as last above
according to will of sd. R. Digges. Obit to be kept at Maidstone according to sd will. My feoffees Edward Hawte,
William Kemp, Thomas Bele gentlemen & Thomas A Denne
thelder to stand seised of my manor of Yoke to use of heirs
of my son John according to fine of entail of Sir Roger Nor-
wode knight, & of my manor of Netherhardes to same uses
in recompense for manor of Wycherlyng which I sold to the
Savoy of my manor of Fokeham & lands in Frenobede &
Leneham, Kent which was late Thomas Cobhams & John
Payfrere, also lands John Nethersole late had to farm unto
use of John D., my son & Mildred his wife & their heirs
male, in default to my son Leonard etc., & of my manor of
Popeshall iuxta Dover, manor of Brome next Byrton etc.,
to use of my wife for life, remainder to sd Leonard in tail
male, in default to heirs male of sd son John, in default to
heirs male of sd cousin Thomas Digges, in default to right
heirs. *Witnesses* Augustine Wormyll, clerk, John Foste de
Cant., Bartelmewe Berham, Thomas Ladde, Robert Watson,
Robert Hawkynge etc.
Proved 24 Nov. 1540 by Leonard Digges & Phillippa the rebet,
the ex'ors. Power reserved to the other ex'ors.
Proved 25 June 1544 to Robert Brent ex'or.

JOHN FLETE of Bedenden co. Kent.

Will dat. 8 Aug. 1556. To my wife Margaret half of household stuff & other half to all my sons equally at 21 or marriage. To s'd wife £80. To my 3 sisters 20s. a piece & to every of their children 20s. a piece. To every of the sons of my brother William F. & to his dau'rs 20s. each. To my brother's wife 20s. To my son William F. gold ring at 21. To my s'd 4 sons plate at 21, if they die same to dau'r Alice or, if she die, to my bro. William F. Ex'ors to purchase lands with residue of goods. My wife to put all my sons to school until 15. Wm. Flete my brother & William F., my son, ex'ors. My wife to be overseer will of lands. To my wife Margaret yearly rent of £20 out of lands in Kent, for life in bar of ½ my land to which she is entitled under custom of the county. To my elder son William F., lands etc. in Charing, Westwell, Little Chart, Pevington & 2 mills called Ford Mill, in fee, but if he die under 21, same to all my s'd sons in fee. To Thomas Flete my lands in Halden & Bedersden & fee simple rent I bought of Bone & Padyam that Richard Stedman doth hire & £110, in fee. If he die under 21, same to my 3 sons in fee. To my third son John F., house etc I now dwell in, the 3 fields I bought of Stephen Harlackenden, woods I bought of Lawrence Day at Marden, in fee 6 £200. If he die under 21, same among my 3 sons. To my 4th son Samuel F., annuities etc., save one fee simple bought of Rooper & £170 in ready money etc., if he die under 21 same to my 3 sons. My 4 sons to pay to their mother £5 a piece for life. To my daur Alice wife of Robert Gibben (*ends here*).
Proved 9 Dec. 1558 by William Flete senior ex'or. Power reserved to William Flete junior also exor now a minor.
12 July 1560 commission to William Flete jun. William Flete senior present.

Helles 14.

[The son or brother William Fleet named in this will was probably identical with the William Fleet who married Katherine Honeywood, of Kent, and died between 1584 and 1586. They were grand-parents of Henry Fleet who emigrated to Virginia. See this Magazine II, 71 &c, V, 253, 254.
John Fleet, whose will follows was evidently son of a citizen of

Worcester, since he leaves his father's portrait to that city. William and Katherine (Honeywood) Fleet had a son Thomas, possibly father of this John.]

JOHN FLEETE, of Hallowe, co. Worcester, Esq.
  Dated 20 Oct. 1618.

Codicil 28 Dec. 1618
Proved 16 Feb. 1618-19

To be enterred in the parishe churche of St. Ellyn in the Citie of Worcester.

And as concerning the greatest parte of my Landes Tenements and Leases, the same are already passed and Conveyed at the marriage of my Sonne THOMAS and I doe confirme and corroborat the same.

To my sonne THOMAS FLEETE, one silver Bason and Ewer etc., which were given unto me by my Father Mr. THOMAS FLEETE.

To my sonne JOHN FLEETE, my lands, meadowes, and pastures lying in the parishe of St. Johns in Bedwardine, co., Worcester called Colewicke or Colemans Land. Also my Lease of Rouckswood Farms, he paying yearlie out of the profitts thereof, unto my neiphue RAFE TWIGFALL, £5. Also my Lease of St. Hellens Harbor, with the meadowe thereunto belonging and one other meadow adjoining graunted by my Cosin Mr. ROBERT STEYNOR, and now in the occupation of JOHN SMYTHE. Also one parcell of grounde lying neere Perry wood, co. Worcester, called Ryngswood als the Harp.

To my Daughter ANNE ACTON, one silver salt

Whereas I have before my marriage, conveyed unto my Brother in lawe EDWARD BOUGHTON of Litle Lawford in Co. Warwick, Esq., and others my Lease of Perry Courte, neere the City of Worcester for the benefitt of my wife. Now yf my wife shall decease before the expiracon of the said Lease then the Residue unexpired shall remain to my said Sonne JOHN FLEETE.

Residuary Legatee & Sole Executrix: ANNE, my wife.
THOMAS DANFORD; EDMOND COWLINGE; THOMAS PENSON; JOHN SMYTHE; Witnesses.

Parker 18.

Codicil dated 28 Dec. 1618.

To my Grandchilde, ANNE ACTON, £50 to be paied unto her at the age of Seventeene yeres.

To my Godsonne, JOHN ACTON, £10.

To my daughter ANNE ACTON, her other two Children, £5 a peece, to be paied unto them at the age of twentie and one yeres.

To my Grandchilde, JOHN FLEETE, £5 to be paied at like age.

To my Sonne in Lawe, Mr. THOMAS ACTON, £10.

To my Brother Mr. EDWARD FLEETE, 40s.

To my Sister COWCHER and my Sister MITTON, 40s. a peece.

To my Neiphues Mr. THOMAS NASHE, Mr. THOMAS FLEETE, Mr. THOMAS COWCHER, Mr. JOHN COW-CHER & Mr. JOHN NASHE and to my Neece Mrs. MARY HALL 40s. each to make them Rynges.

To my Cosins Mr. THOMAS HALL & JANE wife of Mr. ROGER FARLEY, 40s. apeece to the same Intent.

To the City of Worcester, my Father's Picture and my owne picture to be set up over the "Tollsey" of the said Citie amongst the other pictures there.

To the anncient Clerke, WILLIAM YOUNGER, £3. 6. 8d.

To my servant THOMAS DANFORD £5.

To my servant JOHN PERKINSON, 40s.

To my servant GEORGE JACKMAN, the "Estraye" Mare and Colte which he tooke up at Ridmarley.

To my servants, THOMAS PENSON & EDWARD COW-LINGE, 40s. apeece.

To my servant, JOHANE BIDLE, £10.

To the poore of Hallow, 40s.

JOHN PARKINSON
GEORGE JACKMAN
THOMAS DANFORD
Witnesses

Proved 16 Feb. 1618-19 by the Sole Executrix named.

Parker 18.

VIRGINIA GLEANINGS IN ENGLAND

Contributed by Reginald M. Glencross, 176 Worplee Road,
Wimbledon, London, S. W. 20, England.

(Continued from XXX, 367.)

14 Nov. 1640. Admon. of JANE BARHAM of p'ish of Lin-
sted, Arch. Cant. Widow to Richard B. son of dec.

"Lodovicus" (Lewis) Lee of p'ish of Eastlinge, Kent, gent
& Charles Barham of city of Canterbury, innholder, *bondsmen.*
£40.   *Canterbury Archdeaconry A. B.* 34, 3.

[A number of wills of the Kentish family of Barham, to which
Anthony Barham of Virginia undoubtedly belonged, have been printed
in this series.]

Admon. 30 Oct. 1641, of ROGER EPPS of p'ish of Elmested,
Archd. Cant. to brother William E.

Bondsmen John Soones of p'ish of Elmested, co. Kent, yeoman & Edward Cloake of same, yeoman.

28 Oct. 1641. Ellen Epps widow relict of above, renounced.
Archdeaconry of Canterbury, A. B. 34, 66.

[The Virginia family of Eppes, Epps, Eps, bears the arms of the
Kentish family of the name. The name of Francis Eppes, the emigrant,
has not yet been found in the wills so far examined.]

Admon. 14 Mar. 1642-3, of DUDLEY SENTLEGER of St. Johns
in Isle of Thanet, Archd. Cant., gent., to Anne S. widow of dec.

Bondmen: Geo. Crayford of Middle Temple, London, Esq.
& Jo. Quilter of St. John's af's'd yeoman, in £800.
Canterbury Archdeaconry, A. B. 34, 132.

[Dudley St. Leger was no doubt the person of the name who was
the brother of Ursula St. Leger, wife of Rev. Daniel Horsmander.
He was probably ancestor of Capt. Dudley St. Leger, of Deal, who
was a friend of the first William Byrd during his visit to England.]

From Vol. XXXI, No. 2 (April 1923), p. 164.

Mr. John Bayne of Virginia bur. at St. Nichs., Liverpool, Dec. 1700.

Justinian Cooper died in Virginia. P. C. C. Admon. 18 Sep. 1655, to uncle William C. only next of kin.

[For a note on Justinian Cooper, of Isle of Wight County, Va., see this Magazine XXI, 63. His will dated March 26, 1650 is of record in Isle of Wight and an abstract has been printed in this Magazine.]

Nicholas Dickson, formerly of York Town in Virginia but late of Bristol, dec. P. C. C. Admon. 20 Apr. 1770, to relict Charlotte D., widow.

Simon Keich *of Virginia*. P. C. C. Admon. 22 Aug. 1655, to relict Sarah K., widow.

John Kidby in ship "Providence" coming from Virginia. P. C. C. Admon. 3 July 1655, to relict Joan K., widow.

Richard Low of Virginia, bachelor. P. C. C. Admon. 13 Sep. 1655, to Jane Allen *als.* Low, mother of dec.

Edmund Ludham of Ratcliff, but died at Virginia. P. C. C. Adm. 26 July 1655, to relict Margaret L., widow.

Robert Parsons of James Frigate, in Virginia. P. C. C. Admon. 19 June 1655, to mother Sarah Butler *als.* P.

William Rogers of Truro, Cornw., widower. P. C. C. Admon. 17 Nov. 1733, to Isaac Milner, attorney of Robert R., only bro. & n. of k. of dec., now residing at Virginia in America.

Ludovic Rowzee of Virginia. P. C. C. Admon. 16 July 1655, to John Catlett, half brother of Ralph R., now resident in Virginia, eldest son of dec., late of Ashford, Kent, to use of sd. R. R. & of Edward & Martha R., all children of dec., now beyond seas.

[Dr. and Mrs. W. C. Stubbs of New Orleans, La., in their genealogy of the Catlett family (included in their *History of Two Virginia Fam-*

ilies), printed from the Canterbury marriage licenses, one dated Sept. 19, 1626, for Lodowick Rowzie, of Ashford, Doctor of Physic, bachelor, aged about 36, and Sarah Catlett, of St. Peters, Canterbury, widow, aged about 24, relict of John Catlett, late of Sittingbourne, gentleman. Col. John Catlett, her son by the first marriage, came to Virginia, and gave the name Sittingbourne—now in Essex—to the parish in which he settled. His half brothers and sister, Ralph, Edward and Martha (perhaps mistake for Sarah) Rowzie came to Virginia with him. The family of Rowzie, Rowzee or Rowzey was long resident in Essex and has now many descendants in various parts of the county. For a short notice see *Two Virginia Families,* p. 98.]

RICHARD WILLIAMS of Limehouse, but died at Virginia. P. C. C. Admon. 3 July 1655, to Susan Stocke, aunt & guardian to Richard, Jane, Anne, Mary & Stephen W., minors, children of dec. during minority.

EDWARD AISKLEY of Ratcliff, but died at Virginia. Adm. 18 Aug. 1656, to James Shawe, curator of Elizabeth A., minor, only child of dec.

MARY BLISSE of Virginia. Adm. 7 Nov. 1655, to Martha Ward *als.* B. (wife of John W.) sister of dec.

RICHARD BURTON of Virginia, bachelor. Adm. 23 Oct. 1656, to Elizabeth Vaughan *als.* Cooke (wife of Hugh V.) & Martha C., spr., sisters of dec.

MARY HARRIS als. CRUMPE of Virginia. Adm. 12 June 1656, to Martha Jennings (wife of John J.) daur. of dec.

HENRY EDWARDS in ship "Dove" at Virginia. Adm. 10 June 1656, to Christopher Goulding, cousins german & n. of k. of dec.

SAMUEL FRY, bachelor, died in Virginia. Adm. 2 Mar. 1655-6, to mother Anne F., widow.

ROBERT GAYLARD of Virginia, bach. Adm. 24 Apr. 1657, to mother Mary G., widow.

EDWARD HANNYFORD of Virginia. Adm. 28 June 1656, to relict Marchebell H., widow.

JOHN HUMPHREYS of Haniton, Devon., but died in Virginia. Adm. 2 Sep. 1656, to bro. Henry H.

WILLIAM OWEN of Limehouse, but died in Virginia. Adm. 26 Oct. 1655, to Anne Bascombe, guardian of William O., minor, only child of dec., during min.

ANTHONY RICHARDSON of Limehouse, but died in Virginia. Adm. 11 Sep. 1656, to relict Sarah R., widow.

DANIEL SALTER in ship the "Seven Sisters" going to Virginia. Adm. 24 June 1656, to Avis Nutt (wife of John N.) sister of dec.

ROBERT TAYLOR of Stepney, but died in Virginia. Adm. 21 Oct. 1656, to Sarah Bidmore als. T. (wife of John B.) relict of dec.

FRANCIS TOWNSEND in States service at sea, bachelor. Adm. 5 Sep. 1653 to bro. Richard T.

[It was thought, when a copy of this Adm. was asked for, that he might be the son of Richard Townsend of Virginia. Richard Townsend had, however, only two sons, Robert of Stafford Co., Va., and Francis, who removed to London, where he died. Richard Townsend died in or before 1652, when his son Francis obtained a regrant for part of his land. As Rd. Townshend of Va. had no son Richard, the Francis of the text could not have been the son of that name, who lived in London.]

VIRGINIA GLEANINGS IN ENGLAND

Contributed by Reginald M. Glencross, 176 Worplee Road, Wimbledon, London, S. W. 20, England.

(Continued)

SIR HENERY WYATTE of Alington, co. Kent, knight.

Will undated. To be buried in church of Mylton besides Gravesend near Dame Anne my wife. My chantry at Mylton to continue as I ordered in book of foundation. My son Thomas to ensure to sd. chantry priests all such lands in Kent & Essex of which they now take profits. Sd. son also to assure following annuities for services rendered viz, to Cervase Franke 10 marks, to George Multon 4 marks, to Christopher Dyconson 40 s., to Edward Westlye 20 s., to John Sayvell 20 s., to Edward Fatersalk 20 s., to Arthur Loffekyne 40 s., and to John Mores the baillywick which he now occupies—all for life. Son T. to pay to Henry Sayvell during life of his mother 5 marks. To Henry Lee yearly during marriage £10, same to Robert Lee his brother 10 marks yearly during marriage to find him to school. To Walter Hendley, gent., for good counsel 5 marks yearly for life. Right Hon. Thomas Lord Cramwell, my son & heir, Thomas W., & Walter Hendley gent. to be exo'rs. To sd. Lord Crumwell cup with mine arms. Same to sd. W. Hendley.

Proved 21 Feb. 1537-8 by Thomas Wayatt an ex'or Power reserved to the other ex'ors.

Adm. c. b. a. Feb. 1559 to Edward Warner, knight, & Dame Eliz. his wife, d. b. n. a. by sd. ex'ors. & on 17 July 1576 grant to George Wyat next of kin dec.

[The father of the poet. See below.]

From Vol. XXXI, No. 3 (July 1923), p. 237.

ALLINGTON CASTLE

From a view made about 1840.

FRANCIS WYAT of Boxley Abbey, co. Kent, knight.

Will dat. 6 Aug. 1644. To poor of p'sh of Boxley, Kent, £60, of Sowthfleete £4. Whereas there is now owing me several sums of good value but how far forth they may prove good & sperall debts I know not, if on payment of same my personal estate exceed £500, excess to my son Edwyn & my dau'r Elizabeth W. viz. 1-3 to my son & 2-3 to my dau'r. As to lands, to my son Edwyn, for life, my lands called the Gasses (100 acres) now in occup'on of John Parish, tenmt. 62 acres called the Harpe in same occup'on. My lands sometime in occup'on of Christian Sayer & now of sd. J. Parish, 60 acres sometime in occup'on of John Gouldsmith & now of sd. J. Parish, 5 acres, sometime in occup'on of Robert Smith now of sd. J. Parish, lands called Shawes (provost-Ruffe) (?) & Redpitt woods, in my own occup'on, my house etc (4 acres) sometime in occup'on of John Stockwell now of Thomas Newman, house & lands (11 acres) now in occup'on of Robert Gubberd, formerly of John Johnson, all in p'shes of Boxley & Milford (& ? Alisford). Whereas some part of the premises are conveyed & assured to my neice Eleanor Wyat for securing £125. 10., my son Edwyn to pay same. My manor of Boxley & lands purchased therewith from Mr. Stephen Alcocke in p'ishes of Boxley & Alisford, to my wife Dame Margaret W. for life. From deaths of my wife & son, all to my eldest son Henry W. in tail male in default to my youngest son Edwyn in tail male, in default to me & my heirs. Sd. wife & son Henry to be ex'ors. Sd. wife to be a stay to our children in their nonage. Sd. son Henry to have obedience to his mother & love to his brother & particularly his sister. My friend Francis Fynch of Inner Temple London esq. to be overseer & to him a 40 s. gold rong.

Witnesses: John Davy, Jo. Francke, James Birkbecke, Tho. Tomlyn.

Probatum 24 Sep. 1644 euramentis Dominae Margaretae Wyatt viduae relictae et Henrici Wyatt arm. filii dicti def't executorum.

Canterbury Archdeaconry, 70, 640.

[Sir Francis Wyatt, Governor of Virginia. See below.]

ELLINORA WYATT.

Will dat. 1 Jan. 1648. To be buried as my uncle & aunt Sir Nathaniel Finch & Dame Elizabeth his wife think fit. To my cousin Henry Wyatt esq. son of my uncle Sir Francis W. dec. 20 s. ring. To my cousin Mr. John Wyatt son of my uncle Hante W. clerk, dec. £40. To my cousin Mrs. Anne Wyatt, dau'r of my uncle Hante W. clerk, £50. To my cousins Mrs. Ursula Hary 20 s. ring etc. To my cousin Mrs. Phebe Moyle 20 s. ring. To my friend Mrs. Katherine Sidenham 20 s. ring & to Elizabeth Coke, servant to my sd. uncle & aunt Sir N. & Dame Finch 40 s. To my sd. uncle & aunt power to receive moneys on bond due to me & they to see this will fulfilled.

No Witns.

Adm. s. t. a. 25 July 1649 to Dame Elizabeth Finch relict & ex'trix of Will of Nathaniel F. knight dec. uncle & trustee to the sd. Dame E. F. named in Will of E. W. of Covent Garden, Middx., dec. No ex'or being named.

Fairford, 32.

[Eleanor Wyatt was probably the Eleanor Wyatt baptized at Boxley, 1624, a daughter of Henry Wyatt, A. M., who was a brother of Sir Francis and Rev. Hawte. At the time the will was made it is probable that Edward and George, the other sons of Hawte Wyatt, had come to Va. See below.]

HENERY WYATT of Boxley Abby, co. Kent, esq.

Will dat. 12 July 1653. As to land in Boxley &c. Kent, mentioned in indre-tripartite dat. 18 June 1649 beliv. me 1 pt. Dame Jane Duke late of Maidstone widow dec. 2 pt. & Jane Duke one of the dau'rs. of Sir Edward D. Knt. dec. 3 pt. which lands are now assured to sd. Jane Duke my now wife for her life. Sd. lands to her in fee. As to manor of Poole & Poole Wood in p'rshes of Southfleete & Stone, these to my wife for life, remainder to my sd. (sic) dau'r. Frances W. in tail, in default to my sd. wife in fee. My farm called Mates in tenure of Henery Kettlewell, in p'rshes of Southfleete, Swanscombe & Stone, to sd. wife for life, remainder to sd. dau'r F. W. in fee. Lands heretofore mortgaged by Sir Francis W., Knt., my late father, dec., to John Warner, citizen & grocer of London for

626

£500 by indenture dated 31 Act. 1635, my interest therein to my sd. wife for life, remainder to sd. dau'r in fee. If my wife be now with child & it be a son, all land bequeathed to my dau'r. to go to such son in tail, but if it be a dau'r. lands to be divided between sd. 2 dau'rs. To poor of p'rsh of Boxley £5. All goods to my wife Jane W. & she to be ex'trix.

Witnesses: William Dixon, Richard Duke, John Goddin.

Proved 5 Mar. 1654-5, by Jane W., relict & ex'trix.

Aylett, 342.

[Henry Wyatt, son of Sir Francis. See below.]

JOHN WYAT of Boxley, Kent.

Will dat. 27 Apr. 1656. Ex'or my bro. George W. To my wife Elizabeth if she be with child £70, but if it die £50. To my son Stephen £50 at 26. To my son William £30 at 24. To my dau'r. Mary £30 at 20. To wife £10 at my death & £20 in a year et. To Maryan Rogers 20 s. Rest of goods to my bro. George W. to bring up all my children by my first wife. To my dau'r Mary & my son William, sheets etc. Things my last wife wrought as her chest, I give to her. *Testator made his mark.*

Witnesses: Henry Day, Sarah Becket, William Case.

Proved 11 June 1656 by George W. bro. & sole ex'or.

Berkeley, 224.

[This John Wyatt cannot be identified in the pedigree. He was probably descended from some younger son.]

EDWIN WIAT, of the manor house of Boxley, Kent, sergeant at law.

Will dat. 13 Nov. 1713, aged 83. To be buried in Chancel of p'ish Church of B. afsd. My manors etc. are already settled by Deeds on the marriage of my sons Edwin W. & Francis W. Whereas there is a mortgage lease for securing £1,100 on estate fo Sir Thos. Taylor, Bt. made to Anna Gertruy Crispe, my wife's sister, which is vested in my wife Frances W. & her sister & much interest due to sd. wife as ex'trix of sd. A. G.

SIR THOMAS WYATT, POET

Crispe for payment of legacies. My wife knows I have paid such legacies up to £500. Sd. wife with £500 to buy lands to be settled on my dau'r. in law Elizabeth Wiat for her life, remainder to my son Richard W. in tail male, remainder to my son Francis W. in tail male, remainder to my sd. wife Frances in fee. Rest of mortgage money to be paid as by sd. Will of A. G. Crispe, on Maria Adriana Breton & Christopher Clapham. To my sd. dau'r. Elizabeth wife of my son Edwin W. £20 for mourning (she a widow). To sd. M. A. Breton £20. To her husband Richard B. £10. To Sir Edmond Andros £10. To Sir Robert Marsham, Bt. & his Lady, Sir Tos. Palmer, Bt. & his lady, Brooke Bridges, esq. & his Lady & Sir Henry Selby, rings. To my son Francis W. my father's & mother's pictures &c. & £30 for mourning for himself & wife. To my son Richard W. £20 for mourning. To poor of Boxley £10. To my wife Frances W. in fee, my lands in p'ish of St. Olave, Southwark, mortgaged by Friamore Sparke, gent. for £900, my Chambers in Inner Temple & all goods & she to be ex'trix. Sd. sons F. & R. to be dutiful to their mother.

Witnesses: Jane Leche, Dorothy Leche, Anne Leche.

Cod. dat. 8 Sep. 1714. I have now purchased lands in Boxley value £20 a year for £380, I devise same (36 acres) in occup'on of William Champ & John Saunders, & messuage now divided into two, in occupate of Richard Medhurst & Thos. Coxe to my dau'r. Elizabeth W. for life, remainder to my son Francis W. for 60 years if he so long live, remainder to his sons successively in tail male, in default to my son Richard W. for life remainder to his sons similarly, in default to my wife Frances W. in fee. Devise of lands in St. Olave, Southwark, revoked & same to son Richard in fee, he paying his brother Francis £100. Tenements in Boxley in occupation of Mrs. Elizabeth Charlton charged with annual payment of two marks.

Witnesses: John Gore, Eliz. Gore, Thomasin Gore.

Prob. 22 Feb. 1714[-5] by Frances W. relict & ex'trix.

Fogg, 37.

[Sir Henry Wyatt, of a Yorkshire family, was a Lancastrian and resisted the accession of Richard III to the throne. He was imprisoned in the Tower for two years, and, according to his son, was racked in the presence of Richard himself. There was a family tradition that while in prison he was saved from starvation by a Tower cat, who brought him a pigeon each day. Lord Romney, the representative of the Wyatts, has a portrait of Sir Henry, seated in a prison cell with a cat drawing towards him a pigeon through the bars of a window. The biographical sketch in the *Dictionary of National Biography* calls attention to the fact that this portrait represents an old man and must have been painted long after the period of the alledged event.

On the accession of Henry VII, Henry Wyatt was released and admitted to the Privy Council and was one of the executors of that King and guardians of Henry VIII. He was admitted to the Privy Council by the new King in April 1509 and became Knight of the Bath on May 23rd following. He accompanied Henry to the Field of the Cloth of Gold and was in the vanguard at the Battle of the Spurs (August 16, 1513). He purchased in 1492 the castle and estate of Allington in Kent which Henry VIII visited in 1537. He married Anne, daughter of John Skinner, of Reigate, Surry and died March 10, 1537. He had issue: Thomas, Margaret who married Sir Anthony Lee, of Quarendon (and was mother of Sir Henry Lee, K. G.), and Henry, whose descendants were settled in Essex (England). The son, Sir Thomas Wyatt, the poet, was born in 1503 and died Oct. 11, 1542. His seat was at Allington Castle. "Undoubtedly the leader and the acknowledged master of 'the company of courtly' makers who, in the reign of Henry VIII, under Italian influence transformed the character of English poetry. He took a bachelor's degree at Cambridge at 15, was knighted in 1536 and was twice sent as ambassador to the Emperor (Charles V) a strong proof of his repute as a statesman and diplomatist" (*Encyc. Brit.*) He was constantly employed in Henry's service and was apparently in high favor; but was sent to the Tower in 1536, perhaps because it was desired that he should incriminate the Queen, Anne Boleyn, whom he had known from childhood. He was released in the fall of that year. In March 1537 he was knighted. In 1541 he was again imprisoned in the Tower on the old charges; but made an eloquent and manly defence and was released in a few months. He married Elizabeth (who married secondly, Sir Edward Warner), daughter of Thomas Brooke, 3rd Lord Cobham (whose home Cobham Hall, Kent, is still one of the most beautiful places in England), and had a son Sir Thomas Wyatt (born 1530), of Allington Castle, which with Boxley Abbey, Kent, he inherited from his father. From 1543 to 1545 he had a command at Boulougne. In 1554 he joined the conspirators who combined to prevent the marriage of Queen Mary with Philip of Spain. He led a force of Kentishmen to London and entered the city; but his attempt failed and he was captured, imprisoned in the Tower and beheaded on April 11, 1554 and his estates confiscated. He married Jane, daughter and co-heiress of Sir William Hawte or Haute, of Brune, Kent, and had a number of children: George, Richard, Charles, Arthur, Henry, Jacosa, and Ursula, most of whom are said to have d. s. p.

George Wyatt, eldest son of Sir Thomas was restored to his estate of Boxley by Queen Elizabeth in 1570. He married Oct 8, 1582, Jane, daughter of Sir Thomas Finch, of Eastwell, Kent. He died in Ireland and was buried at Boxley Sept. 1, 1624. He had issue: 1. Francis; 2. Haute; 3. Henry "A. M. and minister," buried at Boxley Nov. 10, 1624. (Eleanor "daughter of Henry Wyatt, gent," was baptised at Boxley, Sept. 1, 1624); 4. Thomas, baptized at Boxley, March 4, 1603; 5. Ann, baptized at Boxley, Sept. 7, 1611; 6. Eleanor, married Sir John Finch.

SIR THOMAS WYATT, THE YOUNGER

Sir Francis Wyatt, of Boxley, eldest son of George Wyatt, was born 1588, matriculated at St. Mary Hall, Oxford July 1, 1603 and at Grays Inn 1604. He was knighted July 7, 1618. Sir Francis Wyatt was recommended for the position of governor of Virginia by the Earl of Southampton who stated that he "was well reported of in respect of his parentage, good education, integrity of life and fair fortune." He was Governor of Virginia from Nov., 1621 to Aug. 26, 1625, when a new commission was issued to him and he continued in office until Sept. 18, when he received permission to go to Ireland where his presence was required by business consequent upon the death of his father. He was again Governor of Virginia from November 1626 until February 1641. He was buried in the family vault in Boxley churchyard Aug. 24, 1644. He married in 1618, Margaret, daughter of Sir Samuel Sandys, of Ombersley, and neice of Sir Edwin and George Sandys. The latter died at Boxley. "Copies of letters of Sir Francis Wyatt, with particulars of the history of his family are in the volume of Wyatt MSS. now the property of the Earl of Romney." (*Dict. Nat. Biog.*)

Sir Francis Wyatt had issue: 1. Edwin, Recorder of Rochester, Burgess for Maidstone, etc., who married Frances, daughter of Thomas Crispe, of Quex, Kent. All his children *di s. p.* (His will is given above) ; 2. William, born July 22, 1621 ; 3. George, born Sept. 8, 1620, *d. s. p.;* 4. Henry, married Jane, daughter of Sir Edward Duke, of Copington, Kent; 5. Elizabeth, married Thomas Bosville, of Little Mote, Kent.

Rev. Haute or Hawte Wyatt was born 1594, matriculated at Queens College, Oxford, Oct. 25, 1611 and was a student at Grays Inn. He was minister at Jamestown during his brother's first administration and returned to England with him; served Marston Chapel 1639, became Vicar of Boxley 1632 and died July 31st, 1638. He married 1st, Elizabeth,—who died Oct. 31, 1626, and 2nd, Anne, who died Feb. 1631. By the first marriage he had: 1. Edward; 2. George; 3. Thomas, who was buried at Boxley, April 10, 1627. By the second marriage he had; 4. Anna, baptized Feb. 19, 1631; 5. John. Of these Edward and George came to Virginia and have many descendants. In the church at Boxley is a mural monument erected by Edwin Wyatt (who died in 1714) to the memory of several members of his family. The epitaph names Rev. Hawte Wyatt, and states that he "had issue now living in Virginia."

For notices of this and other families of Wyatt in Virginia see this Magazine, III, No. 2, VII, No. 1, and *The William and Mary College Quarterly* II, No. 3, III, numbers 1 and 2; VI, No. 4; X, numbers 1 and 4; XII, numbers 1, 2, and 4; XVII, No. 1.]

ANTHONY WYATT of p'sh of St. Bartholomew the Great, London, merchant.

Will dat. 4 July 1644. To my sister Margaret (Dingles?) 40 s. To my sister Alice Bradshaw 40 s. To my sister Katherine Smith 20 s. To my kinsman Henry Newton, the eldest son of Francis N. gent 40 s. To John Newton, brother of sd. H. 40 s. To Elizabeth Newton their sister 40 s. To John Math-

ews, brewer, my tenant, 30 s.   To John Troman, my servant
40 s.   To poor of p'ish of St. B. afsd. £5.   The sd. p'ish owes
me much more.   To my son Anthony all lands & goods & he to
be ex'or.   My friend John Dansie, gent. to be overseer & to him
£3.6.8.

Witnesses: John Reeve, James Holmes, Scr(ivener).

Prob. last day of Feb. 1644[-5] by Anthony W. son &
ex'or.   *Rives*, 58.

[The son Anthony Wyatt, named in the will, may possibly have
been the Anthony Wyatt who came to Virginia and settled at "Chaplain's Choice," Charles City (now Prince George) County.   He was
a member of the House of Burgesses 1645, 1653, and 1656.   In the
William & Mary Quarterly X, 261-263, is an account of some of his
descendants who lived chiefly south of the James and Appomattox
Rivers.   The will of a Francis Newton, of London, grocer, bound in
voyage to Virginia, was proved Jan. 11, 1661-2.   He was long engaged
in trade with Virginia.   If he was the person named in the will, his
friendship with Anthony Wyatt, Sr., might have influenced the son
to come to the Colony.

VIRGINIA GLEANINGS IN ENGLAND

Contributed by Reginald M. Glencross, 176 Worplee Road, Wimbledon, London, S. W. 20, England.

(Continued)

CHARLES YEO, of Harton in p'ish of Hartland, Devon.
Will dat. 1 Oct. 1650. To repair of church of H. 20s. To poor there £3, to godchildren 12d, to my cousins Richard Yeo, Charles Yeo, Hugh [and?] Justinian Yeo, Deborah Yeo & Mary Yeo sons & daurs of my bro. Justinian Y. dec. £3 a piece. My son in law William Squire & Deborah his wife, my dau'r. & heir; my exors shall at request of Richard Yeo afs'd lease to him messuage in Harton afs'd wherein my sd. bro. Justinian (*sic*) lately dwelt, from termination of present lease for 99 years if 3 lives to be nominated by sd. R. so long live, at old rent. To my cousin Charles Yeo afs'd. cloke. To sd. Justinian Yeo suit of apparell. To each of the children of my bro. Hugh Yeo 20s. gold ring. To the daur. of my sister Anne 5s. pair of gloves. To each of my sisters in law Mrs. Jane Squire, Mary Isaac & Jane Yeo & also to my cousins Ann Cholwell, Jane Colwell, Ellinor Page & Wilmouth Isaac 5s. pair of gloves. To each of the children of my bro. Peter Isaac dec. that shall be unpaid of their father's legacy at my death 20s. To my cousins Thomas Pruot of Noltacott & Thomas Cholwell of Luttford 20s. gold ring a piece. To my cousins Laurence Deyman of Mockadon & Zachary Deyman 10s. gold piece a piece. To my grandchild Margaret Squire £5 etc. at 21. To my grandchild Deborah Squire £50 etc. at 21. To Nicholas Dennys of Barnstaple esq. & Thomas Prust afsd. my fourth part of messuages & lands in Ermandesworthie in Chemstow . . . . my sixth part of lands in Chemstow, for 1,000 years for use of sd. W. & D. Squire & her heirs. To Margery May 3/4. To servants of my son in law

W. Squire 5s. Rest of goods to sd. W. & D. Squire & they to be exors. *Witnesses*: Tho. Chollwell, Law. Deyman

Strike out name of my cousin Jane Yeo. I gave her certain houses in reversion of her mother for her life

Cod dat. 21 Oct. 1653 of my daur. D. die in life time of son in law W. Squire & sd. W. have a second wife & has issue male by her son that his lands in Parracombe called Foldhayes may not descend to Margaret & Deborah my granddaurs. then to sd. granddaurs £50 a piece on birth of such son. *Witnesses*: Wm. Squire, Edward Poole, Hugh Deyman. Proved 16 Feb. 1654-5 by William Squire & Deborah his wife the exors.

Aylett, 229

[The name Yeo or Yea was numerously represented in Devon, Somerset, etc. The will of George Yeo (published in this magazine XXIX, 39, 40) seemed to indicate the ancestry of Col. Leonard Yeo, of Elizabeth City county. The will of Charles Yeo, given above, undoubtedly gives a clue to the ancestry of Hugh and Justinian Yeo, of Northampton county. About 1649 Hugh Yeo appears as a merchant in Accomac and Northampton counties. In the records of Northampton, 1681, is a reference to Justinian Yeo, of Harton in the parish of Hartland, Devon, brother of Hugh Yeo. Later Justinian Yeo came to Virginia.]

WILLIAM ANDREWES of p'ish of Cote in the parish (*sic*) of Bushopp, Cannings co. Wilts.

Will dat. 16 May 1712. To Elizabeth Andrews of Cote in the p'ish of Bushopp Cannings, Wilts. £50. To my uncle Nicholas Nash his daur. now the wife of Edward Browne £20. To my uncle Nicholas Nash £10. To my aunt Nash £5. To my bro. John A. £5. Rest of my personal estate equally among the children of my uncle Nicholas Nash, Hester, Mary & William N. To poor of Cote £5. My uncle Nicholas Nash & Elizabeth Nash to be ex'ors & ex'trix. *Signs* Wm. Andrews. *Witnesses*: Francis Gilbert, Thomas Skipp, Prescott Pennyston.

Proved 7 Dec. 1721 by Nicholas Nash one of the ex'ors. Power reserved for Elizabeth Nash the other ex'or.

Adm. c. b. a. 19 Aug. 1726 to Hester Brown *als.* Nash one of the resid. legatees named in the will of W. A. late of Cote in p'ish of Bushops Canning Wilts but died in the parts of Virginia a bachelor d. b. n. a. by Nicholas Nash one of the ex'ors.

Buckingham, 215

ROBERT AYLETT, Doctor of Law, Master in Chancery.

Will dat. 28 Jan. 1654. To be buried in Church Yard at Much Braxsted in Essex, place to be designated by Sir Benjamin Ayloffe. My copyhold tenement in Fering, Essex, called Clobbs, to Thomas A. younger son of my late brother dec., in fee. Rest of my copyholds, according to my promise, I leave to descend to William A. my sd. brother's eldest son. Rest of estate, real or personal (except my wife's plate etc. she brought to me, being a widow, which I here declare to be her's) to sd. wife Penelope & she to be ex'trix. If she die before Probate or without naming an ex'or, then John Aylett, my kinsman, third son of my sd. brother to be ex'or. Cloaks & gowns to Sir Benjamin Ayloffe, my brother Eltonhead, Will Aylett, Thomas Juell, & John & Robert Aylett. *Witnesses*: Benjamin Ayloffe, Will Ayloffe, Jo. Sanders. Prob. 22 Mar. 1654[5] by Penelope A. relict & ex'trix.

Aylett, 236

[On account of the destruction of records in the counties where the Virginia Ayletts lived, it is difficult to trace the early generations. So far as any record evidence is concerned the family seems to begin with William Aylett, sheriff of York county 1674. There is, however, a tradition that the emigrant ancestor was John Aylett, a Royalist, who fought at Worcester and then fled to Virginia. The late Col. W. W. Fontaine found, before the Civil War, at the old Aylett home in King William county, a series of letters purporting to be from Sir William and Sir Benjamin Ayloffe, to John Aylett, of Virginia, who was son of the first and brother of the second. The originals have been lost; but Col. Fontaine's copies remain. There is no question that Col. Fontaine did actually find and copy these letters. The doubt is whether the originals were genuine or whether they were written by some one, at a date far later than appears on the face, simply for the amusement of the writer and his family. The chief points in favor of their authenticity are the considerable knowledge shown in regard to people and places in Essex, (Eng.), though, of course, much of which knowledge could be gained from books, and the other favorable point is that the letters had never been made public and no attempt made to create any additional prestige for the family. The principal objection is, plainly, that they are "too good to be true." The supposed writers of the letters give to John Aylett detailed accounts of events in which he took part; but which he would have known of much better than any one else. This is a not uncommon, but awkward device in such compositions. Still, though, any critical reader will seriously doubt their genuineness, the letters may be what they claim and a minute examination in regard to the Essex of this time and especially of the neighborhood of Braxted Magna may sustain them.

Fictitious family narratives are not uncommon in Virginia. An instance is the alleged narrative by the sister of Governor Spotswood's wife. This account makes the two Brayne sisters come to Virginia on the same ship with Alexander Spotswood, when he came to this colony. The writer of this account did not know that Governor Spotswood did not marry until after the expiration of his long administration, and that he met and married Miss Brayne in London. Another of the same type is the story of the wife of John Lewis of Augusta county.

The Ayloffes, Ayliffes and Ayletts of Essex, seem to have been members of a large family, which spelt the name in various ways.]

THOMAS CODDE of Yaldynge co. Kent diocese of Roff [Rochester].

Testament (in Latin) dat. 11 Oct. 1494. To be buried in churchyard of SS Peter & Paul of Y. af's'd. Pr'ous bequests to Y. & West Fawley. To godchildren 6d. each. Rest to my wife Elizabeth to bring up our children. Sd. wife & Richard Trittisham of West Farley, gent. to be ex'ors. Witnesses: "Domino Nicholas None clerico, Thoma. Godyng et multis alus"

Proved 1 Dec. 1499 by ex'ors in will named.

Horne, 35

JOHN CODDE of Ealdyng co. Kent, dioc. Roff. [Rochester].

Testament (in Latin) dat. 7 Feb. 1502. To be buried in churchyard of Apostles Peter & Paul of E. afs'd Pious bequests. To godchildren 4d. a piece. To my dau'r Joan £5 etc. To my dau'r Margaret £5. To my dau'r Agnes 6 marks. To my dau'r Alice 6 marks etc. To my dau'r Isabella £5 etc.

637

Rest of goods to my son Thomas & he to be ex'or. Witnesses:
"Domino Nicho None vicario de Ealdyng, Stephano Nasshe,
Johanne Boold et alys."

Will (also in Latin) of same date to my son Thomas, land
& farm in Ealdyng & Merden for £4 rent & after portions
to children are paid, to him house in which I now live & lands
thereto, also lands lately John Cratfords & meadow lying in
the Denne, all in fee. To my son Robert lands called Bre-
nyngbis Borislands le Risshetts (a meadow in the Denne excepted) in fee. To my son William lands called Asshlakes
& Mellers mede, in fee.

Proved 4 May [1503] by ex'or.

Blamyr, 27

[These Coddes or Codds were early members of the family of
Codd, of Pelicans, Kent, from which came St. Leger Codd of Virginia and Maryland. Several wills of members of the Kentish family
of later dates have been published in this magazine. Yalding and
Ealdyng are different forms of the same name. The earlier Codds
seem to have been substantial "yeomen of Kent," who rose to the
ranks of the gentry about the end of the 16th century.]

FRANCIS EMPEROUR of city of Norwich tobacco merchant.

Will dat. 6 Jan. 1654. To my wife Dorothy, lease of my
house I now dwell in, in parish of St. Saviours, Norwich,
for life & then "Edmond my youngest son & Hannah my
dau'r towards their bringing up & the disposing of it & then
by my ex'ors" (*sic*). To my eldest son John E. £10. To my
son Robert E. £5. To my youngest son Edmond E. £10 at
21. To my dau'r Mary wife of John Bland £5. To my
youngest dau'r Hannah £15 at 20. To my grand child John
Bland £5 at 21. To my sister Susan Lane 5s. To Alice Phillipps 5s. Robert Allred of city of Norwich, schoolmaster, to
be ex'or. Rest of goods to my wife Dorothy. Ex'or to have
20s. for his pains. S'd wife to be supervisor. *Testator made
his mark. Witnesses*: John Bland X, James Reader, Penn
Thurston her mark.

Prob. 5 Apr. 1655 by Robert Allred of city of Norwich, school-master, ex'or in trust named.

Aylett, 350

[In the 16th and 17th centuries there was in Norwich a large family, driven out of the Low Countries by Spanish rule, whose members, originally named Keyser, were turned into Lempereur and Empereur. Francis Empereur, born about 1628, came to Lower Norfolk County, Va. about 1650. An account of his descendants was published in this Magazine in Vols. XXI, XXII, XXIII. A "tobacco merchant" would have been in touch with Virginia, and no doubt the testator, above, was really related to Francis Empereur, of Lower Norfolk.]

THOMAS FAWNE.

Will dat. 25 Dec. 1651. To Robert Williams, chirurgeon, of the ship 'Peter' a watch etc. To my servant William Martin his passage to Virginia & freedom there etc. To poor of Skendley parish, Lincolnshire, 40. To Mr. Hatch, woollen draper, £9. To Mr. Cragford £7. To Thomas Dagger, chest to my father, a pair of silver fringed gloves etc. To my mother, two rings. To Mr. Murrell, gloves etc. To Mr. John Richards gloves, Doctor Presson book and the Life of the Fathers. To Mr. Corbin two holland shirts etc. To Matt Johnson crimson pair of silk stockings. To my bro. Robert my rapier. To John Younge & John Stone whom I have appointed my ex'ors, all debts due to me in Virginia & disposal of all my estate now shipped in the 'Peter,' the return whereof is to be divided among my brothers & sisters whereof Mrs. Frances White is to have one part. To the seamen two cases of drams. *Witnesses*: John Richards, James Furoby.
Prob. 17 Aug. 1652 by John Young, one of the ex'ors. Power reserved to John Stone the other ex'or.

Bowyer, 220

ANNE FINCH, DECEASED.

William . . Archbp. . . . to Charles Norris of Staple Inn in p'ish of S. Andrew Holborn, London, gent. greeting. Whereas it was alleged . . . on part of John Atwood, Alexander Bunyan, Francis Goater, Everard Levitt, Clerk, & Mary Levitt *als,* Doyley (wife of s'd E. Levilt) & Abraham Nicholas, that Philip Finch owing s'd Atwood, F. Goater & M. Levilt (then M. Doyley widow) £133. 11. 8. did with s'd A. Nicholas as his Security enter into a Bond dat. 20 Sep. 1722 of £268 for paym't to sd. J. Atwood. Sd. P. Finch afterward married Ann Cudlip, widow, & in her right became entitled for her life to certain lands keys & landing places in Gaveton als. Gawton in p'ish of Tavistock Devon, then held by Ralph Pike, or at least to an annuity of £24 payable thereout by sd. R. Pike. Sd. P. Finch by Deed Poll dat. 13 Jan. 1723 demised to sd. J. Atwood & A. Bunyan the sd. prem'es & all copper ore therein, in trust inter alia, to discharge s'd £133 11. 8. And whereas it was further alleged that sd. R. Pike soon after dying & Ralph P. his only son, heir at law & admor, refusing to pay sd. yearly sum of £24, sd. prem'es to sd. J. Atwood & A. Bunyan with sd. F. Goater E. & M. Levilt and sd. A. Nicholas exhibited their Bill in Exchequer against sd. R. Pike, P. Finch & Ann his wife, John Cunningham Saunders son & heir of Jacob S. dec., John Edgcombe & William Condy exors. of Will of sd. Jacob Saunders, Robert Edgcombe & Prothesia his wife the relict of sd. Jacob Saunders to compel them to pay sd. rent & arrears. And whereas it was moreover alleged that since, viz. in Feb. 1732 sd Ann Finch died intestate at East Love co. Cornwall & that no Admon has been granted of her goods & further proceeding cannot be had in the cause afsd. on that account sd. Philip Finch her husband now resides in Virginia, so that he cannot be personally served as by an attestation of sd John Atwood of St. Clements Danes Midd'x appears. Admon therefore to thee Charles Norris . . . . Limited to attend the sd suit. Dat. 16 May 1734.

P. C. C., A. A. B., May, 1734

[In 1782 families of the name Finch lived in Charlotte, Mecklenburg, Halifax, New Kent and Stafford.]

VIRGINIA GLEANINGS IN ENGLAND

Contributed by Reginald M. Glencross, 176 Worplee Road, Wimbledon, London, S. W. 20, England.

(Continued)

WILLIAM SYDNOR.

Will dat. 29 Oct. (*sic*) to be buried in Black Friars at Ludgate. To high altar of my parish church of St. Patryk (*sic rectius* Petrock) in Exeter 3s. 4d. My wife to have place she dwelleth in. Sd. wife Joan to have my house in Norgate Street, Exeter, the sign of the crown, valued at 26s. 8d. a year, for life, remainder to our children. To my eldest son Richard S. £40. To my daur. Elizabeth to her marriage £40. To my son Thomas by Joan my wife, on her death, 5 marks yearly in land in Egerton & Bowton [to Kathryn my daur.—*in margin*]. To my son Richard rest of my lands in Egerton & Bowton. To my son Paul £40, he to be in keeping of my ex'ors to lawful age. To my brother Sir Thomas Egerton, Canon of Leeds in Kent £10. To my brother Maister Sir Richard Sydnor silver cup. To my sister Margaret £10. To Roger Sweetornden £10. To each of my brother Swettornden's children 10s. 40. To church of Egerton, white vestments value £10. Rest of goods to my wife & she to be ex'trix. My brother M. Sir Richard Sydnor to be ex'or. *Witnesses*: Sir Thomas Draper, Clerke; Richard Wydder, Salter of the p'ish of All Hallows, Breadstreet & Edward Dormer, haberdasher in same p'ish & others.

Proved 26 Feb 1514 [5] by Master Sydnor ex'or [no mention of Joan. R. M. G.]

Holden 4

[The Paul Sydnor, son of this testator was probably the man of the name who had a grant of the advowson and Vicarage of Brenchley, Kent, in 31st Henry VIII. William Sydnor the testator though he lived in London and was possibly a native of Exeter owned lands at Egerton and Boughton in Kent. See also this Magazine XXX, 44. This family probably removed about 1563 to Suffolk and Norfolk, and later descendants returned to Kent.]

JOHN BANYSTER of London grocer

Will dat. 3 Dec. 1653. I have formerly given £500 a piece & more to my two eldest dau'rs., Mary Crossman & Ann Short to advance them in their marriages which was to the full of my estate, & on latter dau'r my farm & manor called Boones (?) co. Essex from my death. To my youngest dau'r Margaret B. in fee my farm called Softmans (?) in p'ish of Canwedon co. Essex. To my 2 dau'rs Mary Crossman & Margaret B. in fee, remainder in my freehold lands called Colemans in Witham, Folborne & Rivenall co. Essex on death of my sister in law Florence Baldwyn late wife of Alexander Banyster, equally. To my sister Susan Brooks 40s. a year for life. To my cousin John Brookes £5. To my cousin Anne Banyster £5. To my friend Mr. Hancock & his wife 20s. a piece. To my cousin Cressener 50s. To my maid-servant Joan 40s. To my grandchildren & to my godsons Edward Cressener & [blank] Mawdett & to my cousin George Cressener & his wife £30 a piece out of my estate in the Barbados Island. To Mr. William Gore £3. Rest of estate in sd. Island to my 3 dau'rs Mary, Anne & Margaret equally. Rest of goods to my 2 dau'rs Mary Crosseman & Margaret B. equally & they to be exetrices. *Witnesses*: George Stanley, Arthur Hollingworth, G. Cressener, Abraham Stephens.
Prov. 6 Jan 1653 [4] by Mary Crosseman & Margaret B. dau'rs & extrices.

Alchen 37

[As there was frequent intercourse between Virginia and Barbadoes it is possible that the testator was of the same family as John Banister, hte Virginia Naturalist.]

HENRY HERBERT of Cowlebrooke co. Monmouth, esquire

Will dat. 14 Mar. 1654. Whereas on conclusion of my marriage with my wife Mary, my father William H. esq. on

15 May, 1637 conveyed so much of manor of Hardwicke, Monmouthshire, as he was then owner of & all his other lands in H., little thereon to use of me & my wife M. for lives, sd. wife to have same for life. Since sd. 15 May, I have purchased in fee lands in H. afsd. part of John Parry esq, William Johns & John Bennett & one tenement called Skybor Adam etc some time the land of Thomas Parry which I had by will of my aunt Margaret Powle dec., all these & ten'm't. called the Spitty in p'ish of Bergavenny all yearly rent of £64. 13s. to sd. wife M. H. for life. Capital Messuage called Cowldbrooke, capital messuage called Dawkins, my manor of Lanthewy Rotherch & all lands in Bergavenny, Landilor, Pertholy, Lanthewy Rotherch, Lanwenarth, Lanover, Lanellen, Glascoode etc. co. Monm. reversion of my manor of Hardwicke etc given to my wife for life, from her death, to my son James H. in tail male, in default to my issue male in tail male, in default to my brother William H. in tail male, in default to my brother Thomas H. in tail male, in default to my brother Charles H. in tail male, in default to my right heirs, but sd. premises to my friends & trustees Evan Seyse of Bowerton co. Glamorgan esq., Thomas Hughes of Moynscourt co. Monm. esq., Edmund Jones of Lansoy in sd. co. esq. Edward Herbert of Magors Grange sd co. esq., & Walter Morgan of Landilor Portholy in sd. co esq. for 11 years from my death on trust to pay to my son James H. £80 a year or if he die to my other issue male. To my 3 daughters Katherine, Priscilla & Elizabeth £1,000 a piece at marriage or 16 & £40 a year apiece meanwhile & on every 15 Jan (not being Lord's day) to meet with accounts. Whereas I have conveyed lands in Hardwicke etc for payment of £50 yearly during life of my brother in law Lawrence Rudyerd & of £800 on his death payable now only (my brother in law William Rudierd being deceased without children) to Elizabeth, wife of my uncle Matthew Herbert & to my wife M. equally, being legacies given to them by my mother in law Mary Rudyerd deceased by will whereof I am executor; now to sd. trustees lands in p'ish of Bergevenny & Landiloe Pertholy, Monm., which I bought of my cousin John Jones since

dec., now in possession of Hugh Watkin John at £52 rent & also parcel of land in Bergevenny purchased of Richard Tue, at £2-10. rent, for 50 years, on trust to pay Mr. Richard Reade & Master Matthew Herbert £50 a year during life of sd. L. Rudyerd & on his death, to pay to sd. E. Herbert her share of the £800. To poor of Bergevenny £10, to my servants 40s. a piece. To my bro. William H. £20, to his daur Elizabeth H. £10. To my sister Jones £5. To my brother Thomas H. £5. To my brother Charles H. £10. To sd. trustees £5 a piece. To my wife Mary H. morety of household goods etc £100. She to live at Cowldbrooke during minority of my son James H. Other morety to sd. son J. H. at 21. Legacies given to my sd. son J. H. & my dau'rs K. & P. by their grandfather William H. & their grandmother Mary Rudyerd to be paid them. To my brother in law Lawrence Rudyerd 40s. To my uncle Matthew Herbert 40s. To his wife Elizabeth H. 40s, my aunt Powle 40s, my aunt Anne Pownall 40s, my aunt Jane Lewis 40s, my uncle John Herbert 40s all for rings. Annuity given to last by my father for his life out of tithe of Lanthewy Rotherch held by lease to be paid. To my aunt Atye my aunt Parker 40s. a piece for rings. My wife & my brother William H. to be ex'ors. Sd. trustees to be overseers. Rest of goods between my sd. wife & 3 daurs. *Witnesses*: Thomas Quarrell, Nicholas Bound, Anthony Potter, Susanna Cardiffe.

Proved 23 July 1656 by Mary H. the relict & William H. the brother, the ex'ors.

Received original will 23 Feb 1656 [7] for exors. Robt. Cattle.

Berkeley, 267

[In the Blandford Churchyard, Petersburg, Va., is a tomb, removed from "Puddledock", Prince George county, bearing arms and crest and the following inscription:

"Here Lyeth Interred the Body of
IOHN HERBERT Son of Iohn Herbert
Apothecary and Grandson of
Richard Herbert Citizen & Grocer
of London who departed this Life
the 17th day of March 1704 in the
46th year of his Age."

The arms and crest on the tomb are the same as those borne by Sir Richard Herbert of Colbrook, youngest brother of William, 1st Earl of Pembroke. Making the ordinary allowance for generations, Richard, grandfather of John Herbert of Virginia, would have been born about 1598. Dr. Lyon G. Tyler has cited the *Visitation of London*, 1634, which shows that William Herbert, of Colbrook, Co. Monmouth, had issue: 1. William, of Colbrook, eldest son (father of Henry Herbert, the testator); 2. Thomas; 3. Matthew, of London, draper, 1634; 4. Richard; 5. John; 6. Cecil; 7. Dorothy; 8. Jane; 9. Margaret; 10. Katherine, wife of Henry Powell. Henry Herbert names his Aunts Margaret Powell, Anne Pownall and Jane Lewis and Uncles Matthew and John Herbert. Dr. Tyler makes the very probable conjecture that another uncle, Richard Herbert, who was living at the *Visitation* of 1634; but probably dead in 1651, was the grandfather of John Herbert of Virginia.]

ROBERT GOOCH of Earsham co. Norfolk, esq.

Will dat. 14 May 1653. To my eldest son Leonard G. in fee my manor of Dubbells in Earsham afs'd. all lands in Yarmouth, Norfolk, Heddenham Norfolk (in occupon. of Fairehead now in Randalls occupation). To my 2 son Robert G. in fee my manor of Weston in Weston co. Suffolk, capital messuage called Weston Hall & lands in Weston Ringfield, Shuckefeild, he to pay to my son Philip at 22, £200 all this in satisfaction of legacies other than the household stuff left for him according to his grand father's Holnes Will, he not to contend with rest of his brothers & sisters, to join lovingly with his brother Leonard to help all other young ones his brothers & sisters. To my son Clement G. in fee, my lands in Ditchingham & Brome which are not already settled on him, lands in Bungay are his already. To my eldest dau'r. Elizabeth G. £400 (beyond that Lease already hers which lease is for £400 more. To my daur. Anne & 2 younger brothers Clement & Philip to share. To my dau'r. Martha £600. To my son Philip £200 more. Ex'ors to look after their younger brothers and sisters. If any of them willfully overthrow themselves in marriage or otherwise against wills of her brother Leonard & Robert, that son or dau'r to lose half legacy. Sd. eldest son Leonard G. to be ex'or. To sd. son Robert G. lease of a farm in Weston late in Williams' occupation mortgaged by Mr. Kempe for £200 & to take all profits between Mr. Kempe junior & me on the release of Mr. Wally & his

wife to my sd. son R. in Weston Hall which was by covenant
to have been procured in a year after the purchase of Weston
Hall, so more is due from Mr. Kempe son of Mr. K. dec.
who first made the mortgage to me. To son Leonard household stuff here & half my books & other half to my son Robert
especially the French Law Books. My son Robert has sufficient househo ldstuff from his grandfather Holnes will. To
my servants William Micleburgh 20s. & others 10s. each. Rest
of goods to my son Leonard & he to be ex'r. [Memorandum
15 Nov. 1652 & 14 May 1653 as to surrenders & additional
legacies & children.] *Witnesses*: [William Carvell, Christopher Jaye 1652] Will Mickleburgh, Roger Turner, Clement
Gooche, Ralphe Jaye X. To my sister in law Anne Warner
£10 7 Dec 1654.
Prov. 13 June 1655 by Leonard G. son & exor.

Aylett, 280

Rorer Gooch of city of Norwich, gent.
    Will dat. 22 Sep. 1656. To poor of p'ish where I shall
die 20s. To poor of p'ish of St. Lawrence, Norwich 20s,
of St. Michael of Costany in Norwich 20c, of Respham co.
Norfolk 10s, of Hackford near Reepham afsd. 10s, of Howe
co. Norfolk 5s. To my wife Martha my freehold & charter-
hold copyhold & customaryhold messuages & lands in Cardeston, Reepham, Hackford, Whitwell, Howe, Brooke & Porringland Norf. for life, thereafter as follows: to my dau'r.
Frances G. 4 acres called Moregate meadow which I late purch'd of one Breese, & all lands in Hackford, Reepham &
Whitwell now in occupation of George Smith, in fee & rest of
lands in Cardeston, Reepham, Hackford & Whitwell afsd. to
my son Edmund G. in fee. To my son Thomas G. lands in
Howe, Brooke & Porringland, in fee, from death of my wife
M. Sd. wife to pay to sd. son Thomas G. £10 yearly. To
sd. son Edmund G. £100. To my dau'r. Frances G. £100.
Whereas I have with my wife M. & son Edmund G. sold
certain houses in p'ishes of St. Laurence & St. Gregory Nor-

wich to Martin Cumber since dec. on condition for payment of several sums of money & whereas one of the sums is to be paid in 1659. Now I bequeath sd. £105 (sic) to sd. son Edmund G. or (if sum not paid) the sd. houses. To my servant Grace Cubitt 40s. Rest of goods to my wife Martha G. & she to be extrix. *Witnesses*: Roger Smith, Grace Cubitt X, Anne Fovie.

Prob. 6 Dec 1656 by Martha G. relict & extrix.

Bulkeley, 449

[The family of Gooch was at one time quite numerous in Norfolk and Suffolk. Governor Sir William Gooch, was son of Thomas Gooch, Alderman of Yarmouth. Major William Gooch and Lt. Col. Henry Gooch lived in York Co., Va., in the latter part of the 17th century. See note on Governor Gooch in this magazine.]

CHRISTOPHER GREENEHOW of Grisdall in p'ish of Graistocke
    Will dat. 16 Aug. 1644. To Agnes Hyne £3. To Thomas Scott & Christopher Scott my nephews 40s. to either at 21. Rest o fgoods to my brother Richard G. & he to be ex'or. *Witnesses*: John Bancke, John Crosthwait.
    Prob. 28 Sep. 1653 by Richard G. brother & ex'or.

JOHN GREENHOW of Murray in p'ish of Graistocke, Cumberland, yeoman.
    Will dat. 18 May 1653. To be buried in p'ish church yard of G. To my brother William G. & his son George G. 20s. To my brother in law Richard Greenhow, Richard & Christopher 20s. To my brother in law John Bristow two sons John & Thomas being turns 20s. To my brother in law William Jacke his son John Jacke one lamb. To everyone whom I am godfather unto male & female 12d. To Hugh Johnson half bushel of rig. To John Gardhouse same. To Thomas Renoldson of Penrith one peck. To Richard Bristow's wife 1s. To Elizabeth Cowman 1s. To my son James G. husbandry gear. To my wife Mabel & my son James G. afsd. rest of goods & they to be ex'ors. Supervisors William Jacke,

John Bristow both of Berriar. *Witnesses*: William Jack X, William Greenhow X, John Brown X.
Prob. 24 Aug. 1653 by Mabel G. relict & James G. son, the ex'ors.

Brent, 91

RICHARD GREENHOUSE of Water in Mungrisedale in p'ish of Graiesbacks co. Cumb. yeoman
Will dat. 3 Nov. 1655. To my eldest son John Greenhowe husbandry gear so that my wife have to serve her necessaries during widowhood. To sd. son John G. 20 sheep at age of 15. To my dau'r Agnes G. £30 at 21, if she die before, same to my dau'r Margaret G. at 21, if she die before, same to my 2 sons Richard & Christopher. My wife Jennett G. to have her widow right of my tenement according to custom of this manor & a third of my goods. Rest of goods to my 3 children Richard, Christopher & Margaret & they to be ex'ors. If wife be with child same to have its portion. Tho. Greenhowe and William Greenhowe and Edward Greenhowe to be overseers. *Testator made his mark.* Christopher Walker, Richard Strickett, Christopher Buckburrowe.
Adm. c. t. a. 26 June 1656 to Thomas Greenhow, William Greenhow & Edward Greenhow, testamentary curators to Richard, Christopher & Margaret G. children & ex'ors of dec., to their use & during their minority.

Berkeley, 229

[The Greenhows or Greenhalghe (as was an early spelling) seem to have lived in several different counties in the north of England, Cumberland, Lancashire and Westmoreland. Those whose wills are given above were Cumberland men. The branch from which John Greenhow (1724-1787) the emigrant to Virginia came, has been traced to his grandfather, John Greenhow, gentleman, 1650-1733) who was buried at Harwich Chapel, Lancashire. Robert Greenhow, father of the emigrant, removed from Lancashire to High House, Stainton, near Kendal, in Westmoreland. See *William and Mary Quarterly,* VII, 17; XVII, 273-275.]

VIRGINIA GLEANINGS IN ENGLAND

Contributed by Reginald M. Glencross, 176 Worplee Road, Wimbledon, London, S. W. 20, England.

(Continued)

JOHN LANIER, of Camerwell, co. Surrey, gent.

Will dat. 21 Nov. 1616. To be buried in chancel of Camerwell church near my mother in law Mrs. Marke Anthony Galliardello. To my wife Mrs. Frances L. messuage and tenement called Suttie Campes co. Cambridge for life. To her household stuff for life. If she can before her death provide the sums of £40 a piece for my 3 sons viz. Marke Anthony, John & Francis, she to have all goods absolutely, otherwise, at her death, goods to be equally divided between my 3 s'd. sons. To my 2 daur's. viz. to Lucretia £50, to my dau'r. Elizabeth £50—both being due by bond from my son Nicholas L. gent at their ages of 18. To sd. 2 daur's £10 a piece more. To my son Nicholas 40s. for piece of plate. To my dau'r. Judith wife of Edward Norgate, gent. 40s. for plate. For poor of C. afsd. 10s. To my servant Katherine Robinson 6s. 8d. My wife Frances L. to be extrix. Overseers my friends Mr. Edward Wilson, vicar of Camerwell, Mr. Peter Danson, vicar of Cashalton & Mr. Henry Harper. *Witnesses*: Henry Harper, Roger Buford.

Proved 21 Dec. 1616 by Frances L. releict & extrix.

Cope. 124.

[See wills of John Lanier (1650), and Elizabeth Lanier (1652), with note in this Magazine, XXVII, 340-342. The John Lanier whose will is given above is the man of the name noted in the third paragraph of the note on p. 341.

Mr. George Cole Scott, of Richmond, whose wife is descended

From Vol. XXXII, No. 3 (July 1924), p. 260.

from the Laniers, has made some investigation in regard to the English family and contributed the following note. It is evident, however, that Graves was mistaken in stating that Nicholas Lanier, born 1588, was son of Jerome Lanier. The baptismal register and the will here printed show that he was son of John Lanier. Walpole made the same error, Whether the family was from France or Italy may be uncertain; but beyond doubt the most distinguished Nicholas Lanier was born in England.]

"In the notes on the Lanier family published in the *Virginia Magazine of History and Biography* (Vol. XXVIII, pages 341 and 342) and in Tyler's *Historical Magazine* (Vol. III, pages 282-287) it is briefly assumed and probably correctly, that all the American Laniers are descended from a common English ancestry, but it is further stated that the English Laniers were of French origin. An investigation, however, of such authorities as are available does not bear this out.

The Laniers of England from the time of Queen Elizabeth through the reign of Charles the second were of more or less prominence at court as musicians and painters and their lineage should not be difficult to trace.

The "Dictionary of National Biography" states them to be of French descent emigrating from near Rouen. J. F. D. Lanier in the notes on his family (privately printed, second edition 1877) states his family were originally French Huguenots from Bordeaux. Sidney Lanier in appendix to the same publication states the Laniers to have originally been French Huguenots which is repeated in the "Encyclopedia Brittanica" in the article on Sidney Lanier.

From an investigation, it would appear that they were not of French origin, but Italian. The most prominent of the family at the court of Charles the first was Nicholas Lanier. His portrait was painted by Vandyke and again by Livensz, both of which were engraved. He was sent abroad by the King to purchase works of art and was a musician of note and is easily identified. Grave's *Dictionary of Music and Musicians* states that Nicholas Lanier was the son of Jerome Lanier, who emigrated with his brother Nicholas from Italy.

"Bryan's Dictionary of Painters and Engravers" also states that Nicolo or Nicholas Laniere was a native of Italy. Horace Walpole in his "Anecdotes of Painting in England" says Nicholas Lanier was born in Italy and in his article on Vandyke gives certain distinguishing marks that were put on paintings and drawings of the King and the Earl of Arundel, and in an edition published with additions by Rev. James Dalaway there is a foot note by him "These marks are on the drawings, often accompanied by the name of the master written in a very fine Italian hand by Nicholas Lanier, who in the early part of his life was employed both by the King and Lord Arundel to purchase paintings and drawings in Italy."

650

Now Horace Walpole was a dilettante in literature, but his "Anecdotes of Painters" was compiled from the manuscripts of Virtue (now in the British Museum and so far as known have not been published) of whom he says in the preface to the "Strawberry Hill Edition."

"Mr. Vertue had for several years been collecting materials for this work: he conversed and corresponded with most of the virtuosi in England: he was personally acquainted with the oldest performers in the science: he minuted down everything he heard from them. He visited every collection, made catalogues of them, attended sales, copied every paper he could find relative to the art, searched offices, registers of parishes and registers of wills for births and deaths, turned over all our own authors, and translated those of other countries which related to his subject. He wrote down everything he heard, saw, or read. His collection amounted to near forty volumes, large and small."

"One satisfaction the reader will have, in the integrity of Mr. Vertue; it exceeded his industry, which is saying much. No man living, so bigoted to a vocation, was ever so incapable of falsehood. He did not deal even in hypothesis, scarce in conjecture. He visited and revisited every picture, every monument, that was an object of his researches; and being so little a slave to his own imagination, he was cautious of trusting to that of others. In his memorandums he always put a quere against whatever was told him of suspicious aspect; and never gave credit to it till he received the fullest satisfaction. Thus whatever trifles the reader finds, he will have the comfort of knowing that the greatest part at least are of most genuine authority. Whenever I have added to the compiler's stores, I have generally taken care to quote as religiously the source of my intelligence."

Be the Laniers originally French or Italian would not seem difficult to positively settle if one had access to original records in England. But the evidence certainly seems in favor of Italy, and until it is proved to the contrary it would seem safe to leave it so rather than trust to the bare statement in the "Dictionary of National Biography," or the family tradition of their French Huguenot origin.

GEORGE COLE SCOTT."

THOMAS LANDON, of Monington Stradle co. Hereford.

Will dat. 28 Mar. 1614. To church of Vowchurch 20s. To chapel of Monington apd 5s. To my brother John L. 6s. 8d. To my sister Anne 6s. 8d. To my sister Johane 6s. 8d. To my sister Margaret 6s. 8d. & 2 ewes. I forgive my father Roger L. debts. To my sd. father & my mother use of one black cow in hands of John Charles. At death of survivor sd. cow to such of my children as survivor shall appoint. To godchildren 12d. a piece. To my dau'r. Johane £60 at 20. To my son Thomas L. £20 at 18. To my son John L. £20 at 18. Last £100 to be delivered to my cousin Henry Phelpotts gent, to give profits to my wife Anne for life. To my wife Anne rest of goods during widowhood, if she marry again, half the goods to her & the other half of my 4 children william, Thomas, John & Johane equally. Table board, etc. after my wife's death to William L. my son & heir. Sd. wife Anne to be extrix. *Witnesses*: John Greene, Henry Phelpott, David ap Hughe, Hoell Watkynne, Roger Landon, William Seyton? Simon Williams.

Proved 5 July 1614 by Anne relict & extrix.

Lowe, 79.

[Most of the information in regard to the Landons, which is in print, has been compiled by Mr. C. P. Keith, author of *The Ancestry of Benjamin Harrison.* Thomas Landon, of Middlesex County, Va. (who died in 1701) was formerly of Credenhill or Crednal, Herefordshire, and was son of Silvanus Landon, of St. Martins-in-the-Fields, Middlesex, Eng. gent. Silvanus was probably son of John Landon, yeoman of the wine cellar to James I and Charles I. Mr. Keith conjectures with great probability that Thomas, of Cridenhill, afterwards of Virginia, was the kinsman Thomas of Credenhill named in the will dated Feb. 6, 1679, of "Thomas Landon, of Monington Stradell in the parish of Vowchurch, county of Hereford, gent." This last named Thomas must have been the son of Thomas, the testator above.

The will (1632) of Benedict Landon, younger son of a Lancashire family was printed in this Magazine, XX, 179, 180. See *Ancestry of Benjamin Harrison*, 88, and this Magazine, II, 430-433.]

WILLIAM SIDNOR

Sentencia pro confirmatione testamenti et codicilli Willelmi Sidnor defuncti.

Auditis meretis negotii testamentarii sine approbacionis testamenti Willelmi Sydnor . . de [blank] in Com. [blank] in diocese Norwici . . inter Willelmum Gwen, curatorem ad lites Thomae Sydnor parlem agentem ex una et Willelmum Sydnor, Franciscum Sydnor, Paulum Sydnor et Edmundum Sydnor executores testamenti antedicti W. S. partes contra quos . . ex altera.

Ideisco Nos dictum W. S. testamentum fecisse pronunciamus.
Dat. 13 June 1616.

P. C. C. *Cope,* 55.

———————————

[Thomas, William, Francis, Paul and Edmund Sydnor, were probably
the children of William Sydnor, deceased, of the diocese of Norwich,
whose will and codicil were in question. Francis Sydnor, whose will,
1653, was printed in this Magazine, XXX, 44, may have been the
Francis named above, and it is highly probable that William Sydnor,
of the diocese of Norwich, named above, may have been the same
person as William Sydner, Esq., of Blundeston, Suffolk, alive 1573,
who was a son of Paul Sydnor, of Brinckley, Kent, 1542. In this
Magazine, XX/II, 175, is the will of William Sydnor (1514) who had
a son Paul. Francis Sydnor, (will 1653) names a kinsman Fortunatus
Sydnor. A Fortunatus Sydnor was the emigrant to Virginia.]

VIRGINIA GLEANINGS IN ENGLAND

Contributed by Reginald M. Glencross, 176 Worple Road,
Wimbledon, London, S. W. 20, England.

(Continued)

WILLIAM HOPKINS.

William—Archbp., etc., to James Hopkins brother of William H., late of Virginia; but in pish of St. Dunstan in the
West, London, bachelor dec. greeting. Whereas sd. W. Hopkins (as is alleged) made his will & left same in Virginia
and is since dead. Grant of Admon. therefore, to you until
original last will or an authentic copy thereof be brought
to the Registry. Ruth Hopkins widow, the mother first renouncing.

Dat. 12 Feb. 1734[5].

P. C. C., A. A. B., Feb. 1734-35.

[In volume I, pp. 122, 123, of the *Virginia Historical Register* for
July, 1848, is printed an account of William Hopkins, an eminent
member of the Virginia bar, taken, originally, from "Sir John Randolph's Breviate Book."

"In a few Days afterwards [in Dec., 1734] in London died William
Hopkins, Esq., who had practice in this Court about 12 years and
in that Time by hard Study and Observation he made a surprising
Progress; became a very ingenious Lawyer and a good Pleader, tho'
at his first coming he was raw and much despised. But he had a
Carelessness in his Nature, which preserved him from being discouraged,
and carried him on till he came to be admired. He had a good Foundation in School Learning, understood Latin and French well, had a
strong Memory, a good Judgment, a Quickness that was very visible;
and a handsome Person, all mighty advantages. But his manner
was awkward, his Temper Sower, if it was to be judged by the Action
of his Muscles; and was given, was too much given to laugh at his
own Discourses.

When he brought himself into good Business, he almost totally neglected it, which I believe was owing to a Desire of Dipping into all
kinds of Knowledge, wherein he had a great Deal of Vanity, and
prevented his Digesting what he had, so well as he would have done
otherwise. He had many good Qualities in Practice; was moderate

From Vol. XXXII, No. 4 (Oct. 1924), p. 351.

in his Fees; Ingenious and Earnest, never disputed plain Points, but was a candid fair arguer, yet he had a failing which brought him to a Quarrel with me. It was an odd Sort of Pride that would not suffer him to keep an Equilibrium in his own Conceits. He could not see himself admired, without thinking it an Injury to him to stand upon a Level with any other. And therefore tho' I was always his Friend, had done him many Kindnesses, and he himself thought himself obliged to me, He came into so ill a Temper, as not to allow me either Learning or Honesty; which broke our acquaintance, and after that I thought I discovered some Seeds of Malice in him. He died in the Flower of his Age, and may be justly reckoned a Loss to this poor Country, which is not like to abound (at present at least) in Great Geniuses."]

EDWARD BRAIE, of Shortmead in p'ish of Bigleswade co. Will dat. 1 Dec. 1612 Beds. [Bedfordshire]. My freehold ten'mt in Nether Calcote in occup'on of widow Browne in p'ish of Northill, Beds., to be sold, also freehold lands in Stratton Holme & Holmeside in p'ish of Bigleswade, Beds. To my second son William B. in fee 20 acres of freeh. land lately purchased of William Retchford & Nicholas Bray. To my eldest dau'r. Annys B. 100 marks at 21 or marriage, also £10 which was the gift of her grandmother Johan Angell. To my second dau'r. Mary B. 100 marks at 21 or marriage, also £20 which was gift of her grandmother John Angell. To my dau'r. Elizabeth Bray 100 marks at 21 or marriage & £10 more which was the gift of her grandmother Johan Angell. My eldest son Mark B. not to enter on copyhold lands till he be 21. To poor of Bigleswade 13s. 4d. & to Ringers 5s. To William Hunt, Edward Retchford & my godson Edwardes & my godson Luke my godchildren 2s. 6d. a piece & Edward Fisher & Edward Sawyer my godchildren 12 (£ or s?) a piece. To my man Thomas Luffe 5 s. & to my maid Elizabeth Lewis 5s. To my maid Annys Ancell 12d. Rest of goods to my wife Elizabeth & she to be ext'rix. My faithful uncle Clarke & cousin his son John C. & my friend John Smarte of Bigleswade to be overseers & to them 5s. a piece. If my wife refuse to prove will, my brother Robert Astwood to be exor. *Witnesses*: Robert Hinde, John Angell X, Thomas Luffe X.
Proved 5 May 1613 by Elizabeth Astwoode ext'rix. in sd.

will named. This was originally written "Johannis Astwood". "Johannis" was crossed out & "Elizabeth" substituted but "Astwood" left in error.

[The Probate Cert. book has a similar faulty correction. Both in Register and in Act Book is a note stating the correction was made in Oct. 1620, but there is nothing in the Act Book for Oct. 1620 referring to this testator.—R. M. G.]

Capell, 44.

[Edward Bray, of Biggleswade, was probably an ancestor, and certainly of the same family as Robert and Plumer Bray, of Lower Norfolk County, Va. See this magazine, XXVI, 280, for will of Edward Bray, of Biggleswade (1656) and note.]

ANTHONY BEHEATHLAND.

Sentencia condemnatoris in negotio Compoti bonorum Anthony Beheathland.

In Dei Nomine Amen. Auditis . . . per nos . . magistrum custodem . . . meritis . . negotii exhibitionis Inventarii . . bonorum . . . Anthony Beheathland nuper . . parochiae Sancti Martini iuxta Lowe in Com. Cornubiae . . quod coram nobis in judicio inter Georgium B. et Robertum B. fratres . . dicti defuncti partes . . promoventes ex una et Ursulam B. relictam et administricem . . . bonorum . . eiusdem defuncti partem contra quem idem negotium promovetur partibus ex altera . . . vertebatur . . . [Procurator dictae U. B. relictae et administratrices] exhibuit An account of U. B. relict & admix of goods . . of A. B. . . of G. M. by C. . . . gent . . . Nos . . . prenominatam U. B. non nulla bona . . dicti A. B. . . ex Compute . . . omisisse . . et . recipisse . . bona . . . extendentia . . ad suman £685 5s. eandem U. B. . . £147 . . per eam indisposita . . pronunciamus . . et condemnamus U. B. . . ad debitam . . solutionem earundem . . 12 July 1617.

Weldon, 73.

[TRANSLATION]

Sentence Condemnatory in the matter of an Account of the goods of Anthony Beheathland.

In the Name of God Amen. We the Master Keeper . . having heard the merits . . of the matter of the exhibiting of an account of the goods of Anthony Beheathland late of the parish of St. Martin by Lord Cornw. which depended before us in judgement between George B. & Robert B. brothers of sd. dec. plffs. of the one part & Ursula B., relict & admi'x of goods of same dec., deft. of the other part . . . [The proctor of sd. U. B. relict & admix] exhibited "An Account of U. B. relict & admix. of goods of A. B. of S. M. by L. . . . gent." We . . pronounce that the sd. U. B. has omitted some of the goods of sd. A. B. from the Account & has received goods amounting to £685. 5 & that the sd. U. B. has £147 by her undisposed of & we condemn the sd. U. B. to their due payment 12 July 1617.

P. C. C., Adm. Act Book, 1615-8, p. 22.

Anthony Beheathland of St. Martin by Lowe Cornw. (Exon.) Adm. 2 June 1615 to relict Ursula B.

22 May 1618 Caveat entered by Robert Beheathland for payment of £80 among the relations of the dec. according to the order of the Lord Judge.
[No further ref. in Calr. to 1618.]

[Members of this Cornish family were early in Virginia. See this Magazine, XI, 363. In 1628, Dorothy Beheathland, step-daughter of Lt. Thomas Flint, was living in Elizabeth City County. She had a grandmother then living in England. Robert Nicholson, of London, merchant, who owned a plantation in Warwick County, gave, in his will, dated Nov. 10, 1651, bequests to Mrs. Mary Bernard, of Warwick County, widow, and to her daughter, Beheathland Bernard. Rev. Thomas Butler, of Warwick County, in his will dated Nov. 20, 1636, made bequests to "Mr. Thomas Barnett" [Bernard] and to his wife, Mary. Their daughter, Beheathland Bernard, married, 1st, Major John Smith (whose real name was Francis Dade, and 2d, Andrew Gilson. See *William and Mary Quarterly,* XXIII, 292, 293.]

WILLIAM SHROPSHIRE of Chateulne co. Stafford, yeoman.

Will dat. 1 July 1612. To be buried in churchyard of Eccleshall. Whereas I have assured all my lands to my sons Simon S. & John S. in bail in default as I sh'd. appoint by will. Same therefore, in such default, to my 2 neices Tymysin

Brimer dau'r. of James B. late of Chebsic, Staffs. dec. & Johane his wife dec. & of [*sic rectus* to] Phillipp Smyth dau'r. of Roger S. late of Breisenhill in p'ish. of Haughton dec. & of Margaret his wife, in fee equally. To my son Simon S. 5s. as his child's part. Rest of goods to my son John S. & he to be ex'or. Dated at Chateulne afs'd. *Witnesses*: Wm. Iremonger, Walter Barbour, John Broughton jun. Proved 13 Feb. 1612-3 by John S. son & ex'or.

Capell, 13.

[It is not known whether the testator was ancestor of this Virginia family of the name, whose emigrant ancestor was a native of Wiltshire. St. John Shropshire, son of Oliver Shropshire, of Marlborough, Wilts., gent, matriculated at Magdalene Hall, Oxford, April 9, 1685, aged 19, and took his B. A. from Queen's College in 1688, as John Shropshire. St. John Shropshire (doubtless the same as the Oxford man) was minister of Washington parish, Westmoreland County, Va., in 1704. In this year he signed an address of the clergy to the Governor as *John* Shropshire. He died in 1718. The inventory of his estate filed in Westmoreland in that year includes "1 large book press" £4, and "a large library of books" £60. On Nov. 16, 1718, Elizabeth, widow of St. John Shropshire, stated to the court that he made no will. Her son, St. John Shropshire, offered for probate a nuncupative will, which was judged not authentic, and therefore the said Elizabeth and St. John were appointed administrators. Elizabeth Stonehouse in her will dated April 14, 1738 and proved in Westmoreland, Dec. 1, 1742, left her estate to her sons, St. John and Winfield Shropshire. Whether she was widow of Rev. St. John Shropshire or of one of his sons is not known. Walter Shropshire gave bond in Orange County Sept. 2, 1751, as guardian of John and Ann Shropshire, orphans of John Shropshire, deceased. Of course this John Shropshire may have had other children. John and Ann were the minors. A license was issued in Orange, Dec. 4, 1757, for the marriage of John Shropshire and Mary Part [portion of word illegible]. On Dec. 17, 1772, Walter Shropshire, of Craven Co., S. C., made a deed, recorded in Orange, to John Shropshire, of Orange County, Va. There is a marriage license, Orange, 1773, for Joseph Bain Johnson and Elizabeth Shropshire.

This is all the record evidence which has been noted. Doubtless a thorough examination of the records of Westmoreland and Orange would give more information.

The Shropshire family has scattered widely through the South and West. Their traditions as regard to the early generations of the family are so confused and contradicting as to be of no value. It should have been added to the record evidence given above, that on Jan. 1, 1778, William Shropshire of Henry County took the oath of allegiance.

An account, dated 1910, from Mr. Franklin Shropshire, of Leesburg, Ky., says, "My father, Col. B. N. Shropshire, was born in Bourbon Co., Ky., Nov. 8, 1798, his father Joe Shropshire was born in Clarke Co., Ky., who was a son of John Shropshire, a native of

Virginia, who afterwards settled in Clark County, Ky. John Shropshire's father was an Englishman."

The following account, dated 1910, is from Mrs. Laura D. Shropshire, Avon, Ky.:

"Record of the Shropshire family of Kentucky as handed down to the present generation by older members of the family.

Tradition says that John Shropshire migrated from England to Virginia and that his wife was a Miss Campbell from Scotland, but we have not the date of his arrival, but know it was far enough back for one or more of his grandsons to serve in the Revolutionary War several years, and his daughter (Mrs. Elizabeth Switzer) is supposed to be the only Daughter of the Revolution now in the state of Kentucky. The son of the above John Shropshire, also named John, migrated from Virginia to Kentucky some time between 1780 and 1790, bringing with him his wife, Mollie Porter Shropshire, eleven sons and two daughters, named as follows: Walker, Abner, James, William, Benjamin, John, Joseph, Jerry, Edward, George, Moses, Nancy and Betsy. Nancy married Lewis Smith and Betsy married Hawkins Smith, but the Smiths were not related by blood.

John Shropshire and his family settled in that part of Kentucky now known as Bourbon, Clark and Harrison Counties. The family is now a very large one scattered over a number of Western states and the Southern states, especially Texas.

The family of Benjamin Shropshire, who was our great grandfather.

Benjamin, son of John Shropshire was born in Orange Co., Va., 1763. Benjamin married Elizabeth Hoyle, of King George Co., Va., who was born July 3, 1767. To this marriage only one son lived. John Elliott Shropshire was born in Bourbon Co., Ky., March 19, 1795 and married Rebecca Hutchinson, also of Bourbon Co., Ky., who was born March 20, 1797.

The children born to John E. Shropshire and Rebecca Shropshire that lived to maturity were:

Augustus Shropshire, born Aug. 18, 1817, died 1896. James H. Shropshire, born May 21st, 1822-1903. Benjamin Shropshire, born March 24, 1826-1867. Augusta Elizabeth Shropshire, born Dec. 8, 1828-1884. Gabriella Rebecca Shropshire, born March 18, 1831-1862. John Samuel Shropshire, born April 23, 1833 and was killed as a Major of his regiment (in 1862) in a part of the Southern army sent to New Mexico.

James H. Shropshire, 1822-1903, was married to Lucy A. Ware in 1850. Lucy Arabella Ware, born 1830-1876. Their children were eight in number, but only five lived to be grown. John Clifton Shropshire, George Ware Shropshire, 1853-1853, Mary Ware Shropshire (Simpson), Nancy Ware Shropshire (Weathers), Ella Shropshire, 1858-1865, Katherine D. Shropshire (Field), James H. Shropshire, Jr., died in infancy, Laura D. Shropshire.

John Clifton Shropshire in 1882 married Sallie Kinnaird, of Fayette Co., Ky. Their only child was James Kinnaird Shropshire, 1884.- He married Nellie Shirley of Mt. Sterling, Ky. in 1904. Their children are: James Shirley Shropshire, 1906-; Lawrence K. Shropshire, 1909-.

Mary Ware Shropshire married James Madison Simpson in 1885 and their only living child is Laurance Shropshire Simpson, born 1888.

Nancy Ware Shropshire married William T. Weathers in 1887.

Katherine D. Shropshire married David I. Field, 1891. Their children are: Lucy Ware Field, 1891-; David I. Field, Jr., 1895-.''

An account from another source also dated 1910, follows:

"Winkfield Shropshire came to America from England as a missionary from the "High Church of England," about the year 1745. His wife came with him (she was a Miss Moore of Welsh descent) and settled in Va. They had thirteen children, eleven boys and two girls. Three of the sons lost their lives in the Revolutionary War in Va. Mrs. Shropshire also died in Va. Winkfield Shropshire moved from Va. to Ga. in 1780. He died in Oglethorpe Co., Ga., in 1798, and was buried on the "Academy Lands," being the first grave made on this plot of ground. His sons were named William, Winkfield, John, Joshua, Bartholomew, Walter and Spencer. (Names of four sons lost to memory.) Names of daughters, Penelope and Sally. Spencer Shropshire married Miss Frances Pollard of Halifax Co., Va., Jan. 8, 1800. Mrs. Frances Pollard Shropshire was a daughter of Mrs. Tabitha Collins Pollard (Collins being her maiden name). Spencer Shropshire with his wife also settled in Oglethorpe Co., Ga. They had six sons, Wesley, Joshua, Jacob, Seaborn, John and Monroe; two daughters, Cynthia and Malinda. Wesley Shropshire married a Miss Swanson. They had two sons, Jack and Francis Callaway. Francis Callaway married Miss Mary Wright, daughter of Hon. F. R. Wright, of Rome, Ga."

A member of the family entering in 1912 says:

Rev. William Shropshire, a native of Virginia, was educated in Europe and returned in 1740 with his wife Susan Collins, of Wales. She soon died, leaving a son, Alexander. Rev. William married 2d, Mary Edris Witherspoon, who died in one year, leaving a son, John Witherspoon Shropshire, whose descendants live in Aberdeen, Miss., Centa, Ala., and at Washington and Rives, Tenn. Rev. William married about 1743-44 Cynthia Winkfield of Henry Co., Va. [a county not in existence until about 30 years later] and died at the home of his son William Shropshire, Jr., at Washington, Wilks Co., Ga., in 1788. [The fact that there was a Winfield Shropshire in Westmoreland in 1738 makes this third marriage very doubtful—that is as to the name of the 3rd wife.] Winkfield Shropshire, son of Rev. William Shropshire, by his 3rd marriage, married, in 1770, Abigail Spencer Moore, widow of Frederick Moore of Westmoreland, daughter of John Spencer, of Cobham, Albemarle, and granddaughter of John Spencer, of Westmoreland. [There was a family of Moore in Westmoreland; but the name Frederick does not appear in any abstracts of wills. In Albemarle in 1781 John Spencer sold a tract of land on Moore's Creek.] Mrs. Shropshire died in Albemarle in 1779. The eldest son of Winkfield and Abigail Shropshire, Spencer Shropshire, was born in Fairfax County, Va., in 1774, and died at Cuthbert, Randolph Co., Ga., in 1833. Spencer Shropshire, youngest son, W. M. Shropshire, aged 95, now [1912] lives in Rome, Ga. Spencer Shropshire's eldest son, Wesley Shropshire, was born April 3. 1800, near Lexington, Oglethorpe Co., Ga., and died in Chatooga Co., Ga., aged 98 years and 0 months. (The account was from Wesley Shropshire's granddaughter, Mrs. W. C. Henson, of Cartersville, Ga.).

This same lady gave an account, evidently traditional, that Rev. Wm. Shropshire was born in Va. about 1708 and after the death of his father, Rev. St. John Shropshire, went to England with his mother "Marie de Sarentine," widow of Lewis de Sarentine of France. [As Rev. St. John Shropshire's widow was named Elizabeth, it is difficult to see how such a tradition as this one could have originated.]

The accounts of members of the family living as late as the Revolution are no doubt correct, as well as those of their descendants. The John Shropshire who emigrated to Kentucky was probably the John Shropshire, orphan of John Shropshire referred to in the Orange Co. records in 1751. Benjamin, son of the emigrant to Ky., was born in Orange. William Shropshire, whose ministerial designation may have come from tradition, confusing him with Rev. St. John Shropshire, was probably the William Shropshire, of Henry County, 1778, as "Rev. William Shropshire" is said to have married Miss Winkfield, of Henry. Only the Westmoreland records could show how William Shropshire descended from St. John.]

JOHN GOOCHE of Great Yarmouth co. Norf., marchant.

Will dat. 25 July 1617. To my wife Margaret for bringing up of my children all my messuages & lands, fishowses, salthowses, etc. in Y. afsd, which I purchased of John Felton, for her life, remainder to my son Robert G. in fee. To sd. wife M. for same purpose my 2 messuages I lately purchased of Augustin Youngs, late of Y. afsd. dec. & of Gilbert Hill of same town, the former till my son Robert be 21, the latter till my son John be 21. Robert at 21 to have former messuage during life of my wife M. & on her death, sd. messuage to my son John in fee. My son John to have latter messuage during life of my sd. wife & at her death sd. messuage to my son Robert in fee. Rest of estate to my wife M. to pay debts etc, surplus to be paid to my overseers for benefit of my wife & children. Sd. wife M. to be ext'rix. She to permit all personal estate that shall come to her by death of Nicholas Dannock her late father dec., to remain for performance of my will. If she refuse all her legacies etc. to William Gooche, Robert G., Clement G. my brethren & to Charles Rawlyns my brother-in-law whom I ordain supervisors & to be ex'ors on sd. wife's refusal. *Witnesses*: Charles Gooche, Thomas Holland, Roger Gooche.

Proved 21 Aug. 1617 by Margaret relict & ex'trix.

Adm. c. t. a. 4 May 1621 to Charles Rawlins husband of Anne R. sister of Margaret G. relict & ex'trix *d. b. n. a.* by sd. M. G. dec. during min. of Robert, John, Anne, Margaret, Bridget & Mary G. childre nof dec.

Weldon, 80.

WILLIAM GOOCH of Metfeld co. Suffolk, the younger.
Nuncupative. Will dat. 25 Feb. 1604. *Oratio obliqua.* All goods to his wife Jane towards bringing up of his children & she to be ex'trix. Nicholas Gooch & Bartholomew Style his brother & brother in law to be supervisors. Bartholomew Stiles clerk, Gregory Smithe & Robert Kepus to be witnesses. *Signed by these.*
Proved 13 June 1605 by Jane G. relict & ex'trix.

Hayes, 48.

[The two Gooch wills above are additional material towards a genealogy of the family to which Governor Sir William Gooch and (probably) Major William Gooch and Henry Gooch, of York County, belonged. John Gooch, of Yarmouth, was doubtless nearly related to Governor Gooch. See this Magazine, XXXII, 125, 142, 143, 179-181. The two wills show that Robert Gooch (p. 179) had a son Clement, and John Gooch (above) had a brother Clement. John (1617) names a son Robert.]

VIRGINIA GLEANINGS IN ENGLAND

Contributed by Reginald M. Glencross, 176 Worple Road, Wimbledon, London, S. W. 20, England.

(Continued from Vol. XXXII, p. 359)

HUGH BROADHURST, bachelor, died at Virginia.

Adm. 28 June 1659 to brother John B.

[The John Broadhurst who was administrator of his brother Hugh, was probably the man of the name who was a London merchant and a Virginia planter. John Broadhurst's will was dated Sept. 13, 1699 and proved in Princess Anne County in 1700. He styles himself "the younger, of London, factor". He bequeaths real estate at "Hoesfield near Macksfield in the county of Chester". The Probate Act P. C. C., calls him "John Broadhurst of St. Albans, Woodstreet, London; but in Virginia deceased."]

ANDREW HARWOOD of Virginia.

Adm. 1 Aug. 1659 to Edmund Pike curator to Sarah, Margaret and James H., minors.

NICHOLAS HEYRNE, ALS IRON in ship James Town coming from Virginia, a bach'r.

Adm. 19 Dec. 1659 to brother William H., *als*. I.

EDWARD JAMES, died in Virginia.

Adm. 29 June 1659 to Margery Price wife of Christopher P., Eleanor Richardson wife of John R. & Mary J. spr. sisters of dec. By Order of Court.

WILLIAM LANGSTON, of Virginia, widower.

Adm. 16 Dec. 1659 to brother Henry L. for use & during absence of Anthony, Judith, Francis & Mary L., children of dec.

[For note on Anthony Langston, of Virginia, see this Magazine, XXVIII, 139, 140.]

From Vol. XXXIV, No. 4 (Oct. 1926), p. 339.

DANIEL RUSHER, of Wapping, but died at Virginia.

Adm. 28 June 1659 to relict Joan R., widow.

HENRY WARD, of Stepney, Middx., but at Virginia dec.

Adm. 9 June 1659 to relict Sarah W., widow.

ROBERT WEBB, of Virginia, bachelor.

Adm. 1 Aug. 1659 to cousin german William Webb. William Webb, uncle of dec. having renounced.

THOMAS ARGALL, of East Sutton, co. Kent, son of Richard A., Esq., deceased.

Will dat. 10 Dec. 1604. To my wife Katherine, jewels, £1,000 due to me on sundry bonds as well in lieu of certain lands of her inheritance sold by me as for other her deserts. To my brethren Richard & Samuell £50 a piece. My exors to pay to Mistress Bowe of Clinkford in Essex £20 I have received from her. To my sisters Jane & Sara at their marriage silver basen etc., a piece. To poor of East Sutton £10. £10 for new glasing windows in body of church of E. S. £10 for stone over place where my father lies whereto I doubt not but my mother according to her words will contribute for the framing of a more competent memorial of our deceased predecessor. Rest of goods & lands to my brother John in fee & he to be exor.

Proved 16 Mar. 1604-5 by John A., brother & exor.

Hayes, 19.

[Thomas Argall, of St. Faith-the-Virgin, London, Esq., died in 1563, leaving, with others, a son Richard, of East Sutton, Kent, who married Mary, daughter of Sir Reginald Scott, of Scottshall, Kent, and died in 1588, leaving many children. Among these were Thomas, Sir Reginald and Richard, whose wills are given here, Samuel, Governor of Virginia, Elizabeth, who married Sir Edward Filmer, (and was ancestress of Henry Filmer, who emigrated to Virginia) and others. The Argall family was one of the group in Kent and Essex so closely connected with the settlement of Virginia.]

Sir Reginald Argall, of Higham Hill, in pish. of Waltham-stowe, co. Essex, knight.
Will dat. 12 Sep. 1610. To my wife lease that I have of the grounds which John Gaskyn occupies & holds of me in recompense of that small quantity of ground being parcel of her jointure which I sold to Richard Garnett. To sd. wife jewels, etc., £100, she to ratify to William Holliman the elder the lease of Tringe parsonage according to grant to him made. To every of my sisters married & their husbands £10 in plate. To my brother Edmond Randolph £10 similarly. To my sister Sarah A., £50. To my brother Richard A., my lease of Under-hill farm in Isle of Oxney in Kent & £200. To my aunt Argall £3. To servants 20/ a piece except John Wilson to whom £5 & to Francis Jepson 5 marks. To poor of Waltham-stowe £5. To wife plate etc., during widowhood. All my manors etc. to my wife for life, remainder to my brother John A in fee. To my brother Samuel A £50 annuity from death of my wife, also £200. To sd. brother John A & to my sister his wife Damask suit & Damask cloth which my brother Richard gave me. Rest of goods to my brother John A. & he to be exor. Whereas by great care taken by Sir Henry Rowe knight myself & Francis Phillips auditor nominated by Sir Henry Rowe, account of all receipts had by my wife in her widowhood & by me since our marriage of estate of William Rowe dec., late of Higham Hill afsd. from death of sd. William to 24 June 1608 hath been framed according to apptment of sd. William by his Will And whereas for contentment of the children of the sd. William a general meeting of persons hereafter named was had at house of Sir Henry Rowe afsd. then Lord Mayor of London when Francis Phelipps afsd. auditor did make plain sd. account & sd. Sir H. Rowe did then affirm the like as one of the exors of will of sd. W. Rowe his brother, did with Sir Robert Leigh knight & Thomas Chapman, scrivener, 2 of the overseers of sd. will. William Rowe Esq. & Nathaniel Duckett gent that have married 2 of the daurs. of sd. William dec. & Francis Phelipps auditor sub-scribe their names thereunder. And whereas I have in my

665

hands £100 given by Dame Marie Rowe dec. to such uses as in the will of sd. William Rowe are expressed. To such therefore of my wives children as shall accept sd. account, £15 a piece. *Signs*: Reynold Argall. *Witns.*: Samuell Argall, L. Bohune, Jo. Reynoldes vic. of Walthamstoe.

Proved 2 Dec. 1611 by John Argall Esq., the exor.

Wood, 101.

RICHARD ARGALL, of Colchester, co. Essex.

Will dat. 31 Mar. 1614. My brother John A. to be exor. Whereas my brother Samuell is gone a voyage to the seas, if he returns alive into England, to him £500. To my brother John A. & my sister his wife, profit of my lease of Underhill firme in the Isle of Oxney in Kent, for life & then to Richard Argall, my godson, second son to my sd. brother John A. or if dead to sd. brother's other children equally for rest of term. To my sisters £5 piece of plate each. To my faithful friend Mr. John Parsons £100 of debt he owes me. To my sister my brother John A's wife, watch & £20. Rest of goods to my brother John A. *Witns.*: Humphry Lowthe, John Strutt.

Proved 14 Nov. 1614 by John A. brother & exor.

Lowe, 117.

EDWARD COTTINGTON, of pish. of Lye upon Mendipe in dioc. of Bath & Wells, gent.

Will dat. 16 June 1608. To p'ish. church of L. upon M. 20s. To poor of p'ish. there 20s. To my cousin James Cottington the son of John C. dwelling in London £100. To my neice Sarah Cottington his sister £100, to both when 21 or for Sarah at her marriage, they to sign a release for legacies under their father's will. To my cousin Henry Cottington goods in my custody which were his father's & some of my own household goods at my overseers' discretion. Rest of goods & my mansion house at L. upon M. & my lands to my cousin James Cottington son of my brother Philip C. of Godmiston & he to be heir of my lands in Lye, Coleford, Mells & Kilmesdon

& exor. My brother Philip C. & my cousin Thomas Walton of Baltisborough, gent. to be overseers. To my sd. brother my black gelding with a shorn tail & to my cousin 20s. *Witnesses*: Meredith Evans, Minister, Henry Fitz, Henry Erbery.

Proved by sentence 20 June 1609 by James Cottington the exor. Sworn 26 June inst.

Sentence for validity of will. Testator of Leigh, co. Somerset. Parties: Henry C. son of a brother of dec. Plff & James C. also son of a brother of dec. & exor of will & also [James C., John C., George C. & Richard C. next of kin of dec. & all others etc.] Defts.—those in brackets not appearing. Dat. 20 June 1609.

[The accounts of the Ludwell family of Virginia which have been published, state that Thomas and Philip Ludwell the emigrants, were natives of Bruton, Somerset, England, and grandsons of James Cottington who was the son of Philip Cottington of Godminster and a brother of Lord Cottington.

In 1892 the present writer obtained from England and contributed to the *William and Mary Quarterly* the following extract from English Chancery Proceedings which shows the correctness of the account given above.

"Chancery Proceedings—Charles I—Bills and Answers, L, 55 Bundle. Ludwell *vs.* Worsley,

3 May, 1632. Thomas Ludwell of Brewton, in Co. Somerset, Mercer, and Jane, his wife, sole daughter of James Cottington of Discoe in the pish of Brewton aforesd. gent, deceased, and Grace his wife, sheweth. That whereas one Philip Cottington, gent, and Jane his wife, and Maurice Cottington gent sone and heir apparent of the sd Philip, by deed dated 4 Oct. 1631. [?] 8th Yeare of King James I. did demise unto the sd James Cottington his Exors, admrs and assigns all that Captl. messuage fframe house scituate in Discoe in Co. Somersett, and also all those 6 acres and a half of arable lands lyinge in the fields of Brewton, whereof 4½ acres lye in the North field of Discoe neere Deyden Wale, and the other 2 acres nygh the conduct meade there; and also all that close of meadowe conteigneinge 8 acres, And one other close of meadowe, one called little meadow 2 acres, and fower closes of pasture, one called long meade 2½ acres, one other is called the grove 3 acres, one other called fferme close 1½ acres, and the last is called yean ap haye [?] one acre, and those 2 acres and a yard of pasture newly inclosed lyinge in the comon of Discoe, and also conteyne arrable lands called Pulu land 16 acres, together with all houses, buildings orchards, gardens and other the premises etc., belonging to the sd Captl Mess [uage] or frame house and tenemt belonging, all w'ch were late in the tenure of one Roger Walt and his assignes * * * * and James Cottington had issue 2 children of Grace his wife, id est yr Oratrix, Jane, and Roger Cottington deceased, and having executed certain trust deeds of the above property etc. unto John Parham of

Pointington, in Co. of Somersett, Esqr. Sr Edward Parham sonne and heire apparent of the s'd John Parham, Gyles ffthrs, late of Carscombe in the Co. of Dorset gent., and Francis Popleye, late of Chilton Cantile, in Co. Somersett gent, for the benefit of his wife Grace which trust should close in event of issue * * * * now Grace Cottington hath married with one John Worsley, and they deny yr Oratrix any manner of maintenance * * *."

In Vol. 8 of Dwelly's Parish Registers is included the parish of Pitcombe, Somerset, in which is situated Godmister, now called Godminster, the old home of the Cottington family. Various entries from the Register and account of Godminster are quoted here. We are also indebted to this distinguished genealogist (now of Church Road, West Ewell, Surry, England) who specializes on families from Somerset and Devon, for two pictures of Godminster House.

Mr. Dwelly says, "Many of the earlier entries in the Pitcombe registers refer to the Cottington family who came to Godmister during Queen Elizabeth's reign. The greatest scion of their house was Francis, Lord Cottington of Hanworth, who was Chancellor of the Exchequer to Charles I, and is frequently mentioned by Clarendon. He was the fourth son of Philip and Jane Cottington who were married at Pitcombe 18 Aug. 1572.

The old home of the Cottingtons at Godminster still exists and is an unusually good and typical specimen of the smaller manor houses of the late 15th century. The whole of the original main building is intact, with its great hall, solar, old spiral stone staircase and other features of the period. Indeed, the only addition of architectural importance that has since been made is as follows: About 1700 the west side of the house was extended in a northerly direction, the principal entrance placed there, and the whole re-fronted in the style of the period (Wren's) probably by John Cottington."

The first Cottington entry is of the marriage of Mr. Philip Cottington and "Mres." Jane Byflett. Of course, "Mistress" might mean either a single woman or a widow. The pedigree of Bifleet of Somerset in Phillip's Visitation (not accessible here) might show who she was. Philip Cottington was buried Sept. 7, 1615.

The christenings were: "Mres." Elizabeth Cottington, Nov. 9, 1575; Mrs. Jane Cottington, daughter of Mr. Maurice Cottington, March 29, 1604; Jane, daughter of James Cottington, May 31, 1610; Ann, daughter of Maurice Cottington, June 2, 1610; Francis, son of Maurice Cottington, June 26, 1614 (Francis was buried July 2, 1616); Philip, son of Mr. Maurice Cottington, Nov. 7, 1616. Edward Cottington Gent. was buried June 22, 1608.

On a broken tomb at Pitcombe Church is the following inscription: "Hic Jacet Edwardus Cottington nuper de . . . Mindip, generosus, qui obit vicessimo Junii Anno Domini 1608"

Edward Cottington whose will is given above and whose epitaph is in this note was a brother of the first Philip Cottington of Godminster.]

GODMINSTER MANOR, BRUTON, SOMERSET, ENGLAND
Upper—West Front. Lower—South Front.

Courtesy of Mr. E. Dwelly

VIRGINIA GLEANINGS IN ENGLAND

Contributed by Reginald M. Glencross, 176 Worple Road,
Wimbledon, London, S. W., England.

(Continued from XXXIV, 344)

WILLIAM ANDERSON, CITIZEN OF THE STATE OF VIRGINIA,
U. S. A., but now resident of Vauschall in pr'sh of Lam-
belt, G. B.

Will dat. 20 July 1793. To my wife Mary in fee my right
in real & personal estates formerly of Samued Gist, Esq.,
which were vested in my s'd wife by an Act of Gen. Assembly
of Virginia passed in 1782 to her, household furniture etc.
To her for life my leasehold estate which I purchased of Richard Foster Esq. at Vauxhall, afs'd called Belmont House,
trusting my wife & promises of her good father that they
will mkae proper provision for our neice Maria Gist Anderson
whom my wife took an infant & adopted with the fondness
of a mother. Sd leasehold, after death of my wife, to my
nephew Francis Anderson, but if he die s. p. under 22, same
to my neice Maria Gist Anderson, but if she die s. p. same
t boe sold & money equally among my residuary legatees.
Ex'ors to convey to Samuel Gist Esq. of Gower Street in fee,
two tracts of land I purchased of ex'ors of John Bickerton dec.
& Thomas Massie, the one in Hanover Co. of 600 acres, the
other in Goochland Co. of 2,285 acres, both in Virginia, s'd
S. Gist to pay money I gave etc., otherwise same to be sold
& s'd S. Gist to pay rent for time they have been cultivated
for him. Ex'ors to sell tract in Louisa Co. which I purchased
of Robert Harris & my share of lands in Albemarle Co. which
descend to me under will of my grandfather Mills, both in
Virginia. Ex'ors to sell my 2 houses in the Strand & Holy

From Vol. XXXVII, No. 1 (Jan. 1929), p. 39.

Well Street in city of Westminster. Negroes given me by my late father, to my mother for life she to treat them humanely & kindly. On her death all to be set free. £200 to my nephew Anderson Barrett. Purchase money of s'd estates etc. & rest of estates to be divided into three. First part to my brothers & sisters that were living on 25 Dec. last. Equally, one having died since already, shares of those dead at my death to their children. The other two thirds to Samuel Gist Esq. & my wife Mary in trust till my nephew Francis Anderson be 22 to employ same in trade either on present plan in partnership with Messrs. Birkett Shore & Keeves or otherwise. Profits for wife for maintenance of s'd nephew & neice M. G. Anderson. Second third part to s'd nephew at 22 but if he die to my neice M. G. Anderson at 21, otherwise at share 1. Part 3 on 1 June 1800 to go as part 1, meanwhile to be used in trade. My wife Mary A. to be ex'trix, my friend Samuel Gist Esq. my brothers Nathaniel A. & Thomas A., my brother in law Dabney Minor & my nephew Overton Anderson to be ex'ors. Signed in the City of London G. B. *Witns.* Joseph Bowden, No. 6 Fower Dock, Henry Smith Shore, No. 10 Crosby Square, Aiskew Birkett, Rodney Street, Pentonville, Lionel Bradstreet, No. 10 Crosby Square, Bishopsgate Street.

1 Codicil dat. 23 Sep. 1795. My friend Wm. Fowke Esq. of Weston Hall co. Suff'k to be joint trustee with my friend Samuel Gist Esq. & my wife M. A. Considering that having a number of ex'ors that reside in different countries may occasion a clashing of interests I revoke such apptment & appoint my wife, S. Gist, W. Fowke, John Anderson Esq. of Philpot Lane, London & my nephew Overton Anderson to be ex'ors. My brother David A. having conveyed to me a tract in upper end of Hanover Co. Virginia where he lately resided for securing part of a debt due from him to the old concern of William Anderson & Co., ex'ors to sell same & pay money to s'd Company. Signed in town of Chesterfield co. Derby. *Witn's* Elizabeth Fowke, Mary Bard, John Sapton.

2 Codicil dat. at Chesterfield 15 Dec. 1795. To my ex'ors 5 gua's each for ring. *No witn's.*

Proved 23 Jan. 1796 by Samuel Gist Esq., William Fowke & John Anderson Esq. four of the ex'ors. Pewer reserved for Mary A. widow, the relict & Overton Anderson Esq. the

P. C. C., Harris, 1.

nephew the other ex'ors.

[William Anderson, a native of Virginia, removed to London where he became a merchant and acquired a considerable estate. He was son of David Anderson (died 1791), who removed from Louisa county to Albemarle. David Anderson had issue: William, Nathaniel, Thomas, Richard, David, Matthew, Edmund, Samuel, Ann married Dabney Minor of Hanover county, Sarah married Christopher Hudson, and a third daughter who married ———— Barrett and was the mother of Anderson Barrett of Richmond.

A copy of William Anderson's will is on file in the Virginia Archives Department, among the papers laid before the General Assembly in connection with the emancipation of the Anderson negroes.]

ELIZABETH GRAMER OF GERRARD STREET in pr'sh of St. Ann, Westminster, co. Midd'x, widow.

Will dat. 6 July 1772. Samuel Turner, the elder, Esq. Alderman of City of London & Samuel T. the younger, his son, to be ex'ors. To be bur. in same vault in p'rsh church of Islington, co. Midd's, in which my late parents & other relations are deposited. To Charity School at Islington afs'd £100. To Miss Mary Adee the eldest dau'r of Dr. A. 10 guineas & to Miss Olivia, Miss Martha & Miss Catherine Adee the three youngest daur's of sd Dr. A. 5 gu'as each. To Mrs. Priscilla Blake widow & her dau'r Miss Penelope B. 20 gu'as each for ring. To Samuel Brownless (one of the sons of George B., merchant, & Susanna his wife) £300. To Miss Elizabeth Bullock, dau'r of Rev. Mr. Richard B. of Drayton in Cambs. 20 gu5as. To Mary Claiborne, wife of Augustine C., of Virginia, esq., if living at my death, £2,000 to her separate use, but if dead same to all her children equally. To s'd A. Claiborne £500 which he owes me on bond. To sd ex'ors £200 in trust to pay such debts as Cornet Richard Cooke (grandson of my late uncle William Cooke, dec.) shall owe at my death & residue to sd. R. Cooke's advantage. To

Anne Corne, widow of John C., the younger, dec. £20. To
Mary Dobbins one of the daurs. of James D. late of Gravelais
co. Glouc. dec. £10, to Ann Dobbins another of his daurs
£10, to Hannah Dobbins another of his daurs. £10, to Sarah
Dobbins another of his daurs £10 & to James Dobbins his
youngest son £50. To sd exors £100 orphans stock on trust
for education & apprenticing Thomas Wheatley son of Mary
W. daur. of my cousin William Cooke late of Chatham, Kent
& to pay what remains to sd T. Wheatley at 21 or if he die
to his sd mother M. W. notwithstanding her coverture. To
sd M. Wheatley £100 orphans stock. To sd exors £100 orphans stock on trust for educating & apprenticing Thomas
Joseph Forrest son of Robert F. & Elizabeth his wife or if
sd T. J. F. die, same to his sd mother. To sd E. Forrest
£20. To Elizabeth Day daur. of Thomas Staight of Fwyning
co. Glouc. ston ecutter & great grand-daur. of my late aunt
Mary Dobbins £50. To John Dax son of John D. the elder
of Cooks Court, Cary Street, gent. 10 guas. To William
Fowle of Red Lyon Square, Middx. apothecary 20 guas. To
Rev. Robert Nicholas clerk 10 guas. To Joanna Greening
wife of M. G. of Gretton in Gloucs. £10. To Miss Sarah
Ham daur. of John H. of Spittal Square weaver 20 guas. To
David, Jonathan & John Hatchman grandsons of my late cousin
Dorothy Church £20 a piece. To sd exors. £30 in trust for
apprenticing John David Hatchman son of sd David H.. To
Joan Horton Bary Horton Hannah Horton & Elizabeth Hor-
ton of Dumbleton in Gloucs. children of Elizabeth Horton
£10 each. To Judith Hughes wife of Robert H. £15. To
Mr. John Markham ? £50, to Rev. Mr. Samuel Markham
£50, to Miss Elizabeth Markham £50. To Miss Sarah Marriott one of the daurs. of Rev. Randall M., D. D. £50. To
Miss Elizabeth Marriott daur. of Capt. John M. & Mary his
wife 20 guas. To Miss Susannah Meredith now living at
my house £50. To my servant Elizabeth Paton clothes. To
Miss Frances Selwyn & Miss Louisa Selwyn 20 guas. each.
To Miss Elizabeth Selwyn daur. of William S. of Licolns
Inn esq 20 gu'as. To all the children of Mary Smith late
of Spinnage co. Glouc. dec. £10 each. To Susanna Stinton

another daur. of my sd cousin William Cooke late of Chatham Kent £100 stock if alive at my death, free from debts etc. of her husband, if dead for her child or children. To sd exors £300 a piece. To Elizabeth wife of sd S. Turner the elder £100 for ring & to Elizabeth T. & Jane T. daurs of sd exor S. T. sen. £100 stock a piece. To Miss Elizabeth Turner daur of sd S. T. the younger 50 guas. To Mrs. Deborah Tylden widow of late Rev. Richard Osborn T. £400 stock & to Richard Tylden eldest son of sd Deborah T. £100 stock. To Rev. Thomas Biker clerk 50 guas. To Charles Gramer Biker £200. To Rev. Dr. Hind, rector of St. Ann Westm. 10 guas. To Charles Shuttleworth Priest son of William Shuttleworth P. of Coventry gent 10 guas. To Rev. Mr. Arthur Miller of Manchester co. Warw. 10 guas & to Catherine Worcester wife of James W. £5. To my servants (except sd. J. Hughes & except coachman who shall drive me to whom £5) a years wages. Exors to retain legacies to persons under age. To sd exors for life of sd Richard Cooke grandson of my late uncle William Cooke dec. £100 a year for sd R. Cooke with spendthrift clause. To Mary Dobbins widow of sd James D. late of Gravelais afsd. dec. £10 a year for life then to sd Mary D. her eldest daur. for life. To exors £20 a year for life of sd Elizabeth Forrest for her separate use & then to sd Thomas Joseph Forrest £10 a year & to Robert Forrest £10 & Elizabeth Forrest her younger children each £5 a year, for lives. To Sarah Farr widow of George F. dec. £20 a year for life. To Mary Hawkes who was formerly my servant £10 a year for life. To my exors £20 a year for Elizabeth Horton wife of [blank] H. the daur. of John Dobbins late of Spinnage afsd. dec. for her life & to her separate use. To exors £40 a year for life of Sarah Jennings widow in performance of a bond by me. To sd Miss Susanna Meredith £20 a year for life. To exors. £10 a year for life of Mrs. Amelia Forenght daur. of Stephen Wood late pish clerk of Low Layton co. Essex dec. by Elizabeth his last wife, independent of control of her present husband. To exors for life of sd Catherine Worcester £10 a year (couverte). To exors £10 a year for life of sd Sus-

anna Stinton (couverte). To exors £10 a year for life of sd
Mary Wheatley (couverte). To Mary Croft my mantua
maker of Southampton Street Covent Garden widow £10 a
year. To sd. Samuel Brownless £10 a year for 10 years. To
Jonathan Brownless the other son of sd George B. & Susanna
his wife £10 a year until he be 21. To John Dobbins son of
John D. of Winchcomb co. Glouc. £10 a year for 10 years.
To sd John David Hatchman son of sd David H. £10 a year
for 10 years. All sd annuities out of lands in Westminster
Middx only. To sd Augustine Claiborne & heirs for life of
Ann Mitchell wife of [blank] M. of Virginia & daur. of my
late cousin Martha Cock dec. £30 a year for her separate use.
To my servant William Corne for life £30 a year & then to
Jane his wife during widowhood. To sd Ann Corne widow
of sd. John C. the younger, for life £30 a year beyond £20
a year. I have already settled on her for life. To exors for
life of sd Susanna Brownless wife of sd George B. £ 40. To
sd John Dobbins the father of Winchcomb for life £10 a year.
To sd servant Elizabeth Paton £20 a year for life. To exors
£20 a year for life of sd Judith Hughes wife of sd Robert H.
To Sarah Harris, lately my housemaid, for lfie £10 a year.
These last 8 annuities out of lands in Stepney, St. George,
Wapping, Shadwell & Whitechapel Middx. All my real estate
in city of Westminster [subject as above] to my exors in fee
in trust to pay sd annuities & subject thereto in trust for sd
Deborah Tylden in fee. Lands in Stepney etc subject to sd
eight last annuities, to my exors in fee in trust to pay annuities
& subject thereto as sd. Mary Claiborne wife of sd Augustine
C. may appoint in default, for her or her children equally in
fee. My estate at Lambeth etc. co. Surrey to my exors in
trust as Mrs. Mary Filewood wife of Mr. Richard F. of Lam-
belt afsd may appoint in default, for her in fee, charged with
£100 to sd R. Filewood & £100 a piece to Mary F. & Elizabeth Ann F., their daurs. Rest of personal estate to my exors
equally. *Witns.* Richd Fawson, St. Paul's Church Yard, Griffith Jones, Red Lyon Square, Jno. Dax Cooks, Court Carcy
Street.

Proved 31 Mar 1773 by Samuel Turner esq. as Alderman of city of London & Samuel Turner the younger esq the exors.

P. C. C., Stevens, 110

[Col. Augustine Claiborne, of "Windsor", Surry county (born 1721, died May 3, 1787, married Mary, daughter of Buller Herbert, of Prince George county, Va. An account of this branch of the Claibornes by John Herbert Peterson states that Mrs. Claiborne inherited from "her aunt", Mrs. Grammer, a block of houses in London, which were sold by Augustine Claiborne for £80,000. The amount received is probably greatly exaggerated. The will, above, does not state the relationship between Mrs. Grammer and Mrs. Claiborne. The "Cousin Martha Cocke" named in the will was the daughter of John Herbert (died 1704), of "Puddledock", Prince George county, and wife of James Powell Cocke. A copy of a long deed from Augustine Claiborne and Mary his wife in regard to property in London is in existence and will be printed later in this Magazine.]

MICHAELL MUSGRAVE of p'r'sh of Pienketanck in the River Rappahannock in co. Middlesex, Virginia.

Will dat. 21 Dec. 1697 1679 (*sic*). Debts to be paid; if anw overplus same to my daur. Elizabeth M. who troubles me to think of what a poor condition she is here left in England leaving her here in this city of London in the house of John Holmes in Plumetree Court near Holborne Bridge in p'rsh of St. Andrews there to be nurst, taught & brought up. My brother Mr. Thom. M., minister of Woolbed co. Sussex near town of Midhurst & my friend Mr. Will. Newton, grocer, in p'rsh of St. Giles Criplegate, to be exors. *Witns.* Edmond Tribby, Michaell Pitman, Samuel Tribby.

Proved 26 Jan 1697[8] by Thomas Musgrave one of the exors. Power reserved for William Newton the other exor.

P. C. C., Lort, 15.

VIRGINIA GLEANINGS IN ENGLAND

Contributed by Reginald M. Glencross, 176 Worple Road, Wimbledon, London, S. W. 20, England.

(Continued)

WILLIAM CRASHAWE, bachelor of Divinity, Preacher of God's word, first at Bridlington, then at Beverley in Yorkshire, afterwards at the Temple, since then Pastor of Church of Ay Burton in diocese of York, now Pastor of that too great parish of Whitechapel in suburbs of London.
Will dat. 1 Nov. 1621. Long tirade against "Popery". "This my Confession of my Faith is unknown & hath been this 24 years since I first begun it concealed from all men & so shall be by me whilst I live." To library of St. John's Coll., Cambridge, as dear nurse & spiritual mother, "Biblia greca in 2 bus vol. editionis Venetis fol. which cost 40 s., missale Romanum, printed more than 100 years ago in great 4 to, which is at London, a book very rare & hard to be gott." To public Library of Camb. Univ. Pontificale magnum Romanum, in fol. of the old edition (as a jewel) for so it is, Constitutiones Pont. Rom. cum Cemmentar-Petre Matthei & Simauche Constitutiones Catholice. To public library of Oxford Univ. founded or augmented by Sir Tho. Bodley, knight, books to value of 40s. To public library of the College in Ireland Gorsonis opera or other books to 40s. To public library of St. Paul's, London, Book of Martyrs or other book. To public library of St. Peter's, York., Liber Conformitatum beate Francisci which cost 20s, Missale Romanum, fo., '75, which was taken in York Castle, etc. To public library of college church of Rippon, books at Burton (specified). To p'ish of Hansworth co. Ebor. [Yorkshire] where I was born, my own works to be bound to lie in the Church & 40s. for poor.

From Vol. XXXVII, No. 2 (April 1929), p. 139.

To p'ish church of Sheffield & ministers of Beverly & of St.
Mary's Church there & of Bridlington, all co. Ebor., to each
my works. To sizars in St. John's Camb., £13, 4s. To sub-
sizars 20s. To my brother Thomas all my civil law books he
hath not & 20s. for a fair Bible for my sister his wife. To
every of my 2 sisters' sons & daurs that can read a little
bible of 5s. To my brother Francis a bible & Calvin's Institutions. I forgive him what he owes me. To him £10. To
my aunt Rowthe my own works. To my cousin Edw. & his
wife the same. To my cousin Wasnesse & his wife, to my
uncle Stringer & his wife, to my uncle Smithe & his wife, to
my young cousin Eyre & his wife, & to my cousin Fretcharlie
& his wife, the same. To my goddau'r Jane Gee a 7s. Bible.
To my Lord Sheffyld & his children, bibles—my Lady Swift's
in black velvet. To Mr. Henry Alvay my father in Christ,
silver pot. To the Lady Gee my own works. To Mr. Mar.
Brigges & to Mr. Micklethwayte & Mr. Swifte, books. To
Mr. John Warter of Beverley & his wife, my own works.
I forgive Mr. Kitchen of Beverley 6s. 8d., Mr. Utye 12s.,
James Peacocke 2s., John Whrighte 2s. 6d., Roger Moore
2s., widow Coulson 1s., George Nelson 2s., Simon Fletcher
6s. 8d., Mocrofte 5s. 7d., my cousin Sweetinge 20s. of the
£3, Timperley of Cambridge 20s. of £3, 15, godwife Gilderson
of Cambridge 20s. of 40s, Ed. Elton 20s. of £3. 6. 8, Sir H.
Ashbey 20s. of £7, Mr. Chambers 6s. 6d, Mr. Cerford the
Scot 2s, Mr. Wiseman 10s. & Mr. Cardavies 10s. they owe
me. Whereas I have next avoidance of Ay Burton taken in
my brother's name (for which he knows what hath been
offered) same to my sd. brother Thomas, he to pay to Mr.
Eldred, Mr. Johnston or some such other honest merchant
of London (whom Sir Edwin Sandes shall like) £105 for
stipend for preachers of St. Antholines, London.

Codicil dat. 10 June 1622. Ex'ors to sue King that the
suit his majesty gives to his late cupbearer John Hall esq. may
be sequestered into hands of some indifferent gent. to discharge his debts, for which I am bound viz: £140 to Le Ferye,
£200 to Ellis, for Sir Edward Villers £100, to Mr. Porte

£105, to Mr. Gassett £106, to Mr. Benet a receiver of the King £7 or £8, to Mr. Russell in Cheapside £30 or £40, to Mrs. 7yres at the Counter £20. To Mr. Nott all principal debt, these being discharged, the rest to himself. To virtuous gentlewoman Mrs [blank] Sheffyld, ring that was her Lady Grandmother's. To her my late wife's (ring). Mr. Robert Dixon & my son Richard to be ex'ors.

Proved 6 Oct. 1626 by Robert Dixon one of the ex'ors. Power reserved to Richard C. son & the other ex'or.

P. C. C. Hele, 97.

[Rev. William Crashaw, D. D., was a member of the Virginia Company and a staunch friend of the Colony. He was son of Richard Crashaw, of Handsworth, near Sheffield, Yorkshire, and was bapitzed there, Oct. 26, 1572. He entered St. John's College, Cambridge, as a sizar on May 1, 1591; was B. A., 1591-2; M. A., 1595 and B. D., 1603. After holding clerical charges in Yorkshire, he was appointed preacher at the Inner Temple and in Nov., 1618, was admitted to the church of St. Mary Matfellon, or Whitechapel, London. He was the author of many works, the one of most interest to Virginia being "A Sermon Preached Before the Right Honorable the Lord Lawarre, Lord Governor and Captaine Generall of Virginia and Others of His Maiesties Counsell for that Kingdome, and the Rest of the Adventurers in that Plantation, Feb. 21, 1609", London, 1610, 4 to. This sermon, containing about 27,000 words was printed in 1610 and a long abstract is given in Alexander Brian's "Genesis of the United States", pp. 360-375. It concludes with a "Salutation to Virginia":

"And thou Virginea, whom though mine eies see not, my heart shall love; how hath God honoured thee! Thou hast thy name from the worthiest Queene that ever the world had: thou hast thy matter from the greatest King on earth: and thou shalt now have thy forme from one of the most glorious Nations under the Sunne, and under the conduct of a Generall of as great and ancient Nobility as ever was ingaged in action of this nature. But this is but a portion of thy honour: for thy God is coming towards thee, and in the mean time sends to thee, and salutes thee with the best blessing heaven hath, even his blessed Gospell. Looke up therefore, and lift up thy head, for thy redemption draweth nie: and he that was the God of Israel, and is still the God of England, will shortly I doubt not bring it to passe, that men shall say, Blessed be the Lord God of Virginea: and let all Christian people say. Amen.

And this salutation doth my soule send thee, O Virginea, even this poore New-yeeres gift, who though I be not worthy to be thine Apostle, yet doe vow and devote myselfe to be in England thy faithfull factor and solicitor, and most desirous to do thee any service in the Lord Jesus Christ our Saviour and thine: whom we beseech for his standard amongst you, and that you may once crie for yourselves as we do now for you, Even so come Lord Jesus."

Though William Crashaw was a Puritan his only child, Richard, became a devout Catholic. He was a poet of note.]

ANNE BEDELL, of Oundle, co. North[ampt]on, widow.
Will dat. 21 Nov. 1650. To be bur. in church or chancel
of Oundle. My son Gabriel B. to be ex'or. My cousin Christopher Pickering of Titch'm'ch co. North'ton gent. & my cousin
Henry Bedell of Catworth co. Hunt. gent. to be overseers.
As to my small portion of goods. To my son William B. my
wedding ring. To my daur. Lettice my son Brinckhurst's wife
a cradle cloth. To my son William Larkin's children, viz. to his
two sons & two daurs. my grandchildren, a silver spoon each.
More to my goddaur. Anne Larkin a chair etc. which I wrought
myself. To my daur Anne Clement, chair etc. To her daur.
Marie C. my grandchild & goddaur. my least Bible. Anne's
legacies at her death to go to Marie. To my daur. Bridget
B., bedstead etc. etc. bearing cloth she wrought herself. To
my daur. Antonina Maydewell, kettle. To my daur. Elizabeth
B. bed etc. etc. napkins she wrought herself. To my daur.
Rebecca B. my son Gabriel B's wife my biggest Bible. To
their daur. Anne B. my goddaur. & goddaur. best silver spoons
& pictures her father gave me. To poor of town of Oundle
40s. To my cousin Thomas Collins' son who is my godson
a silver spoon. To my six sons, viz. William B., Gabriel B.,
James B., Francis B., Henry B. & Edward B. £5 a piece. If
I die at a time when I shall have spent the most part of my
annuity, goods to be sold for sd £5 legacies. Rest of goods to
my daur. Bridget B. If she die unmarried, same among my
five daurs. viz. Lettice, Jane, Anne, Antonina & Elizabeth.

Witns. Borface Pickering, John Pickering.

Proved 12 Sep. 1657 by Gabriel B. son & ex'or.

[Anne Bedell was daughter of James Pickering, Esq., of Tichmarsh,
Northamptonshire, and wife of Silvester Bedell, who, at the Visitation
of Huntingdonshire, 1613, was eldest son of William Bedell, of Moldsworth and Catsworth, Huntingdonshire. This William Bedell was
the father of Dorothy, who married 1st, Edward Burwell, of Harlington, Bedfordshire (and was mother of Lewis Burwell, of Virginia) and 2nd, Roger Wingate, treasurer of Virginia, 1639-41. The
will of William Bedell, above, is printed in this Magazine, XXIV,
262-265; that of his brother, Sir John Bedell, of Hameston, Huntingdonshire, XXIV, 265-267, and of Sir Thomas, son of Sir John,
XXIV, 267-268.]

VIRGINIA GLEANINGS IN ENGLAND

Contributed by Reginald M. Glencross, 176 Worple Road, Wimbledon, London, S. W. 20, England.

(Continued)

DAME JUDITH BARRINGTON, of Barrington Hall in p'ish of Hatfield Broadoakes co. Essex, widow.

Will dat. 1 May 1655. To be buried in Knebworth church, Herts., to be laid by my father Sir Rowland Litton, knight, dec. Rectory & parsonage of Hamsteed, Herts., leased by King James to George Smith then esq., afterwards knight from Lady Day 1628 [*sic*] for 31 years & lands freehold & copyh. in Hamsteed, co. Herts., purchased by me in names of others of Robert Foodham, clerk, to Sir Thomas Hewett of Pishveburie, Herts., knight, Robert Wallopp of Farley Wallopp, Hunts., esq. & William Heaviningham of Heaviningham, Suff'k, esq. for rest of term & in fee resprly [?] in trust to use of my sister Dame Jane Crofts wife of Sir Charles C. of Bardwells, co. Suf'k, knight, sd husband not to meddle. Rectory etc. of South Elkington, Lines advowson of Vicarage there & freehold lands in S. E. etc. Lines purchased by me in names of others, of Sir Charles Bowles of sd. co., knight, to Robert Barrington of Tofts in Little Baddow, Essex, Esq., John Wilsby of Spalden Lines, esq., & Thomas Goodwynn of South Wild, Essex, clerk, in fee, in trust for use of Marie Barrington, widow, late wife of John B., esq., dec., one of the sons of Sir Francis B., knight & Bt., dec., for life, remainder to sd. Dame Jane Crofts in fee similarly. To my neice the Lady Hewet, wife of Sir Thomas H., knight, £500. To my nephew Rowland Litton of Knebworth, Herts., esq., £400. To my goddau'r, Mrs. Judith Litton the dau'r of sd Rowland L.

From Vol. XXXVII, No. 3 (July 1929), p. 253.

esq. £100. To my godson John Wendham of Felbrick, Norfolk, esq., £100. T omy son in law Robert Barrington of Tofts in Little Baddow, Essex, esq. £400 & little silver inkhorn that was his father's, Sir Francis B., dec. To poor of p'ish of Knebworth, Herts., if burial there, £10, otherwise to p'ish where I am buried £5. Rest of goods & lands to sd Sir T. Hewett, R. Wallopp & W. Heaviningham. To separate use of sd Dame J. Crofts in fee to my nephew Sir Thomas Hewett knight to be ex'or & to him £100. *Witnesses*: Robert Whych, N. Bernard.

Codicil dated 9 May 1655. To my brother Sir William Litton, knight, my wedding ring by Sir George Smith set round with little table diamonds. To my nephew Robert Wallop esq. ring that was his grandmother Littons. To my nephew William Heaviningham, esq., next best ring. To my neice the Lady Postwick, bed etc. To my neice the Lady Barrington, £30 I lent her. To my neice Scroggs, damask & hangings in my London house. To my neice Dodington, silver plates without Aims etc. To my neice Theodosia Wallop, tankard etc. To my dau'r Mrs. Lucie Tyrrell, Indian embroidery which her grandmother Barrington gave me to make a bed of. To my brother in law Sir Charles Crofts, knight, ring. To my dau'r Lucie Barrington, wife of my son Robert B. silver chafing dish her husband gave me, with his Arms. To my friend (whom I call my child) the Lady Elizabeth Tyrrell, wife of Sir Timothy T. knight, all what sd Sir T. T. owes me, sd. Sir T. to pay £200 thereof to my French sister Mrs. Marie Barrington, widow. To Sir Timothy Tyrrell his wives picture. To my chief domestic man servant £5 etc. To my two ancient servants Richard Deane & John Heymon £20 each. To my footboy or footman (if any at my death) £1 & wages due—if I give him any wages at all. To my chief chambermaid £3. To Marie Tavenor (my domestic servant) £10. To other inferior maid servants of years standing £1 each. To my goddau'r Judith King £10 if unmarried at my death. To my son Rowland Smith's goddau'r Judith Staines,

£10 if unmarried at my death. *Witnesses*: Robert Volych, N. Bernard.

Proved 22 Sep. 1657 by Sir Thomas Hewett knight the ex'or.

Ruthen, 262.

[The testator was Judith, daughter of Sir Rowland Lytton, of Knebworth, and widow of Sir George Smith, of Annables. She married, secondly, as his second wife, Sir Francis Barrington, of Barrington Hall, Essex, Bart., who was M. P. in the reigns of Elizabeth, James I and Charles I. Sir Francis married 1st, Joan, daughter of Sir Henry Cromwell, of Hinchinbrook, and aunt of the Protector. Joanne Barrington, youngest daughter of this marriage, married Sir Richard Everard, and was ancestress of Sir Richard Everard, Governor of North Carolina, whose daughter married David Meade, of Virginia.]

Armstrong, John (Capt.)
  245
Army, John 133
Arnal, Ann 271
  Benjamin 271
Arnall, Thomas 26
Arnold, Ann 414
  Benjamin 271
  Edward 503, 504, 505
  George 194, 575
  Samuel 99
  Thomazine 504
  Ursula 159
Arran, (?) (Lord) 339,
  341
Arryes, Edward 147
Arthur, David 276
Artis, (?) 442
Arundel, (?) (Earl) 650
  (?) (Lord) 650
  John 113
  Thomas (Earl) 566
Arundell, Miles 282
Asbe, Simon 51
Asen, Brigett (Mrs.)
  496
Ashbey, H. (Sir) 678
Ashbourne, (?) 197
Ashbye, Geo. 497
  Hen. 497
Ashe, Mary 42
  T. A. (Capt.) 534
  William 253
Ashefield, (?) (Lady)
  438
Ashenden, John 420
Ashhurst, Anne 593
  Cassandra 593
  Francis 594
  Henry 593, 595
  John 593
  Margaret 593
  Mary 593
  William 593
Ashley, Joane 86
  John 86
Ashlie, Thomas 439
Ashpoole, (?) (Dr.) 540
Ashton, Ann 36
  Anne 36
  Charles 36
  Edmond 595
  Edmund 593, 597, 598
  Elizabeth 3
  Henry (Col.) 217
  Isabella 598
  James 2, 3, 431, 593,
  597
  Jane 597
  Jno. (Capt.) 3
  John 2, 3, 360, 431,
  593, 597
  John (Capt.) 3
  Mary 360, 598
  Peter 3, 431, 593,
  595, 597, 598
  Peter (Col.) 3, 431
  Samuel 431
  Thomas 431, 593, 597
  Walter 431, 593, 597,
  598
Ashwell, William 482
Askew, Elizabeth 223, 224
  Robert 223
  Thomas 223
Askewe, Bridget 594
Asope, Richard 78
Asplin, Willm. 211

Aston, (?) 109
  (?) (Lt.-Col.) 392
  Elizabeth 390, 391,
  392
  Henry 188
  Mary 392
  Robert 390, 391
  Sarah 391
  Simon 390, 391
  Susannah 392
  Thomas 391
  Walter 180, 181, 391,
  392
  Walter (Col.) 391
  Walter, Jr. 392
  Walter (Sir) 391
  Walter, Sr. 391
  William 390, 391
Astwood, Elizabeth 656
  Johannis 656
  Robert 655
Astwoode, Elizabeth 655
Athawes, Edward 214
Atherbury, Elizabeth 35
Atherley, Humfrey 468,
  469
Atherold, Anne 577
  Hannah 577
  Martha 576, 577
  Martha A. 577
  Mary 576, 577
  Nathaniel 577
  Nathaniell 576
  Rebecca 577
  Sarah 577
  Susan 577
  Thomas 577
Atherton, Henry 276
Atkins, Abigail (Mrs.)
  152
  Amy 33
  Anne 36
  Edward 32, 33
  Elizabeth 36, 42, 399
  Francis 32, 33, 260
  George 36
  Humfrey 36
  John 32, 35, 36, 399
  Katherine 32, 33
  Lee 36
  Nicholas 33
  Richard 33, 36, 152
  Robert 33
  Thomas 33, 399
  William 32, 33, 36,
  399
Atkinson, John 482
  Letitia 367, 368
  Moses 184
  Raphe 99
  Richard 99, 528
  Thomas 99
  Timothie 423
  William 99
Atterbury, Dorothie 35
  Francis 35
  Richard 35
  Stephen 35
  William 35
Attkins, William 36
Atwood, J. 640
  John 639, 640
Atye, (?) 644
Audley, (?) 431
  Elizabeth 431
  Jane 431
August, Francis 33, 175
Aurelius, John 412

Austen, John 504
  Richard 472
Awbrey, Henry 358, 359
Awdley, (?) (Mrs.) 541
Awgar, (?) (Widow) 555
Axtell, Anne 4
  Daniel 4
  Jeane 4
  Nathaniel 3
  Sarah 4
  Thomas 4
Axtill, Henry 457
Ayarste, Thomas 419
Ayerest, Tho. 148
Ayers, (?) (Mrs.) 274
  George 55
Ayhurst, Anne 387
Aykeroyd, Susanna 580
Aylard, Thomasin 452
  William 452
Aylett, Ann 360
  John 636, 637
  Penelope 636
  Robert 636
  Thomas 636
  Will 636
  William 551, 636
Ayletts, (?) 637
Ayliffes, (?) 637
Aylmer, (?) (Bishop) 292
  Elizabeth 291
  John 291
  Justinian (Rev.) 292
Ayloffe, Benjamin 636
  Benjamin (Sir) 636
  Will 636
  William (Sir) 636
Ayloffes, (?) 637
Aylward, William 35, 46
Ayon, Michael 336
Ayres, Elizabeth 120
  John 525
  Judith Opie (Mrs.) 273
Aysen, Edw. 496
  Henry 496
  John 496
Ayson, Brigett 496
Baab, Thomas 176
Baber, James 58
Bacchus, Ellen 215
  Ellin 215
  Mary 215
Bachellor, James 370
Backhowse, John 533
Backler, Samuel 155
Backwith, Francis 250
Bacon, (?) 158, 225, 378
  Anthony 11, 90, 201
  Elizabeth 201, 202,
  443, 576
  Francis 576
  James 575, 576
  James (Sir) 575, 576
  John 331
  Martha 576
  Nathaniel 107, 443,
  575, 576
  Nathaniel (Pres.) 576
  Nicholas 462, 463,
  544
  Nicholas (Sir) 576
  Thomas (Rev.) 201, 202
  William 201
Bagg, John 86
  Mary 86
Bagge, (?) 122
  Andrew 87, 354
  Ann 354

Bagge (cont.)
  Anna 355
  Cicilia 354
  Edmund 86, 355
  Jo. (Rev.) 354, 355
  John 86, 87, 354, 355
  John (Rev.) 355
  Katherine 87
  Leonard 86, 87, 354, 355
  Luke 86, 354, 355
  Mary 86, 354
  Robert 87, 355
  Susanna (Mrs.) 354
  William 86, 354
Bagley, William 555
Bagnall, Roger 106
Bailey, Arthur 264
  Mary 584
Baily, Arthur 114, 115
  Katherine 114
Bainbrig, Elizabeth 539
Bainton, Henry 294, 295
Baispoole, Richard 533
  William 444
Baker, (?) 161
  Anne 511
  Frances (Dame) 381
  Francis 432
  George 68
  Jane 430
  Jeane 191
  Joane 124
  John 261, 406
  Katherine (Lady) 472
  Mary 432
  Richard 432
  Sarah 432
  Thomas 356, 432
  Thomas (Sir) 381
  William 6, 432, 511, 522
Balding, Mary 209
Baldwin, Cornelius (Dr.) 308
  John 12
  Richard 334, 464
  Tymothie 374
Baldwyn, Anne 95
  Florence 642
  Katherine 334
Baldwyne, (?) 610
Ball, (?) 264
  (?) (Mrs.) 577
  Ellen 351
  Hannah 357
  Jas. 264
  Jos. 264
  Joseph 357
  Joss. 349
  Mary 67, 357
  William 208, 264
  William (Col.) 351, 577
  Wm. 264
Ballantyne, George 14
  Hugh 14
Ballard, (?) 118
  Thomas 119
  William 303
Ballenger, Thomasin 455
Balmol, Elizabeth 104
Baltimore, (?) (Lord) 53
Bambridge, Ann 244
  Joseph 244
Bambrig, (?) 541
Bamfield, (?) 142

Bampford, Lyon 585
Banbriggs, (?) 539
Bancke, John 647
Banckes, John 203
  Rebecca 203
Bancks, John 445
Bandrum, Samuel 277
Banester, Elizabeth 59
  John 59
Banfield, Martha 523
Banister, (?) 545
  Elizabeth (Mrs.) 59, 546
  Francis 276, 526
  John 59, 490, 545, 546, 642
  John (Lt.) 59, 546
  Margaret 546
  Mary 546
Banker, Robert 497
Bankes, Anne 458
  William (Dr.) 2
Banks, (?) 268
  John 203
  Judith 15
  Katherine 269
  Matthias Job 15
Bannaster, Benjamin 215
  Margarett 215
Bannester, Benjamin 215
Banninge, Henrye 295
Bannister, John 545, 546
Banyster, Alexander 642
  Anne 642
  John 642
  Margaret 642
Barber, (?) 182, 568
  (?) (Mrs.) 197
  Agnes 55
  Mary 82, 190
  Susanna 183
  William (Lt.-Col.) 82, 190
Barbon, (?) 568
  Feargod 568
  Praisegod 570
Barbour, Steephen 512
  Walter 658
Barckham, Edward (Sir) 58
Barckley, Henry 290, 291
Barclay, George 353
  Patrick 354
Bard, Mary 671
Barebones, Praisegod 570
Barfields, (?) 523
Barford, Mary 581
Barham, (?) 512, 513
  Alice 511
  Ann 346, 347, 370
  Anne 347, 361
  Annis 511
  Anthony 200, 361, 362, 370, 513, 619
  Arthur 370
  Catherine 395, 513
  Charles 44, 45, 347, 395
  David 511
  Edward 347, 395
  Elizab. 370
  Elizabeth 346, 347, 511, 512
  Jane 619
  Jasper 370
  John 347, 511, 512

Barham (cont.)
  Katherine 346
  Margaret 511, 512
  Marie 512
  Mary 370
  Micoll 370
  Nicholas 512
  Richard 347, 370, 395, 511, 619
  Robert 45, 346, 347, 395, 511
  Susan 346, 347, 513
  Thomas 347, 370, 395
  William 512
Baringer, Thomas 598
Barkclay, Hen. (Sir) 497
Barkeley, Ann 288
  Edwarde 291
  Elizabeth 287
  Elizabeth (Dame) 290
  Gartrude 288
  Henrie 288
  Henry 294
  John 288, 294
  Margaret 290
  Margarett 288
  Maurice (Sir) 293, 294
  Morrys 287
  Richard (Sir) 288
  Robert 287, 288, 290
  Roberte 287
  William 294
Barkeleye, John 287
Barkelie, Morris 291
Barker, (?) 58, 165
  Annis 55
  Elizabeth 598
  Henry 374
  John 125, 551
  Will. 599
  William 31, 484, 598
Barkham, Anne 95, 365
  Edw. (Sir) 95
  Edward 365, 366
  Edward (Sir) 365, 366
  Edw'd. (Sir) 95
  Jane 365, 366
  Margaret 366
  Marg't. 95
  Robert 365, 366
  Stephen 120
  Susan 366
Barkley, Charles 293, 294, 295
  Edward 291, 292, 293
  Elizabeth 294
  Elizabeth (Dame) 290
  Elizabeth (Lady) 292, 293
  Frances 288
  Francis 287
  Harry 291
  Henry (Sir) 292, 293
  Jane 294
  John 288, 294
  Margaret (Dame) 290, 291, 292
  Maurice (Sir) 292
  Morris (Sir) 290
  Robert 288
  William 294
Barklie, Morris 291
Barlow, Ralph 239, 582
  William 393
Barlowe, Anne 393
  Barnaby 393
  John 393
  Julyan 393

689

Baytopp (cont.)
  Thomas 578
Baytup, Daniel 577
  Daniel B. 578
  James 578
  James B. 578
  Mary 577, 578
  Mary B. 577, 578
  Susan 578
  Susan B. 578
  Thomas 577, 578
Beaconsawe, Richard 524
Beadle, Gabriel 403
  Henrye 405
  John 403
Beadles, Henry 378
Beale, (?) 207
  (?) (Dr.) 274
  Anne 61, 105
  George 61
  Hannah 351
  John 44, 61, 250
  Robert 34
  Tho. 105
  Thomas 105
  Thomas (Capt.) 105
Bealy, G. W. (Rev.) 273
Beamond, (?) 609, 610
  John 363
Beane, John 93
Beard, Benjamin 576
  Docke 30
  Dorothy 30
  Margarett 30
  William 30
Beart, Elizabeth 442
Beauchamp, Abel 429
  Abell 231
  John 230, 231, 428,
    429
  Margarett 428
  Richard 231, 429
  William 231, 429
Beauchampe, John 429
Beaumont, John (Sir) 497
Beaver, Nicholas 510
Beavill, Mary 211
Becket, Sarah 627
Beckford, Anne 186
  Edmond 186, 187
Beckwith, Elizabeth 94
  Margaret 94
  Marmaduke (Sir) 96
  Roger (Sir) 96
Bedell, Ann 401
  Anne 680
  Antonina 680
  Bridget 680
  Capell 402, 404, 405,
    406
  Dorothie 404
  Dorothy 205, 401, 402,
    403, 680
  Edward 154, 680
  Elizabeth 400, 401,
    403, 680
  Francis 286, 400, 401,
    403, 404, 405, 680
  Gabriel 403, 680
  Gabriell 402
  George 400, 402, 403
  Harry 405
  Henrie 405
  Henry 402, 403, 404,
    680
  James 680
  Jane 401, 402, 680

Bedell (cont.)
  John 286, 402, 403,
    404, 405
  John (Sir) 402, 403,
    680
  Julius 286
  Lettice 680
  Michaell 286
  Rebecca 680
  Silvester 400, 401,
    402, 405, 680
  Susan 286
  Susanna 286
  Sylvester 401
  Thomas (Sir) 402, 404,
    405, 406, 680
  William 205, 286, 400,
    403, 680
  Willm 401
Bedford, John 32
  Mary 32
Bedingfield, (?) 414
  Edmund 65
Bee, Elizabeth 118
  Robert 118
Beecher, William 454
Beecke, Will 141
Beell, Anne 613
  Thomas 613
Beer, Hercules 354
Beheathland, A. 656
  Anthony 656, 657
  Charles 56
  Dorothy 657
  George 657
  Georgium 656
  John 56
  Richard 56
  Robert 56, 657
  Robert (Capt.) 56
  Robertum 656
  U. 656, 657
  Ursula 657
  Ursulam 656
Bele, Thomas 615
Belfeild, Allen 407, 408
  Catherine 407
  Cicellie 407
  Joane 407
  John 407
  Margaret 407
  Margarett 407
  Marie 407
  Richard 407
  Suzan 407
Belfeilde, Allen 406
  Mary 233
Belffylde, Thomas 408
Belfield, (?) (Dr.) 408
  Alane 408
  Allan 408
  Catherin 407
  Elizabeth 408
  Finney (Rev.) 408
  John 406, 408
  John Finney 408
  Joseph 105, 131
  Joseph (Dr.) 408
  Margaret 408
  Richard 408
  Thomas 408
  Tobias 408
  Toby 408
  Tobye 408
Bell, Anne 384
  Cicely 456
  Ellen 384
  Frances 217

Bell (cont.)
  George 459
  Hollis 384
  Hugh 155
  Humfrey 384
  Humphrey 384
  Humphry 34, 35
  James 217
  John 33, 206
  Robert 33, 384
  Thomas 384
  Thos. 179
Bellamy, William 431
Bellinger, Penelope 394
Bellingham, Edward (Sir)
  372
Bellingrock, Mathew 34
Bellinham, Edwarde 548
Bellowes, (?) 481
Belloye, Thomas (Sir)
  576
Belt, Daniel 34
Benbowe, Frances 409
Bendsteed, (?) 469
Bendysh, Richard 213
  Thomas (Sir) 243
Benefild, Daniel 610
Benet, (?) 679
Benlose, Margaret 58
  Richard 58
Bennet, Richard 107
  Thomas (Sir) 540
Bennett, Ambrose 445,
    447, 448, 449
  Ann 280, 448
  David 448
  Edward 448, 449
  Elizabeth 447, 582
  Frances 280
  Henry 448
  Jane 588
  Joan 445, 447
  John 445, 446, 447,
    448, 449, 643
  John (Sir) 448, 449
  Jone 446, 447
  Margaret 448
  Marie 446
  Mary 281, 446, 447
  Philip 448
  Ralph 448
  Richard 181, 447, 448,
    449
  Robert 448
  Simon 448
  Symon 448
  Symon (Sir) 445, 446,
    447
  Thomas 448
  Thomas (Sir) 446, 448,
    538
  William 495
Bennetts, John 446
Bennison, Eliz'a. 206
Benskin, Frances 410
  Francis 410
  Henry 410
  John 410
  Mary 410
Benskyn, Catherine 410
  Frances 410
  Francis 410
  John 409
  Katherin 410
  Raph 409
  Thomas 409
Benson, Benjamin 265
  Jane 353

Benson (cont.)
William 384
Bensted, (?) 572
Bentley, Isaack 513
Izaacke 514
Richard 455
Robert 57
William 57
Benton, Violett 500
Benwell, Grace 65
Nicholas 65
Strange 65
Beresford, Henry 581
Maud 581
Bereway, John 516
Bergavenny, (?) (Lord)
84
Berham, Bartelmewe 615
Berisford, (?) 250
Richard 134, 250
Berkeley see de Berkeley
Berkeley, (?) 364
(?) (Earl) 289
(?) (Gov.) 292
(?) (Lady) 206
(?) (Lord) 288
Anne 288, 289
Besse 288
Charles 295
Charles (Sir) 295
Eadnoth 289
Edward 287, 291
Elizabeth 289
Frances 289
Francis (Sir) 289
Gertrude 289
Henry (Sir) 288, 291,
295
James 289
John 289
John (Lord) 295
John (Sir) 288, 289
Margaret 288, 289,
291, 295
Maurice 289, 294
Maurice (Sir) 288,
289, 291, 295
Richard 73
Richard (Sir) 288, 289
Thomas (Baron) 289
William 289
William (Sir) 295, 363
Berkett, Thomas 507
Berkley, Edward 291
Henry 294
Margaret 294
Maurice 294
Bermingham, John 336
Bernard, Anna (Mrs.)
415
Anne (Mrs.) 21
Beheathland 524, 657
George 589
Lucy 311
Mary 657
Mary (Mrs.) 657
N. 682, 683
Richard 21, 415
Robert (Sir) 311
Thomas 50, 657
William 311
William (Col.) 589
Berouth, James 130
Berry, (?) 337, 509,
529
(?) (Mrs.) 345
John 262, 362
Richard 568

Besst, Edward 169
Beswick, Mary 7
Betavehompe, Robert 255
Bettes, (?) 531
Edward 414
Betts, James 157
Betty, Parr 326
Robert 300, 301
Beverley, Robert 113
Bevyse, Thomas 452
William 452
Bickerton, Bridgett 186
John 670
Richard 186
Bickford, Ames 407
Amies 407
Gregory 407
Bickley, (?) (Mrs.) 35
Anne 33, 34, 384
Frances 285
Frances (Sir) 602,
603
Francis 33, 34, 285,
286, 384
Francis (Sir) 34
John 34, 285, 286,
384
Joseph 34, 603
Philadelphia 33
Philadelphia (Mrs.)
34
Sarah 285, 286
William 34
William (Sir) 34
Biddle, Abigail 285
Biddlecombe, James 589
Bidle, Johane 618
Bidmore, John 622
Sarah 622
Bidwell, Elizabeth 33
Bigge, John 174
Thomas 111
Bigges, Thomas 293
Biggins, (?) 226
Arthur 226
William 226
Biggs, Richard 53, 54
Sarah 53, 54
Thomas 54
William 54
Bignett, John 406
Biker, Charles Gramer
674
Thomas (Rev.) 674
Billiard, Thomas 117
Billingsbee, Matthew
197
Bills, George 583
Robert 583
Bing, Henry 323
William 281
Bingley, Orator 282
Binne, Margaret 232
William 232
Binnes, Margaret 234
Binns, (?) 392
Elizabeth 392
Bird, Lucy 335
Lucy (Mrs.) 335
William 4
Birkbecke, James 625
Birkett, (?) 671
Aiskew 671
Thomas 533
Biron, John (Sir) 68
Biscoe, Elizabeth 126
Bishop, Christofer 526
John 181

Bishopp, Hellen 370
John 180
Richard 610
William 244
Bispam, (?) 68
Bitham, Richard 318
Bix, John 387
Black, William 206
Blackaby, James 34
Blacke, William 280, 547
Blackman, Jeremia 171
Blackmore, Thomas 48
Blackwell, Thos. 560
Bladder, Marmaduke 200
Blagrave, (?) 133
A. Henry 133
Anthony 132, 133
John 132, 133
Margaret 132
Thomas 132
Blagrove, (?) 133
Benjamin (Rev.) 133
John 133
Blague, Margarett (Mrs.)
147
Blair, (?) 336
(?) (Dr.) 336, 337,
338
(?) (Mrs.) 337
Blake, Penelope 672
Priscilla (Mrs.) 672
William 526, 527
Blakemore, Winfeild 211
Blakeston, Ralph (Sir)
586
Blakiston, Nathaniel
(Col.) 172
Blanchard, Ann 114
Jane 114
John 114
Thomas 114
William 114
Wm. 126
Blancheflower, Benjamin
297
Blanchflower, Alexander
296, 297
Benjamin 296
Blancko, Anne 256
Bland, Alice 523
Anne 524
Esdras 257
Joane 257
John 257, 638
Mary 257, 448
Rebecca 257
Richard (Dr.) 535
Thomas 257, 282, 448
William 533
Blands, Alice 523
Blanshard, Jon. 315
Blaydes, Samuel 15
Bleamire, William 146
Bleeck, Ar. 296
Blenerhasset, Henry 438
Blesshenden, Thos 507
Bleunerhasset, Ambros
440
Dorothie 438
Jane 440
John (Sir) 440
Marie 440
Blewitt, (?) 593
Jane 593
John 593
Katherine 593
Susan 593
Blisse, Martha 621

Bradshaw, (?) 124
  Alice 632
  John 598
  Richard 143
  William 204, 206
Bradshawe, (?) 593
  Cassandra 495
  Elizabeth 593
  John 593
  Robert 593
Brady, Thomas 77
Bragg, Charles 610
Braie, Annys 655
  Edward 655
  Elizabeth 655
  Mark 655
  Mary 655
  William 655
Bramspeth, Elizabeth 269
  Thomas 269
Bramston, Abigaill 8
  Alice (Mrs.) 8
  Anthony 8
  Bridgett 8
  Marie 8
Branch, (?) 259
  Christopher 113
  Christopher, Jr. 112
  Christopher, Sr. 112
  Obedience 259
  Priscilla 259
  Thomas 112
Brand, Jonathan 460
  Mary 250
Brandon, Martin 208
Branston, Edward 219
Braviour, Peter 191
Braxton, Elizabeth 413
Bray, Ann 15
  Anne 82
  Edward 15, 483, 656
  Elizabeth 655
  James 82, 164
  Jane 483
  John 483
  Katherine 483
  Ned 15
  Nicholas 655
  Plumer 656
  Richard 15
  Robert 483, 656
  Ruth 483
Braye, John 483
  Katherine 483
Brayne, (?) 637
Brayning, Arnold 381
  Elizabeth 381
Braynte, John 32
Breaux, Mary 458
Bree, Henry 570
Breeding, (?) 358
Breese, Mary 458
Breesford, Anne 151
Brent, (?) 116
  Benj 357
  George 196
  Giles 16
  Robert 615
  Sara 16
  Sarah 16
  William 16
  Wm. 357
Brente, Robert 614
Bressie, William 6
Bressy, Amy 449
  Hugh 449
  James 449
  Richard 449

Bressy (cont.)
  Thomas 449
Breton, Dennis 265
  M. A. 629
  Maria Adriana 629
  Richard 629
Brett, Alexander 370
  Alicia 370
  Arthur 370
  Benjamin 369
  Catherine 370
  Edmund 207
  Edward 369
  Edward (Sir) 267,
    268, 369
  Elizabeth 207, 369,
    370
  Elizabeth Bush 370
  Elizabeth Highgate
    370
  Frances 369
  Francis 207
  George 370
  James 70
  Johanna 350
  John 141, 369, 370
  Margaret 370
  Mary 269, 369
  Randall 369
  Richard 369, 370
  Robert 148, 369, 370
  Symon 370
  William 269, 369,
    370
  Wm. 369
Bretton, Dennis 265
  Dennys 265
  He. 265
Brewer, John 50
  Mary 50
  William 310, 461, 546
  Willm 461
Brewster, Alice 514, 516
  Ambrose 516
  Amy 516
  Edward (Capt.) 516
  Elizabeth 516
  Ffrauncs 516
  Francis 514, 515
  Grissell 515, 516
  Humfrey 514, 515
  Humphrey 517
  John 516
  Martha 516
  Marye 513
  Richard 516
  Robert 515
  Sackford 516
  Thomas 513, 514, 516
  Thos. 516
  William 516
Brexton, (?) 413
  Cornelius 414
  Francis 414
  Richard 413, 414
  Thomas 414
  William 413
Breynton, John 329
Brian, Alexander 679
  William 191
Briant, Thomas 245
Brice, (?) (Mrs.) 94
  John 94
  Martha 61
  Thomas 61, 62
Brickhead, Jane 275
Bridge, Abell 191
  John 16, 299

Bridge (cont.)
  Thomas 191
Bridger, Joseph (Capt.)
    113
  Margarett 358
Bridges, Brooke 629
  Jane 61
  John 16, 435
  Mary 61
  Thomas 491
Bridgman, Edward 313
  Jacob 554
  James 554
  John 605
  Orlando (Sir) 457
Bridley, Robert 556
Brigges, Ambrose 504
  Mar. 678
  Sam 556
Briggs, Gray 125
  John 138
  Laurence 585
  Thos. 585
Brighouse, Elizabeth 87
  George 87
  James 87
Brilston, Thomas 406
Brimer, James 658
  Johane 658
  Tymysin 657, 658
Brinckhurst, (?) 680
Bringborne, Francis 531
  John 531
Brinley, Laurence 286
  Sarah 286
Brinsden, John 261
Bristow, Anne 114
  Avarilla 114
  Catherine 114
  Elizabeth 114
  Frances 114
  James 16
  John 114, 115, 647,
    648
  Katherine 114, 115
  Rachel 16
  Rebecca 114
  Richard 647
  Robert 16, 114, 115,
    116, 117
  Robert, Jr. 359
  Robert (Maj.) 116
  Thomas 647
  William 114, 115
Bristowe, Robert 539
Bristows, (?) 358
Britten, Driver 5
  Elizabeth 4
  John 4, 5
  Lawrence 5
  Margaret 4
  Mary 5
  Sarah 5
  Sibill 5
  Thomas 5
  William 5, 522
Britton, Charity 20
  John 20, 602
Broadhurst, (?) 62
  Charles 61
  Edward 61, 62
  Elizabeth 377
  Hugh 663
  Jane 377
  John 61, 62, 663
  Margaret 329
  Phyllis 61
  Samuel 62

Chappell, Thomas 59
Charles, George 608
  John 651
Charleton, Anne 210
  Elizabeth 210
  Jno. 210, 211
  Jone 210
  Julyan 420
  Margarett 210
Charlton, Elizabeth
  (Mrs.) 629
  James 103
Charnock, Mary 554
  Mary (Mrs.) 554
Charnocke, Mary 554
Chatfield, Amye 251
Chatham, (?) (Lord) 97
Chaumberleyn, Christian
  468
  Humfrey 468
  Johane 468
  John 468
  Walter 467
  Xpian 468
  Zpian 468
Chaumont, (?) 129
Chaundler, Edward 433
  George 434
  John 136
  Marie 433
  Mary 136
  Richard 433
Chawcroft, William 239
Checkerell, Richard
  577
Cheeseman, Anna 157
  Edmond 157
  John 157
  Margaret 157
  Margarett 157
  Thomas 157
Cheesman, John (Col.)
  158
  Margaret (Mrs.) 158
Chelsham, Jethro 34
  Mary 34
Cheltnam, George 91
Cheriton, Chas. 523
Chernock, Marie 554
Cheshire, (?) (Mrs.)
  380
  Margaret 319, 380
  Silvester 380
Chesley, (?) 118
  Bridget 364
  Edward 364
  Margaret 118, 119
  Philip 118, 119, 364
  Philip (Capt.) 119
  Philipp 119
  Phillip 364
  Thomas 364
  William 119
Chester, (?) (Capt.)
  317, 318
  (?) (Mrs.) 94
  Katherine (Mrs.) 335
  Lucy 344
  Lucy (Mrs.) 335
Chetwyne, (?) (Dr.)
  256, 257
Chew, John 140, 517
Cheyney, (?) 290
  Anne 196
  John 377
  Thomas (Sir) 468, 469
Chicheley, Dorothie 423
  Dorothie (Lady) 423

Chicheley (cont.)
  Dorothy 422
  Dorothy (Lady) 422
  Henry 40, 421
  John 424
  Mary 422
  Thomas 421, 422
Chichely, (?) 554
  Dorothie (Mrs.) 554
  Dorothy (Lady) 553
Chichester, (?) 350
  A. P. B. (Sir) 350
  Anne 385
  Dorothie 385
  Elizabeth 349
  Ellen 349, 350
  Hannah 349
  Hugh 350, 384, 385
  John 349, 350, 351,
    384, 385
  Mary 349, 385
  Richard 349, 350, 351,
    385
  Robert 384
  Sarah 350
  William 384, 385
Chichley, (?) (Lady)
  423
  Anne 423
  Devereux 423
  Devoreux 423
  Dorothie 423
  Henry (Sir) 422, 554
  Henrye 423
  Jane 423
  John 423
  John (Sir) 554
  Mary 422
  Thomas 423
  Thomas (Sir) 422, 423
Chilcott, Robert 244
  William 244
Child, (?) 610
  Ales 610
  Alice 608
  Thomas 572
Childe, Alice 609
  Francis 543
  John 253
  Mary 488
  Rich. 157
Childerstone, John
  330
Chill, Alexander 30
Chilmead, Henry 378
Chilton, E. 174
Chinn, Alice 519
  Anna 351
  Edward 520
  Elinor 519
  Elizabeth 519, 520
  Francis 520
  Grace 519
  Hannah 520
  Isabell 520
  John 520
  Jonathan 520
  Margaret 519
  Martha 520
  Mary 519
  Nathaniel 520
  Rebecca 519
  Richard 519, 520
  Sarah 520
  Thomas 520
  Walter 519
  William 520
Chirgwine, John 183

Chisman, Edmund 158
  Edmund, Jr. 158
  John 157
Chisseldyne, (?) 524
Chistian, Edward 472
Chiversal, Hem. 556
Chollwell, Tho. 635
Cholmely, Robert (Vis-
  count) 449
  Thomas 450
Cholwell, Ann 634
  Thomas 634
Chrashawe, Anne 595
Christ, J. 103
  Jesus 449, 679
Christian, Eliza Ann
  307
Christmas, (?) 307
Christophers, Thomas 537
Church, Dorothy 673
  William 171
Churchey, George 376
Churchill, Anne 424
  Frances 424
  Henry 423, 424
  John 423, 424
  Joseph 423, 424
  Marie 424
  Phillis 423, 424
  Thomas 423, 424
  Tobias 423, 424
  William 423, 424
Churchills, (?) 342
Churchman, (?) 373
Chynn, John 519
  Richard 518
  Rivhard 519
  Thomas 519
Chynne, Dorothy 520
  Elizabeth 519
  Grace 519
  John 519
  Mary 519
  Thomas 518
Claiborne, (?) (Mrs.)
  676
  Augustine 672, 675,
    676
  Augustine (Col.) 676
  Mary 672, 675, 676
  Thomas 41, 357
  William 280
  William Dandridge 218
Clapham, Christopher 629
  George 106
  Henry Lee 106
  Sarah 106
  William 106
  William, Jr. 106
  William, Sr. 106
Clappum, William 133
Clare, Ambrose 40
Clarence, George (Duke)
  453
Clarendon, (?) 668
  (?) (Lord) 188, 321
  Edward (Earl) 243
Claridge, John 218
Clark, (?) (Mrs.) 197
  Francis 80
  Hannah (Mrs.) 557
  Margaret 60
  William 379
Clarke, (?) 135, 139,
  455, 465, 655
  Edward 81, 82, 498
  Francis 230
  Gabriell 402, 403

698

Dickson (cont.)
Nicholas 226, 620
Digby, (?) (Lady) 497
Everard (Sir) 494
John (Sir) 497
Kellam (Sir) 497
Diggens, (?) 414
Digges, (?) 200
Anne 614
Dudley 14, 375
Dudley (Sir) 174, 375,
381, 422, 554, 614
Edward 381, 422, 554,
614
F. 615
Francis 614, 615
Isabel 613
James 613, 614
Joan 614
John 614, 615
Leonard 614, 615
Mary 381, 422
Mildred 615
Philip 614, 615
Phillippa 615
R. 615
Richard 615
Sarah 614
Thomas 174, 381, 614,
615
W. 615
William 614, 615
Wm. 614
Diggs, Dudley 174, 374
Dudley (Sir) 554
Edward 174, 375, 381
Elizabeth 174
Herbert 381
Jo. 174
Leonard 381
Mary 381
Mary (Lady) 553
Thomas 381, 554
Will 174
William 174
Dight, Edward 326
Walter 326
Dillon, Michael 349
Dimock, Alice 595
Lionel (Sir) 595
Dingles, Margaret 632
Dingley, William 118
Dinwiddie, Elizabeth
304
John 304
Lawrence 303
Rebecca 304
Robert 303, 304, 352
Sarah (Mrs.) 303
Dison, Humfrey 473
Dix, Ch. 312
Chr. 312
John 386
Dixey, Bridgett 402
Richard 402
Dixon, (?) (Mrs.) 540
Ann 305, 331
Cornelius 304, 305,
306
Eliza 307
Elizabeth 306
Harriet Peyton 308
John 304, 305, 306,
307, 308, 331
John (Rev.) 304, 305,
306
John, Sr. 308
Lucy 306, 307, 308

Dixon (cont.)
Lyonel 305, 306
Lyonell 304
Mary 307, 308
Mildred 307
Nancy 307
Philip 307
Priscilla 307
Robert 304, 305,
306, 307, 679
Roger 304, 305, 306,
307, 331
Susannah 305, 308
Susannah Ann 306
Thomas 305, 306
Thomas Rootes 307
Tobias 282
William 306, 307,
388, 627
Dobbett, Ann 240, 241
Dobbie, George 245
Sarah 245
William Hugh 245
Dobbins, Ann 673
Hannah 673
James 673, 674
John 674, 675
Mary 673, 674
Sarah 673
Ursula 456
Dobbs, Richard 131
Dobie, John (Rev.) 245
Dobson, Drue 506
Dockinge, Robt 516
Dod, (?) 391
Dodd, Anne 450
John 450
Lucilia 390
William 450
Dodington, (?) 682
Dodson, George 517
Dogett, John 58
Doggett, (?) (Widow)
424
Richard 423, 563
Domelawe, Richard 70
Donnelly, Patrick 18
Doodes, Thos. 463
Thos., Jr. 463
Dorington, John 504
Dormer, Edward 641
Fleetwood 149
Fleetwood (Sir) 148,
149, 569
Mary 569
Robert 267
Dorney, Joseph 58
Dorny, Thomas 58
Dorrell, William 169
Zachary, Sr. 169
Dorrington, (?) 153
Doughtie, John 257
Doughty, John 392
Douglas, Charles 316
Charles (Capt.) 316
Charles (Col.) 316
Douglass, Charles 316
Downall, William 568
Downe, Ann 362
Edmond 437
George 362, 437,
438
Jane 362
Joane 437
Nicholas 362, 437
Thomas 6
Downeman, Alice 435,
436

Downeman (cont.)
Anne 436
Christopher 436
Elizabeth 437
James 435
John 78, 437
Judith 436
Million 437
Prudence 436
Raleigh 436
Robert 436
William 435, 436, 437
Zachary 436
Downer, William 172, 173
Downes, Alice 437
Ann 437
Beatrice 41, 42
Edward 41
Elizabeth 41
George 362, 438
Jane 362
John 42, 437
Margarett 437
Mary 41
Nicholas 362, 438
Robert 41, 42
Susan 41, 42
Downman, (?) 436
Dorothy 437
Raleigh 437
William 437
Wm. 437
Downum, Thomas 195
Dowre, Alice 525
Dowse, (?) 153
Winifred 526
Doyle, Edward 442
Doyley, Charles 87, 88
D'oyley, Charles 88
Doyley, Cope 87, 88
D'oyley, Cope 88
Doyley, Cope, Jr. 87
Cope (Rev.) 87, 88
Elizabeth 88
M. 640
Mary 640
Robert 87, 88
D'oyley, Robert 88
Robert (Rev.) 88
Doyly, Charles 327
Drabble, Edward 284
Drake, Edward 78
Francis 267
Franck 267
Gilbert 33
Drakeford, Gregory 260
Drakote, (?) 260
Mary 260
Drannte, (?) 234
Draper, (?) (Mrs.) 134
Darcis 133
Darkis 134
Elizabeth 133
Josias 264
Lettice 40
Matthew 40
Nathaniell 78
Thomas (Sir) 641
Vincent 133, 134
Draycott, Thomas 242
Drewe, Joseph 126
Driver, (?) 192
Drome, Emanuell 504
Drummond, Sarah 535
William 535
Drury, John 108
Drys, Mary (Mrs.) 297
Ducket, Barbery 70

Fleetwood (cont.)
William (Sir) 92,
148, 149
Fleming, John 557
Jontia. 94
Fleminge, Mich. 184
Fletcher, Simon 678
William 85
Flete, Alice 616
John 616
Margaret 616
Samuel 616
Thomas 616
William 616
William, Jr. 616
William, Sr. 616
Wm. 616
Flint, Mary 49
Thomas 49, 50
Thomas (Capt.) 49
Thomas (Lt.) 657
Flood, Walter 49
Flower, Edward 86
Edwd 414
Geffrey 17
Jeffrey 17
Lucie 17
Flowre, Thomas 374
Fludd, Francis 206
Fluellinge, Thomas 152
Flute, Michael 259
Foissin, John 19
Folliot, Edward 292
Edward (Rev.) 291
John (Sir) 291
Thomas 291
Folliott, Catherine 292
Thomas 292
Fontaine, (?) (Col.)
636
W. W. (Col.) 636
Foodham, Robert 681
Foord, (?) 197
Nathaniel 51
Foot, Simon 564
William 564
Foote, Elizabeth 564
Humfrey 564
Johan 563, 564
John 564
Margaret 564
Margarett 564
Richard 564
Symon 564
Thomas 59
William 564
Forby, Benjamin 100
Felix 100
Jane 100
John 100
Ursula 100
Ford, (?) 360
Alice 360
Hannah 32
Richard 124, 165
W. 173
Forde, John 548
Mary 103
William 212
Fordham, Nathaniel 366
Forenght, Amelia (Mrs.)
674
Forman, Elizabeth 440
Forrest, E. 673
Elizabeth 673, 674
Robert 673, 674
T. J. 673

Forrest (cont.)
Thomas Joseph 673,
674
Fortescue, Henrie 76
William 76
Fortesue, Nicholas (Sir)
473
Fortre, Samuel 135
Samuell 135
Fortree, John 135
Samuel 135
Fortrie, James 136
Samuel 136
Samuell 137
Fortune, (?) 232
Anne 232
Blanch 232
John 232
Mary 232
Morris 232
Walter 232
William 232, 234
Forward, John 375
Fossaker, Elizabeth
196
John 196
Richard 28, 196
Fossett, Thomas 80
Foste, John 615
Foster, (?) (Bishop)
102
(?) (Mrs.) 197, 198
Alice 216
Betty 197
Frances 263
Jane 216
John 2, 3, 104, 216
Margarett 216
Philip 125
Phillip (Capt.) 176
Ralph 278
Richard 137, 670
Robert 87, 569, 570
Thomas 286
Fotherbuy, Henry 473
Fothergill, Gerald 4
Fotherstone, Edward 93
Foulefford, Jane 212
Foulkes, Nathaniell 393
Fouls, Cordelia (Lady)
148
Fovie, Anne 647
Fowke, Adam 585
Ann 584, 585
Ann (Mrs.) 584
Anne 585
Anthony 584
Chandler 357
Dorothy 584
Elizabeth 584, 671
Francis 416
Francisco 584
Gerrard 416, 584,
585
Gerrard (Col.) 584
J. 584
James 416
Jane 267, 584
Joan 416
John 583, 584
Joyce 382
Judith 584
Margery 584
Mary 584, 585
Robert 584
Roger 382, 416, 583,
584
Susanna 584

Fowke (cont.)
Thomas 416, 584
W. 671
Walter 416
William 584, 585, 672,
673
Wm. 671
Fowkes, Francis 158
Fowler, Daniell 300
Elizabeth 300
James 300
Roarry 300, 301
William 259
Wyatt 369
Fowles, David 92
David (Sir) 92
Henry 92
Fowlis, James 143
Fowlsham, Eliz. 553
Fox, (?) 154
Ann 162
Anna 351
David 52, 130, 141
Geo. 214
Mary 156
Peter 156
Robert 162
Sam'l 261
Stephen 156, 157
Thomas 156
William 157
Foxall, Ambrose 602
Anne 602
Bridget 602
Elizabeth 601, 602
John 170, 171, 601,
602
Mary 602
Sara 602
Ursula 601
William 601, 602
Foxe, Laurence 394
Foxhall, John 170, 602
Martha 170, 602
Foxley, (?) 120
Foye, Edward 80
Foyle, Ja. 528
Frampton, Thomas 411
Francin, Henry 111
Francis, John 590
Richard 12
Susannah 13
William 415
Francke, (?) 155
Jo. 625
Richarde 454
Uenys 381
Francklin, John 150
Francklyn, Thomas 385
William 385
Franes, James 243
Franke, Robt. 585
Franklyn, Gilbert 201
Frauncis, John 288
Frazier, Daniel 245
Freake, (?) 607
Freckelton, Robert 12
Sarah 12
Frederick, John (Sir)
203
Mary (Dame) 203
Fredericke, John (Sir)
203
Leonora 203
Rebecca 203
Thomas 203
Fredway, Elizabeth 455
Freebody, John 159

Gipps, Jane 61
  Richard 61
Gist, S. 670
  Samuel 670, 671, 672
Glanvell, Alice 89
Glascock, John 430,
  431
Glascocke, John 452
Glass, Thomas 557
Glassbroke, William
  171
Glasse, (?) (Dr.) 201
  Samuel (Dr.) 201
Glegg, John 188
Glemham, Henry (Sir)
  440
Glencross, (?) 561
Gleson, Israel 501
Glocester, Anne 41
  Christian 41
  Edmund 41
  Elizabeth 41
  Joseph 41
  Mark 41
  Mary 41
  Robert 41
  Sarah 41
  Thomas 41
Glover, Charles 19
  Euseby 569
  John 226
  Richard 19, 39
  Thomas 102
Glubb, Walter 436
Glyde, (?) 482
Goater, F. 640
  Francis 640
Gobert, John 464
Godbold, John 527,
  528
Goddard, (?) 232
  Bridget 415
  Edward 415
  Vincent 513
  Willm 397
Goddart, Margaret (Dame)
  538
  Margaret (Lady) 541
Godderde, Edward 414
Goddin, John 627
Godfrey, Henry 401, 403
  Rere 463
  Veare (Mrs.) 256
Godson, William 10
Godstall, Anne (Lady)
  199
Godwin, (?) 306
  Thomas 193
Godwyn, Katherine 189
  Ralph 189
  Thomas 441
Godyng, Thoma. 637
Goffe, (?) 452
Gofton, Francis 473
  Francis (Sir) 474
Goidd, Judith 58
Gold, Robert 10, 528
Goldsmith, C. 606
  Charles 606
  Judith 606
  Mathias 606
Goldstone, Alice 51
  Charles 51
  Edward 51
  Sara 51
  Sarah 51, 52
  Susannah 51
  Thomas 51

Golley, Tho. 506
Gomond, James 475
  Mary 475
Gonge, Thomas 327
Gonne, Margaret 256
  William 256
Gooch, (?) (Gov.) 647,
  662
  Anne 645
  Clement 645, 662
  Edmund 646, 647
  Eleanor 20
  Elizabeth 645
  Frances 646
  Henry 662
  Henry (Lt.-Col.) 647
  Jane 662
  John 662
  Leonard 645, 646
  M. 646
  Martha 645, 646, 647
  Nicholas 662
  Philip 645
  Robert 645, 646, 662
  Roger 463
  Rorer 646
  Thomas 646, 647
  William 19, 662
  William, Jr. 20
  William (Maj.) 105,
    589, 662
  William (Sir) 20, 647
  William, Sir (Gov.)
    662
Gooche, Anne 661
  Bridget 661
  Clement 646, 661
  John 661
  M. 661
  Margaret 661
  Mary 661
  Robert 661
  Roger 661
  William 661
Gooch-Lewis, Eleanor
  (Mrs.) 14
Goodacre, Henry (Sir)
  260
Goodall, Richard 525
Goodart, Rebecca 345
Goodaye, Richard 451
Goodday, George 5
  Margaret 5
  Sarah 5
Goode, Bennett 190
  Martha 190
  Will. 263
  William 263, 483
Goodfellow, Allan 222
  Anne 222
  Chris. 222
  Christopher 222
  Elizabeth 222
  John 222
  Mary 222
  William 222
Goodfellowe, Edward 222
Goodgyon, Henry 585
  Rob. 585
Goodlad, William 208
Goodlade, William 208
Goodman, (?) 528
  James 265
  Richard 459
Goodrich, (?) 20
  Thomas 20
Goodrick, Margarett
  442

Goodrick (cont.)
  Richard 442
Goodridge, Nicholas
  (Capt.) 296
Goodwin, John 132, 300,
  301
  Thomas 441
  William 38
Goodwyr, George 577
  Mary 439
  Theordore 439
  Thomas 440, 442
Goodwyne, Thomas 439
Goodwynn, Thomas 681
Goodyae, Roger 451
Goodyeare, Thomas 58
Goodyer, James 410
  John 12
Gookin, Daniel 196
Gookins, Daniel (Capt.)
  140
Gordon, William 535
Gore, Eliz. 629
  John 629
  Thomasin 629
  William 642
Gorford, Joan 574
Gorges, Ferdinando
  (Capt.) 477
  Thomas 374
Gorsuch, Alice 249, 250
  Ann 249
  Anne 249, 250
  Daniel 249, 251
  Daniell 250
  Edward 250
  John 249, 250
  John (Rev.) 251
  Katherine 250
  Richard 250
  Robert 250
  William 250, 251
Gos, Mary 251
Gosnol, Anthony 158
Gosnold, (?) 458
  Anthony 158
  Bartholomew 158, 159
  John 158
  Robert 158
  Thomas 158
Gosnoll, Robert 257
Gosnould, George 457
Gossage, (?) 549
Gostellowe, John 462
Goswell, Elizabeth 20
  John 20
Goudrey, William 147
Gouge, (?) 30
  Thomas 30
  William 29
  William (Rev.) 30
  Wm. (Rev.) 30
Gough, (?) 182
  Giles 183
Gould, Henry 480
Goulder, William 262
Gouldes, William 443
Goulding, Christopher
  621
Gouldsmith, Charles 606
  John 625
  Morrel 430
Goulsborrow, Myles 138
Gounter, (?) 242, 243
Gower, (?) 106
  Abel 69, 258
  Abell 258
  Amie 257

Gwyn, Edmund 311
John (Rev.) 277
Lucy 311
Gwynn, Elizabeth 91
Gyfford, (?) 575
Gyle, Dorothy 216
Gylson, George 523
Hacker, (?) 581
Anne 581
John 581
William 581
Hackett, Thomas 34
Haddocke, (?) (Mrs.)
168
Richard 168
Haddon, Elizabeth 608
Francis 608
Judeth 607
Judith 608, 609, 610
Marie 608
Richard 608
Haecker, Ann 581
John 581
Haines, Katherine 249
Haistwell, Thomas 122
Hale, (?) 433, 434
Robert 433
Hales, Edward 546
James 546, 547
Steven 464
Haley, Richard 594
Halfhead, (?) (Widow)
10
Halfhide, William 117
Halford, Jane 101, 102
John 102
Richard 102
Thomas 102
Hall, (?) 59, 234, 476
(?) (Mrs.) 223
Alice 251
Ambrose 445, 446
Anne 482
Augustin 256
Francis 596
Henry 494
James 320
Jane 596
Jno 333
John 251, 262, 678
Joseph 203, 577
Margaret (Mrs.) 319
Mary (Mrs.) 618
Mother 250
Nevill 34
Prudence 262
Robert 196
Sarah 203
Susannah 203
Thomas 618
William 151, 243
Wm 383
Hallam, Anne 109
James 106
Margaret 110
Robert 110
Robert, Jr. 110
Samuel 110
Sarah 110
Thomas 110
Thomas, Sr. 110
William 110
Hallams, (?) 110
Halley, (?) 155
Halliman, Josiah John
42
Halliwell, James 460
Hallom, Robert 109

Hallome, Robert 109
Hallywell, John, Jr.
263
Halmer, (?) 469
Halybell, Thomas 613
Ham, El zabeth 550
Hierom 550, 551
Hierome 551
Jerom 551
Jerome 551
Jeromie 551
John 673
Sarah 673
Sibella 551
Hambden, (?) (Lady)
232, 233
Hamilton, (?) (Rev.)
303
Archibald 303, 304
Christian 303
Walter (Hon.) 336
Hamlin, Elizabeth 43,
44
Stephen 44
Hammer, Anne 210
Hammon, (?) 374
Anthony 381
Hammond, (?) 556
Ann 381
Anthony 381
Mainwaring (Col.) 557
William 563, 603,
604
Hamond, Henry 326
James 524
John 178, 326
M. 603
Mainwaring (Col.)
556
Man. (Col.) 556
Mary 603
Hamonds, John 523
Hamor, (?) 30, 79
Hampden, Ann 456
George 456
Griffith 456
John 458
Hamper, John 86
Hampshewe, John 327
Hampson, Anne (Mrs.)
447
Rebecca 447
Thomas 445, 447
Hanbury, Osgood 266
Hanchet, (?) 372
Hancock, (?) 192, 194,
642
Hancorne, William 504
Hand, Katherine 189
Thomas 189, 190
Handford, (?) 129
Anne Rake 129
Catherine 129
Elizabeth 227
Francis 129
Hugh 128
Humfrey (Sir) 472
Humphrey (Sir) 129
John 128, 129, 227
John (Sir) 129
Margaret 129
Mary 227
Richard 227
Thomas 129
Tobias 128, 129, 227
Walter 128
Handson, Henry 496
Mary 497

Handson (cont.)
Mary (Mrs.) 496
Richard 171
Hane, Jose 462, 463
Jost 256
Haney, Elizabeth 358
Maximilian 358
Hanford, (?) 129
(?) Slingsby 129
Charles 129
Compton 129
Edward 129
Eleanor 129
Elizabeth 129
Elizabeth Hurst 129
Frances Compton 129
Humphrey (Sir) 474
James 129
Thomas 129
Walter 129
Hanger, Phillip 236
Hannsworth, (?) 179
Francis 178, 179
Hannyford, Edward 622
Marchebell 622
Hansford, (?) 129
Humphrey (Sir) 129,
474
John 129
Tobias 129
Hanson, Robert 31
Hanwell, Andrew 526
Harbin, William 536
Harborough, Edmond 278
Hardford, Charles, Sr.
275
Hardich, (?) 217
Margarett 216
Thomas 216
William 216
Hardidge, (?) 217
Elizabeth 217
Elizabeth Sturman 217
William 217
Hardie, Roose 514
Hardier, (?) (Mrs.) 442
Harding, Edward 147
John 331
Margarett 147
Simon 474
William 147
Hardwick, (?) 363
Hardy, Elizabeth 275
Hugh 118
John 118
Robert 572
Hardyn, Christopher 78
Harecourt, (?) 467, 572
Harewell, Fra. 556
Harford, Charles 276
Hargrove, Ann 307
Elizabeth Mildred 307
John 307
Haridene, Sara 256
Harinston, William 224
Harlackenden, Stephen
616
Harley, James 138
Harman, Fra. 206
Henery 207
Hennery 177
William 287, 410
Wm. 206
Harmar, Anthony 572
Arthur 571, 572, 573
Bridgett 571
Charles 573
Elizabeth 572, 573

711

Haywood, Samuel 2
Hazlewood, Elizabeth
    (Mrs.) 20
Heale, Elizabeth 264
    Ellen 264
    George 264
    John 264
    Joseph 264
    Nicholas 264
    Sarah 264
Heane, Thomas 498
Hearle, Charles 188
    John 188
Heath, Anne 450
    James 460
    John 257
    Richard 450
    Robert 473
    Robert (Sir) 205,
        320
    William 548
Heathe, Robert (Sir)
    609
Heather, Jane 447
    Joan 445
    John 280, 547
Heaviningham, W. 682
    William 681, 682
Hedge, (?) 277
    Margaret 51
Hedgies, William 249
Hedgman, Peter 16
Hele, William 575
Hellier, Alice 526
    John 142
    Mary 526
Hellinger, Anne 378
Helmes, (?) 58
Helpes, William 520
Hely, Jn 355
    Nic. 425
Hemsley, E. 607
    Ellen 609
Hemying, Thomas (Sir)
    582
Hendere, (?) 319
Henderson, Henry 82
    James 331
    Susanna 82
Hendley, W. 623
    Walter 623
    William 512
Henley, John 517
    Walter 487
Henman, John 579
Henshaw, Francis 111
Henshawe, Edward 186,
    187
    Frances 186
    Tho. 187
Hensman, Thomas 256
Henson, W. C. (Mrs.)
    660
Henworth, Thomas 495
Herbert, Buller 676
    Cecil 645
    Charles 643, 644
    Dorothy 645
    E. 644
    Edward 643
    Elizabeth 643, 644
    Gressell 322
    Henry 642, 645
    Iohn 644
    J. 644
    James 643, 644
    Jane 645
    John 644, 645, 676

Herbert (cont.)
    K. 644
    Katherine 643, 645
    Margaret 645
    Mary 642, 643, 644,
        676
    Matthew 643, 644, 645
    P. 644
    Priscilla 643
    Richard 644, 645
    Richard (Sir) 645
    Thomas 643, 644, 645
    William 642, 643,
        644, 645
Hercy, Edward 207
Herdmeate, William 249
Hering, Oliver 224
Herman, Jno. 206
    John 579
Herndon, Edmond 523
Herne, Elizabeth 203
    John 203, 377
    Joseph 203
    Joseph (Sir) 203
    Judith (Dame) 202
    Nathaniel 202, 203
    Nathaniel (Sir) 202
    Nathaniell 202
    Nicholas 202, 203
    Thomas 203
Hernon, Mathew 583
Hersey, Richard 446
Hesseter, James 520
    Richard 520
Heton, Anne 583
    Martin 583
Hewet, (?) (Lady) 681
    John (Sir) 77
    Thomas (Sir) 75, 681
    William 77
Hewett, John 76
    John (Sir) 76
    Samuel 76
    T. (Sir) 682
    Thomas (Sir) 681,
        682, 683
    William 7, 76
    William (Sir) 75, 76
Hewit, George 62
    Thomas (Sir) 76
    William 77
Hewitt, Rachel 7
    Rich. 206
Heycock, Joane 296
Heyes, Alice 215
    Hugh 215
    James 215
    John 215
    Margerie 215
Heylin, (?) 383
    Joyce 383
    Mercy 383
Heyling, Francis 383
    Grace 383
Heylyn, Edward 383
    Peter 383
Heyman, (?) (Mrs.) 109
Heymon, John 682
Heynes, Joseph 330
Heyrne, Nicholas 663
    William 663
Heyward, John 276
    Margaret 49
Heywood, Raphe 485
Hickes, Adye 386
    George 386
    John 600
Hickman, Henry 86

Hicks, Thomas 472
Hide, Barnard 610
    Leonard (Sir) 524
Higford, Margaret 129
    William 129
Higgens, John 232
Higgins, (?) 540
    Edward 33, 384
    John 384
Higginson, Dorothie 469
    Robt. 276
Highgate, Elizabeth
    370
    Reginald 370
Highings, Edward 118
    John 118
Highlord, (?) 232
    John 232
High Lord, John, Jr. 235
Highlord, Zacharie 235
Hill, (?) 361, 389, 497
    (?) (Mrs.) 389
    Ann 117
    Dorothy 120
    Edward 161
    Edward (Col.) 161, 392
    Elizabeth 161, 201
    George 296, 314
    Gilbert 661
    Grace 495
    Hannah 392
    Henrietta Maria 161
    Higham 665
    Humphrey (Col.) 271
    Jo. 58
    John 20, 54, 329, 406,
        496
    Marmaduke 54
    Mary 81
    Merriall (Mrs.) 507
    Molly 271
    Nathaniel 58
    Nicholas 448
    Paule 533
    Phillipp 57
    Richard 201, 477, 478,
        485, 561
    Robert 495
    Sara 161
    Silvester 448
    Thomas 505
    William 507
Hilles, (?) 533
    Merriel 507
Hillhouse, James 67
Hilling, Hierome 572
Hills, John 484
Hillson, Amice 251
    Robert 251
Hilpes, Richard 520
    William 520
Hind, (?) (Rev.) 674
Hinde, Frances 432
    Henry 169
    John 423
    Robert 655
Hine, Richard 156
Hinshaw, Edward 469
Hinsman, Thomas 49
Hinton, (?) 332
    William 423
Hions, Richard 326
Hiscoke, John 520
Hitchcock, (?) 150
Hitson, Nicholas 320
Hixon, Mary 593
Hlwoet, Nathaniel 516
Hobart, William 562

713

Jackman (cont.)
  Dorothy 324, 553
  Elizabeth 43
  George 618
  J. J. 43
  Joseph John 42, 43
  Mary 43
  William 43
Jackson, (?) (Dr.)
    553
  Anne 283, ∠84
  Arthur 89
  Barnaby 496
  Blanche 233
  Francis 253
  Henry 283
  Jo. 24
  John 154, 237
  Myles 283
  Patrick 432
  Robt. 357
  Thomas 188, 283
Jacksonne, Ann 284
  Magarett 283, 284
Jacob, Matthew 354
Jagoe, Robert 600
James, (?) (Mrs.) 293
  Anne (Mrs.) 549
  Edward 33, 504, 663
  Edward Wilson 25
  Elisha 3
  Jane (Mrs.) 549
  Jo. 180
  John 181, 361
  Joseia 78
  Mary 663
  Thomas 469
  William 549
Janson, (?) (Mrs.) 173
Jarary, William 34
Jarrard, Catherine
    292
  Robert 292
Jarrell, Thomas 302
Jarrett, Johanra 43
Jarvis, Thomas 69
Jauncy, James 109, 230,
    231
Jay, Thomas (Sir) 194
Jaye, Christopher 646
  Ralphe 646
Jeay, Benjamin 194
  Will. 155
Jeffereyes, John 51
Jefferies, Jeffery 143
  John 174
Jefferson, Dorothy 412
  Elizabeth 412
  John 411
  Martin 411
  Mary 412
  Nathaniel 412
  Nathaniell 412
  Thomas 259, 566
  Went gen 412
  Weyntge 411
Jeffery, Alice 191
  Dorothy 191
  Edmond 435
  Jane 386
  John 191
Jefferys, John 52
Jeffrey, John 62
Jeffreys, (?) 505
  Ann 52
  Edward 52
  Geoffrey 28
  Jeffrey (Sir) 52

Jeffreys (cont.)
  John 28, 52
  Watkyn 52
Jelliffe, John 285
Jenings, (?) 94
  Edmond 366, 585
  Edmond (Sir) 366
  Edmund 96, 97, 144,
    586
  Edmund (Gov.) 310
  Edmund (Pres.) 94
  Edmund (Sir) 94, 586
  Edmund (2nd) 97
  Edmund (3rd) 97
  Eliz. 585, 586
  Elizabeth 586
  Frances 310
  Jonathan 585, 586
  Jonathan (Sir) 586
  Peter 585, 586
  Richard 183
Jenkin, Petherick 558
Jenkins, Daniel 277
  Henry 276, 277
  Henry (Capt.) 277
  Mary 192
Jenkinson, Margaret 447
  Sarah (Dame) 347
Jenkly, Judith 504
Jenkyns, William 188
Jennett, Richard 461
Jenney, Thomas 432
Jenning, Thomas 546
Jennings, (?) 94, 230
  (?) (Pres.) 96
  Agnes 298
  Ambrose 566
  Ambrose (Sir) 443
  Ariana 94, 96
  Edmd. J. 95
  Edmond 298, 585, 586
  Edmond (Sir) 298
  Edmund 93, 94, 95,
    96, 299, 586
  Edmund (Gov.) 299
  Edmund (Sir) 95
  Eliz. 96
  Elizabeth 95, 96,
    298
  Frances 96
  Jane 298
  John 621
  Jonathan 95, 96, 585
  Jonathan (Sir) 95,
    96
  Martha 621
  Mary 298
  Peter 95, 299
  Peter (Col.) 281
  Pieter (Col.) 298
  Sarah 674
  Tho. 132
  Will 177
  Will. 208
  William 177, 208,
    298
Jennison, William 147
Jenny, Thomas 432
Jenyngs, Robert 542
Jepp, Elizabeth 263
Jepphson, John (Sir)
    320, 321
Jepson, Francis 665
  Robert 147
  Susan 147
Jermyn, (?) (Lord) 98,
    243
  Robert (Sir) 438

Jermyn (cont.)
  William 438, 442
Jermyns, (?) 439
Jerrard, Catherine 292
Jerrell, Sarah 302
Jervis, Abigail 63
  Lindsey 306
Jett, Thos 360
Jewell, Richard 518
  Thomas 434
Jewer, Benjamin 70
Jewes, (?) (Capt.) 608
Jnnys, Martin 193
Joanes, John 158
  Richard 518, 519
Jodrell, Edmond 189
John, Hugh Watkin 644
Johns, William 643
Johnson, (?) 228, 540
  (?) (Dr.) 310
  (?) (Mrs.) 609
  Alder 473
  Alderman 474
  Anne 59
  Edward 410
  Ewen 282, 283
  George 369
  Hassard 609
  Henry 132
  Hugh 647
  James 24
  Jo. 362
  John 138, 440, 625
  Joseph Bain 658
  Luke 59
  Margaret 283
  Margarett 282
  Matt 639
  Richard 550, 556
  Solomon 406
  Thomas 47, 255
  Thos. 585, 586
Johnston, (?) 678
  Allen 490
  Ben. 348
  Christopher (Dr.) 97
  Jno. 314
  Robert 314
Jolliffe, John 285
  William 280, 547
Jones, (?) 536
  (?) (Mrs.) 125
  Alice 313
  Allen 125
  Ann 209
  Anne 313
  Arnold Elzey 583
  Charlotte 125
  Constance 327
  Cutbert 331
  Eben 40
  Edmond 191
  Edmund 643
  Edward 517
  Elizabeth 313
  Frances 12
  George 436
  Gilbert 257
  Gilberte 258
  Griffith 675
  Henry 57
  Jane 239, 519
  Jaques 313
  John 105, 326, 415,
    643
  John, Jr. 21
  John, Sr. 21
  Marie 313

Jones (cont.)
Martha 21, 109, 110, 126
Mary 518
Morgan 52
Nebuchudnezor 105
Orlando 12
Richard 55, 57, 111, 432
Robert 22, 125
Robert, Jr. 125
Roger 556, 573
Sarah 111, 125
Silverster 519
Thomas 55, 111
Willian 475
Willie 125
Winifr-(?)-d 517
Jongh, William Ende 411
Jonson, Ben 321
Jordan, Christian 498
Edward 601
George 122, 231
Robert 498
Jorden, George 231
Joseph, Tho. 601
Josiaffant, (?) 473
Joslyn, Susan 592
Joy, Wm. 148
Joye, Roberte 148
Thomas 425
William 148
Joyner, Mathewe 232
Judge, Cecilia 355
Thomas 355
Judrey, Katherin 223
Juell, Thomas 636
Jurner, Mary 279, 547
William 279, 547
Juye, Thomas 425
Karmichell, Anne 105
Keane, Nicholas 515
Kearney, Edward 351
Keat, Ann 529
John 529
Kebelthwaite, Thomas 525
Kedge, (?) 459
Keeble, John 310
Robt. 378
Keen, (?) 264
Anne (Mrs.) 272
Sarah (Mrs.) 272
Keene, Elizabeth 158
Henry 158
Newton 24
Thomas 158
Keeves, (?) 671
Keich, Sarah 620
Simon 620
Keith, C. P. 652
Kelley, Richard 105
Kelly, John 225
Kelsey, Ann 150
Elizabeth 150
George 150, 151
Simon 150
Susan 150
Thomas 150
Kelsies, (?) 150
Kely, Mary 86
Kemp, (?) 124, 553
Amy 596
Ann 554, 597
Anthony 552
Arthur 324, 552
Bridget 325
Dorothy 322, 324, 554

Kemp (cont.)
Edmond 323, 324, 325
Edmund 324, 552, 597
Edward 322, 323, 324, 552
Elizabeth 324, 554
F. H. 323, 324
John 554
Mathew 325
Mary 554, 614
Peter 324, 325
Richard 31, 111, 323, 324, 325, 552
Robert 552, 323, 324, 325
Robert (Sir) 111, 323, 324
Robt. 552
Thomas 323, 324, 325, 554
Thomas (Sir) 554, 596, 614
William 615
Kempe, (?) 11, 30, 645, 646
(?) (Lady) 324, 553
Anthony 11
Arthur 322, 323, 552
Dorothie 322, 553
Dorothy 321, 322, 323, 422
Dorothy (Lady) 421
Edmond 322, 553
Edmund 323, 325
Edward 322, 323
Elizabeth 322, 323
Jane 322
Jane (Dame) 322
John 323
Margery 10, 11
Richard 107, 111, 323
Robert 321, 323
Robert (Sir) 322, 323, 324, 553
Thomas 322
Thomas (Sir) 422, 553
Tom 553
William 11
Kemple, Edmund 597
Kemps, (?) 11
(?) (Lady) 554
Kempthorne, John (Sir) 168
Rupert 168
Sarah 600
Kendall, Dorothie 555
Edward 555
Frances 555
Hellen 555
Henry 555
Jane 555
John 322, 555, 556
Judith 555
Margarett 555
Mary 555
Richard 555
Rose 555
Stephen 555
Thomas 555, 556
William 555, 556
Kenion, Mary 103
Kenner, Benjamin 490
Henry 490
Marie 490

Kenner (cont.)
Martha 490
William 490
Kennet, (?) 386
Kennett, Sampson 546
Kennon, Richard 69
Kennor, Joane 489
John 489
Richard 489
Kennyon, Mary 103
Kensington, William (Lord) 126
Kent, (?) 34
Alice 328, 329
Elizabeth 556
Jas. Hen. 210
Kente, Paule 422
Kepus, Robert 662
Kerby, Thomas 336
Thos. 336
Kerrill, Sampson 120
William 120
Kersey, Henry 42
Kersley, Henry 42
Kerton, Thomas 363
Kestin, Elizabeth 42
Richard 42
Thomas 42
Keston, Elizabeth 42
Francis 42
Ketchmaye, Davye 212
Ketchmore, John 481
Kettlewell, Henery 626
Key, John 32
Keydon, Mordica 610
Keyser, (?) 639
Kibble, Owen 259
Kidby, Joan 620
John 620
Kidder, Joane 545
Kidley, (?) 561, 562
Anne 561, 562
R. 561
Richard 561, 562
Kighte, Hen. 181
Killegrew, Elizabeth 295
Robert (Sir) 295
William (Sir) 294, 295
Kimpton, (?) 250
Kincade, Margaret 12
King, Alice 107
Arnold 266
Dorothy 456
Hen. 222
James 154
Jno 333
John 15, 107
Judith 682
Richard 266
William 2
Kinge, (?) 195
(?) (Dr.) 572
Edward 400
Simond 285
Kingmill, (?) 81
Richard 81
Kingsmill, Andrew 414
Kinnaird, Sallie 659
Kinnesman, Ha. 568
Kirke, Robert 242
Kirkham, Fra. 113
Francis 113
Richard 108
Robert 108
Kirle, Ann 455
Kirton, Mary (Mrs.) 107
Kitchen, (?) 678

721

Moore (cont.)
Thomas 255
William 171
Mooreton, (?) 454
Moorey, (?) 309
Morce, William 519
Mordant, Bedingfield 65
Castle 65
Castles 64
Charles 65
Cleere 65
Frances 65
George 64, 65, 66
Henrie 64
Henry 64, 65, 66
John 64, 65
Lestrange 64, 65, 66
Mary 64, 65
Riches 65
Robert 64, 65, 66
Robert (Sir) 65
Roger 65
Tallemage 65
Mordaunt, George 66
Lestrange 66
Lestrange (Sir) 66
Robert (Sir) 66
Morden, Fraunces 84
Morder, Richard 56
More, Earon 132
Geo. 610
John 31
Kate 610
Robert 610
Susan 31
Valentine 31
William 132
Morecroft, Edmund 171
Morecrofte, Elizabeth 171
Marie 171
Morecrosse, Ferdinando 250
Moreland, Thomas 277
Mores, John 623
Moreton, (?) (Dr.) 573
(?) (Earl) 316
Morgaine, (?) 496
Morgan, (?) 484
Christopher (Capt.) 43
Edward 59
James (Capt.) 43
Richard 56
Temperance 56
Walter 643
Morgaine, (?) (Dr.) 497
Morison, Fines 321
Richard (Sir) 320
Morley, (?) (Dr.) 102
Mary 188, 233
Morrice, (?) (Mrs.) 581
Mary 496
Thomas 496
Morris, George 173, 253
Matthew Robinson 214
Thomas 116, 214, 253, 415
Morrison, (?) (Mrs.) 59
Fynes 321
Richard (Sir) 321
Morse, Benjamin 261
Thomas 322

Mortimer, Margaret 289
Roger 289
Morton, (?) (Dr.) 572
Elizabeth 245
Richard 59
William 503
Moryson, Charles 575
Francis 321
Francis (Col.) 321
Fynes 321
Henry (Sir) 321
Letitia 321
Richard (Maj.) 321
Richard (Sir) 321
Robert (Capt.) 321
Moseley, Edward 536
Edward (Col.) 536
Edward (Sir) 496
Mary 123
William 123
Moses, William 203
Mosley, (?) 402, 496
Brudenell 403
Willm 402
Moss, Alexander 604
Mothe, John 437
Mott, George 196
Mottram, Ann 130
Frances 130
John 130, 131
John (Col.) 130
John, Jr. 131
John (Maj.) 131
Ruth 131
Mouce, Alex. 159
Moule, Isaac 570
Moulsen, Peter 146
Moulson, (?) (Dame) 147
Foulke 146
Peter 147
Moulton, Robert 168
Mouncke, Katherine (Mrs.) 574
Moundeford, Edward 213
Mounte, Marie 233
Mountjoy, Catherine 288
William (Lord) 288
Mountney, Richard 472
Mourton, George 249
Mowlson, (?) (Lady) 58
Moy, John 66
Moye, John 150, 151
Richard 150
Moyle, Phebe (Mrs.) 626
Mullard, Joshua 362
Mullet, George 249
Multon, George 623
Muncke, (?) 445
Mundy, Alis 209
Suzann 51
Mundye, Arthur 489
Munsers, James 213
Murdock, William 350
Murr, James 143
Rachell 143
Murray, James 316
Murrell, (?) 639
Mus, Hannce 434
Haunce 434
Muse, Elizabeth 180
Musgrave, Christopher 585
Elizabeth 676
Michaell 177, 676
Thom. 676

Musgrave (cont.)
Thomas 676
William 286
Mvnford, Edward 211
Mydleton, William 530
Myghtin, Willm 329
Myldmay, Anthony 373
Myles, Arthur 168
Myllynton, Griffin 92
Mynn, John 265
Mynne, Charles 34
Jane 211
Robert (Capt.) 215
Sarah 215
William (Sir) 212
Mynterne, Alice 91
Bynger 91
John 91
Nathaniel 91
Samuel 91
William 91
Nagus, John 155
Namdred, Richard 244
Nanson, John 481
Napier, Robert (Sir) 609
Narbrow, (?) 392
Nares, George 217, 218
James 217, 218
Nash, Elizabeth 635
George 235
Hester 635, 636
Mary 635
Nicholas 635, 636
Stephen 560
William 635
Nashe, John 618
Thomas 618
Nasshe, Stephano 638
Nayler, Geo. 586
Neadle, Mary 604
Neale, (?) 35
(?) (Mrs.) 260
Bartholomew 294
Francis 596
William 384
Nean, Henry 314
Nedham, Barbara 23
George 23
James 23
Neede, William 85
Needham, Anne 518
Eustace 28, 599
Frances 517, 518
John 28, 599
Lettice 28, 599
Margaret 29, 599
Mary 518
Neele, Georg 574
George 574
Margaret 574
Marie 574
Neill, (?) 30
Nellson, Heugh 246
Nelme, Richard 390
Nelms, Elizabeth 278
Nelson, Bridget 145
Bridgett 246
Dorothy 145, 146
Elizabeth 247
George 247, 678
Hugh 145, 146, 246, 247
Hugonis 146
John 145, 146, 246, 247
Richard 586
Sarah 145, 247

723

728

744

ADDITIONS